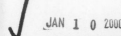

AFRICAN HISTORICAL DICTIONARIES
Edited by Jon Woronoff

32. *Ethiopia*, by Chris Prouty and Eugene Rosenfeld. 1981. *Out of print. See No. 56.*

33. *Libya*, 3rd ed., by Ronald Bruce St John. 1998.

34. *Mauritius*, by Lindsay Rivire. 1982. *Out of print. See No. 49.*

35. *Western Sahara*, by Tony Hodges. 1982. *Out of print. See No. 55.*

36. *Egypt*, by Joan Wucher King. 1984. *Out of print. See No. 67.*

37. *South Africa*, by Christopher Saunders. 1983.

38. *Liberia*, by D. Elwood Dunn and Svend E. Holsoe. 1985.

39. *Ghana*, by Daniel Miles McFarland. 1985. *Out of print. See No. 63.*

40. *Nigeria*, 2nd ed., by Anthony Oyewole. 1999.

41. *Côte d'Ivoire (The Ivory Coast)*, 2nd ed., by Robert J. Mundt. 1995.

42. *Cape Verde*, 2nd ed., by Richard Lobban and Marilyn Halter. 1988. *Out of print. See No. 62.*

43. *Zaire*, by F. Scott Bobb. 1988. *Out of print. See No. 76.*

44. *Botswana*, 2nd ed., by Fred Morton, Andrew Murray, and Jeff Ramsay. 1989. *Out of print. See No. 70.*

45. *Tunisia*, 2nd ed., by Kenneth J. Perkins. 1997.

46. *Zimbabwe*, 3rd ed., by Steven C. Rubert and R. Kent Rasmussen. 1998.

47. *Mozambique*, by Mario Azevedo. 1991.

48. *Cameroon*, 2nd ed., by Mark W. DeLancey and H. Mbella Mokeba. 1990.

49. *Mauritius*, 2nd ed., by Sydney Selvon. 1991.

50. *Madagascar*, by Maureen Covell. 1995.

51. *The Central African Republic*, 2nd ed., by Pierre Kalck; translated by Thomas O'Toole. 1992.

52. *Angola*, 2nd ed., by Susan H. Broadhead. 1992.

53. *Sudan*, 2nd ed., by Carolyn Fluehr-Lobban, Richard A. Lobban, Jr., and John Obert Voll. 1992.

54. *Malawi*, 2nd ed., by Cynthia A. Crosby. 1993.

55. *Western Sahara*, 2nd ed., by Anthony Pazzanita and Tony Hodges. 1994.

56. *Ethiopia and Eritrea*, 2nd ed., by Chris Prouty and Eugene Rosenfeld. 1994.

57. *Namibia*, by John J. Grotpeter. 1994.

58. *Gabon*, 2nd ed., by David Gardinier. 1994.

59. *Comoro Islands*, by Martin Ottenheimer and Harriet Ottenheimer. 1994.

60. *Rwanda*, by Learthen Dorsey. 1994.

61. *Benin*, 3rd ed., by Samuel Decalo. 1995.

Historical Dictionary of Democratic Republic of the Congo (Zaire)

Revised edition of
Historical Dictionary of Zaire

F. Scott Bobb

African Historical Dictionaries, No. 76

The Scarecrow Press, Inc.
Lanham, Maryland, and London
1999

SCARECROW PRESS, INC.

Published in the United States of America
by Scarecrow Press, Inc.
4720 Boston Way
Lanham, Maryland 20706
http://www.scarecrowpress.com

4 Pleydell Gardens, Folkestone
Kent CT20 2DN, England

Copyright © 1999 by F. Scott Bobb

British Library Cataloguing in Publication Information Available

Library of Congress Cataloging-in-Publication Data

Bobb, F. Scott, 1950–
    Historical dictionary of Democratic Republic of the Congo (Zaire) /
F. Scott Bobb.
       p.   cm.
    Rev. ed. of: Historical dictionary of Zaire. 1988.
    Includes bibliographical references (p.).
    ISBN 0-8108-3571-1 (cloth : alk. paper)
    1. Congo (Democratic Republic)—History—Dictionaries. I. Bobb, F.
Scott, 1950– Historical dictionary of Zaire. II. Title.
DT650.17.B63   1999   98-34189
967.51'003—dc21   CIP

This book is dedicated to my family, without whose support it would not have been possible.

CONTENTS

EDITOR'S FOREWORD

One of Africa's largest, most populated and potentially richest countries, located strategically at its core, the Congo (previously Zaire) has both dominated the surrounding region and been affected by it. For three decades, its position was regionally predictable, under the control of a strong (if anything, too strong) leader, Mobutu Sese Seko, who brought political stability, but also economic decline and a stultifying system of government that undermined any durable stability. With his passing, it is now less clear in which direction the Congo will turn. Some factors are promising and others less so, under the new ruler (yet old politician) Laurent Kabila.

Still, this is a good time to take stock. And that is the main purpose of this *Historical Dictionary of the Congo (Zaire)*. It looks back at 30 years of Mobutism, nearly 40 years of independence, over a century of colonial rule, and even earlier kingdoms and groups that shared the territory. It does so through numerous entries on politics, the economy and society, the geography and ethnic makeup, noteworthy figures and significant events. It cannot tell us what will come, but the "new" Congo is growing out of these older elements and, no matter what the regime desires, it too will be shaped by them. This gives added interest to the lengthy chronology, comprehensive introduction, substantially expanded dictionary and truly impressive bibliography. This volume should quickly become a privileged tool in understanding what happens in the heart of Africa.

The *Historical Dictionary of the Congo (Zaire)* was written by F. Scott Bobb, who also wrote its predecesor, the *Historical Dictionary of Zaire*. The same care and effort have gone into it. Brought up by missionary parents in the then-Belgian Congo, Bobb spent a decade living in various regions before and after independence. He has returned many times since and followed events while away. Beginning in 1977, Bobb worked as a reporter-broadcaster for the Africa Division of the Voice of America and wrote articles on African topics for *Africa Report*. More recently, he was chief of the news division of the VOA, and is now returning to the field, this time in Cairo as Middle East correspondent. But his interest in the Congo remains, and we can look forward to future editions that will answer many of today's open questions.

Jon Woronoff
Series Editor

ACKNOWLEDGMENTS

A work of this nature owes a great deal to the research and scholarship of others which, in some cases, was carried out decades ago. However, a number of works deserve special mention: The country studies edited by W. MacGaffey, G. McDonald, H. Roth, and Meditz and Merrill, respectively, and the works of T. Callaghy, G. Nzongola-Ntalaja, C. Young and T. Turner, J. Vanderlinden, and E. Dungia.

The assistance of a number of Congolese in government and academia is gratefully acknowledged in the preparation of the dictionary. The staff of the US Library of Congress was particularly helpful in researching the bibliography. Nevertheless, any errors in this work are my responsibility, and any opinions, however unintentional, are entirely my own.

F. Scott Bobb

NOTE TO THE READER

Given the varied orthography and nomenclature used by scholars of Congo/Zaire, a few clarifications on the use of names and spellings in this work are in order. During the past century, many names have changed, some more than once. The name of the country itself was changed a half dozen times. Under the banner of "authenticity" from 1966 to 1971, many names were changed to "authentic" African ones. Zairians dropped their Christian names in the early 1970s (i.e., Joseph-Désiré Mobutu became Mobutu Sese Seko). The Congo became Zaire. Cities and provinces lost their colonial names and the names of numerous organizations were changed to reflect these realities. A guide provides a reference to the major changes of geographical names (see p. xix). In passages referring to specific times, I have tended to use the name(s) in current use at that time (i.e., the "Katanga Secession" or the "Shaba Wars"), but in general or multiple time-frame references, I have opted for the name in use at the time of this writing. On first reference, I have given the full name of all individuals except for Mobutu Sese Seko, to whom I refer to simply as Mobutu.

It should be noted that the use of certain names has taken on political connotations. With the advent of multipartyism, some members of the opposition rejected appellations adopted under authenticity. As a result, many Zairians resumed using their Christian names in public. More importantly, some opposition members rejected the name "Zaire" and preferred to use "Congo." With the fall of Mobutu and the installation of the Kabila government in May 1997, the name of Zaire was changed back to Democratic Republic of the Congo. Some regions also regained names in use prior to the Mobutu coup and many organizations changed their names as well. I have made these changes where I could, although the transition from the immediate post-Mobutu era is not over. I have used "Congo" when it was in current use and Zaire when it was the official name. For general reference, I have tended to use Congo/Zaire or Congo/Kinshasa, in part to differentiate from the former French Congo, which I call Republic of Congo or Congo/Brazzaville. I underscore that my intent is historical and not political.

Considerable political baggage at one point was attached to whether one used "National Conference," which was viewed as controlled by pro-Mobutu forces, or "Sovereign National Conference," which was controlled by the opposition. Again, I have used these names in their historical context, with no political connotations intended.

I have used the name "Congo River" to describe the country's major river, because it was the term always used by international cartographers.

Concerning the names of ethnic groups, I have adopted the increasingly common anglophone practice of dropping prefixes, thus using "Kongo" instead of "Bakongo" and "Zande" instead of "Azande." However, I have used "Kikongo," "Lingala," and "Tshiluba" to distinguish these languages from the groups that speak them. I have also avoided for the most part the use of the term "tribe," since it is considered pejorative by many Africans. When the term is used, however, it is meant in the sense of ethnic group or nation with no negative connotations intended.

I have used English spellings of French names that are well known in English, a practice that has meant dropping some orthographic accents. For example, in general I use "Zaire" and "Leopoldville" as opposed to "Zaïre" and "Léopoldville." However, I have used French spellings when referring to official names of organizations such as "Office National du Café" and "Université Nationale du Zaïre," unless they have commonly used English translations, as with "Central Committee" and "Organization of African Unity."

Where clarity is not sacrificed, I have used standard abbreviations for units of measurement, for example, "km" for "kilometers" and "MW" for "megawatts."

An attempt has been made to cross-reference all major entries in the dictionary. Words which have their own entry are entered in **boldface**. However, a word is only cross-referenced if its entry relates to the topic under discussion. For example, in "Belgian government," the word "government" would only be cross-referenced if it related in some way to the Congolese government.

At the time of the final editing of this book, the post-Mobutu transition was still underway in Congo and historians and journalists were still updating their lexicographies. I apologize for any oversight.

ABBREVIATIONS AND ACRONYMS

ABAKO	Alliance des Bakongo
ACMAF	Association des Classes Moyennes Africaines
AFDL	Alliance des Forces Démocratiques pour la Libération du Congo/Zaïre
ANC	Armée Nationale Congolaise
AND	Agence Nationale de Documentation
ANI	Agence Nationale d'Immigration
ANR	Agence Nationale des Renseignements
APIC	Association de Personnel Indigène de la Colonie
APL	Armée Populaire de Libération
ASADHO	Association Africaine de Défense de Droits de l'Homme
AZADHO	Association Zaïroise de Défense de Droits de l'Homme
AZAP	Agence Zaïroise de Presse
BALUBAKAT	Association des Baluba du Katanga
BNC	Banque Nationale du Congo
BNZ	Banque Nationale du Zaïre
CADR	Corps des Activistes pour la Défense de la Révolution
CAR	Central African Republic
CCCI	Compagnie du Congo pour le Commerce et l'Industrie
CDC	Coalition Démocratique Congolaise
CEEAC	Communauté Économique des États de l'Afrique Centrale
CELZA	Cultures et Élevages du Zaïre
CEPGL	Communauté Économique des Pays des Grands Lacs
CETA	Centre d'Entraînement des Troupes Aéronautiques

CFA	Communauté Financière Africaine (franc zone)
CFL	Chemin de Fer des Grands Lacs
CFM	Chemin de Fer de Mayombe
CFMK	Chemin de Fer Matadi-Kinshasa
CFS	Congo Free State
CGTC	Confédération Général de Travailleurs Congolais
CIMA	Cimenterie Nationale
CIZA	Société des Ciments du Zaïre
CMC	Compagnie Maritime du Congo
CMZ	Compagnie Maritime du Zaïre
CN	Conférence Nationale
CND	Centre National de Documentation
CNECI	Caisse Nationale d'Épargne et de Crédit Immobilier
CNL	Conseil National de Libération
CNRI	Centre National de Renseignements et d'Investigation
CNS	Conférence Nationale Souveraine
CONACO	Confédération Nationale des Associations Congolaises
CONAKAT	Confédération des Associations Katangaises
CPG	Compromis Politique Global
CRISP	Centre de Recherche et d'Information Socio-Politiques
CSK	Comité Spécial du Katanga
CSLC	Confédération des Syndicats Libres du Congo
CSN	Conseil de Securité National
CVR	Corps des Volontaires de la République
CVZ	Chemin de Fer Vicinaux du Zaïre
DSP	Division Spéciale Présidentielle
ECOCAS	Economic Community of Central African States
ECC	Église du Christ au Congo
ECZ	Église du Christ au Zaïre
ENA	École Nationale d'Administration
EU	European Union
FAC	Forces Armées Congolaises

FAZ	Forces Armées Zaïroises
FGTK	Fédération Générale du Travail du Kongo
FLEC	Frente para a Libertação do Enclave de Cabinda
FLNC	Front pour la Libération Nationale du Congo
FNL	Front National de Libération
FNLA	Frente Nacional de Libertação de Angola
FODELICO	Forces Démocratiques pour la Libération du Congo
FPC	Forces Politiques du Conclave
FRF	Forces Républicaines et Fédéralistes
GDP	Gross Domestic Product
GECAMINES	Générale des Carrières et des Mines
GECOMIN	Générale Congolaise des Minérais
HCR	Haut Conseil de la République
HCR/PT	Haut Conseil de la République/Parlement de la Transition
IAA	International African Association
IAC	International Association of the Congo
IBRD	International Bank for Development and Reconstruction (World Bank)
IDA	International Development Association
ILO	International Labor Organization
IMF	International Monetary Fund
INEAC	Institut National pour l'Étude Agronomique du Congo
INEP	Institut National d'Études Politiques
INERA	Institut National pour l'Étude et la Recherche Agronomique
JMPR	Jeunesse du Mouvement Populaire de la Révolution
KDL	Chemin de Fer Kinshasa-Dilolo-Lubumbashi
LJV	Ligue des Jeunes Vigilants

MARC	Mouvement d'Action pour la Résurrection du Congo
MIBA	Société Minière de Bakwanga
MNC	Mouvement National Congolais
MNC/L	Mouvement National Congolais/Lumumba (wing)
MPLA	Movimento Popular de Libertação de Angola
MPR	Mouvement Populaire de la Révolution
NZ	New zaire (nouveau zaïre) currency
OAU	Organization of African Unity
OBMA	Office des Biens Mal-Acquis
OCAM	Organisation Commune Africaine et Malgache
OCS	Office du Chemin de Fer du Sud
OGEDEP	Office de Gestion de la Dette Publique
OKIMO	Office des Mines d'Or de Kilo-Moto
ONATRA	Office National des Transports
ONC	Office National du Café
ONDE	Office Nationale pour le Développement de l'Élevage
ONS	Office National du Sucre
ONP	Office National de Pêche
ONR	Office Nationale de la Route
OTRAG	Orbital Transport und Raketen Gesellschaft
OZRT	Office Zaïrois de Radio et de Télévision
PALU	Parti Lumumbiste Unifié
PDSC	Parti Démocrate et Social Chrétien
PLC	Parti de Libération Congolaise
PRP	Parti Révolutionnaire du Peuple
PSA	Parti Socialiste Africain
PSA	Parti Solidaire Africain
PSND	Projet des Services des Naissances Désirables
PSZ	Projets Sucriers au Zaïre
PT	Parlement de la Transition
PUZ	Presses Universitaires du Zaïre
RCD	Rassemblement Congolais pour la Démocratie
RDL	Rassemblement des Démocrates Libéraux

REGIDESO	Régie de Distribution d'Eau et d'Électricité
RPC	République Populaire du Congo
RTNC	Radio-Télévision Nationale Congolaise
SADEC	Southern Africa Development Community
SARM	Service d'Action et de Renseignements Militaire
SGB	Société Générale de Belgique
SGM	Société Générale des Minérais
SMK	Société Minière de Kisenge
SMTF	Société Minière de Tenke-Fungurume
SNCZ	Société Nationale des Chemins de Fer Zaïrois
SNEL	Société Nationale d'Électricité
SNIP	Service Nationale d'Intelligence et de Protection
SOCIR	Société Congo-Italienne de Raffinage
SODIMIZA	Société de Développement Industriel et Minier du Zaïre
SOMINKI	Société Minière et Industrielle du Kivu
SONAS	Société Nationale des Assurances
SOZACOM	Société Zaïroise de Commercialisation des Minérais
SOZIR	Société Zaïro-Italienne de Raffinage
UDEAC	Union Douanière et Économique de l'Afrique Centrale
UDI	Union des Démocrates Indépendants
UDPS	Union pour la Démocratie et le Progrès Social
UEAC	Union des États de l'Afrique Centrale
UFERI	Union des Fédéralistes et des Républicains Indépendants
UGEC	Union Générale des Étudiants Congolais
UMHK	Union Minière du Haut-Katanga
UN	United Nations
UNAZA	Université Nationale du Zaïre
UNHCR	United Nations High Commissioner for Refugees
UNIMO	Union Mongo
UNISCO	Union Nationale des Intérêts Sociaux Congolais
UNITA	União Nacional para a Independência Total de Angola
UNTC	Union Nationale des Travailleurs Congolais

UNTZA	Union Nationale des Travailleurs Zaïrois
URD	Union pour la République et la Démocratie
USAID	US Agency for International Development
USORAS	Union Sacrée de l'Opposition Radicale et Alliés et Société Civile
UTC	Union des Travailleurs Congolais
VSV	La Voix des Sans-Voix pour les Droits de l'Homme

GUIDE TO NAME CHANGES

Most name changes occurred between 1966 and 1971.
Names marked with an * were changed back in 1997.

Former Name	Name under Mobutism
Albert, Lake	Mobutu Sese Seko, Lake*
Albertville	Kalemie
Bakwanga	Mbuji-Mayi
Banningville	Bandundu
Bas-Congo (province)	Bas-Zaïre (region)*
Baudoinville	Virunga
Centime (currency)	Likuta (plural: makuta)*
Congo, Democratic Republic of the	Zaire, Republic of*
Congo Franc (currency)	Zaire*
Congo River	Zaire River*
Coquilhatville	Mbandaka
Costermansville	Bukavu
Districts	Subregions*
Élisabethville	Lubumbashi
Jadotville	Likasi
Katanga (province)	Shaba (region)*
Leopold II, Lake	Maï-Ndombe, Lake
Luluabourg	Kananga
Ministers	State Commissioners*
Ministries	Departments*
Orientale (province)	Haut-Zaïre (region)*
Paulis	Isiro
Port Francqui	Ilebo
Provinces	Regions*
Stanley Pool	Malebo Pool
Stanleyville	Kisangani
Thysville	Mbanza-Ngungu

CHRONOLOGY

c. 1000 BC Arrival in western and southwestern regions of the forerunners of Bantu-speaking people from West Africa.

1000 BC to Bantu-speaking peoples spread throughout Congo
AD 200 Basin.

500 to 1000 Bantu-speaking people spread to the savannas and toward the Indian Ocean through what are now the Kasai, Kivu and Shaba Regions.

900 Migration of other ethnic groups from Lake Chad region into central Zaire.

1200 to Emergence of the Kongo, Kuba, Luba and Lunda
1500 kingdoms and the Zande and Mangbetu dominions.

1483 Portuguese admiral Diogo Cão arrives at the mouth of the Congo River, which he names the Zaire. Cão returns in 1485 and 1487 to establish trading posts.

1500 Zande people arrive in north and central Zaire. Nilotic people migrate into northeastern Zaire.

1640 Dutch replace the Portuguese as leading traders. The French and English establish a large presence, leading to the decline of Portuguese power toward the end of the 1600s and the departure of many missionaries.

1700 The slave trade with the Americas begins to flourish.

1789 José Lacerda e Almeida makes the first scientific

	exploration of the Congo Basin, penetrating as far as Katanga where he discovers copper mines.
1800	The Afro-Arab trade begins to flourish in eastern Zaire.
1816	British expedition led by James Tuckey sails up the mouth of the Congo River.
mid-1800s	Slavery is officially abolished in most European countries.
1854	Scottish missionary/explorer David Livingstone reaches Lake Dilolo in Katanga and crosses the Kasai and Kwango river basins into Angola.
1858	British explorers Richard Burton and John Speke, traveling from East Africa, reach Lake Tanganyika.
1860	Explorer Samuel Baker reaches Lake Albert.
1865	The defeat of the Confederacy in the United States ends slavery throughout the country and closes the largest market for slaves in North America.
1867-68	Livingstone reaches Lakes Mweru and Bangwelu, arriving at Lake Tanganyika in 1869. Seeking the headwaters of the Nile, he sails down the Lualaba River and reaches Nyangwe in southern Kivu in 1871.
1870s	Christian missionaries begin returning to Zaire.
1870-88	Slavery is abolished in South and Central America.
1871	Journalist/explorer Henry Morton Stanley locates Livingstone at Ujiji on November 10 after an expedition of 236 days.
1874	Stanley, commissioned by the *New York Herald* and *Daily Telegraph* newspapers to continue Livingstone's

explorations, sets out to sail down the Congo River, in part to prove that the Lualaba is not the headwater of the Nile. The trip takes 999 days. Stanley arrives at the Atlantic Ocean on March 12, 1877.

1878-87   Stanley, hired by Belgium's King Leopold II, sets out to establish trading posts and make treaties with local chiefs along the Congo River. He eventually returns with 450 treaties.

1884   The Berlin Conference begins on November 15 with the participation of 13 European governments and the United States as an observer. It ends on February 26, 1885, with the signing of the Act of Berlin, through which the European powers partition Africa. Leopold obtains personal sovereignty over the Congo, which soon becomes the Congo Free State (CFS).

1890-94   Military campaign drives Afro-Arab traders from Zaire and ends slave trade with the Middle East.

1904-05   Reports by missionaries and diplomats in the CFS of forced labor and brutalities by authorities of the Congo Free State lead to public outcry and legislative hearings in Europe and the United States.

1908   Faced with international condemnation of human rights abuses in the CFS, Leopold II agrees to turn it over to the Belgian government and the Belgian parliament reluctantly agrees to annex the territory as a colony on September 9. On November 15, the CFS becomes the Belgian Congo.

1910-25   A large portion of the existing railway network is completed at great cost and with heavy human sacrifice.

1914-45   The economic fortunes of the colony largely follow the world economy, experiencing a boom in the 1920s and a depression in the 1930s. Congolese minerals help the

Allied war efforts and Congolese soldiers fight with the Allies in the African Theater in World Wars I and II.

1945-55   The *évolués* class of educated and primarily urban white-collar workers begins to emerge. Although political activity is banned, évolués gather in "associations" based primarily on ethnic and alumni affiliations. Calls are made for greater equality and advancement opportunities for African workers. Trade unionism begins to emerge.

1957   The colonial authorities allow elections for local urban districts and colonial councils. However, authorities say independence is at least 30 years away.

1958   Belgium holds the Brussels World Fair and brings hundreds of Congolese to Brussels. Charles De Gaulle, speaking in Brazzaville, offers France's colonies autonomy within a French community. The All-Africa People's Conference is held in December in newly independent Ghana. Patrice Lumumba and other Congolese leaders attend and return home fired up with the idea of independence.

1959   At a rally in Leopoldville on January 4, Lumumba calls for independence for the Belgian Congo. A confrontation with police leads to the arrest of Joseph Kasavubu and two weeks of rioting in the capital and several other cities. The colonial authorities agree to hold local elections. Elections are held in December but are boycotted by many of the emerging parties. The Belgian government, in the face of continued unrest, agrees to hold a Round Table Conference in Brussels.

1960   The Round Table Conference begins on January 20 with 45 delegates from various Congolese parties in attendance. The Belgian delegates reluctantly agree to set June 30 as the date for independence. Elections are held on June 25th, but they are inconclusive. Talk of secession is heard in various regions. A compromise is struck through which Kasavubu becomes president and Lumumba becomes prime minister. The Congo becomes independent on June 30. On July 4, the Force Publique mutinies for higher pay and better promotion opportunities. The violence leads to the evacuation of foreigners and the arrival of Belgian paratroopers. The Congolese government, fearful of Belgian occupation, asks the United Nations for military and administrative assistance. On July 11, Katanga secedes, followed by South Kasai. During a political standoff between Kasavubu and Lumumba, Armed Forces Chief of Staff Joseph Mobutu "neutralizes" the government. Lumumba is dismissed on September 5 and is later captured while trying to join supporters in Stanleyville. A College of Commissioners is installed on September 29.

1961   Lumumba and two colleagues are killed on January 17 shortly after arriving in secessionist Elisabethville under Armée Nationale Congolaise (ANC) custody. The assassinations lead to the secession of Orientale and Kivu Provinces. The College of Commissioners is dissolved on February 9 with the formation of the Ileo government. Cyrille Adoula negotiates an end to the secession of South Kasai. He is named prime minister on July 25. UN relief efforts are necessary to aid victims of famine and internecine fighting in Kasai and Katanga. UN Secretary-General Dag Hammarskjöld dies in a plane crash in Katanga on September 17.

1963   Following UN military intervention, the Katanga secession is ended on January 14 and Moïse Tshombe goes into exile.

1964   Tshombe is appointed prime minister at the head of a southern-dominated coalition on July 6. The country's first constitution is passed on August 1. The secessionist People's Republic of the Congo is proclaimed in Stanleyville on September 7 and is recognized by 13 foreign nations. Reports of atrocities by Stanleyville-based soldiers against Congolese and foreign hostages leads to a Belgian paratroop drop on Stanleyville on November 24. Over the next several weeks, the central government regains control over most of eastern Congo. Meanwhile, the Kwilu rebellion led by Pierre Mulele gathers force.

1965   Elections are held in March in which Tshombe's CONACO party makes significant gains. Tshombe is dismissed by Kasavubu on October 13 and Évariste Kimba is named prime minister. Parliament refuses to endorse the designation. An attempt by Joseph Ileo is also thwarted. Amid the political standoff and a resurgence of the eastern rebellion, the military decides to take command on November 24 and installs Mobutu as head of state with powers of decree. The Kwilu rebellion is put down. Mobutu consolidates his power with support from the Binza Group and the Corps des Volontaires de la République.

1966   The Mouvement Populaire de la Révolution (MPR) is formed on April 17. City names are Africanized on May 3. Kimba and three other alleged coup plotters are publicly hanged in Kinshasa on June 2. An army rebellion in Orientale Province is put down by the central authorities.

1967   Union Minière du Haut-Katanga (UMHK) is nationalized on January 2. The N'Sele Manifesto is issued on May 20. An attempt by Katangan Gendarmes and mercenaries to return Tshombe to power by fomenting a rebellion in eastern Congo is thwarted by the central authorities. The second constitution is promulgated on June 24, reducing regional autonomy and granting increased powers to the president. Tshombe is kidnapped on June 30 while on a flight in Spain and is imprisoned in Algeria. Kinshasa hosts the

Organization of African Unity (OAU) summit and Mobutu becomes OAU chairman. Mulele accepts Mobutu's offer of amnesty on September 29, but is killed on October 8 upon returning to Congo. The last eastern rebellion is ended, although the Parti Révolutionnaire du Peuple (PRP) continues to control some territory in Kivu.

1969   Kasavubu dies. Tshombe dies in an Algerian prison on June 29.

1970   Elections are held in November and Mobutu, the sole candidate, is elected president. The MPR is declared the sole political party and supreme institution of the country on December 23.

1971   The Congo becomes the Republic of Zaire on October 27. The three private universities are nationalized following student unrest.

1973   Zaire breaks relations with Israel October 4. Mobutu announces the Zairianization of major foreign-owned companies on November 30. Thirty-one religious publications are banned.

1974   The third constitution is promulgated on August 15. It further centralizes power in the presidency and creates a party-state. Retrocession is decreed on December 30, returning portions of Zairianized farms and companies to private ownership.

1975   Following a drastic fall in copper prices, economic recession sets in and the government begins to fall in arrears on its foreign debt. The Movimento Popular de Libertação de Angola (MPLA) faction that is fighting a civil war for control of Angola takes control of Luanda in June. Zaire, which opposes the MPLA, continues to support two other factions.

1977   Front pour la Libération Nationale du Congo (FLNC) guerrillas enter Shaba Region from bases in Angola on March 8. They advance to the outskirts of Kolwezi but are forced back into Angola by Zairian and Moroccan troops 80 days later. Foreign Minister Nguza Karl-I-Bond and other Lunda leaders are imprisoned and convicted of complicity. Nguza is later pardoned and returned to government. Zaire holds national and local elections in October. Mobutu is elected to a second term on December 2.

1978   FLNC guerrillas attack Kolwezi on May 3 and occupy the town. Reports of looting and killing lead to a paratroop drop by Zairian, French and Belgian troops. They regain control after two weeks and the rebels flee back into Angola. A Pan-African peacekeeping force is established in the region and the government, stung by international criticism of its economic and political policies, enacts some reforms.

1980   Thirteen parliamentarians, led by Étienne Tshisekedi, publish an open letter to Mobutu, urging political and economic reforms and the establishment of a multiparty democracy. Pope John Paul II visits.

1981   Nguza resigns unexpectedly in April and goes into exile. The Zairian government comes under severe criticism in the US and West European legislatures.

1982   Zaire reestablishes diplomatic relations with Israel on May 13. Legislative elections are held on September 18 and 19 in which multiple candidates are allowed. Three-fourths of the incumbents are turned out. The 13 former parliamentarians form a second party, the Union pour la Démocratie et le Progrès Social (UDPS), and are arrested and convicted of treason. Kengo wa Dondo is named prime minister on November 5, charged with fighting corruption in government and imposing economic reforms.

1983   Mobutu proclaims a general amnesty on May 21
            whereby exiled dissidents may return if they cease
            opposition activities. On September 9, following nearly
            a decade of recession and debt arrears caused by low
            copper prices and mismanagement, the government
            announces a monetary reform, floats the currency on
            the free market, and removes overall subsidies on
            petroleum and agricultural products. Annual inflation
            reaches 100 percent. Labor protests are put down.

1984   Mobutu is elected to a third term on July 29. PRP
            guerrillas attack Moba in November demanding the end
            of the Mobutu government. The army reoccupies the
            town two days later.

1985   Zaire celebrates 25 years of independence on June 30.
            Many former exiled dissidents, including Nguza, are
            present. However, PRP guerrillas attack Moba on the
            eve of the celebrations. Annual inflation is reduced to
            20 percent, drawing praise from international creditors.
            The pope pays a second visit.

1986   Following a month-long meeting of the MPR Central
            Committee, the government says economic stabilization
            programs are strangling the economy and announces it
            will limit payments on its foreign debt to 10 percent of
            export revenues and 20 percent of government
            revenues. Kengo is sidelined and the post of prime
            minister is abolished. Responding to persistent criticism
            of Zaire's human rights record, Mobutu announces the
            creation of a ministry of citizens' rights.

1987   Zaire announces a major agreement with the Paris Club
            on May 22. In June, clashes are reported along the
            border with Uganda. Legislative elections are held and
            are dominated by young party cadres because the MPR
            Central Committee has become the primary forum for
            legislative debate.

1988   Tshisekedi is obliged to submit to a psychiatric examination and on February 8 is declared to have a "disturbed personality." On October 1, South African President Pieter Botha meets Mobutu in Gbadolite.

1989   A new economic reform plan is announced and new agreements are reached with the International Monetary Fund (IMF) and World Bank.

1990   The UDPS leads a popular demonstration for multipartyism. In a speech on April 24, Mobutu announces the end of the single-party state and says he is resigning as president of the MPR. He backtracks in a speech on May 3, saying only two additional parties will be allowed. Nevertheless, dozens of opposition parties are formed. Security forces attack a UDPS rally on April 30, killing two. On the night of May 11, soldiers invade dormitories of the Lubumbashi campus. Human rights organizations say as many as 100 students are killed. Protests are staged in Kinshasa on May 28. The United States, Canada and the European Union suspend all non-humanitarian aid. Mobutu pledges no limits on the number of political parties on October 6 and the decree on party registration is passed on November 25. An opposition rally is attacked on November 4 and police kill four during protests over rising food prices. Inflation reaches 81 percent for the year.

1991   The Sacred Union is formed to press for a national conference and the departure of Mobutu. It eventually groups more than 200 opposition parties. Mobutu resumes the presidency of the MPR and announces a National Conference will be allowed. It convenes on August 7, but collapses on August 15 over accreditation disputes and political wrangling. On the night of September 23, soldiers, angry over low and late salaries, loot containers at Ndjili airport. The looting spreads to Kinshasa's commercial district and to some residential areas. Civilians join in. Order is restored on September 25 after the arrival of French and Belgian troops. Thirty people are killed and 10,000 expatriates are evacuated. Damage is estimated at $1 billion. Mobutu names Tshisekedi prime minister on September 29, but dismisses him when he refuses to sign an oath of allegiance to the president. Violence and looting occur from October 21 to 27 in a number of regional cities. Bernadin Mungul Diaka is named prime minister on October 23. The Sacred Union forms a parallel government on October 31. Nguza is named prime minister on November 25 and expelled from the Sacred Union. Inflation reaches 2,154 percent.

1992   Nguza reopens the National Conference on January 17, but closes it two days later saying it is too expensive. Twenty-nine soldiers seize the radio station in Kinshasa on January 22 demanding democracy; the mutiny is quickly crushed. Security forces attack a group of protesters following church on Sunday, February 16, killing 46. The National Conference reconvenes on April 6, declares itself sovereign on the 17th and renames itself the Conférence Nationale Souveraine (CNS). In a victory for the opposition, Archbishop Laurent Monsengwo Pasinya is named chairman on April 21. On August 14, he proposes the Transitional Act aimed at overseeing the transition period and reducing presidential interference in the process. Tshisekedi is elected prime minister on August 15. Mobutu accepts Tshisekedi's appointment on August 19, but his decree makes no mention of the Transitional Act. Inflation accelerates to 4,130 percent. In an attempt to curtail the printing of banknotes to meet government expenses, Tshisekedi names new heads of the central bank and customs collection agency, but these are vetoed by Mobutu. Troops are stationed outside the bank, prevent Tshisekedi from entering his offices, and seal off the CNS. The CNS drafts a constitution that considerably reduces the powers of the president. Mobutu announces he is convening the single-party legislature to draft another constitution more to his liking. The CNS establishes the Haut Conseil de la République (HCR) and dissolves itself on December 6.

1993   The central bank issues new five-million-zaire notes, worth about $1 US each. Tshisekedi condemns them as inflationary. Some merchants refuse to accept them from recently paid soldiers. Troops go on a looting spree on January 28 and 29, battled by troops of the Division Spéciale Présidentielle. More than 100 people, mostly soldiers, are killed, including the French ambassador who is shot while looking out his office window. Tshisekedi is dismissed on February 5 after calling for foreign military assistance in overthrowing Mobutu. Troops surround the legislative chamber on February 24 and hold HCR members hostage until they accept the five-million-zaire banknotes, which they do on the 26th. Mobutu names Tshisekedi's senior advisor Faustin Birindwa prime minister in March, leading to his expulsion from the UDPS. In October, negotiations lead to the merger of the CNS and the MPR parliament into the 745-member Haut Conseil de le République / Parlement de la Transition (HCR/PT). Monetary reform is enacted on October 22. Three million zaires are exchanged for one new zaire (NZ). Annual inflation reaches 2,000 percent.

1994   The presidents of Rwanda and Burundi are killed on April 6 in a suspicious plane crash. Rwandan militias in two months massacre an estimated 500,000 Tutsis and moderate Hutus. The Tutsi-led Rwandese Patriotic Front (RPF) seizes control of Kigali causing two million refugees to flee into neighboring countries. Within a few weeks, more than one million of them arrive in eastern Zaire. Birindwa resigns. Kengo is elected prime minister on June 17, 1994, in a vote contested by Tshisekedi and is charged with combating inflation and reviving the economy. He announces a number of austerity measures including the closing of 64 embassies around the world. The World Bank declares Zaire in default on December 7 and closes its office in Kinshasa. Annual inflation reaches 6,000 percent.

1995   An outbreak of the Ebola virus in March causes 244 deaths. On June 30, the HCR/PT votes to extend the transitional period and postpone national elections until July 9, 1997. A few weeks later Monsengwo is ousted as chairman of the HCR/PT, although he calls the dismissal illegal. Inflation officially is reduced to 382 percent, although prices for basic commodities are disproportionately higher.

1996   On January 8, a cargo plane taking off from Ndolo airport crashes into a crowded market killing 350 people. The four crew members survive. On March 18 the electoral commission is formed and announces national and local elections will be held in May and June 1997, following a constitutional referendum. The UDPS splits over whether to participate in the vote, with Tshisekedi's supporters vowing to boycott. The HCR/PT drafts a new constitution. On August 22, Mobutu undergoes prostate surgery and treatment for cancer in Switzerland. On October 18, rebels of the Alliance des Forces Démocratiques pour la Libération du Congo/Zaïre (AFDL) launch an offensive in Sud-Kivu and capture Bukavu on October 30 and Goma on November 1. Mobutu returns on December 17, shakes up the military high command and reshuffles the cabinet. On December 30, Mobutu signs a decree calling for the constitutional referendum in February.

1997   On January 5, the government introduces new banknotes of up to one million zaires. On January 17, the United Nations and the European Community pledge $250 million to help finance elections. The government announces a counteroffensive on January 20, but rebels capture Kisangani on March 15 despite stiff resistance from government troops and foreign mercenaries. Mobutu dismisses Kengo on March 24 and names Tshisekedi prime minister on April 2. Rebels take Mbuji-Mayi on April 4. A state of emergency is declared on April 5. After rebels take Lubumbashi on April 9, Mobutu dismisses Tshisekedi. He appoints General Bolongo prime minister and General Mahele defense minister on April 11. Kananga and Kolwezi fall on April 12. Kikwit falls on April 29. As rebels approach Kinshasa, Mobutu leaves on May 16 for Togo. Mahele is killed that night at Camp Tshatshi. The rebels enter Kinshasa on May 17. Kabila is sworn in as president on May 29 and pledges to hold elections by April 1999. He announces the country's former name, Congo, will be restored and the zaire will be replaced by the Congolese franc. Reports of massacres lead the United Nations in July to appoint a special investigative team. Fighting erupts in Brazzaville between forces loyal to President Pascal Lissouba and former President Denis Sassou Nguesso. Tensions in Kivu lead to clashes in which thousands are killed. Mobutu dies in a hospital in Rabat, Morocco, on September 7. In October, four months of fighting in Brazzaville peak and artillery shells from the devastated capital land in Kinshasa, killing 21 people. The Kabila government sends troops to Brazzaville. Nguesso forces take control of Brazzaville and, backed by Angolan troops, seize Pointe Noire and consolidate control over most of the country. The Kabila government asks South Africa to extradite exiled Mobutu officials, including 20 generals. The arrest of Kabila's senior military advisor causes a day of shooting on November 28 in which three people are killed. On November 30, the government bans foreign broadcasts on local radio stations but lifts the ban four days later. Kabila announces a reorganization of the military on December 2. A donors conference ends on

December 4 in Brussels pledging to disburse $180 million in frozen aid to help rebuild the economy. On December 5, the ex-director of Air Zaïre goes on trial, the first of 34 detained Mobutu barons facing charges of corruption. Kabila returns from a week-long visit to China on December 23 saying China will be the model for Congolese development. Heavy rains cause flooding in cities along the Congo River, displacing 20,000 residents of Kisangani.

1998   Kabila reshuffles his cabinet on January 3, naming Katangan Governor Gaetan Kakudji interior minister. He also orders officials to return property seized from former officials. Security forces break up a UDPS meeting on January 17. Tshisekedi is arrested on February 12 and banished to his home village. Three newspapers editors are detained for questioning in April after publishing articles critical of the government. In a speech on May 17 marking his first year in power, Kabila reaffirms his pledge to organize a constitutional referendum during his second year in office and lift the ban on political parties. He creates a 300-member transitional assembly which drafts a new constitution later in the year. In late May, the government arrests five ministers and the directors of state electricity, water and oil companies for questioning as part of a corruption investigation. The ministers are sacked in a cabinet reshuffle on June 1. The three editors are released on June 24. The Congolese franc replaces the new zaire beginning June 30. Tshisekedi is released on July 1. Kabila visits Cuba in July. On July 27, Kabila orders 100 Rwandan officers commanding Congolese troops to return home. A new rebellion is launched in eastern Congo on August 2 by Banyamulenge, former Mobutu officials and disaffected Kabila supporters. The rebels take Goma on August 3 and fighting breaks out at a barracks in Kinshasa. Bukavu falls on August 5. Rebels claim to capture the western port of Moanda on August 7 and

Matadi a few days later. Kabila flies to Lubumbashi to meet with southern African leaders and announces a counterattack on August 8. The rebels announce the formation of the Rassemblement Congolais pour la Démocratie (RCD) on August 12 and the broader Coalition Démocratique et Fédéraliste (FRF). They say they want to replace Kabila, whom they accuse of corruption and nepotism. Kisangani falls to the RCD on August 23. Fighting breaks out near Ndjili airport on the outskirts of Kinshasa. Angolan forces help government troops retake Matadi on August 29. Government forces, backed by troops from Zimbabwe and Namibia, drive the rebels from Kinshasa. There are reports of mass lynchings of captured rebels and Tutsi civilians in the capital. In September, Kabila announces he will hold elections by April 1999. Tshisekedi proposes a government of national unity with elections in two years. On November 28, Kabila attends the France-African summit as an acting head of state. There are various attempts to mediate the conflict in the following months, but they are stymied by Kabila's refusal to meet with the rebels.

1999   The RCD, attempting to broaden its support, on January 13 creates a "nationally representative assembly," to act as a parliament in exile, and a government with an eight-person collective presidency. On January 31, Kabila signs a decree allowing political activity, but the UDPS criticizes the requirements for registering political parties as too restrictive. The UN human rights representative returns to Congo on February 16 and after a week-long tour announces there are 20 distinct armed groups in the country. Calls arise for an international peacekeeping force for the Great Lakes region. Kabila forms a new cabinet on March 14, in an attempt to attract opposition leaders into his government, and one week later says he is launching a "national debate" on the country's future.

Political Map of Democratic Republic of the Congo (Zaire)

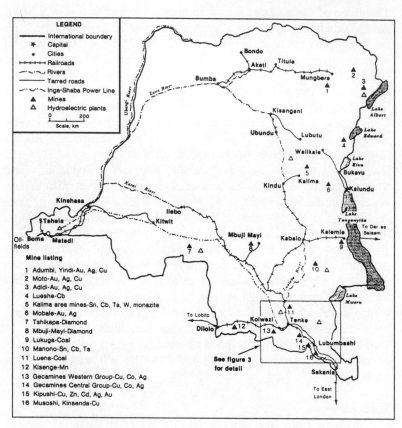

LEGEND

──────── International boundary
✳ Capital
● Cities
├┼┼┼┼┼┤ Railroads
‒‒‒‒‒ Rivers
──────── Tarred roads
‒‒‒‒ Inga-Shaba Power Line
▲ Mines
△ Hydroelectric plants

0   200
Scale, km

Mine listing

1 Adumbi, Yindi-Au, Ag, Cu
2 Moto-Au, Ag, Cu
3 Adidi-Au, Ag, Cu
4 Lueshe-Cb
5 Kalima area mines-Sn, Cb, Ta, W, monazite
6 Mobale-Au, Ag
7 Tshikapa-Diamond
8 Mbuji-Mayi-Diamond
9 Lukuga-Coal
10 Manono-Sn, Cb, Ta
11 Luena-Coal
12 Kisenge-Mn
13 Gecamines Western Group-Cu, Co, Ag
14 Gecamines Central Group-Cu, Co, Ag
15 Kipushi-Cu, Zn, Cd, Ag, Au
16 Musoshi, Kinsenda-Cu

Map of Congolese Mines and Infrastructure

xxxviii

INTRODUCTION

The shape of Congo/Zaire has often been compared to that of a heart. And although the physiological comparison may be debated, there is no doubt that it is the heart of Africa. Its 2,344,895 square kilometers of territory cover one-half of the Congo Basin, an area with some of the heaviest rainfall in the world. The basin is drained by the mightiest river in Africa, the Congo River, which is second in volume of flowing water only to South America's Amazon River. Because of its location, Congo/Zaire has long been considered one of the most geopolitically strategic countries in Africa. It borders nine countries: Angola (including the enclave of Cabinda), Zambia, Tanzania, Burundi, Rwanda, Uganda, Sudan, Central African Republic, and Congo/Brazzaville. It also borders the lakes of the Great Rift Valley, which form the headwaters of the White Nile River. Congo/Zaire possesses great natural resources. The hydroelectric potential of the Congo River and its tributaries is 100,000 MW, or more than that of the rest of Africa combined. Its mineral wealth is also considered of strategic importance. At its peak, it produced one-third of the world's cobalt (used to produce super-alloys), a major portion of the world's industrial diamonds and 7 percent of its copper. In addition, environmentalists said Congo/Zaire was one of the largest remaining repositories of primary, tropical rainforest in the world and contained significant portions of the world's remaining elephants, gorillas and wildfowl, as well as hundreds of thousands of species of animal and plant life still unknown to science.

Topography

Ranging from five degrees north of the equator to 14 degrees south of the equator, a great deal of Congolese territory is characterized by the hot, humid climate of the Congo Basin, where an average of more than 2,000 mm of rain falls each year. The low-lying terrain generally contains relatively poor soils but the region is rich in game, fish and hydroelectric potential. In the southeast, the terrain is characterized by more temperate savannas and woodlands which allow the cultivation of maize and millet as well as the raising of cattle. Cattle raising is not possible in the basin because of the presence of the tsetse fly and numerous parasites. Woodlands and savannas also cover the northernmost

1

parts of the territory. Fertile, densely populated forests cover the eastern highlands, where the temperate climate allows the growing of seasonal crops. The terrain lying to the west of the capital, Kinshasa, is low, flat plains, an ancient seabed that is relatively fertile and in the westernmost Bas-Congo Region far enough away from the parasites of the rainforest to allow animal husbandry. Several mountain ranges cross the territory: the Ruwenzori Mountain range in the northeast, the highest range in Africa; the Virunga Mountains in the eastern Kivu regions; and the Crystal Mountains in Bas-Congo. The mountains are largely responsible for the three stretches of cataracts that truncate the 3,000 navigable kilometers of the Congo River: between Kongolo and Kindu in Maniema Region, between Ubundu and Kisangani in Haut-Zaïre Region, and between Kinshasa and Matadi in Bas-Congo Region. Despite the cataracts, which disrupt transportation between the Atlantic Ocean and most of the country, the 14,000 km of navigable waterways in the country provide a natural transportation system that may be used year-round. Railways were constructed between the 1890s and 1930s to circumvent the unnavigable portions of the river system and, during the first half of the 20th century, 140,000 km of roads were constructed to provide a system to bring agricultural and mineral products to market.

Early History
    Little is known about the early inhabitants of Congo and archeological research has been hindered in many parts of the territory by the rainforest. However, anthropologists believe the first humans to arrive in the region were Bantu-speaking peoples from West Africa who moved into the western and southwestern parts of the Congo Basin area beginning in 1000 BC. Over the next 2,000 years they are believed to have spread throughout the basin and toward the Indian Ocean and southern Africa. Migrations and counter-migrations helped produce the considerable mixture of West African, North-Central African and East-Central African strains of Bantu-speakers that are found today. Sudanic and Nilotic clusters of ethnic groups are believed to have begun migrating into northern Congo in AD 1500. They intermingled with Bantu-speaking groups in the areas, creating a mosaic of ethnic cultures. Meanwhile, the great kingdoms of the Kongo, Kuba, Luba and Lunda, with established hierarchies of paramount kings and lesser, tribute-paying kings and chiefs, began to rise in western and southern Congo. It was these kingdoms that the European explorers encountered when they

began arriving after the Portuguese explorer Diogo Cão sailed up the Congo River in 1483 and encountered the Kongo people. The Kongo, unlike some of the peoples further inland, welcomed the European visitors. The reigning king was converted to Christianity, becoming Affonso I, and the kingdom exchanged ambassadors with several courts in Europe. The Kongo also welcomed missionaries and traders. The former arrived seeking to save souls. The latter came at first seeking gold and silver but eventually settling for ivory and slaves in exchange for cloth, manufactured goods and luxuries brought from Europe. The Europeans ventured a certain distance into the interior, but found the terrain and people there inhospitable and sometimes dangerous. As a result, they tended to prefer to trade with African middlemen who brought goods from the interior. Meanwhile, Africans and Arabs based in east Africa began developing overland trading routes into eastern Congo. In the late 1600s, the greed of the traders, warfare between competing tribes, and fighting among the European powers led to a decline of the European presence. The abolishment of slavery in the western hemisphere in the mid-1800s also contributed to the decline, although the trade continued in the western part of the territory until the 1880s and in the eastern part of the territory until the late 1890s.

Congo Free State
European interest revived in the mid-1800s and the writings of explorers such as David Livingstone, Richard Burton, John Speke, Samuel Baker and Henry Morton Stanley whetted the appetites of European political leaders for markets and sources of revenue. One of the wiliest of the leaders at the time was Belgium's King Leopold II, whose dreams and ambitions far exceeded the boundaries of his relatively small kingdom. Under the mantle of associations like the International African Association and the Survey Committee for the Upper Congo, which espoused noble goals such as the exploration of central Africa and the abolition of slavery, Leopold financed a number of expeditions into central Africa to explore the Congo Basin and negotiate trading agreements with local chiefs. As a result, when 13 European governments, with the United States as an observer, met in Berlin in November 1884 in an effort to "negotiate an end to international rivalry over Africa and promote civilization and trade on the continent," Leopold was able to produce more than 400 treaties signed in his name with chiefs primarily along the Congo River. The treaties, the king's influence through the associations, and the preoccupation of Britain, France

and Germany with the more accessible coastal African territories, led the powers to agree to accept the Congo as the personal domain of Leopold, a decision codified in the Act of Berlin on February 26, 1885.

Shortly thereafter the Congo Free State (CFS) was formed and an administrative system was established to govern and develop the territory and "civilize" its indigenous inhabitants. Leopold decided, however, that the cost of developing the territory should be born by the territory itself. Consequently, the CFS granted European companies exclusive rights to trade and operate on large tracts of land in exchange for a percentage of the profits. More significantly a labor law was passed that allowed the companies and CFS agents to forcibly employ indigenous laborers or oblige them to provide a certain amount of marketable produce, particularly rubber, as payment of a "state tax." The labor law was abused to such an extent that entire villages were forced into bondage and the atrocities committed by agents of the CFS against groups that failed to meet their quotas raised a storm of international protest. The outcry led a reluctant Belgian government to annex the territory in 1908 and the CFS became the Belgian Congo.

Belgian Congo

Under the Colonial Charter established by the Belgian parliament, the territory became a colony of the government. The king remained sovereign, although his decrees had to be countersigned by the minister of colonies, who was answerable to parliament. Despite avowed intentions to improve human rights abuses in the Congo, the harsh labor laws persisted until the 1920s and numerous rebellions, harshly put down, occurred. In addition, political activity was prohibited and a policy of paternalism evolved that regarded Congolese essentially as children, well-intentioned and potentially good citizens but needing supervision and a firm hand. During the two world wars, Belgium was occupied by German forces. Congolese material contributed to the Allied war effort and Congolese soldiers fought with distinction in the African Theater.

Following World War II, colonial authorities and private companies began to regard Congolese labor as a resource to be developed and cultivated and many of the harsher labor practices were abolished. Basic literacy was encouraged and the colonial government subsidized many mission schools. Training for Congolese, however, was aimed primarily at filling semiskilled labor or clerical jobs. As a result, secondary education was reserved for a small minority and the colony had no university until 1954. In addition, contact with Africans from other colonies was considered dangerous. As a result, few Congolese were allowed to travel outside the colony until the Brussels Worlds Fair of 1958, when the Belgian government, eager to display its good works in the colony, brought hundreds of them to Belgium.

Congolese were prohibited from forming political organizations, but in the early 1950s, they began forming alumni associations and ethnically based "interest" groups. In addition, Congolese workers began organizing and calling for pay and advancement opportunities equal to those granted expatriate workers. Some Congolese began advancing their views in local periodicals. These were avidly read by the Congolese urban elite. They were tolerated for the most part by the authorities who felt their audience to be too small to matter. These activities were encouraged by missionaries and "progressive" Belgian political leaders who argued that the Congolese should be preparing to assume control of their country one day. However, the activities were opposed by other Belgian leaders and many colonial administrators, who felt they were premature. For example, a report in the late 1950s that suggested independence might be possible in 30 years was considered daring.

Events began to move rapidly in 1958 following French President Charles de Gaulle's offer of autonomy to France's colonies and the convening of the All-Africa People's Conference, held in newly independent Ghana. Several Congolese leaders, including a fiery orator named Patrice Lumumba, attended the Accra conference and upon their return began calling openly for independence. During a rally in Leopoldville on January 4, 1959, a confrontation with security forces erupted into violence that led to two weeks of rioting. The Belgian government, in an effort to calm emotions, offered to move toward limited forms of self-government in the colony and elections were held for local councils in December of that year. The campaign for the elections led to the emergence of numerous parties, many of them based on ethnic associations. However, some of the most influential parties boycotted the elections. In the face of continued unrest, the Belgian government called for a Round Table Conference in January 1960 to discuss some form of autonomy for the colony. Forty-five Congolese delegates from various parties attended. However, they surprised the Belgian delegation by making two demands before the conference: first, that a date for independence be set at the conference and secondly, that all of the conference's resolutions be binding. Under pressure from both domestic and foreign sources, the Belgian government gave in. As a result, independence was set for June 30, five months away, and the Fundamental

Law was hastily drawn up to serve as a temporary constitution for the new nation.

As independence approached, political activity blossomed and more than 100 political parties were formed. Attempts to form nationally based parties foundered on ethnic tensions and personality conflicts and the larger coalitions splintered. Ethnic tensions degenerated into fighting in Kasai and Katanga Provinces and caused friction in the political parties and the ranks of the army. Elections were held in May 1960 but no single party received a majority. A compromise was struck whereby Joseph Kasavubu of the Alliance des Bakongo (ABAKO) party was elected to the ceremonial office of president and Lumumba of the Mouvement National Congolais (MNC) was elected prime minister. The election of Kasavubu ended talk of secession in the ABAKO stronghold of Bas-Congo, but southern-based parties, particularly the Confédération des Associations Katangaises (CONAKAT), led by Moïse Tshombe, left Leopoldville in anger over its relatively small representation in the Lumumba government.

Independence

The Belgian Congo became the Republic of the Congo on June 30, 1960, as many expatriate technicians and professionals were leaving the country for their annual summer vacations. Five days later elements of the army, angry over low pay and the lack of promotion opportunities, mutinied. The looting and violence that followed made headlines around the world, caused the evacuation of most of the remaining foreigners in the Congo, and led to the occupation by Belgian paratroopers of a number of Congolese cities. Fearful that the Belgian government intended to retake control of its former colony, the Congolese government asked the United Nations for security and administrative assistance. The United Nations subsequently began its first, and for 30 years only, "police action" in Africa. Following a series of resolutions, the UN Secretariat sent troops and police to reestablish security in the country and administrators, judges and technicians to reactivate government operations. In addition, relief supplies were sent to refugees who had fled famine and internecine fighting in Kasai and Katanga.

The mutiny by the army brought a pay raise and promotions. Master sergeants, the highest-ranking Congolese soldiers at the time, overnight became colonels. One of these, a bright former journalist named Joseph-Désiré Mobutu, was appointed army chief of staff. Meanwhile, Tshombe, whose CONAKAT party had swept the provincial elections in Katanga, led Katanga into secession and, encouraged by foreign commercial interests, declared the Independent State of Katanga on July 11. Albert Kalonji, a southern leader who had split from the MNC, declared South Kasai an independent state.

At the same time, the central government was finding it difficult to function. The Fundamental Law had established numerous checks and balances in government but had failed to specify the division of powers between the presidency and the parliament. On September 5, Kasavubu dismissed Lumumba after he threatened to seek military aid from Soviet-bloc countries to put down the secessions. However, Lumumba refused to accept his dismissal and his cabinet voted to "dismiss" Kasavubu.

The constitutional crisis led Mobutu to "neutralize" all political activity and form a College of Commissioners, composed of young intellectuals and technocrats, to run the government. Lumumba was placed under house arrest. In November, he escaped and was heading to Orientale Province to join his supporters, led by former Vice Prime Minister Antoine Gizenga, when he was captured and imprisoned in a military camp in Bas-Congo. In a move that was never fully explained, the Congolese government ordered Lumumba and two senior officials flown to Elisabethville. Subsequent investigations revealed the prisoners were severely beaten by their army guards during the flight and were killed shortly after their arrival in Elisabethville on January 17, 1961. Lumumba's assassination halted any further overtures by the Congolese government to the Soviet bloc, but provoked an international outcry and led to the secession of Orientale Province and parts of Kivu Province.

In February 1961, the College of Commissioners handed power back to a civilian government headed by Joseph Ileo. Kalonji ended the South Kasai secession and joined the government. Gizenga and several MNC leaders were also named to the cabinet but did not immediately leave Stanleyville. In December 1962, UN troops took military action against foreigners believed to be aiding the Katangan government and the Katangan secession ended on January 14, 1963.

Tshombe went into exile but returned to head a southern-dominated government in July 1964. The United Nations ended its action in the Congo that month. However, the Stanleyville group consolidated its hold on eastern Congo and gained control of more than one-third of Congolese territory. It declared the People's Republic of the Congo in September and received diplomatic recognition from 13 countries. On November 24, 1964, amid reports of widespread atrocities committed against foreigners and the local population in the east, Belgian paratroopers dropped on Stanleyville from US military transport planes. They recaptured the city but not before 200 foreigners and several thousand Congolese "hostages" had been killed. The intervention prompted further indignation among supporters of the Stanleyville government and a rebellion began in Kwilu Province that included terrorist attacks in Leopoldville.

Ascendance of Mobutu

A constitution was promulgated in 1964 and elections were held in 1965. Tshombe's Confédération Nationale des Associations Congolaises (CONACO) party made sizable gains. Kasavubu dismissed the Tshombe government in October 1965. Like Lumumba before him, however, Tshombe and his supporters in parliament refused to accept the dismissal and blocked the appointment of his designated successors, Évariste Kimba and subsequently Ileo.

Amid the latest constitutional crisis, the 14 senior military commanders on November 24, 1965, took over the government. The coup d'etat was carried out at dawn without bloodshed and Mobutu was named head of state with powers of decree. During the following months, civilian political institutions were stripped of their powers, the army was purged and military operations were launched to regain control of territory still under rebel control. In April 1966, the Mouvement Populaire de la Révolution (MPR) was launched and eventually proclaimed the sole legal party. Political power was gradually centralized by decree in the presidency and codified in the Constitution of 1967. Many of the early political leaders accepted the new regime. A number of them, however, did not and went into exile or were imprisoned.

By 1967, the Mobutu government had regained control over most of the territory. It began a program called "Authenticity" aimed at abolishing tribalism and regionalism and developing a sense of nationhood among the people. Under Authenticity, former colonial names were changed to "authentic" African ones. The Congo was renamed "Zaire" and citizens exchanged their Christian names for Zairian ones. In addition, European-style dress was discouraged and Zairian fashions were promoted. Efforts were made to rewrite Zairian history from a Zairian point of view and develop political institutions that better reflected traditional patterns of leadership. The Constitution of 1974 codified the decrees of previous years, centralizing government in the presidency and creating a party-state.

Economic Centralization

Historically, the Congolese economy, based at first on agriculture and subsequently on mineral exports, had always tended to follow the business cycles of the world economy. It grew in the 1920s, experienced severe depression in the 1930s, and rebounded following World War II. With the sudden rise of mineral prices following the first Arab oil embargo of 1973, the Zairian economy experienced a rapid expansion which led to heavy borrowing and spending on international markets. In November 1973, at the height of the economic boom and amid popular support for Authenticity, the Zairian government nationalized all businesses with annual revenues of more than one million zaires ($2 million US) and all foreign-owned businesses in certain strategic sectors. The large mining consortia had already been nationalized as early as 1967. "Zairianization" led to a flight of foreign capital. In addition, the nationalized establishments were redistributed primarily on the basis of political connections rather than business acumen. As a result, productivity declined.

In 1974, the price for copper, Zaire's major export, plummeted to one-third its level of the previous year. Government revenues tumbled and the government was obliged to borrow increasingly large sums to cover a growing balance-of-payments deficit. "Retrocession" was decreed in December 1974, which allowed up to 40 percent and later up to 60 percent foreign ownership in Zairianized businesses. Despite these and other incentives, foreign capital was slow to return. In the meantime, accusations of mismanagement and corruption in government were growing. The Zairian government signed a number of economic stabilization agreements with the International Monetary Fund (IMF), but for the most part it was unable to meet its goals. Annual inflation reached 100 percent. Production continued to fall and foreign exchange became scarce enough on occasion to hinder production at the state-owned mining companies, which provided more than one-half of government revenues.

Shaba Insurrections

Amid this background of economic difficulties and political centralization, the first insurrection occurred against the Mobutu government since the end of the post-independence rebellions. On March 8,

1977, guerrillas of the Front pour la Libération Nationale du Congo (FLNC) invaded southern Shaba Region from bases in Angola and over a period of several weeks marched to the outskirts of Kolwezi which, after Lubumbashi, was the most important mining center in the country. The Zairian army initially put up little resistance and only with the aid of Moroccan troops was it able to drive the guerrillas back into Angola 80 days later. The incursion focused world attention on the Zairian government's political and economic problems. It led to a degree of political liberalization and the launching of the Mobutu Plan for economic revival. The incursion also led to new purges of the army, the arrest of several prominent leaders from Shaba, including then-Foreign Minister Nguza Karl-I-Bond, and renewed efforts to induce exiled dissidents to return home.

In May 1978 the FLNC attacked again. This time, however, instead of marching through the sparsely populated countryside of southwestern Shaba, the guerrillas infiltrated Kolwezi and in a surprise attack seized the town and stopped work at the mines. The guerrillas then went on a looting spree. Amid reports of killings and atrocities, a force of Zairian, French and Belgian paratroopers landed on Kolwezi and nearby towns and drove the guerrillas out. Two hundred foreigners and 1,000 Zairians were killed during the two-week occupation. Work at the mines, however, quickly resumed. A Pan-African peacekeeping force, composed of troops from Morocco, Senegal and Togo, was formed and efforts were made to address some of the grievances of the local population, which to a certain degree had supported the FLNC. In the same year, an insurrection also occurred in Idiofa, in Bandundu Region. It was harshly put down and 14 village chiefs were publicly executed.

Political Developments

The Zairian government began a concerted effort to improve its image abroad. The effort was hampered by accusations of authoritarianism, corruption and human rights violations leveled by exiled Zairians and by some members of the US Congress and Belgian and French parliaments. However, with the upsurge of fighting in Chad, Ethiopia, Somalia, Western Sahara, Namibia and Angola, public attention was diverted elsewhere. Meanwhile, the Zairian government made an uneasy truce with the government in Angola, which it had opposed during the Angolan civil war and which it suspected of backing the FLNC. The truce led to the establishment of diplomatic relations between the two neighbors in 1978 and an agreement not to support each other's dissidents.

The advent of the Reagan administration in 1981 and its focus on combating the Soviet "evil empire" brought greater appreciation for Zaire's staunch pro-Western stance and less concern for internal policies. And after the departure of the Carter administration, which had sharply criticized Mobutu's authoritarianism and human rights record, some of the political reforms began to be circumvented. Nevertheless, legislative elections were held in September 1982 in which multiple candidates were allowed within the MPR party and three-fourths of the incumbents were turned out. By that time, however, Zaire had become a party-state. The Central Committee of the MPR had assumed most of the legislature's role as the primary government body for consultation and debate and the legislature, known as the Legislative Council, had evolved into a body that met primarily to approve party initiatives. Under a system which had been evolving since the early 1970s, the Political Bureau, consisting of a score of trusted Mobutu collaborators, assumed policymaking functions and undertook most legal initiatives. The Executive Council of high commissioners, or ministers, became primarily an administrative body, equivalent to a ministerial cabinet. And the Judicial Council, composed of senior judicial officials and Supreme Court members, became a politicized organization, the independence of which was frequently questioned. Mobutu was elected to a third term in July 1984 by 99 percent of the vote in elections which were rife with irregularities but were accepted by the international community.

Some political dissidence continued. Most of it was based outside the country and most of it was pacifist, except for the Parti de Libération Congolaise (PLC), which in the late 1980s staged sporadic attacks in northeastern Zaire from bases along the Ugandan border. Two groups, however, were active within Zaire. The most notable was a group of 13 parliamentarians which in 1980 issued an open letter to Mobutu calling for a multiparty system. Members of this group in 1982 formed a second party, the Union pour la Démocratie et le Progrès Social (UDPS), which by law was an act of treason. They were arrested, convicted and sentenced to lengthy prison terms. They were amnestied the following year but, when they refused to cease their activities, were sent into internal exile. Over the next few years, they were imprisoned and released a number of times. The second group, the Parti Révolutionnaire du Peuple (PRP), consisted of guerrillas who split from the Gizenga regime in Stanleyville in 1964 and established control over a remote portion of mountainous territory in northern Shaba and Sud-Kivu near Lake Tanganyika. The PRP seized four foreign students in Tanzania in 1975 and held them for a number of months. It also staged attacks on the port town of Moba in November 1984 and June 1985. These attacks, quickly repelled by the Zairian army, appeared intended primarily to embarrass the government.

In 1986, the government acknowledged human rights abuses had occurred and announced the creation of a ministerial-level post, State Commissioner for Citizens Rights, to attend to complaints of abuses of personal freedoms. However, the office was largely ineffectual. Elections for the Legislative Council were held in 1987, but because of the predominance of the MPR Central Committee, they attracted few influential politicians and were contested primarily by young party cadres.

Economic Decline

Although political reforms were rolled back during the 1980s, attempts at economic reform continued intermittently. In the mid-1980s, faced with continued inflation, high indebtedness and low productivity, the Zairian government made its first significant move to liberalize the economy. In September 1983, the currency was floated on the free market, ending 23 years of profiteering on the parallel market, where the currency sometimes traded at rates as low as 15 percent of the official exchange rate. Overall subsidies on petroleum and agricultural products were ended and private participation was allowed in the mining, air transportation and diamond industries. In addition, government budget deficits were reduced, imports were slashed and greater efforts were made to service the foreign debt, which had surpassed the annual gross domestic product. The measures impressed the international economic community but also caused severe recession in the country. Real purchasing power fell drastically, affecting all but the wealthiest. The measures caused some labor unrest and many Zairians expressed concern over the declining ability of the government to provide health, educational and social services.

In October 1986, following a month-long meeting of the Central Committee, the Zairian government announced it could no longer abide by IMF stabilization programs, which it said were "strangling" the economy. The government said it no longer would devote 50 percent of revenues to servicing its $4.5 billion foreign debt and would henceforth limit servicing to 10 percent of export revenues or 20 percent of government revenues. The move to peg foreign debt repayments to export revenues was unprecedented in Africa. Peru had taken similar steps in 1985 that had virtually ended new infusions of foreign capital. However, many foreign donors initially expressed understanding for Zaire's situation and what they called its "heroic" effort to redress its economy. During the late 1980s, Zaire's economic situation worsened. Although gross domestic production grew by 1 to 2 percent per year, per capita production declined because of a population growth rate of more than 3 percent. The government failed to meet requirements for a series of stabilization agreements with the IMF, primarily targeted at reducing the deficit and controlling inflation. It also fell further behind in servicing its external debt, leading the IMF to declare it in "noncompliance" and suspend its drawing rights in 1989. Inflationary pressure rose during the period, as the government increasingly resorted to printing money to pay the salaries of soldiers and civil servants.

Return of Multipartyism

In the late 1980s, a number of Francophone West African nations made moves toward abandoning the single-party political systems which had been widely adopted across the continent in the 1970s. The moves came amid pressure from Western donors and a decline of military dictatorships around the world. French President François Mitterrand expressed the mood publicly when he announced during the French-African summit at Le Baule in July 1990 that henceforth France would link development assistance to progress on political reform. Several West African nations held national conferences. Opposition groups made inroads in Benin and Niger, but were defeated in Gabon and Cameroon.

Mobutu, under pressure at home and abroad to institute democratic reforms, announced the end of single-party rule in a speech on April 24, 1990, and said he was resigning as head of the MPR. A number of parties, including the UDPS, announced their intention to register and many leading politicians announced they were leaving the MPR to form their own parties. Mobutu backtracked in a speech on May 3, saying only two additional parties would be allowed, but his remarks were largely ignored. On October 6, following months of demonstrations, Mobutu pledged that there would be no limits to the number of parties and the decree on registration of new parties was passed November 25.

National Conference
The opposition began to focus its efforts on pressing the government to hold a national conference to draft a new constitution and prepare national elections. An opposition alliance called the Sacred Union was formed, led by the UDPS, the Parti Démocrate et Social Chrétien (PDSC), and the Union des Fédéralistes et des Républicains Indépendants (UFERI). It began pressing for political reforms through a series of popular demonstrations and labor strikes. By mid-1991, more than 200 parties had joined the alliance. Many critics accused Mobutu of encouraging the proliferation of opposition parties and splinter groups within them in a maneuver to fragment the opposition, a practice that came to be called "multi-Mobutism."

In April 1991, Mobutu agreed to hold a national conference and named Crispin Mulumba Lukoji prime minister to organize it. The conference opened on August 7, 1991, but quickly degenerated into chaos as nearly 8,000 delegates laid claim to the 2,800 seats. Conference leaders sought to settle the conflicting claims over accreditation, and the generous per diem that came with it, through vetting committees. However, the Sacred Union boycotted the conference, saying its leadership was controlled by Mobutu. The conference collapsed on August 15, causing a rising sense of frustration among the general population.

On the night of September 23, 1991, elements of the airborne brigade mutinied over low pay and salary arrears and began looting containers at the international airport on the outskirts of Kinshasa. Over the next 36 hours, the looting spread to the downtown commercial district and some wealthy suburbs. Thirty people were killed in the violence, which caused an estimated $1 billion in damage and the collapse of many businesses. French and Belgian troops were sent to evacuate 10,000 expatriates. Between October 21 and 27, similar incidents occurred in a number of regional cities, including Lubumbashi, Kolwezi, Kisangani and Mbuji-Mayi. Human rights organizations estimated the overall death toll at 250 people.

Embarrassed by the violence that had severely shaken his authority and brought yet another foreign military intervention, Mobutu named one of the leading opposition figures, Étienne Tshisekedi of the UDPS, prime minister on September 29. However, he dismissed Tshisekedi two weeks later after the latter refused to sign the customary oath of allegiance to the president and, in an interview with a Belgian newspaper, called Mobutu a "monster." Mobutu named Bernadin Mungul Diaka prime minister on October 23 and the Sacred Union formed a parallel government, leading to months of political stalemate. Another prominent opposition leader, Jean Nguza Karl-I-Bond, was named prime minister on November 25, leading to the expulsion of the UFERI from the Sacred Union. Nguza reopened the national conference on January 17, 1992, but closed it a few days later, saying it was costing too much money.

After weeks of political wrangling, the national conference was reconvened on April 6. In what was viewed as a victory by the opposition, it renamed itself the Conférence Nationale Souveraine (CNS) on April 17 and declared that henceforth its decisions would be legally binding, a resolution which was never acknowledged by Mobutu. The archbishop of Kisangani, Laurent Monsengwo Pasinya, was elected chairman on April 21. Combining a talent for political compromise with considerable parliamentary skills, Monsengwo pushed and cajoled the often unruly delegates through a broad agenda of topics, including the principles governing a future central government and a new constitution. In August 1992, Monsengwo drafted the Transitional Act to govern the transitional period and the Compromis Politique Global (CPG), which stated that no organ of state could be used to undermine the authority of another. It was a move aimed at neutralizing the military, which had been used on numerous occasions to intimidate the delegates and break up opposition rallies.

Tshisekedi was elected prime minister on August 15. Mobutu ratified his nomination on August 19 but made no mention of the Transitional Act. Confrontation between Mobutu and Tshisekedi began almost immediately. Tshisekedi, citing a need to put the country's economic house in order, sought to replace the governor of the central bank and the head of the customs collection office, who were viewed as conduits for unlimited funds to the president and his colleagues. Mobutu refused to accept the dismissals and stationed troops around central bank headquarters.

During the following months, the CNS adopted a number of resolutions that reinstated the flag, national anthem, name and political system established by the Constitution of 1964 and in principle called for a return to the Congo that existed prior to the Mobutu coup. As the draft constitution began to take shape, however, Mobutu declared his opposition to it and convened the MPR parliament, elected in 1987 but suspended in 1990 as part of the democratic transition, to draft an alternate document. As the standoff intensified, troops stationed around the bureau of the prime minister barred Tshisekedi from entering his office and sealed the People's Palace where the CNS met. Nevertheless, the CNS completed its work. It formed the Haut Conseil de la République (HCR) to act as a transitional parliament, with Monsengwo as its chairman, and on December 6 disbanded itself.

Economic Collapse

The confrontation between the Tshisekedi government and the presidency was also intensifying over economic policy. In the early 1990s, due to mismanagement and the political uncertainties of the democratic transition, Zaire's economic problems reached crisis proportions. Inflation, which had reached 81 percent in 1990, rose to 2,154 percent in 1991, due largely to the enormous number of banknotes issued in higher and higher denominations to pay the salaries of soldiers and civil servants. Counterfeiting also flourished. Moreover, an estimated two-thirds of the diamond trade was being conducted outside official channels. By 1993, the value of the currency, the zaire, plummeted to a rate of five million zaires to one US dollar.

In January 1993, the central bank issued a new banknote of five million zaires. Tshisekedi called it inflationary and urged his supporters to reject it. When merchants in Kinshasa refused to accept the notes from recently paid soldiers, the latter went on a looting spree on January 28-29. Members of the presidential guard tried to suppress the rioting, leading to clashes in which an estimated 100 people, mostly soldiers but also including the French ambassador, were killed. The violence affected a large portion of what remained of the economically productive sector. From 1990 to 1992, gross domestic product declined nearly 25 percent and urban unemployment rose from 20 to 80 percent. The government decreed monetary reform on October 22, 1993, creating the "nouveau zaire" which was exchanged for three million old zaires and initially was valued at about $1 US.

Stalemate over Democratic Transition

Tshisekedi was dismissed on February 5, 1992, after calling for foreign military assistance to overthrow Mobutu. On February 24, troops surrounded the People's Palace and for two days held delegates of the HCR hostage until they accepted the five-million-zaire notes. Mobutu, capitalizing on dissatisfaction among moderate opposition leaders over Tshisekedi's hardline policies, appointed as prime minister Faustin Birindwa, Tshisekedi's senior economic advisor. The hardline opposition refused to accept Tshisekedi's dismissal and continued to view his as the legitimate government. Foreign donors, led by Belgium, France and the United States, began a policy of diplomatically isolating Mobutu and members of his government. The political standoff, characterized by two rival governments, lasted until early 1994, when negotiations led to the merger of the HCR and the MPR parliament into what was named the Haut Conseil de la République / Parlement de la Transition (HCR / PT). Foreign donors, disturbed by the declining authority of the central government and increasingly desperate living conditions of most citizens, pushed for a compromise between Mobutu and the opposition. When Tshisekedi refused to negotiate with Mobutu, they backed the election by the HCR / PT of Léon Kengo wa Dondo as prime minister on June 17. Kengo had served as prime minister in the 1980s and his economic reforms had achieved some success before they were overturned. However, his election was dismissed as illegal by the hardline opposition.

Following his election, Kengo announced a number of austerity measures, including the closing of 64 Zairian embassies around the world and the privatization of a number of government-owned corporations. He was allowed to name the governor of the central bank and sought to halt the unofficial printing of banknotes and the extraofficial marketing of diamonds. When Kengo took office, annual inflation was estimated at 6,000 percent. In 1995, it declined to 382 percent, largely at the expense of average Zairians who, if they worked at all, earned a wage of less than $15 per month.

Crisis in Eastern Zaire

Zaire made the front pages of international newspapers in mid-1994, when more than one million Rwandan refugees arrived in eastern Zaire after fleeing genocide and the takeover of the Rwandan government by the Tutsi-led Rwandese Patriotic Front (RPF). The RPF takeover caused France to send troops to southern Rwanda, using Kisangani as a staging area. And the flight of the Rwandan refugees created a humanitarian crisis. In August 1995, the Zairian government announced its intention to expel the Rwandan refugees, saying they were creating too large a burden on the local population in the region. The decision met with loud approval in the Zairian press, but except for one attempt late in the year, it was not implemented. In January, however, the government began closing certain refugee camps which, it said, were being used by leaders of the deposed Rwandan government to stage attacks in Rwanda.

Growing tensions in the region led to an offensive in October 1996 by the Alliance des Forces Démocratiques pour la Libération du Congo/Zaïre (AFDL). The offensive, led by Zairian Tutsis and supported by Tutsis in neighboring countries, caused most of the Rwandan refugees to return home. However, an estimated 100,000 hardline opponents of the RPF and their families moved deeper into Congo/Zaire, away from the border area. The AFDL by December had seized a 500-km stretch of Zairian territory along the border, including the cities of Bukavu and Goma. Mobutu, who had undergone surgery for prostate cancer in Switzerland on August 22, returned home December 17, reorganized the army high command, and reshuffled the cabinet. He also signed a decree authorizing a constitutional referendum in February 1997 which called for elections in May and June 1997.

However, the AFDL continued to advance, encouraged by the weakness of the Zairian armed forces and the vacuum of political leadership in Kinshasa. Its troops were supported by fighters from Rwanda, Uganda and Burundi, and subsequently by Angola and the Katangan Gendarmes which had been behind the Shaba incursions in the 1970s. The Zairian army, backed by Serb mercenaries, attempted to make a major stand at Kisangani but collapsed, allowing the rebels to take the city on March 15. In an effort to draw the opposition to his side, Mobutu again appointed Tshisekedi prime minister on April 2, but dismissed him after the AFDL took Mbuji-Mayi on April 4 and Lubumbashi on April 9. Negotiations were hastily announced, but neither Mobutu nor AFDL leader Laurent Kabila appeared anxious to talk. South African President Nelson Mandela brought the two together on a ship moored at Pointe-Noire in Congo/Brazzaville in May, but by then the AFDL had taken Kikwit and were advancing on the capital.

Post-Mobutu

Mobutu and his entourage left Kinshasa on May 16 for Togo and subsequently Morocco. AFDL forces entered the capital the following day. Kabila was sworn in as president on May 29 and announced a referendum would be held in 1998 on a new constitution leading to national elections in 1999. He also said the name of the country would be changed back to Democratic Republic of the Congo and the Congo franc would replace the zaire. The national anthem and flag of the early 1960s were also restored and it became clear that Kabila intended to remove symbols of the Mobutu government, which many viewed as illegal. Mobutu died of cancer in a hospital in Rabat on September 7 and was quietly buried in Morocco. He was remembered in newspaper obituaries abroad as the last great African dictator but his death went largely unheralded in Congo/Zaire.

Kabila's problems were just beginning. Reports had been surfacing since May 1997 of massacres by AFDL troops in eastern Congo/Zaire of Rwandan refugees who had refused to return home. Relief workers and local eyewitnesses told of mass graves in the forest. Humanitarian agencies at times were prevented from evacuating people from the refugee camps. Human rights organizations charged that Tutsi soldiers of the Rwandan army, which had backed the AFDL, were committing the atrocities. A UN investigation was launched but investigators were kept from traveling to the region. Western governments and the United Nations threatened to impose sanctions. Clashes erupted in the east between local militia and fighters from Rwanda, Uganda and Burundi.

Kabila was also under pressure in Kinshasa. He had excluded Tshisekedi and most opposition politicians in Kinshasa from his government. He had banned political meetings after UDPS demonstrations ended in violence. And he was under criticism from local politicians who accused the AFDL of being a government of foreigners. Tensions soon arose between different supporters in his government, including Tutsis from the east, former Katangan Gendarmes, Ugandan and Rwandan fighters who had played major roles in the AFDL's military successes, and independent elements that suddenly emerged proclaiming themselves part of the Congolese military. And the interethnic violence in the Great Lakes Region, which had been a major catalyst for the offensive that ended the Mobutu era, continued to drain government resources and undermine efforts to restore the authority of the central government.

The economy, however, stabilized somewhat. By 1998, the Kabila government had reduced inflation and stabilized exchange rates, largely by limiting the issue of new banknotes. It carried out a monetary reform on June 30, 1998, replacing the inflation-battered new zaire with the Congolese franc. Congolese in some areas reported some improvement in their lives. They said they no longer were subject to the arbitrary detention and extortion practiced by Mobutu's security forces. However, they complained that the new forces of order had quick trigger fingers and their officers seemed more interested in expropriating the residences and patrimony of the "dinosaurs" of the previous regime than in imposing true change. Resentment grew in Kinshasa against

Rwandan soldiers and Congolese Tutsis, the new barons of the regime, who came to be regarded as a foreign occupation force. Attacks continued against Congolese Tutsis in the east. And relations with Rwanda and Uganda deteriorated because of the Kabila government's inability to halt cross-border raids from Congo/Zaire by opponents of the governments in Kigali and Kampala.

On July 27, Kabila dismissed 100 Rwandan officers, including his armed forces chief, and sent them home, saying their services were no longer needed. A new rebellion was launched on August 2 by Congolese Tutsi, former Mobutu officials, and disgruntled Kabila supporters including Foreign Minister Bizima Karaha. They formed the Rassemblement Congolais pour la Démocratie (RCD) to pressure Kabila to broaden his government, which they accused of corruption and nepotism. Within days their forces took Goma, Bukavu and Kisangani and, backed by Rwanda, Uganda and Burundi, took Moanda on August 7 and Matadi a few days later. As the rebels advanced on Kinshasa, Kabila sought to marshal support from friends in southern Africa. Fighting broke out near Ndjili airport, on the outskirts of Kinshasa, on August 29, but Congolese forces, backed by troops from Zimbabwe, Angola and Namibia, drove the rebels out and retook western Bas-Congo.

In the following months, fighting continued in eastern and northern Congo, including aerial bombardments, atrocities against civilian populations, and widespread looting of industries and businesses. Human rights officials in early 1999 said 20 distinct armed groups were operating in the region. African leaders sought to mediate an end to the violence, but Kabila during 1998 refused to meet with the rebels. On January 31, 1999, Kabila lifted the ban on political activity, but placed stringent requirements for the registration of political parties, leading to objections by the opposition.

As the cycle of violence and despoliation wore on, most Congolese remained preoccupied primarily with surviving in a country where the formal economic infrastructure had collapsed, the currency was not trusted, and politicians were viewed with considerable disdain. Many Congolese said they despaired of ever ridding their country of the mentality of authoritarianism and plunder that had existed in various forms since the days of King Leopold II.

THE DICTIONARY

- A -

ABACOST. The national **dress** for men adopted during **Authenticity**. It consists of a tight-fitting, two-piece suit tailored of dark material, with a high collar buttoned almost to the throat, and highlighted by a silk scarf instead of a tie. President **Mobutu Sese Seko** championed the abacost and for a time virtually all males in Zairian officialdom wore it. When Mobutu announced multipartyism in April 1990, he said the abacost would no longer be mandatory. Subsequently, only hardline supporters of Mobutu and his **Movement Populaire de la Révolution (MPR)** party continued to wear it.

ACQUIRED IMMUNE DEFICIENCY SYNDROME (AIDS). A **disease** first diagnosed in 1980 that destroys the body's ability to fight disease, making it vulnerable to a variety of illnesses. The disease strikes African males and females in roughly equal numbers and consequently is believed to be transmitted in Africa primarily through heterosexual activity and blood transfusions. Studies by Zairian, Belgian and US teams in the 1980s revealed that 5 to 15 percent of the urban populations of Zaire and as much as 30 percent of the prostitute population had been exposed to AIDS, albeit a variety not always lethal. A nonlethal strain of AIDS also was found in a species of monkey inhabiting northern Zaire.

In a country where other health problems already were straining government budgets, AIDS was initially viewed as a disease brought in by foreigners. Its transmission primarily by sexual contact discouraged official recognition of its dangers. As a result, in early 1987 the Zairian government officially acknowledged only 150 cases of AIDS in the country, while doctors at **Kinshasa**'s Mama Yemo Hospital alone said they had recorded 300 cases of the disease and that 12 percent of newborn babies at the hospital carried AIDS antibodies. By the 1990s, continued public awareness campaigns combined with the deaths from AIDS of a number of well-known personalities had raised awareness considerably, although surveys showed the adoption of preventative measures among the general population to be slow. By the mid-1990s, researchers estimated tens of thousands of Zairians had died from the disease and hundreds of thousands were infected. The deterioration of the public **health care** system and the collapse of most blood banks had not helped the situation.

ACTION MOVEMENT FOR THE RESURRECTION OF THE CONGO. *See* MOUVEMENT D'ACTION POUR LA RÉSURRECTION DU CONGO (MARC).

ADMINISTRATION. From independence, the administration of the **government** and state was nominally the responsibility of the various ministries, but the Bureau du Président (Office of the President) retained most of the final authority for policymaking from the mid-1970s until the **democratic transition**. The bureau consumed about one-third of the government's operating budget. In its heyday it was staffed by the best and brightest young professionals and exerted predominant influence over policymaking and the allocation of resources. The administration traditionally was highly centralized in **Kinshasa**, leading to complaints of neglect from the remote regions, particularly in eastern Congo/Zaire. During the reforms of the 1980s, some attempts were made to decentralize by increasing the authority and staffing of the regional administrations. By the 1990s, with the collapse of the formal **economy** and the decline of influence of the central government over the regions, a great deal of local administration became fragmented. Many localities refused to send tax revenues to the central government. Others began levying their own forms of taxation. Local businessmen financed some public works projects, such as **road** repair and public clinics. A number of local governments, in the spirit of **federalism** called for by the **Conférence Nationale Souveraine (CNS)**, issued their own "visas" and charged disembarkation fees to travelers. *See also* Presidency; Provinces; Regions.

ADOULA, CYRILLE. The **prime minister** who headed the Congolese government during most of the period of the **United Nations**

presence in the Congo, Adoula is best remembered for his belief in a united Congo and his tireless efforts to negotiate between the central government and the various secessionist factions. Adoula was an *évolué* who in 1954 joined the Amicale Socialiste. He was a cofounder of the **Mouvement National Congolais (MNC)** and a member of its first executive committee. Following the inconclusive **elections** of June 25, 1960, he was a major architect of the compromise that brought Joseph **Kasavubu** and Patrice **Lumumba** to power. He served as interior minister in the Joseph **Ileo** government formed in early 1961 after the dissolution of the **College of Commissioners**.

He was named prime minister on July 25, 1961, following Ileo's dismissal. During the following three years, he attempted to negotiate an end to the **Katanga secession** and the **rebellions** in northeastern Congo and the **Kwilu**. In June 1964, a few days before the departure of the UN forces, Kasavubu dismissed him and appointed Moïse **Tshombe** to head a new government. He went into exile for two years, but returned following the **coup d'etat** and served as ambassador to Brussels and Washington. In August 1969, he returned to government as foreign minister, but was removed from the post in a cabinet reshuffle shortly thereafter. He died a few years later.

AFFONSO I. King of the **Kongo** from 1506 to 1541, Affonso welcomed the Portuguese explorers, traders and **missionaries** who sailed up the **Congo River** during the first half of the 16th century. He converted to **Christianity**, along with a large number of his people, and sent members of his court to Europe. He established diplomatic relations with a number of European powers and corresponded with European leaders. His hospitality and desire for European goods are said to have led to exploitation by the traders and the spread of **slavery**.

AFRICAN ASSOCIATION FOR HUMAN RIGHTS. *See* ASSOCIATION AFRICAINE DE DÉFENSE DE DROITS DE L'HOMME (ASADHO).

AFRICAN CHARTER OF HUMAN AND PEOPLE'S RIGHTS. A document signed by most African governments, including **Congo/Zaire**, pledging respect for basic **human rights** and individual liberties. Human rights organizations consider it to have been largely unobserved.

AFRICAN DEVELOPMENT BANK (ADB). A multilateral lending institution based in Abidjan, Côte d'Ivoire, the ADB provided loans with easy terms of payment to and was considered one of the lenders of last resort for African governments.

AFRICAN SOCIALIST FRONT. See FRONT SOCIALISTE AFRICAIN (FSA).

AFRICAN SOCIALIST PARTY. See PARTI SOCIALISTE AFRICAIN (PSA).

AFRICAN SOLIDARITY PARTY. See PARTI SOLIDAIRE AFRICAIN (PSA).

AFRICANIZATION. A term used in the late 1950s and early 1960s to denote a policy of advancing Congolese quickly into positions of responsibility in **government**, the military, **civil service**, and private enterprise. However, resistance by entrenched colonial bureaucrats and the lack of preparation for **independence** meant that when the colonial era ended, few Congolese were serving in positions above the clerical level. See also Zairianization.

AFRO-ARABS. Traders and slavers originally from Zanzibar and the East African coast who spread west, reaching the **Congo River Basin** in the second half of the 19th century. Most of the Afro-Arabs were driven out of Congo by 1900. See also Slavery.

AFRO-MALAGASY COMMON ORGANIZATION. See ORGANISATION COMMUNE AFRICAINE ET MALGÂCHE (OCAM).

AGENCE NATIONALE DE DOCUMENTATION (AND) / NATIONAL DOCUMENTATION AGENCY. For years, the name of **Congo/Zaire**'s secret police, in charge of internal **security** and counterespionage. It was renamed the **Service National d'Intelligence et de Protection (SNIP)** in August 1990. It was one of several **intelligence services** endowed with its own network of informants and communications. Its agents reportedly enjoyed special detention authority and answered directly to the president. *See also* Service d'Action et de Renseignements Militaire (SARM).

AGENCE NATIONALE DE RENSEIGNEMENTS (ANR) / NATIONAL INFORMATION AGENCY. The agency responsible for national **security**, adopted after the installation of the Laurent **Kabila** government in May 1997. The ANR replaced the **Service National d'Intelligence et de Protection (SNIP)**, which was formed under **Mobutu Sese Seko**. *See also* Intelligence Services.

AGRICULTURE. Three climatic regions lie within Congo/Zaire: an equatorial region where **palm oil, coffee**, cocoa, **bananas** and **rice** are grown; a tropical region of wooded savannas where **cotton**, peanuts and **manioc** are grown; and the high plains where potatoes, leeks and arabica coffee are grown and **livestock** are raised. Most of the soil is moderately fertile. However, the eastern highlands of **Ituri** and **Kivu** contain fertile soils largely of volcanic origin, and the cooler climate there permits the extensive cultivation of vegetables such as cabbage, onions, tomatoes and even strawberries. Congo/Zaire's major cash crops are palm products, **rubber**, coffee, tea and **sugar** cane. In the large subsistence sector, crops like manioc, **maize**, rice, bananas and to a lesser degree beans, peanuts and cotton are grown.

Twenty-five percent of Congo/Zaire's land is considered arable, but less than 2 percent is under cultivation. An estimated 80 percent of the population is engaged primarily in agriculture, 70 percent at the subsistence level. Less than 3 percent of government expenditures have been devoted to agricultural investment, and these have been allocated primarily to administrative organs.

World Bank figures reveal that annual agricultural production grew at an average rate of 0.4 percent in 1975-79, 3 percent in 1980-85, and 2 percent from 1985 to 1993 (the last year for which figures were available). However, due to **population** growth *per-capita* food production declined steadily by 2.3 percent in the late 1970s, 0.2 percent in the early 1980s, and 1.2 percent in the late 1980s and early 1990s. Food **exports** declined by 5.8 percent in the early 1980s and by 7.6 percent from 1985 to 1993.

Historically the **mineral** sector dominated the Congolese economy, but the severe decline in mineral production in the 1990s caused the proportion of agricultural production to rise from one-sixth of gross domestic product (GDP) in the 1980s to one-third of GDP in the mid-1990s.

At independence, the country had achieved net self-sufficiency in food, partly through the use of taxation schemes and forced growing programs, and cash crops earned 40 percent of total foreign exchange. Following independence, political instability and the flight of experienced technicians caused a rapid fall in production and private investment in agriculture. Contributing to the decline were mismanagement and the failure by the government to invest in the **transportation,** agricultural extension and **communications** networks needed to support the sector.

The development of agriculture and the achievement of self-sufficiency in **food supply** were the "priority of priorities" of the **Mobutu** government from the mid-1970s. However, a nationalization program, **Zairianization,** further aggravated the situation. In November 1973, the government, concerned over falling production, announced it was nationalizing agricultural operations with annual revenues of more than one million zaires. More than 100 farms and plantations were affected. In less than two years, however, Zairianization was judged a failure and was reversed. The failure was attributed to several factors. The Zairians who received the Zairianized properties were generally politically well-connected individuals who knew little about farming. They came to be known as *acquéreurs.* In addition, the operations often were divided up among several *acquéreurs* and there was little coordination among them. The departure of experienced managers led to the disruption of the marketing system. And the *acquéreurs* tended to view their new property merely as a source of revenue and did not invest in its maintenance and long-term growth.

Production continued to decline and in December 1974, the government announced the policy of **Retrocession,** whereby 40 percent foreign participation would be allowed in the large operations but smaller plantations would be reserved for Zairians. The lack of response to these measures led the government a few years later to allow up to 60 percent private ownership in the sector. Continued stagnation led the government in mid-1977 to announce the Agricultural Recovery Plan of 1978-80. Capital expenditures for agriculture, which had fallen from 15 percent of gross domestic product (GDP) in 1958 to 3.7 percent, were gradually increased and reached 13 percent of GDP in 1977.

In 1983 a series of measures were announced to encourage Zairians to invest in farming. Price controls on food products were eased and foreign currency disbursements by the central bank for imported food were severely restricted. The government also instituted programs to increase the production of rice, manioc, vegetables and meat, and launched projects to improve **roads** and bridges, particularly in western Zaire, in order to improve the farm-to-market network.

As a result, in 1985 Zaire was producing 50,000 tons of wheat per year, according to government figures, or roughly one-half of total demand, and 1.5 million head of cattle or three-fourths of demand. Zairian officials said production had returned to pre-independence levels. However, population growth continued to outpace production gains and a severe setback in the early 1990s, brought on by **inflation**, looting and shortages of fuel and spare parts, caused per-capita production in the formal sector to decline sharply. The loss of purchasing power by salaried workers also lessened demand. As a result, many farmers could not afford to take their produce to market and subsequently reduced production. The government of Laurent **Kabila**, in the months after it took power in 1997, launched an appeal for low-cost farm implements and inputs in an effort to revive the sector.

Today, Congo is a net importer of food, and during disasters it often receives emergency relief aid from international donors. The decay of the transportation infrastructure and **banking** system, inflation, **unemployment** and the loss of individual earning power have fostered the growth of subsistence cultivation, even in urban areas. *See also* Crops; Plantations.

AIR FORCE. The Congolese air force is a small branch of the **armed forces** with 1,800 active members. Its primary mission is to provide close support in skirmishes and transportation for the much larger ground forces. The force consists of one fighter squadron of French-supplied Mirage Vs; one counterinsurgency squadron of Italian-supplied Aermachi MBs and US-furnished ATs; one helicopter squadron of French Alouettes, Pumas and US

Bell 47 helicopters; and a transport wing of US-made aircraft that included several C-130s. In the 1980s and 1990s, maintenance problems and a lack of spare parts tended to keep most of the fleet grounded.

AIR TRANSPORTATION. Because of the size of the country and the poor condition of some **roads**, air **transportation** is an important link to parts of Congo/Zaire and at times has been used to transport **minerals** and food. The national **Air Zaïre** airlines (renamed **Lignes Aériennes Congolaises** in 1997) officially provide service to 40 airports. Three of these, **Kinshasa**, **Lubumbashi** and **Kisangani**, are international airports and can accommodate wide-body aircraft. One hundred fifty mostly unpaved airfields and landing strips, some of which are privately maintained, also are available primarily for small planes. Missionary and relief agencies also operate small fleets of single- and twin-engine planes. The state-owned **Société Nationale d'Électricité (SNEL)** operated a fleet of several planes and helicopters to maintain the Inga-Shaba power line.

During the first 20 years of independence, air service was dominated by Air Zaïre (originally Air Congo), which at its peak in the mid-1970s operated one dozen aircraft, including four large jets. In the late 1970s, domestic air service was opened to private carriers and a number of small companies emerged. One of the first was **Scibe Airlift**, which was formed in 1982 and operated routes between Kinshasa and northern Zaire, **Belgium**, and several neighbors in East Africa. **Shabair** was launched in the early 1990s and operated routes between Lubumbashi and Kinshasa, **Mbuji-Mayi** and Johannesburg. Blue Air Lines was formed in 1993 and served four cities. Express City was formed in the mid-1990s and served nine Zairian cities. The number of private air companies surpassed 100 in the mid-1990s, fueled in part by trafficking in arms, diamonds and **currency** dealings, but declined to 10 by 1998.

Maintenance generally has been considered lax by international standards. On December 18, 1995, a Lockheed leased by Trans Service Airlift crashed in northern Angola, killing 141 people. A Russian-operated Antonov-32 belonging to African Air on January 8, 1996, crashed upon takeoff from **Ndolo Airport** into a market in central Kinshasa, killing more than 300 people on the ground. In June 1996, a cargo Ilyushin-76 crashed upon takeoff at **Ndjili Airport**, killing 12 crew members.

AIR ZAÏRE. Congo/Zaire's national air carrier, called Air Congo until 1971. At its peak, in the 1970s, Air Zaïre operated one DC-10, two DC-8s and a fleet of small jet and propeller planes. However, it consistently lost money, due in part to **Mobutu**'s propensity for commandeering its aircraft for official and personal travel by his family and entourage. Its planes were also used to transport **coffee** from **Kivu** in early 1978 and **cobalt** from **Shaba** in 1979-80. The carrier depended on substantial government subsidies and with the government's growing financial woes in the 1970s, it began to decline. A number of capital infusions were announced, often with foreign participation.

In January 1985, Mobutu announced Air Zaïre would be partially privatized and a group of Israeli investors, headed by Leon Tamman, said they would invest $400 million to rebuild the fleet and restructure its operations. The French company Union des Transports Aériens (UTA) managed it for a time under an agreement announced in 1986. However, by the 1990s, the airline was struggling and operated only a few flights on an erratic basis using a DC-10 and a Boeing 737. In 1995, it jointly operated a few external flights with Cameroon Airlines. On several occasions, its craft were seized for payment arrears when they landed at foreign airports, creating diplomatic strains between Zaire and the local authorities. It was declared bankrupt by a Belgian court in 1995. It resumed operations in November 1997 under a new name, **Lignes Aériennes Congolaises**, and utilizing initially one Boeing 737. Its director, General Kikunda Ombela, was put on trial in December on charges of corruption. *See also* Air Transportation.

ALBERT I (1875 - 1934). Third king of **Belgium**, who visited the **Belgian Congo** as crown prince, and advocated a more humane colonialization. Albert I ascended the throne in 1909 upon the death of his uncle, **Leopold II**. He ruled during World War I and the Great Depression until his death in a mountain-climbing accident on February 19, 1934.

ALBERT II (1934 -). Younger brother of King **Baudoin**, he acceded to the throne of **Belgium** upon Baudoin's death on July 31, 1993. Albert II served in the Belgian navy beginning in 1953 and attained the rank of admiral. In 1959, he married an Italian princess, Donna Paola Ruffo di Calabria. He served in the Belgian senate and as president of the Belgian Red Cross. He visited the **Democratic Republic of the Congo** on February 18, 1969.

ALBERT, LAKE. *See* LAKE ALBERT.

ALLIANCE DES BAKONGO (ABAKO). One of the major political parties to wield power in the five years between **independence** and the **coup d'etat** that brought **Mobutu** to power. ABAKO was one of a number of groups that formed in **Kinshasa** and a few other urban areas following World War II as Congolese leaders began to press for an end to restrictions on trade unions and political gatherings. Its original purpose was to defend the rights and interests of the **Kongo** people. At times its leaders also advocated recreating the ancient kingdom of the Kongo by combining portions of **Congo/Kinshasa**, **Angola** and **Congo/Brazzaville**. On August 23, 1956, following the publication of the *Conscience Africaine* manifesto calling for a greater African voice in the affairs of the **Belgian Congo**, ABAKO issued its Declaration of Civil Rights, calling for immediate freedom of speech, association and press for Congolese. ABAKO adopted relatively tough positions against the colonial administration and even boycotted the local elections of 1959. Its leaders were considered radical by the colonial authorities and were frequently imprisoned.

ABAKO drew most of its strength from **Bas-Congo**. However, the relatively large numbers of Kongo living in the capital, **Leopoldville**, added to its influence. ABAKO scored impressive victories in the legislative elections leading up to independence. However, these were not enough to give it a majority in the legislature. In a compromise, ABAKO's leader, Joseph **Kasavubu** assumed the primarily ceremonial post of president, and another major winner in the elections, Patrice **Lumumba**, became prime minister. ABAKO was dissolved with all other political parties following the coup d'etat in which Kasavubu was overthrown.

The party quickly reformed following Mobutu's announcement of the **democratic transition** on **April 24, 1990**. Although subsequently split by internal rivalries, ABAKO for the most part opposed Mobutu and allied with the **Sacred Union**. Although many members initially allied with **Nguza Karl-I-Bond's Union des Fédéralistes et des Républicains Indépendants (UFERI)**, they left the alliance when Nguza was named prime minister and expelled from the Sacred Union in November 1991. ABAKO adherents maintained a deep grudge against the Mobutu government for refusing to acknowledge the historical significance of Kasavubu, the country's first president.

ALLIANCE DES FORCES DÉMOCRATIQUES POUR LA LIBÉRATION DU CONGO/ZAÏRE (AFDL) / ALLIANCE OF DEMOCRATIC FORCES FOR THE LIBERATION OF CONGO/ZAIRE. An alliance of four small political parties which launched an offensive in eastern **Congo/Zaire** on October 18, 1996, and in seven months took over the government in **Kinshasa**, one day after the flight into exile of **Mobutu** on May 16, 1997. The AFDL, of which the best known member group was the **Parti Révolutionnaire du Peuple (PRP)**, initially appeared intent primarily on driving out armed militia of the deposed government of Rwandan President Juvenal Habyarimana, which had been harassing the local population and attacking installations in **Rwanda** from refugee camps around **Goma** and **Bukavu**. In four months the AFDL seized the cities of Uvira, Bukavu, Goma, Bunia and **Kalemie**. One of the first effects of its offensive was to send an estimated 800,000 Rwandan **refugees** back home. An estimated 200,000 hardline supporters of Habyarimana and the **Hutu** militias involved in the massacre of one-half million Rwandans in 1994 did not return, however, fearing retaliation. Instead they moved west, deeper into Zairian territory.

The AFDL subsequently announced through its spokesman, PRP founder and veteran **dissident** Laurent **Kabila**, that it did not seek secession, but rather the overthrow of Mobutu. Kabila emerged as the leader of the political wing of the alliance. He was one of the few dissidents who had never joined in a Mobutu government and his credentials as a guerrilla leader and early supporter of Patrice **Lumumba** enhanced his appeal to exiled opponents of Mobutu. Weak resistance from Zairian troops and a vacuum of leadership in Kinshasa caused by Mobutu's illness bolstered the alliance and brought statements of support from **opposition** parties in the capital. In what was viewed as the major victory of the offensive, the AFDL on March 15, 1997, took **Kisangani**, where the Zairian army, backed by Serb mercenaries, had mounted a major defense. AFDL forces took the diamond mining center of **Mbuji-Mayi** on April 4 and **Lubumbashi**, the capital of mineral-rich **Shaba Region**, on April 9.

The international community, fearing a bloodbath if the AFDL reached Kinshasa, sought to organize mediation talks. South African President Nelson Mandela brought Mobutu and Kabila together in early May, but no agreement was reached and the negotiations were overtaken by the AFDL offensive. Mobutu and his entourage left Kinshasa on May 16 as the AFDL forces neared the capital. Zairian **armed forces** commander **Mahele Lieko Bokoungo** that evening persuaded Mobutu's elite presidential guard to lay down their arms, for which he was killed, and the AFDL met little resistance when it entered Kinshasa on May 17. Kabila was sworn in as president on May 29 and in his inaugural address pledged to hold free **elections** in 1999.

The AFDL sought to remove symbols of the Mobutu era. The name of the country was changed back to **Democratic Republic of the Congo**, the Congo franc replaced the **zaire**, and the flag and national anthem of the country prior to the Mobutu coup were reinstated. The Kabila government said it wished to reeducate Congolese and change the national mentality which developed under the 32 years of **corruption** and authoritarianism which had marked the Mobutu regime. However, it also came under criticism for excluding respected opponents of Mobutu, in particular Étienne **Tshisekedi**, and for allowing interethnic violence to continue in the east.

ALLIANCE DES FORCES PATRIOTIQUES (AFP) / ALLIANCE OF PATRIOTIC FORCES. A political alliance of about 30 parties, many from the **Sacred Union**, formed by **Nguza Karl-I-Bond** after he was named **prime minister** and expelled by the Union in November 1991. It attempted to form a moderate **opposition** bloc at the **National Conference**, saying it espoused political change but rejected extremism. However, it was dismissed for the most part as pro-**Mobutu** and collapsed the following year when Nguza was dismissed as prime minister.

ALLIANCE OF DEMOCRATIC FORCES FOR THE LIBERATION OF CONGO/ZAIRE. *See* ALLIANCE DES FORCES DÉMOCRATIQUES POUR LA LIBÉRATION DU CONGO/ZAÏRE (AFDL).

ALLIANCE OF PATRIOTIC FORCES. *See* ALLIANCE DES FORCES PATRIOTIQUES (AFP).

ALUMINUM. Congo/Zaire is known to have deposits of alumina ore in **Haut-Uélé District** and the **Bas-Congo** Province of the country. However, interest has focused primarily on Bas-Congo, where deposits estimated at 132 million metric tons have been found near **transportation** routes and adequate sources of manpower and electrical power. In the 1970s, the Zairian government drew up a project to build an aluminum complex in the proposed Inga Free Trade Zone and a consortium of foreign companies was formed to participate in joint ventures in the area. However, richer deposits were found in neighboring countries and oversupply of aluminum on the world market, combined with the deterioration of the **economy**, led in the mid-1990s to the indefinite postponement of any commercial attempts at exploitation. *See also* Aluzaïre.

ALUMNI GROUPS. Groups of former students of **Catholic Church** mission schools which, with trade unions and social/ethnic associations, began pressing for changes in the colonial system, including equal pay for equal work, better representation in local government, and an end to various forms of racial discrimination. Many members of the alumni groups became leaders in the **independence** movement and subsequent political parties. Some of the most notable alumni groups were formed by the Jesuits, Christian Brothers, Scheut Fathers and Marists.

ALUR. An ethnic group of Nilotic origin living in a remote part of northeastern Congo/Zaire, northwest of **Lake Albert**. Ethnologists say it is the only major group in Congo/Zaire that speaks an Eastern Sudanic **language**, although Zairian ethnologists cite the Kakwa, Logo and Lugbara as equally important groups of Nilotic descent. Less warlike than some neighbors such as the **Zande** and **Mangbetu**, the Alur gained influence in their region because of a reputation for being able to mediate interlinear disputes. The group is characterized by relatively small political groupings. **Chiefs** are religious figures who, through intercessions with the ancestors, mediate disputes and are believed to control natural phenomena such as rain.

ALUZAÏRE. A consortium of nine companies formed in 1981 to construct an **aluminum** smelter with planned production capacity of 150,000 to 200,000 metric tons per year. The smelter, to be built at Moanda, was one of several projects aimed at utilizing surplus electrical capacity of the **Inga Hydroelectric Complex** east of **Matadi**. However, the consortium announced in April 1985 that it was suspending the project for the "indefinite future" because of low prices for aluminum on the international market and **transportation** problems within Congo/Zaire.

ALVARO I. King of the **Kongo** who is credited with returning the kingdom to stability following the **Jaga** invasion of 1568-70. However, under his successors, Alvaro II, Alvaro III and **Garcia II**, the Kongo kingdom continued to lose influence and suffer rebellions from outlying subkings.

AMNESTY INTERNATIONAL. An international **human rights** organization which has frequently accused the **government** of Congo/Zaire of detaining, torturing and killing political opponents, as well as ordinary criminals. The government usually denied these charges and often blamed them on information that was outdated or obtained from **dissidents** trying to discredit the regime. In 1986, however, **Mobutu** acknowledged that "some abuses" had occurred and formed a government ministry to deal with them. The portfolio was abolished a few years later in an austerity reform. In the 1990s, the Zairian government maintained that Amnesty delegates could visit anytime they wished. However, the organization said its investigators were prevented from traveling to Zaire by diplomatic and bureaucratic obstacles. In 1993, the organization issued a report that said human rights in Congo/Zaire were as bad as during the chaos following **independence**. In 1997, Amnesty also helped publicized reports of massacres of **Hutu refugees** from **Rwanda** by fighters for the **Alliance des Forces Démocratiques pour la Libération du Congo/Zaïre** during its offensive beginning in October 1996.

AMNESTY OF 1983. On May 21, 1983, the Zairian government announced a general amnesty for political **dissidents**, whereby exiled dissidents would be allowed to return home and would be pardoned if they ceased their antigovernment activities. Although the response was cautious at first, a number of prominent exiles eventually took advantage of it. These included former Prime Minister **Nguza Karl-I-Bond**, former Foreign Minister Thomas **Kanza**, former Ambassador to **Belgium Mungul Diaka**, **Tshombe Ditenj** (son of the late Moïse **Tshombe**), former Ambassador to **France** Mbeka Makosso, and former leader of the **Stanleyville secession** Christophe **Gbenye**. In addition, a number of the **Group of Thirteen Parliamentarians** sentenced to prison or internal exile for subversion also were pardoned.

ANCIENS, LES. A term, roughly translated as "veterans," given in the revolutionary days of the 1970s to citizens who had been involved since **independence** in Congolese politics, business, administration, the military or other leadership positions. Some Congolese admired them for the ability to survive. Others did not. See also Dinosaurs, The.

ANGOLA, RELATIONS WITH. Relations between Congo/Zaire and Angola were mutually suspicious since Angola gained independence from **Portugal** in 1975. Zaire supported the **Frente Nacional de Libertação de Angola (FNLA)** and **União Nacional para a Independência Total de Angola (UNITA)** movements which fought against the **Movimento Popular de Libertação de Angola (MPLA)** during the Angolan civil war. It continued its support of the opposition movements after the MPLA gained control of the capital of Luanda and was subsequently recognized by a large portion of the international community. The **Mobutu** government also supported the **Frente para a Libertação do Enclave de Cabinda (FLEC)**, which sought independence for the oil-rich Angolan enclave north of the Congo River.

Angola, with a population of nine million people spread sparsely over its 800,000 square km of territory, has a 1,400-km-long border with Congo/Zaire. Portuguese **explorers** arrived at the Angolan coast at the same time as in Congo and trading and **missionary** activities were carried out jointly in the area for centuries. The colonial period in Angola is considered to have been at least as harsh as that in Congo, but when calls for independence began to be heard in Angola in the late 1950s, they were suppressed. After the **Belgian Congo** obtained its **independence**, it supported Angolan independence movements and allowed many Angolan **refugees** to live in western Congo. The Zairian government initially supported the FNLA whose leader, Holden Roberto, was Mobutu's son-in-law. The FNLA was based in the **Kongo** ethnic area of northern Angola and **Bas-Zaïre**.

Following the end of the Portuguese military dictatorship in 1975, Portugal granted independence to Angola and the three factions began a civil war for control of the country. The Soviet-backed MPLA took control of Luanda in June 1975 and installed a Marxist-based regime that was admitted to the **Organization of African Unity (OAU)** on February 11, 1976, and to the **United Nations** on December 11, 1976. However, the FNLA and UNITA factions, backed primarily by the **United States, South Africa** and Zaire, continued a guerrilla war against the Luanda government. Following the Shaba incursions, in which former members of the **Gendarmerie Katangaise** based in Angola occupied parts of **Shaba Region**, Mobutu and then-Angolan President Agostinho **Neto** met and agreed to end hostilities. Zaire and Angola established diplomatic relations in July 1978. Neto visited **Kinshasa** in August and Mobutu returned the courtesy in October. Relations improved slowly thereafter. However, mutual suspicions remained and were heightened by the Cuban and Soviet military presence in Angola and by the economic ties between Zaire and South Africa.

Attempts were made to reopen the **Benguela Railway**, which until its closure in 1974, provided the most efficient route to the sea for Zaire's **mineral exports**. However, UNITA kept the railway out of operation through sabotage. In April 1987, UNITA announced it would no longer sabotage the Benguela, but the railway remained largely closed because of continuing clashes between the factions and physical decay of the line and rolling stock. In December 1985, relations were strained when an Angolan plane carrying 40 Cuban and three Angolan soldiers to **Cabinda** landed in Zairian territory 280 km southeast of Kinshasa and subsequently was set afire.

In the late 1980s, relations were soured by press reports that the Zairian government was allowing the US **Central Intelligence Agency (CIA)** to use a military airfield at **Kamina** in **Kasaï Occidental** to supply UNITA forces. A ceasefire was negotiated, leading to elections in September 1992 won by the MPLA and rejected by UNITA. After a period of renewed fighting, a second agreement was reached in 1995 whereby UNITA leader Jonas **Savimbi** was to assume the vice-presidency. Relations remained cool into the 1990s because of Zairian support for UNITA during the protracted peace negotiations and because of extensive **diamond** smuggling from northwestern Angola to the southern Kasai area and the use of Zairian territory to supply arms to UNITA forces.

Angolan troops backed the **Alliance des Forces Démocratiques pour la Libération du Congo/Zaïre (AFDL)** in its offensive to overthrow the Mobutu government. Following the installation of the Laurent **Kabila** government in May 1997, Angola sought to cut off UNITA's supply lines through Congo/Zaire and clashes intensified in northern Angola. UNITA began using the **Republic of the Congo (Brazzaville)** as a conduit for the arms and diamond trade, leading the Angolan government to back the militia of former president Denis Sassou-Nguesso against President Pascal Lissouba. In October 1997, 3,000 heavily armed Angolan troops entered Congo/Brazzaville from Cabinda and helped the Sassou-Nguesso fighters take control of the country. Their purpose was to destroy FLEC bases in Congo/Brazzaville and end the use of airstrips in the territory as transshipment points for UNITA arms and diamond shipments.

APRIL 24, 1990. The date **Mobutu** announced the transition to multiparty democracy and the end of party-state controls over **labor** unions, the print **news media**, and other elements of **society**. The transition was to last one year. During this period local councils were to continue to operate, but the Council of Ministers was considered to have resigned. Mobutu initially called for three political parties, one of which would be the **Mouvement Populaire de la Révolution (MPR)**. He also said Zairians could abandon their "authentic" names and **dress**, and that he was resigning as head of the MPR in order to head a caretaker government. Analysts said the president was reacting to pressure from creditors, **opposition** groups, foreign governments and **human rights** organizations, as well as to a growing trend in Francophone Africa. Many said Mobutu envisioned a three-party system, with the MPR and the **Union pour la Démocratie et le Progrès Social (UDPS)** on either end of the political spectrum and a centrist group, headed by former barons like **Nguza Karl-I-Bond** and **Kengo wa Dondo**, which he expected he could draw into a dominating coalition. However, the move was roundly rejected and demonstrations ensued pressing for a **national conference** and the complete removal of controls on political organization.

Mobutu eventually acquiesced to these and other demands, but only after debilitating civic unrest, acts of repression, and extended periods of political crisis and governmental paralysis. Political infighting, the disturbances of 1991 and 1993, delaying tactics by hardline elements, and obstacles erected by the **president** himself slowed progress and in mid-1995 the transition was extended for a third time, until July 9, 1997. The offensive by the **Alliance des Forces Démocratiques pour la Libération du Congo/Zaïre (AFDL)**, beginning in October 1996, disrupted the process, but following the AFDL takeover its leader, Laurent **Kabila,** announced at his inauguration on May 29, 1997, that his government would hold a constitutional referendum in 1998 and free national **elections** in 1999, thereby extending the **democratic transition** to virtually the end of the decade.

ARAB COUNTRIES, RELATIONS WITH. Congo/Zaire's relations with Arab countries were largely affected by its relations with **Israel**, which have been substantial since **independence**. On October 4, 1973, during the Arab oil embargo that followed the Israeli-Egyptian conflict known as the Yom Kippur War, **Mobutu** announced before the **United Nations** General Assembly that Zaire was breaking relations with Israel. A number of African governments followed suit. Relations with Arab countries improved markedly in the following years. Zaire signed agreements with a number of Arab governments exchanging oil for **minerals** and timber. In 1976, however, Zaire voted against expelling Israel from the United Nations and refrained from condemning Israeli ties with **South Africa**. Nevertheless, relations with moderate Arab governments, particularly **Morocco**, Saudi Arabia and Iran (until the Shah was overthrown) remained warm.

On May 13, 1982, Zaire reestablished relations with Israel, saying the Israeli return of the Sinai Peninsula to **Egypt**, a fellow member of the **Organization of African Unity (OAU)**, had ended Africa's quarrel with Israel. Zaire began to receive Israeli assistance in the areas of **security, agriculture** and **transportation**. It also received support from the Jewish lobby before the US Congress, which had been holding embarrassing hearings on Zairian economic mismanagement and **human rights** violations. Although Zaire had received $444 million in aid from Arab countries from 1973 to 1982, the government was said to be disappointed by what was characterized as a lack of serious Arab investment in the country's **economy** and the lukewarm Arab support for African issues such as the efforts to end apartheid and South Africa's occupation of Namibia. A number of Arab governments, including Saudi Arabia, Qatar, **Libya** and South Yemen, broke relations with Zaire. Others reduced their diplomatic missions and virtually all aid was cut off in 1986. Zaire's renewal of Israeli relations was followed that same year by Liberia and by Côte d'Ivoire.

Relations with Arab nations were gradually restored as virtually all African governments recognized Israel. In the 1990s, Zaire's relations were warm with most Arab states, although they remained hostile with Iraq, Iran and Libya, which viewed Mobutu as a puppet of the West. Relations with Libya improved under Laurent **Kabila**, who visited in 1998.

ARMED FORCES. The Forces Armées Congolaises (FAC) include a 1,300-member **navy** (including 600 marines) and a 1,800-member **air force**, but they are dominated by the army, which consists of 25,000 men and (since 1976) women. They also formerly included the **Gendarmerie Nationale** of 20,000 persons which exercised **police** functions in the country since it absorbed the national police in 1972 and a **Civil Guard** estimated at 10,000 troops. The purpose of the armed forces as written in the **constitution** is to defend the territory against external aggression and to maintain internal order. In the years following **independence**, the officer corps was dominated by soldiers from southern Congo, but since the 1970s the army has attracted troops from all over the country. A conscious attempt was made during the 1970s to assign soldiers and officers to areas outside their home **regions**. The policy was aimed at preventing the development of regional power bases, but it also contributed to incidents of abuse of the local population and was eased in the 1980s.

The chief of staff of the armed forces reports through the minister of defense to the **president** who is the commander-in-chief. **Mobutu** held the portfolio of minister of defense from 1969 until 1993, when he acceded to opposition demands and allowed the **prime minister** to name a civilian to the post. The army was divided into five infantry brigades, a counterinsurgency/ commando brigade, an airborne brigade, and an elite presidential guard, the **Division Spéciale Présidentielle (DSP)**. The infantry brigades have operated primarily in the southern and eastern areas of Congo/Zaire. The airborne brigades are deployed primarily at **Kinshasa's Ndjili Airport** and the presidential guard was billeted near the presidential palace, with elements detailed in the 1990s to **Shaba Region**. Military training was received at different times from **Belgium, France**, the **United States, China**, North Korea, **Israel**, and more recently, **South Africa**. The FAC's equipment reflects the diverse military assistance programs.

The Congolese armed forces trace their history back more than 100 years to October 1885, when King **Leopold II** created the **Force Publique**. More commonly known as the "Bula Matari," which means "stone-cruncher," the Force Publique was a feared corps, officered by Europeans, that in the 1890s drove the Arab traders out of eastern Congo and established control over **Katanga**. According to historians, conditions were harsh in the corps and there were three mutinies by 1900. During World War I, the Force Publique was reinforced with Belgian soldiers and sent to Cameroon and Tanganyika to join the Allied war effort against Germany. It was highly commended. During World War II, after Belgium surrendered to Nazi Germany, the corps was sent to Ethiopia. In 1942, it went to Nigeria as part of the West African Frontier Force and also fought in Egypt. Four thousand Belgian troops remained in Congo following World War II, primarily as officers. In the 1950s, the colonial administration launched a system designed to prepare young Congolese for officers commissions.

At independence, however, when the Force Publique became the Armée Nationale Congolaise (ANC), there were no Congolese above the rank of master sergeant. Following the independence festivities, there was some grumbling in the corps over low pay and the lack of promotion opportunities. Five days after independence, the Belgian commander, Emile Janssens, on July 5, 1960, responded by summoning the men and writing on a blackboard the famous phrase: "After Independence = Before Independence." The mutiny that followed spread rapidly. The attacks committed primarily against Belgians caused panic among the European population and prompted the Belgian government to send paratroopers to a number of cities to restore order. The Patrice **Lumumba** government quickly raised salaries, sent most of the Belgian officers home, and promoted M-Sgt. Victor **Lundula** to general and commander of the army. M-Sgt. Joseph-Désiré Mobutu was promoted to colonel and made chief of staff.

The new commanders visited garrisons around the country to quiet the troops. They succeeded in large part, but the task of re-organizing the forces in the face of new challenges proved more difficult. Ethnic tensions were rising within the corps as in the country in general. Increasingly talk was heard of secession in Katanga and other **provinces** that felt left out of the central government. The subsequent instability brought many foreign soldiers to Congo, including **United Nations** troops from African, Asian, European and American nations as well as foreign **mercenaries**. By late 1965, although the secessions in Katanga and **South Kasai** had been ended and UN troops had left Congolese soil, the country still faced a **rebellion** in eastern Congo and **Kwilu**, guerrilla bomb attacks and organized banditry in **Leopoldville**, and yet another political crisis caused by a standoff between the president and prime minister. In the face of these events, official Congolese history recounts that the armed forces senior command met on the night of November 24 and asked Mobutu to take charge of the government. The bloodless **coup d'etat** carried out that night appeared to have the backing of most of the armed forces.

Following the coup, greater efforts were made to improve the effectiveness of the armed forces. Training programs were increased and a National Security Council was established in 1969. There were purges within the armed forces and, in 1975, seven senior officers were executed after a reported coup attempt. The armed forces were renamed the **Forces Armées Zaïroises (FAZ)** when the Congo became Zaire in 1971. In March 1977, former members of the **Gendarmerie Katangaise**, who had been based in Angola following two unsuccessful rebellions in the east in 1966 and 1967, led an incursion into southern Katanga Province. The Zairian armed forces responded slowly and 1,500 Moroccan troops were flown in on Egyptian planes to help them repel the incursion in what came to be known as the **Eighty-Day War**. One year later, the Gendarmerie Katangaise returned, only this time they seized the important mining town of **Kolwezi**, causing most of the **mining** operations to shut down, and called for the end of the Mobutu government. French and Belgian paratroopers in US military planes were sent to the region. Zairian paratroopers landed in Kolwezi and distinguished themselves in a bloody battle to regain control of the airport. A Pan-African peacekeeping force of Moroccan, Senegalese and Togolese troops remained for several months after "Shaba II" and France, Belgium and North Korea began new training programs with the demoralized Zairian forces.

In subsequent years, the armed forces were called to respond to surprise attacks by small opposition groups which continued to operate in remote areas of the country. Examples include the seizure for two days of a garrison at **Moba** on **Lake Tanganyika** in 1984 and again in 1985 by about 50 guerrillas of the **Parti Révolutionnaire du Peuple (PRP)** and attacks by fighters of the **Parti de Libération Congolaise (PLC)** in northern **Kivu** and northeastern **Haut-Zaïre** which intensified in 1992. The armed forces were mostly used during the period to quell civil disturbances but also came to be known for their excesses. One that caused an especially virulent outcry was an attack on **student** dormitories at the University of **Lubumbashi** on May 11-12, 1990. Intended as a disciplinary act, the operation caused scores of deaths. An antigovernment demonstration in Kinshasa on February 16, 1992, was attacked, causing 46 deaths. **Human rights** organizations frequently accused the armed forces of preying on the populace in general and targeting members of the **opposition**.

In the early 1990s a shadowy paramilitary group known as *Les Hiboux*, carried out a primarily nighttime campaign of urban terrorism through bomb attacks, beatings, kidnappings and occasionally murder.

On September 23, 1991, forces based at the aeronautics school at Ndjili Airport rampaged over late pay and launched several days of intense looting in which other soldiers and members of the general population eventually joined. Officially 30 people were killed. Most factories and major businesses were stripped of their stock and equipment. Many small businesses and private residents were also looted. French and Belgian paratroopers landed and evacuated 10,000 expatriates. In October, similar incidents occurred in Lubumbashi, **Mbuji-Mayi** and several other cities.

On January 23, 1993, soldiers angry because merchants refused to accept a new five-million-**zaire** note, which the opposition had called on the populace to boycott, rampaged and killed several merchants who refused to accept the bill. The incident degenerated into another round of looting, this time focused in working-class neighborhoods in central Kinshasa. It led to another evacuation of expatriates and seriously damaged the country's economic production. Economists estimated that as much as 80 percent of the industrial productive capacity was destroyed or crippled. Employment and economic activity was reduced by 80 percent.

By the mid-1990s, the Zairian military was viewed by the populace as the main cause of criminality and violence in the country. Armed groups in uniform set up barricades and extorted money or valuables from motorists. Businesses were obliged to "donate" goods or money to soldiers, often at gunpoint. Many citizens sympathized with the plight of the soldiers who, like themselves, were rarely paid and tended to blame their behavior on the **government** and the political paralysis caused by bickering politicians. The FAZ put up only token resistance to the offensive of the **Alliance des Forces Démocratiques pour la Libération du Congo/Zaïre (AFDL)**, which began in October 1996. As a result, casualties were light except in a few early battles and many elements of the FAZ were incorporated into the new military structure, established by the AFDL after it took power in May

1997 and renamed the Forces Armées Congolaises. A young AFDL general named Masasu Ngilima was named armed forces chief of staff. Tensions remained high between various elements within the military and the detention of Masasu in November 1997 caused a day of shooting in which three people were killed. Kabila announced a reorganization of the armed forces on December 2, 1997. Soldiers in Matadi and Boma looted stores on January 22, after their pay reportedly was diverted by superior officers. *See also* Conscription; Military Assistance.

ARMÉE POPULAIRE DE LIBÉRATION (APL) / POPULAR LIBERATION ARMY. The official name given to the loosely organized fighters of the **Orientale Province** who waged an armed struggle against the central **government** during the eastern **rebellions** of 1961-67. More popularly known as "Simbas" (Kiswahili for "lions"), the fighting force was composed primarily of adolescents who were given amulets and taught chants to protect them from bullets. Tens of thousands of Congolese and hundreds of foreigners were killed during their reign of terror and the military campaign to end it.

ARMS TRAFFICKING. During the mid-1990s, **human rights** groups and Western intelligence services expressed growing concern over arms trafficking through Zaire, saying it threatened stability in the entire region. Journalists arriving in **Goma** in October 1996, after it was taken by rebels of the **Alliance des Forces Démocratiques pour la Libération du Congo/Zaïre (AFDL)**, discovered documents showing arms were being shipped clandestinely through Zaire to military elements of the deposed **Hutu**-led government of **Rwanda** as part of a plan to launch a counteroffensive against the government that took power in Kigali in 1994. Intelligence services said arms were also being transshipped through Zaire to groups bordering **Angola, Burundi, Uganda** and possibly **Sudan**. The lack of government control over airports and airspace was cited as a major factor.

ARMY. *See* ARMED FORCES.

ASSEMBLY OF LIBERAL DEMOCRATS. *See* RASSEMBLEMENT DES DÉMOCRATES LIBÉRAUX (RDL).

ASSOCIATION AFRICAINE DE DÉFENSE DE DROITS DE L'HOMME (ASADHO) / AFRICAN ASSOCIATION FOR HUMAN RIGHTS. Originally founded as the Association Zaïroise de Défense de Droits de l'Homme (AZADHO), in 1991, the ASADHO by the late 1990s had become the country's leading **human rights** organization. It was particularly courageous in speaking out against human rights violations in eastern Congo during the **ethnic cleansing** that began in 1993 and the rebellions beginning in 1996.

ASSOCIATION DE PERSONNEL INDIGÈNE DE LA COLONIE (APIC) / ASSOCIATION OF INDIGENOUS PERSONNEL OF THE COLONY. A civil servants' trade union founded in **Leopoldville** in 1946 that was one of the first to begin lobbying for better pay and working conditions for Congolese workers.

ASSOCIATION DES BALUBA DU KATANGA (BALUBAKAT) / ASSOCIATION OF BALUBA OF KATANGA. An association founded by Jason **Sendwe** in the 1950s to represent the interests of the **Luba** in **Katanga**. BALUBAKAT was the main rival of Moïse **Tshombe**'s **Confédération des Associations Katangaises (CONAKAT)** party in the municipal **elections** of 1957 and the 1960 elections for the provincial assembly. In the 1960 elections, CONAKAT won 25 seats, BALUBAKAT won 22, and independent candidates won the remaining 13. The independents joined with CONAKAT, giving Tshombe a majority. BALUBAKAT delegates walked out of the assembly on June 1. However, the Belgian parliament, acting on an appeal from the Katangan colonial governor, amended the **Loi Fondamentale**, thereby allowing the assembly to convene and Tshombe to gain control of the provincial institutions. Tshombe declared the **Katanga secession** on July 11, leading to a revolt by BALUBAKAT in the northern part of the province and a short-lived declaration of secession in January 1961 from the (seceded) Katangan Republic.

BALUBAKAT allied with Patrice **Lumumba**'s wing of the **Mouvement National Congolais (MNC)**, which espoused a unified Congo. The Luba of **Kasai**, despite strong ethnic affinities with the Luba of Katanga, supported the **Fédération Kasaïenne**, which was at odds with the MNC/Lumumba wing because of a perception that it was dominated by **Lulua** elements in the region. In 1964, however, BALUBAKAT representatives in the **parliament** joined with CONAKAT under the **Confédération Nationale des Associations Congolaises (CONACO)** banner to elect Tshombe **prime minister**. When then-**President** Joseph **Kasavubu** dismissed Tshombe on October 13, 1965 and appointed another BALUBAKAT leader, Évariste **Kimba**, to form a government, CONACO twice blocked approval of the Kimba government, leading to a government crisis and the **Mobutu coup d'etat**.

The term "**Balubakat**" also came to characterize the Luba of Katanga in general.

ASSOCIATION DES CLASSES MOYENNES AFRICAINES (ACMAF) / ASSOCIATION OF AFRICAN MIDDLE CLASSES. The ACMAF was an association of Congolese small businessmen and farmers that was founded in 1954 with encouragement from the colonial government. Some of its representatives were appointed to colonial, consultative government councils. It was one of the **labor** and professional organizations that began pressing for an end to discrimination against Africans and greater Congolese participation in government.

ASSOCIATION DES LULUA-FRÈRES / ASSOCIATION OF LULUA BROTHERS. An association formed in **Kasai** in 1953 in reaction to the growing political and economic influence of the rival **Luba** Kasai. The **Lulua** had driven the Luba from western Kasai in the late 19th century. As a result, many Luba had migrated to **Katanga** where they took jobs in the mines and colonial government. The colonial authorities began to view the Luba as radicals and encouraged the Lulua to convene a congress in 1959 during which they called for autonomy rather than independence.

ASSOCIATION INTERNATIONALE DU CONGO. *See* INTERNATIONAL ASSOCIATION OF THE CONGO (IAC).

ASSOCIATION OF AFRICAN MIDDLE CLASSES. *See* ASSOCIATION DES CLASSES MOYENNES AFRICAINES (ACMAF).

ASSOCIATION OF BALUBA OF KATANGA. *See* ASSOCIATION DES BALUBA DU KATANGA (BALUBAKAT).

ASSOCIATION OF INDIGENOUS PERSONNEL OF THE COLONY. *See* ASSOCIATION DE PERSONNEL INDIGÈNE DE LA COLONIE (APIC).

ASSOCIATION OF LULUA BROTHERS. *See* ASSOCIATION DES LULUA-FRÈRES.

AUTHENTICITY. A concept emphasizing the value of all things Zairian that at one point was declared the official ideology of **Congo/Zaire**. **Mobutu** first mentioned Authenticity in February 1971 in a speech in Dakar, Senegal, during which he defined it as "being conscious of one's own personality and values and being at home in one's culture." In interviews Mobutu said he formally launched the movement on February 12, 1972. The concept began to emerge during the late 1960 and early 1970s, partly in reaction to colonialism and the continuing dominance of European and other non-African customs and values. It was also partly due to rising nationalism and the idealism, optimism and growing expectations that characterized the early years of the Mobutu regime.

Authenticity sought to create a truly Zairian identity by developing Zairian institutions and Zairian forms of expression in the nation's political, economic and cultural life. Colonial names of cities, streets, bridges and boats were changed to Zairian ones. Christian names were dropped. Citizens were encouraged to abandon European **dress** for more traditional clothes, a policy that launched a wave of new fashions such as the *abacost* (for "à bas le costume," meaning "down with the suit"), the bou-bou and other clothes made from Zairian-designed **cloth** and prints. The **constitution** was modified. Christian liturgy and influence in **education** and **society** were challenged. Educational curricula were changed. School and history books were rewritten. Foreign-owned businesses were taken over by Zairians under

Zairianization and companies were urged to replace expatriate personnel with Zairian trainees. Hundreds of studies, monographs and documentaries on Zaire by Zairians were commissioned and published.

By the late 1970s, Authenticity had lost some of its luster, in part because of Zaire's waning economic fortunes and in part in reaction to its excesses (at one point, visitors who arrived at **Kinshasa**'s airport had their ties cut off with scissors). Friends resumed calling each other privately by their Christian names and dropped the requisite title of "citizen." The need for expatriate expertise was acknowledged and many nationalized firms were returned to their previous owners in a move called **Retrocession**. In the 1990s, with the advent of multiparty politics and the decline in popularity of Mobutu, Authenticity came to be viewed with some skepticism by the **opposition** at least. Nevertheless, many of the changes brought by Authenticity remain. Authenticity helped form the concept of a national character, served to unify the country in many ways and was widely admired and imitated in other African countries.

- B -

BAKAJIKA LAW / LOI BAKAJIKA. Promulgated on June 7, 1966, the Bakajika Law granted all wealth above and below the ground to the Congolese state. The law was aimed primarily at ensuring that public **mineral** rights went to the **government**.

BAKER, SAMUEL (1821 - 1893). A British explorer who reached **Lake Albert** in 1864, traveling from East Africa's Tanganyika coast.

BAKWANGA. Capital of secessionist **South Kasai** and center of the **diamond mining** trade. Its name was changed to **Mbuji-Mayi** in 1966.

BALADOS. A term in vogue during the 1980s to describe the young men and women who populated the streets of **Kinshasa**, surviving by doing odd jobs or in some cases engaging in petty theft.

Derived from the French *se ballader*, meaning to roam or "hang out." Other, older names include *nguembo* and *bill*.

BALANCE OF PAYMENTS. Congo/Zaire registered balance-of-payments surpluses in the 1950s, a mixture of surpluses and deficits during the 1960s, and increasingly large deficits beginning in the 1970s. The small deficits of the early 1970s were offset by capital inflows from abroad due to high **mineral** prices and **foreign investment**. In the mid-1970s, growing budget deficits were offset by large borrowings from foreign creditors. The balance-of-payments situation improved somewhat in the 1980s, but remained under pressure from low mineral prices and the large amount of **foreign exchange** exported to service the external **debt**. In the late 1980s, the government fell repeatedly into arrears on debt repayments. Although these were rolled over in new agreements on a number of occasions, by 1990 the government had ceased virtually all foreign debt servicing, leading to its expulsion from the **International Monetary Fund (IMF)**.

The *Economist* Intelligence Unit (EIU) reported that despite continuing government budget deficits, high **inflation** and a valueless local **currency**, Zaire's balance of trade improved in the mid-1990s, partly because the government was no longer servicing the external debt. **Exports** reportedly rose by 8 percent from $1.1 billion in 1993 to $1.2 billion in 1994 and **imports** continued to fall, reaching $605 million in 1994. The EIU said that as a result Zaire recorded a trade surplus of $633 million in 1994, up from $531 million in 1994. It attributed the surplus to scarcity of foreign exchange and the continued contraction of the **gross domestic product**.

BALESE. A small ethnic group living in northeastern **Congo/Zaire** speaking a Central Sudanic **language**. Sometimes grouped with the **Mamvu**, the Balese have relatively small political structures and, according to some, even lack chiefs.

BALUBAKAT. The name frequently used to describe **Luba** who migrated to **Katanga** before colonial times, fleeing clashes with the **Lulua** in western **Kasai** and seeking employment and educational opportunities. They frequently were resented for their success in business and administration. Following **independence**, they often were at odds with the **Lunda**-dominated **Confédération des Associations Katangaises (CONAKAT)**, led by Moïse **Tshombe**. During the **Katanga secession** the Balubakat were persecuted to the point where many took refuge in camps protected by **United Nations** forces.

The term resurfaced in 1992, when the governor of **Shaba**, **Kyungu wa Kumwanza** launched a program to drive the Luba from the region. In what came to be called "**ethnic cleansing**," after the term used in the former Yugoslavia, tens of thousands of Luba were ousted from homes and jobs and obliged to camp at railway stations and public buildings until they could obtain passage to **Kasaï Oriental**.

The term is also the acronym for the **Association des Baluba du Katanga**, a political party formed following independence by Luba residents of Katanga.

BANANA (CITY). A **port** town near the mouth of the **Congo River** that is one of Congo/Zaire's three deep-water ports and a major base for the **navy**. In the early 1980s, the Zairian **government**, in an effort to ease congestion at **Matadi** and **Boma**, enlarged the port and improved the **road** connecting it to Matadi.

BANANAS. Primarily a subsistence crop grown in the wet lowlands, bananas and its cousin, the plantain, are viewed by the government as a potential **export** crop. However, poor **transportation** links with the areas where the banana tree grows best continue to impede exploitation for all but domestic consumption.

BANDA. A large cluster of **ethnic groups** speaking a **language** of Adamawa-Eastern origin, living in northernmost **Congo/Zaire** near the **Ubangi River**. The group is characterized by a relatively structured hierarchy with a strong lineage system.

BANDIYA. One of two major groups of the **Zande** nation living in northernmost **Congo/Zaire**, speaking a Sudanic, Adamawa-Eastern **language**. The Bandiya live in the western part of Zande land near the confluence of the **Uele** and **Ubangi Rivers**, between the towns of Ango and Bondo. The other major Zande group is the **Vungara**.

BANDUNDU. Bandundu is the name of the province formerly known as Kwilu Province, as well as the name of its capital (**Kikwit** was the capital of Kwilu Province). The topography of Bandundu Province, lying in the west-central part of **Congo/Zaire**, consists primarily of sandy and relatively infertile soils of the **Congo River Basin** in the southern part of the region. The northern part encompasses 100 million hectares of tropical **rainforest** containing hardwoods that are considered prime **export** material. Although a number of agreements have been signed with foreign companies to exploit the reserves, the forests have been largely untouched because of **transportation** difficulties. The fertile areas are conducive to the cultivation of **palm oil** and **manioc**, and the raising of cattle and hogs. A great deal of the estimated **population** of 5.8 million (4,141,758 in 1982) lives primarily from river **fishing** and trade.

Bandundu city lies 400 km upriver from **Kinshasa**, near the confluence of the **Kwango** and **Kasai Rivers**. Formerly called Banningville, it was a small river **port** and fishing town until the government made it a regional capital, partly in retaliation against Kikwit, which was the center of antigovernment activity in the region following **independence**. *See also* Livestock.

BANGU-BANGU. A subgroup of the **Songye** living east of the **Kasai River**, sometimes classified as part of the **Luba**-Kasai.

BANKING. Congo/Zaire's banking system historically has been small and utilized primarily by the *élite*. At its peak in the 1980s, it consisted of the **central bank** and 17 private banks and investment organizations. Several of these were affiliated with large multinational banks, but the most important were those with significant **government** participation, including two development institutions: the **Caisse Nationale d'Épargne et de Crédit Immobilier** (CNECI) and the Société Financière de Développement (SOFIDE). Congo/Zaire's banking system collapsed in the early 1990s because of the economic crisis. Most banks were closed by 1993 and the central bank acted primarily as the distributor of newly printed **zaire** notes to those with political connections or who were willing to pay a considerable fee for the service. In contrast, an informal banking system was booming, in offices and on the streets of major cities, sustained by the large informal sector. *See also* Economy; "Wall Street."

BANQUE NATIONALE DU CONGO (BNC). The name of Congo/Zaire's **central bank** since 1997. The bank had previously been named the Banque Nationale du Zaïre in 1971, when the Congo became Zaire.

BANQUE NATIONALE DU ZAÏRE (BNZ). The name of Congo/Zaire's **central bank** from 1971 until 1997.

BANTU. As much as 80 percent of the Congolese **population** is considered to belong to the Bantu grouping of African people. Although debate still continues over the origins of the Bantu, many anthropologists believe they immigrated into the **Congo Basin** as early as 1000 BC from the Nigeria/Cameroon/Chad area and over the next 2,000 years spread south and east along **Congo River** tributaries, eventually reaching both coasts and developing a **language** system that could be called "Bantu." Later, some began to emigrate toward southern Africa, while others moved back through the forest in the direction from which their ancestors had come. Hunters, gatherers and cultivators, they initially formed small villages, usually organized loosely around **clan, descent** or lineage groups.

By the 1500s, some of the groups had evolved into large states such as the **Kongo** kingdom and, later, the **Luba** and **Lunda** empires. The Bantu encountered the **Pygmies**, believed to be the first settlers of the **rainforest**, and utilized them as workers or slaves. They developed stone and iron tools. Sometime after 1500, two groups of non-Bantu speakers entered the savanna north of the Congo Basin. Some were assimilated by the Bantu and some were repulsed, leading to the mosaic pattern of **ethnic groups** in northern Congo/Zaire. According to oral tradition, Bantu groups entered the **Kasai/Katanga** area from the north about 1500 AD and formed small states. Others entered the Sankuru/**Lulua** area about the same time, perhaps fleeing the **Jaga** wars. They hunted and fished and eventually developed buildings and methods of food storage. By 1700, Bantu speakers were established along the Congo River from **Malebo Pool** to Bolobo, above the confluence with the **Kasai River.**

Bantu in the coastal areas entered into contact with Europeans in the late 15th century. **Afro-Arab** traders from the East African coast penetrated into eastern Congo in the 1800s, trading cloth, guns and other goods for **gold, ivory** and slaves. By the time the Bantu came into contact with Europeans, their **societies** had developed political systems that varied considerably in the hierarchy of their **chiefs**, their degree of authority and their religious or ritual responsibilities. Chiefs were chosen or established their authority through wealth, war and judicious distribution of riches. Though often authoritarian in demeanor and feared by their subjects, they frequently ruled through consultations and by consensus. They usually made decisions upon the advice of counselors and after spiritual consultations with their ancestors. Another common characteristic was the tradition of paying tribute to a higher **king**. Some groups had officials with judicial powers in addition to a chief with ritual responsibilities. Others had a war leader or other officers with specific responsibilities. *See also* Slavery.

BANYAMULENGE. A group of primarily ethnic **Tutsis** who before **independence** migrated from **Burundi** and **Rwanda** into the Mulenge Mountains of **Sud-Kivu**. Like the **Banyarwanda** living primarily in **Nord-Kivu**, the Banyamulenge were drawn into the interethnic violence that spilled into **Zaire** from Rwanda and Burundi in the 1990s. Facing attacks by **Hutu**-led militia which had been driven into eastern Zaire in 1994 by the Tutsi-led Rwandese Patriotic Front, the Banyamulenge spearheaded an offensive in Sud-Kivu beginning October 18, 1996, and with the **Alliance des Forces Démocratiques pour la Libération du Congo/Zaïre (AFDL)** took power in **Kinshasa** in May 1997. Clashes reportedly continued in the region, causing 2,000 deaths the following year, according to **human rights** organizations. In August 1998, Banyamulenge leaders formed the **Forces Républicaines et Fédéralistes**, under Joseph Mutambo, and joined the **Coalition Démocratique Congolaise** in its rebellion against the Laurent **Kabila** government.

BANYARWANDA. The name given in Congo/Zaire to the people who migrated primarily to **Nord-Kivu** Province of eastern Congo from **Rwanda** before **independence**. Some arrived in the 1800s.

Others, called the *déplacés,* arrived in the 1930s, brought in by colonial authorities to work on the **plantations**. Dynamic and commercially astute, they advanced rapidly under the colonial administrative system. By 1990, their **population** had reached two million, roughly one-half of the total population of the province. However, they were resented by indigenous groups and were considered foreigners. Although the **constitutions** of 1964 and 1967 recognized their right to Congolese nationality, a decree passed in 1971 restricted citizenship to those who had been living in Kivu since before 1960. A 1981 law that was never implemented further restricted citizenship to those who could demonstrate their ancestors had lived in Congo before August 1, 1885.

In 1991, Banyarwanda delegates were excluded from the **national conference** and their status was never resolved. Angered over their exclusion, the Banyarwanda threatened to refuse to pay taxes. In March 1993, then-governor of Nord-Kivu Jean-Pierre Kalumbo Mboho launched a program of **"ethnic cleansing"** (a term first used in the former Yugoslavia, but widely adopted by Zairians) aimed at driving the Banyarwanda back to Rwanda. He was suspended in July but his speeches led to clashes in which hundreds of villages were destroyed, an estimated 7,000 people were killed, and an estimated 350,000 people were made homeless. The Banyarwanda were among those who supported the **Alliance des Forces Démocratiques pour la Libération du Congo/Zaïre (AFDL)**, which launched an offensive in the east in October 1996 and took power in **Kinshasa** the following May.

BANZA-MUKALAY NSUNGU. Vice president of the **Mouvement Populaire de la Révolution (MPR)** and its main spokesman during the **democratic transition**, Banza-Mukalay was named minister of mines in the **Kengo** government of December 1996.

BAS-CONGO. **Congo/Zaire**'s most developed province after the capital **Kinshasa** and **Katanga**, Bas-Congo is the westernmost province, covering territory roughly from Kinshasa to the Atlantic Ocean. Bas-Congo boasts three ports, **Banana**, **Boma** and **Matadi**, which are major gateways for Congo's external **trade**. The province produces **manioc, maize, palm oil, sugar** cane, **coffee** and some cocoa. It is a major producer of **livestock** and a major supplier of food for Kinshasa. The **Mayombe** Forest contains 20 million hectares of tropical hardwood trees, a major source of **timber exports**. **Petroleum** wells and a refinery off the Atlantic coast also provide jobs and cash for local markets. The province produces one-third of Congo/Zaire's manufactured goods and is home to industries in the metal, woodworking, **cement**, textile, iron and **steel**, and sugar refining sectors. The construction of the **Inga Hydroelectric Complex** 40 km upriver from Matadi contributed to economic development in the area. In the 1970s, the Zairian **government**, seeking to utilize a surplus of **electrical power** and take advantage of **transportation** links and human resources in the region, proposed a free trade zone in the Inga area. The project initially attracted only modest interest from foreign investors.

Bas-Congo already was a densely populated area with a structured **society** and an educated *élite* when the Portuguese arrived in 1483 and made contact with the kingdom of the **Kongo**. The residents were farmers, herders and merchants who traded with other peoples further inland. Considerable contact with **missionaries** and educators from Europe and the Americas over the centuries contributed to the region's status at **independence** as one of the largest sources of professional and skilled **labor**. It also was one of the most politically active regions and one of the earliest to form associations to lobby against discrimination and other inequities of colonialism. Bas-Congo was renamed Bas-Zaïre from 1971 to 1997.

BASHI. Ethnic group of **Bantu** origin living in eastern **Congo/Zaire**. It was one of the groups that came into conflict with the **Banyarwanda** of **Nord-Kivu** in the mid-1990s.

BAS-UÉLÉ. A district of northern **Orientale Province**, lying south of the **Uele River**, the Bas-Uélé is a remote area with a sparse **population** estimated at 750,000 in 1995 (567,040 in 1982). Its inhabitants are mostly **Zande**, engaged primarily in subsistence farming, hunting and some river commerce.

BAS-ZAÏRE. The name given to **Bas-Congo** province in 1971, when **Congo**'s name was changed to **Zaire**. The name was changed back by the Laurent **Kabila** government after the fall of **Mobutu** in 1997.

BAUDOIN (1930 - 1993). The Belgian monarch who reigned during the time of **Belgium**'s greatest interest in and influence over **Congo/Zaire**. He assumed the throne on July 17, 1951, following the abdication of his father, King **Leopold III**, and oversaw with tact and diplomacy the end of the Belgian colonial experience in the 1950s and the debate it caused in Belgian society. The only reigning Belgian monarch to visit the territory, King Baudoin paid an official visit to the **Belgian Congo** in 1955, during which he foresaw **independence** in a speech, but said, "Before we realize this high ideal, much remains to be done." In December 1959, he returned to consult with Congolese leaders on independence, and he returned again in 1960 to witness the lowering of the Belgian flag in the **Congo**.

Baudoin was born on September 7, 1930, in Brussels, the son of Leopold III and Queen Astride, who died in a car accident when he was four years old. After the Belgian surrender to Germany in World War II, he accompanied his father and family to Austria. Following the war, the Belgian government, angry over what was viewed as Leopold's collaboration with Nazi Germany, refused to allow the royal family to return to Belgium. As a result, the family lived in Switzerland until 1950, when Leopold asked the parliament to pass a law delegating his powers to his son. His abdication allowed the royal family to return to Belgium. Baudoin married Doña Fabiola de Mora y Aragón of Spain on December 15, 1960. He died of a heart attack on July 31, 1993, while vacationing in Spain. He was succeeded by his younger brother **Albert II**.

BAYONA WA MEYA. Former Supreme Court president, prosecutor-general and minister of sciences and research. In March 1996, he was appointed president of the **Electoral Commission** charged with organizing a constitutional referendum and national **elections** aimed at ending the **democratic transition** period in 1997. Bayona was quickly rejected by the **opposition** as a puppet of the **Mobutu** government who would not be able to ensure free elections. His commission was abolished with the arrival of the Laurent **Kabila** government in May 1997.

BELGIAN CONGO. *See* CONGO, BELGIAN.

BELGIUM. The **Belgian Congo**'s colonial ruler from November 14, 1908, until **independence** on June 30, 1960. The Belgian parliament annexed the territory from King **Leopold II** who had ruled as sovereign over the **Congo Free State** following the **Berlin Conference** of 1885. It administered the colony until independence.

Belgium is a Western European constitutional monarchy bordered by the Atlantic Ocean to the northeast, the Netherlands to the north, France to the south, and Germany and Luxembourg to the east. A small country of 30,507 square km with 10 million inhabitants, it is densely populated. Belgium is deeply divided along ethnic and linguistic lines between the majority Flemish, who are related to the Dutch, and the Walloons, who are a French-speaking minority.

Belgium, small and militarily weak, was dominated over the years by the Romans, the Dutch, the German monarchy, Spain, France, and in the early 1800s, the Netherlands. A revolt, not the first, in 1830 brought independence, as Belgian teachers in the **Belgian Congo** were fond of saying, "after 2,000 years of colonial rule." A constitutional monarchy was established in 1831 with executive power invested in the king and legislative power invested collectively in the house of representatives, the senate and the monarchy.

The primary motors of the Belgian economy are agriculture from the plains of northern Flanders and coal mining and heavy industry in southern Walloons. Belgium is also an international banking center and Brussels, the capital, is headquarters of the North Atlantic Treaty Organization (NATO) and the **European Union (EU)**. Belgium, like many Western European countries, was preoccupied in the 1980s and 1990s by declining industrial productivity, high taxes, a heavy social service burden, and immigration issues.

BELGIUM, RELATIONS WITH. Relations between **Congo/Zaire** after **independence** and **Belgium** varied between normal and stormy. As the former colonial power, Belgium was still resented in Congo/Zaire and often blamed for domestic problems for which it may have been only partly responsible. Relations suffered under populist leaders such as Patrice **Lumumba** and prospered under such moderate leaders as Moïse **Tshombe**. Following the **Mobutu coup d'etat**, relations were initially good. However, over subsequent years they frequently were disrupted by crisis and confrontation. In 1966, in what was to be a precursor of the wave of **nationalism** soon to strike the continent, Congo broke relations with Belgium over the restructuring of the **Union Minière du Haut-Katanga (UMHK)**, the major **mining** company and source of government revenues. In December 1966, Congo announced the nationalization of the UMHK and formed the Générale Congolaise des Minérais (GECOMIN) to replace it. Under agreements signed later, Belgian companies continued to provide technical assistance and marketed some of the **mineral** products. Many minerals continued to go to Belgium for refining.

In the late 1960s, relations improved. Mobutu visited Belgium in June 1968 and was received as a house guest by King **Baudoin**. The Belgian monarch and his wife visited Congo in June 1970. Later that year, however, relations deteriorated when Belgian companies were accused of dealing in the Congo's parallel **currency** market. The imprisonment of some Belgian executives during the scandal created an uproar in Belgium until the issue was resolved. Relations suffered again in 1974 when **Zairianization** was launched and numerous Belgian properties were seized. Relations were strained yet again in the late 1970s and early 1980s by the activities of Zairian **dissidents** based in Belgium.

Relations briefly improved when a number of vocal Zairian dissidents living in Belgium returned home under the **amnesty of 1983**. However, they soured in April 1986 when a Belgian judge, responding to a complaint by a Belgian former pilot of **Air Zaïre** that he had been unfairly dismissed, ordered an Air Zaïre DC-8 passenger plane grounded at Ostende airport. The judge ordered Air Zaïre to pay $100,000 in damages and back pay. The Zairian government accused Belgium of humiliating its former colony, banned all flights to Zaire by the Belgian national carrier Sabena, and threatened to sever all **trade** links.

In the late 1980s, pressured by international **human rights** groups and the local Zairian dissident community, Belgium began to publicly criticize excesses of the Zairian government and to express support for political liberalization. It welcomed Mobutu's announcement of the **democratic transition** in April 1990. However, following the attack by Zairian troops on students at **Lubumbashi** University in May 1990, it suspended all non-humanitarian aid, as did the **European Union, Canada** and the **United States**.

During the 1990s, Belgium joined **France** and the United States in a group that pressed for more rapid democratic reforms. Called the "troika" by the Zairian **news media**, the group frequently criticized Mobutu for blocking the democratic transition and during the early 1990s backed his major opponent, Étienne **Tshisekedi**. During this period, the troika adopted a policy of diplomatically isolating Mobutu, and many barons of the regime were refused visas, even for personal travel. However, Belgium began to view Tshisekedi and his followers as too obstructionist and sought a more accommodating posture toward Mobutu. It offered to end its policy of isolating the regime and to support a moderate or centrist government leader in exchange for progress toward free **elections**. The process was slow.

As a result, Belgium, along with most Western nations, welcomed the pledge by the Laurent **Kabila** government to reform the system after its installation in May 1997 and hold elections in 1999. Many Belgians were tired of Congo/Zaire and its seemingly eternal crises. Commercial ties had eroded because of the looting incidents and economic decline. Nevertheless, interest continued on the part of some political and civic leaders because of historical ties and a sense of at least partial responsibility for the Zairian debacle.

BEMBA. A **Bantu ethnic group** living near northern **Zambia** west of **Lake Tanganyika** and **Lake Mweru**. Ethnologist Jan Vansina identifies the Bemba as one of three "clusters" or sets of similar communities that include the **Hemba** and Bemba-**Haut-Katanga**.

BEMBA, JEAN-PIERRE (1962 -). Son of Jean **Bemba Saolona** and owner of the cellular telephone company, COMCEL. He formed the Movement de Libération Congolais (MLC) in 1998 and launched a **rebellion** in his home region of northern Congo.

BEMBA SAOLONA, JEAN. One of Congo/Zaire's wealthiest citizens and owner of the Association National des Entrepreneurs food marketing group and **Scibe Airlift** airline. From **Équateur** Province, he was a close collaborator of **Mobutu**. He remained in the country after the fall of Mobutu, however, and in 1998 rejected the rebel movement of his son, Jean-Pierre. In March 1999 he was appointed minister of economy and industry in the Laurent **Kabila** government.

BENGUELA RAILWAY. A **railway** built by the Portuguese in the 1920s and opened in 1931, the 1,400-km-long Benguela links **Katanga Province** to the Angolan port of Benguela, near Lobito, on the Atlantic coast. At **Dilolo**, the railway meets a Congolese rail network that links **Katanga** and the **Kasai** provinces to **Zambia** and southern Africa. The Benguela route is the most cost-effective way to transport **minerals** from Katanga to the coast. However, it was closed in 1974 by guerrillas fighting against the Portuguese colonial administration of **Angola** and the Angolan government that took power following independence in 1975. When Zaire and Angola established relations in 1978, they officially reopened the route and a few trains traveling under heavy guard passed through. However, guerrillas of the **União Nacional para a Independência Total de Angola (UNITA)** demonstrated they could sabotage the track at will. UNITA announced in 1987, however, that it would allow the reopening of the railway and again in 1991 said it was reopening the route with help from **Belgium**. Nevertheless, it remained closed for many years because of tensions between UNITA and the government. As a result, minerals from Katanga were exported primarily via the **National Way** and through **Tanzania** and southern Africa.

BENUE-CONGO. A term used by linguists to denote a group of African **languages** that include the **Bantu** tongues. Bantu and Adamawa-Eastern, spoken by a small portion of the Congolese **population**, form the Niger-Congo linguistic division of Benue-Congo.

BERLIN CONFERENCE (1884-1885). The meeting that led to the European partition of Africa and the granting to King **Leopold II** of personal sovereignty over the Congo. On November 15, 1884, 13 European nations gathered in Berlin, with the **United States** as an observer, to settle border disputes and "ensure the peaceful exploitation of Africa." During the meeting, they divided the **Congo River Basin** among **France**, **Portugal** and the Belgian monarchy. The participants recognized Leopold II's **International Association of the Congo** and acknowledged him as sovereign of the territory that would become of the **Congo Free State**.

The conference ended with the General Act of Berlin, signed on February 26, 1885, under which the powers agreed the Congo should be governed by certain principles: freedom of trade and navigation, neutrality in the event of war, suppression of slave traffic, and improvement of the condition of the indigenous people. History shows that these principles were widely disregarded in the Congo as well as in many other colonies. The Act of Berlin formally ended the scramble for Africa and launched the **colonial era**. It also institutionalized a partition that left as its heritage 52 balkanized African states, whose borders cut across traditional African political and ethnic boundaries, and created on the continent a mosaic of linguistic, judicial, political and economic systems.

BINDO. A pyramid scheme also called "Masamuna," Bindo became popular in **Zaire** in mid-1990 by promising financial returns many times an original investment. Its collapse led to unrest, as people tried to retrieve their investments. Two people were killed in **Kinshasa** and dozens were injured. The government issued an arrest warrant for its organizer, Michel Bindo Bulembo, who reportedly fled the country. It also seized the assets of the organization, but little of the investors' money was returned.

BINZA GROUP. Named after a suburban neighborhood of **Kinshasa** in which a number of wealthy Congolese leaders lived, the Binza Group was an association of young, educated intellectuals considered close to **Mobutu** which gathered in the years prior to the 1965 **coup d'etat**. The group included Cyrille **Adoula**, Justin **Bomboko**, Cléophas **Kamitatu** and Victor **Nendaka**, some of whom had served in the **College of Commissioners** that replaced the **parliament** for six months in 1960-61. The Binza Group was critical of the Joseph **Kasavubu** presidency and the fractiousness of parliament. It is said to have been used by Mobutu to bolster support for his coup. Following the coup, many of its prominent members were sent abroad as ambassadors, ostensibly to explain the goals of the new regime but in reality to reduce any threat to the new regime. Some of the members were later arrested and accused of plotting against the Mobutu government. Many remained in politics.

BIRINDWA, FAUSTIN. A technocrat who in the early years of the **democratic transition** was a senior advisor to **opposition** leader Étienne **Tshisekedi** and the **Union pour la Démocratie et le Progrès Social (UDPS)**. He was designated finance minister in the Tshisekedi government of October 1991, which never assumed office, and foreign minister in the government of August 1992, which did. After **Mobutu** dismissed Tshisekedi in February 1993, Birindwa was named **prime minister** by the pro-Mobutu **Forces Politiques du Conclave** in March. He was expelled from the UDPS and the **Sacred Union**. His government, which included six former activists in the Sacred Union, attempted to address Zaire's economic crisis. In September 1993, it announced monetary reform and launched the "new **zaire**" **currency**. Birindwa's government also tried to organize **elections** but was continuously challenged by the Sacred Union, which refused to recognize its authority and maintained Tshisekedi was still the legitimate prime minister.

The Birindwa government was replaced following the accord that created the **Haut Conseil de la République / Parlement de la Transition (HCR/PT)** which elected Léon **Kengo wa Dondo** prime minister in June 1994 in a vote that also was disputed by the opposition.

BIRTH CONTROL. Birth control is not widespread in Congo/Zaire because of the value and social support derived from large families. Despite a government **family planning** program launched in the 1980s, only 5 percent of the population in 1995 was estimated to use some form of contraceptive. One form of birth control, the condom, achieved considerable exposure because of education campaigns to limit the spread of **Acquired Immune Deficiency Syndrome (AIDS)** and other sexually transmitted diseases.

BLACK MARKET. *See* CURRENCY.

BLUMENTHAL, ERWIN. A former director of West Germany's central bank, Blumenthal was the first foreigner appointed principal director of Zaire's **central bank**, the Banque Nationale du Zaïre, as part of an **International Monetary Fund (IMF)** agreement in 1978-79. He later provided evidence of **corruption** in the Zairian **government**. Blumenthal's job was to help bank officials control irregularities in the disbursement of Zaire's **foreign exchange**. However, it turned into a quixotic attempt to prevent the barons of the regime from raiding the state coffers. In December 1978, Blumenthal shocked Zairian business and political leaders by prohibiting 51 prominent Zairian businessmen from drawing foreign exchange from the central bank because of debts and irregular dealings with the bank. One of those affected was **Litho Moboti, Mobutu's** uncle and head of the family financial empire. Seven others were members of the **Political Bureau** of the **Mouvement Populaire de la Révolution (MPR)** party.

Blumenthal left in 1979 and was replaced by another, less flamboyant IMF executive. In 1983, however, Blumenthal again shook the Zairian government in a report detailing incidents of corruption by senior Zairian officials and the presidency. The report was meant to be confidential but was leaked to the public and became an important piece of evidence in hearings by the US Congress. During the 1980s and 1990s, Zairians more intimately involved with the inner workings of the system wrote about what came to be known as the Zairian "kleptocracy," but Blumenthal provided one of the first documented insights into official Zairian corruption.

BOA. An influential ethnic group living near **Kisangani** in **Orientale Province**. In an extensive study, ethnologist Jan Vansina noted that the Boa are primarily a patrilineal group that has no **clans** but operates on a system of lineages, each with its senior male member and usually including slaves. Newcomers to the region, if in a large enough group, are allowed to form their own lineage.

BOBOLIKO LOKONGA MONSE MIHOMO, ANDRÉ (1934 -). A union leader considered by many to be the father of trade unionism in Congo/Zaire. Boboliko was born August 15, 1934, at Lobamiti in **Bandundu** Province. He attended Catholic secondary schools in **Leopoldville** and worked at a printing shop there until he was sent on a scholarship to Louvain, **Belgium**, to study social work. In 1959, he returned to Congo and was elected secretary-general (*administrateur national*) of the Confédération de Syndicats Chrétiens du Congo, a major union. In 1960, Boboliko was elected secretary-general of the Union des Travailleurs Congolais (UTC), one of three major Congolese trade unions. He was a member of the **College of Commissioners** that replaced **parliament** in 1960-61 and was elected president of the UTC in 1961. When the trade unions were united by the government under the banner of the **Union Nationale des Travailleurs Congolais (UNTC)** in 1967, Boboliko was elected secretary-general of that organization. He was appointed to the **Political Bureau** of the **Mouvement Populaire de la Révolution (MPR)** in 1968 and a member of its **Central Committee** in 1980. With the advent of multipartyism in 1990, Boboliko joined the **Parti Démocrate et Social Chrétien (PDSC)** of Joseph **Ileo** and was elected vice president. Following Ileo's death in 1994, Boboliko assumed the presidency of the PDSC and Ileo's post of vice president in the **Haut Conseil de la République / Parlement de la Transition.**

BOBOZO SALELO, LOUIS (GENERAL) (1915 - 1982). A war hero who was one of the commanders who approved the **Mobutu coup d'etat** of November 1965 and who commanded the Zairian **armed forces** from the 1970s until his death in July 1982. Bobozo began his army career in the **Force Publique** in 1933 at the age of 18. He rose through the ranks and at **independence** was one of the highest-ranking Congolese officers. He was a warrant officer stationed at Camp Hardy in Thysville when the army mutinied following independence. Following the mutiny, he was promoted to colonel and made commander of Camp Hardy.

BOKELEALE ITOFO, JEAN (ARCHBISHOP). Head of the **Église du Christ au Congo** that groups most **Protestant Church** denominations in the country. Originally from **Équateur Province**, Bokeleale was educated and ordained in the Disciples of Christ denomination. Opposition leaders criticized him for not speaking out about the excesses of the **Mobutu** government as did the **Catholic Church** and its more vocal leader, Archbishop Joseph **Malula**. However, supporters pointed out that under his guidance the smaller Protestant Church prospered and stayed out of fractious politics. Bokeleale was due to retire in August 1996 but a committee searching for his replacement had yet to complete its work.

BOLIKANGO AKPOLOKAKA-ABUKULU-NZUBE, JEAN (1909 - 1982). An early political leader who attended the **Round Table Conferences** and served in a number of governments following **independence**. Bolikango was born in February 1909 in **Leopoldville** to parents originally from **Équateur Province**. He studied and later taught with the Scheut Fathers. He joined the **Mouvement National Congolais (MNC)** and led its conservative wing for a short time, but split to form the Parti de l'Unité Nationale (PUNA) of which he became president. In 1960, Bolikango ran for **president** under the PUNA banner. He was arrested when Patrice **Lumumba** declared martial law in August 1960. He later served as vice prime minister and information minister in the Joseph **Ileo** government, and as vice prime minister in the Cyrille **Adoula** government. Following the **Mobutu coup d'etat**, he served as minister of public works in the government of Léonard **Mulamba** and was appointed to the **Political Bureau** of the **Mouvement Populaire de la Révolution (MPR)** in 1968 and to its **Central Committee** in 1980. He died of illness in February 1982.

BOMA. A **Bantu ethnic group** living in the Mai-Ndombe area along the **Congo River** north of the **Kwa/Kasai River**. The Boma are considered a relatively heterogeneous group that traces its origins to the **Tio Kingdom** of the precolonial era.

BOMA (CITY). An early capital of the **Congo Free State** and one of **Congo/Zaire**'s three **ports** accommodating ocean-going ships, Boma lies on the north side of the **Congo River**, about halfway between **Matadi** and the Atlantic Ocean. As part of the administrative reorganization of 1978, Boma was made an urban subregion. With an estimated **population** of 250,000 in 1995 (182,930 in 1982), Boma is larger than Matadi, but Matadi's location at the head of the **railway** leading to **Kinshasa** makes it a more important commercial center. Boma acts as a transport center for the agricultural and textile products arriving from the Bas-Fleuve subregion and its links to Kinshasa were improved in the 1980s by the paving of the **road** to Matadi and the construction of a bridge over the Congo River at Matadi.

BOMBOKO LOKUMBA IS ELENGE, JUSTIN-MARIE (1928 -). Foreign minister during the 1980s who headed the **College of Commissioners** in 1960-61. Bomboko was born September 22, 1928, in Boleke, **Équateur Province**, and attended **Catholic Church** schools in the region before studying at **Lovanium University**'s administrative school from 1945-51. He studied political science at the Université Libre de Belgique and was head of the **student** association there before returning to Congo shortly before **independence**. He headed the College of Commissioners, a group of young intellectuals who governed in 1960-61 during the period of "neutralization" of **parliament** following the first standoff between President Joseph **Kasavubu** and Prime Minister Patrice **Lumumba**. He served as foreign minister in the Joseph **Ileo** government after Lumumba's death. Except for the period in 1964-65 when Moïse **Tshombe** was prime minister, Bomboko remained as foreign minister until 1969, when he was named ambassador to Washington. He was recalled in 1970 and was arrested following the unrest of 1971. Bomboko remained out of politics for nearly 10 years thereafter, devoting himself primarily to business, although he was appointed vice first state commissioner (equivalent to deputy prime minister) in 1981 for a brief period.

BOSHONGO (or BUSHONG). A major subgroup of the **Kuba** nation living in **Kasai Province** around Dekese, north of **Ilebo**. Ethnographers say the Boshongo (the spelling used by official Zairian ethnographers) initially were fishermen, but in the 17th century they began to grow **maize**, **manioc** and tobacco, and eventually conquered some of the neighboring **Lulua** and **Mongo** groups.

BRAZZAVILLE. The capital of the **Republic of the Congo/ Brazzaville**, Brazzaville lies across the **Congo River** from **Kinshasa**, at **Malebo Pool**. Brazzaville was heavily damaged and thousands of its residents were killed during four months of fighting between militias of several political leaders from July to October 1997.

BRUSSELS, TREATY OF (1890). A treaty signed following a conference convened in Brussels to address the problem of **slavery** in the **Congo Free State (CFS)**. The conference was called partly in reaction to the public outcry in Europe and the **United States** over reports of mistreatment of Congolese by officers of the CFS and private companies. In the treaty, **Leopold II** agreed to reforms but also won the right to impose a 10 percent import tax to defray administrative costs.

BRUSSELS WORLD FAIR. The Brussels World Fair was held in the fall of 1958. Belgian leaders, anxious to show their accomplishments in one of Africa's largest colonies, brought large numbers of Congolese to Brussels to participate. These individuals ranged from traditional **chiefs** to the up-and-coming *évolués*. During the fair, young Congolese such as Patrice **Lumumba** and **Mobutu** began to realize how isolated they had been kept from the rest of the world. They came into contact with Africans from other colonies: with leaders from Ghana, which had been granted independence the previous year, and with leaders in the French colonies that had elected representatives to the French government and were on the verge of receiving some form of autonomy. The contact with more-mature independence movements is said to have been a major factor in setting the stage for the demands by Congolese beginning in late 1958 for immediate **independence**.

BUKAVU. The capital of **Kivu Province** until the province was divided into three regions as part of administrative reforms in 1988. Bukavu, located on the southern shore of **Lake Kivu** near the border with **Rwanda**, became the capital of **Sud-Kivu Region**. With an area of about 60 square km and an estimated **population** of 250,000 in 1995 (158,465 in 1982), Bukavu lies in one of the most densely populated areas of **Congo/Zaire**. Located in the mountains along a major **trade** route with East Africa, Bukavu was a major trading center until the 1970s, but by the 1980s had been replaced as the major urban center in the region by **Goma**, capital of **Nord-Kivu**, lying on the northern tip of Lake Kivu. In 1994, Bukavu became a major **refugee** center after being inundated by 200,000 refugees fleeing the civil war in Rwanda. In October 1996, rebels of the **Alliance des Forces Démocratiques pour la Libération du Congo/Zaïre (AFDL)**, led by veteran **opposition** leader Laurent **Kabila**, seized Bukavu in one of the first victories of the offensive that overthrew the **Mobutu** government in May the following year.

"BULA MATARI." A colloquial name, meaning "stone crusher," given to members of the **Force Publique**. The expression, also used to denote a tough and forceful individual, an enforcer, was given as a nickname to Erwin **Blumenthal**, a German banker who was designated by the **International Monetary Fund** in the early 1980s as a director of the **central bank** as part of fiscal austerity measures.

BUMBA. A river **port** on the **Congo River** in northern Congo/Zaire. Bumba, sometimes called the gateway to the northeast, was located between the two regional capitals of **Mbandaka** and **Kisangani** and was the port of embarkation for goods traveling by **railway** to Isiro, Buta and Bombo in the northeastern corner of the country.

BURTON, RICHARD (1821 - 1890). An English explorer who, with John **Speke**, was the first European to reach **Lake Tanganyika**, in 1858, by crossing eastern Africa from the Indian Ocean.

BURUNDI, RELATIONS WITH. Burundi is a small, densely populated country with a population of 6.2 million in 1994, originally colonized by the Germans but administered by **Belgium** after World War I. It lies along **Congo/Zaire**'s eastern border and on the banks of **Lake Tanganyika**, where its remote location caused it to be somewhat neglected by Belgian colonial authorities. Relations between Congo/Zaire and Burundi have been close since the two countries gained **independence** in 1960. **Mobutu** helped mediate a dispute between Burundi and **Tanzania** in 1972 after a group of dissidents took refuge in Tanzania following a failed attempt to overthrow the government of Burundian president Michel Micombero. Relations were further strengthened in 1976 when Burundi joined Zaire and **Rwanda** in forming the **Communauté Économique des Pays des Grands Lacs (CEPGL)**.

In the 1980s, President Mobutu exchanged numerous visits with Presidents Jean-Baptiste Bagaza and his replacement, Pierre Buyoya. Mobutu also supported Burundi's bid to host the France-Africa summit in December 1984, which was attended by nearly two dozen heads of state. Zaire supported Burundi's democratic transition, in which President Buyoya's **Tutsi**-dominated military handed power to an elected civilian government led by **Hutu** politician Melchior Ndadaye.

The assassination of President Ndadaye in 1993 by military elements led to a series of interethnic clashes in which hundreds of people were killed and tens of thousands were forced to flee to eastern Zaire. President Mobutu joined other East African presidents in trying to mediate the conflict. In mid-1996, in the face of rising instability due to clashes between Hutus and Tutsis, Buyoya was returned to power in a military coup. Burundi's neighbors imposed tough economic sanctions against the country and refused to allow Buyoya to attend regional conferences. In October 1996, rebels of the **Alliance des Forces Démocratiques pour la Libération du Congo/Zaïre (AFDL)**, led by Congolese Tutsis, launched an offensive in eastern Congo/Zaire, near the Burundian border, and in seven months seized **Kinshasa**, driving Mobutu into exile. Relations between Burundi and the government of Laurent **Kabila**, installed in May 1997, initially were excellent, but soured the following year, when Burundi backed a rebellion against the Kabila government.

BUSHONG. *See* BOSHONGO.

- C -

CABINDA. The Angolan enclave of Cabinda encompasses a mere 600 square km of territory along the Atlantic coast north of the 30-km strip of Congolese coastline surrounding the mouth of the **Congo River**. The port of Cabinda was a major Central African Atlantic port during the 18th and 19th centuries and competed with Pointe-Noire before being destroyed by the French in 1783. Cabinda formally came under Portuguese rule in 1885 and was administered separately until 1956, when it began to be administered as part of **Angola**. The area contains considerable offshore deposits of **petroleum** that provide the Angolan government with most of its foreign exchange earnings. Two hundred wells were operating in the 1990s as a joint venture by the state-owned SONANGOL (51 percent ownership) and the US company Chevron (49 percent ownership), which bought the original partner, Gulf Oil Corp., in 1984.

A nationalist liberation group calling itself the **Frente para a Libertação do Enclave de Cabinda (FLEC)** was formed in the 1970s aimed at liberating the territory from Portuguese rule. Following Angola's independence, FLEC guerrillas continued their attacks, primarily against the oil installations. Zaire supported FLEC until after the **Shaba** wars, when Angola and Zaire agreed to stop supporting each other's **opposition** movements. From the 1970s until their departure in the 1990s, contingents of a 25,000-strong Cuban military presence in Angola guarded the oil installations against attacks by FLEC and the **South Africa**-backed **União Nacional para a Independência Total de Angola (UNITA)**. FLEC activity, including some incidents of hostage-taking, continued sporadically through the 1990s.

CABINET. *See* EXECUTIVE COUNCIL.

CADRES. A French term denoting the executive staff of an **administration** or the officer corps of a military unit. In Zaire, the term took on a broader meaning with political connotations: young intelligent *élites* who were being taught how to actuate the levers of power and who, through political fidelity and purity, expected and were expected to attain senior positions by rising through the political ranks.

CAISSE NATIONALE D'ÉPARGNE ET DE CRÉDIT IMMOBILIER (CNECI). Congo/Zaire's national savings and loan institution, established by the **government** to promote savings and to help citizens purchase homes or finance mortgages. The CNECI, which tended to favor the wealthy *élite*, was bankrupted by the **inflation** of the early 1990s and by 1993 had virtually ceased to operate.

CÃO, DIOGO. A **Portuguese explorer** who was the first European to land at the mouth of the **Congo River** in 1483, a decade before Columbus reached America. In the 1480s, Cão visited the area several times, establishing contacts with the **Kingdom of Kongo**, bringing Portuguese **missionaries** to the kingdom, and taking nobles from the Kongo's court to **Portugal**.

CASABLANCA GROUP. The name given in the 1960s to what were considered the "radical" African nations: Ghana, Guinea, Mali, **Morocco** and the United Arab Republic (**Egypt**). The Casablanca Group supported a strong central **government** in the Congo, as advocated by Patrice **Lumumba**. Following Lumumba's death, they met in Casablanca, Morocco, and announced they were withdrawing their troop contingents that had been taking part in the **United Nations** operation in the Congo. All except Ghana did so.

CASEMENT, ROBERT (1864 - 1916). British consul to the **Congo Free State (CFS)** who was commissioned by the British government in the early 1900s to report on **labor** conditions. His report, published in 1904, was one of those that, along with **missionary** reports and the works of Edmund D. **Morel**, aroused public opinion in the **United Kingdom** and the **United States** against abuses in the CFS and **Leopold II**'s sovereignty over it.

CASSAVA. *See* MANIOC.

CATARACTES. A district of **Bas-Congo Province** named after the cataracts formed by the **Crystal Mountains** that render the **Congo River** unnavigable for some 200 km and contribute to the country's status as a "semi-enclave" state. The district is a relatively fertile area with an estimated **population** of 800,000 in 1995 (590,793 in 1982) that engages in farming, **livestock** raising and some trading.

CATHOLIC CHURCH, ROMAN. The Catholic Church has been the largest organized religious system in Congo/Zaire since the turn of the century. The Vatican's *Annuario Pontificio* states that 40 percent of the **population** of Congo/Zaire is Catholic. The Church has played a significant role in political life, sometimes acting as the conscience of the nation.

Catholic **missionaries** first arrived in Congo in the 1480s and heavily influenced life in the **Kongo Kingdom** for nearly 100 years. They converted a number of **kings** and **chiefs** to **Christianity** and established missions, churches and schools. The missionaries' influence declined in the 1600s, but organized missionary activity resumed in 1870 as European interest in Africa reawakened. Irving Kaplan writes, "Most Catholic missionaries, themselves Belgians, shared the view of the colonial authorities that they had a civilizing mission, the task of inculcating in Congolese those virtues . . . the capacity for hard work, decency, and reliability . . . that would mark them as black Belgian burghers."

The main task conferred upon the missions by the colonial authorities was in the field of **education**. Hundreds of parochial schools were set up during the first decades of the 20th century and beginning in 1925 the colonial government further encouraged the efforts by subsidizing (primarily Catholic) missions schools to train Congolese. The Catholic Church also founded Congo's first **university, Lovanium,** in 1954. In addition to the educational work, the Church established clinics and hospitals, carried out large-scale baptism programs, and built many churches.

Many sects arose around the Catholic teachings, most notably the **Jamaa** and the Katete, which attempted to meld Catholic principles with African sensibilities and customs. However, these were frowned upon. In 1917, the first Congolese priest was ordained and the first bishop was installed in 1956. In the 1980s, there were more than 700 missions in the country, working primarily in education, **health care** and to a lesser degree in **agriculture.**

The Catholic Church has long been a political power in Congo/Zaire and **alumni groups** of the mission schools were among the first to condemn discrimination against Congolese and other abuses of colonialism. However, the Church as an institution usually worked with the authorities, both before and after **independence,** and often played a stabilizing social role. The Church came into open conflict with the state in the 1970s. The state nationalized Lovanium University in 1971 following **student** unrest. The **Authenticity** program also irritated the Church, particularly the decree ordering Congolese to abandon their Christian names for "authentic" African ones and the attempts to convert parochial schools into lay institutions. The decrees outlawing all **youth** movements except the **Jeunesse du Mouvement Populaire de la Révolution (JMPR)**, the youth wing of the **Mouvement Populaire de la Révolution (MPR)**, and ordering the establishment of JMPR branches in all schools and seminaries also irked the Church. The Church responded by threatening to close its seminaries.

On January 12, 1972, the journal *Afrique Chrétienne* questioned the policy of Authenticity and was closed down. The leader of the church, Cardinal Joseph **Malula**, also objected at that time to the use of hymns with the word "**Mobutu**" substituted for "God" in the lyrics. Malula was forced to leave the country and his residence was sacked. In March 1972, the **Political Bureau** of the MPR announced religious services would no longer be a part of official state functions. Later in the year, the government banned all religious television and **radio** broadcasts and prohibited religious church groups from meeting. In February 1973, 31 religious publications were banned. The antireligious moves came at a time when Zairian political leaders, influenced by the People's Republic of **China** and North Korea, wished to establish the unquestioned supremacy of party and state in Zaire. However, the measures were resented by many Zairians who remained highly religious and many of the decrees were eventually relaxed.

Church-state relations soured again a few years later when the Catholic Church condemned **corruption** and the decline of morality in the country. However, efforts were made to accommodate some government policies and Pope **John Paul II**'s visit in 1980 signaled a rapprochement. The pope paid a second visit to Zaire in 1985, this time beatifying a Congolese nun who was killed by **Simba** rebels during the eastern **rebellions** of the early 1960s.

During the late 1980s, Catholic leaders became increasingly critical of Zairian **government** and **society**. A group of priests wrote a public letter in 1987 decrying the moral degeneration of the society. Similar letters were issued in the 1990s. A march by priests and their followers in **Kinshasa** on a Sunday following mass on February 16, 1992, was violently quashed by security forces, resulting in 46 deaths and a domestic and international outcry.

Malula died on June 14, 1989, at the age of 72 years, in Louvain after a lengthy illness. The bishop of **Mbandaka**, Monsignor Frédéric **Etsou**, was named archbishop of Kinshasa in 1990, then raised to the rank of cardinal, replacing Malula as titular head of the Catholic Church in the country.

The Interdiocesan Center in Kinshasa is the primary coordinating body of the Church in Congo/Zaire. Major orders present in the country include Jesuit, Dominican, Paulist, Sacred Heart, Capuchin, Maris Brothers, Brothers of the Christian Schools, Sisters of Mary, Sisters of the Sacred Heart of Mary, and Sisters of Saint Joseph.

CEMENT. Five cement companies operate in Congo/Zaire with a total capacity of 1.1 million tons per year. However, output in the 1980s and 1990s was less than 50 percent of capacity because of fuel shortages and the economic recession.

CENTER FOR AERONAUTICAL TRAINING. *See* CENTRE D'ENTRAÎNEMENT DES TROUPES AÉRONAUTIQUES (CETA).

CENTRAL AFRICAN CUSTOMS AND ECONOMIC UNION. *See* UNION DOUANIÈRE ET ÉCONOMIQUE DE L'AFRIQUE CENTRALE (UDEAC).

CENTRAL AFRICAN REPUBLIC, RELATIONS WITH. A small landlocked country of 2.5 million people and 241,313 square km of territory lying along Congo/Zaire's northern border, the Central African Republic (CAR) has historically maintained good relations with the government of Congo/Zaire. Because of its isolation and smaller size, it has usually been a junior partner in any endeavors. The government in Bangui had warm ties with the government of **Mobutu**, who was from a small town on the southern side of the **Ubangi River,** which forms a great part of the border between the two countries, and whose family is said to have originated in part from the CAR. The CAR depends on the Ubangi and **Congo Rivers** (the former only navigable between six and eight months of the year) for most of its overland transportation and commerce, and as a result it tries to maintain good relations with Congo/Zaire and **Congo/Brazzaville**, its other neighbor downriver. *See also* Chad, Relations with.

CENTRAL BANK. The **government**'s central **banking** and clearing house for **currency** and **foreign exchange**, the central bank was called the Banque Centrale du Congo Belge et du Ruanda-Urundi during the **colonial era**. The bank was called Conseil Monétaire du Congo from 1961 to 1964, when it was changed to Banque Centrale du Congo. During the **Mobutu** years, when Congo was called **Zaire**, the bank was called the Banque Nationale du Zaïre (BNZ). The name was again changed to Banque Nationale du Congo (BNC) after the fall of Mobutu in 1997.

In the late 1970s, as part of an economic stabilization agreement with the **International Monetary Fund (IMF)**, Zaire permitted an official chosen by the IMF to assume the position of principal director (second to the director) in order to curb excessive and unofficial disbursements of scarce foreign exchange. The bank adopted austerity measures and restricted purchases of foreign exchange for luxury items. The attempts, however, were considered largely ineffective until 1983 when, as part of a package of fiscal and monetary reforms, the government began to allow private banks to sell foreign exchange and the **currency** was floated on the free market. Following the collapse of the formal economic sector in the early 1990s, the BNZ became known for issuing larger and larger currency notes, which were used to pay soldiers and civil servants and frequently ended up directly on the parallel market in exchange for foreign currency. *See also* "Wall Street."

CENTRAL COMMITTEE. A 120-member body of the **Mouvement Populaire de la Révolution (MPR)**, established on September 2, 1980, which during the 1980s assumed legislative functions within the party-state. It became the basic consultative body for the **president** and the **Political Bureau**, responsible for debating laws proposed by the latter. Members were appointed by the Political Bureau. The **Legislative Council**, the members of which were chosen in popular elections, remained but primarily as an organ that ratified the laws emanating from the executive branch and the party. The Central Committee declined in influence following the announcement in 1990 of the **democratic transition**, in part because the **National Conference** increasingly became the forum for legislative-style debate and because many of the Central Committee's members left to form their own political parties.

CENTRAL INTELLIGENCE AGENCY (CIA). **United States** government intelligence agency that was linked by researchers and the news media to many events in Congo, particularly in the early 1960s when, according to declassified cables, it had license to engage in covert activities to counter communist activities in the country. Declassified secret documents reveal that the CIA in 1960 ordered its bureau chief, Lawrence **Devlin,** to study ways to eliminate Patrice **Lumumba**. Devlin said he never carried out the plans. Congolese **dissidents** say **Mobutu** was recruited by the agency and used and was used by it. Mobutu on occasion accused the CIA of seeking to destabilize his government. In 1975, he accused the agency of involvement in the "Ndele" plot, for which three Zairian generals and two army majors were executed. The charges were never substantiated. At other times, the agency was credited with warning Mobutu of impending plots against him. Sean Kelly, in his 1993 book, *America's Tyrant: The CIA and Mobutu of Zaire*, details accounts of CIA officials supporting the government's war against the eastern **rebellions** and uses declassified cables to demonstrate collaboration between Mobutu and officials of the US Embassy in **Kinshasa** in efforts to manipulate events and public opinion.

CENTRE D'ENTRAÎNEMENT DES TROUPES AÉRONAUTIQUES (CETA) / CENTER FOR AERONAUTICAL TRAINING. The training center for **Congo/Zaire**'s airborne forces, based at **Ndjili Airport** on the outskirts of **Kinshasa**. CETA gained notoriety for sparking the looting which began on September 23, 1991, and spread to various urban centers. The violence began over dissatisfaction with low and late pay but became generalized when the local population joined in the **"pillages."** It brought a Franco-Belgian military intervention and the evacuation of 10,000 expatriates. *See also* Air Force.

CHAD, RELATIONS WITH. **Congo/Zaire** and Chad have had close relations since they became independent. Congo sent troops to Chad in the late 1960s to bolster the François Tombalbaye government in the face of a northern rebellion. In 1981, Zaire supplied troops as part of the **Organization of African Unity (OAU)** peacekeeping force sent to Chad to protect the government of Goukouni Oueddai. In 1983, Zairian troops, including the **Kamanyola Division**, were dispatched again and remained for two years after the Goukouni forces, driven from Ndjamena by supporters of Hissen Habre, threatened to return in an offensive backed by **Libya**. Chadian soldiers were frequently sent to Zaire for training and **Mobutu** visited Chad many times. In the economic sector, Congo/Zaire, Chad joined Zaire in 1968 in forming the Union des États de l'Afrique Centrale (UEAC), but the move was greeted with hostility by Cameroon, **Congo/Brazzaville**, and Gabon, which had already joined Chad and the CAR in the **France**-backed **Union Douanière et Économique de l'Afrique Centrale (UDEAC)** customs union. The organization disbanded in the 1970s. Chad and Zaire eventually joined UDEAC in the 1980s. Both were founding members in September 1983 of the 11-nation **Economic Community of Central African States**.

CHANIMETAL. The largest metal works in Congo/Zaire, which builds and repairs river boats at its yards in **Kinshasa** and makes a variety of consumer items ranging from pots and pans to farming tools. *See also* Steel.

CHARTE COLONIALE. *See* COLONIAL CHARTER.

CHIEFS. The titular head of a traditional political entity ranging in size from a small village to feudal state. Anthropologists note that with few exceptions, every community in Congo had a chief of some kind. Often the chief's most important function was to perform religious rituals or settle disputes. Among the **Alur** of northeastern Congo, for instance, chiefs controlled the weather and interceded with the ancestors to settle disputes. Some societies developed elaborate chieftaincy structures. For example, in the **Luba** and **Teke** empires, groups of villages formed chiefdoms, several chiefdoms formed a province, and all of the provinces formed a kingdom. Chiefs rarely made decisions alone and usually only after consulting a council of elders. A notable exception was the **Zande**, who developed a system of supreme chiefs who delegated their power and privileges to subordinates. Some chiefdoms, such as among the Lopwe and Teke, were hereditary. Some were appointed, as in some Luba societies. Others were assumed on the basis of wealth. Some were elected and some were chosen through a combination of the above.

Frequently, a major duty of the traditional chief was to collect tribute for a **king** or higher chief. In the **colonial era**, chiefs were expected to provide links between the administration and the traditional societies. Before World War I, the Congo was divided administratively into chiefdoms (*chefferies*). The chiefs were appointed and paid by the administration and were given administrative and police powers. The chiefs' major responsibility was to administer **customary law**, which was a separate legal system from colonial law. A European could not be tried under customary law, but an African could be tried under either of the two, depending on the nature of the charges. In the 1920s, the chiefdoms were consolidated into sectors. These did not coincide with traditional boundaries and, as a result, created confusion.

Following **independence**, chiefs continued to exercise their functions although the extent of their influence depended on their personal prestige and amount of influence over local administrative authorities. During the administrative reforms of 1972-73, the Zairian government tried to transfer traditional chiefs to other areas, as it had been doing with regional governors and military commanders, but it was obliged to abandon the policy because of public protest. After that, the government for the most part avoided centralized attempts to develop policies toward or regulate the activities of traditional chiefs. Instead it tended to approach chiefs individually, or as a group in a certain area, to help solve specific problems and achieve specific goals, such as acquiring land for public use or obtaining local manpower for public works. Although not always visible to outsiders, traditional chiefs could influence **government** policy, especially if they had experience in dealing with government officials. Traditional chiefs were officially recognized in the **democratic transition**. A large number of them attended the **National Conference** of 1991-92, some as representatives of their officially recognized civic association.

CHINA, PEOPLE'S REPUBLIC OF, RELATIONS WITH. Following **independence**, relations between the Congolese **government** and China were cool because of Chinese support for the **Mulele** uprising and other **rebellions.** In 1972, however, several years after the rebellions were ended and as China was being admitted to the **United Nations,** Zaire established diplomatic relations with China. The friendship between Zaire and China deepened when they discovered they both opposed the **Soviet**-backed **Movimento Popular de Libertação de Angola (MPLA)** faction in the Angolan civil war. **Mobutu** visited Beijing and North Korea in 1973 and upon his return announced he would radicalize the Zairian revolution. He said that henceforth he would be addressed as "citizen" and that he would establish cooperative systems of production. The **nationalization** of foreign-owned businesses with annual gross incomes over one million **zaires** and an increased emphasis on cultural **Authenticity** followed shortly thereafter.

The Chinese government backed Zaire during the **Shaba** invasions saying they were the work of the Soviet-backed government in **Angola.** The Chinese built a convention hall called the "People's Palace" in **Kinshasa** which was the venue for the **National Conference** of 1991-92, and it provided assistance and training in agricultural, particularly **rice,** projects in Zaire. The Zairian government appreciated China's support, which did not fluctuate with international opinion and the ups and downs of Zairian relations with Western governments. The Chinese government saw many parallels between Congo/Zaire and its own large nation of disparate, struggling peoples.

CHOKWE. A **Bantu ethnic group** related in many ways to the **Lunda,** with whom they are often at odds. The Chokwe were originally a seminomadic, matrilineal society of hunters and some traders from northeastern **Angola** who were largely unknown to Europeans until the mid-1800s when they began expanding rapidly into **Katanga, Kasai** and the upper **Kwango** and **Kasai River** areas. A people of the savannas, they were organized into groups of small chiefdoms that, according to some, enabled them to raid

Lunda settlements and at one point to take over the Lunda capital near what is now the Congo-**Zambia** border area. The Lunda halted the Chokwe expansion in the 1890s but did not move them back.

Following **independence**, the Chokwe were an important political force in southern Congolese politics. For a time, they allied themselves with the **Association des Baluba du Katanga (BALUBAKAT)** because of their conflicts with the Lunda, who dominated the **Confédération des Associations Katangaises (CONAKAT)**. In later years, however, their politics were characterized primarily by resentment against the national **government** in **Kinshasa**, which they felt appropriated the wealth of the region for its own uses and returned little of it to the region.

CHRISTIANITY. An estimated 50 to 65 percent of the Congolese **population** is considered Christian, though Christianity is often mixed with local religious practices and liturgy. The **Catholic Church** predominates, claiming adherence of 60 to 70 percent of the country's Christians. Twenty to 30 percent are estimated to belong to **Protestant** denominations, and the remainder adhere to African offshoots of Christianity like **Kimbanguism**.

Christianity arrived in Congo during the 1480s when **missionaries** brought by explorer **Diogo Cão** converted the reigning **king**'s brother, who later became King **Affonso I.** Affonso proved receptive to Catholicism as well as to aspects of European culture. Christianity began spreading slowly eastward with European missionaries and traders. Its influence, however, declined in the 1600s with the rise of **slavery** and the **ivory** trade. However, it returned beginning in 1880 with the arrival in **Boma** of the **France**-based Fathers of the Holy Spirit and the Order of Missionaries in Africa ("White Fathers") on the shores of **Lake Tanganyika**. **Belgium**'s Scheut Fathers arrived in 1888 and by 1900 the number of Catholic missions had grown to 17.

The first Protestant mission was founded in 1878. Following the **Berlin Conference**, Protestant missions expanded quickly with British, American, Swedish, French and Belgian churches sending missionaries to build schools, churches and hospitals. There were 46 Protestant missionary groups in the country at **independence**. That figure has nearly doubled. Kimbanguism, the church of followers of Simon **Kimbangu**, mixes African traditions with Christianity. Kimbanguism was harshly repressed in its early years by the colonial authorities but eventually was accepted. It was admitted to the World Council of Churches in 1969. Its membership has grown steadily and may now constitute 10 percent of all Congolese Christians.

The churches have always been influential in politics. With the advent of **Authenticity** and the **nationalistic** policies of the late 1960s and early 1970s, they entered a period of confrontation with the **government**. In 1972, **Mobutu** decreed that all Zairians born after February 16, 1972, would bear the names of their ancestors instead of Christian surnames. In March, the government announced that religious services would no longer be a part of official state functions. Other measures were taken to lessen the influence of the church in politics, including the suspension of the journal *Afrique Chrétienne*, the banning of all Christian broadcasts and the temporary exile of the head of the Catholic Church, Cardinal Joseph **Malula** in 1972. At the peak of the antireligious fervor, some hymns were adapted by the government with the word "Mobutu" substituted for "God," just as early missionaries had substituted "God" and "Jesus" for the names of traditional African gods in indigenous religious songs. In the mid-1970s, the government loosened some of its antichurch policies and in October 1976 rescinded an earlier decision to take over all church schools. In the face of declining government services in the late 1970s, church agencies assumed an increasingly large role in distributing foreign **food** shipments and developing educational texts and facilities.

Relations between church and state had been officially mended by the time Pope **John Paul II** paid his first visit to Zaire in 1980. He visited again in 1985. During the late 1980s and early 1990s, leaders of the Catholic Church were particularly active in pressing for democratic reforms. The **National Conference** was chaired first by a Protestant leader, **Kalonji Mutambayi** and subsequently by **Monsengwo Pasinya,** the archbishop of **Kisangani**. On a number of occasions, Catholic leaders publicly criticized the government for **corruption** and **human rights** abuses and decried the moral decay of **society**. In 1993, the bishops again publicly condemned the regime and accused Mobutu of seeking to maintain control over the political apparatus through state terrorism, **ethnic cleansing** and economic sabotage. Throughout, nevertheless, a great portion of the church devoted itself primarily to tending the needs of those suffering because of urban migration, the loss of family support-systems, and the decline of the public **social services** network. By the 1990s, church aid groups became major conduits for international aid distributions. *See also* Église du Christ au Congo (ECC) / Church of Christ in the Congo.

CHURCH OF CHRIST IN THE CONGO. *See* ÉGLISE DU CHRIST AU CONGO (ECC).

CIMENTERIE NATIONALE (CIMA). A **cement** plant in **Bas-Congo** built in 1978 with 51 percent **government** ownership and the remainder owned by a private West **German** firm. It operated only intermittently in the 1980s and 1990s, hindered by a shortage of fuel and spare parts and low demand.

CITÉ. The term coined by the Belgians to denote the "inner" or indigenous sections of Congo's cities. In the large cities in particular, the *cité* is a teeming neighborhood of crowded homes, some of which are **government**-built housing projects, others individually built. The *cité* is a vigorous economic and political sector of the city and no politician ignores the mood of its residents.

CIVIL GUARD. Following border clashes between Zairian and **Zambian** soldiers in **Shaba Region** in 1983-84, the Zairian **government** announced it would create a new corps, called the Guarde Civile or Civil Guard, which would be responsible for border **security**, combating **smuggling**, controlling terrorism and "re-establishing public order." West **Germany** and **Egypt** assisted with training. Although poorly paid at times, the Guard was viewed as second only to the **Division Spéciale Présidentielle (DSP)** in loyalty to **Mobutu**. Its forces were used on numerous occasions to quash demonstrations and harass the **opposition**. Military analysts estimated in the early 1990s the Guard numbered 10,000 members, based primarily in urban centers. After the fall of Mobutu, the government of Laurent **Kabila** announced in June 1997 it was abolishing the Civil Guard and **Gendarmerie Nationale** and with **South African** assistance was recreating a national **police** force.

CIVIL RIGHTS. *See* HUMAN RIGHTS.

CIVIL RIGHTS, DECLARATION OF / DECLARATION DES DROITS CIVILS. A document published by the **Alliance des Bakongo (ABAKO)** on August 23, 1956, partly in reaction to a more cautious manifesto published in *Conscience Africaine* on June 30, 1956. The declaration called for immediate political rights of association, speech and press for Congolese. It is often considered the first public manifestation of growing pressure from Congolese intellectuals for political freedom and eventually **independence**.

CIVIL SERVICE / FONCTION PUBLIQUE. A system of public employment that was essentially inherited from the Belgian **colonial era** structure but which underwent some modifications following **independence**. The **government**-wide civil service was abolished in 1972 in order to give the state commissioners (ministers) greater leeway in hiring and firing employees within their departments. However, significant constraints were maintained. The Department of Finance and the Permanent Commission for Public Administration continued to oversee employment practices in order to control abuses. The concept of civil service resembled that of many other countries. Government jobs were viewed by many as a reward for political service and political appointments were routine. A job with the government was considered relatively secure, although the paycheck was not always on time. During the 1970s and 1980s civil servants were expected to profess "militancy" within the **Mouvement Populaire de la Révolution (MPR)** party. Like all Zairians, they were automatically members of the MPR.

With the **democratic transition** beginning in 1990, constraints were lifted on party affiliation and many civil servants openly displayed their support for the **opposition** by abandoning the **abacost** and resuming use of their Christian surnames. With the lifting of restrictions on **labor** unions, a number of unions were created in the civil service. These were among the strongest in criticizing the stagnation of wages and loss of buying power. Lengthy strikes were staged during the 1990s and union leaders on occasion were detained. By the mid-1990s, poor pay and the lack of career mobility had led to rampant absenteeism and the unofficial practice of requiring payment for virtually any kind of service. On March 6, 1995, the government of Prime Minister Léon **Kengo wa Dondo** dismissed 300,000 government workers after an audit revealed that one-half of the country's 600,000 civil servants did not exist.

CLANS. Clans are relatively close-knit groups, usually within the extended family, often organized around one or two veteran family members, their children, grandchildren, spouses and sometimes members of the spouse's families. Clans, by most definitions, are usually within the same **ethnic group**, but often spread further out than **descent groups**, particularly for political purposes and in situations where greater numbers were needed for survival.

CLASS. Experts in recent years have argued against a rigid traditional delineation of class in **Congo/Zaire**, saying rather that it should be viewed as a fluid set of groupings that might change depending on situation or individual perception at a given time. They tend to identify the following groups, elaborated by Georges Nzongola-Ntalaja, in descending order of status: the foreign expatriate class whose salaries in foreign **currency** allow an extremely high standard of living; the Congolese political **élite**, or high bourgeoisie, whose political connections allow large and rapid accumulations of wealth; an entrepreneurial class whose members are often uneducated but aggressive and astute and often achieve business success often in the informal sector; an impoverished but still respected professional class that includes doctors, university professors, clergy, high-ranking parastatal managers, and military officers; a subprofessional or lower bourgeoisie whose members include teachers, clerks, junior military officers and low-level civil servants; a working class of urban and rural wage earners; small or individual workers in cottage industries or the informal sector such as tailors, cobblers, small traders, smugglers, prostitutes and petty thieves; and the peasant class that exists on subsistence farming, small plot gardening and small-time trading.

Experts note that because of Congo/Zaire's economic decline, all but the top three classes are impoverished, benefit little from **social services**, and live with little protection from financial catastrophe other than family solidarity. However, they also note that within **society**, members of the subbourgeoisie, informal, and peasant classes sometimes benefit from the middle-status groups, which in turn benefit from the upper classes. In Congolese society it is widely held that it is important to help the less privileged in times of need, whether through monetary assistance or social connections. Failure to do so is considered antisocial. Although economic decline has rendered such responsibilities increasingly difficult to fulfill, members of the more privileged classes are aware of the responsibility and themselves tend to hold similar views about those with higher status than they. This sense of solidarity or philanthropy tends to help "spread the wealth" and has been cited as one reason for the ability of many Congolese to survive the country's many economic crises. *See also* Middle Class.

CLIMATE. **Congo/Zaire**'s climate is tropical. A normal year is usually divided into a long (four months) rainy season of hot, wet weather and a long dry season of cool, temperate weather. Each long season is usually broken up by a short (two weeks) season of alternate weather. The country straddles the equator, with one-third of the territory in the northern hemisphere and two-thirds in the southern hemisphere. As a result, farming, which is centered around the rainy seasons, is carried out year-round in the country and most **rivers** enjoy relatively stable water levels. Average annual **rainfall** is 1,000 to 2,200 mm. Rainfall is usually heaviest north of the equator between May and September and in the southern hemisphere from November to March. With some variations, the dry season in the north is from November to March and from May to September in the south. In some areas, for example, parts of the **Congo River Basin** and central **Kivu**, it rains almost every day of the year. Temperatures generally range from 20 to 35 degrees Celsius, or 68 to 95 degrees Fahrenheit, although temperatures in parts of **Katanga** sometimes fall below 10 degrees C (50 degrees F). Temperatures average 26 degrees C (78 degrees F) in coastal areas and 18 degrees C (64 degrees F) in mountainous areas. Depending on the season and the region, humidity ranges from 35 to 95 percent.

CLOTH. In Congo/Zaire and other Francophone African countries, the word *pagne* is used to denote the colorful print fabrics used to make everything from bed sheets and curtains to clothes and headdresses. The cloth originated primarily in Dutch-controlled parts of Malaysia, where the use of **wax** and dyes to create colorful prints created some of the most valued pieces of cloth in the world. Manufacture of the prints spread through Africa quickly and became identified as one of Africa's major contributions to fashion. Today most African countries, including Congo/Zaire, have textile factories producing the fabrics. The cloth, made in bolts two yards wide, is usually cut for resale into strips two to six yards in length. The cloth may be hemmed and worn as a robe or body wrap, or cut to make shirts, blouses and pajama-style outfits. A staple of African culture and dress, many prints are given a name. Some are designed and marketed for special purposes, whether it be to praise a leader or to mark a special event such as a summit meeting, a soccer tournament, a cultural festival, or a visit by a foreign head-of-state. The gift of cloth between two individuals is considered a major gesture and may often precede a special request.

COAL. **Congo/Zaire** contains deposits of coal estimated at 60 million metric tons. However, many of the deposits are of relative poor quality and are located in isolated areas where **transportation** costs are prohibitive. The country produced 126,000 tons of low-grade coal in 1990, primarily in **Katanga**. High-quality coke and coal used for **mineral** processing is imported from Zimbabwe. Imports averaged 130,000 tons per year in the 1980s, but declined significantly in the 1990s with falling production by the large **mining** companies. Following the completion of the **Inga Hydroelectric Complex** and **Inga-Shaba power line**, **electrical power** has become the preferred form of industrial power.

COALITION DÉMOCRATIQUE CONGOLAISE (CDC) / CONGOLESE DEMOCRATIC COALITION. An alliance of forces dominated by the **Rassemblement Congolais pour la Démocratie (RCD)**, which launched a **rebellion** against the Laurent **Kabila** government on August 2, 1998.

COBALT. Cobalt, a by-product of some **copper** ores, is used to make super-alloys, particularly for the aerospace industry. At its peak, **Congo/Zaire** produced nearly one-half of the world's cobalt (and one-half of US cobalt imports) from two refineries at **Likasi** and **Kolwezi** operated by **Générale des Carrières et des Mines (GECAMINES)**. Production rose steadily during the 1970s, peaking at 14,500 tons in 1980 when prices reached $40 per pound on the spot market. Production fell over the next three years to 5,400 tons, in part because of a lack of spare parts for **mining** equipment and the exhaustion of easily accessible ores. Production began rising again in the 1980s and reached 10,000 tons in 1985. This level was maintained with some fluctuations until 1991, when production began to decline rapidly following the civil unrest in **Shaba** and the slide of GECAMINES toward insolvency. Production fell to 6,000 tons in 1992 and was estimated at a few thousand tons in 1995. Following the fall of **Mobutu**, the Laurent **Kabila** government announced joint ventures with several foreign companies to revive production in **Tenke, Kolwezi** and Kipushi.

COFFEE. In the 1980s, coffee was **Congo/Zaire's** largest agricultural export. Production, in decline since **independence**, began to rise following **government** reforms to the marketing system in 1983. The government agency **Office National de Café** said production reached 100,000 tons in 1985, of which 80,000 tons were "exportable." The **World Bank** reported the country exported 66,000 tons that year and 130,000 tons the following year, due in part to prices that attracted the product from farmers in neighboring countries. **Exports** declined to 68,000 tons in 1988 but rose in subsequent years and remained around 100,000 tons per year through the early 1990s. They declined to 52,000 tons in 1997 and 23,000 tons in 1998 because of tree disease and the rebellions in the eastern part of the country.

Government revenues from coffee were $432 million in 1994, equaling revenues from **diamonds**. Two major varieties were grown in Congo/Zaire: the hearty robusta in low-lying areas of the **Ubangi, Uele, Kivu, Kasai** and **Bas-Congo** areas, and the lighter arabica grown in the higher altitudes of eastern **Kivu** and **Ituri** and constituted one-fifth of the total crop.

COLLEGE OF COMMISSIONERS. A group of young intellectuals formed to direct state affairs after **Mobutu** "neutralized" the Congolese **government** in September 1960, following a constitutional crisis created by the political standoff between Joseph **Kasavubu** and Patrice **Lumumba**. The commission, headed by Justin-Marie **Bomboko**, was formally installed September 29, 1960. Like the government it replaced, it was weakened by factionalism. It was dissolved February 9, 1961, following the formation of the government of Joseph **Ileo**.

COLON. A French term meaning "colonialist." The *colon* was usually an agent or other secular representative of the colonial administration. The term, however, came to be used to describe other non-African residents of the Congo who, through manner and attitude, personalized an attitude of European superiority over Africans.

COLONIAL CHARTER / CHARTE COLONIALE. A law passed on October 18, 1908, by **Belgium's** parliament that formally abolished the **Congo Free State (CFS)** and ended King **Leopold II**'s personal sovereignty over the territory. The charter, passed partly in reaction to the international outcry over **human rights** abuses in the CFS, set out goals for the colonization of what would become the **Belgian Congo**. The goals included a "civilizing" mission of educating and Christianizing the indigenous people and guaranteed that the abuses of the CFS would not reoccur. In order to address the reluctance among some Belgian political leaders to assume so heavy a financial burden, it was also determined that the colony would earn a "profit" for the metropole. Under the charter, Leopold II lost his sovereignty over the territory but still retained a great deal of authority. He governed with the Belgian parliament and executive branch and ruled by decree, although his decrees required the approval of the minister of colonies. *See also* Constitution.

COLONIAL ERA. Although Europeans for centuries had been carrying out colonial activities of exploration, **trade** and evangelization, the colonial period formally began in Africa with the signing of the Berlin Act on February 26, 1885, at the conclusion of the **Berlin Conference**. The Act, often referred to as the European partition of Africa, divided the **Congo River Basin** among **France**, **Portugal** and the Belgian monarchy, and recognized what was to become the **Congo Free State (CFS)** and King **Leopold II**'s personal sovereignty over it. The CFS became the **Belgian Congo** 23 years later on November 15, 1908, when the Belgian parliament annexed the territory following an international outcry over abusive labor practices by traders and corporate monopolies. Under the **Colonial Charter**, the colony was administered by a governor-general, appointed by the king, who acted in consultation with a council but ruled by ordinance. Political activity was outlawed. Colonialism officially ended with **independence** on June 30, 1960.

The topic of colonialism will probably always remain controversial. Most Africans view colonialism as a period of occupation of their soil by a foreign power, a period of humiliation and of repressed rights and freedoms. Many *colons*, however, saw it as a well-intentioned attempt, perhaps flawed, to administer a vast, ungovernable land by dedicated pioneers who helped create Africa's independent states, albeit 20 to 50 years too early. According to many historians, the *colons* considered the African to be a child, superstitious and generally in need of supervision. The role of the colonizer, they felt, was paternal, to educate and prepare their charges for their eventual independence by teaching them the merits of hard work, productivity and responsibility.

The CFS became a colony in large part because of international criticism of its harsh **labor** practices. Its annexation by the Belgian parliament was also due to a growing realization in **Belgium** that the territory could be "economically viable," that is, that its vast riches could help pay for the cost of developing its infrastructure. Belgian colonial rule ended some of the forced labor practices and some of the **mining** and farming monopolies. However, exploitation continued in order to provide revenues to the metropole.

Colonialism ended much earlier than most Belgians expected, because of a revolt by the colonized, who preferred to develop their own version of the modern state. Because the lack of political and personal freedoms had prevented the evolution of political or administrative experience among the colonized, the colonizer was left with a sense of responsibility for having failed to complete a promised duty.

COMITÉ D'ÉTUDES POUR LE HAUT-CONGO. *See* COMMITTEE FOR THE STUDY OF THE UPPER CONGO.

COMITÉ SPÉCIAL DU KATANGA (CSK). A large, private **mining** consortium established by King **Leopold II** on June 19, 1900, to explore **Katanga** for **minerals**. It was one of a number of large companies or "trusts" given authority by the **Congo Free State (CFS)** to administer monopolies over vast areas of territory. The CSK, which held large amounts of stock in the **Union Minière du Haut-Katanga** mining company, was technically dissolved on the eve of **independence** by Belgian decree. However, its affairs were not settled until 1965 following negotiations with the government of Moïse **Tshombe**.

COMITÉ ZAÏRE. A group of opponents of the **Mobutu** government based in **Belgium** with enough financial support to provide a semiregular newsletter detailing **corruption, human rights** violations and abuses of power in **Zaire**. Some Zairian political exiles allied with the Comité Zaïre and utilized its facilities, but most **dissidents** preferred to form their own organizations. *See also* Opposition.

COMMERCE. *See* TRADE; ZAIRIANIZATION.

COMMITTEE FOR THE STUDY OF THE UPPER CONGO / COMITÉ D'ÉTUDES POUR LE HAUT-CONGO. An association of entrepreneurs formed by King **Leopold II** in 1878 to finance expeditions by Henry Morton **Stanley** and other **explorers** aimed at establishing profit-making enterprises in the Congo. At the time of its formation, the committee was viewed as a noble and even daring venture. However, modern historians have called it a maneuver by a wily monarch to grab as much of central Africa as possible under the guise of scientific research. The committee declined in influence after the **Berlin Conference** in 1885, which recognized Leopold II as sovereign of what was to become the **Congo Free State**.

COMMUNAUTÉ ÉCONOMIQUE DES ÉTATS DE L'AFRIQUE CENTRALE (CEEAC). *See* ECONOMIC COMMUNITY OF CENTRAL AFRICAN STATES (ECOCAS).

COMMUNAUTÉ ÉCONOMIQUE DES PAYS DES GRANDS LACS (CEPGL) / ECONOMIC COMMUNITY OF COUNTRIES OF THE GREAT LAKES. An economic community established in September 1976, grouping **Zaire**, **Burundi** and **Rwanda**. With its headquarters at Gisenye, Rwanda, the Community aimed to increase economic integration by harmonizing tariffs, **trade** and economic policies. It was dominated by Zaire and in its early years served primarily to legalize some of the **smuggling** of contraband goods across **Lakes Tanganyika** and **Kivu**. In the 1990s, **Mobutu** sought to mediate the Rwandan civil war and interethnic clashes in Burundi through the offices of the CEPGL.

COMMUNICATIONS. In the early days, communications in Congo/Zaire were carried out mostly orally and over distances by messengers traveling from town to town on foot and by canoe. "Talking drums" were a major form of communication among the indigenous **societies** of the forest and were used by some early **missionaries**. The drum, usually a hardened tree trunk or other form of hollowed wood, in many ways imitated the tones and vowels of some of the **Bantu languages**. As a result, talking drums could be understood by ethnic groups speaking different languages. In the mid-1900s, the two-way **radio** came into use and communications networks were set up by colonial officials, missionaries, and private companies.

Beginning in 1950, telephone line systems were established in some parts of the country, notably **Kinshasa**, **Bas-Congo** and **Katanga Provinces**, but their effectiveness was hindered by heavy rains and dense forest. In the 1970s, the **government** began a program to link major urban centers through a combination of long lines, microwave towers and **satellite** stations. In 1984 the government announced an ambitious program to install thousands of telephones throughout the country by the end of the century. A satellite earth station was installed outside **Matadi** in 1985. In 1990, there were 32,000 installed telephones. Congo/Zaire's major urban areas were the only centers with established **telecommunications** links, and these had deteriorated considerably by the early 1990s, because of a lack of maintenance. As a result, cellular systems and private radio networks operated by embassies and large commercial establishments became the primary forms of two-way telecommunication. A US company installed a cellular phone system in Kinshasa in 1991 with 4,000 subscribers and a few years later a smaller cellular system in **Goma, Nord-Kivu,** which served a few hundred subscribers.

COMMUNISM. Communism never played a large role in Congolese life or politics although its influence was felt in the 1960s and the country was a battleground for the rivalries of the Cold War. Patrice **Lumumba** espoused some tenets of **socialism** but also sought to play Soviet-bloc nations against Western governments. This practice led to his dismissal as prime minister by Joseph **Kasavubu** and was considered a factor in his arrest and death. Following the political polarization due in part to Lumumba's assassination, his deputy, Antoine **Gizenga,** in 1964 declared a **People's Republic of the Congo** based in **Stanleyville,** which was backed by the **Soviet Union** and recognized by 13 governments.

Certain aspects of scientific socialism, such as the concept of communal property and the elimination of the gap between rich and poor, appealed to some Congolese. The concept of revolution and the policy of struggle against colonialism espoused by the Soviet bloc also struck a sympathetic chord. However, most Congolese felt uncomfortable with an ideology that placed the state and a foreign-styled bureaucracy over family and religion. Nevertheless, communist governments found friends among the early Congolese **opposition.** The People's Republic of **China** backed Pierre **Mulele.** The Soviet Union supported Gizenga and Christophe **Gbenye.**

After **Mobutu** took power, relations with the communist powers were poor. During the **Authenticity** campaign of the early 1970s, however, Mobutu sought a nonaligned policy, frequently using the phrase, "Neither to the left nor to the right, but straight ahead." China and North Korea eventually developed **trade** and economic assistance ties with Zaire, but during the 1960s the Soviet Union made few inroads and its ambassadors on several occasions were expelled amid charges of interfering in Zaire's internal affairs.

Following the **Shaba** wars of 1977 and 1978, Zaire accused Moscow of financing the rebel **Front pour la Libération Nationale du Congo (FLNC)** and broke relations with **Cuba** and East Germany, whom it accused of complicity. At the same time, relations warmed with socialist regimes in Asia. Mobutu visited Beijing in 1973 after Zaire recognized the governments of China and North Korea. Chinese Premier Zhao Ziyang visited Zaire during a trip to Africa from December 1982 to January 1983. With *détente* in the 1970s, the Soviet Union was allowed a discreet though sizable diplomatic presence.

The collapse of the Soviet Union and end of the Cold War saw a decline in Zaire's strategic importance in the international arena. Although old ties and commitments remained, major powers found fewer reasons to court Mobutu. An increasing desire to see political and economic liberalization in Zaire began to take priority in the foreign policies of Zaire's Western allies. The overthrow and execution in 1989 of Romanian leader Nicolae Ceausescu, with whom Mobutu had felt a particular affinity, reportedly profoundly disturbed the Zairian leader. The decline of communism, international pressure for political and economic reforms, and a trend toward multipartyism in other African nations are said to be primary reasons for Mobutu's announcement of the **democratic transition** in April 1990.

COMPAGNIE DU CONGO POUR LE COMMERCE ET L'INDUSTRIE (CCCI). A large Belgian holding company noted for its heavy investments in Congo following World War I.

COMPREHENSIVE POLITICAL ARRANGEMENT. *See* COMPROMIS POLITIQUE GLOBAL (CPG).

COMPROMIS POLITIQUE GLOBAL (CPG) / COMPREHENSIVE POLITICAL ARRANGEMENT. A 10-point document proposed on August 14, 1992, by Archbishop Laurent **Monsengwo** at the height of the standoff between **Mobutu** and the **Haut Conseil de la République (HCR)**. The HCR had succeeded the **Conférence Nationale Souveraine (CNS)** in December 1992 after it elected opposition leader Étienne **Tshisekedi prime minister** and drafted a new **constitution**. The CPG established that no organ of the transition could use its powers to prevent another institution from functioning, a measure designed to prevent disruption by the military of the **democratic transition**. Under the terms of the CPG, the parties also agreed to abide by the **Transitional Act**.

The agreement brought a three-month truce to the political confrontation, but Mobutu never acknowledged it. The truce ended when Mobutu determined that the CNS was controlled by the **opposition** and refused to accept its draft constitution. Instead he convened the former single-party **parliament** to draft a new constitution. He eventually dismissed the Tshisekedi government and appointed a new one with Tshisekedi's former economics advisor, Faustin **Birindwa**, as prime minister, leading to another period of political paralysis with two competing governments. It only ended in late 1993 with the merger of the HCR and the parliament into a single body, called the **Haut Conseil de la République / Parlement de la Transition (HCR/PT)**.

CONCLAVE, FORCES POLITIQUES DU / POLITICAL FORCES OF THE CONCLAVE. A coalition formed by **Mobutu** in early 1993 to counter the **opposition** in the **Haut Conseil de la République (HCR)**, particularly the hardline opposition **Sacred Union** and centrist **Union pour la République et la Démocratie (URD)**. Commonly referred to as the "Conclave," it helped to elect as **prime minister** a senior official of the **Union pour la Démocratie et le Progrès Social (UDPS)**, Faustin **Birindwa**, creating a rival government to that of UDPS leader Étienne **Tshisekedi**. Angered by Mobutu's abandonment of a power-sharing agreement outlined in the **Transitional Act** and the **Compromis Politique Global**, the opposition refused to participate. Western governments also charged Mobutu with undermining the **democratic transition** and adopted a policy of diplomatic isolation of his government.

CONCORDAT OF 1906. An agreement between the Belgian government and the Vatican designating **Catholic Church** missions as the primary source of basic **education** in the **Belgian Congo**. Under the agreement, **Belgium** subsidized most mission activity and **missionary** groups appointed representatives to advisory boards of the colonial government.

CONFÉDÉRATION DES ASSOCIATIONS KATANGAISES (CONAKAT) / CONFEDERATION OF KATANGAN ASSOCIATIONS. A political association dominated by **Lunda évolués**, CONAKAT was formed in **Katanga** in the late 1950s by Moïse **Tshombe** and supported by Belgian **mining** and financial interests. It reflected the disaffection with **Leopoldville** that was common in Katanga among Congolese and Europeans alike. In 1959, CONAKAT began advocating autonomy for Katanga within a Congolese federation. With the approach of **independence**, it became a **political party** and in the **elections** of 1960 gained control of the Katangan provincial assembly, despite opposition from the **Luba**-dominated **Association des Baluba du Katanga (BALUBAKAT)**. When BALUBAKAT delegates boycotted the assembly, Tshombe obtained an exception to the **Loi Fondamentale** that allowed the assembly to meet without a quorum and established a one-party provincial government in Katanga. However, CONAKAT was unhappy with its representation in the first **Lumumba** government. Encouraged by Belgian commercial interests and by moves for autonomy in the **Orientale** and **Kasai** provinces, Katanga seceded in July 1960. Following reunification in 1963, CONAKAT helped form the southern-based **Confédération Nationale des Associations Congolaises (CONACO)** party that elected Tshombe **prime minister** in 1964.

CONFÉDÉRATION NATIONALE DES ASSOCIATIONS CONGOLAISES (CONACO) / NATIONAL CONFEDERATION OF CONGOLESE ASSOCIATIONS. A coalition of primarily southern political groups that merged into a **political party** headed by Moïse **Tshombe** upon his return to political life following his exile at the end of the **Katangan secession**. CONACO was an effort to form a nationally based political party by the leaders of the **Confédération des Associations Katangaises (CONAKAT)**, the **Association des Baluba du Katanga (BALUBAKAT)**, Albert **Kalonji**'s wing of the **Mouvement National Congolais** (MNC/Kalonji), and some dissatisfied backers of former **Prime Minister** Cyrille **Adoula**. Although they failed to attract significant support from the northern and western parts of the country, CONACO supporters in **parliament** on July 9, 1964, elected Tshombe prime minister with

Godefroid **Munongo** as interior minister and Albert Kalonji as agriculture minister. Following **elections** in March 1965, in which CONACO won 122 of 167 seats in parliament, President Joseph **Kasavubu** dismissed Tshombe and asked another southern leader, Évariste **Kimba** of BALUBAKAT, to form a government. Kimba tried twice but was blocked by CONACO supporters. The deadlock, combined with renewed uprisings in eastern Congo, helped set the scene for the military **coup d'etat** that ushered in the **Mobutu** era. CONACO's activities were suspended along with those of all political parties following the coup.

CONFÉRENCE NATIONALE (CN). *See* NATIONAL CONFERENCE; CONFERÉNCE NATIONALE SOUVERAINE.

CONFÉRENCE NATIONALE SOUVERAINE (CNS) / SOVEREIGN NATIONAL CONFERENCE. The name given itself by the **National Conference** in April 1992, when it reconvened after nine months of political stalemate. The CNS, which had come under control of the **opposition**, declared its resolutions constitutionally binding and resolved that henceforth the **president** would be obliged by law to carry them out. The CNS adopted a number of measures restoring the flag, anthem and system of **government** under the 1964 **constitution**, which was suspended following the **Mobutu coup d'etat**. It voted to change the country's name back to Congo, drafted a new constitution, and established the **Haut Conseil de la République (HCR)** to oversee the **democratic transition**. In October, Mobutu rejected these measures and, in a move widely viewed as illegal, convened the single-party **parliament** which had been disbanded earlier. When Mobutu dismissed opposition leader Étienne **Tshisekedi** as **prime minister** in February 1993 and appointed his former advisor, Faustin **Birindwa,** as the new prime minister, the country entered a period characterized by two rival governments. The stalemate was ended in late 1993 with the merger of the HCR and the parliament into the **Haut Conseil de la République / Parlement de la Transition (HCR/PT).**

CONGO BASIN. *See* CONGO RIVER BASIN.

CONGO, BELGIAN. The name given to the **Congo Free State (CFS)** when it was annexed by the Belgian parliament on November 14, 1908, and retained until the proclamation of **independence** on June 30, 1960, when it was renamed the **Republic of the Congo**. The government of **Belgium** only agreed to assume control over the territory after heated debate during which many leaders opposed the annexation, saying it would be too costly. Under international pressure because of publicity over **human rights** abuses in the CFS, however, the parliament eventually agreed to assume responsibility for the territory out of what it said was a religious belief in the need to "civilize Africa" and on condition that it operate at a profit. The **Colonial Charter** was passed October 18, 1908, setting up the guidelines for administering the territory.

Under colonial administration, many monopolies were diluted, but a number of large companies, including the **Société Générale de Belgique**, the Comité du Kivu and the **Comité Spéciale du Katanga**, retained special privileges.

The king, as head of state, ruled by decree, but the decrees to be valid had to be countersigned by the minister of colonies and reviewed by the Belgian parliament. In the colony, an advisory council of government composed of older, conservative leaders was established in 1911, but political activity was forbidden. The king was represented by a governor-general who, as chief administrator, issued ordinances with the power of law. The territory was divided into chiefdoms, called *chefferies*, which were grouped into sectors. **Chiefs** appointed by the governor administered **customary law**, which was kept separate from colonial law. There was some resistance to the colonial administration, particularly by the **Yaka, Zande, Luba-Katanga** and **Lele**. Congolese were appointed to the council beginning in 1947. Historians say that in the **colonial era, labor** policies improved somewhat from the harsh practices of the CFS, but nevertheless remained oppressive for decades. *See also* Paternalism.

CONGO/BRAZZAVILLE. The name commonly used for the former French Congo, the **Republic of the Congo** with its capital in Brazzaville, to differentiate it from the former **Belgian Congo**, the

Democratic Republic of the Congo or Congo/Kinshasa, with its capital in **Kinshasa**.

CONGO, DEMOCRATIC REPUBLIC OF THE. **Congo/Zaire** was officially known as the Democratic Republic of the Congo from August 1, 1964, until October 27, 1971, when it became the **Republic of Zaire**, and again beginning in May 1997, after forces led by Laurent **Kabila** took power. It was often called **Congo/Kinshasa** to differentiate it from **Congo/Brazzaville**, the former French Congo. The name was changed from **Republic of the Congo** by the **constitution** of 1964.

The Democratic Republic represented an attempt to set aside the disorder following independence. Although it brought some improvements, political fragmentation and administrative disintegration continued, leading to **Mobutu**'s military **coup d'etat** 15 months after its promulgation.

CONGO, FEDERAL REPUBLIC OF THE. The name given to **Congo/Zaire** under the **constitution** drafted by the **Haut Conseil de la République / Parlement de la Transition (HCR/PT)** to be put to a popular referendum in February 1997, which was never held. The new constitution was due to come into force at the end of the **democratic transition** on July 9, 1997, but the process was disrupted by the military offensive that drove **Mobutu** out of power in May 1997. After the Laurent **Kabila** government was installed, it announced a new timetable, promising a constitutional referendum in 1998 and national **elections** in 1999.

CONGO FREE STATE (CFS) / ÉTAT INDÉPENDANT DU CONGO. The Congo Free State came into existence on November 26, 1885, shortly after the **Berlin Conference** at which 13 European nations recognized King **Leopold II**'s sovereignty over the territory. The Berlin Act stipulated that the territory be governed by the principles of free **trade** and navigation, neutrality in war, and policies aimed at improving the lives of the indigenous people. Leopold II was recognized as sovereign of the territory and ruled by decree with advice from the Belgian ministries of foreign affairs, finance and interior. The territory was divided into 15 districts, each headed by a commissioner. The authority of the local **chiefs** was reduced.

In order to pay for the administration of the territory and render a profit to the king, the CFS was protected from business competition by decrees requiring many commodities produced in the CFS to be sold only to the state. The CFS also decreed that all land not owned by Europeans belonged to it and granted to various private companies exclusive rights for exploitation and trade on large tracts. A **security** force called the **Force Publique** was formed in order to curb the influence of the local chiefs, drive **Afro-Arab** traders from the eastern part of the territory, and prevent disruptions to trade. By 1900, concern was building in the international community over reports of maltreatment of the indigenous populations in the territory. A number of writers, most notably **Edmund D. Morel**, drew on **missionary** reports to describe atrocities in the CFS. A 10 percent **labor** tax, passed in 1890, had become an excuse for demanding large quantities of **rubber** from the African populations. Failure to pay the tax was punished by flogging, execution and occasionally the destruction of entire villages. Soldiers were required to produce the right hand of villagers who had been executed for not paying their taxes.

The procurement of hands became an end in itself, reportedly leaving thousands of maimed victims. An international commission of inquiry and US Congressional hearings substantiated the abuses. Public outcry led the Belgian parliament to annex the territory as a colony on November 14, 1908. Labor conditions improved somewhat during the **colonial era**. Nevertheless, they remained harsh for decades and the end of the CFS did not mean the end of the exploitation of Congo and its people. *See also* Congo, Belgian.

CONGO JAZZ. The name given to the rhythmic **music** popularized by urban orchestras in Congo/Zaire, beginning in the late 1950s that became popular throughout Africa. In the late 1960s, Congo Jazz evolved into "Soukouma" and then diverged into many different forms, some taking inspiration from Reggae, Disco, or Soukous. Others delved into indigenous **languages,** melodies and rhythms.

CONGO/KINSHASA. The name frequently used for the former **Belgian Congo**, which is now officially called the **Democratic Republic of the Congo**, to differentiate it from the former French

Congo, which is also called the **Republic of the Congo** or **Congo/Brazzaville**. *See also* Congo/Zaire.

CONGO, PEOPLE'S REPUBLIC OF THE (PRC) / RÉPUBLIQUE POPULAIRE DU CONGO (RPC). A short-lived people's republic proclaimed on September 7, 1964, during the **rebellion** in eastern Congo. The PRC dissolved following the Belgian-American mission to free **Stanleyville** and Paulis and the mercenary-backed offensive by the Congolese army to retake control of the territory in November 1965. At its peak, however, it was recognized by 13 foreign governments and its delegations were seated at some international conferences. This should not be confused with the People's Republic of the **Congo (Brazzaville)**, which was declared in the former French Congo by Marien **Ngouabi** on June 24, 1973, and which changed its name to **Republic of the Congo** when it renounced Marxism in 1990. *See also* Gizenga, Antoine; Mouvement National Congolais; Simbas.

CONGO REFORM ASSOCIATION. A group formed by Edmund D. **Morel** at the beginning of the 20th century to lobby against the atrocities committed against indigenous populations in the **Congo Free State**. Public pressure that followed the association's reports led to the annexation of the territory by the Belgian parliament and the beginning of the **colonial era**.

CONGO, REPUBLIC OF THE (BRAZZAVILLE), RELATIONS WITH. Called the People's Republic of the Congo until 1990, **Congo/Brazzaville**, as it is commonly known, has always prided itself on being different from its neighbor across the **Congo River**. Relations between the two countries, which for 11 years following **independence**, shared the same name, fluctuated considerably, marked by periods of friendship broken by disputes which were resolved months later.

The former French colony is much smaller than **Congo/Zaire**, with 343,000 square km of territory and a population of 2.5 million persons concentrated in the two urban centers of Brazzaville and Pointe-Noire. Brazzaville was the capital of French Equatorial Africa during the **colonial era** and also was the headquarters of the Free French forces during World War II. Congo became independent on August 15, 1960. A military coup in September 1968 led to Marien **Ngouabi's** assumption of the presidency on January 1, 1969. Congo formalized its affiliation with Marxism-Leninism by becoming a people's republic on June 24, 1973. Nationalization of large private companies followed.

Ngouabi was assassinated on March 18, 1977, by a group of commandos. Former President Alphonse Massamba-Debat was convicted of responsibility and executed for the assassination. Joachim Yhombi-Opango was named president on April 4, 1977, and in June the new government resumed relations with the **United States** after a 12-year break. However, Yhombi-Opango resigned on February 4, 1979, in a power struggle and was replaced by Denis Sassou-Nguesso. The nationalizations hurt the economy in the 1970s, but in the 1980s the country entered an economic boom due to the discovery of significant deposits of offshore petroleum. Congo renounced Marxism in 1990, changed its name to Republic of the Congo, and embarked on its own, sometimes difficult path toward democratization. Disputed elections in 1992 led to violence, while the economy declined because of a government practice of mortgaging future oil production to finance current expenditures in a practice called "forward selling."

Diplomatic relations between Congo/Zaire and Congo/Brazzaville were frequently suspended over various disagreements, and the ferry linking Brazzaville to **Kinshasa** often was closed because of disputes over contraband, gunrunning, **currency smuggling** and illegal immigrants. Ideological and historical differences also frequently played a role in the sometimes stormy relations. Congo/Brazzaville supported the **Stanleyville secession** and became the exile-home of one of its leaders, Antoine **Gizenga**. The Brazzaville government also supported the uprising in **Kwilu** and is said to have been the source of arms and explosives that were used in terrorist attacks in **Leopoldville**. After the Kwilu **rebellion** was put down, its leader, Pierre **Mulele**, fled to Brazzaville. He subsequently accepted an offer of amnesty from **Mobutu**. But upon his return to Kinshasa, he was executed, leading a furious Brazzaville government to break diplomatic relations.

Congo/Zaire and Congo/Brazzaville often voted with opposing blocs at the **United Nations** General Assembly and they supported different factions in the civil war in **Angola**. In the 1970s, as the very different "revolutions" of each nation matured and with *détente* coming to much of the world, some of the mistrust dissipated. In 1976, the Brazzaville government attempted to mediate the differences between Congo/Zaire and Angola by hosting a reconciliation meeting between Mobutu and then-Angolan President Agostinho **Neto**. In 1978, following the second **Shaba** war, the Brazzaville authorities hosted a series of talks that brought an agreement by Zaire and Angola to establish diplomatic relations with one another and to refrain from supporting each other's **dissident** guerrilla groups. In April 1985, Zaire and Congo/Brazzaville signed a protocol agreeing in principle to the construction of a 17-km-long bridge across the Congo River to link the capitals of the two countries. Relations soured in 1989 and 1990 over expulsions of illegal immigrants and were suspended in 1993 following a ferry accident that killed 150 Zairian deportees.

Disputed elections in 1992 and 1993 caused fighting between several political factions in which 2,000 people were killed, but it subsided with an accord under which Pascal Lissouba assumed the presidency in Brazzaville. The fall of Mobutu and installation of the Laurent **Kabila** government in Kinshasa in May 1997 was partly responsible for another period of instability in Congo/Brazzaville. Fighting broke out in Brazzaville on June 5, 1997, when government troops loyal to Lissouba tried to disarm militias led by former president Sassou-Nguesso. During the next four months, artillery barrages destroyed much of central Brazzaville and on several occasions reached Kinshasa. In one two-day period in September, mortar shells killed 21 people in Kinshasa, causing the Kabila government to send troops across the river. In Brazzaville, the fighting killed thousands of people and caused nearly one-half of the population of one million to flee.

Some analysts said the fighting was aggravated by elements of the former Zairian military which had fled across the river after Mobutu's fall and had thrown their support behind Lissouba. In October, 3,000 Angolan troops entered Congo/Brazzaville from **Cabinda** and helped the Sassou-Nguesso militias take control of the most of the country. The Angolan government was angry at the Lissouba government for allowing its territory to be used by the **União Nacional para a Independência Total de Angola (UNITA)** opposition group as a base for **arms trafficking** and **diamond smuggling**. The number of Angolan troops was reduced to 1,500 by December and from January 5 to 14, Sassou-Nguesso chaired the National Peace and Reconciliation Forum in Brazzaville and pledged to oversee elections within two years.

CONGO, REPUBLIC OF THE (KINSHASA). **Congo/Zaire** was called the Republic of the Congo from **independence** on June 30, 1960, until the promulgation of the first **constitution** on August 1, 1964. During that time, the country was governed by the **Loi Fondamentale**, a charter modeled on the Belgian system of government.

CONGO RIVER. **Congo/Zaire**'s major **river** and Africa's largest flowing body of water, the Congo River is 4,300 km long and carries the second largest volume of water in the world, after the Amazon River. It provides an average flow at its mouth of 40,000 cubic meters per second with estimated hydroelectric potential of 100,000 MW.

The river was called the **Zaire River** in the newly renamed **Republic of Zaire** beginning in 1971, when many names were changed. The river continued to be called the Congo by **Congo/Brazzaville** and most international cartographers and the original name was restored following the overthrow of **Mobutu** in 1997. The name "Congo" was originally given to the river by **explorers** who named it after the **Kongo** people they met when they landed at its mouth in the 15th century. The Mobutu government said the name "Zaire" was derived from the name actually given by the people to the river. Scholars believe it was an adaptation of the word "nzadi," which in the Kikongo **language** means "big river."

CONGO RIVER BASIN. Known in French as the *Cuvette Centrale*, the Congo River Basin is a topographical depression, lying at an altitude of about 400 meters above sea level, which covers three million square kilometers, including nearly two-thirds of **Congo/Zaire** and parts of the **Republic of the Congo**, the **Central African Republic**, and southeastern Cameroon. The basin is the most sparsely populated area in Congo/Zaire, with five persons or less per square kilometer. It is inhabited primarily by **Bantu-language** speakers primarily of the **Mongo** group, **pygmies**, and some speakers of Adamawa-Eastern languages. The basin is drained for the most part by the **Congo River** and its tributaries. An area of heavy **rainfall**, averaging 2,000 mm per year, it is covered by swamps, marshes and a lush tropical **rainforest**, where the primary means of **transportation** is by boat or dugout canoe. At higher elevations, the ground is covered by clay-like topsoil which allows some forms of **agriculture**. However, the sandy soil with generally poor **mineral** content that covers most of the **region** makes farming difficult. The basin contains an estimated 100 million hectares of forest, but only 60 percent of it is considered accessible for **timbering**.

CONGO/ZAIRE. The name sometimes used to identify the **Democratic Republic of the Congo** (République Démocratique du Congo), which was reinstated after the Laurent **Kabila** government took power in May 1997 and abandoned the name **Republic of Zaire** and other symbols of **Mobutism**. Although the changes were quickly accepted by the international community, some **Mobutu** adherents maintained they were imposed illegally. As a result, "Congo/Zaire" has sometimes been used to indicate neutrality in the dispute. This book uses the term to avoid confusion with the former French Congo, which it refers to as the **Republic of the Congo** or **Congo/Brazzaville**. *See also* Congo/Kinshasa.

CONGOLESE DEMOCRATIC COALITION (CDC). *See* COALITION DÉMOCRATIQUE CONGOLAISE.

CONGOLESE RALLY FOR DEMOCRACY. *See* RASSEMBLEMENT CONGOLAIS POUR LA DÉMOCRATIE (RCD).

CONSCIENCE AFRICAINE. A **Leopoldville**-based newspaper that was one of the first to employ Congolese on its editorial staff and the first to voice, albeit cautiously, Congolese perspectives and complaints about colonial rule. The newspaper's endorsement of a monograph by Belgian Professor Van Bilsen that **independence** for the Congo was 30 years away, prompted the Declaration of Civil Rights of the **Alliance des Bakongo (ABAKO)** in 1956 which was the first public call for immediate independence. *See also* Colonial Era; News Media.

CONSCRIPTION. Conscription into the **armed forces** by law is allowed of males aged 18 years and above. However, it has not been necessary because the armed forces represent a relatively good source of **employment** for less-affluent and less-educated citizens and for some it is a way into the power structure. **Student** unrest on several occasions provided conscripts for the army. Dozens were inducted following antigovernment demonstrations in 1969, 1971 and 1982. Other methods of recruitment reportedly included roundups of young, unemployed males in urban centers and offers of freedom to prison inmates in exchange for service in the army.

CONSEIL DE SECURITÉ NATIONAL (CSN) / NATIONAL SECURITY COUNCIL. A little-publicized organ established in 1969 to advise the **president** on internal and external **security** matters. According to diplomatic observers, the organization remained primarily an informative body since most security decisions were made by the **armed forces** high command and the **intelligence services**.

CONSEIL DU GOUVERNEMENT. *See* COUNCIL OF GOVERNMENT.

CONSEIL EXÉCUTIF. *See* EXECUTIVE COUNCIL.

CONSEIL JUDICIAIRE. *See* JUDICIARY COUNCIL.

CONSEIL LÉGISLATIF. *See* LEGISLATIVE COUNCIL.

CONSEIL NATIONAL DE LIBÉRATION (CNL) / NATIONAL LIBERATION COUNCIL. A body formed in the **Republic of the Congo (Brazzaville)** in late 1963 which claimed to group all Congolese revolutionary organizations. The council was created at a time of heightened interest by the People's Republic of **China** in central Africa and claimed Antoine **Gizenga** and Pierre **Mulele** as members. It faded from view, however, as relations improved between the governments in **Kinshasa** and Brazzaville and as China lost interest in promoting peasant revolution in Africa and turned its attention to its own Cultural Revolution.

CONSTITUTION. **Congo/Zaire** was governed during the 20th century by three constitutions and two charters. The first document, the **Colonial Charter** (Charte Coloniale), was adopted by the Belgian parliament on October 18, 1908, to guide the administration of the **Belgian Congo**. The second charter, the **Loi Fondamentale** (Fundamental Law) was passed May 19, 1960, six weeks before the Belgian Congo attained **independence**. It was designed to guide the **Republic of the Congo** during its early years.

Congo/Zaire's first constitution, which created the **Democratic Republic of the Congo**, was drafted partly in reaction to the weaknesses in these charters. Promulgated on August 1, 1964, the constitution creating the "First Republic" gave the **president** greater powers and made it clear that he was above the **prime minister** and had the authority to appoint and dismiss the cabinet. The Constitution of 1964 merged the two houses of **parliament** into one national assembly. It eliminated the provincial assemblies and, in an effort to diffuse separatist sentiment, divided the **provinces** into 21 provinces. The 1964 Constitution, however, failed to adequately address the eventual power struggle between president and prime minister. A subsequent standoff created yet another power vacuum which was a major reason for the decision by the military to stage the **coup d'etat** of 1965 and suspend political activity.

Congo/Zaire's second constitution was promulgated on June 24, 1967, less than two years after the coup that brought **Mobutu** to power. It responded to what many saw as the failures of the previous document. The new constitution, which was approved by 98 percent of the voters, provided for a unicameral legislature and a strong presidency. It removed most powers previously granted to the provinces. The president was given the power to suspend parliament and political activity and rule by decree. Armed with the power of decree, Mobutu moved quickly to consolidate his authority and launched a personality cult, which he felt was needed to provide the country with strong leadership and a sense of nationhood.

Using his decree powers, Mobutu made many de facto constitutional changes. The **Mouvement Populaire de la Révolution (MPR)** party, which had been launched in 1966, became the sole legal **political party** on December 23, 1970, the same year Mobutu was elected unopposed to his first term. The number of provinces was gradually reduced. As part of a move toward "**authenticity**" and to bury the trauma of the years following independence, the **names** of government institutions, cities and even the nation itself were changed. The ministries became **departments**, ministers became secretaries. **Leopoldville** became **Kinshasa**. The Congo became the **Republic of Zaire**.

The third constitution, promulgated August 15, 1974, codified the decrees of the previous seven years. It further concentrated power in the office of the president. It eliminated the separation of powers, since members of the **judicial system** and executive branches and candidates for the legislature were appointed by the president. The third constitution removed any distinction between party and government and established "**Mobutism**" as the official ideology and doctrine. Under the constitution, most terms of office were for five years in length, except for the president's, which was raised to seven.

The political process was liberalized somewhat in 1977-78, reportedly under pressure from Western donors following the **Shaba** wars. Local party cells were allowed a voice in the selection of legislative candidates and for a brief time the legislature was allowed to summon ministers for questioning. Multiple candidates were allowed in the legislative **elections** of 1982 and for a brief period, some members of the **Political Bureau** were elected. In the 1980s, however, many reforms were circumvented or phased out. The constitution was rewritten in 1983 to incorporate these changes. Zaire became the party-state. All citizens were declared party members from birth until death. The 120-member **Central Committee**, created in 1980, became the de facto legislative body. The Political Bureau was the main policy-making body and inner core of political leadership and power. The legislature's role became one primarily of approving decisions of the Central Committee, while the **Executive Council** in essence became a committee of senior administrators. Critics said the constitution discouraged dissent and invited excesses. Supporters argued that channels existed within the party structure for new ideas and proposals and that it provided political stability and more closely resembled traditional Zairian political structures.

When Mobutu announced the transition to multipartyism in April 1990, many of the tenets of the constitution, such as the supremacy of the MPR, were mooted. Restrictions on political parties, trade unions, and newspapers were lifted. Many of the institutions of the party-state atrophied because of defections by politicians forming their own political organizations. Nevertheless, Zaire continued to operate under the 1974 constitution until the **Conférence Nationale Souveraine (CNS)** passed the **Transitional Act** in August 1992, which was to serve as a provisional constitution. Under this act, the CNS established a transitional government composed of a figurehead president, an independent judiciary and a transitional parliament called the **Haut Conseil de la République (HCR)**, which elected the prime minister.

The transitional government was to govern for two years during which time a new constitution was to be drafted and national elections were to be held. However, progress was stalled by political infighting, disruptive tactics by Mobutu, and the **pillages** in 1991 and 1993. Following protracted negotiations, pro-Mobutu forces and the **opposition** agreed on a compromise joining the HCR and former parliament into a single body, called the **Haut Conseil de la République / Parlement de la Transition (HCR/PT)**, to draft a new constitution and organize national elections.

The HCR/PT voted on June 30, 1995, to extend the transitional period until July 9, 1997, and to postpone elections by two years. The 1974 constitution continued in effect but primarily as a source of reference, subject to amendment by presidential decree and political negotiation among the various parties. In August 1996, the HCR/PT completed a draft constitution creating the Federal Republic of the Congo. It was to be submitted to a national referendum in February 1997. This timetable was disrupted, however, by the military offensive that overthrew Mobutu in May 1997 and brought the Laurent **Kabila** government to power. The Kabila government announced a new timetable, saying a constitutional referendum and national elections would be held by 1999.

CONSUMER PRICE INDEX. *See* INFLATION.

COPPER. At the peak of world copper prices in the mid-1970s, copper was **Congo/Zaire**'s major **export**, supplying one-half of the **government**'s revenues and two-thirds of its **foreign exchange**.

During that period, Zaire was the seventh largest producer of copper in the world and supplied 7 percent of total world output. However, lower prices caused a gradual decline of production in the late 1980s. Then the collapse of the formal **economy** in the early 1990s idled many **mining** companies and caused production to fall sharply, such that in 1996 it was one-tenth of its peak level of 500,000 tons in the mid-1980s.

Most of Congo/Zaire's copper is found in a rich lode 100 km wide, called the Zambia Copper Belt, which runs for about 400 km through the southern part of Congo/Zaire's **Katanga Province** between **Kolwezi** and Sakamia. Important mines are located at Kolwezi, **Lubumbashi**, **Likasi**, **Tenke**, Kipushi and Musoshi. In the 19th century, tales of rich copper lodes brought **explorers** from the east and west coasts of Africa, but surveys determined the deposits were not commercially viable. However, discoveries by a British exploring team in 1901 led King **Leopold II** to send engineers and to start building a **railway**. Production began in 1911. It reached 100,000 tons in 1928 and 300,000 tons in 1960.

During the first half of the 20th century, copper production was virtually monopolized by the **Union Minière du Haut-Katanga (UMHK)**, which operated a dozen mines. The UMHK was nationalized in 1967 and replaced first by the **Générale Congolaise des Minérais (GECOMIN)** and in 1971 by the **Générale des Carrières et des Mines (GECAMINES)**. A second venture, **Société de Développement Industriel et Minier du Zaïre (SODIMIZA)**, also owned by the government but operated by a Canadian company, produced 80,000 tons per year. In 1970, a consortium of British, French, Japanese and US companies organized a third venture with 20 percent state participation. Called the **Société Minière de Tenke-Fungurume (SMTF)**, the venture received a 1,500-square-km concession. The company was liquidated in 1984, but in November 1996 a Canadian company announced a joint venture with GECAMINES to resume production by the year 2000.

The first and only smelting plant, owned by GECAMINES at Lubumbashi, was started in 1911 and produced 100,000 tons of refined copper by 1928. In the mid-1980s, it was producing 150,000 tons of refined copper per year, 70 percent of which was for export and 30 percent of which was for anode production locally. The plant produced 98.5-percent-pure ingots of 225-250 kg. A wire plant and rolling mill in Lubumbashi produced approximately 1,500 tons of wire and rolled products a year.

During the boom years of the early 1970s, the government sought to expand copper production, despite warnings that its emphasis on mineral extraction for foreign exchange was undermining **agriculture**. An expansion program brought copper production to 460,000 tons in 1974. Prices for copper rose sharply in 1973-74, following the Arab oil embargo, and reached $1.75 per pound. The following year, however, they dropped to $.50 per pound. By the end of 1986, prices were in the $.60-.70 range, but production had stagnated because of oversupply on the world market.

Congo/Zaire's copper exports were also hindered by high **transportation** costs. The most efficient route, the **Benguela Railway**, has been closed since 1974 because of the civil war in **Angola**. The **National Way** system, entirely within the national territory, became increasingly difficult because of deteriorating **rail** and **river** transport systems. On occasion, the government reportedly transported refined copper by air from **Shaba** to customers in Europe. The collapse of major underground shafts in the 1990s and the insolvency of GECAMINES severely reduced production in the 1990s and what copper was produced, 40,000 tons in 1996, came from the large stock of previously refined ore.

Following the overthrow of **Mobutu** in 1997, the Laurent **Kabila** government signed a number of agreements establishing joint ventures with foreign companies to revive production. One venture sought to restore production levels to 100,000 tons per year by the year 2000 using ore at the **Tenke-Fungurume** concession. Another sought to refine ore tailings at Kolwezi and Kipushi.

COQUILHATVILLE CONFERENCE. A conference organized by the Congolese central **government** in Coquilhatville (now **Mbandaka**) in April and May of 1961, as part of negotiations aimed at ending the secessions in the **provinces**. The conference followed a meeting in Tananarive (now Antananarivo), Madagascar, the **Tananarive Conference**, which called for a confederal system of government in the Congo that would have granted a large measure of autonomy to the provinces. The Coquilhatville Conference rejected confederalism in favor of a

federalist system. Neither system was adopted, but some elements of the two were used in drafting the Congo's first **constitution** in 1964.

CORN. *See* MAIZE.

CORPS DES ACTIVISTES POUR LA DÉFENSE DE LA RÉVOLUTION (CADR) / CORPS OF ACTIVISTS FOR THE DEFENSE OF THE REVOLUTION. Officially the enforcement wing of the **Jeunesse du Mouvement Populaire de la Révolution (JMPR)**, CADR was an organization primarily of young toughs used primarily in the 1960s and 1970s to intimidate opponents of the regime and their families. Its members were not noted party ideologues and reportedly requested payment for their missions.

CORPS DES VOLONTAIRES DE LA RÉPUBLIQUE (CVR) / VOLUNTEER CORPS OF THE REPUBLIC. A group created on January 9, 1966, to galvanize the people into helping rebuild the Congo after the chaos and deterioration following **independence**. Conceived to mobilize the people behind the **Mobutu** government, the CVR prepared the way for the formation of the **Mouvement Populaire de la Révolution (MPR)** and the single-party era.

CORRUPTION. Congo/Zaire has had a tradition of plunder since the 16th century, when trading by Arabs and Europeans began. It reached notorious levels during the **Congo Free State** era and continued during the **colonial era** under the system of large private monopolies. It was no accident, then, that many Congolese came to perceive the public coffers as a source of personal enrichment.

Corruption is seen in many forms, ranging from the acceptance of gifts for official favors and personal services, to officially sanctioned (or sponsored) **smuggling**, to outright diversion of public funds. During the 1970s, Zaire gained considerable renown for its institutionalized system of "**matabish**" (**Lingala** for "tip"). However, it was not until the 1980s that a dossier of documented evidence began to confirm suspicions that the Zairian state had become a "kleptocracy."

Former **World Bank** official Erwin **Blumenthal**, who served in the Zairian **central bank** in the late 1970s, estimated that less than one-third of the revenues from **diamond** sales were processed through the bank. The rest, he said, were smuggled. He also estimated that as much as one-half of Zaire's revenues were not officially recorded. Other officials from international institutions monitoring the Zairian **economy** said the budget of the **president** was virtually indistinguishable from the president's private accounts. **Dissidents** published documents from the central bank detailing transfers of funds from the bank to private Swiss accounts. They also published receipts purportedly showing that payments for **exports** such as diamonds, **copper** and **cobalt** had been made to private accounts in Europe.

Émmanuel Dungia, a former intelligence official and counselor in the foreign ministry, detailed numerous examples of how **Mobutu**'s financial empire was built and maintained in his 1992 book, *Mobutu et l'argent du Zaïre*. Sources of income reportedly included direct shipments of copper, cobalt, diamonds and **gold** from **government**-owned **mining** companies to purchasing agents primarily in Europe. Payments for these were made by direct deposit to private bank accounts in various international banking havens. Dungia recounts how emissaries, traveling on jets commandeered from the fleet of **Air Zaïre**, the national carrier, bought blue-chip properties and made bank deposits in the name of Mobutu in Europe, Asia, and the Americas. Colette Braeckman in her 1992 book, *Le Dinosaure: Le Zaïre de Mobutu*, described the lavish palace built by Mobutu in his home village of **Gbadolite**, where a lifestyle that included virtually nightly banquets was maintained at a cost of millions of dollars per month.

The situation led the **Catholic Church** on a number of occasions to express concern over the decline of morals in private and public life. Whether viewed as a blight on the state or as a modern version of the traditional practice of spreading the wealth, the practice of diverting funds for personal use seriously affected the ability of the government to administer the country, especially after the fall in **mineral** prices in the mid-1970s.

The Zairian government launched several drives to halt what was euphemistically called "mismanagement." In 1978 and 1982, dozens of lower and mid-level officials were tried and dismissed

for corruption. In 1983, 150 relatively senior officials were tried and punished. In September 1983, amid a major reform program, state commissioners were made personally accountable for overspending in their **departments** and the government began to carry out audits. In the late 1980s and early 1990s, each successive government announced measures to curb corruption. However, these crackdowns did not last. And the main reason, many believed, was the example set by the president, who in the decade following his **coup d'etat** became one of the wealthiest individuals in the world and whose lavish lifestyle was well known, despite the fact that he received no official salary.

Many Zairians shrugged their shoulders at these practices and, invoking traditional culture, noted that a supreme **chief** was expected to accumulate wealth. They noted the wealth was not resented as long as it was shared, and Mobutu was well known for rewarding friends and supporters. However, as the country's economic infrastructure decayed, many blamed the culture of avarice and called for some form of restitution like that seen after the departure from power of the Philippines' Ferdinand Marcos.

Following Mobutu's overthrow in 1997, the Laurent **Kabila** government, which assumed power, announced a campaign against corruption. It created the **Office des Biens Mal-Acquis (OBMA)**, or Office of Ill-Gotten Gains, and arrested more than three dozen former officials and prominent businessmen on corruption charges. It offered to release those who repaid the money they had taken from the state and several individuals were transferred to house arrest after they reportedly agreed to make restitution. Others were put on trial. The Kabila government also asked foreign governments to provide information on the bank accounts and properties of Mobutu and his collaborators. Some documents were provided relatively quickly, but these revealed only a fraction of what was believed to have been looted from the state.

COTTON. Cotton became a principal commercial crop in Congo during the **colonial era**, when it was promoted by colonial administrators as a crop to be grown by individual Congolese. The crop was traditionally reserved for them and was grown extensively on small plots of land of one-half to one hectare in size. Production surpassed 100,000 tons before **independence**,

but fell steadily thereafter to less than 10,000 tons in 1993. In the 1980s, the Zairian **government** attempted to revive cotton production but failed due to a lack of inputs, such as fertilizers and pesticides, and a preference by farmers for growing the more-lucrative **coffee**. By the late 1980s, Zaire imported cotton for its **cloth** industry.

COUNCIL OF GOVERNMENT / CONSEIL DU GOUVERNEMENT. A consultative group set up by the colonial authorities following World War II to provide a source of ideas and information from persons outside the colonial power structure. The body was composed primarily of **civil servants** but also included **missionaries** and social workers who were considered the primary representatives of the Congolese.

COUP D'ETAT. Congo/Zaire experienced a successful coup d'etat by the **armed forces** on **November 24, 1965,** which brought **Mobutu** to power. As with many coups, the military decided to seize power following a political crisis exacerbated by bickering among political leaders and the inability of the civilian **government** to deal with threats to the **security** of the territory. Mobutu had briefly assumed power on September 14, 1960, during a political standoff between President Joseph **Kasavubu** and Prime Minister Patrice **Lumumba**. However, he then made a point of stating he was not staging a coup, but only "neutralizing" the politicians until passions cooled and political order could be restored.

Mobutu assumed power a second time in 1965 during a similar standoff between Kasavubu and Moïse **Tshombe**. It was an especially tense time. **Leopoldville** was being rocked by urban terrorism and banditry and another **rebellion** was beginning in the east. Although Mobutu used the military to wield and remain in power, he did not establish a military regime. Rather, he announced a civilian cabinet and vowed to bring a new political order. This soon became a "revolution" that brought the single-party state to Zaire with Mobutu as its undisputed leader.

There were a number of plots to overthrow the Mobutu government, usually with collaboration from some elements of the Zairian military. All failed, in part because of the **president**'s

efficient internal security network and his practice of offering handsome rewards to informers.

COURTS. *See* JUDICIAL SYSTEM.

CRIME. The Congolese **government** publishes no statistics on crime, court cases, or **prison** populations, so it is impossible to know exactly the extent of criminality or its incidence relative to other countries. Crime of all sorts is present in Congo/Zaire and, as in most of the world, appears to be worst in the cities, where poverty makes burglaries, pickpocketing and petty theft common occurrences. Most **middle-class** and upper-class households are protected by high walls and guards. Tight controls on firearms made their use relatively rare until the 1990s. However, following the economic collapse of the early 1990s, crime skyrocketed throughout Zaire. The **pillages** of 1991 and 1993, led by elements of the **armed forces**, were never punished and as the crisis worsened, the practice grew among some of the **security** forces of relying on the **population** to supplement their declining **incomes**.

By the mid-1990s, most civilians lived in fear of shakedowns at checkpoints by gunmen in military uniform. Another form of crime that arose was sweeps through neighborhoods by security forces who robbed, looted and raped, and shot anyone who resisted. **Arms trafficking** was also on the rise. Large quantities of weapons were being shipped through the country, initially to rebels of the **União Nacional para a Independência Total de Angola (UNITA)** in exchange for **diamonds** and, in the mid-1990s, to belligerents in the interethnic violence in **Rwanda** and **Burundi**. And arms began to appear in the possession of civilians, who used them to protect their families and police their neighborhoods.

After the fall of **Mobutu**, the Laurent **Kabila** government announced a crackdown on crime and the forces of order subsequently were criticized at times for their overzealous punishment of alleged criminals. On January 27, 1998, military firing squads in Kinshasa publicly executed 21 people convicted of murder and armed robbery. Thirty-nine others were executed in similar fashion in **Goma, Bukavu** and **Lubumbashi** in early 1998.

CROPS. Congo/Zaire's major crops include **bananas, coffee, cotton, maize** (corn), **manioc** (cassava), **palm oil, rice, rubber** and **sugar** cane. Other crops include cocoa, millet, peanuts, potatoes, sorghum, tea, tobacco and vegetables. For subsistence farming, the major crops are manioc, bananas and, in the savanna, maize. These are supplemented in some cases by vegetable gardens.

Traditionally, the ground is cleared toward the end of the dry season and the crops planted just before or just after the first **rainfall**. Crops are harvested toward the end of the rainy season or when mature. The hardy manioc is often grown throughout the year. Some years, when the rainy season is long, two crops may be planted and harvested. When the rainy season runs short, the crops are harvested early. There is little crop rotation, but fields are sometimes left to lie fallow for several seasons.

During the **colonial era**, commercial farming, along with **mining**, was the major source of **income** for the administration. Coffee, cotton, palm oil and, in the earliest days, rubber, tea and cocoa, were major cash crops. However, many plantations deteriorated following **independence**, extension services declined, and the maintenance of crop strains suited to the Zairian **environment** often suffered. *See also* Agriculture.

CRYSTAL MOUNTAINS. A small **mountain** chain in **Bas-Congo** province between **Kinshasa** and **Matadi**. The rugged terrain contributes to the cataracts that make the **Congo River** unnavigable between the two cities.

CUBA, RELATIONS WITH. **Congo/Zaire's** relations with Cuba were cool and at times even hostile following **independence**. Cuba was among the **Soviet**-bloc nations that supported the eastern **rebellions**, in particular the **People's Republic of the Congo** in **Stanleyville**. A Cuban contingent, led by Ernesto "Che" **Guevara**, fought against **government** troops in eastern Congo in the mid-1960s. During the Angolan civil war, Cuba sent an estimated 15,000 troops and advisers to **Angola** to back the **Movimento Popular de Libertação de Angola (MPLA)** faction against a rival faction, the **Frente Nacional de Libertação de Angola (FNLA)**, which was supported by the Zairian government. Despite recognition of the MPLA government by the **United Nations** and the **Organization of African Unity (OAU)** in 1976,

Zaire continued to back the FNLA's guerrilla war against the MPLA. Following the first **Shaba** incursion in March 1977 by guerrillas of the **Front pour la Libération Nationale du Congo (FLNC)** from bases in Angola, Zaire severed relations with Cuba.

Relations improved gradually after Zaire and Angola established diplomatic relations in late 1978 and the activities of the FNLA diminished. However, tensions remained as the Angolan civil war continued and Zaire switched support to another rival of the MPLA, the **União Nacional para a Independência Total de Angola (UNITA)** led by Jonas **Savimbi**. During the early 1980s the Cuban presence in Angola increased to more than 25,000 soldiers and a sizable Cuban contingent guarded petroleum installations in the Angolan enclave of **Cabinda**, only a few kilometers from the Zairian border. Cuba began withdrawing its troops and advisors in the late 1980s because of the weakening Cuban economy and a decline of popular support in Cuba for the intervention.

CULTURE. Congolese **government** policy seeks to preserve the traditional culture of the hundreds of **ethnic groups** in the country. As a result, the government has sponsored numerous studies, exhibitions, films, seminars and performances. In addition, some Congolese artists make concerted efforts to propagate aspects of traditional culture in their work, whether literature, **music**, painting or **theater**. Nevertheless, many Congolese feel that a lack of funds and the disruption of traditional transmission patterns caused by **urbanization** are eroding traditional culture. Modern urban Congolese culture, however, is vibrant. Drawing on aspects of the traditional past and melding them with influences from contemporary city life, contemporary culture influences fashion, music and the arts throughout Africa and increasingly in parts of Europe and the Americas. The influence of central African sculpture on modern art is well documented. Today, Congolese influences are regularly felt on the international fashion and music scenes as well. *See also* Cloth; Congo Jazz; Dress; Sports.

CURRENCY. The currency of the **Kingdom of Kongo**, when the Europeans arrived, was a certain kind of shell that could only be found in the **king**'s fisheries. During the **colonial era** and for a number of years after **independence**, the currency was the Congolese **franc**, pegged at a 1:1 ratio to the franc of **Belgium**. The currencies were de-linked at independence. The Congolese franc began to lose its long-standing value of 50 francs to one US dollar and was devalued a number of times. In September 1967, a currency reform was decreed and the currency was changed to the **zaire**. One zaire became the equivalent of and could be exchanged for 1,000 francs, equal to two US dollars. A smaller unit, the likuta (plural: makuta), was worth 1/100th of one zaire. Originally an even smaller unit, the sengi, equaling 1/100th of a likuta, was issued, but it quickly went out of circulation. The zaire, never strong, declined steadily in value during the 1970s and 1980s, and plunged during the 1990s to less than one-millionth of its original value.

The weakness of the currency was due in part to Zaire's historically negative **trade** balance, but primarily to the **government**'s tendency to borrow from the treasury to meet its budget deficits. Shortages of **foreign exchange** also gave rise to a thriving parallel market where the US dollar often traded at three to seven times its official rate of exchange.

On September 9, 1983, the Zairian government again announced monetary reforms. These allowed private banks for the first time to trade in currency through auctions and in essence floated the zaire on the free market. Under the new system, banks met weekly to set the exchange rate, based on supply and demand. After an initial plunge to one-fourth its previous level, the zaire remained stable for a number of years and for a time the parallel market was virtually eliminated.

During the late 1980s, the decline of the zaire resumed and accelerated, due primarily to rising budget deficits and shortages of foreign exchange. It also fluctuated depending on supply and demand at the central bank auctions. According to **World Bank** figures, one US dollar equaled 2.8 zaires in 1980, 50 zaires in 1985, 718 zaires in 1990, 15,587 zaires in 1991, 645,549 zaires in 1992 and five million zaires in 1993. On October 22, 1993, the government introduced a new currency, the new **zaire** (NZ), or nouveau zaïre, one unit of which was to be exchanged for three million "old" zaires. The **opposition** accused the government of printing money to pay its expenses and thereby fueling **inflation**. Inflation was reduced in 1994 and 1995 and the value of the new zaire stabilized somewhat, but it continued to fall. In early 1997, the new zaire was trading at 180,000 to one US dollar. Following the fall of **Mobutu** in May 1997, President Laurent **Kabila** announced the new zaire would be replaced by the Congo franc. The reform was delayed until 1998. However, the Kabila government was able to stabilize exchange rates as part of a vigorous anti-inflation effort and in January 1998, the dollar was being exchanged for 110,000 NZ in **Kinshasa** and about 130,000 in the major provincial commercial centers. The Kabila government reintroduced the Congolese **franc** (CF) on June 30, 1998, exchanging it at the rate of one CF for 100,000 NZ. When introduced, the new currency was exchanged at a rate of 1.4 CF to the US dollar, but it declined to 4.5 CF to the dollar by March 1999.

CUSTOMARY LAW / LOI COUTUMIÈRE. The name for the laws and traditional courts which governed Congolese during the **colonial era**, as opposed to the Belgian-style system which governed Europeans. Customary law was part of a two-tiered **judicial system** that allowed Congolese accused of offenses to be judged under their own traditional systems. **Chiefs** often acted as judges in these "people's courts." The **government** officially ended the dual system on July 10, 1968, incorporating customary law into the national judicial system. Professional judges replaced local chiefs. However, the system was never fully implemented and many citizens continued to seek arbitration and justice through elders and other traditional leaders.

CUVETTE CENTRALE. *See* CONGO RIVER BASIN.

- D -

DE GAULLE, CHARLES (1890 - 1970). President of **France** during the African **independence** period. De Gaulle's speech in Brazzaville on August 24, 1958, in which he offered autonomy to France's African colonies, dramatized the different prospects for independence in the **Belgian Congo** and those in its French-ruled neighbors. De Gaulle's speech, along with the **Pan-African Conference** in Accra and the **Brussels World Fair** that same year, fueled the independence movement and the riots in **Leopoldville** beginning **January 4, 1959**, which set into motion the move toward independence.

DEATH PENALTY. According to the **constitution**, the death penalty may be accorded for the crime of murder and other, extremely serious offenses, usually involving the death of the victim or victims. *See also* Penal Code.

DEBT, EXTERNAL. Congo/Zaire was one of the first casualties of the developing world's debt crisis, caused in part by falling commodity prices and rising interest rates, but also by liberal lending policies by banks. During the early 1970s, as **mineral** prices soared following the Arab oil embargo, prices for **copper** and **cobalt** rose to historic heights. Foreign banks lent large sums to Zaire for large-scale **development projects**. As a result, the external debt, which had more than tripled from 1967 to 1973, tripled again during the following two years, reaching $5 billion or roughly the equivalent of the country's annual **gross domestic product (GDP)**. In 1974, copper prices fell to one-third their level of the previous year and the Zairian government began to fall behind in debt repayments. The government signed a series of stabilization agreements with the **International Monetary Fund (IMF)**, but most of the IMF "standbys" were suspended because of the failure of the Zairian government to reduce its budget deficit and control **inflation**.

In 1983, Zaire undertook a series of drastic fiscal and monetary reforms that included floating its **currency** on the free market and slashing its budget. These measures caused a severe recession, but they also brought renewed confidence and expressions of support from the IMF and foreign creditors. After several years of recession and few signs of economic revival, the government in 1986 said it feared a social upheaval and therefore would begin limiting debt repayments to 10 percent of **export** earnings. It failed to meet this target. It negotiated another reform program in 1987, and yet another in 1989. These programs usually included a rollover of payment arrears, rescheduling of outstanding loans, and infusions of new money. In exchange, the government agreed to anti-inflation and budget reduction measures.

By 1990, Zaire's external debt had exceeded $10 billion and virtually all foreign lenders had frozen their aid programs because of mismanagement, failure to service existing loans, and **human rights** violations. In February 1992, the IMF declared Zaire "noncooperative," thereby making it ineligible for further borrowing. In July 1993, the **World Bank**, which until then had been the one multilateral institution receiving payments from Zaire, froze all lending because of service arrears and closed its office in **Kinshasa**. In 1995, Zaire's external debt was $11 billion, or nearly twice its annual GDP. It was estimated at $14 billion in 1997, when the government of Laurent **Kabila**, after deposing **Mobutu** called for forgiveness of the debt, saying it had all gone into the private accounts of Mobutu, his family and the barons of his regime. *See also* Economy; London Club.

DECLARATION OF CIVIL RIGHTS / DECLARATION DES DROITS CIVILS. *See* CIVIL RIGHTS, DECLARATION OF.

DEMOCRACY. Like many African nations, Congo/Zaire was a multiparty democracy at **independence**, modeled on Western European principles of government. However, during the 1970s and 1980s, it adopted a single-party system that contained limited democratic principles. In 1990, for a variety of ethnic, economic and cultural reasons, the country began a transition back to multiparty democracy that was extended several times because of political infighting.

The **Loi Fondamentale** (Fundamental Law) which established the political institutions at independence was largely influenced by the political system in **Belgium**. It provided for a bicameral legislature with a **president** and **prime minister**. Both president and prime minister were elected by **parliament**, but the Loi Fondamentale did not define the power-sharing relationship between the two leaders and the institution that chose them. The explosive growth of regionally and ethnically based **political parties**, estimated to number 125 prior to the **elections** of 1960, and the fact that no party or group obtained an absolute majority aggravated regional tensions and made governing difficult.

The **constitution** of 1964, which followed the end of the early secessions and **rebellions**, addressed some of these problems. In addition, as parliamentary politics began to mature, some political coalitions began to emerge, leading to significant victories by the **Confédération Nationale des Associations Congolaises (CONACO)** in elections in 1965. However, power struggles between the president and prime minister continued and regional tensions kept the political climate unsettled. Amid new rebellions and another constitutional crisis caused by a political standoff between the president and the ruling parliamentary coalition, **Mobutu** took power on **November 24, 1965**. The new president ruled by decree, suspended all political activity and promised to hold elections in five years. Following purges in the military and the exile of many **opposition** leaders, Mobutu founded the **Mouvement Populaire de la Révolution (MPR)** party and established a single-party system modeled primarily on the Chinese model. In what was to become a trend in many African countries, the sole legal party became the institution of state and the presidency increasingly assimilated political and administrative powers.

Mobutu was elected to seven-year terms in 1970, 1977 and 1984. Each time, he ran unopposed and received more than 99 percent of the vote. During the elections, observers noted many irregularities, such as a dearth of "No" ballots and the active presence at the polls of "pressure" groups of party militants and soldiers. By the late 1970s, Zaire had officially become a party-state. Candidates for public office had to be party members in good standing and were chosen by the **Political Bureau** or the president himself. The president appointed members of the Political Bureau as well as the occupants of most senior-level positions in party and government. All Zairians were made party members automatically from birth.

In the late 1970s, under pressure from Western donors, some liberalization was enacted. This included allowing some members of the Political Bureau to be elected, permitting multiple candidates for legislative elections, and giving local party members a voice in selecting the legislative candidates from their region. Parliament (officially called the **Legislative Council**) was unmuzzled and allowed to summon state commissioners (ministers) for questioning on their **department** budgets.

Parliamentary freedom led to raucous political debate. In part to counter this loss of control, Mobutu in 1980 created the MPR **Central Committee**, which gradually assumed responsibility for major debate and lawmaking functions in government. The Legislative Council's role became of one of approving decisions by the Central Committee, the Political Bureau and the presidency. Many other reforms were circumvented and control of the political process once again was returned to the president and a small group of close associates. Many Congolese felt a harsh dictatorship was being hidden behind the trappings of democracy. However, others noted that the institutions had brought political stability to a country which had spent its early years in virtually constant crisis. Controversial legislative elections were held in 1987 and a new parliament was convened. But it was viewed as weak and occupied by Mobutu *cadres*. Nevertheless, pressures began building for change and following several years of demonstrations and international pressure, Mobutu announced on **April 24, 1990**, the end of the party-state and the beginning of a transition to multiparty democracy. *See also* Democratic Transition.

DEMOCRATIC AND SOCIAL CHRISTIAN PARTY. *See* PARTI DÉMOCRATE ET SOCIAL CHRÉTIEN (PDSC).

DEMOCRATIC FORCES FOR THE LIBERATION OF THE CONGO. *See* FORCES DÉMOCRATIQUES POUR LA LIBÉRATION DU CONGO (FODELICO).

DEMOCRATIC REPUBLIC OF THE CONGO. *See* CONGO, DEMOCRATIC REPUBLIC OF THE.

DEMOCRATIC TRANSITION. In the 1980s, the people of **Zaire** suffered under a declining **economy,** repeated acts of repression and the effects of a decaying leadership. Yet the international community, preoccupied with rising pressure for political and economic reform in Eastern Europe, Latin America and China, did not pay much attention to Zaire. However, the collapse of the **Soviet Union** in 1989 and increasing pressure by Western powers for movement toward multiparty **democracy** in Africa brought pressure to bear on the somnolent autocracy in Zaire. In addition, some Congolese, at times backed by the **Catholic Church**, staged protests and public demonstrations for greater individual freedoms. On **April 24, 1990**, **Mobutu** announced the Third

Republic. He said Zaire would enter a transitional period of one year, during which two additional **political parties** would be allowed, leading to **elections** in 1991. Some of the restrictions of the single-party state were dropped, freedom of the press was allowed, and a number of **dissidents** were released.

Mobutu's speech, rather than easing pressure for political reform, brought an explosion of political activity and calls for a complete liberalization of the political process. After months of protests and negotiations, Mobutu agreed to remove limits on the number of political parties. In a matter of months more than 200 were announced. All embraced multipartyism and most said they were opposed to the Mobutu **government**. The **opposition**, backed by loud and sometimes irresponsible **press** that began to emerge, rejected the offer of elections in one year and instead called for a **national conference** to lay the foundation for a new political order. A number of Francophone African countries were planning national conferences, with mixed results. Threatened with a cutoff of Western aid and weakened by the loss of alliances provided by the Cold War rivalry, Mobutu acceded to many demands, but only after lengthy periods of confrontation, often accompanied by harsh repression of civic unrest.

Alliances were formed and betrayed as the parties jockeyed for position. Nevertheless, several political blocs emerged: the **Mouvement Populaire de la Révolution (MPR)** and its allies; the **Sacred Union** (Union Sacrée) of more than 200 opposition parties led by the **Union pour la Démocratie et le Progrès Social (UDPS)**, the **Parti Démocrate et Social Chrétien (PDSC),** and the **Union des Fédéralistes et des Républicains Indépendants (UFERI)**; and a group of parties espousing the nationalistic, socialistic tendencies of the martyred Patrice **Lumumba**.

Many parties were led by nationally known political figures, most of whom had served in previous governments. However, these leaders had to contend with young challengers who criticized the old political ways and called for a new political mentality. In addition to the "generation rift," a number of parties split over whether they supported Mobutu's plans for the transition. There was speculation that the **president** encouraged and financed factionalism in order to sow disorder and create what some pundits called "Multi-**Mobutism**." Nevertheless, agreement eventually was reached to hold a national conference. It opened on

August 7, 1991, with veteran politician Isaac **Kalonji Mutambayi** as president. But it quickly slid into chaos as nearly 8,000 "delegates" laid claim to the 2,800 seats. The work of the conference was disrupted dozens of times by boycotts, government-ordered lockouts, and the **pillages**, or lootings, of September 1991.

Following the riots, Mobutu named UDPS leader Étienne **Tshisekedi prime minister** but dismissed him one week later after he refused to sign an oath of allegiance. Mobutu then designated a supporter, **Mungul Diaka**, to be prime minister, leading Western nations to announce a cutoff of economic aid to Zaire. Four weeks later, Mobutu appointed as prime minister UFERI leader **Nguza Karl-I-Bond**, a former prime minister with strong support among Western governments.

The competing claims to the seats were eventually resolved and the National Conference was reconvened on December 11, 1991, chaired by the archbishop of Kisangani, Laurent **Monsengwo Pasinya**. In April 1992, the body proclaimed itself the **Conférence Nationale Souveraine (CNS)**, whose decisions were law and were to be carried out without question by the executive. This measure led to protests by Mobutu partisans and a comment by the president that there had been a civilian coup d'etat. On August 15, 1992, the CNS elected Tshisekedi prime minister and passed the **Transitional Act**, which was to guide the nation until a new **constitution** could be drafted and elections could be held. The CNS concluded its work and dissolved itself on December 6, 1992. One of its final acts was to establish the **Haut Conseil de la République (HCR)**, with Monsengwo as its president, to act as an interim **parliament**.

Mobutu's term had officially ended in December 1991, but he stayed on under terms of the transition. By the end of 1992, he had determined that the reforms voted by the CNS had gone too far, that the HCR was controlled by the opposition, and that the constitution it had drafted posed a threat. In October he announced he was convening the former parliament, the **Legislative Council**, which had been elected under single-party rule and had not met since the transition was announced. He said the Legislative Council would draft a new constitution. The country entered a period called "*bicéphalisme*," or "two-headedness," during which the two rival legislatures claimed to be the legal government.

In January 1993, the HCR passed a measure declaring Mobutu guilty of treason because of his mismanagement of the economy and refusal to carry out its orders. Mobutu convened a group of political parties which came to be called the Forces Politiques du **Conclave**, boycotted by the opposition, to take over the reigns of the transition. He "dismissed" the Tshisekedi government, which under the Transitional Act he did not have the authority to do, and named Faustin **Birindwa**, a senior Tshisekedi advisor, prime minister of a "government of national salvation." Birindwa was expelled from the UDPS and the Sacred Union for accepting the post but managed to take a number of minor opposition leaders with him. However, his government was not recognized internationally and Western governments began a policy of diplomatic isolation of Mobutu. The **United Nations** named a special envoy to Zaire in July 1993, but he was rejected by the opposition after he visited **Gbadolite** (which for the opposition had become a symbol of cooperation with Mobutu).

In late 1993, after nearly a year of political paralysis during which the economic crisis worsened, the parties agreed to a compromise whereby the HCR and the MPR parliament were merged to form the **Haut Conseil de la République / Parlement de la Transition (HCR/PT)**. This body of 745 members was to oversee the transition, draft a constitution, and organize elections, which under the Transitional Act were scheduled to be held in December 1994.

In June 1994, the HCR/PT elected as prime minister Léon **Kengo wa Dondo**, a former prime minister who headed a coalition of "centrist" parties. The hardline opposition denounced the vote as taken without a quorum and therefore illegal. It formed the **Union Sacrée de l'Opposition Radicale et Alliés et Société Civile (USORAS)** and refused to recognize the Kengo government. Western governments, frustrated by the lack of progress, backed the Kengo government as a compromise and eased their policy of isolating the Zairian government. Kengo visited Europe and Washington in October 1994, where he was urged to press ahead with political and economic reforms. Kengo, who had overseen as prime minister the economic reforms of the mid-1980s, was viewed within Zaire as a technocrat created by Mobutu and had little popular support.

The HCR/PT voted on June 30, 1995, to extend the transitional period by two years and postpone elections until July 9, 1997. A few weeks later, USORAS and pro-Mobutu forces joined to dismiss Archbishop Monsengwo, whom each side viewed as favoring the other. The **Electoral Commission** was appointed in March 1996. A new constitution was drafted by the HCR/PT in August and a referendum was scheduled for February 1997.

This timetable was disrupted by the offensive launched in October 1996 by the **Alliance des Forces Démocratiques pour la Libération du Congo/Zaïre (AFDL)** from eastern Zaire. In seven months, the AFDL took power, sending an ailing Mobutu into exile and installing Laurent **Kabila** as president. In his inauguration speech on May 29, 1997, Kabila pledged to complete the transition by holding a constitutional referendum in 1998 and national elections in 1999. However, he excluded Tshisekedi and the major opposition parties from his first government and banned political demonstrations shortly thereafter, leading to fears that his government would seek to control the political process and the political stalemate would continue. The ban on political parties was lifted on January 31, 1998, but burdensome requirements for their registration led to protests.

DENARD, BOB. A French **mercenary** who was hired by the Katangan government during the **Katangan secession** of 1960-61 and subsequently by the **Mobutu** government in the mid-1960s to put down the eastern **rebellions**. Denard, who also fought in Nigeria's Biafran civil war, later moved to the Comoros, where he was involved in a number of coups. In the 1980s, he was convicted in absentia for murder in France. On October 4, 1995, he surrendered to authorities in the Comoros after a fourth coup attempt and was extradited to France.

DEPARTMENTS. On January 5, 1973, the ministries of the executive branch were renamed departments, the ministers were renamed state commissioners, and the Council of Ministers became the **Executive Council.** The names and functions of the departments changed over the years and their number varied between 20 and 30, but their basic responsibilities (interior, defense, foreign affairs, education, agriculture, etc.) and their staffs remained. As the power of the **presidency** became institutionalized another trend developed. The departments became increasingly subordinate to the party and the Office of the President, both of which maintained organizational substructures similar to the executive branch. The Office of the President, in particular, attracted the brightest *cadres* and appeared to experience the fewest restraints on spending.

The names of the departments were changed back to ministries following the installation of the Laurent **Kabila** government in May 1997.

DÉPLACÉS. A term, meaning "displaced," coined to describe the **Rwandan** immigrants who were brought by Belgian colonial authorities to **Kivu** in the 1920s and 1930s to work on the **plantations**. They should not to be confused with the **Banyarwanda**, who immigrated to **Sud-Kivu** before the **colonial era**. *See also* Ethnic Cleansing.

DESCENT GROUPS. Although the nature and role of descent groups vary considerably among **ethnic groups**, it is generally agreed that to many central Africans, ancestry is one of the most important aspects of heritage and individual identity. Descent groups are important in the personal development of the individual and usually center on two to as many as dozens of previous generations. In traditional society, lineage groups sometimes assumed political functions, particularly in areas where a chieftaincy structure was not present.

The descent/lineage group often spread over a large area because of the practice of marrying from another group and taking the spouse to the father's or mother's village. In the *patrilineal* **societies**, descent was traced primarily through the male members of the society. The man would marry and often take his wife to his father's village. In the *matrilineal* societies, when a woman married, the husband often moved to the village of his mother-in-law's brother, who usually had more authority over him than his own father. In these societies, a matrilineal uncle often took care of the upbringing and coming-of-age rites of young males and children often took the name of their mother or maternal uncle.

DEVELOPMENT PROJECTS. As a large nation with a history of close ties to Western Europe and the Americas, Congo/Zaire was the recipient of numerous development projects from **independence** until the 1990s. Many of these focused on improving infrastructure, such as **roads, railways, electrical power,** and water supplies. Others focused on improving **agricultural** productivity. A few focused on **industry** and the service sector. Under the **Politique des Grands Travaux** policies of the 1970s, large projects were launched, including the **Inga hydroelectric complexes,** on the **Congo River** 40 km from **Matadi;** the **Inga-Shaba power line** that could carry up to 520 MW of electricity from Inga to the **Shaba** mining region; the deep-water **port** at **Banana** on the Atlantic Ocean; the Matadi-Banana railway project aimed at providing a rail link from eastern Congo/Zaire to the Atlantic Ocean; the suspension bridge over the Congo River at Matadi; the electrification of the Matadi-Kinshasa railway to make use of unused electrical potential at Inga; the Kinshasa-**Ilebo** railway link aimed at supplementing the traditional river link; the **Voix du Zaïre telecommunications** and broadcasting center which produced and transmitted **radio** and television programs via **satellite** to the country; the World Trade Center aimed at providing a major central African trading forum; the **Maluku steel mill** near Kinshasa; **cement** factories in **Bas-Zaïre;** the Kaniema-Kasese **Maize** Project and Gémène Agro-Industrial Complex aimed at installing agribusiness in distant and sometimes neglected regions; and various projects to refurbish and improve airports, roads, bridges, telephone networks, and water and electrical distribution systems. Development experts in the 1980s increasingly favored projects that set relatively simple goals and tended to have a higher success rate than complex projects.

DEVLIN, LAWRENCE. Station chief of the **Central Intelligence Agency (CIA)** of the **United States** during the 1960s. Devlin publicly admitted the CIA had a plan to assassinate Patrice **Lumumba** and had even made initial preparations to implement it, but said it was never carried out. After his retirement, he became a successful businessman in **Kinshasa.**

DHANIS, FRANCIS (BARON). One of the leaders of the military campaigns from 1894 to 1896 against Arab **slavers** and **ivory** traders in eastern Congo and particularly against supporters of the **Mahdi**, prophet of **Sudan**.

DIAMONDS. Congo/Zaire has produced an estimated one-third of the world's industrial diamonds and in the mid-1990s was the world's third-largest producer after Australia and Botswana. The diamonds, a small percentage of which were of gem quality, come primarily from the **Mbuji-Mayi** and **Tshikapa** areas in **Kasaï Orientale** and nearby areas of northeastern **Angola**, where they originate in kimberlite deposits along several **rivers**, but especially along the Lubilash River. The **government**-owned **Société Minière de Bakwanga (MIBA)** concession was the main producer. However, wildcat artisanal digging and panning was a tradition in the area and on occasion led to clashes. Total official production averaged 12 million carats in the 1970s but fell to six million carats in 1981, due to theft, **smuggling** (which reached 70 percent of total production according to estimates), and shortages of spare parts for **mining** equipment. During the 1960s and 1970s, the Zairian government was the sole legal diamond trader. Diamonds were marketed by the De Beers Central Selling Organization except for a period from 1981 to 1984, when a government-owned company, **Société Zaïroise de Commercialisation des Minérais (SOZACOM)**, was responsible for marketing.

In 1982, the government legalized artisanal mining in certain areas and established a system of trading counters that privatized marketing. MIBA continued to market its diamonds through De Beers, while Lebanese, Belgian, Israeli and Zairian groups operated counters that bought diamonds from local miners and middlemen. Official production increased, reaching an estimated 24 million carats in 1990. They declined to an estimated 15 million carats in 1995, but rose again, to 23 million carats, in 1998. Earnings were estimated at $500 million in 1994. Rumors of rich finds created a small diamond rush in the **Kisangani** area in 1995.

The industry was rocked by a number of scandals in the early 1990s. The government of Étienne **Tshisekedi** in 1992 closed two major counters after it was revealed that the **central bank** was granting them **foreign exchange** with which to purchase diamonds at a 30 percent discount. This concession effectively allowed them to corner the market. In addition, Angola protested diamond smuggling from fields in its territory and in mid-1995 announced military patrols were authorized to shoot "suspicious" foreigners in the border area on sight.

Following the takeover of the Laurent **Kabila** government, which was supported by the Angolan government, Angolan troops launched a major offensive in the diamond-mining area in northern Angola, controlled virtually since independence by the **União Nacional para a Independência Total de Angola (UNITA)**. As a result, several thousand Congolese prospectors were driven back home in January 1998.

DIANGIENDA KUNTIMA, JOSEPH. Son of the prophet Simon **Kimbangu** and founder of an offshoot of the Congolese **Protestant Church** called the Church of Jesus Christ on Earth by the Prophet Simon Kimbangu (Église de Jésus-Christ sur la Terre par le Prophète Simon Kimbangu). The church grew following Kimbangu's death in 1951 and was the first independent African church to be admitted to the World Council of Churches.

DIET. The diet of the Congolese varies depending on where they live. The most common staple is **manioc**, or cassava, but **maize** is preferred in the savanna regions and **rice** is the staple of choice of urban dwellers who can afford it. The diet is supplemented with meat, fish or vegetables when they can be afforded or acquired through artisanal hunting, **fishing** and farming. Many families in the cities have vegetable gardens and the practice of forays into the countryside to gather **bananas**, fruits and berries is common. Congo/Zaire has one of the lowest per-capita **incomes** in the world and according to UN figures, one-fourth of its children are undernourished. During the economic crisis of the 1990s, characterized by high **inflation** and **unemployment** of up to 80 percent, the rate of **malnutrition** rose markedly. In the cities, more than one-half of the **population** did not receive the minimum daily nutritional requirement and families frequently could not afford one meal a day. *See also* Food Supply.

DIKEMBE MUTOMBO (1966 -). Congolese basketball star who played for the US National Basketball Association's Denver Nuggets in the early 1990s and from 1996 with the Atlanta

Hawks. Dikembe was born on June 15, 1966, in **Lubumbashi** and attended secondary school in **Kinshasa**. He played for Georgetown University in the 1980s before joining the NBA.

DILOLO. A town of about 50,000 inhabitants lying in western **Katanga Province** along the border with **Angola** where the southern **Katanga railway** system connects with the **Benguela Railway**. During the first **Shaba** incursion, Dilolo was the first town to be taken by the guerrillas of the **Front pour la Libération Nationale du Congo (FLNC)** and the last to be retaken by Zairian and Moroccan troops nearly three months later. The **Lunda ethnic group** predominates on both sides of the border in the area. As a result, there were reports of reprisals by Zairian troops who felt residents had aided the rebels.

DINOSAURS, THE / LES DINOSAURES. A term that came into use during the late 1980s to denote the barons of the **Mobutu** regime. Belgian journalist Colette Braeckman published a book in 1992 entitled *"Le Dinosaure: le Zaïre de Mobutu,"* which detailed numerous excesses by members of the regime.

DIOMI, GASTON. One of the founders of the **Mouvement National Congolais (MNC)** party through which Patrice **Lumumba** rose to prominence. Diomi attended the **Pan-African Conference** in Accra, Ghana, in December 1958 with Lumumba. He was one of the speakers who reported on the conference at a rally in **Leopoldville** on **January 4, 1959**, which led to two weeks of rioting in Leopoldville and accelerated the movement toward **independence**. Diomi, along with Joseph **Kasavubu**, was imprisoned following the riots.

DISEASE. According to UN figures, disease accounts for one-half of the deaths in Congo/Zaire and is an important factor in the low national life expectancy rate of 52 years (1992) and high infant mortality rate of 147 per thousand for children under five years of age. Major diseases are malaria, measles, diarrheal diseases, diphtheria, pertussis, poliomyelitis, tuberculosis, gonorrhea, trypanosomiasis (sleeping sickness), onchocerciasis (river blindness), schistosomiasis and leprosy. Many of these diseases are curable and preventable but continue to flourish because only one-third of the **population** has access to **health care** services and only a fraction of them can afford it. Public health services, which were considered among the most advanced in Africa at **independence**, have declined markedly. To the list of major diseases has been added **Acquired Immune Deficiency Syndrome (AIDS)**, which has attained pandemic proportions in the cities. Studies in the 1980s revealed that 5-15 percent of the urban population and up to 30 percent of prostitutes carried the virus, for which a cure has yet to be found. In addition, outbreaks of rare but deadly diseases, such as the **Ebola** fever in 1976 and 1995, Lassa fever in the 1980s, and Monkey Pox in 1996, have received widespread international attention.

DISSIDENTS. Dissidents, organized and unorganized, have been perceived to be a threat to political stability virtually from **independence**. In fact, popular reaction against the factionalism and secessions of the early 1960s were one reason for the military **coup d'etat** in 1965 and the considerable support it initially received. However, authoritarianism and the establishment of a one-party system led to increased **opposition**.

Some of the better-known exiled dissident groups in the 1970s included the **Mouvement National Congolais (MNC)** led by supporters of Patrice **Lumumba**; the **Forces Démocratiques pour la Libération du Congo (FODELICO)**, led by Antoine **Gizenga**, which were involved in the **rebellions** in northeastern Congo/Zaire; the **Mouvement d'Action pour la Résurrection du Congo (MARC)**, led by **Munguya Mbenge**, which was involved in the **university student** demonstrations of the 1970s; and the **Front pour la Libération Nationale du Congo (FLNC)** led by Nathaniel **Mbumba**, which was involved in the **Shaba** incursions in 1977 and 1978.

In the 1980s, two dissident groups could be described as internally based. The first was the **Union pour la Démocratie et le Progrès Social (UDPS)**, formed in 1982 as a second **political party**, which pressed for a multiparty system and in 1990 became a major opposition party. The second was the **Parti Révolutionnaire du Peuple (PRP)**, which attacked an army garrison at **Moba** in 1984 and 1985.

During the 1980s, the UDPS was the most important opposition force and its members suffered for it. Some of the founders of the UDPS had published a 52-page letter on December 31, 1980, accusing the **Mobutu government** of authoritarianism and **corruption** and calling for multiparty **democracy** in Zaire. In 1982, they were convicted of treason. They were later amnestied, but were imprisoned again when they resumed their activities. They were released once more on June 30, 1985, as part of the festivities marking Zaire's 25 years of independence, but were detained yet again when they still refused to halt their activities.

On May 21, 1983, Mobutu issued the general political **amnesty of 1983**, in which he offered to allow exiles to return to Zaire unmolested if they gave up their antigovernment activities. Over the next two years, many took advantage of the amnesty.

With Mobutu's announcement of the **democratic transition** on **April 24, 1990**, dissent was legalized. Political activities were freed in principle and political parties were allowed to hold rallies. However, many rallies and demonstrations were harshly dispersed by **security** forces and the homes of many politicians were attacked. Political parties were allowed to form in November and many exiled dissidents returned to launch or affiliate with one of the more than 200 parties that sprouted over the following year. Although the government continued to monopolize the broadcast **news media**, the print media was liberalized and dozens of newspapers began to appear, mostly in **Kinshasa**. In October 1996, the PRP led a group of rebels that launched an offensive from eastern Zaire and, backed by fighters from **Rwanda**, **Uganda**, **Burundi** and **Angola**, overthrew Mobutu and took power in the country. *See also* Human Rights.

DIVISION SPÉCIALE PRÉSIDENTIELLE (DSP) / SPECIAL PRESIDENTIAL DIVISION. The elite **security** unit that guarded **Mobutu** and was the most loyal of **Congo/Zaire**'s security forces. The DSP was formed in 1986 from the Brigade Spéciale Présidentielle, which had been created after the second **Shaba** incursion, and was trained initially by **Israeli** officers. Formed primarily of soldiers from the **president**'s **Ngbandi ethnic group** and usually led by a close relative of the president, the DSP was the best and most regularly paid of the security forces. It was based at a camp surrounding the presidential palace. The DSP was used to quell the looting in **Kinshasa** in 1991 and 1993. It was also used in the attack on **students** at **Lubumbashi** University in 1990. One of its most notorious units, "**Les Hiboux**," or "The Owls," carried out a campaign of terrorist attacks against the **opposition** during the 1990s.

The DSP was disbanded following the overthrow of Mobutu and the installation of the Laurent **Kabila** government in May 1997. A number of its senior officers reportedly were executed.

DRESS. In Congo/Zaire, dress and fashion tend to follow central African and European patterns. The Arab-style robe as seen in north and west Africa is rare. For Congolese women, it includes a traditional wrap of two to four yards of African print **cloth**, or *pagne,* with a blouse and matching headdress worn with sandals or high heels. African-style garb for men includes the bou-bou or dashiki, loose-fitting shirts made from colorful **wax** cloth, slacks, sandals, and rarely a hat. During the heyday of **Authenticity**, Zaire pioneered the modernistic, urban version of the traditional woman's garb, whereby the ample, loose folds of the *pagne* were turned into a long, tight skirt and blouse that emphasized the hips. For men, the **abacost** (for "*à bas le costume,*" meaning "down with the suit") was created. The abacost was a tight-laced two-piece suit usually of dark, formal material, with a Mao-type collar that was buttoned to the throat. Ties were not worn, but among the stylish, a silk scarf was permissible. For the politically correct, the party lapel pin of the **Mouvement Populaire de la Révolution (MPR)** was a required accessory. In the late 1980s, European business suits returned as common dress among the apolitical. Among well-to-do youth, sleek French and Italian styles of casual dress were popular, as were American jeans and sneakers. With the announcement of the transition to multiparty politics in April 1990, dress was liberalized for the political class. Most members of the **opposition** abandoned the abacost, which, however, remained de rigueur for supporters of the president.

DUTCH INFLUENCES. The Dutch arrived in the Congo area in the early 1600s and, along with the Portuguese, helped destabilize the **Kongo Kingdom**. Motivated by a need for **slaves** which could not be satisfied through commercial dealings with local African traders, the Dutch increasingly came into confrontation with Kongo leaders. They took Luanda in 1641 and for a time replaced the Portuguese as the leading slave traders along the central African coast. The Portuguese retook Luanda in 1648, however, and Dutch influence declined.

The major Dutch contribution to central African **society** was the printed **"wax" cloth** introduced by traders returning from Asia. The print, originally made using the lost-wax method, was first imported from Indonesia and Java. Today, virtually every African nation possesses a textile **industry** which manufactures "wax" and it is a popular cloth for dresses, shirts, suits, tablecloths, mats and bedding among most Congolese families. It was long a major component of Congolese fashion and by the 1990s had gained popularity in the Caribbean and parts of Europe and the Americas.

- E -

EAST KASAI PROVINCE. *See* KASAÏ ORIENTAL PROVINCE.

EASTERN HIGHLANDS. The highest and most rugged region of **Congo/Zaire**, the Eastern Highlands range for 1,500 km along the **lakes** of the **Great Rift Valley** and include the headwaters of the White Nile. A series of **mountain** ranges 80 to 560 km wide extend from the **Ruwenzori** chain in northeastern Congo/Zaire through the **Virunga** volcanic range in the **Kivus** to the **Mitumba** chain in northern **Katanga**. The hills and mountains range in altitude from 1,000 to more than 5,000 meters, giving the region a cool **climate** which led some to call it the Switzerland of Africa. The region produces **gold**, **tin**, iron ore, **sugar**, textiles, methane gas, **palm oil**, tobacco and **coffee**. Some light **industry** was developed around the two main urban centers of **Bukavu** and **Goma**.

The Eastern Highlands region is also known for its independent attitude toward the central **government** in distant **Kinshasa**. The government at various times tried to reduce the area's isolation, but economic decline and deteriorating infrastructure led to a strengthening of commercial ties with neighboring countries in East Africa. The offensive of the **Alliance des Forces Démocratiques pour la Libération du Congo/Zaïre (AFDL)**, which overthrew **Mobutu** and took power in Kinshasa in May 1997, began in the Eastern Highlands in October 1996 and was widely supported by the local populace.

EASTERN WAY. The term given to the **transportation** route for **mineral exports** from **Katanga** through **Tanzania** to the port of Dar es Salaam. The **government** viewed this route less favorably than the **Benguela Railway** through **Angola**; the **National Way**, which passes entirely through Congolese territory; or the **Southern Way** through **Zambia** and Zimbabwe to the **South African** port of Durban. The Eastern Way required shipping goods by rail 1,300 km from **Lubumbashi** to **Kalemie** on **Lake Tanganyika**, by boat across the lake, and by the Tazara Railway to Dar es Salaam. The Eastern Way, 2,715 km long, was no shorter than the National Way and required several transshipments. Goods were often delayed by maintenance problems with the rolling stock and by congestion at the port. During the 1980s, according to government figures, 11 percent of the country's **copper** was exported via the Eastern Way. However, that figure declined significantly during the mid-1990s.

EBOLA. A highly **contagious disease** of viral origin causing high fever and hemorrhaging of the internal organs with a mortality rate approaching 80 percent. The first recorded outbreak occurred in 1976 in Yambuku near the Ebola River, in northern Congo/Zaire, and caused 211 deaths. A second outbreak was reported in southern **Sudan** in 1979. A third, first detected in March 1995 in **Kikwit**, a city of 400,000 residents in **Bandundu Province**, caused considerable alarm because of fears it might spread to **Kinshasa**, the capital of five million people 185 km to the west. International medical workers rushed to help Zairian teams contain the epidemic. Virologists from Zaire, **Belgium**, and the **United States** collected more than 3,000 samples of insects and birds in the hope of discovering the host of the virus during its periods of inactivity. In August, scientists announced the outbreak was over. Of the 310 people infected, 244 died. Doctors said transfusions of blood from infected individuals who had survived increased survival rates, pointing toward a possible form of treatment until a cure could be developed. The virus reappeared in Gabon in 1996, causing 46 deaths.

ÉCOLE NATIONALE D'ADMINISTRATION (ENA) / NATIONAL SCHOOL OF ADMINISTRATION. A professional school in **Kinshasa**, founded in the early 1960s by the Congolese **government** and private foundations in order to train Congolese for careers primarily in the **civil service**.

ECONOMIC COMMUNITY OF CENTRAL AFRICAN STATES (ECOCAS) / COMMUNAUTÉ ÉCONOMIQUE DES ÉTATS DE L'AFRIQUE CENTRALE (CEEAC). Modeled on the larger and more established Economic Community of West African States (ECOWAS), ECOCAS was first proposed in the early 1980s by **Mobutu** and Gabonese President Omar Bongo, in an attempt to form a Central African common market. The organization seeks to integrate the disparate **economies** of nations ranging from the relatively large **Congo/Zaire** and Cameroon to small, landlocked **Rwanda** and **Burundi** and the island nations of Equatorial Guinea and São Tomé and Principe. In September 1983, 10 nations formally signed the agreement to form the community: Burundi, Cameroon, **Central African Republic**, **Chad, Republic of the Congo**, Equatorial Guinea, Gabon, Rwanda, São Tomé and Principe, and Zaire. Economists predicted many obstacles to establishing a common market in the region, such as a lack of infrastructure and widely diverging economic and political policies. Nevertheless, progress by the smaller, Francophone-dominated **Union Douanière et Économique de l'Afrique Centrale (UDEAC)** has given central African leaders some hope of implementing at least initial steps, such as an alignment of customs tariffs and free movement within the region by citizens of member-nations.

ECONOMIC COMMUNITY OF COUNTRIES OF THE GREAT LAKES. *See* COMMUNAUTÉ ÉCONOMIQUE DES PAYS DES GRANDS LACS (CEPGL).

ECONOMY. **Congo/Zaire**'s formal economy, with a **gross domestic product (GDP)** of $4.6 billion in 1995, depends heavily on the extraction of raw materials such as **copper, cobalt**, industrial **diamonds** and, to a lesser degree, **rubber, timber, coffee, palm oil** and related products, cocoa and tea. During the first three decades following **independence**, copper alone accounted for one-half of **government** revenues and nearly two-thirds of **foreign exchange** earnings. Cobalt, derived from some copper ores, was an important by-product. Congo/Zaire was self-sufficient in **food** at independence, but by the 1980s was importing large quantities of food products, consumer goods, and **transportation** and construction equipment. Less than one-third of the population participated in the formal economy and that proportion declined significantly after the **pillages** of 1991 and 1993 closed many factories and businesses.

Historically, the Congolese economy has tended to follow the economic fluctuations of the world economy: severe depression in the 1930s, recovery after World War II, and a boom during the early 1970s. However, there were several exceptions. One was a recession in the early 1960s following independence caused by secessions and **rebellions** and the departure of many technicians. In the early 1970s, buoyed by high copper prices and encouraged by lending institutions, the government launched the **Politique des Grands Travaux**, or Great Works Policy, which focused on building large **development projects** aimed at transforming the country into a modern industrial state. With the fall of **mineral** prices in 1974-75, the Zairian economy entered a period of stagnation. Productivity declined on a per-capita basis through the 1980s, despite various attempts at economic reform. In the early 1990s, political uncertainty, loss of control over fiscal and monetary policies and civil unrest brought a period of hyperinflation and economic collapse.

GDP, which had stagnated during the 1980s, declined by 10 percent in 1992 and again in 1993, but the decline slowed to 7 percent in 1994, according to government figures. During this period, industrial activity declined from about 30 percent of capacity to 10 percent. Per-capita **income**, which during the 1980s fluctuated between $200 and $250 per year, declined to $125 in 1994.

Inflation, a constant problem, began to accelerate in the early 1980s, reaching 100 percent in 1983. It was reduced considerably in the mid-1980s through austerity measures, but began to rise again in 1986. Rapid expansion of the money supply in the early 1990s led to several years of uncontrolled inflation, which reached an annualized rate of 12,000 percent during several months in 1994, but declined the following year.

High inflation and widespread counterfeiting caused the value of the **currency**, the **zaire**, to collapse. Exchanged at a rate of 700 zaires to one US dollar in 1990, the exchange rate declined to five million zaires to the dollar in 1993. The government issued greater numbers of bills in ever-larger denominations until popular rejection of the five-million-zaire note in January 1993 led to rioting by troops who were unable to spend their pay. A new currency, the new **zaire** (NZ) or nouveau zaïre, was introduced on October 22, 1993, at a rate of three million zaires to one NZ, or 1.5 NZ to the dollar. By early 1997, the currency was being exchanged at a rate of 2,000 NZ to the dollar. By then, most commercial activity was being conducted in US dollars or French and Belgian francs and the new zaire was being used for official transactions only. The crisis also caused many businessmen to flee to the informal sector, which according to some estimates had grown to several times the size of the formal economy.

The late 1970s saw the beginning of Zaire's external **debt** crisis, which was characterized by an inability to meet debt repayment schedules or the goals of repeated stabilization agreements with the **International Monetary Fund (IMF)**. More than one dozen agreements were negotiated during the 1970s and 1980s, but the government could not fulfill the conditions for more than a few months. In 1986, Zaire announced it would limit debt repayments to 10 percent of **export** earnings, but it failed to keep that commitment and virtually ceased to service the debt. In 1992, the IMF declared Zaire "non-compliant," thereby excluding it from any new loans. The **World Bank** closed its office in **Kinshasa** the following year.

Zaire's external debt grew from $5 billion in 1975 to $14 billion in 1997, or roughly twice the annual GDP and 10 times export earnings. The economic crisis had a positive effect, however, on Zaire's balance of **trade. Imports**, which historically had exceeded exports by 10 percent or more, declined by one-half to $600 million in 1994, while exports, bolstered by rising revenues from diamonds and coffee, remained relatively constant at $1 billion.

Economists predicted in mid-1995 that the worst had passed and that under Prime Minister **Kengo wa Dondo**'s austerity measures there was cause for hope. They noted there were proposals to export Zairian **electrical power** from the **Inga** hydroelectric complex in **Bas-Zaïre** to southern Africa and even to **Egypt**, and that new deposits of **petroleum** had been discovered off the coast. However, there was little optimism for a recovery of the state-dominated **mining** industry, historically the driving force of the economy. Most mining companies were operating at less than 10 percent of capacity and technically insolvent and were expected to require massive infusions of new capital to reactivate collapsed mines and old equipment. **South African** companies were the first to express interest in investing in this sector and in November 1996 a Canadian company announced plans to revive production at a major copper concession. Following the installation of the Laurent **Kabila** government in May 1997, after the overthrow of Mobutu, several joint ventures were announced with South African, Canadian, European and **United States** companies. *See also* Agriculture; Arms Smuggling; Balance of Payments; Corruption; Employment; Energy; Fishing; Industry; Labor; Manufacturing; Nationalization; Privatization; Retrocession; Smuggling; Trade; Transportation; Unemployment; Zairianization.

EDUCATION. Education in Congo/Zaire made considerable progress following **independence**, but was hindered by a lack of funds, qualified instructors, and curricula designed to train individuals to address the country's most pressing needs. During the **colonial era**, considerable emphasis was placed on primary school programs and, at independence, the **Belgian Congo** boasted one of the highest **literacy** rates in Africa. Officially, 70 percent of all school-age Congolese were enrolled in primary school, although studies showed that less than one-half of these went beyond the first several grades. The main purpose of the colonial education system was to prepare Congolese for clerical and secretarial jobs. Few Congolese were able to attend secondary schools or **universities**. As a result, at independence there were less than 30,000 enrolled secondary **students** (2 percent of total enrollment), fewer than 200 high school graduates, and only about two dozen Congolese with university degrees.

An emphasis on education following independence raised the literacy rate by 1985 to 79 percent of males and 45 percent females, according to UNICEF figures. In this case literacy was defined as those individuals over the age of 15 years who could write. According to UNICEF figures published in 1987, the proportion of Congolese children enrolled in primary school who completed first grade was 65 percent, while 33 percent of eligible males and 13 percent of the females were enrolled in secondary school. By 1985, there were 20,000 university graduates, some of whom had been educated abroad but many of whom had received their degrees from Zairian universities.

Primary education during the colonial period was handled primarily by religious organizations, although lay, "official" schools were later established in urban centers. The dual system was maintained after independence, but the government established certain standard curricula. The schooling consisted of six years designed to impart literacy, computational skills, and basic knowledge of **health care**, sanitation and nutrition. Textbooks were developed which used Congolese as role models and the village and *cité* as locations. However, many schools were hampered by the poor quality of teachers, who were seriously underpaid, and a lack of basic teaching materials. There was some instruction at the primary level in the four "national" **languages**, Kikongo, **Lingala**, Swahili and Tshiluba, depending on the region.

Secondary education, available to a much smaller proportion of the population, was conducted entirely in French, the "official" language. A great many of the secondary school teachers were expatriates until the mid-1970s when many left because of a lack of funding for salaries and pressure for more Congolese teachers to take their place. Secondary sequences consisted of either a four-year university preparatory course or a two-year vocational course. Secondary schools were afflicted with many of the material and human resource problems of primary schools.

In the early 1970s, most primary and one-half of secondary schools were staffed and managed by religious groups, although their administration was centered in the **government**'s Department of Education and they received government subsidies. In 1974, however, during the height of **Authenticity**, theological faculties were abolished and religious instruction was phased out of primary and secondary schools. By 1976, the government had assumed full administrative control. Beginning with the decline of the Zairian **economy** in the late 1970s, a lack of government revenues left many public schools underequipped, sometimes even without desks and blackboard chalk. Teachers were often paid months late. As a result they often left classes during the day to engage in commerce or charged fees to issue grades. Parents often were called upon to help provide equipment and subsidize teachers' salaries. In the face of the deteriorating conditions and as relations with the churches improved in the late 1970s, the Zairian government returned control of many primary and secondary schools to the churches. As state-supported schools declined, private schools proliferated.

One university existed at independence, at **Lovanium** outside **Kinshasa**, founded in 1954 by the **Catholic Church**. A **Protestant** university, the Université Libre du Congo based in **Kisangani**, was founded in 1963. A state-run institution, the Université Officielle du Congo, was founded in 1964 in **Lubumbashi**. The average length of course-of-study at the universities was three to seven years. Students were obliged to pass a nationally administered state examination before they could receive the equivalent of a bachelor's degree. Students benefited from government stipends and subsidies. Two institutions trained teachers: the Institut Pédagogique National/Kinshasa and the Institut Pédagogique National/**Bukavu**. Vocational and professional education was carried out by more than one dozen schools which focused primarily on **agriculture** and **administration**. They generally offered programs lasting two to four years.

In August 1971, following a period of antigovernment student unrest, the universities were nationalized and renamed **Université Nationale du Zaïre (UNAZA)**. Their faculties were reorganized on the three campuses in existence at the time. In the following years, the universities were closed a number of times because of student unrest, primarily over low stipends, poor food, and difficult living conditions. The **National Conference** in 1992 called for the return of universities to the churches which had founded them.

With the decline of government support for higher education, local governments and businessmen began to establish privately funded campuses. In 1985, the Université de **Kananga** was founded and in the 1990s other private universities opened in **Mbuji-Mayi**, **Bas-Zaïre**, **Bandundu** and **Bukavu**. By 1996, more than 180 private institutions of higher learning were reported in various stages of operation. However, many educators said the economic decline of the 1980s and 1990s had so undermined the quality of education in Congo/Zaire that they called the children of that period the "lost generation."

EDWARD, LAKE. *See* LAKE EDWARD.

ÉGLISE DE JÉSUS-CHRIST SUR LA TERRE PAR LE PROPHÈTE SIMON KIMBANGU. *See* KIMBANGUIST CHURCH.

ÉGLISE DU CHRIST AU CONGO (ECC) / CHURCH OF CHRIST IN CONGO. An organization grouping most of the **Protestant churches** in Congo/Zaire, with 83 member churches in 1982. The ECC evolved out of a series of organizations formed in the early 20th century to avoid duplication and competition among Protestant churches working in the **Belgian Congo**.

The Comité de Continuation Congolais (CCC) was formed in 1911 by Protestant missions in the Congo to encourage contact and cooperation among the various denominations. The Conseil Protestant du Congo (CPC) was created in 1924 from the CCC. In 1934, members of the CPC voted to rename it the Église du Christ au Congo. With 62 members, it became the ECZ when the Congo's name was changed to Zaire in 1971. The 1960s witnessed an **Africanization** of the leadership of the organization. Rev. Pierre Shaumba was elected the first Congolese secretary-general following **independence**. He was succeeded by Rev. Jean **Bokeleale** in 1968, who became archbishop in 1970. Bokeleale was due to retire in August 1996 and a commission headed by ECZ Vice-President Pierre Marini Bohdo was named to choose a successor. The organization changed its name back to ECC when Zaire became Congo once again, after the fall of **Mobutu** in 1997.

EGYPT, RELATIONS WITH. **Congo/Zaire** historically maintained warm relations with Egypt, in part because of a general similarity of policies on international issues and in part because of joint enmity with such **Arab countries** as **Libya**, Iran and Iraq. Following **independence**, Egyptian judges formed part of an international corps of magistrates that presided over Congolese courts until Congolese jurists could be trained. Egypt also sent 50 pilots to aid the Zairian **government**'s counteroffensive against rebels of the **Front pour la Libération Nationale du Congo**

(FLNC) during the first **Shaba** incursion. In 1990, the two governments signed a military cooperation agreement under which Egypt trained Zaire's **Civil Guard** and provided Egyptian-built military equipment to the Zairian **armed forces**. In 1992, the two countries signed an agreement to build a high tension **electrical power** line from **Inga** to Egypt's Aswan area. The proposal benefited from a feasibility study funded by the **African Development Bank** but was viewed by many as unrealistic.

EIGHTY-DAY WAR. The name often used by the Zairian **government** to denote the first **Shaba** incursion, from March 8 until the end of May 1977. During the war, also called "Shaba One," **Angola**-based guerrillas of the **Front pour la Libération Nationale du Congo (FLNC)** took the border town of **Dilolo**, in western Shaba **Region**, and marched east to the outskirts of the mining center of **Kolwezi**. The attack took the authorities by surprise and because of the remoteness of the region, it was several weeks before a counteroffensive could be organized. The second Shaba incursion, frequently called "Shaba Two," was more costly. One year after Shaba One, FLNC guerrillas infiltrated the region and on May 3 seized Kolwezi and its **mining** installations. One thousand Zairians and 200 foreigners died in the ensuing violence, which was only ended weeks later after a bloody counteroffensive by Zairian and French paratroopers. *See also* Katanga.

ELECTIONS. The first elections held in **Congo/Zaire** were the municipal elections of 1957 that followed reforms enacted by the **colonial era** authorities to give Congolese a voice in the running of local affairs. Congolese candidates were allowed to run for posts in the "communes," or urban districts. In December 1959, elections were held to elect representatives to territorial and communal councils. The elections were inconclusive because they were boycotted by the **Mouvement National Congolais (MNC)**, the **Alliance des Bakongo (ABAKO)**, and several other major parties, but several leaders emerged during the campaign who would play significant roles following **independence**: Joseph **Kasavubu**, Patrice **Lumumba**, Moïse **Tshombe** and Albert **Kalonji**.

In May 1960, as part of the preparations for independence, more than 100 **political parties** competed for seats in **parliament** and the provincial assemblies. The MNC received the largest number of seats, but no clear majority. Lumumba and Kasavubu tried to form a coalition government but failed. Lumumba succeeded on his second attempt, backed by a group of smaller parties, and formed a cabinet of 23 ministers. Under a compromise agreement, Kasavubu was elected **president** on June 25, 1960, ending talk of secession in **Bas-Congo**. Tshombe, angered by the exclusion of his party, the **Confédération des Associations Katangaises (CONAKAT)**, withdrew to **Katanga**. Kalonji eventually split with Lumumba and took his wing of the MNC to **Kasai**. Katanga and **South Kasai** seceded a few months later.

The Congo held its first elections as an independent nation in March 1965, under the newly promulgated **constitution**. In that vote, Tshombe's alliance of primarily southern-based parties, called the **Confédération Nationale des Associations Congolaises (CONACO)**, won a majority in parliament. The CONACO ascendancy led to tensions with Kasavubu's ABAKO party and a constitutional crisis which contributed to the military **coup d'etat** that brought **Mobutu** to power in November 1965.

By the time elections were held next on November 11, 1970, the **Mouvement Populaire de la Révolution (MPR)** had been declared the sole legal party. Mobutu ran unopposed and won by an official vote of 10,131,699 to 157. Legislative elections were scheduled for November 1975, but were canceled by presidential decree. Instead, the names of the MPR candidates were read in public and approved by popular applause. In October 1977, following a series of liberalization measures, elections were held for the **Legislative Council** (parliament) and urban councils and some members of the MPR's **Political Bureau**. Any citizen was allowed to run, but party officials eliminated many candidates on technicalities. On December 2, 1977, Mobutu was reelected president for a second seven-year term.

Legislative elections were held again on September 18-19, 1982. Under the liberalization process, multiple candidates were allowed within the party structure. Candidates were nominated by local MPR cells, then approved first by regional party leaders and ultimately by the Political Bureau. Considerable changes were made to some of the lists. Nevertheless, the campaign was lively. About one-half of the incumbents failed to make the list of nominees and, of those who did, half were not reelected. The results led to the youngest legislature in the country's history, with an average age of 35 years, and reflected popular dissatisfaction with the party barons. Many of the defeated incumbents, however, received positions in the party hierarchy. In July 29, 1984, Mobutu again ran unopposed and was reelected by more than 99 percent of the vote in elections that were held six months early because, according to the announcement, "The will of the people made it evident that further campaigning was not necessary." Legislative elections were held in 1987, but were dominated by young party *cadres*, because by then the **Central Committee** of the MPR had taken over as the main organ of state for debate and consultation.

In these elections, there were many reports of irregularities, including a shortage of "No" ballots to be used by voters against the MPR candidates, surveillance and harassment of voters at the polls by soldiers and party militants, and a lack of observers during the ballot counting. Nevertheless, the results were recognized by the world community.

Elections scheduled for 1991 were delayed by the transition to multipartyism announced in April 1990 and were postponed a number of times because of disputes over power-sharing between pro-Mobutu and **opposition** forces. After five years of political stagnation, elections were announced for May and June 1997. An **Electoral Commission** was appointed in March 1996, a constitution was drafted in August, and a constitutional referendum was scheduled for February 1997. However, many opposition leaders said they would boycott the process because they said it was being rigged and the country's **transportation** and **communications** networks had deteriorated to such a degree that a massive reconstruction program was needed first.

The offensive by the **Alliance des Forces Démocratiques pour la Libération du Congo/Zaïre (AFDL)** disrupted the timetable. When the AFDL assumed power in May 1997, following the overthrow of Mobutu, it pledged to hold elections in 1999.

ELECTORAL COMMISSION. An electoral commission was established March 18, 1996, to organize national **elections** in May and June 1997, as part of the **democratic transition** called for by the **Haut Conseil de la République / Parlement de la**

Transition (HCR/PT) which was acting as an interim legislature. **Bayona wa Meya,** a former president of the Supreme Court and minister of justice, was named chairman of the commission. However, the hardline **opposition** dismissed him as a puppet of **Mobutu** and said it would not participate in any elections organized by his commission. The commission was disbanded by the Laurent **Kabila** government, which pledged to establish an independent organ before holding elections in 1999.

ELECTRICAL POWER. Congo/Zaire is estimated to hold 13 percent of the world's, and one-half of Africa's, hydroelectric potential, or 100,000 megawatts (MW). Total installed capacity in the early 1990s was 2,400 MW, 90 percent of it at hydroelectric complexes and the remainder at small, thermal units, many of which had fallen into disuse by the 1990s. One-half of the country's electrical generating capacity was at the **Inga hydroelectric complex,** 40 km upriver from **Matadi** in **Bas-Congo,** where two phases of an original three-phase project operated with a capacity of 1,300 MW. **Katanga** Province was the second-largest producer of electricity, with three complexes on the **Lualaba River** north of **Kolwezi** and two on the **Lufira River** northeast of **Likasi.** Smaller hydroelectric complexes provided power to other areas. These included complexes on the Inkisi River near **Kinshasa,** on the Tshopo River near **Kisangani,** on the Aruwimi River near Bunia, on the **Ruzizi River** supplying **Bukavu** and **Burundi,** and small stations near Punia, Piana, **Mbuji-Mayi, Tshikapa, Kalima,** Sanga and **Zongo.** A line linking Bukavu to **Goma** via Katana was completed in 1985 and a hydroelectric unit at Mobayi supplying **Gbadolite** was inaugurated in 1989.

The **Inga-Shaba power line,** built at a cost of more than $1 billion, was completed in 1982. A 500-kilovolt direct-current, high-tension line with an installed capacity of 560 MW, it links the Inga complex in Bas-Congo to **Shaba** 1,750 km away. The **Société Nationale d'Électricité (SNEL)** was established on May 16, 1970, to exploit and market power from Inga. In February 1974, the government ordered that six private or mixed-ownership electrical complexes still operating in Zaire be absorbed into SNEL. In 1979, the **Régie de Distribution d'Eau et d'Électricité (REGIDESO),** the national water management corporation, turned over to SNEL a number of small thermal units which supplied about 30 Congolese cities in the interior.

Congo/Zaire potentially is a major exporter of hydroelectric power. In the 1990s it supplied about one-third of Congo/Zaire's electricity and also sold power to **Rwanda**, Burundi, and **Zambia**. In 1992, Zaire and **Egypt** proposed to construct a high-tension line carrying 600 MW from Inga to the Aswan dam. A $4 million feasibility study, funded by the **African Development Bank (ADB)**, was completed in 1992. Despite the logistical difficulties of constructing the 5,400-km line and upgrading the facility at Inga, the project, with an estimated cost of $28 billion, received some support. In August 1995, the Southern Africa Development Community (SADEC) announced an electrical power-sharing agreement that would include Congo/Zaire.

ELEPHANTS. Before the 18th century, Congo/Zaire had one of the largest elephant populations in the world, numbering in the millions. However, the **ivory** trade has seriously reduced the population, which was estimated in the 1990s in the tens of thousands. Only herds in the remotest areas were spared. Poaching reportedly was carried on virtually unmolested in more-accessible areas because of **corruption** and a lack of patrols. A worldwide ban on trading in ivory in the 1990s lessened demand considerably, but poaching continues, fueled by demand from clandestine markets abroad.

ELISABETHVILLE. The former name of the capital of **Katanga** Province. Elisabethville, now called **Lubumbashi**, was best known internationally as the capital of secessionist Katanga in 1961-63.

ÉLITE. A French term, now widely used in English, denoting the educated, often wealthy **middle-class** and upper-class Africans usually engaged in business, politics or the professions. In Congo/Zaire, the *élites* sprang in part from the colonial *évolués*, but were joined following **independence** by Congolese who rose to professional and political positions in the new state. In Zaire, the term assumed some negative connotations because of the conspicuous wealth of the *élite* and the presumed involvement of many of its members in **corruption**.

EMÉRY, FRANÇOIS (1952 -). The son of Patrice **Lumumba** and one of the exiled leaders of the Lumumba wing of the **Mouvement National Congolais (MNC)** party from the mid-1960s, Eméry was perhaps best remembered for an article he wrote in *Afrique-Asie* magazine commemorating the 17th anniversary of his father's death, in which he called for the overthrow of **Mobutu**. Following the political liberalization of 1990, Eméry returned to Zaire for a visit and received an emotional welcome. Most of the Lumumbist parties later joined in the **Parti Lumumbiste Unifié (PALU)** under Antoine **Gizenga**.

EMPLOYMENT. Congo/Zaire's **labor** force in the mid-1990s was estimated at 16 million out of a total **population** of 43 million. The International Labor Organization reported that in 1995, 37.5 percent of the total population was "economically active," defined as including the military, the employed, and the unemployed, but excluding **students** and housewives. However, most work was performed in the informal sector. **World Bank** figures showed slightly more than one million people were active in the formal **economy**, 80 percent of these in the public sector. The number is believed to have fallen with the decline of the formal economy in the 1990s. Employment rates during the 1980s were estimated at 60 percent in **Kinshasa** and the urban centers and 20 percent in most other cities. Following the **pillages** (lootings) of 1991 and 1993, many factories and businesses were closed and employment is estimated to have fallen to 20 percent of the labor force or less. It recovered to an estimated 40 percent in 1996, but many of those working in **government** or public services were paid irregularly.

As a result, the informal economy was believed to employ several times the work force of the formal economy, although there were no official statistics. In rural areas, according to UNICEF, 80 percent of the population lived mainly from subsistence farming and hunting. In urban areas, activities included trading, **smuggling**, small-scale businesses such as tailoring or tire and auto repair, and individually contracted services such as house or yard work.

Historically, labor in Congo/Zaire has not been organized. Trade unions were not permitted to form until after World War II. Following **independence**, however, several emerged. They were joined by decree in 1967 into the Union Nationale des Travailleurs Congolais (UNTC), which in 1971 was renamed the **Union Nationale des Travailleurs Zaïrois (UNTZA)**, or National Union of Zairian Workers. Their leaders generally followed the party line and there were few **strikes** until the liberalization of 1990, when UNTZA lost its monopoly of the trade union movement. At that time, several early unions reemerged and were joined by a number of new organizations, formed by profession or economic sector. Strikes became frequent and prolonged, especially by workers in the public sector whose salaries had been reduced by **inflation** to a few dollars per month.

ENERGY. Congo/Zaire possesses relatively abundant energy, 95 percent of it hydroelectric. However, the lack of infrastructure hinders delivery of **electrical power** to remote areas. Hydroelectric potential is estimated at 100,000 MW, nearly one-half that of all of Africa. Installed capacity is 2,400 MW, most of this from the **Inga hydroelectric complex** near **Matadi**.

Known **petroleum** reserves are relatively poor, estimated at 180 million barrels of heavy-grade crude in the mid-1990s. There was no oil production until 1975 when several wells off the Atlantic coast came on line and production was begun on an island in the mouth of the **Congo River**. Total production reached nearly 10.7 million barrels in 1990, but declined subsequently until 1995, when new discoveries boosted production to 11 million barrels. Explorations in the **Mbandaka** area in the early 1980s were not fruitful but there was some hope in the early 1990s of finding new fields in eastern Zaire near the border with **Tanzania** and **Uganda**. A refinery with an installed capacity of 750,000 tons was built with Italian participation near Moanda, but it could not refine the heavy grade of crude produced in the territory and, as a result, crude oil was imported from Nigeria for refining.

There were significant deposits of low-grade **coal** located in the north, but exploitation was uneconomic because of **transportation** costs. Small coal deposits in **Katanga** Province, between **Likasi** and **Kamina** and near **Kalemie**, produced 125,000 tons per year until the 1990s. All of it was used by local **industry**. Higher-grade coke and coal needed to power the **copper** refineries was imported from Zimbabwe.

The government historically has maintained a heavy presence in the energy sector and was sole owner from the mid-1960s until the 1980s. With the reforms of 1983, however, it began to allow partial participation by private investors. It deregulated prices in 1983 and in 1985 lifted the state monopoly on the marketing of petroleum products. During a severe fuel shortage in 1992, the government took over foreign petroleum companies, but it returned them with compensation a few months later.

ENVIRONMENT. Environmentalists tend to view Congo/Zaire's exotic animal life as a resource that is most at risk. The gorillas of the **Virunga Mountain** range have received considerable attention in the mass media, as has the threat to the country's populations of **elephants**, rhinoceros and other large game caused by poaching and human encroachment. A broader concern is the potential threat to the country's 120 million hectares of **rainforests**, representing roughly 6 percent of the world's remaining forest cover. Unlike those of many African countries, Congo/Zaire's forests were considered 85 percent intact in the mid-1990s. However, environmentalists warned in 1995 that the government had signed **timber** concessions covering one-third of the country's forests. They expressed particular concern over **Bas-Congo's Mayombe Forest**, which is relatively accessible to ocean **ports**. Some said the Mayombe had virtually no primary vegetation left. Another major concern was damage to the environment caused by urban pollution, particularly in **Kinshasa** and densely populated areas of Bas-Congo.

ÉQUATEUR. One of eight **provinces**, Équateur lies in the northwestern corner of **Congo/Zaire**, in the heart of the **Congo River Basin**. Its **topography** is dominated by vast **rainforests** and numerous swamps, **rivers** and streams. However, in the northernmost parts along the border with the **Central African Republic**, the terrain is higher and drier and covered by some wooded savanna. With an area of 403,293 square km and an estimated **population** of 4.6 million in 1995 (3,288,353 in 1982), Équateur is one of the most sparsely populated regions in the territory. The region is largely inhabited by members of the **Mongo ethnic group** with some groups of Sudanic origin present in the northern parts. Most live from hunting and **fishing**, although some have a tradition of gathering and cultivation.

The provincial capital is **Mbandaka** with an estimated population of 300,000 (153,440 in 1982). Of the administrative districts of Équateur District, Tshuapa and Mongala are the most populated, with roughly one-half million persons each. Major economic resources include **palm oil**, **timber**, **livestock**, and some cocoa and **rice** farming from irrigated projects. The region is believed to have large deposits of iron ore, but these have yet to be exploited. Originally one of the more remote and neglected areas of Congo/Zaire, Équateur received more attention during the **Mobutu** years, in part because it was the home region of the president and many of his close collaborators and in part because of a **government** policy of attempting to develop less-prosperous provinces of the country.

ÉTAT INDÉPENDANT DU CONGO. *See* CONGO FREE STATE (CFS).

ETHNIC CLEANSING. A term coined to describe efforts by belligerents in the former Yugoslavia to rid disputed areas of rival **ethnic groups**. The term came to be used in Zaire during the early 1990s to describe expulsions and violence in **Shaba** and **Nord-Kivu** and to a lesser degree in **Bandundu** and **Orientale** provinces.

The incidents in Shaba began in August 1992 after Jean **Nguza Karl-I-Bond**, a **Lunda** from Shaba, was replaced as prime minister by Étienne **Tshisekedi**, a **Luba** from neighboring **Kasaï Occidental**. The governor of Shaba at the time, Gabriel **Kyungu wa Kumwanza**, was a member of Nguza's **Union des Fédéralistes et des Républicains Indépendants (UFERI)** party that had allied with **Mobutu** and saw a threat to its base from Tshisekedi's **Union pour la Démocratie et le Progrès Social (UDPS)**. Kyungu, who preferred to call the region by its original name of **Katanga**, for months had been making fiery speeches advocating "Katanga for Katangans." The speeches raised long-standing resentments among Lundas and other original settlers of the region against the Luba. Some Lubas had immigrated to Katanga before the **colonial era**. They came to be called **Balubakat**. Others, called Balubakasai, had immigrated during the colonial period to work in the mines. Both groups had prospered due to an affinity for business and were characterized by a strong sense of ethnic solidarity. Following Kyungu's speeches, attacks began on the Luba and their property by youth militias. An estimated 500 people were killed and more than 100,000 were forced to flee their homes. Many camped for months at **railway** stations and public buildings awaiting **transportation** to **Kasai**. Their homes and businesses were reportedly occupied by local UFERI supporters.

In March 1993, violence broke out in Nord-Kivu between members of the **Nyanga** and **Hunde** ethnic groups and the group known in Congo/Zaire as the **Banyarwanda**. The Banyarwanda, primarily of **Tutsi** extraction, had immigrated from **Rwanda** as early as the 18th century but were never viewed as Congolese by the indigenous populations. Like the Luba in Katanga, they prospered during colonialism. They were granted citizenship at **independence**, but it was rescinded by a decree in 1981 that was never implemented. A commission of the **National Conference** in 1991 never resolved the matter and as a result the Banyarwanda were not represented at the conference. The clashes in Nord-Kivu erupted after Governor Jean-Pierre Kalumbo Mboho began making speeches calling for the extermination of the Banyarwanda and promising support from **security** forces. These clashes caused 7,000 deaths and made 350,000 homeless.

Opposition leaders and **human rights** groups accused Mobutu and his supporters of instigating the clashes in order to clear certain regions of opposition voters prior to national elections. Sentiments ran especially high after Mobutu announced he could not assure the safety of Luba in Shaba. However, outrage grew domestically and internationally. In July 1993, Kalumbo was suspended and a contingent of the **Division Spéciale Présidentielle** was dispatched to the region to quell the fighting. Kyungu was dismissed as governor on April 19, 1995, after being accused of illegally marketing **cobalt** from Shaban mines and of stockpiling arms for a planned secession of the region.

In mid-1997, reports surfaced of massacres of Rwandan **Hutu**s in eastern Congo/Zaire by fighters of the **Alliance des Forces Démocratiques pour la Libération du Congo/Zaïre**. The **United Nations** announced an investigation into the reports. However, the investigation was blocked for several years by the

AFDL government which criticized it for not including the atrocities committed under ethnic cleansing. Continuing interethnic violence led to another rebellion in eastern Congo beginning in August 1998 that included numerous incidents of ethnically motivated massacres.

ETHNIC GROUPS. Although estimates vary, ethnologists say at least 200 distinguishable ethnic groups live in **Congo/Zaire**, speaking as many distinct **languages** and another 250 dialects. Most of these belong to the **Bantu** people that dominate central Africa. Although no single ethnic group is believed to exceed 10 percent of the total **population**, a number of major groupings or "clusters" have been identified. These include the **Kongo, Luba, Lulua, Lunda**, Maï-Ndombe, **Mongo** and **Zande**. There are other ethnic groups with only a few thousand members, but who are distinguishable by language, customs and traditions.

Under **Mobutu**, official Zairian ethnographers cast the northwestern-based Mongo group as one of the largest ethnic clusters in the country, classifying as Mongo societies living as far away as the **Kasai**s and **Katanga**. Although some of the groups could trace their origins from the Mongo area, other ethnologists viewed the Mongo as living in a much smaller range of territory. They tended to view the more homogenous societies of the Kongo, Luba and Lulua as being the largest. The Lunda and **Chokwe** were other large societies, but with a considerable proportion of their populations living in neighboring countries. *See also* Afro-Arabs; Alur; Balese; Balubakat; Banda; Bandiya; Bangu-Bangu; Banyamulenge; Banyarwanda; Bashi; Bemba; Boa; Boma; Boshongo; Fuleru; Hemba; Hunde; Hutu; Jaga; Kanioka; Kazembe; Kete; Kuba; Kunda; Kusu; Kwese; Lele; Lia; Lungu; Mamvu; Mangbetu; Mbala; Mbanza; Mbomu; Mbun; Mvuba; Nande; Ndembo; Ngala; Ngbaka; Ngbandi; Ngombe; Njembe; Nku; Nkutshu; Ntomba; Nyamwezi; Nyanga; Pende; Pygmies; Sambala; Sengele; Shi; Songye; Soonde; Suku; Teke; Tembo; Tetela; Tio; Tutsi; Vungara; Yaka; Yeke.

ETHNICITY. Ethnicity, the concept of identity based on **ethnic grouping**, is as much a product of the European tendency to classify groups of people on the basis of their most discernible traits (physical appearance, **language**, religious practices, etc.) as it is a product of a natural human tendency toward parochialism and the placing of value on family and ancestry. Ethnicity, or tribalism, was used by colonial authorities to divide the people of the Congo and prevent the rise of a **nationalist** movement. It was also used by some Congolese leaders to build powerbases for their political movements.

After the political disruption following **independence**, most African leaders began to criticize tribalism, calling it a source of friction and factionalism that undermined efforts to build nations. As a result, many sought to remove it from national politics through the promotion of single-party states, while at the same time seeking to preserve its cultural aspects through **Authenticity** and the enhancement of folklore studies.

The return to multiparty **politics**, begun in 1990, aggravated interethnic tensions as well as many other social frictions. Although **political parties** sought broad national bases that would transcend ethnic and regional lines, they frequently became associated with a particular ethnic group, often that of their leader. And these leaders, in their desire to build a political base, often played on long-standing ethnic suspicions and rivalries.

Despite efforts to eliminate ethnicity, it continues to be a factor in political appointments, business contracts and, to a degree, housing patterns. However, with successive generations, the concept of national identity continues to rise and "tribalism" is increasingly recognized as a social malady not unlike racism.

ETSOU, FRÉDÉRIC (CARDINAL). Former bishop of **Mbandaka**, who upon the death of Cardinal Joseph **Malula** in 1989 became Archbishop of **Kinshasa** and head of the **Catholic Church** in **Congo/Zaire**.

EUROPEAN UNION (EU). Called the European Economic Community and then the European Community until 1994, the EU has become one of **Congo/Zaire**'s major trading partners, supplying more than one-half of the country's **imports** and purchasing nearly three-fourths of Congolese **exports**. **Belgium** was the largest individual trading partner, although trade with Belgium and the EU declined in the 1980s in favor of the **United States, Germany, France** and **Japan**. In 1975, Zaire signed the **Lomé Convention**, the first trade agreement between the EU and the countries of Africa, the Caribbean and the Pacific (ACP). Zaire also signed three subsequent Lomé agreements in 1979, 1984 and 1989. Each agreement increased European aid in exchange for lower trade barriers in ACP countries. Beginning in the late 1980s, EU governments begin pressuring the Zairian **government** for economic and political liberalization and greater respect for **human rights.** Aid was suspended in 1990 following an army attack on **students** at the **Lubumbashi** campus of the national **university,** and again in 1992 after **Mobutu** nominated a rival government to that of elected **prime minister** Étienne **Tshisekedi.** Following the fall of Mobutu in May 1997, the EU pledged to support the government of Laurent **Kabila** if it pursued the **democratic transition,** but criticized the Kabila government's initial crackdown on political rallies and the **news media** and its obstruction of a **United Nations** investigation into alleged massacres in eastern Congo/Zaire during the offensive that brought it to power.

ÉVOLUÉS. A term used primarily in the 1950s and 1960s to describe Congolese who were the most assimilated into European-style society and lifestyles, usually because of **education** or training and experience at European firms. The term contained more social connotations than *immatriculés,* which had legal implications. Most *évolués* were educated urban dwellers. Some appeared or feigned to be largely disassociated from their traditional **societies.** Following independence they quickly moved into positions of leadership.

EXECUTIVE COUNCIL / CONSEIL EXÉCUTIF. The rough equivalent of a ministerial cabinet, the Executive Council was officially created on January 5, 1975, by merging the Council of Ministers and the National Executive Council of the **Mouvement Populaire de la Révolution (MPR)** party. Members were appointed by the **president.** The formation of the council began in 1972 and was one of the first moves to merge party and state. As the party became the supreme organ of state, its governing bodies, the **Political Bureau** and **Central Committee,** assumed increasing importance and the Executive Council became primarily a committee of the chief administrators of the executive branch. Moreover, with the increasing centralization of powers in the presidency, the Executive Council in the 1980s frequently was overshadowed by the Office of the President until the **democratic transition** was announced in 1990.

EXPLORERS. Recorded history knows little about the African and Arab explorers who traveled and traded across central Africa well before the arrival of the Europeans in the late 1400s. **Tippo Tib** was perhaps the best known of these. The Europeans, beginning with Diogo **Cão** who arrived at the mouth of the **Congo River** in 1483, are better known. These include José **Lacerda e Almeida** of **Portugal** and the British explorers David **Livingstone**, Henry Morton **Stanley**, Richard **Burton**, John **Speke**, James **Tuckey** and Samuel **Baker**. At home, these hardy adventurers were forgotten while they were gone and adulated when they returned. Nevertheless, their explorations and mappings helped spark European interest in the continent. Greater knowledge of the region came later with the traders, **missionaries** and colonialists.

EXPORTS. Congo/Zaire's **economy** is primarily export-driven and during most of the years following **independence** has depended primarily on **minerals**, especially **copper**, **cobalt**, **diamonds**, **gold**, zinc and **tin**. Until the deterioration of the **mining** sector in the early 1990s, more than 80 percent of export revenues came from minerals, 65 percent from copper alone. During this period, **agricultural** products, primarily **coffee** and **palm oil**, formed the second-largest export sector. Other agricultural exports included **timber**, **rubber**, cocoa, tea and **cotton**. Following independence, agricultural exports declined for many years because of mismanagement, **Zairianization** and the lack of investment. **Privatization** and more liberal policies beginning in 1983 spurred agricultural production. The subsequent decline of the mineral sector caused agricultural exports to reach one-third of total exports in the mid-1990s. **Smuggling** has been a perennial problem, but the **government** attempted to address it in 1983 by removing price restrictions on domestically marketed commodities and by allowing the overvalued **currency** to float freely on the open market.

According to government figures, export earnings, after a decline of 15 percent during the 1980s, returned in 1990 to their 1980 level of $2.2 billion. However, with the economic crisis, they again declined to $1.2 billion in 1994. Copper, historically the dominant export, declined by nearly 90 percent in the 1990s, due to the collapse of the state-owned **Générale des Carrières et des Mines (GECAMINES)** mining conglomerate. Production fell to 40,000 tons in 1996 from a historical high of 500,000 tons in the mid-1970s and mid-1980s. Cobalt over the same period declined by 60 percent to 3,600 tons. Diamond exports declined by 20 percent in the 1990s to 15 million carats, but nevertheless became the major mineral export in the mid-1990s because of the collapse of copper mining. Coffee also began to decline from a peak of 100,000 tons in 1992 because of **crop** disease in northern **plantations**. However, coffee earnings replaced copper as the highest export earner and, at $430 million in 1994, were three times those of copper.

Zaire's major export markets in the 1990s were **Belgium**, the **United States**, **South Africa**, **Italy**, **Japan**, **Germany**, the **United Kingdom** and **France**. Exports to African nations other than South Africa averaged 1 percent of total exports and were primarily to neighboring countries and traditional partners such as Cameroon, **Kenya**, **Morocco** and Zimbabwe. *See also* Imports; Trade.

- F -

FAMILY PLANNING. Because of the traditional value placed on large families by Congolese **society**, high infant mortality rates, and relatively low life expectancy, family planning has never been popularized in Congo/Zaire. With the average Congolese woman giving birth to six or seven children, Congo/Zaire has one of the highest **population** growth rates in the world, more than 3 percent per year. The high proportion of rural poor living on subsistence **agriculture**, high **unemployment** rates in the cities and the absence of an effective **social services** system meant that a large family was the only security net for most couples or single mothers.

The Congolese **government** began to express interest in limiting the size of families in 1973, when it issued a decree establishing an agency to disseminate information on family planning. A nongovernment organization called the Association

Zaïroise pour le Bien-Être Familial (ASBEF) / Zairian Association for Family Well-Being was established in 1978 and began working with international agencies on family planning programs. Another organization called Santé Rurale (SANRU) / Rural Health was given responsibility for coordinating projects in the countryside.

Alden Almquist, in his *Country Study of Zaire*, described the first large-scale family planning effort in the country, the Projet des Services des Naissances Désirables (PSND) / Project for Planned Birth Services, which was launched in 1982. The PSND targeted 800,000 women in 14 urban areas and sought to increase the use of contraception from 1 percent to 12 percent by 1986. By the end of the period, he reported, only 4 percent of the targeted women were using contraception. A number of other projects attempted to target women in rural areas and promote family planning through clinics and pharmacies. Aggressive public awareness campaigns and the distribution of condoms in an effort to limit the spread of the **Acquired Immune Deficiency Syndrome (AIDS)** virus also was seen as advancing family planning.

Nevertheless, the efforts to promote family planning continued to be frustrated by traditional values and high infant mortality rates. They were further stymied by the economic crises of the 1990s, which made the purchase of contraceptives a luxury many families could not afford.

FEDERAL REPUBLIC OF THE CONGO. *See* CONGO, FEDERAL REPUBLIC OF THE.

FEDERALISM. The concept of federalism, that is, **provinces** or **regions** with considerable autonomy in local affairs but joined together in national affairs, was frequently advanced as a way for Congo/Zaire's disparate regions to coexist in a modern state. At **independence** many **political parties**, in particular those with power bases in the east and south, espoused federalism although they differed widely on what powers should be granted to the regions and what should be retained by the central government. The **constitution** of 1964 institutionalized a form of federalism, but this was displaced by the military **coup d'etat** of 1965, the subsequent centralization of power in the **presidency** in the constitution of 1967, and the creation of the party-state by the constitution of 1974.

The **democratic transition** period beginning in 1990, however, brought a resurgence of federalist sentiment. Some political parties, notably **Nguza Karl-I-Bond**'s **Union des Fédéralistes et des Républicains Indépendants (UFERI)**, made federalism a pillar of their platform. The **National Conference** drafted a constitution that reestablished a form of federalism similar to that of the 1964 constitution. However, **Mobutu** refused to recognize the document. Nevertheless, the collapse in the 1990s of central services, the formal **economy** and the authority of the central government led to a de facto form of federalism. Many regional and local **governments** began collecting their own taxes and duties and refused to send them to **Kinshasa**. Although the local military commanders continued to take orders from the central command, some worked closely with regional authorities on day-to-day matters and established ways of subsidizing soldiers' wages, which frequently failed to arrive from the capital. And travelers arriving in some regions were obliged to purchase entrance permits and have their passports stamped, as if they were entering a foreign country.

In August 1996, the **Haut Conseil de la République / Parlement de la Transition (HCR/PT)** passed a draft constitution that would have granted a large measure of autonomy to the regions and established the **Federal Republic of the Congo**. A referendum on the constitution was scheduled for February 1997, but it was never held because of the offensive of the **Alliance des Forces Démocratiques pour la Libération du Congo/Zaïre (AFDL)** beginning in October 1996. When the AFDL assumed power after the fall of Mobutu in May 1997, it pledged to draft a new constitution and submit it to a national referendum in 1998 but this was postponed because of the rebellion against Laurent **Kabila** government beginning in August 1998.

FÉDÉRATION DES ENTREPRISES CONGOLAISES (FEC) / FEDERATION OF CONGOLESE ENTERPRISES. An association of businessmen and entrepreneurs formed after the takeover of the **government** by Laurent **Kabila** in 1997. In January 1998, the FEC complained to the government that the

Congolese judiciary was strangling economic revival in the country. It said overly zealous fiscal inspections and excessive fines were hurting business and urged the government to get rid of corrupt judges.

FÉDÉRATION KASAÏENNE. A political alliance of **Luba** in **Kasai** Province at **independence**. It wanted considerable autonomy for Kasai.

FETISHISM. *See* SPIRITUALISM, FETISHISM, SORCERY AND WITCHCRAFT.

FIOTE. A major dialect of Kikongo, spoken by the **Kongo** people of **Bas-Congo** and **Congo/Brazzaville**. It evolved as a **trade** dialect during the **colonial era**. Sometimes called Kituba, it was used by Europeans and came to be considered the "official" Kikongo.

FISHING. Congo/Zaire's vast network of **lakes** and **rivers** endows it with an abundant supply of fish, an important source of protein in the Congolese **diet**. A great deal of fishing is at the subsistence level or on a small commercial scale. There were some commercial fishing operations by European-owned companies on the great lakes, but these virtually disappeared after **Zairianization**. Fuel shortages in the years following **Retrocession** hampered a revival. The Société des Pêcheries Maritimes du Zaïre (PEMARZA) in the 1980s operated a small fleet of fishing boats at the mouth of the **Congo River**, supplying **Bas-Zaïre** and the **Kinshasa** area. The **Agriculture** Department estimated total fish production in the 1980s at 180,000 tons per year, of which approximately two-thirds was from rivers, 20 percent from lakes and 10 percent from ocean waters.

FONCTION PUBLIQUE. *See* CIVIL SERVICE.

FOOD SUPPLY. **Congo/Zaire** was self-sufficient in food at **independence**, but the civil unrest of the 1960s disrupted extension services and harvests and a deteriorating **transportation** sector reduced productivity. In addition, new investment in **agriculture** during the period fell to negligible levels, choking off the establishment of new farms. During the years following the **Mobutu coup d'etat**, **agricultural** production grew by 4 percent per year and by the early 1970s, overall production had returned to pre-independence levels. Agriculture was deemed the "priority of priorities" by Mobutu in 1973 and **government** expenditures, traditionally 1-2 percent of total expenditures, were increased for a time. In the late 1970s growth of food production slowed to a rate of less than 1 percent per year. It rose again following the liberalization of price controls in 1983 and averaged an annual growth rate of 3 percent in the 1980s, then declined severely in the 1990s because of hyperinflation and shortages of fuel and spare parts.

Production never kept pace with **population** growth, however, and as a result, Congo/Zaire was forced to **import** many food items, ranging from **rice** and **maize** to fish, meat and dairy products. Zaire imported an average of $220 million worth of food per year during the 1970s and 1980s, according to official figures, but this declined to $100 million in 1992. The amount spent on food imports outside official channels was estimated to be several times the official amount. The country also received food aid from many donors: a total of 68,000 tons in 1980, 177,000 tons in 1988 and 121,000 tons in 1992, according to **World Bank** figures.

FORCE PUBLIQUE. The name of the **armed forces** of the Congo prior to **independence**. The Force Publique was created in 1885 by **Leopold II** to **police** the newly created **Congo Free State**. A feared corps of Congolese soldiers led by European officers, it was charged with maintaining order in the territory and ensuring compliance by local villages with tax and **labor** laws. Excesses by the force led to an international outcry that was responsible in large part for the annexation of the territory by the Belgian parliament in 1908.

FORCES ARMÉES CONGOLAISES (FAC). *See* ARMED FORCES.

FORCES ARMÉES ZAÏROISES (FAZ) / ZAIRIAN ARMED FORCES. Official name of the Zairian **armed forces**, changed from Armée Nationale Congolaise (ANC) when the **Congo** became **Zaire** in 1971. The name was changed to the **Forces Armées Congolaises (FAC)** when Zaire became the **Democratic**

Republic of Congo following the overthrow of Mobutu in May 1997.

FORCES DÉMOCRATIQUES POUR LA LIBÉRATION DU CONGO (FODELICO) / DEMOCRATIC FORCES FOR THE LIBERATION OF THE CONGO. An **opposition** movement founded by Antoine **Gizenga**, leader of the eastern **rebellion** and successor to Patrice **Lumumba**. Gizenga announced the creation of FODELICO after going into exile following the end of the rebellion. Gizenga's primary support was said to have come from Marxist and radical nationalist African regimes, but he claimed to be a nonaligned, leftist African patriot. The movement for a time was based in **Congo/Brazzaville**. It faded after Gizenga returned to Zaire after the ban on opposition **political parties** was lifted in 1990. He subsequently emerged as the head of an alliance of Lumumbist parties called the **Parti Lumumbiste Unifié (PALU)**.

FORCES POLITIQUES DU CONCLAVE (FPC). *See* CONCLAVE, FORCES POLITIQUES DU.

FORCES RÉPUBLICAINES ET FÉDÉRALISTES (FRF) / REPUBLICAN AND FEDERALIST FORCES. A group of primarily **Banyamulenge** rebels formed in August 1998 and, led by Joseph Mutambo, joined the insurrection against the Laurent **Kabila** government.

"FORCES VIVES." Literally translated as the "Live Forces" or "Forces of Life," the term was used by the **Sacred Union** to mobilize supporters from all walks of life for public demonstrations and **strikes** against the **Mobutu** government in the 1990s. Several hundred civilians were killed during dozens of such protests.

FOREIGN AID. Historically **Congo/Zaire** has been one of the largest recipients of foreign aid in sub-Saharan Africa. From 1980 to 1990, the country received a total of $4.5 billion in aid, according to **World Bank** figures. In 1990, aid reached $898 million, but declined to $476 million in 1991 and $271 million in 1992, because of **human rights** abuses and delays in the **democratic transition**. Primary donors were Western governments, led by the **United States**, **France**, **Belgium**, **Germany** and the **United**

Kingdom. However, other nations, including the People's Republic of **China, Japan**, North Korea, **Egypt** and **Morocco**, also funded important programs.

FOREIGN EXCHANGE. For 23 years following **independence**, **Congo/Zaire**'s **currency** exchange rate was set at unrealistically high levels and consequently foreign exchange, whether Belgian francs, US dollars or French-backed Communauté Financière Africaine (CFA) francs, was always in high demand and short supply. The shortages at the **central bank** led to a flourishing parallel market where hard currency was exchanged at three to seven times the official rate. The parallel market enriched the political *élites* for nearly a quarter-century. Those with political connections would acquire foreign exchange through the central bank at the official rate, ostensibly to import essential goods. Many used the hard currency, however, to purchase consumer goods and luxuries which were subsequently sold at parallel market rates. In some cases, the hard currency was merely dumped on the parallel market for an instant profit.

In September 1983, the government adopted a series of monetary reforms that allowed private banks for the first time to buy and sell foreign exchange at weekly auctions held by the central bank. The rate of exchange was set according to supply and demand. Overnight, the value of the currency plunged from a rate of six **zaires** to one US dollar, to 30 zaires to the dollar. The value of the zaire continued to drift downward, but at a relatively stable rate until the 1990s.

In 1991, due to political uncertainties and a swelling money supply, the value of the currency plummeted. From August 1991, when it was exchanged at 100 zaires to the dollar, it fell to five million zaires to the dollar by the end of 1992. A currency reform on October 22, 1993, introduced the new **zaire** (NZ), one unit of which was exchanged for three million "old" zaires. The decline of the new currency was slowed for a time by austerity measures but nevertheless, by mid-1995 the new zaire was exchanging at a rate of 5,000 NZ (equivalent to 15 billion old zaires) to the dollar and by early 1997, at a rate of 200,000 NZ to the dollar. The Congo **franc** (CF), which had been used from independence until 1967, was reintroduced on June 30, 1998, and initially was exchanged at a rate of 1.4 CF to the dollar. It declined to 4.5 to the dollar by early 1999.

During periods of instability, banks frequently would not or could not provide currency to customers. As a result, free-market traders, often operating from stools on the streets of downtown **Kinshasa** in a section that came to known as **"Wall Street,"** became a major force in the exchange market. During some periods, analysts said, their activities amounted to one-fifth of the country's total foreign exchange transactions. Businessmen and diplomats admitted to being obliged at times to send their couriers to the free market to purchase the currency needed for their operations. A free-market exchange system also thrived in the wealthier regions of the country, where rates often varied considerably from those in the capital.

FOREIGN INVESTMENT. Foreign investment in Congo/Zaire fluctuated from colonial times with world economic and business cycles and according to policies provided by the **government** in power at the time. It reached its peak in the late 1960s and early 1970s, when foreign banks granted large loans for ambitious infrastructure and industrial **development projects** based on projected revenues from Zairian **mineral exports**, which at the time were enjoying historically high prices. Following the collapse of commodity prices and the subsequent recession in 1975, new investment virtually disappeared despite increasingly attractive terms offered by the Congolese government and a trend toward **privatization** of the economy. Following economic and monetary reforms in 1983 and a subsequent stabilization of the **currency**, some foreign investors began to return. Agreements were signed with Japanese and European firms for mineral exploration and international consortia were formed to examine investment in various **industries**.

Foreign investors continued to invest in Zaire through the 1980s, but were often discouraged by the need for political connections and by business practices which in their countries were considered unethical or illegal. With the **democratic transition** beginning in 1990, a period of political uncertainty ensued. Following the **pillages** of 1991 and 1993, large foreign investors absorbed their losses and waited for future possibilities. New investment, however, was put on hold. Following the fall of

Mobutu in May 1997, the Laurent **Kabila** government sought to encourage the return of foreign investors and a number of joint ventures were signed in the subsequent months.

FOREIGN RELATIONS. During the Cold War, **Congo/Zaire** pursued a foreign policy of nonalignment and maintained diplomatic relations with such ideologically diverse governments as **Belgium**, **France**, the **United States**, North Korea, the People's Republic of **China** and most East European nations. Relations with the **Soviet Union** during this period, however, were generally poor. Zaire tended to side with the moderate conservative group of African nations. Radical regimes called it a US puppet, although it often was criticized by the US government for authoritarianism, economic mismanagement and **human rights** violations.

With the end of the Cold War, relations with Western nations became strained as these governments increased pressure on Congo/Zaire for political and economic reforms. Most Western nations cut off non-humanitarian aid following the massacre by **security** forces of **students** at the **University** of **Lubumbashi** in May 1990. When **Mobutu** dismissed the transitional government of **opposition** leader Étienne **Tshisekedi** in early 1993 and appointed a rival government, three major allies, Belgium, France and the United States, adopted a policy of diplomatically isolating the Mobutu government. They withdrew their ambassadors and refused to issue visas to senior Congolese officials. Their support for Tshisekedi cooled by 1994, however, and they switched support to more moderate opposition leaders. They also adopted a policy of accommodation with Mobutu which, it was hoped, would help revive the much-delayed **democratic transition**. During this period, Zaire's relations continued largely unchanged with **Arab**, Asian, and South American nations, which espoused a policy of noninterference in its internal affairs.

In sub-Saharan Africa, the government saw itself as a regional and subregional leader. It was the first sub-Saharan African nation to break relations with **Israel** following the 1973 war and it was the first to reestablish relations in 1982 after Israel completed its withdrawal from **Egypt**'s Sinai Desert. Zaire was an early backer of such regional organizations as the **Economic Community of Central African States** and the Institute for Bantu Studies. It also proposed the creation of an international organization of black-

African states to supplement the activities of the **Organization of African Unity**, which for a time was seen as focusing too much on Arab problems. During the 1980s, Zaire increased its profile among Africa's Francophone countries, particularly after it hosted the France-African Summit in 1982. In the 1990s, African governments tended to avoid official reference to the power struggle between Mobutu and the opposition. Many of them faced similar difficulties, as they struggled with political and economic reforms and shifts in traditional alliances brought on by the new world order. *See also* entries on relations with: Angola; Arab Countries; Burundi; Central African Republic; Chad; Congo, Republic of the (Brazzaville); Cuba; Germany; Italy; Japan; Kenya; Libya; Morocco; Portugal; Rwanda; South Africa; Sudan; Switzerland; Tanzania; Togo; Uganda; United Kingdom; United Nations; Zambia.

FORESTS. More than one-half of Congolese territory, 1.2 million square kilometers, is covered by forests, which contain the world's largest reserves of African hardwoods. The forests dominate the **Congo River Basin** area in the heart of **Congo/Zaire**, but also can be found in western **Bas-Congo** and the mountainous areas of the **Eastern Highlands**. Exploitation of the forests was centered primarily in Bas-Congo, which by 1995 had been heavily deforested, and the most accessible parts of the Congo River Basin. In the 1990s, 400,000 cubic meters of **timber** were being cut per year, of which an average of 150 million cubic meters was exported, according to government figures. Production was considered relatively small, contributing less than 0.3 percent of **gross domestic product (GDP)**, and the **industry** was considered "underdeveloped." However, timber concessions covering one-third of the forests had been signed by the early 1990s, leading some environmentalists to classify Congo/Zaire's great **rainforests** as at risk. *See also* Trade.

FRANC, CONGO. The Congo franc was introduced in 1919. Linked to the Belgian franc, it was the Congolese **currency** for nearly 50 years. As part of a monetary adjustment in 1967, the name was changed to the **zaire** and one zaire was exchanged for 1,000 Congolese francs. After the fall of **Mobutu**, the government of

Laurent **Kabila** reintroduced the currency on June 30, 1998, as part of a broad monetary reform.

FRANCE, RELATIONS WITH. It could be said that France's interest in **Congo/Zaire** dates from the "scramble for Africa" of the 1880s when, following the **Berlin Conference**, the French government sent Count Pierre Savorgnan De Brazza to central Africa on a territory-claiming expedition aimed at countering the expeditions by Henry Morton **Stanley** financed by **Belgium**'s King **Leopold II**. The **Belgian Congo**'s **colonial-era** experience was considerably different from that of the French colonies, but from the late 1950s it began to develop an affinity with the French colonies and closely followed their affairs. France included Congo/Zaire in the special relationship it reserved for the Francophone nations of the world and of Africa in particular, and liked to say Zaire was the second-largest French-speaking country after France. Charles **de Gaulle**'s offer of autonomy to France's African colonies in a speech in **Congo/Brazzaville** in August 1958 was one of several developments that led Africans in the Belgian Congo to begin pressing for **independence**.

Congolese relations with France, though friendly, were relatively underdeveloped in the early years following independence, but they increased steadily after the second **Shaba War**, when France sent 700 French paratroopers to **Kolwezi** to help Congolese soldiers drive out guerrillas of the **Front pour la Libération Nationale du Congo (FLNC)**. Relations grew closer because of Zaire's mercurial relations with Belgium and because of France's much-greater ability to provide **foreign aid**. The entrance into the French "family" was sealed in October 1982, when Zaire hosted the ninth France-African summit in Kinshasa.

During the 1980s, relations with the François **Mitterrand** government were initially cool and suspicious, primarily because of the Socialist president's criticism during his campaign of France's close ties with authoritarian regimes in Africa. However, within two years of Mitterrand's inauguration, a policy of pragmatism evolved and Mitterrand mended fences with **Mobutu** and other traditional friends of France, including Togo's Gnassingbe Eyadema and Gabon's Omar Bongo. The Socialists began to appreciate the support of moderate African governments for French policies in Africa and their receptive markets for

French exports. Later, it would be Mobutu and other moderate African leaders who would persuade a reluctant French government to send military forces to **Chad**, exert moderation in the face of the revolution in Burkina Faso, and press for forgiveness of the continent's external **debt**.

Relations began to cool in the 1990s after France began linking aid to political and economic reforms in Africa, a policy formally announced by Mitterrand in a speech to the France-African summit at Le Baule in July 1990. Following the attack on **students** at **Lubumbashi University** in May 1990, France joined the Western cutoff of aid to Zaire and later joined Belgium and the **United States** in a pressure group called the "Troika," which pressed for democratic reforms. Following the **pillages** of September 1991, France sent troops to evacuate the estimated 4,000 French expatriates in Kinshasa. During another round of violence and looting in January 1993, the French ambassador, Philippe Bernard, was killed in his office by a stray bullet.

France was Congo/Zaire's major foreign partner in **telecommunications**. It built the **Voix du Zaïre** complex in Kinshasa, which when it was completed in 1976 at a cost of $1 billion, housed some of the most up-to-date television and **radio** broadcasting equipment in the world. France also funded military equipment and training, humanitarian assistance and economic **development projects**. French aid to Zaire reached $180 million in 1990 when France replaced Belgium as Zaire's largest provider of foreign aid. France became a major trading partner in the late 1980s after Belgium, the United States and **Germany**. However, it lost ground in the 1990s to **South Africa**, **Italy** and **Japan**. In 1994, Zairian **exports** to France totaled $16 million, mostly **coffee**, cocoa, and **timber**, and **imports** from France totaled $18.5 million, mostly machinery, vehicles, and consumer items.

FRANCK, LOUIS. The Belgian minister of colonies in the 1920s who was credited with enacting changes in the **colonial-era** administration of Congo/Zaire following World War I which consolidated the chiefdoms into sectors. The measures Europeanized, or de-Africanized, the colonial administration by separating it from the traditional African political and judicial structures.

FRENCH CONGO. *See* CONGO, REPUBLIC OF THE (BRAZZA-VILLE).

FRENTE NACIONAL DE LIBERTAÇÃO DE ANGOLA (FNLA) / NATIONAL FRONT FOR THE LIBERATION OF ANGOLA. One of three major guerrilla groups that fought for the independence of **Angola** and, after it was attained, fought each other for control of the national government. The FNLA was a group based primarily in northern Angola with strong ties to the **Kongo** people of **Bas-Congo**. Its leader was Holden **Roberto**, **Mobutu**'s son-in-law. The smallest of the three factions, the FNLA was backed by Zaire during the civil war and for a number of years after the **Movimento Popular de Libertação de Angola (MPLA)** took control of Luanda. Following the **Shaba** invasions, which were backed by the MPLA government, the Congolese and Angolan governments established diplomatic relations and Congolese support for the FNLA officially ended. In the 1980s, the FNLA virtually disappeared, while a second group, the **União Nacional para a Independência Total de Angola (UNITA)**, continued its guerrilla war against the MPLA. Nevertheless, the FNLA sometimes resurfaced seeking financial support and demanding to be included in any power-sharing arrangement between the MPLA and UNITA.

FRENTE PARA A LIBERTAÇÃO DO ENCLAVE DE CABINDA (FLEC) / FRONT FOR THE LIBERATION OF THE ENCLAVE OF CABINDA. A group that surfaced in the 1970s demanding independence for **Cabinda**, at first from **Portugal** and after 1974 from independent **Angola**. Cabinda, an enclave of 600 square kilometers, was a special Portuguese possession until it was attached administratively to Angola in 1956. It lies along the Atlantic coast, separated from Angola by the mouth of the **Congo River** and the Congolese territory that surrounds it. The Zairian government began supporting FLEC in 1974 and was rumored at the time to be interested in annexing Cabinda, which had considerable offshore **petroleum** reserves. Support for FLEC was officially halted following an agreement between Zaire and Angola in Brazzaville on February 26, 1976. FLEC activities ceased for a time, but resumed in the mid-1980s. A sizable contingent of Cuban troops guarded Cabinda's oil installations from FLEC attacks until **Cuba** withdrew its troops from Angola in the late 1980s.

FRONT FOR THE NATIONAL LIBERATION OF THE CONGO. *See* FRONT POUR LA LIBÉRATION NATIONALE DU CONGO (FLNC).

FRONT NATIONAL DE LIBÉRATION (FNL) / NATIONAL LIBERATION FRONT. An antigovernment group created in **Congo/Brazzaville** in the late 1960s. It was said to be linked to the **Conseil National de Libération**, which had been formed earlier and was reportedly headed by Antoine **Gizenga**. The FNL was accused of responsibility for alleged plots against the Congolese government in 1970 and 1971. It faded from view in the 1970s with the consolidation of **Mobutu**'s power and the warming relations between Zaire and Congo/Brazzaville.

FRONT POUR LA LIBÉRATION NATIONALE DU CONGO (FLNC) / FRONT FOR THE NATIONAL LIBERATION OF THE CONGO. An **opposition** group headed by Nathaniel **Mbumba**, a former member of the **Gendarmerie Katangaise**, which supported the **Katanga secession** and participated in an invasion of eastern Congo in 1967 aimed at returning Moïse **Tshombe** to power. After 1967, the Gendarmerie moved to **Angola**, where it fought with the Portuguese against guerrillas fighting for Angolan independence. When independence was attained in 1974, it fought with the Angolan government against two rival factions.

The FLNC was best known for launching the **Shaba** invasions of 1977 and 1978, which were only repulsed by Zaire with the aid of foreign military troops and equipment. The FLNC included younger individuals, primarily of the **Lunda ethnic group**, who resented the imposition of authority from distant **Kinshasa**. The FLNC expressed little ideology or political orientation other than a desire to overthrow **Mobutu**. The attention it initially received faded considerably after the Shaba incursions, although it still was considered a major opposition group in the mid-1980s. Mbumba returned to Zaire after the end of single-party rule in 1990 and was a delegate to the **National Conference**.

FRONT SOCIALISTE AFRICAIN / AFRICAN SOCIALIST FRONT. An exiled **opposition** group, affiliated with the **Parti Solidaire Africain (PSA)**. It was formed by Cléophas **Kamitatu** in the late 1960s after the end of the eastern **rebellions**. The group disappeared after Kamitatu accepted **Mobutu's amnesty of 1983** and returned to Zaire.

FULERU. A small **Bantu ethnic group** living between **Bukavu** and Uvira in the **Eastern Highlands**. Ethnologists say it was organized into a single state, in contrast with other groups of highland Bantus in the region, which tended to be divided into several political groupings, each with its own **king** and **chiefs**.

FUNDAMENTAL LAW. *See* LOI FONDAMENTALE.

FUNGURUME. A small town in **Katanga** west of **Likasi** located in an area containing large deposits of high-grade **copper** and **cobalt**. A consortium of British, US, French and Japanese **mining** companies in 1970 formed the **Société Minière de Tenke-Fungurume (SMTF)**, with 20 percent government participation, in order to exploit the deposits. Low prices for copper and the closure of the **Benguela Railway** in 1974 led to the liquidation of the company in 1984. In November 1996, a Canadian company announced a joint venture with the **Générale des Carrières et des Mines (GECAMINES)** aimed at resuming production in the area by the year 2000. The agreement was overtaken by the offensive of anti-**Mobutu** forces a few months later. It was renegotiated following the installation of the Laurent **Kabila** government in May 1997 and was renegotiated again in 1998, when the Kabila government, facing accusations of favoritism, reopened the bidding and brought in companies from Europe, South Africa and the United States.

- G -

GARCIA II. **King** of the **Kongo** from 1641 until his death in 1661, Garcia II ruled over what many historians believe were the twilight years of the Kongo empire. He faced problems reconciling recently introduced **Christianity** with traditional

Kongo religious practices. After his death, war broke out in 1665 between the Kongo and Portuguese-ruled **Angola**, resulting in the defeat of the Kongo and a weakening of allegiance by sub**chiefs** in distant parts of the kingdom.

GAULLE, CHARLES DE. *See* DE GAULLE, CHARLES.

GBADOLITE. A town on the **Ubangi River** in **Équateur** Province, 400 km upriver from Bangui, the capital of the **Central African Republic (CAR)**. The **Mobutu** family traces its origins to Gbadolite, although its most famous son, Mobutu Sese Seko, was born and raised in **Lisala**. During the Mobutu years, Gbadolite became a model town with electricity, paved **roads** and well developed **health** and **social care** facilities. It also was home of the shrine to Mobutu's mother, Mama **Yemo**.

GBENYE, CHRISTOPHE. Interior minister in the Patrice **Lumumba government** of 1960, Gbenye was a lieutenant of Antoine **Gizenga**, who assumed control of the breakaway **Stanleyville** government in its brutal, final days and in 1964 became president of the short-lived **People's Republic of the Congo** (not to be confused with the People's Republic of the Congo which was established later in **Congo/Brazzaville**). Fearing an offensive by government troops and **mercenaries** in late 1964, Gbenye took hostage the 2,800 Europeans and Americans living in the region. Reports of atrocities led to the Belgian paratroop drop from US military planes on Stanleyville on November 24, 1964. An estimated 10,000 Congolese and 200 foreigners were killed during the final days of the **rebellion**. Gbenye fled to **Uganda** and Europe, but returned to Zaire in 1984 following the general **amnesty of 1983**. In the early 1990s, he headed the Lumumba wing of the **Mouvement National Congolais/Lumumba**.

GENDARMERIE KATANGAISE. A group of well-trained paramilitary units that helped maintain law and order in **Katanga** before **independence**. The Gendarmerie Katangaise, formed primarily of members of the **Lunda ethnic group**, supported the **Katanga secession** in 1961. After the end of the secession in 1963, the Gendarmerie was integrated into the Congolese **armed forces**. Many members, however, subsequently became disillusioned with the **Mobutu** government and went to live in **Angola**. They were implicated in the mutinies of the Congolese Army in 1966 and were part of a group of **mercenary**-led rebels that occupied **Bukavu** for 100 days in 1967 in an attempt to return Moïse **Tshombe** to power. The Gendarmerie's leader, Brigadier General Nathaniel **Mbumba**, formed the **Front pour la Libération Nationale du Congo (FLNC)** in 1968 in Paris. The Gendarmerie fought for the **Portuguese** colonial authorities against pro-independence guerrillas in Angola in the early 1970s, and following Angola's independence in 1974, fought with Angolan government troops against opposition guerrillas supported by Zaire.

Members of the Gendarmerie Katangaise formed the core of the FLNC guerrillas who staged the **Shaba** incursions in 1977 and 1978. Some observers said they were supported directly by the Angolan government, which was angry at Mobutu's support for Angolan opposition movements. The rapprochement between Zaire and Angola following the second Shaba War ended most of the Gendarmerie's activities until 1996, when elements of the Gendarmerie supported the **Alliance des Forces Démocratiques pour la Libération du Congo/Zaïre (AFDL)** in its offensive to overthrow Mobutu. Following the fall of Mobutu in May 1997, the Gendarmerie Katangaise became a major force in the government of Laurent **Kabila**.

GENDARMERIE NATIONALE. A paramilitary **police** force of 20,000 members formed from the colonial **Troupes en Service Territorial** in 1959. During the years following **independence**, the Gendarmerie was placed administratively in the Defense Ministry and its commander reported to the **armed forces** chief of staff. On August 1, 1972, **Mobutu** dissolved the National Police, which had been under the Interior Ministry, and its members were absorbed by the Gendarmerie. The decree essentially moved police responsibilities from the Interior to the Defense Ministry (renamed "**departments**" the following year) and made the commanders of all the **security** forces answer directly to the **president**.

In June 1997, one month after the fall of Mobutu, the Laurent **Kabila** government announced it was disbanding the Gendarmerie and with assistance from **South Africa** was recreating a national police force.

GENERAL MOTORS - ZAÏRE. A company jointly owned by the US General Motors Corp. and the Zairian **government** that assembled cars and trucks. Production began in 1975 at a plant in **Kinshasa** with a production capacity of 4,000 vehicles. During the economic recession of the 1970s and 1980s, production averaged 10-25 percent of capacity. General Motors sold the enterprise to a group of Zairian businessmen in 1987. Production was irregular in the 1990s.

GENERAL UNION OF CONGOLESE STUDENTS. *See* UNION GÉNÉRALE DES ÉTUDIANTS CONGOLAIS (UGEC).

GÉNÉRALE DES CARRIÈRES ET DES MINES (GECAMINES). More commonly known by its acronym GECAMINES, the Générale des Carrières et des Mines was Congo/Zaire's largest corporation. GECAMINES traced its origins to October 30, 1906, when it was formed as the **Union Minière du Haut-Katanga (UMHK)** by the **Société Générale de Belgique (SGB)** and the British Tanganyika Concessions, Ltd., to exploit deposits of **copper** and other **minerals** in southern **Katanga**. The name was changed to **Générale Congolaise des Minérais (GECOMIN)** on January 2, 1967, when the UMHK was nationalized following the refusal by its officers to move the company headquarters from Brussels to **Kinshasa**.

Negotiations on compensation took several years, but were resolved for the most part by the early 1970s in an agreement through which a Belgian company, the **Société Générale des Minérais**, assumed responsibility for technical operations in exchange for a portion (about 6 percent) of revenues. In 1971, GECOMIN was renamed GECAMINES. The company had a dozen subsidiaries operating several dozen mines and several refineries. Historically, it provided the **government** with one-half of its total revenues and two-thirds of its **foreign exchange**. The size of the company and its power made it virtually a state-within-a-state and it dominated the economic affairs of such cities as **Lubumbashi** and **Kolwezi**. From 1975 until the early 1980s, GECAMINES was crippled by low prices for copper and a shortage of foreign exchange and spare parts. In 1976, the Zairian government granted the company the right to use one-half of its foreign exchange earnings to refurbish and modernize its plants. In 1983, faced with mounting shortages of spare parts and supplies needed for refining, it was granted de facto permission to purchase foreign exchange on the parallel market.

GECAMINES was restructured in 1984 and a great deal of the top-heavy central management was redistributed among three entities: GECAMINES-Exploitation, responsible for the extraction, processing and transport of the minerals to embarkation points; GECAMINES-Commerciale, charged with marketing the minerals; and GECAMINES-Développement, responsible for developing **agricultural** and **livestock** units to feed company workers. The three legally and financially independent entities were grouped under GECAMINES-Holding. At its peak in 1984, GECAMINES produced 500,000 tons of copper, making it the seventh-largest producer in the world, and 9,000 tons of **cobalt**, 50 percent of world production of that element. It also produced 70,000 tons of **zinc** in raw and semirefined form, 1.2 million ounces of **silver**, 80,000 ounces of **gold**, and 300 tons of cadmium. The company employed 33,500 persons, of which less than 300 were expatriate technicians. Revenues exceeded $1 billion in 1984.

From its peak in the mid-1980s, GECAMINES began a slow decline. Production of all minerals except cobalt fell during the late 1980s, although the work force increased to 37,000. Receipts were often diverted to government coffers in Kinshasa or to private bank accounts in Europe. Equipment and the physical plant deteriorated. The political infighting in Kinshasa following the advent of multipartyism in 1990 accelerated the decline. During the civic unrest of October 1991, equipment was looted and expatriate technicians were evacuated. Copper production declined from 335,000 tons in 1990 to an estimated 40,000 tons in 1996. Zinc production, in decline since the 1980s, fell to less than 20,000 tons. Cobalt, which had remained at relatively high levels during the 1980s, began to fall, from 10,000 tons in 1990 to an estimated 3,000 tons in 1996.

By 1995, GECAMINES was considered insolvent. In the mid-1990s, several **South African** firms expressed an interest in reviving the enterprise. On November 30, 1996, the **Switzerland-**

based Group Lundin announced that an agreement had been signed between GECAMINES and its Canadian affiliate, Eurocan Consolidated Ventures, to resume production at **Tenke-Fungurume** in southern **Katanga**. Under the agreement, GECAMINES would own 45 percent of the venture, which planned to produce 100,000 tons of copper and 8,000 tons of cobalt by the year 2000. *See also* Mining; Société Zaïroise de Commercialisation des Minérais (SOZACOM).

GERMANY, RELATIONS WITH. Relations between Congo/Zaire and the former West Germany were generally good and from the mid-1970s Germany was an important donor and trading partner, especially before reunification with East Germany. In 1976, a West German rocket manufacturer, **Orbital Transport und Raketen Gesellschaft (OTRAG)**, signed a contract with the Zairian **government**, reportedly for $50 million, giving it exclusive access to nearly 100,000 square km of territory in a remote part of northern **Shaba** near **Lake Tanganyika**. The purpose was to develop and test commercial rockets to place **satellites** into orbit. However, **Tanzania** and other nations in the region protested and the government canceled the contract the following year. West Germany helped train the **Civil Guard** when it was formed after the **Shaba** wars. A bilateral investment agreement was signed in the 1980s. Trade increased between the two countries and, by 1993, Germany had become one of Zaire's top three trading partners. That year, it bought $39 million worth of Zairian **exports** and provided $35.7 million of Zaire's **imports**.

Relations with the former East Germany, which supported Patrice **Lumumba** and the **Stanleyville secession**, did not exist until 1972, when Zaire recognized it along with **China** and North Korea as part of an effort to burnish its membership credentials in the Non-Aligned Movement. Commercial ties, however, never developed.

GHENDA, RAPHAEL (1946 -). Information minister in the early governments of Laurent **Kabila**, Ghenda is a lawyer of the **Tetela ethnic group** from eastern **Congo** who spent years as a political exile in **France** and **Belgium**. He was a representative of Kabila's **Parti Revolutionnaire du Peuple (PRP)** in Brussels from 1990 until 1996, when he joined the anti-**Mobutu** offensive.

GIZENGA, ANTOINE. Vice prime minister in the Patrice **Lumumba** government of 1960 and chief lieutenant of Lumumba's wing of the **Mouvement National Congolais (MNC)**, Gizenga was dismissed along with Lumumba by President Joseph **Kasavubu** on September 5, 1960. Gizenga left for **Stanleyville** on November 13 to form a secessionist government. Lumumba was captured and subsequently assassinated while trying to join him. Lumumba's assassination caused an outcry among many nations of the "Afro-Arab" and Soviet blocs.

Following negotiations with the **Leopoldville** government, Gizenga agreed in 1961 to participate in a federally structured central government. He was made first vice prime minister of Cyrille **Adoula**'s government of reconciliation although he remained in Stanleyville. He was arrested on January 16, 1962, with support from the **United Nations,** and was imprisoned on Bula-Bemba Island at the mouth of the **Congo River**. When Moïse **Tshombe** became prime minister in July 1964, he released Gizenga, but in October placed him under house arrest. He was freed by **Mobutu** following the **coup d'etat** in November 1965. Gizenga was rumored to be involved in the **Congo/Brazzaville**-based **Front National de Libération**. In the early 1970s, he formed the **Forces Démocratiques pour la Libération du Congo (FODELICO)** in exile.

In 1977, Mobutu invited him to return to Zaire to oppose him in **elections**, which Gizenga declined. Nevertheless, he did return after the **democratic transition** was announced in 1990 and by 1993 had brought together a number of Lumumbist parties under the **Parti Lumumbiste Unifié (PALU)**. In July 1995, 10 people were killed when **security** forces broke up an unauthorized protest march by PALU in **Kinshasa**. Gizenga was arrested and his home was looted following the incident. He was released five days later.

Following the fall of Mobutu in May 1997 and the installation of the government of Laurent **Kabila**, who had also been a Lumumba supporter, Gizenga and PALU remained in the opposition and PALU marches on several occasions were harshly put down by security forces. *See also* Kashamura, Anicet.

GOLD. The search for gold was one of the main reasons for the exploration of the interior of the Congo, particularly **Katanga**, by

Europeans. However, the explorers found none and so turned to trading in **ivory** and **slaves**. Gold was discovered in 1903 near Bunia, in the **Ituri District** of **Orientale**, and later in northern **Kivu**.

Official production of gold peaked in the 1930s and 1940s at 16,000 kg per year, and fell thereafter, reaching 958 kg in 1983. That year, the Zairian **government** legalized artisanal **mining** and in 1985 launched a large-scale reinvestment program. In 1988, it awarded contracts to rehabilitate two mines to a Brazilian and a British firm. Official production rose to 2,000 kg in 1988, but declined to less than 100 kg by 1993.

Congo/Zaire had known gold reserves of 100 tons. The major gold-mining operation was the **Office des Mines d'Or de Kilo-Moto (OKIMO)**, nationalized in 1973, which worked alluvial and underground deposits in an 83,000-square-km concession in the Bunia area. Two other companies also were involved in gold production, primarily in Katanga Province: **Générale des Carrières et des Mines (GECAMINES)** and the **Société Minière et Industrielle du Kivu (SOMINKI)**. A fourth, Bureau de Recherches Géologiques et Minières (BRGM), of mixed private and state ownership, undertook feasibility studies in 1985 of two sites in **Haut-Congo** but production never began.

Historically, a great deal of Congo/Zaire's gold was lost to **smuggling** out of the country, most often through east Africa. During the 1970s, for example, **Uganda** became a major exporter of gold, although it produced none. And in the mid-1990s, Kenya became an exporter although it too had no gold mines.

GOMA. The capital of **Nord-Kivu Province**, Goma and its population of several hundred thousand people, was living a relatively quiet existence as a regional trading and administrative center in 1994, when one million **refugees** fleeing the **Rwandan** civil war arrived and in a few weeks set up camps around the town. World attention subsequently was riveted on Goma, as relief agencies tried to distribute emergency aid flown in by troops from donor nations. The presence of officers and soldiers from the deposed Rwandan government and members of militias that had carried out mass killings of 500,000 people in Rwanda, created considerable insecurity in the region. In August 1995, the Zairian government announced it would expel the refugees, saying local populations could no longer support the strain. It relented under international pressure, but **security** in the area deteriorated because of attacks by Rwandan militias based in the refugee camps against installations in Rwanda and against Congolese of Rwandan origin, called **Banyarwanda**. In October 1996, rebels of the **Alliance des Forces Démocratiques pour la Libération du Congo/Zaïre (AFDL)** launched an offensive in the region. They drove the Rwandan militias deeper into the interior and over the next seven months moved west, taking **Kinshasa** on May 17, 1997. Goma was seized on August 2, 1998, by rebels of the **Rassemblement Congolais pour la Démocratie (RCD)**, the first victory of their drive to unseat the AFDL.

GOODYEAR ZAÏRE. A subsidiary of the US company, Goodyear Zaire produced tires for automobiles, trucks and bicycles at plants in **Kinshasa** and **Kisangani**. Like many industries, production was hindered in the late 1970s and 1980s by low demand and a shortage of **foreign exchange** needed to **import** equipment and materials. Production rarely exceeded 20 percent of capacity. Goodyear sold the operation to a group of local businessmen in 1987. The plant was stripped during the **pillages** of 1991.

GOVERNMENT. Through the years, **Congo/Zaire** has seen a variety of governmental systems, ranging from monarchy and dictatorship to parliamentary and highly centralized presidential systems. A tendency toward authoritarianism was a major characteristic of virtually all of these.

After the partition of Africa at the **Berlin Conference** of 1885, Congo was recognized as a sovereign territory of King **Leopold II** and was ruled by him for 23 years as the **Congo Free State**. Some argue the king only continued **trade** patterns set centuries earlier by European and **Afro-Arab** traders. Nevertheless, the excesses of his rule caused the Belgian parliament to annex the territory in 1908 and ushered in the **colonial era**, during which the king exercised considerable authority but the colony was officially administered by a colonial governor appointed by the parliament.

With **independence** in 1960, Congo/Zaire adopted a bicameral parliamentary system which considerably diluted executive powers and left unclear how power was to be shared by the **president** and **prime minister**. The goal of the system was to provide checks and balances and prevent abuses. However, it led to confusion and a series of confrontations between the president and prime minister. When the authority of the central government broke down following independence, a variety of federal and confederal systems were contemplated and the first **constitution**, promulgated in 1964, granted considerable autonomy to the provincial governments. However, following the military **coup d'etat** in 1965, Congo entered a period during which power gradually became concentrated in the presidency.

In the 1980s, the president enjoyed broad powers of decree and controlled virtually all aspects of **security**, legislation, economic policy and the **judicial system**. Zaire evolved into a party-state, modeled on the Chinese system. The concept of **chieftaincy** was also retained and a personality cult was developed around the president and his family. Multiple candidacies within the ruling **Mouvement Populaire de la Révolution (MPR)** party were allowed during the 1980s, but control over the process was retained by the president and the party hierarchy.

Under the third constitution, promulgated in 1974, the party was the supreme body of state and sole legal party, to which all Zairians automatically belonged from birth to death. There were seven basic organs of state: the president, who was the "center for decisions and control of the activities of the MPR" and who presided over all of the state organs; the **Political Bureau** of the party, which was the central policy and decision-making organ; the **Central Committee** of the party, which was the major forum for "debate and discussion of ideas emanating from the Political Bureau"; the Congress of the Party, which was the broad-based forum for consultations with party members; the **Legislative Council**, or legislature, which essentially was a consultative body; the **Executive Council**, which was the equivalent of a ministerial cabinet; and the Council of the Judiciary, which grouped the senior judges and members of the Supreme Court.

A system for political **succession** in the case of the president's death existed but was never tested. Under the constitution, in the absence or incapacitation of the president, the dean of the MPR Central Committee would assume the presidency for a period of 30-60 days, during which time the Political Bureau would organize elections and choose the party's candidate for president.

Administratively, Congo/Zaire was organized into 10 **provinces** (called **regions** from 1972 to 1997) and the autonomous capital district. The provinces were divided into districts (called subregions from 1972 to 1997), urban and rural, and the rural districts were divided into zones.

The judicial system consisted of five levels of courts. Independence of the judiciary was guaranteed by the constitution, but was weakened considerably because of the omnipotence of the party and the president.

The system of government began to change on **April 24, 1990**, when **Mobutu** declared the birth of the Third Republic and announced he was launching a one-year transition to a multiparty system. He initially said two other **political parties** would be allowed (later amended to allow an unlimited number of parties) and that he was lifting restrictions on public gatherings and the print **news media**. Until then, calling for a second party was a treasonous offense punishable by death. The president also said all aspects of the current constitution and government would continue in effect unless specifically repealed or amended.

The following years were characterized by political jousting between an **opposition** convinced that real **democracy** could only be achieved with the removal of Mobutu, and the president, who was determined to stay on at all costs. The opposition used popular and international pressure to seek concessions from the president, while Mobutu utilized parliamentary maneuvers, his patronage powers, and force when necessary to keep the opposition on the defensive. As a result, government was largely paralyzed during the 1990s, while a fractious **National Conference** struggled to draft a constitution (which was eventually rejected by the president), the authority of the central state decayed, and the formal **economy** was shaken by **hyperinflation** and recession. Although the Zairian government continued to be recognized internationally, at home the government commanded little authority or popular respect.

In August 1996, the transitional parliament which had emerged following years of bickering drafted a constitution calling for a **federalist** system and renaming Zaire the **Federal Republic of the Congo**. National **elections** were scheduled for May and June 1997. However, the process was slowed by political infighting and Mobutu's deteriorating health. In October 1996, the **Alliance des**

Forces Démocratiques pour la Libération du Congo/Zaïre launched an offensive in eastern Zaire which led to the exile of Mobutu in May 1997 and the installation of Laurent **Kabila** as president. At his inauguration on May 29, Kabila pledged to hold national elections in 1999. He sought to revive the **administration** of government and promised to pay salary arrears of **civil servants**. *See also* Democratic Transition; Mobutism.

GOVERNORS, COLONIAL. The governors of the **Belgian Congo** were appointed by the government of **Belgium** and although they were responsible to the king and the Belgian parliament, they exercised considerable individual power because of the distance and slowness of communications between **Leopoldville** and Brussels. The governors implemented the **colonial era** policy of **paternalism**, which included isolating Congolese from other Africans and preventing the formation of political organizations. The last colonial governors were: Eugène Jungers (1946-52), Léon Pétillon (1952-58), and Hendrik Cornelis (1958-60).

GREAT CITY OF THE KING. *See* MBANZA KONGO DIA NTOTILA.

GREAT LAKES REGION. The area around the **lakes** of the **Great Rift Valley** which form **Congo/Zaire**'s border with **Uganda, Rwanda, Burundi** and **Tanzania**. Rwanda and Burundi in September 1976 joined Zaire in forming the **Communauté Économique des Pays des Grands Lacs (CEPGL)**, an economic **trade** zone with its headquarters in Gisenye, Rwanda. The region was destabilized in the mid-1990s by interethnic violence in Rwanda and Burundi, which spread into eastern Zaire and continued after the fall of **Mobutu** in 1997.

GREAT RIFT VALLEY. A geographical fault dividing east Africa from the rest of the continent. The western edge of the rift, characterized by rugged **mountain** ranges and deep **lakes**, lies in eastern **Congo/Zaire** and helps form **Lakes Tanganyika, Kivu** and **Albert**.

GREAT WORKS POLICY. *See* POLITIQUE DES GRANDS TRAVAUX.

GROSS DOMESTIC PRODUCT (GDP). Congo/Zaire's gross domestic product, the total of goods and services produced per year by the **economy**, in 1994 was estimated at $4.6 billion according to official figures, after declining from more than $7 billion in 1988. Historically, GDP has tended to fluctuate with the world economy and demand for Congolese **exports**. GDP rose in the 1920s and 1950s, and declined during the 1930s and part of the 1940s. GDP also declined during the political unrest of the 1960s, but recovered at a rate of 5-8 percent per year following the return of political stability in 1967. Following the drop in **copper** prices and the world recession caused by the rise in **petroleum** prices in the mid-1970s, GDP declined by an average of 3.2 percent per year from 1975 to 1979, and only resumed growth in the 1980s, following economic reforms that included lifting **price controls** and restrictions on **currency** exchange markets and business. From 1980 to 1985, GDP rose by an average of 1.9 percent per year, peaking at $7.7 billion in 1988, according to the **World Bank**. However, it declined by a similar amount in the late 1980s and during the economic crisis of the early 1990s fell by as much as 10 percent per year, returning to the level of the mid-1970s.

Historically, the **mining** sector produced 25 percent of GDP. **Agriculture**, **industry** and **transportation** contributed roughly 10 percent each; **trade** contributed 15 percent. Services, including the **government**, contribute 31 percent. However, in the 1990s, the severe decline of mineral production, particularly copper, made agriculture a major contributor once again, and it produced one-third of GDP in 1995.

GROUP OF THIRTEEN PARLIAMENTARIANS / GROUPE DES TREIZE PARLEMENTAIRES. This group of 13 members of **parliament** published a 52-page open letter to **Mobutu** on November 1, 1980, listing numerous abuses of power under the single-party system and calling for the creation of a multiparty **democracy**. Members of the group in 1982 founded an **opposition** party, the **Union pour la Démocratie et le Progrès Social (UDPS)**, which under the **constitution** of 1974 was considered an act of treason. As a result, the members of the group, who included Étienne **Tshisekedi**, Joseph **Ngalula** and

Gabriel **Kyungu wa Kumwanza,** were convicted of conspiracy in 1983 and sentenced to prison terms ranging from 15 years to life. They were later pardoned but continued their activities and were frequently subjected to various forms of detention. In the 1980s, the parliamentarians, mostly from **Shaba** and **Kasai Regions,** were the most prominent internal **dissidents** in Zaire. Following the announcement of multipartyism on **April 24, 1990,** they were freed. The UDPS was one of the first parties to be registered after multipartyism was formalized in November and quickly became a leading opposition party and pillar of the **Sacred Union** alliance. *See also* Democratic Transition.

GUARD, CIVIL. See CIVIL GUARD.

GUEVARA, ERNESTO "CHE" (1928 - 1967). The Argentine revolutionary who became a legend for his attempts to bring communism to Latin America, Guevara in 1965 headed a contingent of 100 **Cuban** troops dispatched to eastern Congo to help rebels fighting the **Kinshasa** government. He complained about the quality of the rebel forces and left after a few months. One of the rebel leaders was Laurent **Kabila,** who became president after the fall of **Mobutu** in 1997. Guevara was killed in Bolivia in October 1967. His mission to **Congo** was revealed for the first time in a documentary on his life broadcast by Cuban television in 1987.

GULF OIL ZAÏRE. Part of a consortium led by Gulf Oil (called Chevron-Gulf after the purchase of Gulf Oil by Chevron in 1984) with participation by the Zairian **government,** Japan Petroleum, and the Belgian **Société du Litoral Zaïrois.** The consortium engaged in offshore **petroleum** production near the mouth of the **Congo River** beginning in 1975. Production averaged 17,000 barrels per day in the 1970s, but rose to 25,000 in the late 1980s and 30,000 in 1995. The crude extracted was too heavy for the country's sole **refinery** and consequently was exported.

- H -

HAMMARSKJÖLD, DAG (1905 - 1961). Secretary-General of the United Nations from April 11, 1953, until his death on September 18, 1961, in an airplane crash while en route to **Ndola**, Northern Rhodesia (now **Zambia**), in an attempt to mediate an end to the **Katanga secession**. The cause of the plane crash was never fully determined. It could have been accidental, but anti-UN sentiments were high in the Katangan government, which had a small air force. The Katangans were bitter over the armed intervention by UN troops in the area and the attempts to expel Belgian advisors and **mercenaries** from the territory. As a result, many UN officials believed the plane crashed either after being hit or while being harassed by a Katangan fighter plane that was reported in the air over the region that day.

HASSAN II (1929 -). King of **Morocco** who maintained close relations with the **Mobutu** government virtually since it came to power. Morocco sent 1,500 troops to help Zairian forces repel the first **Shaba** incursion in 1977. They returned in 1978 following the second Shaba incursion and remained for several months, forming the backbone of an **Organization of African Unity (OAU)** peacekeeping force deployed until Zairian troops could be retrained and reorganized. The Mobutu government consistently supported Morocco's claim to the Western Sahara. When the Polisario Front's Saharan Republic, which was fighting Morocco for control of the former Spanish territory, was admitted to the OAU in 1984, Morocco left the organization. Zaire, in a show of support, suspended its participation for two years, the only member to do so. The friendship between Hassan and Mobutu remained strong. When Mobutu fled Zaire in May 1997, he was granted asylum in Morocco, where he died on September 7.

HAUT CONSEIL DE LA RÉPUBLIQUE (HCR) / HIGH COUNCIL OF THE REPUBLIC. The transitional **parliament** established in December 1992 by the **Conférence Nationale Souveraine (CNS)** to oversee the transition to multiparty **democracy**. As part of the **Transitional Act** approved by the CNS in August 1992, the 453-member HCR was to draft a new **constitution** and oversee its submission to the people in a national referendum. However,

Mobutu felt the HCR was dominated by the **opposition** after it elected Étienne **Tshisekedi** as **prime minister** in August 1992 and, in October, announced he was reconvening the **Legislative Council**, the parliament of the defunct single-party state. The Legislative Council had been inactive since the announcement of the **democratic transition** in April 1990, but had never formally been dissolved. When the HCR presented the draft constitution, Mobutu rejected it and ordered the Legislative Council to draft an alternate document. In March 1993, Mobutu dismissed Tshisekedi and appointed a rival government, headed by his former advisor Faustin **Birindwa**. It was a clear violation of the Transitional Act. Western governments began a policy of diplomatic isolation of the Birindwa government. Months of political confrontation passed before the various parties agreed in September 1993 to merge the two bodies into a new transitional parliament with 780 members, called the **Haut Conseil de la République / Parlement de la Transition (HCR/PT)**.

HAUT CONSEIL DE LA RÉPUBLIQUE / PARLEMENT DE LA TRANSITION (HCR/PT) / HIGH COUNCIL OF THE REPUBLIC/PARLIAMENT OF THE TRANSITION. A 780-member provisional **legislature** established in September 1993 to end a standoff between pro-**Mobutu** forces and the **opposition**. The agreement merged the **Haut Conseil de la République (HCR)**, viewed as controlled by the opposition, and the **Legislative Council**, which had been elected under single-party rule and was controlled by Mobutu. The transition quickly entered another standoff in January 1994, when the HCR/PT failed to reconfirm opposition leader Étienne **Tshisekedi** as **prime minister**. He had been elected to the post by the HCR in August 1992, but had been dismissed by Mobutu the following year. On June 14, 1994, the HCR/PT instead elected a centrist candidate, Léon **Kengo wa Dondo**. The hardline opposition, known as the **Sacred Union**, called the vote illegal and boycotted the Kengo government. In July 1995, the Sacred Union representatives allied with pro-Mobutu delegates to oust the president of the HCR/PT, Laurent **Monsengwo**. The body subsequently was governed by two vice presidents, one from the Sacred Union and one from the pro-Mobutu camp, called the Forces Politiques du **Conclave**. The HCR/PT went on to appoint an **electoral commission** and draft a

constitution to be submitted to a popular referendum prior to national **elections** scheduled for May and June 1997. However, its work was overtaken by the offensive of the **Alliance des Forces Démocratiques pour la Libération du Congo/Zaïre (AFDL)**, which overthrew Mobutu in May 1997 and brought the government of Laurent **Kabila** to power.

HAUT-UÉLÉ DISTRICT. A remote district of **Orientale Province** in the northeastern corner of **Congo/Zaire**, the Haut-Uélé's main economic activities include **agriculture** and some **mining** of iron ore and **gold**. It is linked to the rest of the country by the **Ubangi** and **Uele Rivers**, navigable only part of the year, and a small-gauge **railway**. As a result, traditional trading patterns are with southern **Sudan** and the **Central African Republic**. One of the most sparsely populated regions in the country, the Haut-Uélé, north of the Uele River, had an estimated 1.3 million inhabitants in 1995 (1,063,202 in 1982). The **Bas-Uélé District**, south of the river, had about one-half of that **population**.

HAUT-ZAÏRE. The name given to the northeastern **Orientale Province** in 1971. The provincial capital, **Stanleyville**, had been renamed **Kisangani** in 1966. "Orientale" was restored after the fall of **Mobutu** in 1997.

HEALERS, TRADITIONAL. Traditional healing, not to be confused with sorcery and witchcraft, is a profession that is gaining respect and legitimacy in modern Africa and other parts of the world. The **government** of Congo/Zaire supported the scientific study of herbs, plants and methods used by traditional healers. Scientific testing had proven some traditional plants and herbs to be effective against malaria, amebic dysentery, infections and parasites. In addition, traditional healers successfully performed a variety of surgical operations under clinical scrutiny using traditional instruments with little or no medication or anesthesia. As a result, members of the international medical community, including the World Health Organization, supported scientific study of healers and their methods.

HEALTH CARE. Public health care in Congo/Zaire is relatively poor and limited primarily to urban centers. In the mid-1990s, approximately 20 percent of the **population** had access to health services, according to UN figures, and government expenditures on health care averaged $1 per person. There were two hospital beds for every 1,000 persons and one doctor per 15,442 persons. These are relatively high figures compared to other countries in the region. However, the statistics are misleading. Because of a lack of supplies, families of patients usually were obliged to furnish virtually all medicine, bandages and surgical material and to pay hospital staff for routine care. The public health system was dysfunctional. Besides the lack of supplies, poorly paid staff members were often absent, obliged by financial hardship to engage in commerce or other money-making activities outside their jobs.

Historically, the **government** allocated 2 to 3 percent of its total budget to health care, but this figure in the 1990s declined to less than 1 percent. Approximately one-fifth of children under one year of age receive the four major immunizations (against polio, diphtheria, tuberculosis, and measles) and up to one-half receive at least one of them. A great deal of health care is supplied by religious missions and during emergencies by foreign relief agencies. Some large commercial concerns provide health care facilities for their employees. Members of the general public use private clinics or traditional methods when they can afford them. The wealthy go abroad for treatment.

HEMBA. A cluster of **ethnic groups**, identified by Jan Vansina as living in the savanna area straddling **Katanga** and the **Kasai Provinces**. A matrilineal group said to be related to the **Luba**, the Hemba lived along the **Lualaba River** near Kongolo, Kasongo and Manono. A Hemba **kingdom** once flourished in the highlands and may have formed part of the Luba empire or may have been an offshoot of it. The kingdom came to an end before the 20th century.

"HIBOUX, LES." / "THE OWLS." A shadowy paramilitary group that engaged in nocturnal terrorist acts against **opposition** leaders and their supporters during the 1990s. *Les Hiboux* were heavily armed and traveled in unregistered expensive all-terrain vehicles, leading to the belief that they were sponsored by the military and supported by powerful elements in the **government**.

HIGH COUNCIL OF THE REPUBLIC. *See* HAUT CONSEIL DE LA RÉPUBLIQUE (HCR).

HIGHWAY BOARD. *See* OFFICE DES ROUTES.

HUMAN RIGHTS. Under **Mobutu**, the **government** of **Zaire** signed the **African Charter of Human and People's Rights** and the **United Nations** International Covenant on Civil and Political Rights. Guarantees of individual freedoms and rights were also enshrined in its **constitution**. However, the government on numerous occasions has been severely criticized by human rights organizations and foreign governments for human rights violations. These accusations included summary execution, detention of political opponents without charge, disappearance of political **dissidents**, torture and inhumane conditions in prisons and the existence of secret detention camps. Human rights advocates also accused the government of failing to guarantee a free and independent **judicial system** and of harassing the **opposition news media**.

The government denied the charges and for a brief period in the 1980s it appeared more contrite. At a public meeting on November 2, 1986, following a month-long meeting of the **Central Committee** of the **Mouvement Populaire de la Révolution (MPR)**, Mobutu acknowledged some human rights abuses had occurred. He said steps were being taken to address the problem and announced the creation of the post of State Commissioner for Citizens' Rights and Liberties. However, human rights organizations said that despite these developments, the abuses did not stop. With the advent of multipartyism in the 1990s, violence and terrorism were frequently used to intimidate the opposition and press and instill fear in the **population**.

Beginning in 1990, the Zairian government officially tolerated the activities of major Zairian human rights organizations, of which there were three: the Ligue Zaïroise des Droits de l'Homme (Zairian League of Human Rights), the Association Zaïroise de Défense des Droits de l'Homme (Zairian Association for the Defense of Human Rights), and the **Voix des Sans-Voix pour les Droits de l'Homme** (Voice of the Voiceless for Human Rights). The government, however, did not allow international human rights organizations to visit and rejected their reports as attempts to destabilize the country. This did not prevent activists from issuing frequent and detailed reports on abuses committed under the Mobutu regime, charges which were supported by the UN Commission on Human Rights, the **European Union**, the **United States** State Department, and the governments of **Belgium**, **France**, **Germany** and several Scandinavian countries.

Amnesty International in its 1995 annual report on Zaire said hundreds of civilians had been extrajudicially executed by soldiers; scores of political opponents and hundreds of soldiers suspected of disloyalty had been detained without trial; scores of dissidents had "disappeared"; and torture and ill-treatment of prisoners were widespread. In a report issued on September 16, 1993, Amnesty International said, "Zaire is undergoing its worst human rights crisis since the end of the civil war in the early 1960s. The crisis has been marked by the ruthless brutality of government security forces . . . who have murdered or tortured thousands of civilians and members of the peaceful political opposition." Another prominent group, Human Rights Watch, published several reports in the 1990s on prison conditions, violence against **Luba** in **Shaba**, and efforts to subvert the **democratic transition**. The Lawyers Committee for Human Rights in 1990 published a comprehensive summary of the abuses in a 200-page volume, *Zaire: Repression as Policy.*

Religious organizations also spoke out. In 1992, the Washington Office on Africa, affiliated with the US National Council of Churches, issued a report, *Zaire Held Hostage,* in which it detailed 38 incidents or periods of abuse since 1964, as reported by a variety of human rights investigators. According to the document, nearly 3,000 people were killed or died in detention under the Mobutu government. The figures did not include the period during the **rebellions** of the 1960s, when **security** forces backed by foreign **mercenaries** massacred thousands of civilians believed to support the rebels. Nor did it include the incidents of **"ethnic cleansing"** in Shaba, **Nord-Kivu**, and **Bandundu** beginning in 1992 in which thousands of people were killed and hundreds of thousands driven from their homes and jobs.

Human rights investigators said casualty tolls in many incidents were higher than actually reported because families of the victims were afraid to speak out for fear of reprisals. The government frequently defended the actions of its security forces, saying they were seeking to prevent violence and to preserve law and order. No public investigation of any allegation of abuse was carried out and if any members of the security forces ever were punished for their actions, it was in secret.

In 1994, with the arrival of more than one million **refugees** fleeing interethnic violence in **Rwanda** and **Burundi**, the human rights situation in eastern Zaire deteriorated severely. Attacks by Rwandan militia based in the refugee camps brought retaliation from local groups who, backed by neighboring countries, formed the **Alliance des Forces Démocratiques pour la Libération du Congo/Zaïre (AFDL)**, which launched an offensive that in 1997 brought the overthrow of Mobutu and the installation of the Laurent **Kabila** government.

The Kabila government immediately faced charges that its forces had carried out reprisals against the refugees in which thousands were believed to have been massacred. For months it blocked travel to the region by UN investigators, leading to threats of international economic sanctions and a cutoff of reconstruction aid. The Kabila government also came under criticism for banning meetings and demonstrations by **political parties** and for detaining and harassing independent journalists and church leaders. In January 1998, the government began publicly executing criminals and by March had put a total of 60 people to death in **Goma, Bukavu, Kinshasa** and **Lubumbashi**. Human rights organizations expressed concern that most of those executed were civilians and that their trials were before military tribunals. However, the Kabila government responded by saying they were repeat offenders of whom an example had to be made in order to curb rampant criminality in the country.

Human Rights Watch in December 1997 expressed concern that "things are headed in the wrong direction . . . and there is no hint of democracy anywhere in the practice of the new government." And Congolese critics expressed the fear that the struggle to oust Mobutu had merely served to replace one harsh dictatorship with another. When a rebellion against the Kabila government began in August 1998, abuses became more generalized. Human rights organizations reported numerous attacks against ethnic **Tutsis**, sometimes by members of the civilian population, and widespread atrocities by armed forces against civilians caught in zones of conflict.

HUNDE. An **ethnic group** living in the **Kivus** which clashed with **Banyarwanda** groups during a period of **ethnic cleansing** in the mid-1990s. The clashes began after local politicians urged the Hunde and **Nyanga** to exterminate the Banyarwanda, who had immigrated during the **colonial era** but for the most part had never been granted full citizenship. The cleansing was officially ended in 1994, but the Hunde continued to clash with **Tutsi** elements from **Rwanda,** which entered with troops of the **Alliance des Forces Démocratiques pour la Libération du Congo/Zaïre (AFDL)** in 1996.

HUTU. One of two socio-**ethnic groups** in **Rwanda** and **Burundi** whose age-old conflicts have erupted on numerous occasions in recent history, leading to widespread massacres. In Rwanda, a civil war and inflammatory rhetoric inspired in no small part by the advent of multiparty politics led to the massacre of an estimated 500,000 **Tutsis** and moderate Hutus in 1994 following the death of Rwandan President Juvenal Habyarimana in a suspicious airplane accident. The advance of Tutsi-led rebels of the Rwandese Patriotic Front caused more than one million Rwandans, including officials, soldiers and supporters of the Habyarimana government to flee to eastern Zaire in June 1994. In several weeks, they created some of the largest **refugee** camps in the world, primarily around **Goma, Bukavu**, and Uvira. The situation caused insecurity in **Nord-Kivu**, which for a number of years had been experiencing conflict between indigenous groups and **Banyarwanda** immigrants who had arrived from Rwanda decades before.

The violence was responsible in part for the formation of the **Alliance des Forces Démocratiques pour la Libération du Congo/Zaïre (AFDL)** which, backed by Rwanda, Burundi and **Uganda**, launched an offensive that toppled the **Mobutu** government in 1997. During the offensive, AFDL troops reportedly massacred thousands of Hutu refugees, leading to international condemnation and the threat of international sanctions against the new government. *See also* Ethnic Cleansing.

HYPERINFLATION. A term used to describe the uncontrolled rise in **prices** and the precipitous fall in value of the **currency** in 1992-93. At one point, annualized **inflation** reached 12,000 percent. During this period, prices for basic commodities doubled virtually overnight and **wages** were reduced to a few dollars per month in real terms.

- I -

IDIOFA. A small town of about 50,000 inhabitants in **Bandundu Province**, 100 km east of **Kikwit** between the **Kasai** and **Kwilu Rivers**. The area was a center of **opposition** to the central **government** in the 1960s and 1970s. An uprising in January 1978 was harshly put down by government troops. **Human rights** groups said as many as 2,000 people reportedly were killed and 14 local **chiefs** were publicly executed.

IKEFA. A secret concentration camp located in the forest of **Équateur Province**. According to **human rights** organizations, it was built primarily to hold political **dissidents**.

ILEBO. A **river port** town of 60,000 inhabitants, formerly called Port Francqui, lying on the **Kasai River** near its confluence with the **Sankuru River**. The most important port for the **Kasai provinces**, it was an important link to **Katanga**. Goods arriving by riverboat from **Kinshasa** were transferred to a **railway** line that traveled through **Kamina** and **Likasi** to the **mining** centers of **Lubumbashi** and **Kolwezi**. It formed an important link in the **National Way** by which a large portion of **Congo/Zaire**'s minerals were **exported**.

ILEO, JOSEPH (1922? - 1994). A political leader active in the **independence** movement and **government**, who was considered one of the grand old men of Congolese politics. Ileo headed the editorial committee of the *Conscience Africaine* newspaper that in 1956 published the first known public demand by Congolese for political liberalization. Elected to **parliament** at independence, Ileo was considered a moderate pro-Belgian leader. Following the dismissal of Prime Minister Patrice **Lumumba** on

September 5, 1960, President Joseph **Kasavubu** named Ileo to form a new government. However, his government was not approved by parliament, which backed Lumumba. Ileo tried a second time, but that government was "neutralized" by **Mobutu** on September 14, 1960, and replaced by the **College of Commissioners** on September 29th. The College was dissolved in January 1961 and on February 6, 1961, Ileo became **prime minister** at the head of a provisional government. However, he was unable to draw the major secessionist leaders into his government and stepped down on August 1 to allow the formation of the Cyrille **Adoula** government-of-reconciliation. He served in the Adoula government as information minister and following the end of the **Katanga secession**, as minister of Katangan affairs. During the 1970s and 1980s, Ileo was a member of the **Political Bureau** and **Central Committee** of the **Mouvement Populaire de la Révolution (MPR)**.

Following Mobutu's announcement of the transition to multipartyism in 1990, Ileo formed the **Parti Démocrate et Social Chrétien (PDSC)**. It allied with the **Union pour la Démocratie et le Progrès Social (UDPS)** led by Étienne **Tshisekedi** and the **Union des Fédéralistes et des Républicains Indépendants (UFERI)** led by Jean **Nguza Karl-I-Bond** to form the **Sacred Union**, which eventually attracted more than 200 **opposition** parties. Though he was considered more moderate than Tshisekedi, Ileo, like Tshisekedi, resisted Mobutu's attempts to woo him away from the Sacred Union, unlike Nguza, who was expelled from the Sacred Union after he accepted the post of prime minister in November 1991. Ileo was named vice president of the **Conférence Nationale Souveraine (CNS)** and later the **Haut Conseil de la République (HCR)**. He died on September 19, 1994, at a clinic in Brussels at an age reported to be between 72 and 75 years. **Boboliko Lokonga** was elected president of the PDSC and assumed Ileo's post in the HCR.

IMMATRICULÉS. Congolese who served in the **armed forces**, missions, **industry** and other colonial institutions. Unlike the term *"évolués,"* which carried primarily socio-economic connotations, the *immatriculés* benefited from a legal distinction accorded by the Immatriculation Decree of 1952. The decree gave them the same legal status as Europeans and recognized them as special

Africans whose children would lead future generations of Congolese leaders, eventually to **independence**.

IMPORTS. Congo/Zaire's **economy** historically was based on the **export** of raw materials, first from the **agricultural** sector but after **independence** increasingly from the **mining** industry. A great deal of the country's **foreign exchange** went to import fuel, industrial equipment and consumer goods. International financial institutions often criticized the government's import policies saying the large amount of imported consumable and luxury goods aggravated the **balance-of-payments** deficit and weakened the **currency**. In the early 1980s, 40 percent of Zairian imports were consumable goods, 25 percent were raw materials and semimanu-factured goods, 20 percent were capital goods, and 15 percent were **energy** products. Undeclared imports by the government and state-owned companies during these years often reached 65 percent of the total. Principal imports were food items such as **rice, maize** and wheat; consumer goods; raw and semiprocessed material used in the food and clothing industries; equipment; and spare parts. According to government figures published by the **World Bank**, imports totaled $1.5 billion in 1980, but fell to $850 million in 1982. Following the economic reforms of 1983, they began to rise again, reaching $1.2 billion in 1985 and $1.5 billion in 1990. With the economic crisis of the 1990s, however, imports declined to an estimated $600 million in 1994. In 1991, 72 percent of Zaire's imports were from the **European Union**, 9 percent from North America, 3 percent from sub-Saharan Africa and 16 percent from the rest of world (primarily Asia), according to World Bank figures. Major exporters to Zaire in 1994 were **Belgium**, **South Africa**, **Germany** and Hong Kong. Major sub-Saharan exporters to Zaire were Nigeria, Zimbabwe, Cameroon, **Kenya**, and **Morocco**.

INCOME. Per-capita income in Congo/Zaire averaged $200 per year during the first 20 years after **independence**, although during the austerity policies of 1983-85 and the period of **hyperinflation** of the 1990s, it fell markedly. The minimum **wage** historically has been in the range of $20-40 per month. Professionals generally earn 10 to 20 times the minimum wage. Senior **government** officials earn 25 to 50 times the minimum wage in addition to benefits such as food, housing and entertainment allowances. Economists say the income gap between rich and poor is one of the widest in Africa. Recession and austerity measures during the 1980s seriously eroded standards of living.

The economic crisis of the early 1990s, characterized by annual **inflation** as high as 6,000 percent and the contraction of economic production by nearly 30 percent, drove all but the *élites* into poverty. The minimum wage fell to the equivalent of a few dollars per month. Professionals employed by the state, when paid, received $10-20 per month. At the same time, the removal of most **price controls** meant that workers could not afford a healthy **diet**, much less medicine, **transportation**, and school costs. The situation led many Congolese to supplement their incomes through small trading, second jobs and, in some cases, graft and **corruption**. Many depended on family gardens and foraging expeditions into the countryside for their food.

INDEPENDENCE. The **Belgian Congo** became independent on **June 30, 1960,** after a century of European dominance and after a brief transitional period that saw the emergence of more than 100 **political parties** based primarily on **region** and **ethnic group** and national **elections** that failed to give a clear mandate to any one party or coalition. At the time, it was said that the most progressive colonial administrators envisioned independence in 1990 at the earliest. Lack of preparation, the sudden removal of restrictions on political activities after decades of repression, and a splintered political structure resulting from interethnic and regional tensions led to the rapid erosion of central authority. The secessions and **rebellions** that followed were partly responsible for the military **coup d'etat** of 1965 that led to the single-party state. Africanists note that many African nations experienced peaceful and orderly transitions to independence, but few had such large and remote territories, such diverse **populations**, and so little time to forge them into a nation as did the Congo. *See also* Constitution.

INDUSTRY. The **manufacturing** sector historically accounts for 10 percent or less of total **gross domestic product (GDP)**, most of it concentrated in the **Kinshasa**, **Katanga**, and **Bas-Congo** provinces. The sector primarily produces goods for local consumption, including processed foods, textiles, beer and tobacco products.

In the 1970s, efforts to launch heavier industries such as metallurgy, auto assembly and tire manufacturing were made. Despite substantial investment, however, these never produced at more than 30 percent of capacity because of weak markets, heavy **government** controls, poor **transportation** networks and a lack of **foreign exchange** for fuel and spare parts. By the mid-1980s, most factories were producing at an estimated 10 percent of capacity and many **foreign investors** had sold out. During the **pillages** of 1991 and 1993, many plants were stripped bare and closed for a number of years. Some in consumer-oriented industries reopened relatively quickly, but continuing political uncertainties slowed the capital investment needed for solid revival. As a result, industrial contribution to GDP was negligible in the mid-1990s.

Small-scale companies, frequently in the informal sector and usually employing less than one dozen workers, continue to operate, however, making clothes, furniture, jewelry and crafts. However, these are frequently subjected to extortion by **security** forces and attacks by bandits. *See also* Cement; Cloth; Nationalization; Privatization; Retrocession; Steel; Zairianization.

INFLATION. Inflation was kept to moderate levels during the **colonial era** and the early years of **independence**. However, it began to grow in the mid-1960s, reaching 40 percent in 1973. With the jump in **petroleum** prices in the mid- and late 1970s, inflation rose to 60 percent in 1976 and reached 100 percent in 1983. Subsequent austerity measures reduced it to 50 percent in 1984 and to 20 percent in 1985. However, it began to rise again in the late 1980s. In 1990, political uncertainty caused by the **democratic transition** and the **government**'s practice of printing banknotes to pay **wages**, sent inflation soaring. It reached 81 percent in 1990, 2,154 percent in 1991, 4,130 percent in 1992, 2,000 percent in 1993, and 6,000 percent in 1994. For several months in 1994, annualized inflation was 12,000 percent. Inflation was reduced to 600 percent in 1995 and 1,000 percent in 1996. It has remained a constant complication in business planning and transactions and has led many companies and traders to transact business in US dollars. *See also* Currency; Economy; Hyperinflation.

INFORMAL ECONOMY. *See* ECONOMY.

INGA HYDROELECTRIC COMPLEX. Congo/Zaire's major hydroelectric complex, named after a nearby village, located on the **Congo River** 40 km upriver from **Matadi**. The complex is located on a stretch of the river that falls 100 meters in less than 2 km, creating 50,000 megawatts (MW) of hydroelectric potential. A bend in the river allows for construction of dams in stages without diverting the river. Studies for an **electrical power** plant were made in the 1950s, but work was not begun until 1968. The first phase of the complex, called Inga I and containing six turbines generating 58 MW each, was completed in 1972. Inga II, containing eight turbines generating 175 MW each, was completed in 1982 with participation by US, West German, French and Italian companies. Construction of Inga III is not envisioned in the near future, since a great deal of the 1,750 MW capacity of the first two phases is still not being used. Construction of the **Inga-Shaba power line** allowed the transmission of up to 560 MW to **Shaba** beginning in 1983. The potential of the complex continues to attract the attention of economic planners and in the 1990s **Egypt** and the Southern Africa Development Community (SADEC) funded studies of projects to exploit the energy from Inga.

INGA-SHABA POWER LINE. One of the world's longest, direct-current, high-tension power transmission lines, the Inga-Shaba Power Line was capable of carrying up to 560 megawatts (MW) of direct current across 1,750 km of Congolese savanna, **mountain** and **rainforest** from the **Inga hydroelectric complex**, near **Matadi**, to southeastern **Katanga Province**, where it ties into a grid powering the region's **mining** installations. The line was built at a cost of $1 billion between 1973 and 1983. Construction was hindered by logistical problems, a lack of infrastructure, two rebel attacks in **Shaba**, and considerable cost overruns. Its two lines, each with three strands of wire, required the construction of 8,500 steel pylons, 8,000 km of permanent and temporary roads, and 2,000 permanent and temporary bridges. It also required the construction of special railroad cars and **river barges** to transport material and, at its peak, a fleet of six planes and two helicopters. Built by the Idaho-based Morrison-Knudsen company with large portions of work contracted to French and Italian companies, the line was completed in July 1983 and inaugurated by **Mobutu** on November 24.

The project was criticized from the beginning as costly and unnecessary, since studies had revealed that the shortage of **electrical power** in Shaba could be resolved by construction of several medium-sized hydroelectric plants on local rivers. The project was also criticized because initially it did not provide electricity to any areas along the way.

By the mid-1990s, lack of maintenance and a shortage of **foreign exchange** for spare parts had taken its toll on the line and it was reported on a number of occasions to be out of commission. When it was functioning, it transmitted power at one-fourth of capacity. Nevertheless, the potential exists for better utilization of the line. The Southern Africa Development Community (SADEC) announced in 1995 it would include Zaire in plans to develop a region-wide electrical grid in southern Africa. A study was also made to construct a 500-MW power transmission line from Shaba 5,400 km to Aswan, **Egypt**. And the Zairian government was seeking financing to build converter stations along the line to provide electrical power to cities in **Bandundu** and the **Kasai provinces**.

INSTITUTE FOR BANTU STUDIES. Proposed by Gabon's Omar Bongo and supported by **Mobutu**, the Institute was founded for the study and dissemination of knowledge about **Bantu** culture. Headquartered in Libreville, Gabon, the institute was inaugurated in 1984.

INTELLIGENCE SERVICES. Under **Mobutu**, the **government** operated a number of intelligence services. The primary national **security** service was called the **Service National d'Intelligence et de Protection (SNIP)** until 1997 when following the fall of Mobutu, the government of Laurent **Kabila** renamed it the **Agence Nationale de Renseignements (ANR)**. Called the Sûreté Nationale at **independence**, the service was renamed the Centre National de Documentation (CND) in 1969 and the **Agence**

Nationale de Documentation (AND) in the early 1980s. It reported directly to the **president**. Military intelligence was furnished by the **Service d'Action et de Renseignements Militaire (SARM)**. The Agence Nationale d'Immigration (ANI) was responsible for border security. The **Civil Guard** and **Gendarmerie Nationale** also had intelligence units. A shadowy unit called *"Les Hiboux"* ("The Owls"), reportedly related to the military, appeared in 1990 and engaged in kidnappings and terrorist acts against the **opposition**.

INTERNATIONAL AFRICAN ASSOCIATION (IAA). A European organization created in 1876 ostensibly to encourage the exploration of Africa and to seek the abolition of **slavery**. **Leopold II** made his move into central Africa as president of the IAA from 1876 to 1880. During that time, he founded the **Committee for the Study of the Upper Congo** (Comité d'Études pour le Haut-Congo) and hired Henry Morton **Stanley** to explore the **Congo River**. The committee became the **International Association of the Congo** one year later and its work, combined with Stanley's explorations, led the European powers to grant Leopold II sovereignty over the Congo at the **Berlin Conference** in 1885.

INTERNATIONAL ASSOCIATION OF THE CONGO (IAC) / ASSOCIATION INTERNATIONALE DU CONGO. Association established by **Leopold II** in 1877 as an outgrowth of the **Committee for the Study of the Upper Congo** to explore the **Congo River Basin** and encourage **trade** and the "civilization" of the indigenous people in the area. The association was recognized by the **United States** government and subsequently by 13 European nations which partitioned Africa at the **Berlin Conference** in February 1885. The association adopted its own flag but was disbanded shortly thereafter to allow the formation of the **Congo Free State**. According to historians, the association met only once in its brief history.

INTERNATIONAL BANK FOR RECONSTRUCTION AND DEVELOPMENT (IBRD). *See* WORLD BANK.

INTERNATIONAL DEVELOPMENT ASSOCIATION (IDA). An affiliate of the **World Bank,** which specializes in granting "soft" loans to the world's least-developed nations. The IDA grants loans at near-zero interest rates, with long grace periods and long repayment schedules for projects such as a $9 million program in Zaire in 1978 to rehabilitate **plantations** that deteriorated following **Zairianization.**

INTERNATIONAL MEMBERSHIPS. Congo/Zaire is a member of the **United Nations** and most of its agencies, the **Organization of African Unity (OAU),** the Non-Aligned Movement, the **Union Douanière et Économique de l'Afrique Central (UDEAC),** the **Communauté Économique des Pays des Grands Lacs (CEPGL),** and the **African Development Bank (ADB).** In 1984, Zaire and nine other central African nations signed an agreement in Libreville, Gabon, forming the **Economic Community of Central African States (ECOCAS),** which was aimed at harmonizing customs, tariffs and visa policies and ultimately at establishing a common market in the region. Zaire signed the **Lomé Conventions** providing for greater **trade** and economic cooperation between the **European Union** and more than 70 developing nations of Africa, the Caribbean and the Pacific. It also regularly participates in the annual France-African summit meetings. *See also* International Development Association (IDA); International Monetary Fund (IMF); World Bank.

INTERNATIONAL MONETARY FUND (IMF). The sister institution of the **World Bank** formed at Bretton Woods, New Hampshire, in 1948. Originally designed to help stabilize the European economies following World War II, the IMF increasingly was called upon to assist governments with cash liquidity problems, in particular following the leap in oil prices of the 1970s. In exchange for the implementation of economic stabilization programs which usually includes severe austerity measures, the IMF provides infusions of hard currency to governments needing new capital or experiencing problems repaying their foreign **debts.**

Zaire negotiated more than one dozen agreements with the IMF after its debt crisis began in 1975. The programs began as relatively modest "standbys," or loans, of $150 million over one year's time to the record (at that time) $1.1 billion standby over three years accorded in 1981. Initially, Zaire was unable to meet the programs' targets, which included budget cuts, **currency** devaluations and regular payments to the IMF. In 1983, Zaire met most of the targets of the current stabilization plan, including floating its currency on the free market and removing subsidies on **petroleum** and **agricultural** products. However, on October 29, 1986, the government announced that certain international organizations were "strangling" the **economy** and creating severe human suffering. As a result, the government said it would limit foreign debt repayments to 10 percent of **export** revenues.

Several agreements with the IMF were negotiated in subsequent years, but the government failed to meet their targets and by the late 1980s had virtually ceased to service its debt to the fund. In 1992, the IMF issued a "Declaration of Non-Compliance," ending any further disbursements to Zaire and effectively expelling it from the organization. *See also* London Club.

ISLAM. Although eastern Congo experienced considerable Islamic influence during the 18th and 19th centuries, spread by Arab and eastern African traders, Islam never became entrenched in Congo as it did in East and West Africa. Muslims are estimated to compose just 1-2 percent of the **population**. Congolese are free to espouse any belief and there is no known repression of Muslims because of their religion. *See also* Afro-Arabs.

ISRAEL, RELATIONS WITH. In the early years of the **Mobutu** government, relations with Israel were friendly and Israeli advisors helped train Zaire's **armed forces**. In the early 1970s, Mobutu even made some attempts to mediate the Middle East dispute. On October 4, 1973, however, following the Yom Kippur War and the Arab oil embargo, Mobutu announced before the **United Nations** General Assembly that Zaire was breaking off diplomatic relations with Israel because of its occupation of the Sinai Peninsula, which belonged to **Egypt**, a member of the **Organization of African Unity (OAU)**. All African nations except Lesotho, Malawi, Swaziland and apartheid-ruled **South Africa**, followed his lead. Zaire's relations with Israel, however, remained strong though clandestine, and Israeli products frequently were seen on the shelves of Zairian stores during the period.

On May 13, 1982, the Zairian government announced the reestablishment of relations, saying Israel had returned the Sinai to Egypt as called for in the Camp David accords and, as a result, Africa's quarrel with Israel had ended. Certain internal pressures were also at work. Mobutu hoped to benefit from Israeli military training once again and make use of the Jewish lobby in the **United States** before the US Congress, which had cut **foreign aid**. The massacre of Palestinians at the refugee camps of Chabra and Shattila that year, reportedly by Israeli-backed Southern Lebanese Christian militia, embarrassed the Zairian government. Mobutu said Zaire would not accept military equipment captured from the Palestine Liberation Organization and it was not until August 1983 that a second African nation, Liberia, reestablished relations with Israel. Zaire received military assistance from Israel in the 1980s and 1990s, primarily training for the **Division Spéciale Présidentielle (DSP)** and Mobutu's personal guard. Israeli advisors are also said to have aided in training Zairian **security** services. A number of private Israeli businessmen invested in various enterprises in Zaire, most notably **transportation** and **diamond** marketing.

ITALY, RELATIONS WITH. Italy has been a significant trading partner of Congo/Zaire. The Italian government also has helped train Congolese **armed forces**, particularly the **air force**. An Italian **petroleum** company engaged in a joint offshore oil exploration venture. Another company participated in the **Société Congo-Italienne de Raffinage (SOCIR)** oil refinery near Moanda. An Italian contractor helped build the **Inga-Shaba power line** and an Italian company held part interest in the iron and **steel** works at **Maluku**.

ITURI DISTRICT. One of five districts of **Orientale Province**, the Ituri district covers 65,658 square km of territory bordering **Uganda**. With an estimated population of 2.3 million in 1995 (1,673,727 in 1982), it is the most populated administrative subdivision of the province. It also is one of the most remote and least developed areas of the country.

ITURI FOREST. The Ituri **Forest** is one of the most dense and least explored tropical **rainforests** in the world. It is named after the Ituri River which flows westward from the border with **Uganda**, north of **Lake Albert** to join the **Congo River** below **Kisangani**. The Ituri Forest covers most of the northeastern corner of **Congo/Zaire** and is inhabited by **Bantu**, **Pygmy**, Nilotic and Sudanic peoples. Ranging from the highlands below the **Ruwenzori Mountains** along the Ugandan border to the swampy lowlands of the **Congo River Basin**, the Ituri is rich in **timber**, **gold** and **fish** and reportedly contains unexploited deposits of iron ore.

IVORY. The highly valued tusks of the **elephant** were one of the riches that drew foreign traders to Congo/Zaire as early as the 16th century. Although the ivory trade was banned by international convention in the 1990s, **smuggling** continues. There are no official estimates of ivory production.

- J -

JAGA. A group of warriors of unknown origin who invaded the **Kongo Kingdom** from the east in the 1560s. Some historians believe the Jaga were distant Kongo people opposed to the Kongo **king** who perhaps were joined by non-Kongo peoples in an effort to take over the coastal **slave** trade. Others believe that theory may have been a European myth. The Jaga were driven away with Portuguese help in 1573 and the debt owed by the Kongo contributed to the increased slave trade with **Portugal**.

JAMAA. A Swahili word meaning "family," Jamaa was the name of a religious movement established in 1953 in **Katanga** by the Belgian Franciscan priest Placide Tempels. The movement combined African mysticism and **spiritualism** with Catholicism and some of the priest's own thoughts. Doctrine stemmed in part from African roots, although the movement reportedly opposed sorcery and instead emphasized emotionality and mystical experiences. It also downplayed the importance of hierarchy and academia. The movement was always linked to the **Catholic Church**, but many church leaders became wary of it. Tempels was ordered back to **Belgium** in 1962 and obliged to break his ties with his followers.

JANSSENS, ÉMILE. The commander of the **Force Publique** at **independence** who according to legend sparked the mutiny of the Force on July 5, 1960, by responding to soldiers unhappy over low salaries and the lack of Congolese officers that "After Independence = Before Independence," writing it in the form of a mathematical equation on a blackboard. The mutiny that followed spread to **Leopoldville** and other regional capitals and brought the first deployment of Belgian troops in Congolese history. The mutiny also brought the departure of Janssens and the other Belgian officers and the appointment of a Congolese officer corps that within weeks would face interethnic violence and several **rebellions**.

JANUARY 4, 1959. The date on which the popular movement for Congolese **independence** was launched. On a Sunday, following a fiery rally by Patrice **Lumumba**, recently returned from Europe, the **Alliance des Bakongo (ABAKO)** party had scheduled a pro-independence rally in **Leopoldville** at which Joseph **Kasavubu** was to speak. The colonial authorities, fearing such a gathering would lead to violence, banned the rally and detained Kasavubu. The move sparked two weeks of civil unrest that led to the imposition of emergency **police** measures and clashes in which scores of people were killed. After order was reestablished, colonial authorities opened negotiations which led to the **Round Table Conferences** during which Congolese delegates demanded immediate and complete independence and the date was set for **June 30, 1960**.

JAPAN, RELATIONS WITH. Relations between **Congo/Zaire** and Japan are based primarily on commercial ties which grew steadily during the 1970s and 1980s, then waned in the 1990s. **Trade** was virtually nonexistent after **independence** but, by the early 1980s, Japan had become a major supplier of Zairian **imports** such as automobiles, trucks, appliances and electronic equipment. Japan imported some **minerals** and **timber** from Zaire, but enjoyed a large trade surplus. The Japanese carried out a modest bilateral **development program**, building the suspension bridge over the

Congo River at Matadi in 1982-83 and assisting in the rehabilitation of roads and bridges in Bas-Zaïre and Bandundu provinces. On the commercial front, a Japanese company participated in a mining consortium in Shaba and a company called Japan Petroleum Zaïre was involved in a consortium operating offshore oil wells near the mouth of the Congo River.

JEUNESSE DU MOUVEMENT POPULAIRE DE LA RÉVOLUTION (JMPR) / YOUTH OF THE POPULAR REVOLUTIONARY MOVEMENT. The youth wing of the Mouvement Populaire de la Révolution (MPR), Zaire's sole legal political party from 1967 to 1990. Under the party-state system, all Zairians were automatically members of the JMPR from birth until they reached the age of 30 years, at which time they automatically became members of the MPR. The JMPR was made the sole youth organization by decree in 1968. Other youth-oriented organizations such as the YMCA, scouting, and church groups were banned and their assets taken over by the JMPR. The monopoly of the JMPR over the country's youth was ended with the abolition of the MPR as the sole legal party in 1990. The Conférence Nationale Souveraine (CNS) in 1992 returned many properties to their former owners.

JOHN PAUL II (POPE) (1920 -). Pope John Paul II visited Zaire in May 1980, the first pontiff ever to do so. The visit officially ended eight years of strained relations between the Roman Catholic Church and the Zairian government which were caused primarily by the Authenticity policies of the 1970s. Mobutu, a widower, married for the second time shortly before the visit and asked for a papal blessing of the union. The pope reportedly was dismayed by the degree to which he found African traditions had been incorporated into church liturgy and litany. However, Zaire statistically was home to the largest Catholic population in Africa and both sides appeared anxious to make the visit a success. The pope visited a second time in August 1985 and beatified a Congolese nun who was killed by Simba rebels during the eastern rebellions in the mid-1960s.

JUDICIAL SYSTEM. During the colonial era, two judicial systems existed. The first applied written law primarily to Europeans, but on occasion to Congolese. The second applied oral **customary law**, as practiced by traditional **ethnic groups**, to Africans only. Under the system, the findings of each court were subject to review by the next higher court of a five-tier system. In 1958, a decree attempted to end distinctions between the systems.

After **independence**, the judicial system virtually collapsed because of the departure of expatriate judges and professionals following the civic unrest. The **United Nations** called in jurists from **Egypt**, Syria, Lebanon, Greece and Haiti to preside over courts and act as attorneys. They gradually were replaced by Congolese. Under the **Loi Fondamentale** (Fundamental Law), the judiciary was independent of the **legislative** and executive branches of **government**. The provision was maintained in the **constitution** of 1964 but the **president** was granted the power to appoint all judges. In 1968, a presidential decree restructured the court system under the Code d'Organisation et de Compétence Judiciale, allowing customary law to be valid and relevant as long as it was "compatible with public order." A decree on February 11, 1972, called for reform of the civil code in order to make it more authentically Zairian. The reform was implemented on May 5, 1975. The constitution of 1974 created the **Judiciary Council**, presided over by the president. In theory, magistrates were free and independent, but they were required to be party members and owed their positions to the president.

As Zaire became a party-state and the **Mouvement Populaire de la Révolution (MPR)** became the supreme body of government, the party became the source of legality and the judiciary's role evolved into one of interpreting it. The president of the Supreme Court and the attorney-general were automatically members of the **Political Bureau** of the MPR, and the heads of the regional courts belonged to regional committees of the party. The court system reflected the administrative and political organization of the country and ascended in importance in the following order: urban and rural subregional tribunals; regional tribunals; three tribunals of the first instance (appeals) in **Kinshasa**, **Lubumbashi** and **Kisangani**; and ultimately the Supreme Court of Justice based in Kinshasa. A system of juvenile courts was created by decree in 1987 but never fully implemented.

Although independence of the judiciary is guaranteed by the constitution, jurists said the application of justice could be influenced by the party and certain powerful individuals. Following the political reforms of 1990, some magistrates demonstrated a measure of independence, ruling in several instances against the government and in favor of trade unions and the **opposition**. However, these rulings were usually overturned or circumvented through appeals or other judicial maneuvers. Magistrates staged a lengthy **strike** in 1991 over low pay and a lack of facilities.

JUDICIARY COUNCIL / CONSEIL JUDICIAIRE. A group of senior judges of Zairian courts and the Supreme Court, presided over by the **president**. It was created by the **constitution** of 1974 and designated one of the main organs of **government**. *See also* Judicial System.

JUNE 4, 1969. The date on which a group of **university** and professional school **students** staged a demonstration in **Kinshasa** against the **Mobutu** government, primarily to protest poor living conditions and delays in payment of their stipends. The demonstration degenerated into violence and vandalism. The clashes that followed led to more than 100 deaths and the closing of the schools. Dozens of student leaders were arrested and inducted into the **armed forces**. A group of students and professors formed the Mouvement du 4 Juin (Movement of June 4th) which later evolved into the **Mouvement d'Action pour la Résurrection du Congo (MARC) opposition** group. June 4 became the date for demonstrations in commemoration of those killed in 1969 and marches were held in 1971, 1977, 1981 and 1982. These were also harshly repressed by **security** forces.

JUNE 30, 1960. The day of Congo/Zaire's **independence** on which King **Baudoin** formally handed power to an elected Congolese **government** and ended 52 years of colonialism. June 30 was also the date in 1956 of the publication of the *Conscience Africaine* manifesto demanding greater political freedom for Congolese, and the date of publication in 1982 of a manifesto by former Prime Minister Jean **Nguza Karl-I-Bond** criticizing what he called the political, economic and moral bankruptcy of the **Mobutu** government and calling for free, multiparty **elections**. And on this day in 1995, the **Haut Conseil de la République / Parlement de**

la Transition (HCR/PT) voted to postpone by two years the already delayed multiparty elections and extend to seven years the **democratic transition**.

- K -

KABANGA SONGA SONGA, EUGÈNE (ARCHBISHOP). The archbishop of Lubumbashi who issued one of the first public critiques of **Mobutism**. His pastoral letter in 1976 denounced excesses of the **Authenticity** movement and the moral decline of Zaire's leaders.

KABILA, LAURENT-DÉSIRÉ (1939 -). A left-leaning leader from **Katanga** who supported Patrice **Lumumba** following **independence**, opposed the **Mobutu** government from remote guerrilla camps in the east, and became the country's third **president** on May 29, 1997, after a seven-month military offensive. Kabila was born on November 11, 1939, in Jadotville (now **Likasi**) in southern Katanga Province. He received his basic **education** locally and later studied in **France** and East **Germany**.

Kabila was an early member of the **Association des Baluba du Katanga (BALUBAKAT)** party. He joined Lumumba's **Mouvement National Congolais (MNC)** at independence and participated in the **Stanleyville**-based government of Antoine **Gizenga** during the eastern **rebellions**. However, he quarreled with Gizenga and, in 1964, left to form the **Parti Révolutionaire du Peuple (PRP)**, based in the **Lake Tanganyika** area. Kabila received military training in the People's Republic of **China** during the 1960s and at various times was reported to be living in **Tanzania**, **Uganda** and Europe. Ernesto "Che" **Guevara** worked with the Kabila forces for several months in the mid-1960s but left, criticizing the guerrillas as ineffectual and their leadership as interested primarily in living a comfortable life outside the country.

Although the PRP was small and relatively unknown, it retained control over a remote area west of the **Mitumba Mountains** throughout the Mobutu era. In 1984 and 1985, the PRP seized the **port** town of **Moba** on Lake Tanganyika, but was driven out or left after a few days by a government counteroffensive.

On October 18, 1996, the PRP joined with three other parties to form the **Alliance des Forces Démocratiques pour la Libération du Congo/Zaïre (AFDL)**, whose troops, reportedly backed by **Rwanda, Burundi,** Uganda and **Angola,** launched an offensive. Initially, Kabila was the spokesman of the AFDL, but he rapidly emerged as its president and most visible representative. The AFDL forces moved quickly, seizing **Bukavu, Goma, Kisangani, Mbuji-Mayi, Lubumbashi** and **Kikwit** by April 1997. **South African** President Nelson Mandela hosted two rounds of talks between Mobutu and Kabila as the AFDL troops closed in on **Kinshasa,** but these were overtaken by events. Mobutu left the capital on May 16, 1997, and the AFDL forces entered the following day. Kabila was sworn in as president and announced national **elections** would be held in 1999. He failed to obtain the support, however, of major Congolese **opposition** leaders, in particular Étienne **Tshisekedi,** and as a result formed a government composed of young technocrats, including the daughters of Lumumba and former President Joseph **Kasavubu.**

Kabila sought to project the image of a moderate, but his early sympathies with Lumumba and the leaders of the eastern **rebellions** surfaced on occasion. He visited Beijing in late 1997 and upon his return announced that China would serve as a model for Congolese development. He delivered a speech to the nation on the anniversary of the death of Lumumba, saying his government knew who Lumumba's assassins were and urging them to come forward to accept the nation's forgiveness.

Kabila was criticized by opposition leaders as heading a government controlled by neighboring countries. He was also attacked by **human rights** organizations for banning political demonstrations and for obstructing a **United Nations** investigation into alleged massacres of Rwandan **refugees** during the AFDL offensive. Kabila's critics called him an opportunist who was named leader of the AFDL because he was one of the few opposition leaders who was never co-opted by Mobutu.

Kabila's greatest challenges were to consolidate control over the vast territory and enact political and economic reforms, while addressing rivalries among the various factions in the alliance that brought him to power. In western Congo and particularly in

Kinshasa, he was viewed a puppet of the Ugandan and Rwandan governments. Nevertheless, many Congolese initially said they were prepared to give him a chance, especially since there was little alternative, given the military strength of AFDL and the moral bankruptcy of most of the Kinshasa-based opposition.

Within months, however, Kabila found himself increasingly at odds with Rwandan army officers, who had been the core leadership of the AFDL, and with **Banyamulenge** who had provided important initial support. These elements increasingly were resented by the local population, which considered them to be a foreign occupation force. In July 1998, Kabila announced the Rwandan officers had accomplished their mission and were returning home. The following week, a group of them, including Foreign Minister Bizima **Karaha**, announced an offensive to overthrow the Kabila government, which they said had become corrupt and authoritarian.

KAKUDJI, GAETAN. A cousin and close advisor to Laurent **Kabila** and a senior officer in the **Alliance des Forces Démocratiques pour la Libération du Congo/Zaïre (AFDL)**, which took power in May 1997. Kakudji was a spokesman for Kabila's **Parti Revolutionnaire du Peuple (PRP)** and was named governor of **Katanga** after the AFDL took **Lubumbashi** on April 9, 1997. He became interior minister in the cabinet of January 3, 1998.

KALALA ILUNGA. According to legend, Kalala Ilunga was one of the early kings of the **Luba** empire. A nephew of **Kongolo**, he led the Balopwe into the **Kasai** area around 1500 and by 1550 controlled a large portion of territory. His relative, **Kibinda Ilunga**, in 1600 moved away to found what was to become the **Lunda** empire.

KALEMIE. A town in northern **Katanga Province** lying on **Lake Tanganyika**. Kalemie was linked to Katanga and the **Kasai**s by the Chemin de Fer des Grands Lacs (CFL) railway which joined the Chemin de Fer Kinshasa-Dilolo-Lubumbashi (KDL) system at **Kamina**. Some **coal** deposits are located near the town. Major industries include a **cement** plant and textile factories. Kalemie's **port** made it a center for trade across the Lake with **Tanzania** and **Burundi** and a small naval base supports lake patrols by the **navy** and border officials. The CFL deteriorated in the 1980s, but was refurbished in the mid-1990s by a consortium of **Belgian** and **South African** companies called **Sizarail**.

KALONJI DITUNGA, ALBERT (1927 -). An early **independence** leader and president of the secessionist Independent Mining State of **South Kasai** from 1960 to 1961. Kalonji was born June 6, 1927, at Kemotinne, in **Kasai Province**. He was educated by the Scheut Father **missionaries** and attended the Centre Agronomique de Louvain in **Belgium**. In 1949, he was named director of the Institut National pour l'Étude Agronomique du Congo (INEAC). He helped found the **Mouvement National Congolais (MNC)** party in 1956 but, unhappy with the rise of Patrice **Lumumba** in the hierarchy, broke away in July 1959 with several moderate leaders to form a rival group that came to be known as MNC/Kalonji.

At independence, his group allied with Moïse **Tshombe** to form the main **opposition** block in **parliament**. Amidst the collapse of central authority at independence, Kalonji declared South Kasai an independent state and proclaimed himself *mulopwe* or **king**. The secession was ended in 1961, and Kalonji was stripped of his parliamentary functions and found guilty of sedition. He went into exile in Spain in January 1963 but returned in 1964 to serve as minister of agriculture in the Tshombe government. He joined Tshombe's **Confédération Nationale des Associations Congolaises (CONACO)** party and was elected to the Senate in 1965. Following the **Mobutu coup d'etat**, Kalonji abandoned national politics.

KALONJI MUTAMBAYI, ISAAC (1915 -). The first chairman of the **National Conference** and one of the few Congolese politicians to serve in **government** without interruption from **independence** until the **democratic transition**. Kalonji was born on September 9, 1915, at Lusambo in **Kasai** Province. He was educated by Protestant **missionaries** and became an administrator at the École Moyenne de Luebo. He moved to **Elisabethville**, where he became a member of the Conseil de Centre d'Élisabethville and president of the Association des Classes Moyennes du Katanga, two associations of Congolese businessmen and professionals that became cells for political activity prior to independence.

At independence he was elected to the senate and made state commissioner for Kasai in the Patrice **Lumumba** government. He was elected vice president of the senate in 1961 and president of the senate in the Moïse **Tshombe** government. He was a member of the **Legislative Council** until 1982 and a member of the **Central Committee** of the **Mouvement Populaire de la Révolution (MPR)** party until the announcement of the democratic transition. When the National Conference convened in August 1991, Kalonji was elected chairman. Faced with the chaos caused by some 8,000 pretenders to the 2,800 seats in the conference, he organized committees to adjudicate competing claims and select the delegates. Following the **pillages** of September 1991 and under pressure from both pro-**Mobutu** and **opposition** groups, he resigned September 30 and retired from politics.

KAMANDA WA KAMANDA, GÉRARD (1940 -). A lawyer and diplomat who was **Congo/Zaire**'s first senior official in the secretariat of the **Organization of African Unity (OAU)**. Kamanda was born December 10, 1940, in **Kikwit, Bandundu Province**. While a **student** at **Lovanium University** in the 1960s, he was an officer of the Union Générale des Étudiants Congolais, one of the leading student organizations. After receiving his law degree, he served on the **Kinshasa** Court of Appeals, as a professor of law at the Institut National d'Études Politiques (INEP) and as legal counsel to the **president**. He was named assistant secretary-general of the OAU in 1972 and Zaire's ambassador to the **United Nations** in 1981. He served as foreign minister on several occasions during the 1980s and, on January 3, 1983, was named to the **Central Committee** of the **Mouvement Populaire de la Révolution (MPR)**.

With the end of the single-party era in 1990, Kamanda formed an **opposition political party**, the Front Commun des Nationalistes (FCN), joined the **Sacred Union**, and was transportation minister in the Étienne **Tshisekedi** government of 1992. He was expelled from the Sacred Union in 1994 when he joined the **Kengo wa Dondo** government as justice minister. Kamanda subsequently was made interior minister with the rank of deputy prime minister and, in 1994-95, was the major government mediator in the **Rwandan refugee** crisis in eastern Zaire. He was named foreign affairs minister in the cabinet reshuffle of December 24, 1996. When the **Mobutu** government was deposed on May 17, 1997, Kamanda fled the country and from exile announced the formation of a resistance movement, the Conseil National de la Résistance (CNR).

KAMANYOLA DIVISION. Named for a battle during the Congo **rebellions** in which hundreds of army soldiers were killed, the Kamanyola Division (originally called Kamanyola Brigade) was one of the most prestigious divisions of the Zairian **armed forces**. Trained by North Koreans, it participated in the operation to retake **Kolwezi** during the second **Shaba** War. The division was assigned "permanently" to the region following the war, although units were sent to bolster allies such as Hissen Habre during the civil war in **Chad** in 1983 and Juvenal Habyarimana during the **Rwandan** civil war in 1990.

KAMINA. A small city in northern **Katanga Province** lying on the **railway** linking **Lubumbashi** to the **Kasai River port** of **Ilebo**. Kamina is also a junction for the railway linking the towns of **Kalemie** and **Kindu** in **Kivu** to **transportation** networks in Katanga and Kasai. A large air base located nearby was used for military operations during the **Shaba** Wars. During the 1980s, the base was used to transship US **military assistance** to **Angolan** rebels of the **União Nacional para a Independência Total de Angola (UNITA)**. *See also* National Way.

KAMITATU MASSAMBA, CLÉOPHAS (1931 -). An early **independence** leader who was one of the founders of the **Parti Solidaire Africain (PSA)**, which participated in the first Congolese **governments**. Kamitatu was born in June 1931 in Kilamba and educated by the Jesuits. He lead the PSA delegation to the **Round Table Conferences** and was elected a deputy to **parliament** in June 1960. He was interior minister and subsequently planning and development minister in the governments of Cyrille **Adoula** of 1962-64, and he was foreign minister in the Évariste **Kimba** government which was overthrown by the **Mobutu coup d'etat** in 1965. Following the coup, Kamitatu went into exile where he organized the **Front Socialiste Africain** (FSA) **opposition** group and wrote a highly critical biography of Mobutu. He later accepted Mobutu's offer of amnesty and returned to Zaire. He was turned down as a candidate in the 1977 legislative **elections**, but eventually returned to government as minister of **agriculture** in the 1980s and was appointed to the **Central Committee**. With the advent of the **democratic transition**, Kamitatu became a senior official of the **Parti Démocrate et Social Chrétien (PDSC)** led by Joseph **Ileo**, but had a falling out with the central leadership after Ileo's death and in 1995 formed a splinter wing.

KANANGA. The capital of **Kasaï Occidental Province**, Kananga is an administrative urban district with an area of 378 square km and an estimated **population** of more than one million, up from 492,156 in 1982, the date of the last official census. From the **colonial era**, Kananga (then called **Luluabourg**) was the administrative, political, economic and educational center of **Kasai** Province. Its influence began to wane, however, with the creation of the **Kasaï Oriental region** in 1966 and the gradual transfer beginning in the 1970s of **diamond** marketing operations to **Mbuji-Mayi** (formerly Bakwanga). By the 1980s, its infrastructure had decayed severely and Kananga was experiencing a severe recession. Efforts were made in the late 1980s to resolve some of the problems. The installation of a switching station along the **Inga-Shaba power line** brought an infusion of capital and some jobs. Kananga remains an important administrative, **transportation** and milling center in the region.

KANDE, DZAMBULATE (1930 -   ). Journalist and **government** official who headed the Congolese Press Agency in 1964 when the **United Nations** ended its operation in Congo. Kande was born April 23, 1930, in **Kinshasa** and studied at **Lubumbashi**, in Prague and at the École Supérieure de Journalisme de Paris in the 1950s and 1960s. He served as information minister in the Léonard **Mulamba** government formed after the **Mobutu coup d'etat** and in several other subsequent governments.

KANIOKA. One of three clusters of the **Luba-Katanga ethnic group** delineated by Jan Vansina, living in the northwestern region of **Katanga** and southern **Kasaï Oriental Province**.

KANYONGA MOBATELI. Secretary-General of the **Mouvement d'Action pour la Résurrection du Congo (MARC)** who, along with 18 others, was tried in absentia and received the death sentence in 1978 for conspiring to overthrow the **government**. He reportedly died shortly thereafter in a gun accident.

KANZA, DANIEL. Known as "Buta Kanza" (meaning "old man" or "elder" in Kikongo), Kanza was the head of a political family from **Bas-Congo Province**. He was vice president of the **Alliance des Bakongo (ABAKO)** party and a member of its delegation to the **Round Table Conferences** in 1960. He served as mayor of **Leopoldville** from 1960 to June 1962. He was father of Thomas **Kanza**, a prominent political figure in the early 1960s and again in the 1990s.

KANZA, THOMAS. A diplomat, intellectual and reportedly the first Congolese to receive a **university** degree, Thomas Kanza, son of **Daniel Kanza**, served as ambassador to the **United Nations** with ministerial rank in the Patrice **Lumumba** and Joseph **Ileo governments** in the early 1960s, when the debate over the UN intervention in Congo was at its height. He was appointed ambassador to London in the Cyrille **Adoula** government, but resigned and joined the **Stanleyville** government during the eastern secession. He served as its foreign representative from September 1964 to 1966, when he went into exile in London. Disillusioned with Congolese **politics**, Kanza wrote a number of books that bitterly questioned the future of the Congolese state.

Kanza returned to Zaire for the first time following the general **amnesty of 1983**. During the **democratic transition**, he reestablished his family's political base in **Bas-Zaïre**. He ran unsuccessfully as the pro-**Mobutu** candidate against **opposition** candidate Étienne **Tshisekedi**, when the **Conférence Nationale Souveraine (CNS)** chose the **prime minister** for the transitional government in 1992. During subsequent years Kanza frequently sided with pro-Mobutu forces. After the fall of Mobutu, He was named minister of international cooperation in the first Laurent **Kabila** government of June 1997.

KAONDE. *See* KUNDA.

KARAHA, BIZIMA (1968 -   ). Foreign minister in the early **governments** of Laurent **Kabila**, Karaha was a **Banyamulenge** from eastern Congo who spent much of his youth abroad. He was practicing medicine in **South Africa** when named to the government. In August 1998, Karaha broke with Kabila and joined rebels of the **Rassemblement Congolais pour la Démocratie (RCD)**.

KASAI. Originally one of six colonial **provinces**, Kasai was the second richest in **minerals** after **Katanga** and at its peak in the 1960s and 1970s produced two-thirds of the non-Communist world's industrial **diamonds**. Kasai also had the highest per-capita **income** after **Kinshasa** and Katanga. On August 8, 1960, under the leadership of Albert **Kalonji**, the southern portion of Kasai seceded and proclaimed itself the Independent Mining State of South Kasai. Kalonji ended the secession in 1961 and joined the central **government**, but not before a violent interethnic war between the **Luba** and **Lulua** caused thousands of deaths, the destruction of millions of dollars worth of property, and widespread famine in the region. South Kasai was represented when **parliament** reopened on July 25, 1961, at **Lovanium University** under **United Nations** protection. Partly because of tensions between the Luba and Lulua, Kasai on December 24, 1966, was divided into two provinces, **Kasaï Occidental** and **Kasaï Oriental**.

KASAÏ OCCIDENTAL PROVINCE / WEST KASAI PROVINCE. Kasaï Occidental is a province dominated by the **Lulua** and **Kete** **ethnic groups** with an estimated **population** of four million people (2,933,528 in 1982) and an area of 156,967 square km. It represents roughly half of the former **Kasai province** which was partitioned into Kasaï Occidental and **Kasaï Oriental** in 1966. The capital of the province is **Kananga** with an estimated population of one million (492,156 in 1982). The province is divided into the urban district of Kananga and the two rural districts of Kasaï and Lulua. Primary economic activity includes **transportation**, (primarily subsistence) **agriculture**, iron-ore **mining** and some of the **diamond** trade. Like many of the more-remote **provinces**, Kasaï Occidental suffered from recession and a severe deterioration of its infrastructure in the 1980s. The

National Way transportation route, by which a large portion of Congolese **minerals** are exported, crosses both Kasais, by **rail** from **Kamina** to **Ilebo** and by riverboat from Ilebo to **Kinshasa.**

KASAÏ ORIENTAL PROVINCE / EAST KASAI PROVINCE. Kasaï Oriental, with **Mbuji-Mayi** (formerly Bakwanga) as its capital, had an estimated **population** of 3.3 million people in 1995 (2,335,951 in the 1982 census) and an area of 168,216 square km. It represents roughly half of the former **Kasai province**, which was partitioned into Kasaï Oriental and **Kasaï Occidental** in 1966. Kasaï Oriental is the **Luba**-dominated province, divided into the urban district of Mbuji-Mayi and three rural districts of Kabinda, Sankuru and Tshilenge. Mbuji-Mayi, estimated population 800,000 (334,875 in 1982), was a major **diamond** trading center and had considerable banking and commercial services related primarily to the diamond industry. In the 1990s, diamonds smuggled by Angolan rebels from the diamond-rich area of northwestern **Angola,** were marketed through Kasaï Oriental in exchange for arms.

KASAI RIVER. **Congo/Zaire**'s second major **river transportation** route after the **Congo River,** the Kasai River rises from headwaters in eastern **Angola** and flows some 600 km east to **Dilolo** in **Katanga,** then 1,000 km north to **Ilebo** in **Kasaï Occidental,** at which point it turns to the west and flows an additional 600 km before joining the Congo River 300 km above **Kinshasa.** The Kasai River is navigable from Ilebo to the Congo River and forms an important part of the **National Way** transportation route, by which a major portion of **minerals** from Katanga are exported. Several other important tributaries feed into the Kasai River, including the Sankuru, **Lulua**, Kwilu and **Kwango** Rivers.

KASAJI. A small town of about 30,000 people in southern **Katanga Province,** lying on the **road** and **railway** between **Dilolo** and **Kolwezi.** Kasaji was one of several towns captured by guerrillas of the **Front pour la Libération Nationale du Congo (FLNC)** during the first **Shaba** War in 1977.

KASAVUBU, JOSEPH (1917 - 1969). The first **president** of Congo, who governed from **independence** on June 30, 1960, until **Mobutu**'s **coup d'etat** on **November 24, 1965**. Kasavubu surprised many observers by his ability to survive the chaos following independence and the repeated challenges to his authority by **parliament** and his **prime ministers**. Born at Kuma-Dizi, a small town near Tshela in the **Mayombe** district of **Bas-Congo** (renamed **Bas-Zaïre** under Mobutu), Kasavubu received his early **education** from **Catholic Church missionaries** at Kizu. He studied **agriculture** at the Institut Philotechnique de Bruxelles and in 1946 became a member of the Union des Interêts Sociaux Congolais, a "study group" formed to circumvent the **colonial era** ban on political organizations. In 1950, he joined the **Association des Bakongo (ABAKO)**, an organization formed to defend the interests of the **Kongo** people, and was elected its president in 1954.

In the late 1950s, Kasavubu became an increasingly outspoken advocate of greater political and personal freedoms for Congolese. He was elected burgomaster (mayor) of the Dendale Commune (township) of **Leopoldville** in the "consultations" of 1957, the first local **elections** organized by the colonial authorities. He was imprisoned during the riots for independence in Leopoldville in January 1959 but was released two months later. ABAKO won a significant number of seats in the elections of 1960 but did not obtain a majority. Following a brief political standoff, ABAKO and the **Mouvement National Congolais (MNC)**, the other major winner in the elections, agreed to a compromise under which Kasavubu, running against Jean **Bolikango**, won the presidential vote in parliament while MNC leader Patrice **Lumumba** became prime minister at the head of a broad-based coalition government.

Under the **Loi Fondamentale** which served as a **constitution** from 1960 until 1964, the post of president was intended to be largely ceremonial and the powers of government were to be vested primarily in the prime minister and parliament. However, Kasavubu managed to wield considerable power by dismissing prime ministers and designating political rivals to replace them. On two notable occasions, the prime ministers wielded enough influence in parliament to block Kasavubu's designated successor, leading to political standoffs. One such standoff between Kasavubu and Lumumba in September 1960 led Mobutu, then chief of the **armed forces**, to "neutralize" parliament and appoint a **College of Commissioners** to govern the country for four months. Another such crisis, between Kasavubu and Moïse **Tshombe**, brought a period of confrontation that contributed to the Mobutu coup in 1965. After the coup, Kasavubu retired to Bas-Congo where he lived until his death in April 1969.

KASHAMURA, ANICET. A leader of Antoine **Gizenga**'s "radical" faction of the **Mouvement National Congolais (MNC)**, Kashamura was minister of information in the Patrice **Lumumba** government. He was dismissed along with Lumumba and Gizenga by President Joseph **Kasavubu** on September 5, 1960. In early 1961, Kashamura took power in **Kivu Province** in the name of Gizenga's secessionist government in **Stanleyville**. He was a minister in the government of the Stanleyville-based **People's Republic of the Congo** in 1961 but was driven into exile when forces of the central government reestablished control over the region in the mid-1960s. Following the takeover of Congo/Zaire by the **Alliance des Forces Démocratiques pour la Libération du Congo/Zaïre (AFDL)** in May 1997, newly installed President Laurent **Kabila** announced Kashamura would chair a constitutional commission as part of a move to draft a new **constitution** leading to **elections** by 1999.

KASONGO. A city on the **Lualaba River** in southwestern **Kivu** that was a center for the **Afro-Arab slave** and **ivory** trade in the 19th century. It was considered the capital of the **Tippo Tib** empire in the 1870s.

KASONGO KALOMBO. A **Luba king** who ascended the throne in 1860 and allied with **Afro-Arab** traders in eastern Congo against European traders attempting to penetrate the interior from the west. External pressures and internal conflicts during the late 1800s fragmented the kingdom and eroded the authority of the king.

KASONGO NIEMBO. The last of the great **Luba kings** who held out in eastern Congo against the Belgians until 1910.

KATANGA. The **mineral**-rich province that drew European **explorers** into the central African interior in the 1800s and was a major cause of the **United Nations** intervention in the "Congo crisis" following **independence**. **Katanga** has an area of 496,965 square km and had an estimated **population** of 5.5 million in 1995 (3,762,806 in 1982). It is rich in **copper, cobalt, tin**, tungsten, **gold** and other by-products of copper ores and, until the deterioration of the **mining** industry in the early 1990s, its **exports** provided more than one-half of the **government**'s revenues and two-thirds of its **foreign exchange**. Yet Katanga is more closely linked historically, ethnically and economically to southern Africa than to **Kinshasa** and the west African coast.

When **Leopold II**'s agents laid claim to the region in the 1890s, beating out the British colonizer Cecil **Rhodes,** they found local residents already hostile to outside influences. During the early years of the **Congo Free State (CFS)**, the region was run at first by the privately owned **Comité Spécial du Katanga**. In 1910, however, Leopold II placed the territory under a vice governor-general, separate from the rest of the CFS. It was brought under the central colonial administration in 1933 in a move that was widely resented by local and foreign residents. Periodic uprisings during the **colonial era** were harshly put down.

At independence, Moïse **Tshombe**'s **Confédération des Associations Katangaises (CONAKAT)** party swept the local **elections**, leading to the formation of a one-party provincial government. Unhappy with CONAKAT's representation in the central government and encouraged by private commercial interests and an organization of European residents called the **Union Katangaise**, Katanga seceded on July 11, 1960, 12 days after Congo's independence. The **Katanga secession** held world attention during the next two years as Tshombe stalled mediation efforts and frustrated UN attempts at reunification. Congo's first **prime minister**, Patrice **Lumumba**, and UN Secretary-General Dag **Hammarskjöld** died in Katanga and thousands of **Luba** and **Lunda** were killed in interethnic fighting during the secession. After a series of mediation efforts and two military operations by UN forces (Operation Rumpunch and Operation Morthor, the latter widely condemned by some members of the international community), the Katangan secession was declared at an end on January 14, 1963.

Mobutu, following the **coup d'etat** in 1965, sought to strengthen control over the province and renamed it **Shaba** in 1971. The region regained international attention on March 8, 1977, when guerrillas of the **Front pour la Libération Nationale du Congo (FLNC)** occupied a series of towns along the **railway** linking Shaba's mining centers to **Angola**'s **Benguela Railway**. The guerrillas were primarily of the Lunda **ethnic group** and were led by Nathaniel **Mbumba**, a former officer in the **Gendarmerie Katangaise**, which had supported the Katangan secession and invaded northeastern Congo in 1967 in an attempt to return Tshombe to power. Sometimes called the **"Eighty-Day War,"** the first Shaba invasion was not a secession attempt but rather an effort to spark a general uprising in Zaire. However, the FLNC stopped before reaching the important mining town of **Kolwezi** and was eventually driven back into Angola by the Zairian army, backed by 1,400 **Moroccan** troops and logistical support from **France**.

In 1978, the FLNC attacked again. This time, however, it infiltrated the area around Kolwezi and on May 3 seized the city, halting work at the mines. The guerrillas then went on a week-long spree of looting and violence in which 1,000 Zairians and 200 foreigners were killed. Zairian troops, backed by 700 French Foreign Legionnaires, parachuted into Kolwezi and recaptured the city after several days of bloody fighting. More than 1,000 paratroopers from **Belgium** also dropped on the city of **Kamina** to the north. The **United States** government supplied equipment and transport that included 18 C-141 planes. The guerrillas gradually withdrew from the territory with stolen vehicles and looted goods. A peacekeeping force composed of Moroccan, Senegalese and Togolese troops was deployed while Zairian army units were reorganized, reequipped and retrained.

Charges of Angolan and **Cuban** support for the rebels brought condemnation in international forums. The two attacks also focused attention on the inability of the **armed forces** to defend the national territory and the high degree of political and military centralization of the Mobutu government. This led to a measure of liberalization in Zairian **politics** and to diplomatic initiatives to resolve the differences between the Zairian and Angolan governments. Zaire had supported the **Frente Nacional de Libertação de Angola (FNLA)** faction in the Angolan civil war and reportedly was supplying arms to the FNLA for attacks on Angolan installations. After the second Shaba war, however, Zaire and Angola agreed to cease hostilities and stop supporting each other's **opposition** guerrillas. Zaire and Angola established diplomatic relations later that year.

In the early 1980s, a series of clashes and cross-border raids by Zairian and **Zambian** troops raised tensions in the region. However, Presidents Mobutu and Kenneth Kaunda expressed a desire for negotiated solutions to the conflicts and a joint commission was established to resolve disputes.

In 1984 and 1985, guerrillas of the **Parti Révolutionnaire du Peuple (PRP)** based in the **Mitumba Mountains** of northern Shaba, attacked the town of **Moba** in an attempt to embarrass the Zairian government, but government troops quickly regained control of the town.

With the advent of multipartyism in 1990, political activity increased in Shaba. Many residents supported **opposition** parties, in particular the **Union des Fédéralistes et des Républicains Indépendants (UFERI)** of Jean **Nguza Karl-I-Bond**, a former prime minister and favorite son, or the **Union pour la Démocratie et le Progrès Social (UDPS)** of Étienne **Tshisekedi**, a Luba from neighboring **Kasaï Orientale Province**. Political tensions between the two groups increased in 1991, when Nguza was appointed prime minister. The Nguza government appointed the regional president of UFERI, Gabriel **Kyungu wa Kumwanza**, as governor, reportedly the first governor from the region. Kyungu advocated considerable autonomy for Shaba, which he called Katanga, and made a number of speeches advocating "Katanga for Katangans." These heightened historic rivalries between Luba-Kasai, who had immigrated during the colonial era, and more-established **ethnic groups** in the region. When Nguza was dismissed in 1992 and Tshisekedi was elected prime minister by the **National Conference**, attacks began against Luba-Kasai, reportedly by militia of the UFERI **youth** wing. An estimated 500 people died in the violence, which lasted into 1993. More than 100,000 Luba-Kasai lost their homes and returned to **Kasai**. Opposition leaders charged UFERI with **ethnic cleansing** as part of an effort to consolidate its political base by expelling members of Tshisekedi's ethnic group. In April 1995, Kyungu was dismissed amid charges of diverting income from the mines and reports he had stockpiled weapons for an eventual secession of the region. Forces of the **Alliance des Forces Démocratiques pour la Libération du Congo/Zaïre (AFDL)**, led by PRP leader Laurent **Kabila**, took power in the region in early 1997 and Kyungu was placed under house arrest. He was released later that year and made governor once again.

KATANGA SECESSION (1960 - 1963). **Congo/Zaire's** best-known and most successful **rebellion** and the major reason for the **United Nations** first, and for more than 30 years only, unilateral military intervention. Katanga historically was an autonomous-minded part of central Africa. Its local inhabitants resisted the colonial authorities and a number of uprisings during the **colonial era** were harshly put down. Katanga's geographical and ethnic ties to southern Africa and its distance from the capital of **Leopoldville** contributed to a lack of identification with the rest of the **Belgian Congo**. From 1910 to 1933, the province had its own separate administration and vice governor-general, appointed by the king of **Belgium**. Its **mineral** wealth and relatively developed infrastructure was a cause of pride and the fact that it was a major contributor to **foreign exchange** earnings caused resentment toward the rest of the territory.

At **independence**, Moïse **Tshombe's Confédération des Associations Katangaises (CONAKAT)** party swept the local elections, leading to a single-party provincial government. However, CONAKAT received relatively minor representation in the first cabinet of Prime Minister Patrice **Lumumba**. Unhappy with its representation in the central government and supported by private business interests and its sizable expatriate population, Katanga seceded on July 11, 1960, 12 days after independence. For several years, Tshombe stonewalled reunification attempts by Congolese leaders and the United Nations. At the same time tensions between the **Lunda** and **Luba ethnic groups** escalated into fighting, displacing hundreds of thousands of residents and requiring a major UN relief effort.

The United Nations carried out two military operations in Katanga, Operation Rumpunch and Operation Morthor, ostensibly aimed at removing foreign **mercenaries** who were the backbone of the Katangan military forces, but also designed to weaken the Katangan government and its foreign supporters. The Katangan government, though recognized by several countries, was unable to withstand the pressure and the secession was ended on January 14, 1963. Tshombe fled into exile and several CONAKAT leaders were appointed to Cyrille **Adoula**'s government of national reconciliation.

KATANGAN GENDARMES. *See* GENDARMERIE KATANGAISE.

KATANGAN UNION. *See* UNION KATANGAISE.

KAZEMBE. A group of people related to the **Lunda** living in Haut-**Katanga** District in the Luapula Valley near the border with **Zambia**. During the mid-1800s the Kazembe had some control over the **ivory** trade, but their leader, the Mwata Kazembe, was subordinate to the paramount **chief** of the Lunda. Traders from the east eventually bypassed the Kazembe and began dealing directly with the Lunda and **Luba**.

KENGO WA DONDO, LÉON (1935 -). The tough **prime minister** who was called upon to tame **inflation** and revive the Zairian **economy** in 1994, following an economic crisis caused by **hyperinflation** and civil unrest in the early 1990s. Kengo earned a reputation as a rigorous enforcer of economic austerity measures in the mid-1980s, when he implemented a series of fiscal and economic reforms that for a time stabilized the economy but also plunged the country into a severe recession.

Kengo was born May 22, 1935, at Libenge in **Équateur Province**. He studied law and received his doctorate in 1962 from the Université Libre de Bruxelles in **Belgium**. In April 1968, he was named prosecutor-general to the **Kinshasa** Court of Appeals and in August was promoted to attorney-general. He became president of the **Judicial Council** in December 1977 and a member of the **Central Committee** in September 1980. Kengo gained fame in the 1980s as the tough lawyer who prosecuted Jean **Nguza Karl-I-Bond**, the **Group of Thirteen Parliamentarians**, and other Congolese political **dissidents**. He was named first state commissioner (prime minister) on November 5, 1982, charged with cleaning up **corruption** in government and enforcing austerity measures which were part of a package of economic reforms negotiated with the **International Monetary Fund**

(IMF). Kengo was not considered a political threat because, although he was born of a Congolese mother, his father was Polish and under the Zairian **constitution** both parents of the president of the republic must be Zairian.

In 1986, after two years of recession, party members argued forcefully against continued adherence to the IMF-imposed austerity measures and Kengo's policies began to lose favor. The post of prime minister was abolished in October 1986. Kengo was named foreign minister, then demoted to president of the Court of Auditors.

With the advent of multipartyism in 1990, Kengo launched the **Union des Démocrates Indépendants (UDI)** party. The party was meant to be centrist, positioning itself between supporters of **Mobutu** and the **Sacred Union opposition**. At one point, Kengo promised that if elected president he would repay more than $100 million he said he had embezzled during the 1980s, causing consternation among political leaders and a surge of approval from the general population.

In June 1994, after four years of political and economic turmoil, Kengo was elected prime minister by the acting transitional **parliament**, the **Haut Conseil de la République / Parlement de la Transition (HCR/PT)**, and directed to stabilize the Zairian economy and organize national **elections**. His efforts at economic stabilization initially received support from Zaire's major foreign creditors and later that year he paid an official visit to Europe and the **United States**, ending several years of diplomatic isolation. At home, however, his efforts received lukewarm support from pro-Mobutu forces and virulent opposition from the Sacred Union. By 1995, inflation had returned to triple-digit levels and, although Kengo was reappointed prime minister in the cabinet reshuffle of December 1996, his political base was considered to be weak. He fled the country in May 1997 on the eve of the arrival in **Kinshasa** of the **Alliance des Forces Démocratiques pour la Libération du Congo/Zaïre (AFDL)** led by Laurent **Kabila**.

KENYA, RELATIONS WITH. As fellow members of the "moderate" group of African nations, relations between Congo/Zaire and Kenya generally were good, although there was little direct personal contact between the leaders of the two countries. Kenya sent a message of support to the Zairian government during the **Shaba** Wars. And the leaders of both countries tried to mediate the civil war in **Rwanda** and ethnic clashes in **Burundi** in the 1990s. However, with the installation of the Laurent **Kabila** government on May 29, 1997, following the overthrow of **Mobutu**, relations cooled. During the offensive that brought him to power, Kabila had received support from Ugandan President Yoweri Museveni, who was a longtime critic of Kenyan President Daniel Arap Moi. Museveni viewed Moi as one of the corrupt old-style dictators who were strangling African development. The Kenyan government viewed Kabila as a puppet of the Ugandan government and its allies in East Africa until mid-1998, when Kabila's relations deteriorated with Museveni.

KETE. An **ethnic group** living in western **Kasaï Occidental Province** around the city of **Luebo**.

KHOISAN. Khoisan-speakers (sometimes called "Bushmen"), spread into the **Congo River Basin** from eastern and southern Africa, according to some theories. However, to date there is no evidence they settled in Congo and no linguistic traces have been found among **ethnic groups** living in the territory.

KIBASSA MALIBA, FRÉDÉRIC (1939 -). An **opposition** leader who was a prominent figure in the **Union pour la Démocratie et le Progrès Social (UDPS)** party from its founding in 1982. A native of **Katanga**, Kibassa was born on December 28, 1939, in **Lubumbashi** where he was educated and, in his youth, was a well-known boxer. He was elected president of the UDPS when it was formed in 1982 and was detained on numerous occasions in the 1980s for advocating a return to multipartyism. He was named minister of sports and leisure in 1988 during a brief period of *détente* with the **Mobutu government**. In the early 1990s, he was one of four presidents of the UDPS, responsible for internal party matters. However, he was widely viewed as the number-two man of the party after founder Étienne **Tshisekedi**. Kibassa's residence was the headquarters of the **Sacred Union** in the early 1990s and during periods of civil disobedience it was the target of a number of attacks by Zairian **security** forces. His eldest son, Betho, was killed in such an attack on the night of January 31, 1993. In

January 1996, a rift developed between Kibassa and Tshisekedi, in part over whether to participate in national **elections** scheduled for 1997. The dispute took on regional tones because Kibassa was from Katanga and Tshisekedi from neighboring **Kasaï Oriental.**

After the fall of Mobutu in 1997, Kibassa sided at first with Tshisekedi in opposing the government of Laurent **Kabila,** when it failed to reach a power-sharing agreement with senior UDPS leaders. In November, however, Kibassa accepted the post of deputy minister of mines. He was promoted to minister of mines in the cabinet reshuffle of January 1998.

KIBINDA ILUNGA. Brother of the founder of the **Luba** empire, **Kalala Ilunga,** Kibinda Ilunga in 1600 led a group of followers from the Luba lands in southern **Kasai** to an area near the Congo-**Angola** border to found what became the **Lunda** empire.

KIKWIT. A city of 400,000 inhabitants in **Bandundu Province,** lying on the **Kwilu River** and along the major **road** linking **Kinshasa** to the central part of the country. Kikwit prospered during the **colonial era** and was the capital of **Kwilu** Province in the early 1960s. However, a series of uprisings beginning with the **Mulele rebellion** in the mid-1960s caused Kikwit to lose favor with the central government. As a result, considerable attention was devoted to developing Bandundu, a small city lying down the river. During the administrative reforms of the late 1960s, Bandundu became the capital of Bandundu Province and Kikwit became an urban subregion, though still an economically important one. Major economic activity in the area included **palm oil** and vegetable oil processing, **timber** and some **livestock** raising and vegetable farming. In March 1995, Kikwit became the focus of an international medical alert when an outbreak of the **Ebola** virus caused 244 deaths. Authorities, fearing the virus would spread to Kinshasa, for several weeks blockaded roads to the city, disrupting commerce and food supplies.

KILO-MOTO GOLD MINES BOARD. *See* OFFICE DES MINES D'OR DE KILO-MOTO (OKIMO).

KIMBA, ÉVARISTE (? - 1966). One of the founders of the **Association des Baluba du Katanga (BALUBAKAT),** Kimba was foreign minister in the Moïse **Tshombe government** in 1964. Following the dismissal of Tshombe on October 13, 1965, Kimba was asked by **President** Joseph **Kasavubu** to form a government. His first attempt was thwarted by Tshombe's supporters in **parliament**. His second attempt was thwarted by **Mobutu**'s military **coup d'etat**. Five months after the coup, Kimba and three associates were accused of trying to overthrow the Mobutu government in what was called the "Pentecost Plot." They were found guilty in a trial denounced in juridical circles as a sham and were sentenced to death. On June 2, 1966, despite appeals from the international community, the four were publicly hanged in **Kinshasa**.

KIMBANGU, SIMON (? - 1951). Founder of the **Kimbanguist Church**, the first African Christian church to be recognized by the World Council of Churches. Kimbangu was a member of the British Baptist Church who in 1921 decided to found his own church after he dreamed he had been appointed by God to heal and preach. At first he worked with **Protestant** leaders, but broke away when some of them began to express disapproval over reports of his miracles. In June 1921, the colonial authorities tried to arrest Kimbangu during a religious meeting, but he escaped capture, further enhancing his reputation as a miracle worker. However, he turned himself in to authorities in September. He was tried and sentenced to death on charges of crimes against the security of the state, but the sentence was commuted to life imprisonment by **Leopold II**. Despite pleas from his followers to use his powers to escape, Kimbangu died in prison in 1951.

KIMBANGUIST CHURCH. Formally known as the Église de Jésus-Christ sur la Terre par le Prophète Simon **Kimbangu** (Church of Jesus Christ on Earth by the Prophet Simon Kimbangu), Kimbanguism is considered a syncretist group, that is, one which mixes **Christianity** with traditional beliefs and practices. In August 1969, it was the first independent African church to be admitted to the World Council of Churches. The church claimed to have five million adherents in the mid-1990s, or 8 percent of the Congolese **population**, although independent observers estimated membership to be lower.

Kimbanguism is based on the Bible and the concept of spiritual salvation. It mixes some traditional African practices but follows the law of Moses and calls for the destruction of fetishes and an end to sorcery and polygamy. The church was formed by Simon Kimbangu, originally a member of the British Baptist Church, following a vision in 1921. When Kimbangu was arrested in 1921, the church was pushed underground. The period of repression led to many apostles calling themselves prophets and to increased use of animist practices among some of these groups. Kimbangu died in prison in 1951 and was replaced by his son, Joseph **Diangienda**. A church council was organized in 1956 and was granted legal recognition by the colonial government in 1959.

Like many Congolese churches, Kimbanguism was restricted by the Zairian government in the early 1970s. Unlike the Roman **Catholic Church**, however, the Kimbanguist Church did not play an active public role in national **politics**.

KINDU. The capital of **Maniema Province**, Kindu is a city of about 120,000 people lying on the upper **Congo River** in eastern **Congo/Zaire**. It is a major station on the Chemin de Fer des Grands Lacs (CFL) **railway**, which links **Lubumbashi** and **Kamina** in **Katanga Province** to **Kisangani** in **Orientale Province** and to **Kalemie** on **Lake Tanganyika**.

KINGS AND KINGDOMS. In traditional **society**, a king usually was the leader of many **clans** and chieftaincies. Often called a "paramount **chief**," he, or in some rare cases she, usually came to power through one or a combination of several paths: inheritance, designation (usually at death) by the former chief, designation by a council of elders, or a series of tests. The king, once chosen, usually accumulated great wealth, was expected to have many wives and children, and might hold the power of life and death over his subjects. Subordinate chiefs paid tribute to the king of money, goods, wives, **livestock**, **slaves** or other wealth. The king usually ruled until he died or was deposed.

KINLAO. Site of the country's sole **petroleum** refinery, built in 1968 near the mouth of the **Congo River** and the town of Moanda.

KINSHASA. The capital of **Congo/Zaire**, Kinshasa, formerly called **Leopoldville**, is located on the **Congo River** across from Brazzaville, **Republic of the Congo**. Kinshasa was a small village when Henry Morton **Stanley** arrived in the 1880s and signed an agreement with the local **chief** allowing him to claim the area for **Belgium**'s King **Leopold II**. It grew from a city of about 100,000 inhabitants at **independence** to a megalopolis with an estimated **population** of five million in the mid-1990s (2,124,127 in the census of 1982). The city is located in the capital zone of Kinshasa, which covers an area of 2,016 square km and contains an additional one million inhabitants. It occupies an area traditionally dominated by the **Kongo** people and Kikongo was one of the main languages spoken. However, the use of **Lingala** by the **armed forces** and **government** and the presence of sizable communities from all parts of the country has made Lingala the lingua franca.

The political and financial center of Congo/Zaire, Kinshasa is the home of one-third of all of Congolese **industry**, including **textiles**, milling, shipbuilding, **steel**making, **timber**, **palm oil**, chemical and food processing, **motor vehicle** assembly, tires, and footwear and apparel manufacturing. An **educational** center, Kinshasa is also home to the National **University** at Kinshasa (formerly **Lovanium**), the Institut National d'Études Politiques, the **Makanda Kabobi Institute** and many private schools. Kinshasa is a major transshipment point between the deep-water **port** of **Matadi** and the Congolese interior. The country's major international airport and **telecommunications** center are located in the city and it has hosted numerous international meetings, including the summit of the **Organization of African Unity (OAU)** in 1967, the France-African summit in 1982, and the annual FIKIN international fair.

During the 1990s, Congo/Zaire's economic crisis took its toll on Kinshasa and following the **pillages** of 1991 and 1993, a great deal of industry was shut down and public services became available only intermittently. *See also* National Way; Transportation.

KINSHIP. In traditional **society**, kinship is an important factor in the security and well-being of an individual and may provide considerable support in the face of personal hardship. But it can lead to practices that Western societies consider illegal or unethical. Within the tradition of family solidarity, an individual who is well-off is expected to aid less-fortunate members of his or her extended family by providing jobs, financial opportunities and gifts. Such acts absolve the successful individual to a degree of an obligation to that particular family-member, who in turn may be approached by other family members in need. To avoid paying the debt is to risk disfavor and even ostracism. Likewise, an individual experiencing hardship can draw on more fortunate relatives for assistance. The custom sometimes led to offices and businesses staffed virtually exclusively by relatives of the owner or director. It also placed considerable financial pressure on the successful individual and often has been a major reason for favoritism, diversion of funds and other practices considered **corrupt** in Western societies.

KISANGANI. Kisangani, formerly **Stanleyville,** is the capital of **Orientale Province**. An urban district with an estimated **population** of one-half million (328,476 in 1982) covering an area of 1,910 square km located at the confluence of the **Congo** and **Tshopo Rivers**, Kisangani lies at the furthest continuously navigable point upriver from **Kinshasa**. The city is separated by 200 km of cataracts from another navigable portion of the Congo River between **Kindu** and Ubundu. Originally a fishing village and minor **Afro-Arab** trading post, Kisangani became a major river **port** with the arrival of European traders in the late 1800s and was used as a base for the campaign to drive the Arab traders from the territory. Kisangani is linked by **river** to Kinshasa and western Congo/Zaire, by **railway** to **Maniema** and northern **Katanga Provinces**, and by a network of **roads** to the northeastern corner of Congo/Zaire and East Africa.

The **rebellions** following **independence** and the **Zairianization** of large **plantations** in the early 1970s ruined a great many private enterprises in the region. Efforts to revive them in the late 1970s were hampered by widespread shortages of **energy, electrical power** and spare parts.

Kisangani is also home to a regional **radio** station and a campus of the national **university** (formerly the Protestant University of Zaire). In the mid-1980s, the Zairian **government** attempted to revive **agriculture** and **industry** in the area with capital infusions into plantations, the Kilo-Moto **gold mining** operation, and several infrastructure projects. Economic production was hurt, however, by the **pillages** in the early 1990s, and deteriorating **transportation** links caused many of the traders to direct their activities to East Africa. In early 1997, government forces, backed by foreign **mercenaries**, sought to organize a major defense line against advancing troops of the **Alliance des Forces Démocratiques pour la Libération du Congo/Zaïre (AFDL)**. The victory by the AFDL forces on March 15 led to the beginning of the collapse of the **Mobutu** government, which fell two months later with the arrival of the AFDL in Kinshasa. Following the takeover, the government of Laurent **Kabila** announced a major program to rebuild infrastructure and industry in eastern Congo. The city was devastated by floods, when the Congo River burst its banks in December 1997, killing more than 70 people and making 22,000 homeless. In August 1998, Kisangani fell to rebels of the **Rassemblement Congolais pour la Démocratie (RCD)**, who occupied eastern Congo in a drive to overthrow the Kabila government.

KITAWALA MOVEMENT. A syncretist movement combining African and Christian beliefs which emerged in the 1920s in the **mining** communities of **Katanga** from the teachings by **missionaries** of the Watch Tower Bible and Tract Society, or Jehovah's Witnesses. Aside from the traditional teachings of equality and the imminent arrival of God's kingdom, Kitawala evolved into an anticolonial movement, whose adherents refused to pay taxes or salute the flag. The movement was disavowed by the Watch Tower Church and banned by the colonial authorities, but it continued to gain support. After **independence**, it resisted at times the authority of the Congolese government. The appearance of a military unit at a meeting in **Shaba** in 1979 led to a clash in which two soldiers were killed.

KITUBA. *See* FIOTE.

KIVU. One of the original six **provinces**, Kivu was one of the most remote of **Congo/Zaire**'s provinces. Located in eastern Congo/Zaire bordering the smaller **lakes** of the **Great Rift Valley**, it was divided in May 1988 into three **regions**: **Nord-Kivu, Sud-**

Kivu and **Maniema**. A region of primarily mountainous and forested terrain, Kivu is one of the most densely populated regions of the country, with an estimated **population** of more than six million in the early 1990s (4,361,736 in the 1982 census) inhabiting an area of 256,662 square km. The region is rich in **tin**, tungsten, iron ore and **gold**. Large deposits of natural gas were discovered in the 1970s below **Lake Kivu**. In addition, the high altitude and temperate **climate** are excellent for growing tea, tobacco, **sugar** cane, arabica **coffee** and strawberries. Plantains, **bananas** and vegetables are also grown by small farmers. The lakes, except for Lake Kivu, provided freshwater **fish** and there is some **livestock** herding. Tin mines operated until the collapse of tin prices in the 1980s.

During the **colonial era**, Kivu was neglected by the authorities in **Leopoldville** and its people generally had little regard for the central government. At **independence**, Kivu sided with the secessionist government led by Antoine **Gizenga** in **Stanleyville**, but some of its leaders broke away in 1964 to form a separate, highly autonomous group, the **Parti Révolutionaire du Peuple (PRP)**. The PRP controlled portions of remote territory in the **Mitumba Mountains** near **Lake Tanganyika** and in 1975 kidnapped four Western students at a wildlife research center in Tanzania.

The Kivu region, particularly the cities of **Goma** and **Bukavu**, received more than one million **refugees** in mid-1994 during **Rwanda**'s civil war, creating a major humanitarian crisis. In mid-1996, tensions escalated into fighting between **Banyamulenge** immigrants from Rwanda, Zairian government troops and **Hutu** militias that had hidden in the Rwandan refugee camps. In October 1996, forces of a PRP-led alliance, the **Alliance des Forces Démocratiques pour la Libération du Congo/Zaïre (AFDL)**, launched an offensive aimed at overthrowing the **Mobutu** government. By March 1997, they had seized a 1,000-km stretch of territory that included most of Kivu and, with support from Rwanda, **Burundi**, **Uganda** and **Angola**, took over the government on May 17, one day after Mobutu fled into exile. The government of AFDL leader Laurent **Kabila**, which was installed 12 days later, announced a program to revitalize the economies of Kivu and other eastern regions and to rebuild their **transportation** links with East Africa. However, a rebellion led by the

Banyamulenge, backed by Rwanda and Uganda, arose in August 1998 and quickly recaptured most of the region.

KIVU, LAKE. *See* LAKE KIVU.

KOLWEZI. An urban district in southern **Katanga** with an estimated **population** of 500,000 people, lying between **Lubumbashi** and **Dilolo** on a **mineral** lode along the northwestern edge of the **Zambian copper** belt. The city of Kolwezi, which contains most of the population of the district, is primarily a **mining** town. Its **economy** was dominated by the **Générale des Carrières et des Mines (GECAMINES)** company, which was responsible for operating one underground and several open-pit mines.

Kolwezi came to the front pages of the world's newspapers largely because of the **Shaba** Wars. On March 18, 1977, guerrillas of the **Front pour la Libération Nationale du Congo (FLNC)** invaded Shaba from **Angola** and advanced to the outskirts of the city. They withdrew without attacking, however, in the face of a government counteroffensive. On May 3, 1978, they again infiltrated the area from the south and this time occupied Kolwezi on May 12. Amid reports that the guerrillas were engaging in widespread looting and killing, a military operation was launched in which 1,700 Belgian, 700 French and several thousand Zairian paratroopers landed in the area. After two weeks of fighting, they drove the guerrillas out and rescued the population, including 2,000 Europeans, but not before 1,000 Zairians and 200 foreigners had been killed.

Most of the **industry** in Kolwezi was related to the mining operations, including a series of hydroelectric installations outside the city and a **railway** depot on the line linking Lubumbashi to Angola's **Benguela Railway**. A milling plant is located in the city and there is some herding and vegetable farming on the outskirts. However, economic activity in the area was severely reduced in the mid-1990s by the insolvency of GECAMINES and the collapse of most mining operations.

KONGO. A people living in western **Congo/Zaire**, southern **Republic of the Congo** and northern **Angola**, near the Atlantic coast. The Kongo people were among the first to come into contact with European **explorers**, traders and **missionaries**. The **Kongo**

Kingdom was a flourishing empire in 1483 when **Diogo Cão** first sailed up the mouth of the **Congo River** and landed in an area near **Boma**, eight years before Columbus reached America. The kingdom decayed in the 17th century, possibly because of competition between European powers and the rise of the **slave** trade which upset the balance of power among the various tribes and chieftaincies. Nevertheless, the linguistic and cultural influence of the group continued to be felt. A matrilineal people with a highly organized judicial and political hierarchy, the Kongo were spread as far east as the plains of **Kinshasa** and their language, Kikongo, became one of Congo/Zaire's four national **languages**.

The Kongo people's access to **educational** opportunities and their proximity to major cities such as Kinshasa and **Matadi** contributed to their large representation in the **colonial-era civil service** and among the class of *évolués*. The Kongo were among the earliest and most influential advocates of greater personal freedom for Congolese and, later, of **independence**. They were considered by the colonial authorities to be among the more radical pro-independence groups and one of the most anti-**Belgium**. Their leaders formed the Association des Bakongo in 1950 to protect their **culture** from influences of the **Ngala** and **Luba**, who began arriving in **Leopoldville** following World War II. The association later became the **Alliance des Bakongo (ABAKO) political party** which was one of the first groups to press for **labor** rights, political freedoms and, ultimately, independence. ABAKO produced Congo's first **president**, Joseph **Kasavubu**.

Following independence, the Kongo *cadres* continued to dominate the **government** and civil service, occupying more than one-third of the administrative positions. Demographic studies in the 1980s revealed that up to one-third of the **population** of Kinshasa traced its origins to the Kongo and one-fifth of these were Kongo of Angolan origin.

KONGO, KINGDOM OF. The **Kongo** kingdom was the first Congolese nation to make formal contact and develop economic and cultural exchanges with Europe, beginning in 1843. At its peak from the 1400s to the 1600s, the kingdom stretched from the Atlantic coast to the **Kwango River** in the east and the **Kwilu**

River in the north. The kingdom was primarily a loose confederation of sub-**kings** and hereditary **chiefs** who paid homage in varying degrees to the central king in the mythical birthplace of all Kongo, the **Mbanza Kongo dia Ntotila** (Great City of the King).

The Portuguese **explorer Diogo Cão** encountered the Kongo in 1483 when he arrived at the mouth of the **Congo River**. He befriended the reigning king, who converted to **Christianity** and changed his name to **Affonso I**. Affonso I established considerable exchanges with **Portugal** and other European powers. He sent ambassadors to Lisbon, the Holy See and the Netherlands and asked for **missionaries**. Trading posts were set up to ship **ivory** and **gold** to Europe, but **slaving** eventually became the dominant **trade**. In 1570, the kingdom was threatened by **Jaga** invaders from the east, but Portuguese troops restored the reigning king, **Alvaro I**, to the throne. In the early 17th century, Dutch and other European traders and explorers began to arrive. The Kongo allied with the Dutch but were defeated by the Portuguese at the battle of Ambuila in 1665. The king was assassinated. Christian practices faded. By the end of the 17th century, the Portuguese presence in the region had been reduced to a few coastal trading posts. In 1883, as European powers began making territorial claims in Africa, the Kongo kingdom was attached to **Angola**. The territory was later partitioned between Portugal, **France** and **Belgium**'s King **Leopold II**.

KONGOLO. Chief of the legendary Balopwe nobility, who migrated into the **Congo River Basin** from the north around 1500 and founded what became the **Luba** empire.

KONGOLO, MWENZE (1961 -). A lawyer and senior official in the **Alliance des Forces Démocratiques pour la Libération du Congo/Zaïre (AFDL)**. Kongolo was named interior minister in October 1997 in the Laurent **Kabila government**, after the fall of **Mobutu**, and justice minister in January 1998. A native of **Katanga**, Kongolo studied in the United States and worked in the office of the attorney general of the US state of Pennsylvania until he joined the AFDL in 1996.

KUBA. A **Bantu** people driven east, according to some ethnologists, by the **Jaga** invasion of the **Kongo Kingdom** in the 16th century. The Kuba established themselves between the Sankuru River and **Lulua River** in an area bounded by **Luebo** and Mweka to the south and **Ilebo** to the east. The Kuba were primarily cultivators and artisans noted for their tapestries and carvings of angular, diagonal designs. They were ruled by a **king** whose successor was chosen from among his nephews. The kingdom reached its zenith in the 18th century and remained stable until the 19th century, when revolts in the east created a near-civil war. The revolt was quelled harshly by the colonial authorities in the early 1900s. Jan Vansina says Kuba society was the "most complexly organized state with the possible exception of the **Lunda**." The Kuba had a hierarchy of higher and lower **chiefs** and a high degree of differentiation between them. The Kuba "cluster" included the **Lele, Njembe** and a number of groups ruled by the Bashongo.

KUNDA. A **Bantu** people living in Haut-Katanga District of **Katanga Province**, south of **Kolwezi**, identified by ethnologist Jan Vansina as part of the "Haut-Katanga" cluster. Sometimes spelled Kaonde.

KUSU. A **Bantu**-speaking group living along the **Lomami River** in a remote part of **Maniema Province** between Kibombo and Lubao. Congolese ethnographers consider the Kusu to be part of the **Mongo** group, although they were never reported to identify with that group. Some experts believe the Kusu and the **Tetela** sprang from the same group but grew apart as the Kusu came under the cultural influence of the **Afro-Arab** traders, while the Tetela rejected them. **Tippo Tib** used the term "Kusu" to describe the people he met during his trading expeditions in eastern and southern **Congo**. The Kusu were unquestionably influenced by the Afro-Arabs. Many adopted their **dress**, converted to **Islam** and adopted Swahili as their lingua franca. The Belgians called them the *Arabisés*. After driving the Arab traders from the region in the late 1800s, the Belgian authorities drew a provincial border line between the Kusu and Tetela zones of influence, placing the Kusu in **Kivu** Province and the Tetela in **Kasai** Province.

KWA RIVER. The name sometimes given to the lower **Kasai River** between the area where it joins the Lukemie River at Mushie and its confluence with the **Congo River** 100 km downstream.

KWANGO RIVER. A major **river** in western **Congo/Zaire** which rises in central **Angola** and courses north 1,300 km before flowing into the **Kasai River** near **Bandundu**. It is the domain primarily of the **Chokwe** and related peoples.

KWESE. A small **ethnic group** of the **Pende** cluster living between the **Kwilu** and **Kasai Rivers** in the southern Kwango and Kasai districts of **Bandundu** and **Kasaï Occidental Provinces**.

KWILU DISTRICT. A district of **Bandundu Province**, Kwilu was a district within **Leopoldville** Province during the late **colonial era** and early **independence** period. With **Kikwit** as its main urban center, it is relatively densely populated. Its estimated three million inhabitants occupy an area of 78,019 square km and live primarily by **fishing**, hunting and **agriculture**. There is some **timbering**, oil palm cultivation and produce farming. Other than vegetable oil processing plants, however, there is little **industry** and few attempts have been made to develop an economic infrastructure, according to some officials, because of local **opposition** to the central **government**. In January 1964, a **rebellion** began, led by Pierre **Mulele** with backing from **China**. The rebels engaged in acts of sabotage and urban bombings in Leopoldville before the rebellion was ended in 1966. In 1978, another uprising was reported near **Idiofa** in which thousands of people reportedly were killed and following which 14 local **chiefs** were publicly executed. In March 1995, an outbreak of the **Ebola** virus centered in Kikwit caused 244 deaths.

KYUNGU WA KUMWANZA, GABRIEL (1938 -). The governor of **Shaba Region** in the early 1990s whose calls of "**Katanga** for Katangans" are blamed for the expulsions of **Luba** immigrants from **Kasai** beginning in August 1992. Kyungu was born on October 24, 1938, in Ankoro, Katanga, where he received his primary **education**. He attended secondary school in **Lubumbashi**. He was a teacher, union leader and, following **independence**, functionary in the **Office National des**

Transports (ONATRA) and the Société Nationale des Chemins de Fer Zaïrois (SNCZ).

Kyungu was one of the **Group of Thirteen Parliamentarians** who first called for multipartyism in an open letter to **Mobutu** in 1980. He was detained on numerous occasions during the 1980s for supporting the illegal **Union pour la Démocratie et le Progrès Social (UDPS) opposition** party. With the advent of multipartyism in 1990, he joined the **Union des Fédéralistes et des Républicains Indépendants (UFERI)** party of Jean **Nguza Karl-I-Bond** and was elected the party's regional president. He was appointed governor of Shaba when Nguza was named **prime minister** in November 1991.

As governor, Kyungu espoused autonomy for the **region**, which he preferred to call Katanga, and the removal of immigrants, many of whom had settled before or during the **colonial era**. He also argued that revenues from the region's **mining** industry should remain in the region. He was dismissed on April 19, 1995, and placed under house arrest amid allegations of fraudulent reporting of **cobalt** production and reports in **Kinshasa**'s newspapers that his group was stockpiling weapons to back a secession of the region. He publicly expressed support for the **Alliance des Forces Démocratiques pour la Libération du Congo/Zaïre (AFDL)** as its troops approached Lubumbashi during the offensive that overthrew Mobutu. However, the AFDL viewed him as a supporter of Mobutu and he was placed under house arrest for several months. Kyungu was appointed governor once again on March 27, 1997, after he pledged to strengthen **security** in order to halt a wave of looting in the area. He was named ambassador to **Kenya** in 1998. *See also* Ethnic Cleansing.

- L -

LABOR. Labor in **Congo/Zaire** historically was one of the more abused sectors of **society** and at times a major proponent of change. During the **Congo Free State (CFS)** era, private companies and government operators were given virtually free reign to obtain cheap labor. In the late 1800s, the labor tax law allowed operators to require local citizens to work or collect **rubber** and **ivory** for the authorities without remuneration. Failure to meet quotas led to beatings and executions. It also led in some areas to the amputation of hands by **security** agents to prove they had punished workers in uncooperative villages. Outrage in Europe and America over these practices led to reforms in 1906 limiting the labor tax to 40 hours per month, a practice which was not always observed. In 1910, following the **Belgian** parliament's annexation of the CFS, largely because of the outcry over such abuses, the labor tax was abolished. However, the use of forced labor did not stop. Often workers were taken or hired from the villages, housed, fed and clothed. These "expenses" were then deducted from their earnings. Little money was left.

In 1925, the **Union Minière du Haut-Katanga**, in an effort to build a permanent work force, established policies which improved working conditions. A labor association for whites only, the Association de Fonctionnaires et Agents de la Colonie (AFAC) was created in 1926. In 1946, the **government** for the first time authorized unions for Congolese, but these were strictly monitored through a system of councils. In the 1950s, several trade unions arose in urban areas. They were given true bargaining powers in 1957, the same year that multiracial unions were legalized. The Social Pact of 1959 gave full freedom to all unions and these soon became a major force leading the drive for political freedom and, eventually, **independence**.

Following independence, three major trade unions emerged: the moderate Union des Travailleurs Congolais (UTC), the socialist-oriented Fédération Générale du Travail du Kongo (FGTK) and the "liberal" Confédération des Syndicats Libres du Congo (CSLC). A small communist Confédération Générale de Travailleurs Congolais (CGTC) also was formed. Membership in 1966 ranged from 50,000 for the CSLC to 100,000 for the UTC.

In 1967, the unions were merged into the UTC, which became the Union Nationale des Travailleurs Zaïrois (UNTZA) in 1971. Although some labor leaders protested the loss of their autonomy, the government argued that numerous unions were a divisive force in the labor movement, which instead should be devoting its energies to motivating greater productivity and support for government policies. With the ascendancy of the party over state, the lines between labor and government became blurred. The senior leadership of UNTZA was appointed to government policymaking bodies such as the **Political Bureau** of the

Mouvement Populaire de la Révolution (MPR). There were occasional labor protests, particularly in the **transportation** and **banking** sectors, and there were occasional **strikes** for better pay and working conditions. These were often harshly repressed.

Within days of **Mobutu**'s April 1990 speech authorizing political pluralism, the UNTZA leadership met and voted to disassociate itself from the MPR. Some leaders tried to revive the unions that had existed in the 1960s. And a number of unions were formed to represent professional groups, most notably **civil servants**, public sector physicians and **university** professors. During the early 1990s, labor protests increased markedly as unions tested their new found freedom and workers vented frustration over low **wages**, declining benefits and poor working conditions. Public-sector workers, whose wages at times had been reduced by **inflation** to as little as one dollar per month, staged numerous strikes, some of which lasted months. They extracted some concessions from the government. Nevertheless, through the early 1990s wages remained low, averaging $15 per month at the bottom of the salary scale and less than $100 per month for professionals.

In the 1980s, UNTZA reported one million registered members. UNTZA's name was changed to **Union Nationale des Travailleurs Congolais (UNTC)** in 1997, after the fall of Mobutu, but by that time the proliferation of competing labor groups had considerably reduced its membership.

In 1990, the government reported 1.07 million people employed in the formal **economy**. It listed traditional farming as the largest sector, with 24 million workers working on four million farms with an average size of 1.5 hectares. The International Labor Organization (ILO) depicted Congolese labor in a broader manner, using the UN definition of "economically active" people as those who furnished labor to produce goods and services for market, barter or personal consumption, and including individuals in the **armed forces** and the **unemployed** but excluding **students** and housewives. Using its definition, the ILO reported that in 1990, 37.5 percent of the Congolese **population**, or 14 million people, was active, down from 40.3 percent in 1980 and 42.4 percent in 1975. The participation rate in 1990 was classified as 49 percent for males and 26.3 percent for females. Fourteen percent of children aged 10 to 14 were reported to be active.

LACERDA E ALMEIDA, JOSÉ. A Portuguese **explorer** who led the first scientific exploration of the **Congo River Basin** in 1789. He went as far inland as **Katanga**, where he heard stories of rich deposits of **copper** and other **minerals**, leading other Europeans to explore the interior.

LAKE ALBERT. Called Lake **Mobutu Sese Seko** by Congolese cartographers during the 1970s and 1980s, Lake Albert lies on the **Great Rift Valley**, at an altitude of 618 m, north of the **Ruwenzori Mountains** along **Congo/Zaire**'s border with **Uganda**. The country's second-largest lake and the 30th-largest natural lake in the world, it is 160 km long and 50 km wide and covers 5,300 square km with a maximum depth of 50 meters. With **Lake Edward**, it forms the headwaters of the White Nile River.

LAKE EDWARD. Called Lake Idi Amin Dada by Congolese and Ugandan cartographers in the 1970s, Lake Edward lies on the **Great Rift Valley** at an altitude of 912 m, south of the **Ruwenzori Mountains** and north of **Rwanda**, along **Congo/Zaire**'s border with **Uganda**. Eighty-eight kilometers long and 40 km wide, it covers 4,403 square km and with **Lake Albert** forms the headwaters of the White Nile River.

LAKE KIVU. One of **Congo/Zaire**'s largest **lakes**, Lake Kivu is 100 km long and 60 km wide and has a large island at its center. Lying in the **Great Rift Valley** at an altitude of 1,460 m, Lake Kivu drains via tributaries of the **Congo River** into the Atlantic Ocean, while the neighboring **Lakes Albert** and **Edward** drain via the Nile River system into the Mediterranean Sea. The cities of **Goma** and Gisenyi, **Rwanda**, lie on Lake Kivu's northern shore while **Bukavu** lies on its southern shore. The lake contains high levels of methane gas, which prevent the development of any **fish** or other animal life in its waters. Natural gas reserves below the lake are estimated at 60 billion cubic meters. However, the depth of the lake, 250 m, has prevented commercial exploitation.

LAKE MAÏ-NDOMBE. A relatively shallow lake lying in a marshy area near the center of the **Congo River Basin** in a remote, sparsely populated area of northern **Bandundu Province**, between Bandundu city and **Mbandaka**. Lake Maï-Ndombe is 130 km long and about 40 km wide, although its boundaries vary with the seasons.

LAKE MWERU. The largest lake in **Katanga Province**, lying in northern Katanga along the border with **Zambia**. Lake Mweru, 130 km long and 50 km wide, is fed by the Luapula River and drained by the Luvua River, which flows into the **Lualaba River** and eventually the **Congo River**.

LAKE TANGANYIKA. Considered the seventh-largest natural lake in the world, Lake Tanganyika is 670 km long and 100 km wide at its widest point, covering 32,900 square km. The lake lies on the **Great Rift Valley** at an altitude of 772 m, with a maximum depth of 1,435 meters. It is connected to **Lake Kivu** by the **Ruzizi River** and drains via the **Congo River** system into the Atlantic Ocean. Lake Tanganyika was first reached by Europeans in 1858 when British **explorers** Richard **Burton** and John **Speke** arrived from the East African coast. It enjoys a relatively temperate **climate**, good **rainfall** and fertile soils, which helped make the area around it one of the most densely populated in Africa. Lake Tanganyika formed part of the **Eastern Way transportation** route through which **minerals** from **Katanga** were exported by **rail** to **Kalemie**, across the lake to **Tanzania** and by rail once again to the port of Dar es Salaam. A group of antigovernment guerrillas, the **Parti Révolutionaire du Peuple (PRP)**, controlled some territory near the lake from the time of the **rebellions** following **independence**.

LAKE TUMBA. A small lake, 40 km long and 40 km wide, located in a marshy area of the central **Congo River Basin** near the **Congo River** about 80 km downriver from **Mbandaka**.

LAKE UPEMBA. A marshy lake lying in a swampy area of northern **Katanga** near Bukama. The lake lies near the **Lualaba River**, which is the headwater of the **Congo River**.

LAKES. **Congo/Zaire**'s major lakes lie in the east along the **Great Rift Valley**, although several are located in the **Congo River Basin**.

LAND. Congo/Zaire covers 2,345,000 square km, or nearly one million square miles, making it the third-largest nation in Africa after **Sudan** and Algeria. **Forest** and woodlands cover more than 50 percent of the territory. Estimated arable land is 25 percent. However, the **United Nations** Food and Agriculture Organization estimates that only 3 percent of the land is devoted to **crop** cultivation. Other organizations estimate less than 2 percent of the land is under cultivation. One tenth of the land is said to be devoted to pasture, primarily in the west, southeast and northeastern regions. The topsoil of the **Congo River Basin** area that covers more than half of the country is thin and only moderately fertile. The soil covering territory bordering the basin is considered better, while the soils of the highland and savanna areas are considered excellent. *See also* Eastern Highlands; Topography.

LAND LAW AND TENURE. According to the Congolese **constitution**, land technically belongs to the state, which grants or makes it available to individuals, private groups or publicly owned organizations. But the constitution also guarantees individual and collective rights to property which has been acquired by **customary** (traditional) **law** or statutory (written or modern) law. Most land, however, is held by population groups under traditional laws of tenure that considerably predate colonialism and statutory law. Aspects of ownership vary, but they generally are communal, that is the land is owned by the village, the chieftaincy or a **descent group**. The one exception is in urban areas where statutory laws have been applied for longer lengths of time and disputed titles have been settled to some degree. Irving Kaplan says, historically, land tenure was controlled most often by descent groups, called lineages, which acted as agents in distributing the land to families. Individuals often had a right to the fruits of the land accorded them and could pass it on to their descendants, but they were not authorized to sell the land or transfer it outside the lineage group. The lack of outright ownership was said by some to have discouraged farmers from investing in land improvements that would have raised productivity.

The early **colonial era** authorities did not understand land ownership by **clans** and lineages. The **Congo Free State (CFS)** initially laid claim to all land not inhabited or under cultivation. A decree in 1906 liberalized the law to allow villages and communities to own three times the land under cultivation, in order to allow for **crop** rotation. Early CFS legislation allowed Africans to buy and sell land, but the practice never became common. Sales were made to Europeans, but it is likely the Africans saw the sale as more of a lease, that is, compensation for temporary use of the land which eventually would revert back to its owner. In 1938, the colonial government ended sales of land by Africans to private parties, saying land rights could be transferred only to the state and only the state could lease or sell land to private individuals. In 1953, legislation was proposed allowing Africans in urban areas to purchase land, but only three **provinces** implemented the proposals. The potential did exist for Africans to obtain legal ownership under the *paysannat indigène* system suggested by **Leopold III** in 1933, before he became king. The program was aimed at improving **agricultural** productivity, but it did not begin until the 1950s and was ended following **independence**.

In June 1966, the government enacted the **Bakajika Law**, which granted the state ownership of all wealth above and below the ground. At the peak of **Zairianization**, the government claimed ownership of all land through a constitutional amendment enacted on December 31, 1971, and the General Property Law of July 1973. Under the law, individual rights to land were accorded through concessions by the government or through customary land rights. The changes caused considerable confusion, since only a small portion of land was registered and previous laws and customs continued to be observed. The absence of adequate recordkeeping and a high incidence of forged and false claims created a system in which bribery and political influence were frequently required to settle land disputes.

LANGUAGES. The languages spoken in Congo/Zaire come from four major sources. Most indigenous languages are related to the **Bantu** root, which is classified as a branch of the Benue-Congo group. Of the estimated 200 languages and 450 dialects spoken in the country, Bantu-related tongues are spoken by an estimated 80 percent of the people.

Bantu-speakers moved into the area from the north during the first millennium AD and from there spread across the continent. Sometime during the second millennium AD, probably between 1500 and 1600, people speaking languages of the Adamawa-Eastern and Sudanic groups migrated into northern Congo, either driving out earlier settlers or assimilating them. The arrival of Belgian traders, **missionaries** and colonial officials in the 1800s brought French, which became the official language. French is still used in all formal academic, business, diplomatic, legal, political and many social transactions.

Congo/Zaire also has four "national" languages, Kikongo, **Lingala**, Swahili and Tshiluba, which are lingua francas in their respective regions. Lingala, a **trade** language used along the **Congo River**, is descended from the **Ngala** people of northwestern Congo/Zaire and has long been the language of the army as well as the primary national language of the **administration** and **civil service**. Its use by soldiers and civil servants, who frequently were assigned to regions other than their home areas, led to its grudging recognition as the second language of government. Kikongo is the language of the **Kongo** people and the lingua franca of **Bas-Congo**. Its use extends from the Atlantic Ocean to **Kinshasa** and as far east as **Kikwit**. Although it is spoken in a relatively small geographical area, the density of the population in western Congo/Zaire and the use of Lingala in neighboring **Republic of the Congo** contributed to its importance. Tshiluba, the language of the **Luba ethnic group**, is the lingua franca of most of the **Kasais** and part of northern **Katanga**. Swahili, actually a dialectal version of the tongue used in East Africa, is the lingua franca of the eastern part of the country and is heard in **Orientale**, **Kivu** and most of **Katanga**. A fifth language, Lomongo of the **Mongo** people, is widely used in **Équateur Province** of northwestern Congo/Zaire.

Missionaries seeking to produce vernacular versions of the Bible in the early 1900s developed written forms of a number of languages and encouraged the adoption of standardized dialects, especially for the Kongo, Luba, Mongo and Ngala tongues. Pidgin forms, particularly of Lingala, were widely used and all but those Congolese hailing from the most remote villages appeared able to communicate using some combination of the various tongues.

LEAGUE OF VIGILANT YOUTH. *See* LIGUE DES JEUNES VIGILANTS (LJV).

LEGAL SYSTEM. *See* JUDICIAL SYSTEM.

LEGISLATIVE COUNCIL / CONSEIL LÉGISLATIF. The official name of Zaire's national assembly, or **parliament**, from 1972 to 1993. All of its 310 members belonged to the **Mouvement Populaire de la Révolution (MPR)** party, although they competed for their seats against other members in their districts. Under the **constitution** of 1974, which created the party-state, the Legislative Council lost most of its powers to the **Central Committee** of the MPR and became an organization primarily of young party *cadres* whose sessions were devoted primarily to rubber-stamping party initiatives. With the advent of multipartyism in 1990, the Legislative Council was officially abolished and replaced by the **Haut Conseil de la République (HCR)**. In 1992, however, when the HCR drafted a constitution removing many of the laws and tenets of **Mobutism** and elected **opposition** leader Étienne **Tshisekedi** as **prime minister**, **Mobutu** reconvened the Legislative Council and ordered it to draft another constitution. The move was denounced as illegal by the opposition and some foreign governments and led to a period of political stalemate characterized by two rival governments. In late 1993, a compromise was reached and the Legislative Council was merged with the HCR to form the **Haut Conseil de la République / Parlement de la Transition (HCR/PT)**. This organ was to oversee the transitional period, draft a constitution, and organize national **elections**. *See also* Democratic Transition; Legislative System.

LEGISLATIVE SYSTEM. Since **independence**, the legislature has formed one of several major branches of the Congolese **government**. However, it was steadily weakened during the 1970s and 1980s as the presidency and party assumed greater powers. Under the **Loi Fondamentale** (Fundamental Law), in effect from 1960 to 1964, the Congo had a bicameral legislature similar to **Belgium**'s, which elected the **president** to serve as head of state. The **prime minister** and ministers were also chosen by **parliament** and could be removed by it. However, the Loi

Fondamentale failed to adequately specify the powers accorded to the president and prime minister and, as a result, it led to a number of constitutional crises, two of which prompted military interventions, in 1960 and 1965.

Under the **constitution** of August 1964, attempts were made to further define the powers of the two offices. The president was given the power to appoint and dismiss the prime minister with the approval of parliament. Following the **coup d'etat** that brought **Mobutu** to power, the president was granted wide powers of decree and, with the creation of the **Mouvement Populaire de la Révolution (MPR)** as the sole legal party, the presidency began to assume many legislative powers. Parliament was reduced to a consultative body and subsequently was suspended. The constitution of June 1967 accorded the president even greater powers, allowing him to govern by executive order, which carried the force of law. In addition, the bicameral parliament was replaced by a single chamber called the National Assembly.

On July 19, 1972, as part of the **Authenticity** program, the assembly was renamed the **Legislative Council**. In August 1974, following a meeting of the **Political Bureau** and the Legislative Council, a new constitution was enacted that incorporated all changes and ordinances instituted since the 1967 constitution. Under the 1974 constitution, the Legislative Council was subordinate to the party, the president and his appointed ministers. The Legislative Council remained one of five organs of government, but the president was automatically president of all five organs and the party became the supreme institution of state. Members of the Legislative Council had the right to initiate laws "concurrently" with the president.

In the late 1970s, following the **Shaba** invasions and amid pressure from the international community for greater political freedom, a measure of liberalization was enacted. The Legislative Council regained some of its lost powers. The post of prime minister, renamed first commissioner of state, was restored. The Legislative Council was allowed to summon ministers for questioning on budgetary matters. And multiple candidates for legislative seats were allowed within the party structure. By the end of 1980, however, most of these measures had been reversed except for the provision allowing multiple candidates in legislative **elections**.

The influence of the Legislative Council was further reduced by the creation on September 2, 1980, of the MPR **Central Committee**, whose 120 members were chosen by the Political Bureau of the party. The Central Committee eventually assumed most real legislative functions and became the body of "consultation and debate" of the party-state. The Legislative Council's role became primarily one of approving party initiatives. Elections for five-year legislative terms were held in September 1982, during which multiple candidates, proposed at the local level with Political Bureau approval, were allowed. More than three-fourths of the incumbents were turned out and replaced by a youthful body whose average age was 35 years. Elections were held again in September 1987. By then the most influential politicians had moved to the Central Committee.

Following Mobutu's announcement of the transition to multiparty politics on **April 24, 1990**, the Legislative Council was suspended and the **National Conference**, convened in 1991, took over the task of debating and legislating the **democratic transition**. The National Conference proclaimed itself the **Conference Nationale Souveraine (CNS)** in April 1992 and determined that its decisions would be sovereign and by law would be carried out by the executive. This act brought a protest from Mobutu, who accused the body of staging a "civilian" coup d'etat. The CNS drafted a constitution that considerably reduced the powers of the presidency in favor of a prime minister elected by the legislature.

The CNS concluded its work in December 1992 and established the 453-member **Haut Conseil de la République (HCR)** to take over legislative duties and oversee multiparty elections. By then Mobutu had decided the process was under **opposition** control and announced he was reconvening the Legislative Council to draft another constitution. A political standoff ensued characterized by two rival governments. It ended in late 1993 with an agreement to merge the HCR and the Legislative Council into a transitional body of 745 members called the **Haut Conseil de la République / Parlement de la Transition (HCR/PT)**. This body was to oversee the transition, draft a constitution and organize elections by July 1995. However, political infighting and the economic crisis slowed its work and, in June 1995, it voted to extend the transitional period until July 9,

1997, and postpone elections by two years. This timetable was disrupted by the offensive of the **Alliance des Forces Démocratiques pour la Libération du Congo/Zaïre (AFDL)**, which took power in **Kinshasa** in May 1997 and announced elections would be held in 1999.

LELE. A small but independent **ethnic group** of the **Kuba** cluster living in the lower **Kasai Province**. Organized into relatively autonomous villages, often in conflict with each other, the Lele were believed to have been moved by war to the less fertile areas of the Kasai between the **Lulua River** and Loango River. They were among the groups that most strongly resisted the Belgian colonial administration.

LEOPOLD II (1835 - 1909). The second king of **Belgium**, who financed the first explorations of the **Congo** and engineered the territory's exploitation following the European partition of Africa. Leopold II began seeking a source of raw materials for his nation soon after acceding to the throne in 1865. Hearing reports of great **mineral** wealth in Africa, he formed the **International African Association**, over which he presided from 1876 to 1880, to encourage exploration on the continent. After **explorer** Henry Morton **Stanley**'s highly publicized expedition to "find" David **Livingstone,** Leopold recruited Stanley in 1878 and financed an expedition to explore the **Congo River**. The first mission was a near-disaster, but Stanley established that most rivers in central Africa drained through the Congo River system into the Atlantic Ocean and not through the Nile River into the Mediterranean Sea, as believed by many at the time.

Stanley undertook a second expedition to obtain treaties with as many local **chiefs** as possible and to scout for **trading** stations up the river. He returned in 1884 with 450 treaties which Leopold took to the **Berlin Conference** to bolster his claim to be actively engaged in the exploration and "civilization" of central Africa. The conference concluded in February 1885 by recognizing the treaties signed with the **International Association of the Congo** as an independent state with Leopold as its sovereign. In order to pay for the administration of what in 1886 became the **Congo Free State (CFS)**, Leopold granted to private companies large trading concessions called "trusts," which became virtual monopolies. The king also passed a forced **labor** tax that allowed companies to require Congolese to work for them or supply **rubber** and **ivory**.

The brutality with which some companies collected the "taxes" led to a public outcry in Europe and America that forced a reluctant Belgian parliament to annex the CFS in 1908 as a colony, the **Belgian Congo**. Leopold II, who died the following year, is credited with pioneering the establishment of an administration and **transportation** network in the territory. However, he is more frequently remembered as the wily monarch who because of personal ambition allowed a regime of terror, **human rights** abuse and uncontrolled exploitation to develop in what would one day become the Democratic Republic of the Congo. He was succeeded by his nephew, **Albert I**.

LEOPOLD III (1901 - 1983). Fourth king of **Belgium** from February 23, 1934, until July 16, 1951. Leopold III assumed the throne after his father **Albert I** died in a mountain-climbing accident. During World War II, Leopold declared Belgium neutral and refused to join the parliament in a government-in-exile. He surrendered to the Third Reich and spent most of World War II under house arrest in Germany and Austria. Following the war, Leopold III was accused of treason by liberal and socialist members of the Belgian parliament. He lived in exile in Switzerland for a number of years until an agreement was reached whereby he abdicated in favor of his son, **Baudoin**, in order to allow the royal family to return to Belgium. Leopold III did not possess the presence or consuming desire for power of his great-uncle, **Leopold II**.

Leopold III's major contribution to Congolese affairs came in 1933 when, before becoming king, he proposed a system whereby Congolese could obtain legal ownership of **land** by cultivating it regularly, even if it lay fallow for a number of years. The purpose of the proposal was to counter a law in force at the time by which the state assumed ownership of virtually all land not under cultivation. Leopold's proposal, called *paysannat indigène*, was instituted after World War II. *See also* Land Law and Tenure.

LEOPOLDVILLE. The capital of **Congo/Zaire** during the **colonial era** and the first years of **independence**. Its name was changed to **Kinshasa** in 1966.

LEOPOLDVILLE ROUND TABLE. The first of three meetings aimed at ending the **Katanga secession**. The Leopoldville meeting was held in January and February 1961 and preceded the **Tananarive Conference** in Madagascar in March and the **Coquilhatville Conference** in April and May of the same year. None produced an end to the secession, leading to an escalation of **United Nations** military operations later that year.

LIA. An **ethnic** sub**group** of the **Mongo**, living between the Tshuapa and **Lomami Rivers** in the southeastern corner of **Équateur Province**. The Lia are said to differ from most of the Mongo linguistically, culturally and politically. They are headed by a hierarchy of sacred **chiefs** and subchiefs.

LIBOKE LYA BANGALA. Literally translated "bundle of **Ngala**," the Liboke lya Bangala was an association formed in the 1950s to defend the traditions and interests of the Ngala **ethnic group** in **Congo/Zaire**'s large cities. It was outlawed by **Mobutu** following his **coup d'etat**, along with all other ethnically based political organizations.

LIBYA, RELATIONS WITH. Relations between **Congo/Zaire** and Libya historically were poor and Libyan leader Muammar Khadhafi and **Mobutu** were intense rivals virtually since they came to power. Mobutu visited Libya in 1973 as part of a tour of **Arab countries** after he announced he was breaking relations with **Israel**. However, the two leaders backed opposing factions in the **Angolan** civil war and sided with opposing camps in the dispute over Western Sahara. Relations deteriorated further when Zaire recognized Israel in 1982. In 1983, when Libya occupied northern **Chad**'s Aouzou Strip, Zaire sent troops to Ndjamena to bolster the government of Hissen Habre. Khadhafi publicly called for the "elimination" of Mobutu in 1985. Discussions on normalizing relations began in the early 1990s but no major progress was made.

Laurent **Kabila**, who became president in 1997 after the fall of Mobutu, enjoyed good relations with Libya because of close ties to radical African leaders dating from the 1960s. Kabila visited Libya on several occasions and Khadhafi tried to mediate the rebellion by the **Rassemblement Congolais pour la Démocratie (RCD)** which broke out in August 1998.

LIGNES AÉRIENNES CONGOLAISES. The name given to the national airlines in November 1997 by the Laurent **Kabila government** after the fall of **Mobutu**. The airlines replaced **Air Zaïre**, which was declared bankrupt in 1995. *See also* Air Transportation.

LIGUE DES JEUNES VIGILANTS (LJV) / LEAGUE OF VIGILANT YOUTH. A radical **youth** group formed on January 9, 1966, in **Kinshasa** to struggle for "national consciousness" and against imperialism. It declared its ideology to be **nationalism** and economic independence. It was a precursor to the **Mouvement Populaire de la Révolution (MPR)** and an early signal of the nationalistic trend that emerged in the late 1960s and culminated with **Zairianization** in 1973.

LIKASI. A small city in southern **Katanga**, lying northwest of **Lubumbashi** on the road to **Kolwezi**. Likasi is an urban district of 235 square km with an estimated **population** of 250,000. It is the site of a chemical plant that produces sulfuric acid primarily for refineries of the **Générale des Carrières et des Mines (GECAMINES)**. Milling, **cement** and **coal mining** operations are located nearby. It was the scene of some of the worst violence against **Luba**-Kasai during the episode of **ethnic cleansing** in **Shaba** in 1992.

LINEAGE GROUPS. *See* DESCENT GROUPS.

LINGALA. One of four national **languages**, Lingala is used widely in **Kinshasa** and in the northwestern **Congo/Zaire**, as well as by the military and **civil service** throughout the country. A **trade** language which came into use before **independence** along the **Congo River**, it is the language of the **armed forces** and, after French, is the language of the **administration** and **government**. It was the only African language used publicly by **Mobutu**.

LISALA. A small city of about 100,000 inhabitants lying in **Équateur Province** in northwestern Congo/Zaire between **Mbandaka** and

Kisangani, Lisala is also known as the city where **Mobutu** was born and received his early **education**. It is a **river port** that serves as a processing and **transportation** center for **plantations** in the surrounding area where food **crops, palm oil, rubber, coffee**, cocoa and **rice** are grown.

LITERACY. Colonial officials estimated the basic literacy rate in the **Congo** at **independence** to be 60 percent. By 1990, this figure had increased and the **World Bank** reported 72 percent of Congolese were literate, defined as being able to read and write a short simple statement. Literacy among males was reportedly 84 percent and 61 percent among females. If accurate, the figures placed Congo/Zaire among the countries with the highest literacy rates in Africa. Other demographers, however, believed the figures were high and placed functional literacy at 20 to 30 percent. The relatively high rates were believed to be the result of the early colonial emphasis on primary (though not secondary) schooling and the emphasis by many religious groups on **education**. The use of the national **languages** in primary education was instituted in the 1970s as part of the **Authenticity** movement. Critics said the policy contributed to a decline in literacy, but others said the decline was due more to deteriorating facilities, falling enrollment because of financial constraints on parents, and increased absenteeism by underpaid teachers obliged to seek other sources of **income**. *See also* Women.

LITHO MOBOTI NZOYOMBO (1924 - 1982). Uncle of **Mobutu** and head of the family **clan** who, at his death on February 25, 1982, was one of the wealthiest and most powerful men in Zaire. Litho was born on June 22, 1924, at Kawele in **Équateur Province**. He studied at the **Catholic Church** mission of Molegbe and prior to **independence** worked as an agronomist with the Institut National pour l'Étude Agronomique du Congo (INEAC). He was a state secretary in charge of planning at the presidency from 1963 to 1965. From 1965 to 1970, he served as minister of finance and subsequently as minister of **agriculture**. The owner of a major group of **plantations** and food-processing companies, Litho was also president of the Congolese subsidiaries of a number of multinational companies. He was elected to the **Legislative**

Council in 1977 and was named to the **Central Committee** of the **Mouvement Populaire de la Révolution (MPR)** in 1980.

LIVESTOCK. The raising of livestock is carried out primarily in the savanna and highland areas of **Katanga, Orientale, Bas-Congo** and the **Kivu Provinces**. The wet areas of the **Congo River Basin** are not conducive to animal husbandry because of the presence of the **tsetse fly** and numerous other parasites and **diseases**.

At **independence**, cattle numbered one million head. The number dropped by 20 percent during the early 1960s but returned to preindependence levels in the mid-1970s. In 1985, the Zairian government reported that the country produced 50,000 tons of butchered meat whereas demand was 110,000 tons. One-fourth of the shortfall was met by **imports** and the remainder by substitution, primarily of **fish** and game meat.

Most traditional herding is carried out in Orientale and the Kivu Provinces. Commercial herding is more prevalent in Katanga, **Kasaï Occidental**, Bas-Congo, **Bandundu** and upper **Équateur** Provinces. An estimated three million head of sheep and goat are raised, primarily by small-herd owners. Hog production, primarily in Bandundu and Bas-Congo, reached 800,000 head in the 1980s. There is also some commercial raising of chickens and ducks near urban centers, such as at the "model" farm at N'Sele outside **Kinshasa**. Following **Zairianization** in 1973, large foreign-owned ranches were placed under control of a **government** agency, the **Office National pour le Développement de l'Élevage (ONDE)**, and small ranches were leased to Congolese. Under **Retrocession** one year later, however, some ranches were returned to their previous owners.

LIVINGSTONE, DAVID (1813 - 1873). A Scottish **missionary** and **explorer** who was one of the first Europeans to travel through southern and eastern Africa. Livingstone began his explorations searching for the source of the Nile River. He was one of the first Europeans to reach what is now **Congo/Zaire**. He crossed **Lake Mweru** and Lake Bengweulu in 1867-68 and traveled on the **Lualaba River** to reach **Nyangwe** in 1871. His disappearance for two years in the late 1860s was one of the major reasons for the first expedition by Henry Morton **Stanley**. During this trip, Stanley developed the theory that the Lualaba River, which

Livingstone thought to be the headwater of the Nile, was in fact the headwater of the **Congo River**. Stanley met Livingstone at **Ujiji**, on the eastern shore of **Lake Tanganyika**, in 1871, on his way to the Congo River. Livingstone died two years after meeting Stanley without ever leaving Africa.

LOBITO. A port city on **Angola's** Atlantic coast, 30 km north of Benguela, Lobito is on a major **export** route for **minerals** from **Katanga** until the **Benguela Railway** was closed by Angolan rebels in 1975.

LOI BAKAJIKA. *See* BAKAJIKA LAW.

LOI COUTUMIÈRE. *See* CUSTOMARY LAW.

LOI FONDAMENTALE / FUNDAMENTAL LAW. A charter passed by the parliament of **Belgium** on May 19, 1960, to serve as a temporary **constitution** for the Congo during its first years of **independence**. The Loi Fondamentale, which drew heavily from the Belgian system of **government**, provided for a **president** as chief of state and a **prime minister** as chief of government, both elected by a bicameral legislature. However, in its effort to provide checks and balances, the charter failed to adequately define the division of power between the executive and **legislative** branches of government. This deficiency, combined with rising interregional and interethnic tensions, contributed to the political crisis following independence. The Loi Fondamentale was replaced by the first constitution on August 1, 1964.

LOMAMI RIVER. A tributary of the **Congo River**, the Lomami rises in southern **Katanga Province** near **Kamina** and meanders north, almost parallel to the **Lualaba River**, for more than 1,500 km before joining the Congo River some 100 km downriver from **Kisangani**.

LOMÉ CONVENTION. An agreement between the **European Union (EU)** and nearly 80 developing nations of Africa, the Caribbean, and the Pacific (ACP) to foster greater economic cooperation by lowering tariffs and other market restrictions between the developing nations and the EU. The Lomé Convention also included provisions for development assistance. The first convention was signed in Lomé, **Togo**, in 1975 and came into force on April 1, 1976, replacing earlier agreements reached in Yaoundé, Cameroon, and Arusha, **Tanzania**. Zaire was an original signatory. The agreement allowed many **agricultural** products from ACP countries to be exported duty-free to the EU. An **export** stabilization program (STABEX) attempted to compensate countries hurt by the removal of **price controls** and exposure to more competitive economies. Subsequent conventions, signed in 1979, 1984 and 1989, expanded the programs to include virtually all exports to the EU from ACP countries.

LONDON CLUB. The unofficial name of the group of approximately 100 major commercial and private banks which negotiated requests for external **debt** reschedulings by countries in arrears on their debt repayments. According to **World Bank** figures, Zaire in 1980 owed $1.4 billion, or nearly one-third its total external debt, to private creditors. In 1993, this debt had declined to $836 million, whereas total foreign debt had risen to $11.2 billion. The change represented a massive shift in the government's debt from private creditors to multilateral lending institutions and donor governments.

LOOTINGS. *See* PILLAGES.

LOVANIUM UNIVERSITY. The original name of Congo/Zaire's first **university**, founded in 1954 by **Catholic Church missionaries** on hills overlooking **Leopoldville**. The university was nationalized in 1971 following **student** unrest and became the **Kinshasa** campus of the **Université Nationale du Zaïre (UNAZA)**. It was returned to the church in the mid-1990s.

LUALABA RIVER. The name often given to the headwaters of the **Congo River**, the Lualaba rises in the **Katanga** plateau at an altitude of 1,500 m above sea level and courses 1600 km north to **Kisangani**. Although some international cartographers differentiate between the Congo and Lualaba Rivers, official Congolese maps consider the Lualaba to be the upper extension of the Congo River. **Rice** and other food **crops** are cultivated along its banks and two **electrical power** plants near **Kolwezi** furnish 250 kW each to the region and its **mining** installations. The Lualaba is navigable from Bukama to **Kasongo** near the border between Katanga and **Sud-Kivu**, and from **Kindu**, in **Maniema Province**, to Ubundu in **Orientale Province**. **Railways** circumvent the unnavigable stretches of the river, but most **exports** from Katanga go by rail to **Ilebo** and down the **Kasai River** to **Kinshasa**, along what is called the **National Way**, or via **Tanzania, Zambia** and Zimbabwe to ports on the Indian Ocean.

LUBA. A large cluster of tribes living in the **Kasai** and **Katanga Provinces**, the Luba group inhabits territory stretching from the **Kasai River** around **Kananga** and **Mbuji-Mayi** in the west to the **Lualaba** and **Lufira Rivers** near **Bukavu** and Bulundi in the southeast. The Luba are primarily patrilineal and speak Tshiluba, one of Congo/Zaire's four national **languages**. Jan Vansina divides the Luba into three clusters: the Luba-Shaba or Luba-Katanga (which include the Kanioka, Lakundwe and Lomotwa), the Luba-Kasai (which include the **Lulua**, Luntu, Binji, Mputu and North **Kete**), and the **Songye** (which include **Bangu-Bangu** and, according to some, the **Hemba**).

According to legend, the Luba began organizing under local **chiefs** in the 15th century. They were invaded by a foreign **Bantu**-speaking group from the north called the Balopwe, which, led by **Kongolo**, founded a Balopwe-dominated empire, with its capital at Mwibele. At its peak in the early 1600s, the group controlled considerable territory, including most of Katanga and southern Kasai. Ethnographers say the empire was divided into provinces which were divided into chiefdoms, or groups of villages. The **king** retained a great deal of power over appointments and tribute. Occasionally, deposed or disgruntled chiefs would leave with their followers to form a new state. One such split lead to the formation of the **Lunda** empire. Shifts in population and increased **trade** led to a consolidation of the empire in the late 1700s and early 1800s. The Luba empire began to decline in the late 1800s with the rise of the **Chokwe**, who raided many of their settlements.

Independent and ethnocentric, the Luba resisted outsiders, including the **Afro-Arabs** and Europeans. During the **colonial era**, however, many Luba moved to urban areas and **missionary** centers to take advantage of **education** and **employment** opportunities. Many rose to positions of responsibility in business and the **civil service**. Nevertheless, the colonial authorities were said to consider them a source of dissent and as a result supported ethnic rivals such as the **Lulua**. The Luba fought a bitter land war with the Lulua in 1959-60 and they fought Moïse **Tshombe** and the Lunda during the **Katanga secession**. Many fled to eastern Kasai following massacres in Katanga in 1960. Like many southern and eastern groups, they tended to be suspicious of the central **government**.

During the **Mobutu** era, many Luba were critical of his government and suffered because of it, although many others served in senior government and party positions. Nevertheless, the Luba's ethnocentricity and upward mobility caused resentment among other Congolese. In 1992-93, hundreds of thousands of Luba-Kasai were expelled from **Shaba** by local militia in an episode of politically motivated **ethnic cleansing**. The installation of Laurent **Kabila** following the fall of Mobutu in May 1997 brought the first Luba to the **presidency** of the country.

LUBUMBASHI. Formerly **Elisabethville**, Lubumbashi is the capital of **Katanga Province** and Congo/Zaire's second most important city after **Kinshasa**. It was the capital of the secessionist **Katanga** state in 1961-63. A company town long dominated by the **mining** industry and the **Général des Carrières et des Mines (GECAMINES)**, Lubumbashi is an administrative urban district with an estimated **population** of one million, lying on the Katanga high plateau. The city is surrounded by open-pit and underground mines as well as a **copper** refinery and related metallurgical plants. As the second-largest industrial center in the country with the second-highest per-capita **income**, Lubumbashi is also a **manufacturing** center for the cigarette, **cloth**, shoe, metalwork, **palm oil** and food-processing industries.

The city is linked to the Atlantic Ocean by the **National Way** across Congo/Zaire and by the **Benguela Railway** through **Angola**. It is also linked by **railway** through **Zambia** and Zimbabwe to Indian Ocean ports in **Tanzania**, Mozambique and **South Africa**. In many ways closer to southern Africa than to central Africa in geography, traditional **trade** routes, and cultural temperament, Lubumbashi has often felt ignored by the **government** in Kinshasa, which it frequently perceives as a remote capital that profits from its wealth but provides few services in return. After the fall of **Mobutu** in May 1997, the government of President Laurent **Kabila**, which was dominated by easterners, pledged to rebuild **industry** and infrastructure in eastern Congo/Zaire and restore Lubumbashi's importance as the economic capital of the region.

LUEBO. A major town on the **Lulua River** in **Kasaï Occidental**, Luebo is a regional educational and commercial center.

LUFIRA RIVER. A 500-km-long tributary of the **Lualaba River**, the Lufira rises in the highlands between **Lubumbashi** and **Likasi** near the **Zambian** border and flows north, joining the Lualaba River below Bukama. Two hydroelectric complexes located near Likasi supply **electrical power** to **Lubumbashi**, Likasi and **Kolwezi**.

LULUA. An **ethnic group** related to the **Luba** cluster living in **Kasaï Occidental Province** between the **Lulua** and **Kasai Rivers**. The Lulua supplied **Angolan slave** and **ivory** traders in the 19th century and drove the Luba from western Kasai in the late part of the century. They were courted by the Belgian colonial authorities to counter the Luba, who had been victimized by the **Afro-Arab** slave traders and were considered more independent.

During the early **colonial era**, the Lulua were considered relatively complacent and did not seek **education** and **employment** opportunities as actively as did other groups in the region. After World War II, however, they began to organize politically and formed the **Association des Lulua-Frères** in 1953 to defend their interests, primarily in urban centers. In 1959, the Lulua convened a conference during which they called for autonomy rather than **independence**. Some historians have charged that colonial authorities encouraged historical tensions between the Lulua and Luba. These tensions, centered primarily around traditional **land** disputes, erupted into violence in October 1959, resulting in massacres of villages, the displacement of tens of thousands of people and the destruction of millions of dollars worth of property and **crops**. The famine that followed obliged the **United Nations** to mount a million-dollar relief effort in the region in 1960-61.

LULUA RIVER. A large, but mostly unnavigable **river** that originates near the **Zambian** border east of **Dilolo** and flows 900 km north and then west, joining the **Kasai River** between **Luebo** and **Ilebo**.

LULUABOURG. The name of the capital of **Kasai Province** during the **colonial era** and early years of **independence**, renamed **Kananga** in 1966.

LUMUMBA, PATRICE (1925 - 1961). Congo/Zaire's first **prime minister** and a principal advocate of pan-Africanism, who died under mysterious circumstances less than one year after **independence**. Fluent in French, **Lingala** and Kiswahili, Patrice Lumumba was a fiery orator who inspired strong feelings of **nationalism** on a continent that still bore the psychological scars of the "colonial yoke." However, his rhetoric and political overtures to Soviet-bloc nations at the height of the Cold War caused fear among groups with vested interests in Congo, including Western governments, private businessmen and moderate African leaders. His assassination in 1961 aroused anger and consternation, particularly in the socialist world.

Lumumba was born on July 2, 1925, in the village of Onalua in Sankuru district of **Kasai Province**. Of the **Tetela ethnic group**, he received his primary **education** at a local **Protestant missionary** school and attended secondary school in **Leopoldville**. As an adult, he moved to **Stanleyville**, where he became president of the local club of **évolués**, provincial president of the **Association de Personnel Indigène de la Colonie (APIC)**, and a regular contributor to various magazines. In 1956, he was convicted, reportedly for political reasons, of theft and spent one year in prison. He was freed in 1957 with his reputation considerably enhanced. Lumumba worked for a local brewery for two years, rising to the position of commercial director.

In December 1958, he attended the first **Pan-African Conference** in Accra, in newly independent Ghana, where he met Ghanaian President Kwame **Nkrumah** and became further acquainted with the concepts of Pan-Africanism and "active neutralism." He is said to have been the first Congolese leader to openly call for **independence**, at a political rally on December 28, 1958. He helped found the **Mouvement National Congolais**

(MNC) and attempted to make it a nationally based **political party** by attracting a variety of regional and ethnic leaders. He achieved some success, but fighting between the **Luba** and **Lulua** tribes caused a split in the Kasai-based wing of the party and personality conflicts caused some leaders to break away to form their own parties.

On October 31, 1959, riots erupted in Stanleyville after an MNC meeting. Lumumba was arrested the next day and accused of having provoked them. However, he was released in January 1960 in order to attend the **Round Table Conference** in Brussels. The MNC scored significant victories in the **elections** of May 1960, but did not win an absolute majority. Lumumba succeeded in forging a compromise **government** in which he became prime minister and defense minister and Joseph **Kasavubu** of the **Alliance des Bakongo (ABAKO)** party was elected **president**. The agreement lasted only two months, during which time the central government's authority seriously deteriorated and **Katanga Province** and the **South Kasai** region seceded. In late August, Lumumba declared martial law and imprisoned a number of his rivals. He also issued a request for aid from Soviet-bloc nations to help put down the secessions. The request caused consternation in Western capitals and led Kasavubu to dismiss him. However, Lumumba refused to accept his dismissal. Rather, he and his cabinet accused Kasavubu of treason and voted to dismiss him, precipitating a constitutional crisis. The head of the armed forces, Joseph-Désiré **Mobutu**, announced in mid-September he was "neutralizing" the government for six months. A group of young intellectuals, called the **College of Commissioners**, was appointed to govern in the interim.

When the **United Nations** voted to seat the Kasavubu delegation in the General Assembly, Lumumba, with Antoine **Gizenga** and Anicet **Kashamura**, decided to move the MNC's base to Stanleyville. Gizenga and Kashamura arrived, but Lumumba never did. He left Leopoldville on the night of November 26-27 and was traveling by **road** toward the region when he was captured in western **Kivu** by Congolese **armed forces**. He was imprisoned first at Camp Hardy in Thysville in **Bas-Congo**. However, authorities feared he would spark an uprising among the soldiers at the camp and, in what most historians believe was a calculated move aimed at his elimination, ordered him to be flown on January 17, 1961, to **Elisabethville** where his archenemy Moïse **Tshombe** was based. According to reports compiled by investigative commissions, he was guarded during the flight by Luba soldiers, who considered him responsible for the massacre of Luba in Katanga by Congolese troops a few months earlier. According to the investigators, Lumumba and his two companions, ex-Senate vice president Joseph Okito and ex-Minister of Youth and Sports Maurice Mpolo, were severely beaten during the flight. Most believe he died shortly after his arrival in Elisabethville. His body was never found.

The Katangan government announced on February 13 that Lumumba had been killed by "angry tribesmen" following an "escape attempt." Mobutu, in a 1985 interview, said Lumumba was killed on January 17 in Elisabethville, that he was not killed by soldiers and that a Belgian journalist witnessed the execution. Although Mobutu, as armed forces chief of staff, reportedly ordered Lumumba flown to Elisabethville, he denied responsibility for the murder, saying it occurred in secessionist Katanga.

Lumumba's death caused an international outcry and precipitated the **Stanleyville secession**. It also caused the **Soviet Union** and a number of East European states to withdraw recognition of the Leopoldville government, refuse to finance the UN operation in the Congo, and begin covert programs supporting various rebellions in the country. The secessions and **rebellions** eventually were suppressed in the mid-1960s, following the Mobutu **coup d'etat**. Today, Lumumba is still a hero and a martyr for many, and many Africans still believe in his dream of an Africa united in the pursuit of its own political interests and economic development.

LUNDA. A large **ethnic group** related historically to the **Luba**, living in southern **Katanga Province**, northern **Zambia** and western **Angola**. In **Congo/Zaire**, Lunda-related people also live in an area between the Lubilash and **Kasai Rivers**, in southwestern **Kasai** and the southeastern tip of **Bandundu Province**. The Lunda empire was formed by a group led by **Kibinda Ilunga**, which split from the Luba in the 1550s. It flourished during the 17th and 18th centuries and expanded south to straddle what became Congo's border with Angola and Zambia. Unlike the Luba, the Lunda sought to expand their empire by absorbing other peoples. They organized a political structure with related hierarchies and by the end of the 17th century had created the position of paramount **king**, the **Mwata Yanvu**. During the 18th century, the Lunda expanded their empire in search of **copper**, salt, **slaves** and **ivory**. The empire began to decline in the mid-19th century, however, and was attacked by the **Chokwe**, who at one point took the Lunda capital.

Following World War II, a Lunda political organization began to coalesce, formed in part to counter Luba and Chokwe interest groups. It came to be known as the **Confédération des Associations Katangaises (CONAKAT)** party and was headed by Moïse **Tshombe**. The **elections** of May 1960 gave CONAKAT an absolute majority in the Katangan provincial assembly and led to the formation of a one-party government in **Katanga**. However, the Lunda felt excluded from power in the central **government** in **Leopoldville** and eventually opted to support the **Katanga secession**.

The Lunda were a major source of **opposition** to the **Mobutu** government. Lunda members of the **Gendarmerie Katangaise** staged the **Shaba** invasions in 1977 and 1978 from bases in Angola. Lunda villages afterwards suffered reprisals by Congolese **armed forces**. Some Lunda leaders were involved in the expulsions, or **ethnic cleansing**, of Luba-Kasai in 1992-93, which displaced hundreds of thousands of longtime residents of Shaba. Many joined the rebellion led by Laurent **Kabila** in 1996.

LUNDA BULULU, VINCENT. The first **prime minister** of the **democratic transition**, Lunda was appointed by **Mobutu** following the announcement of multipartyism in April 1990. He resigned in March 1991 to pave the way for the appointment of Crispin **Mulumba Lukoji**, a technocrat from the south whose government was meant to appease **opposition** groups rallying around Étienne **Tshisekedi**. Lunda joined rebels of the **Rassemblement Congolais pour la Démocratie (RCD)** in August 1998 and in January 1999 was named a vice president of the group.

LUNDULA, VICTOR. An uncle of Patrice **Lumumba**, Lundula was a leader of the **Mouvement National Congolais (MNC)** who was appointed the Congo's first chief of the **armed forces** following the mutiny of the **Force Publique** in July 1960. Lundula was dismissed by **Mobutu** in September 1960 and placed under house arrest, but broke out and managed to reach **Stanleyville**, where he was made commander of the armed forces of the secessionist government of Antoine **Gizenga**. He later transferred his loyalties back to the central government as part of a reconciliation negotiated by Cyrille **Adoula**. He was an advisor to the Defense Department from 1962-64 and was elected senator from Sankuru district in 1965. Following the Mobutu **coup d'etat**, he occupied a number of defense-related posts.

LUNGU. A relatively small **ethnic group** living near the **Bemba** and **Kazembe** tribes in an area near **Lake Tanganyika**. The Lungu were known for their close relations in the late 1800s with **Tippo Tib** and the **Afro-Arab** traders.

- M -

MABI MULUMBA. An economics professor who was appointed finance minister in October 1986 and **prime minister** on January 22, 1987. Mabi, the author of a book on **banking** and Zaire's external **debt** problems advocated reducing payments on Zaire's debt. With Mabi's appointment, the **government** announced it was limiting repayment of Zaire's external debt to 10 percent of **export** earnings and 20 percent of government revenues. Mabi's appointment ended a period during which Zaire attempted to abide by **International Monetary Fund (IMF)** stabilization measures and, under Prime Minister **Kengo wa Dondo**, set aside as much as 50 percent of government revenues for debt servicing. Mabi lost credibility a few years later, when **inflation** returned and Zaire was once again obliged to seek debt relief.

MAHDI. The name of the prophet who led **Sudan**'s revolt against the British in the 1800s. The Mahdi's supporters controlled trade in northern Congo until 1890, when they were driven out by European forces fighting to end the **slave** trade.

MAHELE LIEKO BOKOUNGO (GENERAL) (1941 - 1997). A popular senior military officer who fought against **rebellions**, served as **armed forces** chief of staff and was killed when **Mobutu** fled Zaire on May 17, 1997, reportedly after urging soldiers not to resist the arrival of rebels in **Kinshasa**.

Born in **Équateur Province** of the Mbuza tribe, Mahele was trained as a carpenter. He was recruited into the army after the Mobutu **coup d'etat** in 1965 and served for a time as Mobutu's personal bodyguard. He received military training in **France**, **Israel** and **Belgium** and fought against eastern-based rebels in the 1980s. As head of the **Division Spéciale Présidentielle (DSP)**, he led the contingent sent to **Rwanda** in 1990 following the outbreak of the civil war there. As armed forces chief of staff, he gained respect among the populace when he ordered troops to fire upon elements of the army when they looted Kinshasa during the **pillages** of 1993. However, he was dismissed on October 2, 1993, after criticizing the armed forces before the **National Conference**.

Mobutu named him chief of staff again on December 19, 1996, to reorganize the armed forces after their losses in eastern Zaire in late 1996 to rebels of the **Alliance des Forces Démocratiques pour la Libération du Congo/Zaïre (AFDL)**. Mahele reportedly accepted on condition he be given command over all military contingents, in particular the DSP, which answered directly to Mobutu. Mahele tried unsuccessfully to counter the rebel offensive, particularly at **Lubumbashi**. On the night of May 17, 1997, after Mobutu left Kinshasa, as rebels closed in on the capital, Mahele went to Camp Tshatshi, headquarters of the DSP. He urged the crack troops to help prevent civilian casualties by laying down their arms. Eyewitnesses report he was shot by soldiers who viewed him as a traitor. After the rebels took over he was buried with full military honors and was widely credited with having avoided a bloodbath in Kinshasa.

MAI-MAI. A legendary group of ethnic warriors in eastern Congo/Zaire, who fought against the central **government** at various times during the 1960s and 1990s. The Mai-Mai backed the **Stanleyville Secession** in the early 1960s. They became renowned as ferocious fighters who, armed only with bows and arrows, amulets, and magical chants, frequently routed government troops in battle. They were subdued by **mercenary-backed** government forces after the **Mobutu coup d'etat**.

They resurfaced again in the early 1990s during a period of **ethnic cleansing** in the **Kivus** and sided with local combatants against perceived outsiders from **Rwanda** and **Burundi**. They fought with troops of the **Alliance des Forces Démocratiques pour la Libération du Congo/Zaïre (AFDL)** when their offensive against the Mobutu government began in October 1996. After the AFDL took **Kinshasa** and installed Laurent **Kabila** as president, however, they began to object to the continued presence of foreigners in eastern Congo, particularly ethnic **Tutsi** fighters from Rwanda and **Uganda**, whom they viewed as an occupation force. Clashes between the Mai-Mai and AFDL forces began in mid-1997 and the Mai-Mai militias sided with the **Rassemblement Congolais pour la Démocratie (RCD)** when it launched its rebellion in 1998.

MAÏ-NDOMBE, LAKE. *See* LAKE MAÏ-NDOMBE.

MAIZE. An important **crop** grown throughout Congo/Zaire. It is most popular in the southeast, where it is the major staple, but is also grown in other parts of the country where **manioc** is favored. Maize was introduced by Portuguese settlers, along with manioc, in the 1500s in western Congo and in central Congo in 1600. It grows particularly well in the higher, cooler climates of **Katanga**. Production steadily increased from 594,000 tons in 1980 to 930,000 tons in 1993, making it the country's third-largest food crop after manioc and **bananas**.

MAKANDA KABOBI INSTITUTE. The academic and ideological training center of the **Mouvement Populaire de la Révolution (MPR)** party and repository of many **government** records, the Makanda Kabobi Institute was founded in August 1975 to train party *cadres* and encourage the study of party doctrine and **Mobutism**.

MALEBO POOL. Formerly called Stanley Pool, Malebo Pool is a stretch of the **Congo River** 25 km wide that extends from **Kinshasa**'s Mont Ngaliema nearly to N'Sele, 80 km upriver. It is caused by the backup of water due to the cataracts that begin below Kinshasa. Brazzaville, the capital of the **Republic of the Congo**, lies across the pool.

MALNUTRITION. Health officials say malnutrition is widespread in Congo/Zaire. The **United Nations** Development Program (UNDP) estimated in the early 1990s that 15 percent of all Zairian infants were underweight, defined as weighing less than 2.5 kg, and 27 percent of all children between the ages of two and five years were stunted, defined as significantly below the standard average weight for children their age. International donors worked with local churches and charity groups to distribute food in the poorest sections of major cities, but the incidence of **disease** and death rates rose in the 1990s because of the reduced caloric intake of many inhabitants. *See also* Diet; Food Supply.

MALUKU STEEL MILL. Part of the ambitious plans of the late 1960s to bring heavy **industry** to **Zaire**, the mill was meant to exploit iron ore deposits from Banalia, Isiro and **Luebo** and make Zaire a **steel** exporter. The plant was built at a cost of more than $250 million near Maluku, a town 100 km upriver of **Kinshasa** near N'Sele. Constructed with **Italian** and **German** participation, the **development project** was completed in 1975 and was billed as a major technological achievement. However, the lack of infrastructure to exploit domestic iron ore reserves obliged the plant to operate with imported scrap metal. Production never exceeded 10 percent of its 250,000-ton capacity and ceased in the 1980s.

MALULA, JOSEPH (CARDINAL) (1917 - 1989). Archbishop of Zaire and the first Congolese head of the country's Roman **Catholic Church** until his death in 1989. Malula, a former president of **Lovanium University**, was elevated to cardinal by Pope Paul VI on March 28, 1969. He encouraged the **Africanization** of church litany and hierarchy, but was best known for his criticism of Zairian **society** under **Mobutu**. He suffered reprisals from the government in the 1970s because he opposed some aspects of **Zairianization**, in particular the dropping of Christian names and the use by the government of secularized religious songs. He fled the country after his residence was ransacked by soldiers in 1972 and later decried **corruption** and moral decay in society. With

Pope **John Paul II**'s visit in 1980, a reconciliation was sealed with the **government**. Malula continued his critiques, but these were usually tolerated. After his death, he was replaced by Monsignor Frédéric **Etsou**, former bishop of **Mbandaka**.

MAMVU. A major **ethnic group** speaking a **language** of central Sudanic origin that lives in **Orientale Province** between Isiro and the border with **Sudan** and **Uganda**. Unlike other groups from northern Zaire such as the **Mangbetu** and **Zande**, who assimilated other peoples and created states with nobles and commoners, the Mamvu remained relatively decentralized. Official Zairian ethnographers classify some of the Mamvu as of the **Bantu** group.

MANGBETU. A group of Zairians speaking a **language** of central Sudanic origin, the Mangbetu migrated into the **forest** of the northern and northeastern **Congo River Basin** in the 1600s or 1700s and currently live between the **Ituri** and **Uele Rivers** near Poko, Isiro and Rungu. They assimilated other **ethnic groups** and established relatively hierarchical **societies** with aristocracies and commoner groups.

MANIEMA PROVINCE. A relatively sparsely populated **province** in eastern **Zaire** that was a subregion of **Kivu** until the administrative reorganization of May 1988. With an estimated **population** of one million people living in an area of 132,250 square km, Maniema is rich in iron, **gold** and **tin**, and its soil is fertile, allowing the cultivation of many cash **crops**. However, the remoteness of the **region** and a deteriorated **transportation** infrastructure has hindered development of the area.

MANIOC. A fast-growing tuberous root, sometimes called cassava, that grows well in relatively poor soil, manioc was brought to Africa from the Americas by the Portuguese in the 1500s. Its cultivation spread slowly eastward, and by the 1800s, it had become a major staple **crop** throughout most of the Congo. An estimated 18.5 million tons were produced in 1993, according to the **World Bank**. After being harvested, the root is usually soaked for several days, then dried and pulverized. The flour is then used to make a dough or paste that is eaten with various sauces and dishes. The high starch and low protein content of manioc can lead to protein deficiencies, in particular kwashiorkor. In addition, some varieties contain poisons such as strychnine, which over time can cause goiter and other **diseases**. As a result, researchers are seeking to develop more nutritious strains.

MANUFACTURING. Manufacturing is a relatively young economic sector in Congo/Zaire. In the early years of the **colonial era**, few attempts were made to establish manufacturing **industries** because of the focus on extraction of **mineral** and **agricultural** products. At the turn of the century, some factories were established to produce **cement**, soap, **cloth** and beer. Growth was depressed first by World War I and then by the Great Depression. The greatest expansion began following World War II using capital-intensive methods and expatriate management and technicians. Plants were constructed in a number of urban areas to process flour, **sugar**, vegetable oil, margarine, **fish**, leather goods, tobacco, chemicals, paint, **palm oil** and **timber** products. A foundry and shipbuilding enterprise was also set up in **Kinshasa**. In the mid-1970s, a **motor vehicle** assembly plant, tire manufacturing plant, and **steel** mill were brought on line. A consortium was formed in the 1970s to construct an **aluminum** complex, but plans were put on hold "indefinitely" in the 1980s because of continuing depressed prices on the world market.

At **independence**, Congo was meeting nearly one-half of its domestic needs for manufactured goods and manufacturing accounted for nearly 10 percent of **gross domestic product (GDP)**. Production declined following independence because of political unrest, but regained preindependence levels by the late 1960s. An investment code passed in 1969 allowed equal benefits for local and foreign investors. However, the **Zairianization** in 1973 of all foreign-owned private enterprises with gross revenues of more than one million **zaires** caused foreign investors to withdraw and production to decline. **Retrocession**, announced one year later, returned partial ownership to private owners, but many foreign investors chose not to return. The fall in **copper** prices and foreign **debt** repayment problems subsequently sent the **economy** into a recession that caused domestic demand to fall. A shortage of **foreign exchange** also hurt production. By the early 1980s many plants, with the exception of those in the food-processing area, were operating at 10-25 percent of capacity, due to shortages of raw materials, spare parts and fuel. In the mid-1980s, production, although still well below capacity, began to increase, primarily because of the stabilization of the **currency** and an infusion of foreign exchange from international lenders. A great deal of manufacturing capability was crippled by the **pillages** of 1991-93 and production was slow to revive because of a lack of foreign capital from risk-conscious entrepreneurs. *See also* Foreign Investment.

MARXISM. Although some espouse Marxist beliefs and the ideology enjoyed considerable popularity in Zairian **universities** in the 1970s, most citizens seem uncomfortable with Marxism's subordination of family and **religion** to the state. Most left-leaning **opposition** groups have tended to choose a nonaligned or **socialistic** ideology. However, a few groups embraced Marxism-Leninism or Maoism, most notably the **Stanleyville** regime and followers of Pierre **Mulele** based in **Kwilu** in the early 1960s. Some exiled groups maintained close ties with the **Soviet Union** until its demise in the early 1990s.

MATABISH. A **Lingala** expression meaning "tip" or "bribe." Similar to "dash" in Anglophone Africa and "baksheesh" in the Arab world, *matabish* is the way many **unemployed** and underemployed Congolese make ends meet. It often is a present given in return for small favors, odd jobs and errands. It can also facilitate access to **government** services or provide speedier passage through the official bureaucracy.

MATADI. **Congo/Zaire**'s major ocean **port**, lying 200 km up the **Congo River** from the Atlantic Ocean, Matadi is the political and economic capital of **Bas-Congo Province**, the third-wealthiest in the country after **Kinshasa** and **Katanga**, and an urban district of the province. The district covers an area of 110 square km and is home to an estimated **population** of one-half million people in the mid-1990s (146,930 in 1982). Lying just below the cataracts that render the Congo River unnavigable to Kinshasa, Matadi is the major transshipment point for goods traveling by rail to the capital. Consequently, it is the gateway to the country's **National Way**, an internal **transportation** network of 14,000 km of **rivers** and 5,000 km of **railways**. Aside from the port installations and a major naval base, Matadi is the site of ship-repairing facilities, a major flour mill and the only bridge over the Congo River. Also nearby are a **cement** factory, **sugar** processing plant and the **Inga hydroelectric complex**.

MAWAPANGA, MWANA NANGA (1952 -). Minister of finance in the first **government** of Laurent **Kabila**, Mawapanga was a researcher at the University of Kentucky and a leader of the Zairian expatriate community in the **United States**. He visited Kabila in eastern Zaire in 1996 and joined the **Alliance Démocratique pour la Libération du Congo/Zaïre (AFDL)**. He was appointed finance minister in May 1997, after the fall of **Mobutu**. In late 1997, he was accused of improprieties in negotiating joint ventures with foreign investors aimed at revitalizing the **mining** industry in **Katanga**. He subsequently was vindicated and continued to pursue a policy aimed at stabilizing **inflation** through the control of monetary growth and rebuilding the Congolese **economy** through **foreign investment**.

MAY 11-12, 1990. The night on which Zairian troops invaded the **Lubumbashi** campus of the **Université Nationale du Zaïre (UNAZA)**, entering dormitories and assaulting **students**. The government said one person was killed in the attack but refused to allow an international inquiry. **Human rights** organizations said 30 to 100 students died. The incident led to the suspension of non-humanitarian aid by the European Community, the **United States** and Canada and marked the beginning of the final withdrawal of Western support for the **Mobutu** regime.

MAYOMBE FOREST. A **forest** located in **Bas-Congo Province** containing significant reserves of **timber**, **minerals**, and soils suitable for **agriculture**. Ecologists in the mid-1990s began to voice concern that heavy timbering was encroaching on the forest and threatening many life forms there.

MBALA. One of several major groups of the **Bantu** family living in the western part of southern **Congo/Zaire** between the **Kwango** and **Kasai Rivers** and speaking a **language** related to the **Kongo** group. The Mbala live primarily along the **Kwilu River** around **Kikwit**. Although critical of the **Mobutu** government, most of the

Mbala opposed the Kwilu **rebellion** of the 1960s because of a perception that it was led primarily by the rival **Mbun** and **Pende ethnic groups**.

MBANDAKA. The capital of **Équateur Province** and major city of northwestern **Congo/Zaire**, Mbandaka (formerly Coquilhatville) is an urban district with an estimated **population** of 400,000 (153,440 in 1982) covering an area of 460 square km in the southwestern corner of the province. Lying near the confluence of the **Congo, Ubangi** and **Tshuapa Rivers**, Mbandaka is a major **port** for the northern **river** system. Low-lying land in the area makes farming and herding difficult, although some **agricultural** activity, particularly upriver, has been successful. **Petroleum** deposits were discovered in the area in the early 1970s. Exploration was begun on several occasions by multinational oil companies, but to date no commercially exploitable deposits have been found. The city was severely damaged in December 1997 by flooding which rendered 6,000 people homeless.

MBANZA. Sometimes called "Mbanja" by ethnographers, the Mbanza form one of the larger groups that speak **Banda**, an Adamawa-Eastern **language**. They live in **Équateur Province**, primarily between the **Congo** and **Ubangi Rivers**.

MBANZA KONGO DIA NTOTILA (GREAT CITY OF THE KING). The mythical capital of the **Kingdom of Kongo** from which, according to legend, all **Kongo** people are descended. The capital was located in northwestern **Angola** around the area that became **São Salvador** in the 1530s. It remains a place for which Kongo people often express nostalgia and longing.

MBANZA-NGUNGU. Formerly Thysville, Mbanza-Ngungu is the capital of the **Cataractes** District of **Bas-Congo** and, with an estimated 500,000 inhabitants, one of the most densely populated in the **region**. The city lies on the **road** and **railway** linking **Matadi** to **Kinshasa**. A farming and herding center, it is a major source of the **food supply** of the Kinshasa area. The city is perhaps most frequently remembered as the site of the **armed forces** mutiny against Belgian officers five days after **independence**. The violence led to the rapid promotion of

Congolese into the officers corps and the appointment of **Mobutu** as army chief of staff.

MBOMU. The name given to commoners in **Zande society**, as opposed to the aristocracy who were called **Vungara**. The Mbomu were primarily hunters from **Sudan** who migrated into northern Congo in the 18th and 19th centuries and intermarried with local **Bantu** inhabitants.

MBUJI-MAYI. The capital of **Kasaï Oriental Province**, Mbuji-Mayi is the commercial center for most of the country's **diamond trade**. Formerly known as Bakwanga and once the capital of the secessionist state of **South Kasai**, Mbuji-Mayi has experienced explosive growth since the mid-1970s, when a great deal of the **banking** and commercial activities related to the diamond industry moved in from **Kananga**. The city at various times also attracted a considerable number of **Luba** immigrants fleeing ethnic tensions in western **Kasai** and **Katanga**. An urban district covering an area of 64 square km, Mbuji-Mayi's **population** grew from 39,038 in 1959 to 334,875 in 1982 and to an estimated 600,000 in 1995.

MBUMBA, NATHANIEL (BRIGADIER GENERAL). Leader of the **Front pour la Libération Nationale du Congo (FLNC)** that launched the incursions into southern **Shaba Region** in 1977 and 1978. Mbumba was an officer of the **Gendarmerie Katangaise** which supported the **Katanga secession** in the early 1960s and in 1966 and 1967 led two **rebellions** in **Kivu** and **Orientale Provinces**. During this period, Mbumba expressed support for Moïse **Tshombe**. However, during the Shaba uprisings, Mbumba said he wished only to bring about the fall of **Mobutu** and the advent of **democracy**. In the 1980s, he was offered amnesty on several occasions but remained in exile and appeared to be retired in the 1990s.

MBUN. A **Bantu** people living in the lower **Kasai** area along the **Kwilu River** near **Idiofa**, the Mbun helped stopped the **Chokwe** expansion in 1885. They were among the most ardent supporters of Pierre **Mulele** who, with the **Pende**, helped launch the Kwilu **rebellion** and the terrorist attacks in **Leopoldville** in the mid-1960s.

MENDE OMALANGA, LAMBERT. Leader of an offshoot of the **Lumumba** wing of the **Mouvement National Congolais (MNC)**, one of the founders of the **Sacred Union**, and a visible force in the hardline **opposition** of the 1990s. However, he left the radical opposition to join the **government** of Léon **Kengo wa Dondo** on December 24, 1996, as vice prime minister and minister of **transportation** and **communications**.

MERCENARIES. A term first employed by Léon **Roget** when sent to organize the **Force Publique** in 1886, the term came to represent the foreign professional soldier who, for money, was willing to participate in invasions and coups against or on behalf of established governments. Moïse **Tshombe** is generally cited, rightly or wrongly, as being the first African leader to employ mercenaries, in order to bolster his forces in the secessionist **Katanga** state. Upon becoming **prime minister** in 1964, Tshombe hired mercenaries to help quash the eastern **rebellions**. **Mobutu** also hired mercenaries to crush rebellions in the east in 1966-67. He hired them again in 1996 in a futile attempt to defend **Kisangani** from advancing troops of the **Alliance des Forces Démocratiques pour la Libération du Congo/Zaïre (AFDL)**.

MERCHANT MARINE. Congo/Zaire has a small merchant marine operated by the state-owned Compagnie Maritime du Zaïre (CMZ). The company operates a number of routes linking **Matadi** primarily to ports in West Africa and Europe. However, a lack of funds and deteriorating equipment by the mid-1980s had considerably reduced operations.

METALLURGIE HOBOKEN-OVERPELT (MHO). A Belgian refining corporation that from the **colonial era** was a major customer for raw and semirefined minerals marketed by the **Générale des Carrières et des Mines (GECAMINES)**, in particular **copper**, **cobalt** and **zinc**.

MIDDLE CLASS. **Congo/Zaire**, like many developing nations, has a small middle **class**, which despite a severely reduced standard of living, retains some influence in the affairs of the nation. Following World War II, Congolese in clerical and low-level administrative positions, part of the *évolué* group, began pressing for better **wages** and working conditions. They founded a number of study groups and **labor** organizations. Two of the most prominent were the **Association de Personnel Indigène de la Colonie (APIC)**, which grouped **civil service** workers, and the **Association des Classes Moyennes Africaines (ACMAF)**, which was composed primarily of small merchants and farmers and sent representatives to the consultative councils of the colonial government. Following **independence**, the middle class grew rapidly as Congolese took over senior administrative and professional positions vacated by expatriates. Except for a period or prosperity in the early 1970s, however, deteriorating economic conditions and high **inflation** steadily eroded the purchasing power and **income** of the middle class. As a result, by the 1980s the middle class of salaried workers, professionals and small businessmen was living close to the subsistence level. For example, teachers and professors could not afford telephones or cars unless they were furnished by the **government**, and many were obliged to engage in secondary **employment**, often in the informal sector, in order to make ends meet.

MIGRATION. Historically, the people of Congo were largely migratory. Families, lineages and entire villages would move to find better farming, hunting or herding land, or sometimes for political or spiritual reasons. In some **societies**, power disputes would be resolved by one of the aspirants leaving with family and supporters to found a new village or **kingdom**. During the **colonial era**, people migrated toward centers of **industry** and farming in search of jobs. Thus large numbers of **Kongo** people moved to the capital of **Leopoldville**. Many **Luba** left **Kasai** for the **mining** centers of **Katanga**. And people from **Rwanda** moved into eastern Congo to work on the **plantations**. The colonial authorities sought to halt migrations of traditional rural groups, since nomadic people were harder to tax and introduce to cash **crops**. Most Africans in the colony had to obtain permission to change residence. Migration to the cities by people seeking jobs, **education** and **social services** began in the 1930s, but intensified following **independence**. In 1970, 30 percent of the **population** was classified as urban. The figure had risen to 40 percent by 1990. *See also* Urbanization.

MILITANTS. A term used in many countries to denote active members of a **political party**. From the early 1970s, however, **Mobutu** used the term frequently in his speeches to address the Zairian people. The major reason was to emphasize the membership of all Zairians in the **Mouvement Populaire de la Révolution (MPR)**. It underscored what was seen as the continuing struggle to end tribalism, regionalism and factionalism, and to erect in its stead a new Zairian state, independent, self-sufficient and authentically "Zairian."

MILITARY ASSISTANCE. Since **independence**, Congo/Zaire has received military assistance from many foreign governments. Following independence, **Belgium** was the main military partner. However, by the mid-1960s agreements for equipment and training had been signed with the **United States, Italy, Israel**, and the **United Kingdom**. In the 1970s, **France** became an increasingly important partner and programs were also launched with North Korea, the People's Republic of **China, Egypt** and **South Africa**. **Morocco** and several other African countries sent troops during the **Shaba** Wars. By the 1990s, Zaire was receiving little foreign military assistance because of **human rights** abuses and lack of progress on democratic and economic reforms. Following the departure of **Mobutu**, several Western governments offered to help the government of Laurent **Kabila** rebuild the Congolese military, but this aid was stalled by the Kabila government's lack of cooperation with investigations into alleged massacres in eastern Congo in the mid-1990s. The Kabila government received military support from **Angola, Chad, Namibia**, and **Zimbabwe** when a **rebellion** backed by **Uganda** and **Rwanda** broke out in 1998. *See also* Armed Forces.

MILITARY SECURITY AND INTELLIGENCE SERVICE. *See* SERVICE D'ACTION ET DE RENSEIGNEMENTS MILITAIRE (SARM).

MINERALS. Congo/Zaire is one of the richest countries in Africa in terms of mineral wealth. Tales of distant kingdoms resplendent with **copper, gold** and **diamonds** motivated **Afro-Arab** and later European **explorers** to venture into **Katanga** in the 1800s. And reports of the region's wealth led **Belgium**'s King **Leopold II** to form the **Comité Spécial du Katanga** in 1890, one of the first of several powerful "trusts" which were given virtual monopolies over tracts of territory in exchange for royalties. Earnings from the **Belgian Congo**'s minerals supplemented the Belgian government's **foreign exchange** reserves during the **colonial era**, supported the government during the World Wars, and provided the **uranium** used to build the first atomic bomb.

During the first decades after **independence**, mineral **exports** provided the Congolese **government** with two-thirds of its foreign exchange. The rapid rise in mineral prices, particularly for copper and **cobalt**, in the mid-1970s created an economic boom in **Zaire**. This was followed by a series of recessions when prices fell in the late 1970s. As the **mining** infrastructure deteriorated in the 1980s because of poor maintenance and a lack of new investments, copper was supplanted first by cobalt and subsequently by diamonds as the major foreign exchange earner. In the mid-1990s, the mining industry had declined to such an extent that **agriculture** replaced mining as the country's top export for the first time since independence.

Following the fall of **Mobutu** in 1997, the government of Laurent **Kabila** negotiated a number of new joint ventures with foreign companies to rebuild the mining industry. *See also* Aluminum; Coal; Silver; Tin; Zinc.

MINING. Since the early 1900s, mining has been a source of a great deal of Congo/Zaire's wealth. Historically, the mining sector contributed an average of one-third of its **gross domestic product (GDP)**, more than three-fourths of its **export** revenues and one-half of **government** revenues. According to historians, Africans knew of **copper** ore deposits long before the arrival of European **explorers** in **Katanga** in the 1890s and reports reaching the coast of great **mineral** wealth are credited with encouraging some of the first explorations into the interior. The deposits found in Katanga initially were judged to be too small for commercial exploitation, until 1900 when **Leopold II** established the **Comité Spécial du Katanga** to explore and develop the region. Ore discoveries in 1901 led to the construction of a **railway** and, in 1908, to the creation of the **Union Minière du Haut-Katanga (UMHK)** which would later become the **Générale des Carrières et des**

Mines (GECAMINES). The first smelting plant began operation in 1911, producing 1,000 tons of copper. Production reached 100,000 tons in 1928 and 460,000 tons in 1985, or 7 percent of total world production. **Diamond** and **gold** mining began in earnest in the 1920s.

The **Bakajika Law** of June 1966 granted all mineral rights to the state and the large mining companies were **nationalized**, beginning with the UMHK. Private companies were contracted to operate the companies in return for a portion of the revenues. In the late 1970s, the Zairian **government** entered into a number of joint mining ventures with private foreign companies and also allowed private traders to participate in the commercialization of gold and diamonds. Nevertheless, government participation in the mining sector remained large and production was dominated by a few companies. GECAMINES, the country's largest company, dominated the mining of copper, **cobalt** and most minerals in Katanga Province, and the **Société Minière de Bakwanga (MIBA)**, the country's second-largest company, dominated the formal diamond mining industry. In addition to its major mineral products of copper, cobalt, diamonds, **uranium, tin**, gold and **petroleum**, Congo/Zaire has also produced **zinc**, manganese, **silver**, cadmium, tungsten, germanium, columbium, tantalum, lithium, monazite and iron ore. With the economic crisis of the late 1980s and early 1990s, production of all minerals except for diamonds declined dramatically. The state-owned mining companies, beset by falling production, decaying equipment and a lack of new investment, were considered insolvent by the 1990s. By 1995, **agriculture** had become an equal contributor to GDP.

Evacuation of the minerals was always a problem. The **National Way** is a tortuous route via rail and **river** to the **port** of **Matadi**, but it lies completely within the national territory. The most economic route, the **Benguela Railway** that links Katanga to the **Angolan** port of **Lobito**, was closed from 1975 by the Angolan civil war. Other routes, to the **Tanzanian** port of Dar es Salaam, the Mozambican port of Beira, and the **South African** port of Durban, were disrupted by railway inefficiencies, port congestion and political issues. *See also* Coal.

MINISTRIES. In early Congolese **governments**, the executive branch was divided into ministries, but these were renamed "**departments**," headed by "state commissioners," on January 5, 1973, as part of a gradual process of introducing an authentic Zairian form of government. Departments were renamed ministries again in 1997, after the installation of the Laurent **Kabila** government.

MISSIONARIES. Missions and missionaries have played a prominent role in the **education** of many leaders and in drawing world attention to **human rights** abuses in Congo/Zaire, first with the campaign against **slavery** during the 1800s, later with the campaign against abusive **labor** practices in the **Congo Free State** and the **Belgian Congo**, and more recently with reports of abuses of power by the Zairian **government**. Missionaries have been praised for introducing **Christianity**, education and **health care** facilities, and criticized for helping colonialists de-Africanize the Congolese people.

Nevertheless, there is no doubt that the missionaries exerted a significant influence. Missionaries first arrived in the **Kongo** area of what is now **Bas-Congo** in the 1480s, brought by the Portuguese expeditions. The Roman **Catholic Church** flourished for a time in the **Kongo Kingdom**, but it did not spread far and began a 200-year decline in the 1600s.

Organized Roman Catholic and **Protestant** missionary activity returned in the 1870s and, by World War II, the missions had become major providers of education and health services in the colony, sometimes subsidized by the colonial administration. Some of the earliest efforts to standardize Congolese **languages** and adapt them to written form were made by missionaries seeking to translate the Bible, hymnals and liturgy into African languages. At **independence**, 65 percent of Congolese identified themselves as Christian and the country's official **literacy** rate was 60 percent, one of the highest in Africa.

The first Congolese priests and pastors were ordained in the 1910s, but in the 1960s, considerable efforts were made to increase Congolese leadership and influence in the church and to Africanize litany and ceremony. The first secretary-general of the **Église du Christ au Congo**, later Église du Christ au Zaïre, which grouped most Protestant denominations in the country, was elected shortly after independence. The first Roman Catholic cardinal was installed on March 28, 1969.

The rise of **nationalism, Authenticity** and party dominance in the early 1970s raised tensions between church and state. Zairians were ordered to abandon their Christian names and replace them with "authentic" Zairian ones. The **universities** operated by Catholic and Protestant groups were nationalized in 1971. Religious observances were removed from government ceremonies and an attempt was made to ban religious teachings in the schools. An exodus of expatriate missionaries began.

In the 1980s, however, relations improved. Missions were still actively engaged in building and running schools, hospitals, printing presses and some agricultural projects and had become major distributors of **foreign aid** such as food and disaster relief supplies. The deterioration of many government-funded **social services** increased reliance on church-supported institutions. Moreover, by the 1990s many schools, hospitals and entire mission stations were run entirely by Zairian staff, which sought heroically in some cases to cope with the lack of funds and the needs of a population suffering increasing economic hardship.

MITTERRAND, FRANÇOIS (1916 - 1996). The president of **France** from 1981 to 1995, Mitterrand was France's longest-governing head of state. Better known for his efforts to unify Europe, Mitterrand also presided over France during the sometimes tortuous efforts at democratization in French-speaking Africa. A socialist, he campaigned on a platform of opposing Africa's dictators, but following his investiture quickly acknowledged that France's foreign policy and business interests required cooperation with them. He attended the France-Africa Summit in **Kinshasa** in 1982 and subsequently paid several official visits to Zaire. In the early 1990s, Mitterrand's government joined the **United States** and **Belgium** in applying diplomatic pressure on the **Mobutu government** for economic reforms and more progress on the **democratic transition**. However, these policies were moderated in the mid-1990s because of what was seen as a need to address Zaire's economic crisis and disappointment over what was viewed as intransigence by hardline **opposition** leaders in the **Sacred Union**. Guarded support was expressed for the economic reforms of Léon **Kengo wa Dondo** and thanks were expressed for Zairian help in the international effort to resolve the **Rwandan refugee** crisis in eastern Zaire in 1994-96.

MITUMBA MOUNTAINS. A **mountain** range in a remote part of northwestern **Katanga Province** that is largely inaccessible except by foot. The **Parti Révolutionnaire du Peuple (PRP) dissident** group controlled a significant amount of territory in the mountains from the early 1960s and the area was the scene of some important early victories by the **Alliance des Forces Démocratiques pour la Libération du Congo/Zaïre (AFDL)** when it launched its offensive to overthrow **Mobutu** in late 1996.

MOBA. A small town of about 60,000 inhabitants on **Lake Tanganyika** in northeastern **Katanga Province**, Moba is the site of an army garrison that was attacked in October 1984 by guerrillas of the **Parti Révolutionnaire du Peuple (PRP)**. The attack caused an estimated 50 deaths. The Zairian **armed forces** recaptured the town two days later and most of the guerrillas disappeared into the surrounding countryside. The Zairian **government** accused **dissidents** living in **refugee** camps across the lake in **Tanzania** and **Burundi** of responsibility. Tanzania acknowledged that a camp of Zairians existed in its territory but denied they were responsible for the attack. A second attack by the PRP in June 1985 was less successful. In early 1997, Moba was one of the first towns to fall to forces of the **Alliance des Forces Démocratiques pour la Libération du Congo/Zaïre (AFDL)**, of which the PRP was a member, when they advanced into **Shaba**. It was the scene of sporadic battles when rebels of the **Rassemblement Congolais pour la Démocratie (RCD)** launched their offensive in mid-1998.

MOBUTISM. At the height of single-partyism, Mobutism was proclaimed the official ideology of the **Mouvement Populaire de la Révolution (MPR)** party and of the Zairian state. Official party documents described the doctrine as the "thought and vision of **Mobutu Sese Seko**." It encompassed all the policies and ideological thoughts of Mobutu, whether, for example, the **Zairianization** of private companies in 1973 or their **Retrocession** in 1975, whether the centralization of political power in the 1970s or the decentralization of local **politics** in the 1980s. With the advent of multipartyism in 1990, use of the term declined and sometimes became a source of derision. In the early

1990s the president was accused of encouraging the creation of hundreds of **political parties** in order to splinter the **opposition** and confuse the electorate in what was called, "multi-Mobutism."

Despite the contradictions, Mobutu and Mobutism are likely to be remembered for several notable influences: the political unification of the country in the late 1960s; the policies of **Authenticity** and Zairian **nationalism** in the early 1970s; mismanagement and the failure of the economic policies in the late 1970s; the half-hearted corrections of the 1980s; and the Machiavellian obstruction of the **democratic transition** in the 1990s. Mobutu dominated Zairian politics during the first quarter-century of its nationhood and virtually until his death, and as a result, Mobutism will be an important topic for students of modern African history.

MOBUTU, BOBI LADAWA. Second wife of **Mobutu**, married in 1980 following the death of his first wife, Gbiatibwa Gogbe Yetene **Mobutu**. From **Équateur Province**, Mama Bobi, as she is known, involved herself in work with **women**, handicapped persons and other **social services**. She accompanied Mobutu into exile and was at his bedside in Rabat, **Morocco**, when he died of cancer on September 7, 1997.

MOBUTU, GBIATIBWA GOGBE YETENE (? - 1977). First and much-loved wife of **Mobutu**. Mama Mobutu was from **Équateur Province**. She married Mobutu on July 26, 1955. They had 10 children before her death due to health reasons on October 22, 1977.

MOBUTU, NYIWA. **Mobutu**'s eldest son. He held a number of official posts including ambassador-at-large and, it was believed, was meant to succeed him. He died in the early 1990s, reportedly from an illness associated with **Acquired Immune Deficiency Syndrome (AIDS)**.

MOBUTU PLAN. A plan announced by **Mobutu** in November 1977 aimed at revitalizing the Zairian **economy**. Inspired by the Marshall Plan to reconstruct Europe following World War II, the Mobutu Plan came after the first **Shaba** War and amid international attention on Zaire's worsening **inflation** and indebtedness. It called for new investments to foster **agricultural** development and improve **transportation** and **communications** infrastructures. It also called for some decentralization of economic policymaking. The plan was to cover the period 1978-82, but became a rhetorical peg on which to hang subsequent economic proposals. The term fell into disuse in the 1980s and during the economic collapse of the 1990s was officially forgotten.

MOBUTU SESE SEKO KUKU NGBENDU WA ZA BANGA (JOSEPH-DÉSIRÉ) (1930 - 1997). One of Africa's longest-ruling heads of state, Mobutu was close to power in the early years following **independence** and dominated Zairian political life after the **coup d'etat** that brought him to power on **November 24, 1965**. His rule was characterized by the heavy centralization and personalization of power. His style of authoritarianism included rewards for those who supported him, punishment for those who opposed him, and forgiveness for **dissidents** who returned to the fold. He is credited with forging a nation from a territory characterized at independence by administrative collapse, secessionism and ethnic and regional rivalry. He was criticized for allowing a political **élite** to plunder the public wealth, for centralizing power in the hands of a few cronies and for failing to prepare his political **succession**. Nevertheless, he dominated political life during the country's first 35 years and he will be remembered by history.

Mobutu was born Joseph-Désiré on October 14, 1930, at **Lisala** in **Équateur Province**. His maternal family, of the **Ngbandi ethnic group**, was originally from **Gbadolite**, a town by the **Ubangi River** across from the **Central African Republic**. Mobutu's father, Gbemani Albéric, was a cook who reportedly died when Joseph-Désiré was eight years old. Young Mobutu attended primary and secondary school at **Mbandaka** and entered the **Force Publique** on February 14, 1950. He began writing articles under the pseudonym "de Banzy" for *L'Avenir* and *Actualités Africaines*, two periodicals published in **Leopoldville**. He left the military on December 31, 1956, and worked as a journalist for *L'Avenir Colonial Belge* and *Actualités Africaines*. He subsequently went to Brussels, **Belgium**, to take courses at the Institut Supérieur d'Études Sociales and work at the Maison de la

Presse. Mobutu met Patrice **Lumumba** and joined the **Mouvement National Congolais (MNC)** in 1958 and attended the **Round Table Conference** in January 1960. When Lumumba became **prime minister** at independence, Mobutu was appointed his state secretary.

After the mutiny of the Force Publique on July 5, 1960, Mobutu was named army chief of staff with the grade of colonel on July 8. He undertook a tour of army garrisons around the country in an effort to pacify the troops. On September 14, 1960, during a standoff between Lumumba and President Joseph **Kasavubu**, Mobutu announced he was "neutralizing" the political leaders and formed the **College of Commissioners**, composed of young intellectuals, to govern the country for six months. The College returned power to the constitutional **government** in February 1961.

On November 24, 1965, during a similar crisis between Kasavubu and Prime Minister Moïse **Tshombe** and in the face of new **rebellions** in eastern Congo, Mobutu took power in a bloodless coup d'etat. Officially he was "called upon by the military high command" to assume the leadership of the country. He said he would govern for five years under emergency measures, then hold **elections**. Over the next few months, the political system was gradually dismantled, **parliament** was suspended and Mobutu gained the power to rule by decree. The **Mouvement Populaire de la Révolution (MPR)** party was formed in 1966 with Mobutu as president and the concept of a Congolese revolution was developed. A program of **Authenticity** was launched. Former colonial names were changed to "authentic" ones. The Congo became the **République du Zaïre**. The MPR became the only legal party and subsequently the supreme organ of state.

With the promulgation of the third **constitution** in 1974, Zaire became a party-state. Power increasingly was centralized in Mobutu, who presided over all organs of government, including the **legislative** and **judicial systems**, and had the power to appoint and dismiss virtually all leaders of party and government. He ran unopposed in presidential elections in 1970, 1977 and 1984 and each time was elected by more than 99 percent of the vote. On December 11, 1982, he was given the title of field marshal.

With the fall of **copper** prices in 1974, the Zairian **economy** began to decline. In 1983, the government launched a series of monetary and fiscal reforms that for a time reduced **inflation** but also caused a severe recession. In 1986, the government said it would severely limit payments on the external **debt**. The late 1980s were characterized by deteriorating relations with foreign creditors, rising inflation and falling standards of living among the people.

On **April 24, 1990**, in the face of growing domestic and international pressure, Mobutu announced the end of single-party rule and the beginning of a one-year transition to multiparty **democracy**. The political liberalization led to confrontation and uncertainty, which aggravated the country's economic problems. A period of **hyperinflation** and civil unrest caused a severe drop in economic production. The frequently extended **democratic transition** was characterized by periods of confrontation and intransigence followed by mediation and compromise. During that time, **opposition** leaders were co-opted to assume political posts to "resolve the Zairian crisis," only to be dismissed later in failure and political disgrace. Mobutu was accused of fomenting the instability in order to sabotage the transition and prove that political pluralism was bad for the country. As throughout his career, he displayed an acute sense of both domestic and international **politics** and genius at manipulating them to his advantage. Though frequently criticized and later ostracized by Western governments for his policies, he frequently obliged them to work with him. For example, he provided staging bases to support **Angolan** rebels during the Angolan civil war in the 1980s and, in 1994, he allowed foreign troops to use Zairian military bases to deliver emergency relief to one million **refugees** fleeing the civil war in **Rwanda**.

In August 1996, amid rumors of failing health, Mobutu flew to Europe. He underwent prostate surgery in Lausanne, **Switzerland**, on August 22 and began treatment for cancer. The interethnic conflict in Rwanda had spilled over into eastern Zaire, but Mobutu's government seemed powerless to counter it. Attacks against ethnic Zairian **Tutsi**s by remnants of the Rwandan **Hutu** militia led to retaliation. On October 18, the **Alliance des Forces Démocratiques pour la Libération du Congo/Zaïre (AFDL)** announced an offensive, which in four months seized control of a

1,000-km-long stretch of territory along Zaire's eastern border. Mobutu returned to Zaire on December 17. He reshuffled the cabinet, naming Léon **Kengo wa Dondo** prime minister, and purged the military high command. The AFDL offensive continued, facing only modest resistance in **Kisangani** and **Lubumbashi**.

As the AFDL forces move closer to **Kinshasa**, African leaders organized a series of mediation talks in Pointe-Noire, **Republic of the Congo (Brazzaville)**, which Mobutu and AFDL leader Laurent **Kabila** attended. On May 16, 1997, as AFDL troops approached the capital and announced the formation of a new government, Mobutu and his entourage left Kinshasa for **Togo** and five days later arrived in **Morocco**, where King **Hassan II** offered him asylum. Reportedly, no other country did so.

The rebels entered the capital on May 17. During the following weeks, defectors from the Mobutu entourage told stories of an ailing former leader, bitter over what he viewed as the betrayal by his supporters and his people. Mobutu underwent surgery for "serious internal bleeding" on June 27. On July 1, he was admitted to Mohammed V military hospital in Rabat, where he died on September 7, 1997, at 9:30 p.m. with his family by his side. He was buried in Morocco.

MOKOLO WA MPOMBO. An official frequently in and out of **government** during the cabinet reshuffles of the 1980s, Mokolo was named state commissioner for foreign affairs in 1985, but was moved to the **Department** of Higher Education and Science in a reshuffle in April 1986.

MONGO. A large **ethnic group** that is considered a major cluster, or subgroup, of the **Bantu** family. Primarily a people of the **forest**, the Mongo live in most of the **Congo River Basin** and part of the southern uplands in a vast area bordered by the Lulonga River in the north, the Sankuru River in the south, the confluence of the **Congo River** and Momboyo River to the west, and the confluence of the **Lualaba River** and Lukuga River to the east. The Mongo **language**, a major lingua franca in northwestern Congo/Zaire, is remarkably homogeneous, lending weight to the legend that the Mongo are descendant from one man. In Mongo **societies**, which can be either matrilineal or patrilineal, **chiefs** are usually chosen on the basis of wealth, rather than kinship. The village is usually the core group, formed around a lineage of which the chief might also be the chief of other, client lineages. Irving Kaplan says Mongo societies in the southwestern groups were organized into hierarchical systems, divided into provinces and headed by a sacred chief.

MONSENGWO PASINYA, LAURENT (ARCHBISHOP) (1939 -). Archbishop of **Kisangani** and president of the Episcopal Conference of Congo, Monsengwo was elected chairman of the **National Conference** on December 12, 1991, following four months of political turmoil and confrontation that prevented the conference from taking any meaningful action and was partly responsible for several periods of social unrest. With a combination of doggedness and parliamentary finesse which he credited to his experience as moderator of the Episcopal Conference, Monsengwo steered the National Conference through 12 months of stormy debate. It produced several dozen reports on the state of Zairian **society** after three decades of **independence** and drafted a **constitution** that repealed many of the laws established under the **Mobutu government**. When the National Conference disbanded in December 1992, Monsengwo was elected president of the **Haut Conseil de la République (HCR)** which replaced it and was charged with overseeing the transition to multiparty **democracy**. On July 1, 1995, the supporters of Mobutu and the **opposition**-led **Sacred Union** both accused him of favoring the other side and entered into an unlikely alliance that ousted him from the chairmanship. He returned to his archdiocese in Kisangani and said he would devote himself to pastoral work, though he retained considerable political support.

MOREL, EDMUND D. A British author who wrote extensively on the atrocities and **labor** abuses in the **Congo Free State (CFS)**. His work led the British government in 1897 to instruct its consul-general in **Leopoldville** to draft a report on labor practices in the CFS. The report aroused public anger and eventually led to the Belgian parliament's annexation of the territory, marking the end of the CFS and the beginning of the **Belgian Congo**.

MOROCCO, RELATIONS WITH. Relations between **Congo/Zaire** and Morocco were close virtually from **independence**, strengthened by **Mobutu**'s friendship with King **Hassan II** and by a similarity of policies on a variety of regional and global issues. Morocco sent 1,500 troops to **Shaba** in April 1977 to help repel an invasion by the **Front pour la Libération Nationale du Congo (FLNC)** in the first Shaba War. Moroccan troops returned to Shaba in 1978 as part of a peacekeeping force to help maintain order following the second Shaba War. Zaire supported Morocco in the Western Sahara dispute and suspended its participation in the **Organization of African Unity** when Morocco withdrew in 1984 because of the admission of the Polisario Front's Saharan Republic. When Mobutu fled Zaire on May 17, 1997, as **opposition** forces prepared to enter **Kinshasa**, he was granted asylum in Morocco, where he died on September 7, 1997.

MOTOR VEHICLES. Registered motor vehicles numbered 362,800 in 1990. One-half of these were registered in **Kinshasa**. More than half were private passenger cars and the remainder were commercial vehicles, although many private vehicles were sometimes used for commercial purposes. Assembly plants owned by **General Motors of Zaire** and British Leyland (Land Rover) were capable of producing 3,000 to 5,000 vehicles each per year. However, most vehicles were imported, primarily from **Japan**, **France**, **Germany** and the **United States**. The government announced on January 10, 1997, a reregistration program aimed at raising an estimated $300 million and recovering vehicles looted during the **pillages** of 1991 and 1993.

MOUNTAINS. Although most of **Congo/Zaire** is located in the lowlands of the **Congo River Basin**, the country also contains several mountain ranges, primarily in the eastern part of the country. The most spectacular of these is the **Ruwenzori**s in the northeast. The highest chain in Africa, the Ruwenzoris rise primarily between **Lake Albert** and **Lake Edward** and vary from 1,000 to 5,000 m in altitude. The **Virunga** Range, north of **Lake Kivu**, and the **Mitumba** Range, in northern **Katanga Province**, are less dramatic but more arable. The **Crystal Mountains**, lying in western Congo between **Kinshasa** and **Matadi**, are relatively low but are associated with the cataracts that render the **Congo**

River unnavigable for 200 km and hinder **transportation** between the Atlantic Ocean and most of the country.

MOUVEMENT D'ACTION POUR LA RÉSURRECTION DU CONGO (MARC) / ACTION MOVEMENT FOR THE RESURRECTION OF THE CONGO. A Brussels-based **opposition** group headed by Munguya Mbenge, a former commissioner in **Shaba Region**, MARC evolved out of the "Mouvement du 4 Juin" ("Fourth of June Movement") which was formed following the **student** unrest of the late 1960s. MARC was accused of fomenting several uprisings and, in March 1978, a military tribunal sentenced 19 alleged plotters to death, five of them in absentia. Thirteen of those found guilty were executed on March 17.

MOUVEMENT DE LIBÉRATION CONGOLAIS (MLC). Small rebel group formed in 1998 by Jean-Pierre **Bemba** in northern Congo.

MOUVEMENT NATIONAL CONGOLAIS (MNC) / NATIONAL CONGOLESE MOVEMENT. One of the major **political parties** at **independence**, the MNC was formed by Zairian *évolués* in **Leopoldville** in July 1956, although some date its launching as October 1958. The founders included Patrice **Lumumba**, Joseph **Ileo**, Joseph **Ngalula**, Gaston **Diomi**, Arthur **Pinzi** and Cyrille **Adoula**. One of the few parties at independence that eschewed regionalism and attempted to develop a national base of support, the MNC tried to develop a cogent ideology and took its inspiration from African **nationalists** such as Ghana's Kwame **Nkrumah** and Guinea's Ahmed Sekou Toure. It sought to establish a nationalistic program of economic, political and cultural development and supported the concept of Pan-Africanism.

By 1959, however, the MNC had begun to splinter. Albert **Kalonji** left following the massacres of **Luba** in **Katanga** with a group that came to be called the MNC/Kalonji. Other leaders left to form their own parties. During the **elections** prior to independence, the MNC and **Alliance des Bakongo (ABAKO)** parties received the largest number of votes, but neither received an absolute majority. Lumumba eventually brokered a compromise whereby he became **prime minister** and the ABAKO candidate, Joseph **Kasavubu**, became **president**.

The MNC, which expressed nationalistic and anticolonial sentiments that were applauded by Soviet-bloc governments and viewed with anxiety by Western governments, was radicalized following the assassination of Lumumba in early 1961. It became the major force behind the eastern **rebellions** from 1961-64, and although it was splintered and weakened by the end of the decade, it remained a prominent **opposition** group in exile. With the announcement of the **democratic transition**, a number of former leaders of the MNC resurfaced and formed parties claiming to be the legitimate heirs to the Lumumba legacy. Some joined the **Sacred Union** but others rejected it as containing too many leaders who had collaborated with **Mobutu** in the past. In the mid-1990s, a number of them regrouped to form the **Parti Lumumbiste Unifié (PALU)** headed by Antoine **Gizenga**, who led the party and the eastern rebellions following Lumumba's assassination in 1961. *See also* Kashamura, Anicet.

MOUVEMENT POPULAIRE DE LA RÉVOLUTION (MPR) / POPULAR REVOLUTIONARY MOVEMENT. Zaire's sole legal **political party** from 1970 until 1990, the MPR was established six months after the **Mobutu coup d'etat** and steadily grew in power until it became the supreme organ of state in 1974.

The party's early roots lay in the **Corps des Volontaires de la République**, a group of young intellectuals called to service by Mobutu in January 1966. The MPR was formally constituted on April 17, 1966. The party's ideology was outlined following a meeting at N'Sele, outside **Kinshasa**, which eventually became party headquarters. The **N'Sele Manifesto**, issued on May 20, 1967, proclaimed an official ideology of **Authenticity** and **Mobutism**, which was defined as "authentic Zairian **nationalism**" and which condemned regionalism and tribalism. The manifesto proclaimed a policy of "positive neutralism" in world **politics** and espoused a path between capitalism and **communism**, characterized by the phrase "neither to the right nor to the left, but forward." The manifesto also established national objectives of fostering economic independence, strengthening the central **government**'s authority throughout the country, building the

Congo's international prestige, and working for the social and economic development of the Congolese people.

The MPR was declared the supreme organ of state and sole legal party on December 23, 1970, and was fused with the government beginning in 1972. The **constitution** of 1974 formally established the Zairian party-state and codified the concentration of power in the **president**. It instituted the "unity" of party, people and government and eliminated any real separation of powers. The party's youth wing, the **Jeunesse du Mouvement Populaire de la Révolution (JMPR)** was particularly militant. From birth, all Zairians were automatically members of the JMPR and at 30 years of age, everyone became a member of the MPR and remained so until death.

During the 1970s and 1980s, the lines between party and state were completely blurred. The **Political Bureau**, a body of several dozen senior leaders, was the senior policymaking body. The Congress of the Party was a larger forum for discussion and debate that met every five years. The **Legislative Council** of 310 members ratified laws proposed by the Political Bureau. The **Executive Council** composed of heads of **departments** (ministries) and the first state commissioner (**prime minister**) formed the executive branch and oversaw the **administration** of government. And the **Judicial Council**, composed of presidents of the highest courts, interpreted the law. In 1980, the MPR **Central Committee**, composed of 120 senior party members, was created and began to emerge as the de facto **parliament** with a mandate to review and carry out the initiatives of the Political Bureau. As a result, the Legislative Council lost most of its power. The president presided over all of the organs. Party congresses were held in 1970, 1977 and 1984 to nominate Mobutu as the sole candidate for presidential **elections** in those years.

Originally, all members of the Political Bureau were nominated by the president. The Political Bureau then selected members of the other institutions and nominated the sole candidates for the Legislative Council. The president, as chief executive, chose the state commissioners, state governors and other senior members of the executive. However, a degree of liberalization was introduced in 1978. A portion of the membership of the Political Bureau was chosen by party members and multiple candidates within the party were allowed in the legislative elections. However, the size of the Political Bureau was changed to maintain a majority of presidential appointees and the legislative candidates, although chosen by local party cells, were subject to review by senior party officials. The election of part of the members of the Political Bureau was later abolished and the Central Committee, whose members were appointed by the Political Bureau, assumed most of the lawmaking duties formerly held by the Legislative Council. In January 1985, in a move aimed at eliminating "conflicts of interest," a by-law was adopted forbidding members of the Political Bureau and Central Committee to hold office in the executive or legislative bodies. Most officials chose to retain their party posts.

The avowed purpose of the MPR was to mobilize and educate the masses and to build support for government policies and actions. Another major goal was to foster unity, which after the fragmentation of the early 1960s remained a major concern. However, political analysts noted that the MPR did not arise from popular roots but was created and imposed from the top. And the main result, according to critics, was to institutionalize a political system that received little input from the masses and concentrated political and economic power in the hands of a small **élite**. The system was also blamed for contributing to the institutionalization of **corruption** and political patronage.

With the end of single-partyism announced by Mobutu in a speech on **April 24, 1990**, more than 200 parties formed and the MPR for a time changed its name to the Mouvement Populaire pour le Renouveau (Popular Movement for Revival) and was separated from government. It also underwent a measure of internal turmoil characterized by competition for leadership positions vacated by members joining the **opposition** and by conflicts along regional and generation lines. Mobutu, in an attempt to position himself above partisan politics following his April 1990 speech, resigned as president of the party for a time. He reassumed the post one year later.

Following the exile and death of Mobutu in 1997 and the installation of Laurent **Kabila** as president, MPR activities were proscribed, along with those of all political parties that had collaborated with Mobutu. *See also* Dissidents; Legislative System.

MOVIMENTO POPULAR DE LIBERTAÇÃO DE ANGOLA (MPLA) / POPULAR MOVEMENT FOR THE LIBERATION OF ANGOLA. One of three guerrilla groups that fought for **Angola**'s independence and afterward waged a civil war for control of that country. Headed by Agostinho **Neto** and backed by **Cuba** and the **Soviet Union**, the MPLA took control of the capital Luanda in 1975 but was subsequently faced with guerrilla attacks from the **União Nacional para a Independência Total de Angola (UNITA)** and the **Frente Nacional de Libertação de Angola (FNLA)** groups and, until 1990, incursions by **South African** forces fighting pro-independence guerrillas in Namibia. José Eduardo dos Santos became head of the MPLA and president of Angola following Neto's death on September 10, 1979. FNLA activity diminished in the 1980s, but UNITA continued to threaten the MPLA government. UNITA controlled large portions of territory in the eastern and southern parts of the country and disrupted the economy by halting mining and agriculture and by sabotaging the **Benguela Railway**, which provided the most efficient **transportation** link between Zairian mines in **Shaba Region** and the Atlantic Ocean.

Zaire supported the FNLA during the 1970s, but after its activity declined, switched support to UNITA. The government allowed Zairian territory to be used for guerrilla bases and arms transshipments to the guerrillas. In 1986, **Zambia** said Zairian territory was being used to supply covert military aid from the **United States** to UNITA. Mobutu denied the charge and declared his support for the MPLA government, although reports persisted of US supplies going to UNITA through Zaire.

A number of attempts were made to mediate the conflict, and elections were held in September 1992, which were won by the MPLA. UNITA subsequently resumed attacks and weeks of fighting in Luanda left an estimated 1,000 people dead. Another agreement was reached in 1995 and, despite sporadic violations, it held. In December 1996, several UNITA leaders assumed positions in the armed forces senior command as part of an agreement to merge the rival forces. The offensive of the **Alliance des Forces Démocratiques pour la Libération du Congo/Zaïre (AFDL)** beginning in October 1996 was backed by the MPLA. The arrival of the AFDL in Kinshasa in May 1997 placed considerable pressure on UNITA, which lost control of a major diamond smuggling and arms trafficking route through southern Congo/Zaire. During 1998, UNITA forces in northern Angola were caught between Angolan and Congolese government troops, leading to a gradual erosion of the Angolan ceasefire and renewed fighting in southern Angola.

MPINGA KASENDA (1937 -). A former **prime minister** and senior party official. Mpinga was born on August 30, 1937, at Tshilomba in **Kasaï Oriental Province**. He received a degree and later a doctorate in political science from **Lovanium University** and studied at the Institut Technique Supérieur d'Études Sociales at **Lubumbashi**. A professor at the **Université Nationale du Zaïre**'s **Kinshasa** campus during the early 1970s, he became a member of the **Political Bureau** of the **Mouvement Populaire de la Révolution (MPR)** party in 1972 and, in 1974, director of the **Makanda Kabobi Institute**, the MPR party school. He served as first state commissioner from 1977 to 1979 and became permanent secretary of the Political Bureau in 1979 and a member of the **Central Committee** on September 2, 1980. He was named defense minister in the Jean **Nguza Karl-I-Bond** government of 1992 and foreign minister in the Faustin **Birindwa** government of 1993.

MSIRI. Legendary king of the Garenganze in **Katanga**.

MULAMBA NYUNY WA KADIMA, LÉONARD (COLONEL). Mulamba was named **prime minister** on November 28, 1965, following **Mobutu**'s **coup d'etat**. The post was eliminated on October 26, 1966, and the duties of head of government were assumed by the **president**.

MULELE, PIERRE. The Chinese-trained guerrilla who lead the **Kwilu rebellion** and brought urban guerrilla terrorism to Congo for the first time. At **independence**, Mulele was the head of the **Parti Solidaire Africain (PSA)** and minister of **education** in the **government** of Patrice **Lumumba**. He left the country following Lumumba's death and went to **China** where he received military training. Mulele and his supporters, who espoused a Maoist form of peasant revolution, began their operations in January 1964 in Kwilu. They destroyed many administrative and **missionary** institutions and set bombs that terrorized **Leopoldville** for a number of months. When the **rebellion** was put down in 1965, Mulele went into exile in Brazzaville, People's Republic of the Congo (presently **Republic of the Congo**). Offered amnesty by the **Mobutu** government, he returned to **Kinshasa** on September 29, 1968, where he was summarily tried for treason and executed on October 8, 1968. Following his execution, the Brazzaville government broke relations with the Mobutu government.

MULUMBA LUKOJI, CRISPIN. The second **prime minister** of the transitional period, Mulumba was named to that post on March 15, 1991, following the resignation of **Lunda Bululu**. He oversaw the opening of the **National Conference** in August 1991. An academic from southeastern Congo/Zaire, his appointment was seen as a move to undercut support for **opposition** leaders Étienne **Tshisekedi** and Jean **Nguza Karl-I-Bond**. However, he quickly fell out of favor with the opposition, which accused him of being pro-**Mobutu**. He resigned on September 30, 1991, amid civil unrest and a political stalemate over the **democratic transition**. He died of a heart attack in Johannesburg, **South Africa**, on March 3, 1997.

MUNGUL DIAKA, BERNADIN. At **independence**, Mungul was a supporter of Patrice **Lumumba** who became Antoine **Gizenga**'s ambassador to **China** during the eastern **rebellion**. He was provincial minister of **Kwilu Province** in 1962-63, minister of the **middle classes** in the Léonard **Mulamba** government, and ambassador to Brussels in 1966-67. He was **education** minister when he resigned from the government in July 1968 and went into exile. He sought asylum in Brussels in the mid-1970s and led a group of exiled **dissidents** until he returned to Zaire under the general **amnesty of 1983**. With the advent of multipartyism, Mungul formed a small party. He was appointed **prime minister** in October 1991 after **Mobutu** refused to accept the first Étienne **Tshisekedi** government but was replaced by Jean **Nguza Karl-I-Bond** in November. In the mid-1990s he served as governor of **Kinshasa**.

MUNGUYA MBENGE. Commissioner (governor) of **Shaba Region** during the 1977 invasion by the **Front pour la Libération**

Nationale du Congo (FLNC), Munguya fled into exile. He was tried and convicted in absentia of collaborating with the FLNC. *See also* Mouvement d'Action pour la Résurrection du Congo.

MUNONGO MWENDA M'SIRI SHYOMBEKA, GODEFROID. Moïse **Tshombe**'s interior minister in the secessionist **Katanga** government, Munongo was head of **security** and one of the most feared members of the Katangan regime. The son of a traditional **chief** of the **Yeke ethnic group**, Munongo was born November 20, 1925, in Benkeya and received his **education** at **missionary** schools in Katanga. He became a provincial judge in 1954 and was elected the first president of the **Confédération des Associations Katangaises (CONAKAT)** in 1959. When Tshombe became **prime minister** after the **Katanga secession** was ended, he joined the **government**, but was dismissed in a cabinet reshuffle on July 9, 1964. Following **Mobutu**'s **coup d'etat**, he was arrested in a general crackdown on December 26, 1966, and subsequently spent several years in detention. He reemerged in **politics** in 1991 as the leader of a group of traditional chiefs accredited to the **National Conference**.

MUSIC. One of Congo/Zaire's greatest contributions to contemporary African **culture** has been its music, particularly the orchestra music that developed in the 1960s. The first Congolese musicians to gain popularity throughout the territory were troubadours in the 1940s and 1950s, who traveled and performed primarily in the remote provinces. Among the early troubadours were Antoine Wendo, born in 1925, who gained recognition with his recording of "Liwa ya Paul Kamba." He traveled as a soloist in the **Kasai**, **Orientale** and Maï-Ndombe areas. Other soloists included Paul Kamba, Tête Rossignol, Polidor, Jean Bosco and Colon Gentil. As the music developed, the solo acts became groups, adding African drums and acoustic guitars. Antoine Kasongo, Tekele Monkango (perhaps the first female music star) and Odéon Kinois were among the first leaders of groups. The second generation left traditional music for new forms and added more instruments.

The first recordings of Congolese music were reportedly made beginning in 1947 by colonial museums. Joseph Kabasele, another founding father, formed the African Jazz Orchestra around 1953 and made a few records. Franco Luambo, born in 1938, formed the O.K. Jazz Orchestra and played cha-chas and rumbas before they became popular. Beginning in the late 1950s, the influence of Cuban and Latin music began to be felt, and a number of Latin American records were adapted and recorded by Congolese groups. These included "Kay-Kay," "Son," "Tremendo," "L'Amor," and "Lolita." The Latin influence led to the composition of songs with Latin rhythms and Congolese lyrics, including such classics as "Indépendance Cha-cha" by Rochéreau to commemorate **independence**, and "Cha-cha-cha de Amor" by Franco. Congolese musicians eventually adopted the term "jazz" to describe their music. Musicologist Michel Lonoh writes that the first instance of use of the term "**Congo Jazz**" occurred in the song called "Pasi ya mokili et Congo Jazz akei" (roughly translated: "Heartache for the homeland and Congo Jazz took off").

By the mid-1960s, the term "Congo Jazz" was generally used to describe Congolese orchestral music, with Franco's O.K. Jazz, Rochéreau and Docteur Nico among the most popular musicians. By the late 1960s, the "soukouma" style of music had entered the lexicon and gradually became the dominant form. By this time, Congolese music was among the most popular in Africa. By the late 1970s, the number of bands had multiplied and the music had become considerably diversified. Some leaders incorporated disco, jazz and blues into their compositions. In the 1980s, reggae, Antilles and rap rhythms grew in popularity. Still other musicians favored ballads and more traditional musical forms. Many **languages** were used in the lyrics, but **Lingala** remained the most common.

Congolese music was primarily dance music, favored in the large, traditional open-air dance clubs where the orchestra played and the beer flowed often until dawn. **Kinshasa** was one of the earliest recording centers in Africa. However, economic difficulties caused a decline in the late 1970s, while other African cities like Abidjan, Lagos, Johannesburg and Nairobi became popular recording sites. Congolese orchestras frequently performed and recorded in Paris, Brussels and London and gained considerable popularity in major cities and on college campuses in the United States.

MUTSHATSHA. A small town in western **Katanga Province** lying on the **railway** connecting Katanga's **mining** centers to **Angola**'s **Benguela Railway**. Mutshatsha gained renown in 1977 as one of the most important conquests of the **Front pour la Libération Nationale du Congo (FLNC)** during the first **Shaba** invasion.

MVUBA. An **ethnic group** of central Sudanic origin living in **Orientale Province** north of the **Uele River**. The Mvuba were said to be primarily a group of decentralized, small-scale political entities, lacking **chiefs** and dominated by the **Mamvu** and **Mangbetu**.

MWATA YANVU. Sometimes written as "Mwaant Yaav," the Mwata Yanvu (meaning "King of Vipers") is the traditional paramount **chief** of the **Lunda**, their political and religious ruler and a strong force in **Katangan** politics.

MWERU, LAKE. *See* LAKE MWERU.

MWINYI, ALI HASSAN. President of **Tanzania** from 1985 to 1995, Mwinyi was vice president under Julius **Nyerere** until the latter's retirement. Mwinyi was reelected to a second term in 1990. Relations between **Zaire** and Tanzania, which were strained under Nyerere, improved under Mwinyi, especially after he declared his government would not allow **opposition** activities against the **Mobutu** government on its territory. In the early 1990s, Mwinyi encouraged talks aimed at improving relations between Zaire and **Angola** and, with Mobutu, sought to mediate an end to the **Rwandan** civil war in the mid-1990s. He was succeeded by Benjamin Mpaka in 1995.

- N -

NAME CHANGES. A number of name changes have been carried out during the history of **Congo/Zaire** that have affected the name of the country, **provinces**, cities and even of the citizens themselves. In 1885, the vast territory with hundreds of ethnic "nations" was given the name **Congo Free State**. In 1908, the Congo Free State became the **Belgian Congo**.

At **independence**, the country was named the **Republic of the Congo (Kinshasa)**, but with the promulgation of the first **constitution** in 1964, it was renamed the **Democratic Republic of the Congo**. In an effort to foster a greater sense of nationhood, Belgian names adopted during the **colonial era** were abandoned in favor of Congolese names. On May 3, 1966, **Leopoldville** became **Kinshasa**, **Elisabethville** became **Lubumbashi**, and **Stanleyville** became **Kisangani**, among others (see guide on page xix).

Following the launch of the **Authenticity** movement, the country became the **République du Zaïre** on October 27, 1971. As part of the movement, countless streets, bridges and buildings were renamed to honor Congolese heroes and leaders. The process culminated in May 1972, when Zairians were ordered to drop their Christian surnames and adopt Zairian ones instead. For example, Joseph-Désiré **Mobutu** became Mobutu Sese Seko Kuku Ngbendu Wa Za Banga.

With the decline in popularity of the Mobutu **government** in the 1980s, many Zairians, especially **opposition** leaders, resumed using their Christian names in public. When Mobutu announced the end of single-party rule and the transition to multiparty democracy in April 1990, the practice spread and came to represent a statement of political affiliation. It was also seen as an expression of dismay by some Zairians over the loss of ethics and morality which had occurred during the Mobutu years. Most Mobutu supporters continued to use their "authentic" names in public. Opponents used their Christian names and those who wished to remain neutral used both.

When the **Alliance des Forces Démocratiques pour la Libération du Congo/Zaïre (AFDL)** took Kinshasa on May 17, 1997, it indicated a desire to remove all symbols of Mobutu, whose regime was viewed as illegal. When AFDL leader Laurent **Kabila** took the oath of office on May 29, he announced that Zaire would henceforth be called by its previous name, the Democratic Republic of the Congo or République Démocratique du Congo (RDC); the **zaire currency** would be replaced by the Congo franc; and the national flag and anthem adopted under Mobutu would be replaced by those of the First Republic.

The names of most cities and regions were not affected, except for **Bas-Zaïre**, **Shaba** and **Haut-Zaïre** Regions, which were changed back to **Bas-Congo**, **Katanga** and **Orientale**, respectively. The names of many companies and public institutions, however, were changed if they were associated with the Mobutu era.

The changes were quickly accepted by the international community and most Congolese, but the adoption of "Congo" brought a return to the old confusion with the **Republic of the Congo (Brazzaville)**, the former French colony across the **Congo River**. Many distinguish the two by adding the name of the capital, as in Congo/Kinshasa and Congo/Brazzaville. This book tends to use the name in use at the time of the reference, whether it is Belgian Congo, Congo or Zaire. In more-general references, it uses Congo/Zaire, Congo/Kinshasa or, upon second reference, Congo.

NAMIBIA, RELATIONS WITH. The government of Congo/Zaire supported Namibia's struggle for independence against **South Africa** and quickly recognized the government when it achieved independence on March 21, 1990. Namibia supported the Laurent **Kabila** government in 1998 when it faced a rebellion by the **Rassemblement Congolais pour la Démocratie (RCD)**.

NANDE. An **ethnic group** living in eastern Congo/Zaire which became a traditional rival of the **Banyarwanda** when the latter began to immigrate to the region during the **colonial era**. Nande clashes with the Banyarwanda during the period of **ethnic cleansing** beginning in 1993 were one of the reasons for the offensive by the **Alliance des Forces Démocratiques pour la Libération du Congo/Zaïre (AFDL)** which deposed **Mobutu** in 1997.

NATIONAL ASSEMBLY. *See* LEGISLATIVE COUNCIL.

NATIONAL CONFEDERATION OF CONGOLESE ASSO-CIATIONS. *See* CONFÉDÉRATION NATIONALE DES ASSOCIATIONS CONGOLAISES (CONACO).

NATIONAL CONFERENCE / CONFÉRENCE NATIONALE (CN). The original name for the Sovereign National Conference, or **Conférence Nationale Souveraine (CNS)**, which was to meet for one month in August 1991 to chart the one-year transition to multiparty **democracy**. The conference opened in on August 7 under the chairmanship of Isaac **Kalonji Mutambayi**, a veteran politician, to draft a new **constitution**, but it quickly degenerated into chaos because of disputes over accreditation and charges by the **opposition** that pro-**Mobutu** forces were trying to load the assembly with their delegates. It was suspended and reconvened a number of times during the next four months, a period marked by political demonstrations, **labor strikes** and the **pillages** of September 23-24. In December 1991, with most of the accreditation disputes resolved, the conference reconvened under the chairmanship of **Monsengwo Pasinya**, the archbishop of **Kisangani**. In April 1992, it proclaimed itself the Sovereign National Conference and subsequently declared its measures would be constitutionally binding and the **president** henceforth would be obliged by law to carry them out. The declaration was ignored by the Mobutu **government**. *See also* Democratic Transition.

NATIONAL CONGOLESE MOVEMENT. *See* MOUVEMENT NATIONAL CONGOLAIS (MNC).

NATIONAL CONGOLESE RADIO AND TELEVISION. *See* RADIO-TÉLÉVISION NATIONALE CONGOLAISE (RTNC).

NATIONAL DOCUMENTATION AGENCY. *See* AGENCE NATIONALE DE DOCUMENTATION (AND).

NATIONAL FISHERIES BOARD. *See* OFFICE NATIONAL DE PÊCHE (ONP).

NATIONAL FRONT FOR THE LIBERATION OF ANGOLA. *See* FRENTE NACIONAL DE LIBERTAÇÃO DE ANGOLA (FNLA).

NATIONAL INFORMATION AGENCY. *See* AGENCE NATIONALE DE RENSEIGNEMENTS (ANR).

NATIONAL INTELLIGENCE AND PROTECTION SERVICE. *See* SERVICE NATIONAL D'INTELLIGENCE ET DE PROTECTION (SNIP).

NATIONAL LIBERATION FRONT. *See* FRONT NATIONAL DE LIBÉRATION (FNL).

NATIONAL LIVESTOCK DEVELOPMENT BOARD. *See* OFFICE NATIONAL POUR LE DÉVELOPPEMENT DE L'ÉLEVAGE (ONDE).

NATIONAL ORDER OF THE LEOPARD. *See* ORDRE NATIONAL DU LÉOPARD.

NATIONAL SCHOOL OF ADMINISTRATION. *See* ÉCOLE NATIONALE D'ADMINISTRATION (ENA).

NATIONAL SECURITY COUNCIL. *See* CONSEIL DE SECURITÉ NATIONAL (CSN).

NATIONAL SUGAR BOARD. *See* OFFICE NATIONAL DU SUCRE (ONS).

NATIONAL TRANSPORT BOARD. *See* OFFICE NATIONAL DES TRANSPORTS (ONATRA).

NATIONAL UNION FOR THE TOTAL INDEPENDENCE OF ANGOLA. *See* UNIÃO NAÇIONAL PARA A INDEPENDÊNCIA TOTAL DE ANGOLA (UNITA).

NATIONAL UNION OF ZAIRIAN WORKERS. *See* UNION NATIONALE DES TRAVAILLEURS ZAÏROIS (UNTZA).

NATIONAL UNIVERSITY OF CONGO. *See* UNIVERSITÉ NATIONALE DU CONGO (UNC).

NATIONAL WAY / VOIE NATIONALE. The National Way is the name given to the only **transportation** route located entirely on Zairian territory linking the **mining** areas in **Katanga Province** to the Atlantic Ocean. Established in 1928, the National Way was intended to replace **export** routes through **Tanzania** and Mozambique to the ports of Dar es Salaam and Beira. A tortuous route 2,750 km long, the National Way involves transporting **mineral** products by **railway** from Katanga to the **port** of **Ilebo** (formerly Port Francqui) on the **Kasai River**, by river to

Kinshasa, and by rail once again to the ocean port of **Matadi**. Although the route required two to six months' transshipment time, it became vital to Zaire's mineral exports after 1975 when the **Angolan** civil war closed the **Benguela Railway**, which had been the most direct route from Katanga to the Atlantic Ocean. The National Way, although more costly and time-consuming than the **Southern Way** through Zimbabwe and **South Africa**, was politically more favorable because it was entirely within Zairian territory. According to government figures, 45 percent of **Shaba**'s minerals were exported via the National Way in 1985. By the 1990s, however, the National Way was used only intermittently because of deteriorating **river** and railway service and the most efficient transportation link between Shaba and western Zaire was by **air transportation**.

NATIONALISM. The nationalist movement began in the 1950s when the colonial authorities began to allow Congolese to form trade unions and ethnic "interest" groups. **Political parties** began to form in the late 1950s. Most of them advocated some form of **independence**. Immediately following independence in 1960, Congo was wracked by ethnic and regional divisions. The colonial restrictions on political activity had suppressed political parties and the development of a sense of nationhood. Once allowed to form, parties grew initially out of the ethnic interest groups, except for the **Mouvement National Congolais (MNC)** and a few others which attempted to attract members from all over the country.

In addition, the **government**, modeled on the Belgian system, sought to provide checks and balances by spreading power between the **president** and **prime minister** and the two houses of the **legislature**. However, this caused further weakness and divisiveness. As a result, one of the major goals of the **Mobutu** government following the 1965 **coup d'etat** was to unite Congolese and instill in them a sense of nationhood. The **N'Sele Manifesto**, the Magna Carta of the **Mouvement Populaire de la Révolution (MPR)**, specifically noted the need to eliminate tribalism and regionalism.

The early years of the Mobutu government were characterized by rising nationalistic sentiment that in the mid-1970s led to the establishment of the party-state and the emergence of the **Authenticity** movement and **Mobutism**. The feelings of national pride and strength were boosted by the rise in Zaire's economic fortunes. In the late 1970s, however, the decline of the Zairian **economy**, the **Shaba** invasions, the emergence of **dissident** groups, and growing resentment by the people against the political oligarchy contributed to a creeping disillusionment with the ideals of the early Mobutu years. The political reforms of 1990 brought multiparty politics and an increase in political rivalries based on personality, **region** and ethnic affiliation. Many in the **opposition** advocated a less-centralized system of government, most often modeled on a **federalist** system, and an increase in interethnic tensions in the east and the rise of a rebel group that in 1997 took control of the country shook the central government. Nevertheless, the sense of nationhood and national identity among most citizens remained strong.

NATIONALIZATION. Nationalization of Zairian **industry** began in 1966 with the **government** takeover of the **Union Minière du Haut-Katanga** (now called the **Générale des Carrières et des Mines**, or **GECAMINES**) **mining** company. It reached its peak in November 1973 with the **Zairianization** of large foreign-owned businesses. The deterioration of the commercial sector, combined with a declining **economy** due to falling **copper** prices, led in 1975 to a partial privatization called **Retrocession**. Further privatization of certain sectors, including **agriculture**, **transportation** and **diamond** and **gold** trading, was enacted during the 1980s. And, in the 1990s, partial privatization was announced of state-owned **river** and **railway** transportation companies.

NAVY. The **government** maintains a small navy of 1,300 persons, including 600 marines, engaged primarily in coastal, border patrols along the Atlantic Ocean in the west and the Great Lakes in the east. The largest ship, commissioned as the *Zaire*, is a 70-ton vessel based at **Matadi**. The remainder of the fleet comprises two dozen light patrol vessels, primarily of French, Chinese, US and North Korean manufacture. The main base is at **Banana** on the coast and includes a training facility. Other bases are located at **Boma** and **Kinshasa** on the **Congo River** and at **Kalemie** and **Moba** on **Lake Tanganyika**. The **United States** government launched a bilateral aid program with the Zairian navy in 1977 that included the supply of patrol boats, spare parts and some training. The program was suspended in the early 1990s.

NDEMBO. An **ethnic group** in western **Katanga Province** related in **language** and **descent groups** to the **Lunda**, but which tend to side with the **Chokwe** in opposing the Lunda in modern-day politics.

NDJILI AIRPORT. Congo/Zaire's largest airport, located near the suburb of Ndjili on the northern outskirts of **Kinshasa**, Ndjili Airport is the home base for a significant portion of the country's **air force**. It is also the headquarters of the national carrier, the **Lignes Aériennes Congolaises** (formerly **Air Zaïre**), and several private carriers. It has been serviced by a number of international carriers, including Air Afrique, Sabena, TAP, Cameroon Airlines, Ethiopian Airlines, Air France and Alitalia. The airport was one of the stops on PanAm's West African coastal route from New York to Johannesburg until the 1980s. On **September 23-24, 1991**, elements of **Centre d'Entraînement des Troupes Aéronautiques (CETA)**, the military air training facility, looted containers to protest late and low wages. The looting, which came to be known as the **pillages**, spread throughout Kinshasa and brought a major military intervention by **Belgium** and **France** to evacuate 10,000 expatriate residents.

NDOLA. A **mining** town in **Zambia**'s **copper** belt that has considerable commercial ties with **Lubumbashi**. Ndola was the destination of UN Secretary-General Dag **Hammarskjöld**'s plane when it crashed over **Katanga** in 1961, killing all of its occupants.

NDOLO AIRPORT. **Kinshasa**'s first commercial airfield, located in the heart of the city in Ndolo commune, a few minutes from downtown Kinshasa. With the opening of **Ndjili Airport** in 1960, Ndolo became a domestic airfield used primarily by private and military aircraft. On January 8, 1996, an overloaded cargo plane crashed upon takeoff into a large market near the end of the runway. More than 300 people were killed, most of them women and children working at the market, making it Zaire's worst aviation accident. The four Russian crew members survived. The airport was closed for two years after the incident, but has since been reopened.

NENDAKA BIKA, VICTOR. An influential figure in numerous Congolese **governments** and a leading member of the **Binza Group**, Nendaka was vice president of the Patrice **Lumumba** wing of the **Mouvement National Congolais (MNC)** and head of the Sûreté secret **police** from September 1960 until 1965, when he became interior minister in first the Moïse **Tshombe** and then the Évariste **Kimba** governments. After Kimba failed to obtain the vote of confidence for his government on November 14, 1965, Nendaka was asked to form a government, but was prevented by the military **coup d'etat** on **November 24, 1965**. He was named minister of **transportation** and **communications** after the coup, then finance minister from 1967 until August 1969 and subsequently ambassador to West **Germany**. Nendaka was recalled in 1970 and placed under house arrest. He was accused, with former foreign minister Justin **Bomboko**, of plotting the assassination of the **president** and sent into internal exile. However, he was rehabilitated in 1977 and became a delegate to the **National Conference** in 1991-92.

NETO, AGOSTINHO (1922 - 1979). The first president of **Angola**, Neto was the poet-liberation leader of the **Movimento Popular de Libertação de Angola (MPLA)** faction in Angola's war for independence and subsequent civil war. A socialist with close ties to the **Soviet Union**, Neto was disliked by **Mobutu**, who supported his rivals. However, following the **Shaba** invasions by guerrillas of the **Front pour la Libération Nationale du Congo (FLNC)** based in Angola, Mobutu and Neto met in Brazzaville and agreed to cease hostilities. Diplomatic relations were subsequently established, although tensions and suspicions remained. Neto died of cancer in the Soviet Union on September 10, 1979.

NEWS MEDIA. Most Congolese receive information by word of mouth and by **radio**, which historically has been the most accessible and most popular of the news media. There were an estimated four million radio sets in Congo/Zaire in the mid-1990s. The **government**-owned station, called La **Voix du Zaïre** from 1976 until 1997, when it was renamed La **Voix du Peuple**, daily broadcast from **Kinshasa** in French and the four national **languages**. Its transmissions were sent via satellite to eight regional stations, which rebroadcast portions of them and added their own programs in local languages. International radio stations, in particular the Voice of America, Radio France Internationale, British Broadcasting Corporation and the national stations of **Switzerland**, **Germany**, Canada, **Egypt** and **South Africa**, provide international news which is closely followed by many.

Television and printed publications reached a more limited audience, primarily the urban-based upper classes. There were an estimated 40,000 television sets in the country in the mid-1990s. International TV broadcasts, mostly from Europe, have been received by satellite since 1990 and some of these are retransmitted locally.

Prior to **independence**, several newspapers, some financed by church groups, published in the colony and for the most part continued to do so during the First Republic. During the years of single-party rule, however, heavy government control of the media and self-censorship by journalists restricted domestic news to information viewed as favorable to the government. In the 1970s, the media contributed extensively to the personalization of **Mobutu**'s power. During that period, two major newspapers were published in Kinshasa: *Salongo*, the party/government daily, and *Elima*, which closely followed the government line. There were a number of weekly magazines devoted to current affairs, **society** and **culture**, most notably *Zaïre* magazine. **Lubumbashi** and **Kisangani** each had a newspaper, *Mjumbe* and *Boyoma,* respectively, which sought to publish on a daily basis.

The advent of multiparty politics produced a growth industry in the printed media reflecting that of the **political parties**. Media-watchers in the early 1990s counted more than 120 printed publications, and by 1996 more than 400 were appearing intermittently. Most published one to several times per week as funds and newsprint allowed, but about one dozen aspired to publish on a daily basis. *Salongo* continued to follow the pro-Mobutu line. *Elima*, however, became a strong government critic. A number of new publications which criticized the government appeared. Some of the most notable were *Le Potentiel, Référence*

Plus, Le Palmarès, Le Phare, Umoja, Forum, Le Standard, La Cité Africaine, Le Grognon (satirical), *Libre Expressions, La Société, Le Soir du Galibot, Perspectives Africaines, Le Compatriote, Graben* and *La Tempête des Tropiques.* Le Soft focused primarily on economics and business. In Lubumbashi, three major publications appeared: *Le Lushois, l'Espoir* and *Le Communicateur.*

Virtually all members of the printed media in the early 1990s were strongly opposed to the Mobutu government and engaged in strongly worded, often personal attacks against the **president** and his supporters. Several dozen journalists were detained during a crackdown in 1992-93. The editor-publisher of *Elima*, Essolomwa Nkoy ea Linganga, was detained in 1991. In 1992, the offices and presses of *Elima, La Réference, Le Phare* and *Le Potentiel* were attacked, as was the home of *Umoja* editor Léon Moukanda Lunyama. The editor of *Le Phare*, Mukengeshayi Kenge, was arrested in 1993.

During the early 1990s, the government retained control over the broadcast media and as a result some of the best reporting on the **National Conference** and the **opposition** came from broadcasts by **Republic of the Congo**-based radio and television, which could be received in Kinshasa. In 1992, a group of journalists at La Voix du Zaïre led a revolt against government censorship of radio and television newscasts, saying the proceedings of the National Conference should be fair and should include the coverage of opposition activities and positions. For a time, this demand was accommodated. However, the military later occupied the station, taking it off the air and causing rumors of a coup attempt. When the broadcasts resumed, increased government control was evident.

In the mid-1990s, several dozen private FM radio stations were licensed in major cities. The following year private television stations were also allowed. These largely avoided reporting on domestic **politics** until the late 1990s, when they began rebroadcasting news and programs relayed by international broadcasters supplemented by their own staff reporting. The government-controlled national news agency, Agence Zaïre-Presse, published a daily summary of government activities until the mid-1990s, when financial problems caused it to close.

When opposition forces led by Laurent **Kabila** took power in May 1997, they said they would tolerate a free press and news media. However, it became clear that the new government did not care for attacks against its leaders. In subsequent months, a number of editors were arrested for criticizing the government or, in once case, forecasting its imminent demise. In June, the Kabila government said it was nationalizing Tele Kin Malebo, a popular private television station, saying it had been established with equipment purchased by the government for the Voix du Zaïre complex and therefore belonged to the people. The Kabila government periodically used legal means to pressure the local media when it became too independent. In February 1999 it announced a major inspection of registration documents and broadcast schedules of local radio stations.

NGALA. One of the major **ethnic groups** of northwestern **Congo/Zaire**, living between the **Congo** and **Ubangi Rivers**, whose **language, Lingala,** is one of the country's four national languages. Most ethnographers consider the Ngala to be of the **Bantu** cluster, although others maintain they belong primarily to the Sudanic group. Both clusters settled in the area and there was considerable intermingling among them, but the Ngala language appears to be related more to Bantu tongues than to any others.

Originally a relatively small tribe, the Ngala gained importance in the minds of many for two reasons. Lingala, based on the traditional Ngala tongue, came into increasing use beginning in the mid-1800s as the **trade** language of the lower Congo River and the language of the military. It became the lingua franca in **Leopoldville** during the **colonial era** and, following **independence**, was adopted as the conversational idiom of the **civil service** and **administration** (as opposed to French, which continued to be the official, written idiom). Secondly, **Mobutu** used Lingala (as opposed to other national languages) to address Zairians. To the rest of Africa, Lingala is probably best known as the language of its vibrant **music**, which gained popularity on the continent beginning in the 1960s.

NGALULA MPANDAJILA, JOSEPH. One of the founding fathers of the **Mouvement National Congolais (MNC)** who attended the **Pan-African Conference** in Accra in December 1958 with

Patrice **Lumumba** and upon his return addressed a rally at which the first calls for **independence** were heard. When the MNC split, Ngalula followed Albert **Kalonji**'s wing and became vice president and prime minister of the secessionist Mining State of **South Kasai**. Following the end of the South Kasai secession, he returned to **Leopoldville** and was appointed minister of **education** in the first and second Cyrille **Adoula governments**. He was dropped from the government in 1963. However, Ngalula remained in Congolese politics and came to attention once again in the 1980s as a signatory of the open letter by the **Group of Thirteen Parliamentarians** to **Mobutu** and one of the founders of the **Union pour la Démocratie et le Progrès Social (UDPS)**. He was tried, imprisoned, banished and pardoned several times during the mid-1980s for advocating the creation of a second **political party**. With the advent of multipartyism, in 1990, he joined the **opposition**-led **Sacred Union**.

NGBAKA. A central-Sudanic **ethnic group** living in the northwestern corner of **Congo/Zaire** along the **Ubangi River** near Zongo.

NGBANDI. A Sudanic people, according to some ethnographers, related to the **Ngala**, living in northwestern **Congo/Zaire** between the **Congo** and **Ubangi Rivers** east of Busingu. The Ngbandi are one of the major **ethnic groups** speaking an Adamawa-Eastern **language**. The most famous Ngbandi son was **Mobutu**, who traced his parental and ancestral origins to the group living around **Gbadolite**. Mobutu, however, was born in **Lisala** and grew up among the **Ngombe** and Ngala people near **Mbandaka**.

NGOMBE. A subgroup of the **Mongo** people living along the **Congo River** north of **Mbandaka** and Basankusu.

NGONGO LUTETE. A Congolese leader who fought in the campaign to drive the **Afro-Arab** traders from eastern Congo in the 1890s and, with the help of the **Sambala** people, pacified and occupied the **Maniema** region west of **Kivu**.

NGOUABI, MARIEN (1938 - 1977). Founder of the Marxist People's Republic of the Congo (presently **Republic of the Congo**) in the former French Congo. Ngouabi headed the National Council of the Revolution, which took power in a military coup d'etat in **Congo/Brazzaville** in September 1968, and was president from January 1, 1969, until his assassination on March 18, 1977. Ngouabi was born at Ombélé and was a member of the Congolese armed forces. Following independence in 1960, he became an admirer of Marxism. His arrest in 1968 led to the military coup d'etat that overthrew Massamba-Debat. Ngouabi, along with Marx and Lenin, was considered one of the heroes of the official Congolese revolution. He led the Congo during a period of hostile relations with **Congo/Zaire**, but was also responsible for organizing the meetings between **Mobutu** and **Angolan** President Agostinho **Neto** in 1976 which eventually brought diplomatic relations between Zaire and Angola. Although Marxism-Leninism was abandoned in 1990 and the country was renamed the Republic of the Congo, Ngouabi remains a national hero.

NGUZA KARL-I-BOND, JEAN (1938 -). A leading political leader from **Katanga** and political heir to Moïse **Tshombe**, Nguza (frequently called "Nguz") spent his career alternating from a staunch supporter of **Mobutu** while in **government** to outspoken critic when out of power. Articulate in French, English and most of Congo/Zaire's national **languages**, Nguza was popular among Western governments. He was one of the most prominent exiled **dissidents** in the early 1980s until he returned to Zaire under the **amnesty of 1983**.

Nguza was born August 4, 1938, in Musumba, near Kapanga in western Katanga, a nephew of Tshombe and related to the **Lunda** paramount **chief**. At an early age, he moved to **Likasi**, where he attended primary school with the Xavier Brothers and then attended secondary school in **Elisabethville** under the Benedictine Fathers. He graduated from **Lovanium University** in July 1965 with a degree in international relations and entered the diplomatic corps. Nguza served as the second-ranking diplomat at the Zairian mission to the **United Nations** until his appointment as foreign minister on February 24, 1972. He was replaced in a cabinet reshuffle on March 8, 1974, but returned to the post on February 4, 1976, during a period when he was touted in the Western news media as a possible successor to Mobutu. He was arrested on August 13, 1977, accused of having prior knowledge of the first **Shaba** invasion, and dismissed as foreign minister six days later. Nguza was sentenced to death for treason but the sentence was commuted to life imprisonment. He was freed one year later, appointed foreign minister once again on March 6, 1979, and promoted to **prime minister** shortly thereafter.

In April 1981, Nguza resigned and went into exile, accusing the Mobutu government of **corruption**, authoritarianism and abuse of power. He published a book in 1982 that documented some of his charges, detailed his trial and torture in 1979, and advocated a return to multiparty **democracy** in Zaire. He launched a tour of Europe and North America, during which he testified before the US House of Representatives Africa Subcommittee. He continued to be an outspoken leader of the exiled **opposition** until he was muzzled by the Belgian government along with other dissidents in a move to improve relations with the Zairian government. In June 1985, Nguza accepted the amnesty of 1983 and returned to Zaire. He was appointed ambassador to the **United States** in September 1986.

A few days after Mobutu's announcement of the transition to multipartyism in 1990, Nguza announced he was forming an opposition party and would run for **president**. He founded the **Union des Fédéralistes et des Républicains Indépendants (UFERI)**, which became one of the three major parties in the **Sacred Union** in 1991. Nguza supported the Étienne **Tshisekedi** government of October 1991, which was never formally installed. However, after Tshisekedi's dismissal, Nguza accepted the post of prime minister and formed a government on November 28, for which he was expelled from the Sacred Union. While prime minister, he formed a "moderate" coalition of about 30 parties called the **Alliance des Forces Patriotiques**. But he was condemned as a traitor by the opposition and was replaced when the **Sovereign National Conference** elected Tshisekedi prime minister in August 1992.

With UFERI's power base reduced primarily to Shaba Region, its militants, led by then-Governor Gabriel **Kyungu wa Kumwanza**, began a campaign of **ethnic cleansing** under the rallying cry of "Katanga for Katangans." From 1992 to 1993, tens of thousands of **Luba**-Kasai, viewed as supporters of Tshisekedi's **Union pour la Démocratie et le Progrès Social (UDPS)**, were expelled and their homes and businesses destroyed or taken over by UFERI supporters. The opposition said the expulsions were instigated by Nguza in order to consolidate his political power base and were supported by Mobutu, who saw it as a way to split the opposition in the southeast. Nguza returned as defense minister in the Faustin **Birindwa** government of 1993 but was excluded from the Léon **Kengo was Dendo** government that replaced it in 1994. He suffered a stroke in 1995 and received extensive treatment in **South Africa**. He returned to Zaire the following year but was excluded from the government of Laurent **Kabila** that took power in May 1997 because of his long-standing connections to Mobutu and largely discredited political class.

NJEMBE. An ethnic subgroup of the **Kuba** living in **Kasaï Occidental Province**.

NKRUMAH, KWAME (1909 - 1972). First president of Ghana and one of the leaders of the Pan-Africanist movement who organized the Union of African States with Guinea and Mali in 1961. Patrice **Lumumba** met Nkrumah at the **Pan-African Conference** in Accra in December 1958. Nkrumah is said to have greatly influenced Lumumba's thinking on such topics as African solidarity, the need for African nations to distance themselves from the colonial powers, and the need to forge a Pan-African union by integrating political and economic systems. Nkrumah was deposed in a military coup d'etat in 1966 and lived in exile in Guinea until his death.

NKU. An **ethnic group** identified by Jan Vansina as of the **Boma-**Sakata cluster living in the Lower **Kasai River** area.

NKUTSHU. Sometimes written "Kuntshu," the Nkutshu are of the **Bantu** group, related to the **Mongo**. They live in the central portion of eastern **Congo/Zaire** between the Lukenie and Sankuru Rivers and are sometimes identified with the **Tetela** and the **Kusu** people of the same region.

NORD-KIVU. A province of eastern **Congo/Zaire** that was a subregion of **Kivu** until it was divided in the administrative reform of May 1988. The province contains some of the country's most fertile soil and its most temperate **climate**. It produces vegetables, **palm oil**, **timber** and **gold**. With an estimated **population** of 2.7 million

(1,861,960 in 1982) living in an area of 59,563 square km, Nord-Kivu is one of the country's most densely populated areas.

In March 1993, tensions began to rise between **Rwandan** immigrants, the **Banyarwanda**, who had settled during the **colonial era**, and more-established groups. They erupted into violence after then-Governor Jean-Pierre Kalumbo Mboho began calling on **Hunde** and **Nyanga** groups to exterminate the Banyarwanda. Entire villages were burned to the ground. Seven thousand people were killed and several hundred thousand were made homeless. **Opposition** leaders said the **ethnic cleansing** was sparked by politicians who wished to consolidate their political base by expelling groups seen as opposed to them.

In 1994, the region was saddled with more than one million **refugees** fleeing interethnic fighting in Rwanda and, to a lesser degree, **Burundi**. The influx severely strained services and infrastructure around the urban centers of **Goma** and **Bukavu** and caused resentment among the local population, which already was suffering from the effects of Zaire's economic crisis. Political and military activity in refugee camps by leaders of the ousted Rwandan government of the late President Juvenal Habyarimana created tensions in the region and strained relations between Zaire and the new government in Rwanda.

In September 1996, a group of Zairian **Tutsis**, led by veteran **dissident** Laurent **Kabila** and reportedly backed by forces of the new government in Rwanda, attacked **Hutu**-dominated militias in Rwandan refugee camps. The attacks caused 500,000 refugees to return to Rwanda in November and led to the occupation by the Kabila forces of Goma, Bukavu and Uvira. Encouraged by the ease of their victories, the Kabila forces continued their offensive against the **Mobutu** government and took the entire country by May 1997. *See also* Banyamulenge.

NOVEMBER 24, 1965. The day the military took power in Congo/Zaire in a bloodless **coup d'etat** and asked then-Lt. Col. Joseph-Désiré **Mobutu** to assume presidential powers. The coup ended a fractious multiparty **democracy** and brought to power a man who became one of Africa's longest-governing heads of state. The takeover was decided in the early hours of Wednesday, November 24, during an all-night meeting of the **armed forces** high command which had gathered in **Leopoldville** ostensibly to commemorate Congolese soldiers who had died fighting the **rebellions**. In the face of an upsurge of rebel activity in the east and yet another political standoff between the **president** and **prime minister**, the 14 senior officers who made up the high command were summoned by armed forces chief of staff Mobutu to discuss a military takeover.

The 14 who signed the proclamation of the coup and became known as the Companions of the Revolution were Generals Mobutu and **Bobozo Salelo Ndembo Aduluma**; Colonels Masiala Kinkela Kulu Kangala, **Mulamba Nyuny Wa Kadima**, Nzyoyigbe Yeu Ngoli, Itambo Munkina Wa-Kambala and Bangala Oto Wa Ngama; and Lieutenant Colonels Ingila Grima, Tshatshi Ohano, Moyango Bikoko Ebatamungama, Singa Boyenge Mosambayi, Basuki Belenge, Malila Ma-Kende and Tukuzu Gusu-Wo Angbanduruka. Among other things, their proclamation dismissed President Joseph **Kasavubu** and prime minister-designate Évariste **Kimba** and underscored that the coup was not aimed at creating a military dictatorship.

Under Mobutu, November 24 was declared the **Republic of Zaire**'s National Day and was celebrated with greater pomp than any other day, including **Independence** Day. Because it was the national holiday, it was often the date for the inauguration of important **development projects** such as the **Voix du Zaïre telecommunications** facility in 1976, the **Inga-Shaba power line** in 1983 and the bridge over the **Congo River** at **Matadi** in 1984.

November 24, 1964, was the day that Belgian paratroopers, using US planes, dropped on **Stanleyville** to free 10,000 Congolese and 1,000 foreigners held hostage by secessionist forces during the eastern **rebellion**. The decree that lifted the restriction on **opposition** parties and officially ended the single-party state was signed on November 25, 1990, a pointed deviation given Mobutu's well-known fondness for the 24th.

N'SELE MANIFESTO. The N'Sele Manifesto was issued on May 20, 1967, following a lengthy meeting of the **Binza Group**, the **Corps des Volontaires de la République** and other intellectuals at N'Sele, the model farm 60 km upriver from **Kinshasa** which was to become the headquarters and retreat of the **Mouvement Populaire de la Révolution (MPR)**. The manifesto became the basis for the centralization of power in the person of **Mobutu** and the one-party state. It was aimed at ending the bickering and political infighting that had characterized the post-**independence** era. The N'Sele Manifesto advocated a revolution to chart a new course for the Congo. It called for "positive neutralism" in world affairs and set as national objectives economic independence, stronger **government** authority throughout the territory, actions to increase the nation's prestige abroad, and the promotion of economic and social development for the Congolese people. It set the major themes of what came to be known as **Mobutism**.

N'SINGA UDJUU ONGWAKEBI UNTUBE, JOSEPH (1934 -). A technocrat who during the 1980s was first state commissioner and member of the **Political Bureau** of the **Mouvement Populaire de la Révolution (MPR)**, N'Singa was born on September 29, 1934, at Nsontin in **Bandundu Province**. He studied theology for one year but received a law degree from **Lovanium University** in 1963. A provincial official in the Lac Leopold II administrative district from 1963 until 1966, he was named to the central **government** in 1966 and was justice minister from 1967-68. He subsequently served in ministerial-level positions in the Interior Ministry and the Presidency. He was named first state commissioner on April 22, 1981, left the government on November 5, 1982, and was named to the Political Bureau on January 3, 1983. With the advent of multipartyism, he joined the **opposition** and was named justice minister in the Étienne **Tshisekedi** government of 1992, foreign minister in the Faustin **Birindwa** government of March 1993, and transportation minister in the Léon **Kengo wa Dondo** government of 1994.

NTOMBA. A relatively large subgroup of the **Mongo** ethnic cluster living along the Maringa River between Basankusu and Djolu in northwestern **Congo/Zaire**. Ethnographers have also identified an Ntomba-related group living southeast of **Lake Maï-Ndombe**. Kaplan says the Ntomba differ from most Mongo peoples in **language** and hierarchical system. Their **chiefs** are considered sacred and their territory is divided administratively into provinces.

NYAMWEZI. A group of East African traders from **Tanzania** that entered Congo in the 16th or 17th century and established the

Yeke Kingdom. The kingdom flourished for 30 years before declining into smaller groups which live in **Katanga Province** around **Kolwezi** and Kasanga.

NYANGA. An **ethnic group** living in the **Kivus** which clashed with the **Banyarwanda** during a period of **ethnic cleansing** after local politicians called upon them to exterminate Banyarwanda in an effort to drive them from the region. The Nyanga had settled the region before the arrival of the Banyarwanda. Nevertheless, they felt the immigrants, despite the fact that they had been living in the region for decades, had usurped jobs and land.

NYANGWE. A small trading city, now called Kibombo, on the **Lualaba River** in **Sud-Kivu Province** that was a major base for **Afro-Arab** traders in the 19th century. David **Livingstone**, searching for the headwaters of the Nile, was the first European to reach Nyangwe in 1871. Verney Lovett Cameron reached the town in 1874, two years before Henry Morton **Stanley**, and by measuring the flow of water, deduced that the Lualaba formed part of the headwaters of the **Congo River** and not of the Nile as Livingstone had supposed. Arab influence diminished following the anti-**slavery** campaign by Commander Francis **Dhanis** in the 1890s. The Arab traders were driven away in 1893 and the city taken over by the **colonial** authorities.

NYERERE, JULIUS (1922 -). President of **Tanzania** from its independence in 1963 until his retirement in 1985. Relations between the governments of Congo/Zaire and Tanzania were officially cordial. However, there were frequently tensions during the **Mobutu** years. These were caused in part by suspicions that Tanzania harbored opponents of the Mobutu government in **refugee** camps near their common border, but were also due to personal distrust between Mobutu and Nyerere because of their considerable differences in ideology, methods of government, and personal lifestyles. Upon leaving office in 1985, Nyerere, known as "Mwalimu" or "Teacher," was replaced by Ali Hassan Mwinyi but he still retained considerable influence in the region. He was called upon to help mediate various conflicts, including the turmoil in the **Great Lakes Region** in the mid-1990s and the fighting in **Republic of the Congo** in 1997.

- O -

OFFICE DE GESTION DE LA DETTE PUBLIQUE (OGEDEP) / OFFICE FOR THE MANAGEMENT OF THE PUBLIC DEBT. A **government** agency formed in January 1977 after Zaire fell seriously behind in its foreign **debt** repayments. The agency's purpose was to oversee debt repayments and participate in government negotiations with foreign creditors.

OFFICE DES BIENS MAL-ACQUIS (OBMA) / OFFICE OF ILL-GOTTEN GAINS. An agency established following the takeover by the Laurent **Kabila government** in 1997 and headed by a leader of the **Alliance des Forces Démocratiques pour la Libération du Congo/Zaïre (AFDL)**, Jean-Baptiste Mulemba. Its purpose was to investigate and prosecute corrupt officials from the **Mobutu** era and seek the return of state assets. These included government loans which were never repaid, taxes and duties which were never collected, funds transferred to private accounts, and state property which had disappeared. More than 30 former officials and businessmen were arrested on **corruption** charges following the Kabila takeover. The first official to be brought to trial was the former head of the bankrupt national airline, **Air Zaïre**, beginning in December 1997.

OFFICE DES MINES D'OR DE KILO-MOTO (OKIMO) / KILO-MOTO GOLD MINES BOARD. Known more commonly as "Kilo-Moto," OKIMO was the major **gold mining** company in Congo/Zaire, employing 5,900 people, of which less than 10 were expatriate. State-owned since **Zairianization** in 1973, the company was located in **Haut-Zaïre Region** (later renamed **Orientale Province**), where it worked both subterranean and alluvial deposits with an estimated 100 tons of reserves in an 83,000-square-km concession around Bunia and Isiro. An additional mine, called Adidi, began operating in 1973 at Mongbwalu. A Brazilian company reportedly discovered sizable deposits in the area in 1986 and was awarded a contract in 1988 to rehabilitate some of the mines. However, the economic problems of the early 1990s caused production to fall to negligible levels by the mid-1990s. Artisanal mining continued in the area and often surpassed total official production. However, most gold produced in this manner was smuggled to East African nations in exchange for hard **currency** or consumable goods. After the **Alliance des Forces Démocratiques pour la Libération du Congo/Zaïre (AFDL)** took control of the region in late 1996, it negotiated contracts with several foreign companies to revitalize production.

OFFICE DES ROUTES / HIGHWAY BOARD. A **government** agency established in 1972 to build and maintain Zaire's **roads**. The Office des Routes began a three-year program in 1985 to rehabilitate existing roads, in particular the highway linking **Kinshasa** and **Matadi**, and to construct new roads, including a new highway from **Kisangani** to **Bukavu**. By the 1990s, the lack of funding had severely crippled the organization and lack of maintenance had caused severe deterioration of the country's road system. *See also* Transportation.

OFFICE FOR THE MANAGEMENT OF THE PUBLIC DEBT. *See* OFFICE DE GESTION DE LA DETTE PUBLIQUE (OGEDEP).

OFFICE NATIONAL DE CAFÉ (ONC) / ZAIRIAN COFFEE BOARD. The **government**'s national **coffee** marketing board, the ONC exported 104,000 tons of coffee in 1992, up from 74,000 tons in 1980, making it the country's largest exporter of agricultural products. **Exports** declined in subsequent years, but a rise in the price of coffee increased revenues to $400 million in 1994. Of 11 state marketing boards created between 1971 and 1974, the ONC was the only one still operating effectively in the 1990s.

OFFICE NATIONAL DE PÊCHE (ONP) / NATIONAL FISHERIES BOARD. The **government** agency that promoted **fishing** in the country and, in some cases, marketed the products of state and privately owned fisheries and fish-processing plants.

OFFICE NATIONAL DES TRANSPORTS (ONATRA) / NATIONAL TRANSPORT BOARD. The state-owned company that dominated **river** transport in Congo/Zaire, ONATRA during the **colonial era** was known as the Office d'Exploitation des

Transports Coloniaux. It was created in 1935 as a **government**-sponsored agency to operate river and sea**port** facilities and to control all water transport in the colony except that of the upper **Congo River** and **Lake Tanganyika**. It was renamed Office des Transports du Congo (OTRACO) at **independence** and became the Office National des Transports du Zaïre (ONATRA) upon its **nationalization** in the early 1970s. ONATRA also operated passenger service along the Congo, **Kasai** and **Ubangi Rivers**. At its peak in 1972, ONATRA operated 700 barges, 100 tugboats and 40 other vessels on Zaire's principal waterways. ONATRA's monopoly of river **transportation** was abolished by government decree in 1977. In the 1980s, economic recession and a shortage of **foreign exchange** and operating capital caused problems, but for a time the company kept most of its fleet in operation despite shipping delays and pilferage of valuable cargo. By the mid-1990s, however, aging equipment and a lack of funds had virtually halted river transport by ONATRA. An audit ordered by the Léon **Kengo wa Dondo** government in February 1995 discovered that large stipends were being paid to directors while worker salaries were as much as six months in arrears and there were insufficient funds to purchase fuel. Charges were brought against several directors. Plans were formulated in early 1996 to revitalize the company through partial **privatization**.

OFFICE NATIONAL DU SUCRE (ONS) / NATIONAL SUGAR BOARD. A **government** agency established by decree on January 1, 1974, as part of **Zairianization**. It grouped all **sugar** refineries and most of the large cane **plantations** in the country. The ONS was disbanded on May 8, 1978, and a sugar development board called **Projets Sucriers au Zaïre (PSZ)** was established. The agency recovered its original name after the fall of **Mobutu** in 1997.

OFFICE NATIONAL POUR LE DÉVELOPPEMENT DE L'ÉLEVAGE (ONDE) / NATIONAL LIVESTOCK DEVELOPMENT BOARD. A **government** agency that took over ownership and operation of many large ranches following **Zairianization** in 1973. Under **Retrocession**, some of the ranches were returned to their former owners. Others were entrusted to private operators while the government retained ownership. *See also* Livestock.

OFFICE OF ILL-GOTTEN GAINS. *See* OFFICE DES BIENS MAL-ACQUIS (OBMA).

OFFICE ZAÏROIS DE RADIO ET DE TÉLÉVISION (OZRT) / ZAIRIAN RADIO AND TELEVISION AGENCY. The **government**'s national broadcasting agency located in the Department of Information and Press. The agency operated the **Voix du Zaïre radio** and television complex in **Kinshasa** and eight regional radio stations. Following the takeover by the Laurent **Kabila** government, the agency was renamed **Radio-Télévision Nationale Congolaise (RTNC)** and the Voix du Zaïre became the **Voix du Peuple**. *See also* News Media; Telecommunications.

OIL. *See* PALM OIL; PETROLEUM.

ONDEKANE, JEAN-PIERRE (1962 -). A career military officer, born January 1, 1962, in **Mbandaka** and raised in **Shaba Region**, who rose through the ranks of the **Mobutu army** to become commander of government troops in **Lubumbashi**. However, he joined the **Alliance des Forces Démocratiques pour la Libération du Congo/Zaïre (AFDL)**, when they took Lubumbashi in 1997. He was made commander of AFDL forces in **Goma**. In August 1998, he joined the **rebellion** of the **Rassemblement Congolais pour la Démocratie (RCD)** and was named commander of the RCD's military forces.

OPÉRATION DRAGON ROUGE. Code name for the joint Belgian-United States parachute drop on **Stanleyville** on November 24, 1964, to rescue expatriate hostages held in the eastern **rebellion**.

OPPOSITION. Opposition **political parties** proliferated during the first five years of Congo's **independence**. They were suspended along with all political activity, however, following the **coup d'etat** that brought **Mobutu** to power in 1965. They were outlawed in 1970 by the decree making the **Mouvement Populaire de la Révolution (MPR)** the sole legal party. According to the 1974 **constitution**, attempting to form a second party was considered treason. As a result, during the 1970s and 1980s most opposition to the **government** was based abroad.

In 1980, however, the **Group of Thirteen Parliamentarians** issued an open letter to Mobutu calling for multiparty democracy. Some of these, including Étienne **Tshisekedi** and Joseph **Ngalula**, in 1982 founded a second party, the **Union pour la Démocratie et le Progrès Social (UDPS)**. They were tried in 1983 and sentenced to prison terms ranging from 15 years to life. They were later pardoned but spent most of the 1980s in various forms of detention.

With Mobutu's announcement of the **democratic transition** on **April 24, 1990**, opposition parties once again began to flourish. More than 200 had formed by mid-1991, many of them grouped in the **Sacred Union** alliance. Their number had surpassed 400 by the mid-1990s. During the 1990s, most opposition leaders displayed a degree of opportunism that earned them the disdain of many citizens. Except for a few, they took turns in and out of power and they engaged in exercises of in-fighting and shifts of alliance that stalled governance and diverted public attention from the country's growing crises.

When the **Alliance des Forces Démocratiques pour la Libération du Congo/Zaïre (AFDL)** took power in May 1997, it banned activity by all parties, saying that whether in power or not they were part of the rotten system established by Mobutu. Some parties, most notably the hardline wing of the UDPS and the **Parti Lumumbiste Unifié (PALU)** led by Antoine **Gizenga**, continued to publicly oppose the government. Their meetings were dispersed by **security** forces and a number of their leaders were detained on various occasions. Tshisekedi was detained briefly in 1997 and again in February 1998. Upon his second arrest, he was sent into internal exile in his home village.

Dissatisfaction with the AFDL led **Banyamulenge** who had helped overthrow Mobutu to launch a **rebellion** from eastern Congo on August 2, 1998. They reached the outskirts of **Kinshasa** in September but were driven back. *See also* Dissidents.

ORBITAL TRANSPORT UND RAKETEN GESELLSCHAFT (OTRAG). A West German company which signed a contract with the Zairian **government** on March 26, 1976, reportedly for $50 million, giving the company virtually complete control over

150,000 square km of a remote northeastern corner of **Shaba Region.** The avowed purpose of the lease was to allow the company to develop and test commercial rockets. However, the secrecy that surrounded the project raised suspicions in the international community and the **news media.** In addition, some of Zaire's neighbors, in particular **Tanzania,** expressed strong disapproval of such a project near their borders. The contract was canceled in 1979.

ORDRE NATIONAL DU LÉOPARD / NATIONAL ORDER OF THE LEOPARD. The major national order of merit, with varying degrees of elevation, established by **Mobutu** in the late 1960s to honor esteemed national and foreign leaders. The order is named for the national animal of Congo/Zaire, which is highly respected in traditional society for its speed and hunting prowess.

ORGANISATION COMMUNE AFRICAINE ET MALGÂCHE (OCAM) / AFRO-MALGASY COMMON ORGANIZATION. One of the first Pan-African organizations created as African nations attained **independence** in the early 1960s to press for economic integration and development on the continent. With the development of regionally oriented economic organizations, however, OCAM gradually declined in membership and influence. Zaire, a founding member, withdrew in 1972. The organization was dissolved in 1984.

ORGANIZATION OF AFRICAN UNITY (OAU). The Pan-African organization founded in 1963 in Addis Ababa, Ethiopia, to unite Africa in its struggle to end colonialism and racial discrimination. As the **colonial era** waned, other struggles gained prominence, including the promotion of economic development and regional integration, the peaceful settlement of African disputes, and the elaboration of joint African positions on international issues. Zaire remained for the most part a member of the "moderate" camp of the OAU. It supported **independence** movements and the struggle against apartheid in **South Africa,** but opposed membership for the Soviet-backed **Movimento Popular de Libertação de Angola (MPLA)** after it came to power in **Angola,** and "suspended" its participation in the OAU in 1984 when the (Western) Saharan Republic was admitted over the protests of

Morocco, Zaire's long-time ally. Zaire hosted the OAU summit of 1967 that elected **Mobutu** chairman for the 1967-68 term. For the event a multimillion-dollar "OAU Village" was constructed in **Kinshasa**, which later was used as an exclusive resort for prestigious gatherings such as the France-African summit of October 1982. The OAU leadership made modest attempts to help mediate disputes such as the violence in **Rwanda** and eastern Zaire in the mid-1990s and the fighting in **Republic of the Congo** in 1997, but it was stymied by provisions in the OAU Charter that prohibited it from interfering in the "internal affairs" of member nations.

ORIENTALE PROVINCE. **Congo/Zaire**'s northeastern **province**, at 503,232 square km the country's largest, and with an estimated **population** of 6.3 million in 1995 (4,524,467 in 1982), its most populous. Orientale is rich in **timber, rubber, coffee, fish, gold**, iron ore and hydroelectric and agricultural potential. There is some cattle and goat herding. However, the **province** is remote and many areas are inaccessible if they are not located near one of several navigable **river** networks. The **road** network is poorly maintained and supplies, particularly fuel and spare parts, are often difficult to obtain. As a result, **industry** has been stagnant, except for areas bordering East Africa, which is the province's historical trading partner.

Some parts of the province lie in the Sudanese savanna and the **Great Rift Valley** highlands, but most of the territory lies in the **Congo River Basin**, where the **forests** tend to isolate communities and make them self-reliant and independent from the central **government**. The region was the scene of three **rebellions** between 1961 and 1967 and sporadic antigovernment activity by armed guerrillas in the 1990s. It was renamed **Haut-Zaïre** in 1971.

The area was economically depressed by **Uganda**'s civil war from the 1970s until the late 1980s and by the civil war in **Rwanda** from 1990 until 1994. After the fall of **Mobutu** in 1997, following a seven-month offensive which began in the east and brought the government of Laurent **Kabila** to power, the original name was restored. The Kabila government pledged to rebuild roads and infrastructure in the region and formed joint ventures with a number of private companies to revive **mining** and **agriculture**.

"OWLS, THE." *See* "HIBOUX, LES."

- P -

PALM OIL. At **independence**, Congo/Zaire was Africa's second largest exporter of palm oil, after Nigeria. It produced 245,000 tons in 1959, of which 75 percent was exported, accounting for 12 percent of total **export** revenues. However, by 1980, production had fallen to 168,000 tons, according to **World Bank** figures, of which 10,000 tons were exported, accounting for less than 2 percent of total export revenues. By 1990, production had risen to 180,000 tons, of which little was exported through official channels, although some reportedly was **smuggled** to neighboring countries for **foreign exchange**. Production was 184,000 tons in 1993.

PALU. The site of the first Belgian settlement on **Lake Tanganyika**, established in May 1883. It was used primarily as a base to drive the **Afro-Arab** traders from the territory, to establish Belgian sovereignty over the eastern Congo, and to explore the **mineral** riches of **Katanga**.

PAN-AFRICAN CONFERENCE. Officially called the All African People's Conference, the meeting came to be more commonly known as the Pan-African Conference because of the concept of Pan-Africanism which it helped to launch. The conference was held in December 1958 in Accra, the capital of newly independent Ghana. Patrice **Lumumba**, Joseph **Ngalula** and Gaston **Diomi** attended. Joseph **Kasavubu** was prevented from going by the colonial authorities. There they came into contact with the **nationalist** ideas of such leaders as Kwame **Nkrumah** of Ghana, Gamal Abdel Nasser of **Egypt** and Ahmed Sekou Toure of Guinea. They also became aware of growing demands for independence by Africans in the French colonies, of Charles **de Gaulle**'s offer of autonomy to France's African colonies, and of the relative isolation of the Belgian colonies.

The Congolese representatives, particularly Lumumba, returned home fired by the passion for **independence**. He first called for independence during a speech at a rally on December 28, 1958. A pro-independence rally on **January 4, 1959**, was disrupted by the colonial authorities who prevented Kasavubu from speaking. It sparked two weeks of rioting that led within a year to the decision by the Belgian government to grant independence to the **Belgian Congo**.

PARIS CLUB. The name given the group of government creditors that since 1962 has met regularly to discuss the external **debt** of developing nations. The club works in conjunction with the **International Monetary Fund (IMF)** and the **London Club** of private creditors to reschedule the foreign debts of financially strapped governments. Zaire's debt to Paris Club members rose steadily during the 1970s and, by 1980, had reached $2.3 billion, or nearly one-half of its total foreign debt. By 1993, the debt to Paris Club creditors had risen to $5.7 billion, according to the **World Bank**, while external debt had reached $11.2 billion. Although some governments wrote off portions of Zaire's debt, it continued to rise because of the government's failure to make payments on principal or interest. When Laurent **Kabila** assumed power after the departure of **Mobutu** in May 1997, he launched talks aimed at renegotiating the debt on more favorable terms.

PARLEMENT DE LA TRANSITION (PT). *See* HAUT CONSEIL DE LA RÉPUBLIQUE / PARLEMENT DE LA TRANSITION (HCR/PT) / HIGH COUNCIL OF THE REPUBLIC / PARLIAMENT OF THE TRANSITION.

PARLIAMENT. Since **independence**, the **government** of **Congo/Zaire** has included a parliament, although it has been called by different names and its power has varied considerably. Under the **Loi Fondamentale** (Fundamental Law), which acted as a **constitution** from 1960 until 1965, the parliament consisted of two chambers: a chamber of deputies and a senate. The **prime minister** was head of government and answered to parliament, but he could also be dismissed by the **president**, who was head of state. The system was aimed at providing checks and balances to power in the government, but it caused a number of political stalemates. The first, in 1960, led **Mobutu** to suspend parliament and appoint a **College of Commissioners** to govern for six months. The last, in 1964, was cited as a major reason for the **coup d'etat** that brought Mobutu to power for 32 years.

Under **Mobutism**, the two chambers of parliament were combined into one and renamed the National Assembly. With the decree of the single-party system in 1970, the assembly's power and influence began to wane. It was formally subordinated to the **Mouvement Populaire de la Révolution (MPR)** party and its name was changed to **Legislative Council**, when the party-state was established in 1972.

In 1992, the **Conférence Nationale Souveraine (CNS)**, controlled at the time by anti-Mobutu groups, drafted a new **constitution** and established the **Haut Conseil de la République (HCR)**, which was to act as a transitional parliament until national **elections** could be held. Mobutu countered, however, by convening the Legislative Council, which had been moribund since the beginning of the **democratic transition** in 1990. He directed it to draft an alternate constitution and oversee the transition. The country lived with two rival parliaments until in 1993, when they were merged into the **Haut Conseil de la République / Parlement de la Transition (HCR/PT)**. The stalemate between pro-Mobutu and **opposition** forces continued until the offensive by the **Alliance des Forces Démocratiques pour la Libération du Congo/Zaïre (AFDL)** drove Mobutu into exile in 1997.

The Laurent **Kabila** government, which was installed after the fall of Mobutu, pledged to draft a new constitution and hold elections by 1999 for a national parliament and local assemblies. *See also* Legislative System.

PARLIAMENTARIANS, GROUP OF. *See* GROUP OF THIRTEEN PARLIAMENTARIANS.

PARTI DE LIBÉRATION CONGOLAISE (PLC) / PARTY OF CONGOLESE LIBERATION. A group formed in 1984 that staged attacks in northeastern Zaire from bases in the **Ruwenzori Mountains** in a no-man's land between the Zairian and **Ugandan** borders. It registered as a **political party** after the end of single-party rule in 1990.

PARTI DÉMOCRATE ET SOCIAL CHRÉTIEN (PDSC) / DEMOCRATIC AND SOCIAL CHRISTIAN PARTY. One of the first **opposition** parties to be launched following **Mobutu**'s speech of **April 24, 1990**, announcing the end of single-party rule. The PDSC was founded by Joseph **Ileo**, a veteran politician who was one of the first to publicly speak out for political freedoms for Congolese in 1956. He was **prime minister** of the provisional **government** formed after Mobutu "neutralized" government in 1960, and during the single-party era he was a member of the **Political Bureau** and **Central Committee** of the **Mouvement Populaire de la Révolution (MPR)**. The PDSC adopted a social-democratic platform with an emphasis on morality and Christian values, which its leaders felt had eroded during the era of secular single-party rule. The PDSC sought to extend its support beyond any single region or **ethnic group** and succeeded in attracting prominent politicians from many parts of Zaire. It was one of the three major parties that formed the **Sacred Union** opposition alliance in mid-1990. Although more moderate than the **Union pour la Démocratie et le Progrès Social (UDPS)**, it allied with it in the early 1990s to oppose the governments of Jean **Nguza Karl-I-Bond**, Faustin **Birindwa** and Léon **Kengo wa Dondo**, which were viewed as puppets manipulated by Mobutu. Upon Ileo's death in September 1994, André **Boboliko** assumed the presidency of the PDSC and was confirmed in the past at the party's national convention in September 1995.

PARTI LUMUMBISTE UNIFIÉ (PALU) / UNIFIED LUMUMBIST PARTY. A union of Lumumbist splinter parties, descended from Patrice **Lumumba**'s **Mouvement National Congolais (MNC)**. PALU was formed by Antoine **Gizenga**, former vice president of the MNC, after his return from exile following the announcement of the **democratic transition** in 1990. In July 1995, a march by PALU supporters to the People's Palace in central **Kinshasa** was attacked by **security** forces. Ten people were killed and Gizenga was subsequently detained for five days.

PARTI RÉVOLUTIONNAIRE DU PEUPLE (PRP) / PEOPLE'S REVOLUTIONARY PARTY. The only known armed resistance to the Zairian **government** based inside the country after the

rebellions of the 1960s were suppressed. The PRP, headed by Laurent **Kabila**, emerged from the **Lumumba** wing of the **Mouvement National Congolais (MNC)** and the first **Stanleyville secession** of the early 1960s. After Kabila broke away from the MNC in 1964, he formed the PRP, which established guerrilla bases in the remote **forests** of **Sud-Kivu** west of the **Mitumba Mountain** range. In 1975, PRP guerrillas kidnapped four foreign **students** from a **Tanzanian** wildlife refuge. They were later released. A reporter for *New African* magazine visited the area and wrote in 1982 that the guerrillas had established a rudimentary social and economic infrastructure and provided indoctrination along communist/socialist lines to people living in the areas under their control.

In November 1984, PRP guerrillas briefly occupied the **port** town of **Moba** in northern **Shaba Region**, calling for Zairians to rise up and overthrow the **Mobutu** government. The Zairian army retook Moba two days later. Official casualty figures were never released but were estimated at between 10 and 50 dead. The government accused Zairian exiles living in neighboring Tanzania and **Burundi** of responsibility. The PRP denied the charge, saying it was based entirely within Zaire. The guerrillas staged a second attack on Moba in June 1985 as Zaire was celebrating the 25th anniversary of its **independence**. The second attack, however, was quickly repelled.

The PRP resurfaced in October 1996 as one of four members of the **Alliance des Forces Démocratiques pour la Libération du Congo/Zaïre (AFDL),** headed by Kabila. The alliance launched an offensive aimed at overthrowing the Mobutu government and establishing **democracy** in the country. Bolstered by disciplined troops from **Uganda**, **Rwanda**, Burundi and **Angola**, it met little resistance as it took over the country and on May 17, 1997, arrived in **Kinshasa**, one day after Mobutu fled into exile. Kabila was sworn in as **president** on May 29.

The PRP's ideological roots were **socialist** and **nationalist** and Kabila made a point in January 1998 to deliver a major speech to mark the anniversary of Lumumba's death. The PRP also advocated the establishment of a new form of government to replace the **corruption** which it felt had become entrenched during the Mobutu era. Nevertheless, it espoused pragmatic policies, negotiated numerous contracts with private foreign companies to revitalize important sectors of the **economy**, and pledged to hold national **elections** in 1999.

PARTI SOCIALISTE AFRICAIN (PSA) / AFRICAN SOCIALIST PARTY. A party founded by Jibi Ngoyi and registered in 1990.

PARTI SOLIDAIRE AFRICAIN (PSA) / AFRICAN SOLIDARITY PARTY. A left-leaning party founded by Antoine **Gizenga** and Cléophas **Kamitatu** in the late 1950s which sent delegates to the **Round Table Conference** in 1960. At **independence**, the PSA joined with Patrice **Lumumba**'s **Mouvement National Congolais (MNC)** to form the first Congolese **government** and received three portfolios, including that of vice prime minister. Its ministers were dismissed with Lumumba on September 5, 1960. They left **Leopoldville** to form a rival government in **Stanleyville** following the **United Nations** recognition of the Joseph **Kasavubu** government and the assassination of Lumumba. The PSA was included in the reconciliation government of Cyrille **Adoula**, with first Gizenga then Kamitatu holding the most senior portfolio. It was ousted when the Moïse **Tshombe** government was elected, and many PSA leaders went into exile. Gizenga later resurfaced in Stanleyville to form the **Forces Démocratiques pour la Libération du Congo (FODELICO)** and lead the second eastern **rebellion**. Pierre **Mulele**, a former secretary-general of the PSA, left for military training in the People's Republic of **China**. He went to the **People's Republic of the Congo** where he joined the Brazzaville-based Conseil de Libération du Congo and launched the **Kwilu** rebellion, which carried out a series of terrorist attacks in Leopoldville. The PSA was banned along with all political parties following the **Mobutu coup d'etat**. Mulele was executed for treason in 1968 after accepting an offer of amnesty and returning to Kinshasa. Gizenga returned from exile after the political liberalization in 1990 and formed the **Parti Lumumbiste Unifié (PALU)**. Kamitatu joined the **Parti Démocrate et Social Chrétien (PDSC)**.

PARTY OF CONGOLESE LIBERATION. *See* PARTI DE LIBÉRATION CONGOLAISE (PLC).

PATERNALISM. The term often used to characterize **Belgium**'s policy toward its African colonies and in particular the **Belgian Congo**. According to the concept, Africans were considered to be like children, well-intentioned but prone to excesses and not to be entrusted with too much responsibility or authority. They were to be "civilized" and given basic **literacy** and **health care**. They were to be taught moral and **Christian** values and gradually would be granted increasing responsibilities. According to the policy, brighter Congolese could aspire to positions such as office clerk, teaching assistant or assistant nurse. In 1959, colonial authorities felt political **independence** and the assumption of senior leadership positions by Congolese were at least one generation away. As a result, with the advent of independence, few Belgians believed the Congolese would be able to govern their country and predicted chaos. Their rapid abandonment of the former colony helped fulfill the prediction.

PENAL CODE. Before the **colonial era, customary law** was the basis for punishment for most crimes among the various **ethnic groups** and foreigners did not tamper with it. With the creation of the **Congo Free State**, however, traditional law came under criticism as savage and brutal. As a result, a penal code was adopted in 1888. Based on the Belgian penal code, it remained in force until a new code was enacted in 1940. The code permitted the **death penalty** for premeditated murder and certain crimes against the state. Lengthy prison terms were given to those convicted of serious crimes such as involuntary murder, kidnapping, rape and aggravated assault which caused disability. Theft, arson, fraud and embezzlement also could draw serious prison terms and fines. However, considerable latitude was given to judges to take into account mitigating circumstances, the extent of damages, the age of the offender and the offender's previous record. Historians note that customary law continued to be used in many cases where the crime did not involve a European.

In 1963, certain crimes were established in the area of state **security** and public order. The Code d'Organisation et de Compétence Judicial (Code of Judicial Organization and Competence) enacted on July 10, 1968, called for the unification of the customary and "official" systems and the abolition of the customary courts. The 1974 **constitution** established a national

judicial system that paralleled the administrative structure. An order establishing a system of juvenile courts was issued in 1987. In the 1970s and 1980s, some changes were enacted which reduced penalties for certain offenses and placed more emphasis on rehabilitation. However, penalties were increased for "political crimes." The death penalty was accorded in many cases to those convicted of treason or subversion. Conviction on charges of plotting against the state could draw lengthy prison terms.

The code continues relatively unchanged today. In principle, an accused has the right to defense counsel and a public trial, and an individual arrested is to appear before a magistrate within 48 hours. However, **human rights** organizations charge that these guarantees frequently are not observed. They note that some prisoners languish for months before appearing in court and others are released without trial upon payment of a bribe. The right of appeal is guaranteed in capital cases except those involving state security, **smuggling** and armed robbery. These come before a special Court of State Security which is frequently used to try political **dissidents**. Military courts can try civilian cases during states of emergency and their rulings cannot be appealed. *See also* Penal System.

PENAL SYSTEM. Congo/Zaire at **independence** inherited a harsh penal system from the Belgian colonial authorities. However, conditions became harsher under **Mobutu** and **human rights** organizations repeatedly criticized the country's penal system for being poorly funded, harsh and corrupt. Neglect and maltreatment of prisoners are widespread. Beatings are common, as is death by **disease** and starvation. Some efforts are made to isolate juvenile offenders from adults, but a common practice is to induct young, chronic offenders into the **armed forces**. Most observers say the harshness of the penal system in the case of all but political **dissidents** is due primarily to poor management, **corruption** and a lack of funds. Most inmates, in order to survive for any length of time, depend on their families to provide food, clothing and medicine, which are usually transmitted through prison officials for a fee or a portion of the provisions.

The prison system is administered by the minister of justice and keeper of the seals. Most prisons are located in urban areas and three of the largest are in **Kinshasa**: Makala, Ndolo and

Linguela. Dissidents accuse the **government** of building in remote areas several secret prisons and "reeducation camps" for habitual offenders and political opponents. Some report spending time in a detention center called "Kota-Koli" near Mobutu's home town of **Gbadolite** and a labor camp called Ikafela in the northwestern forest.

PENDE. A cluster of **Bantu**-speaking people living between the **Kwilu** and **Kasai Rivers** south of Gungu in southern portions of **Bandundu** and **Kasai Provinces**. One of four diverse **ethnic groups** living in the area, the Pende joined the **Mbun** and **Njembe** in the 1880s to stop the expansion of the **Chokwe** nation. Closely related to the Mbun, the Pende supported the Pierre **Mulele** rebellion in Kwilu in 1964-65.

PEOPLE'S REPUBLIC OF CHINA. *See* CHINA, PEOPLE'S REPUBLIC OF.

PEOPLE'S REPUBLIC OF THE CONGO. *See* CONGO, PEOPLE'S REPUBLIC OF THE; CONGO, REPUBLIC OF THE (BRAZZAVILLE).

PEOPLE'S REVOLUTIONARY PARTY. *See* PARTI RÉVOLUTIONNAIRE DU PEUPLE (PRP).

"PER DIEM." The monthly stipend paid to delegates of the **National Conference** in 1991-92 which, because of the economic crisis, became a major source of **income** and competition for credentials and an example by critics of excesses on the part of conference organizers.

PETRO-CONGO. The government-owned **petroleum** company (called Petro-Zaïre until 1997) which was formed following the **nationalization** in December 1973 of the five private oil companies operating in Zaire. A settlement was reached in 1978 through which the companies were allowed to operate under a partnership with the state retaining one-half ownership. Petro-Zaïre enjoyed a monopoly on importation and distribution of refined petroleum products until reforms in 1985 removed **price controls** and allowed competition by foreign companies.

PETROLEUM. Congo/Zaire has proven deposits of petroleum reserves estimated at 150 million barrels and unexploited deposits in remote parts of the country that have prompted exploration by international oil companies. To date, all of the country's exploitable petroleum has been located in the central African basin that has also made **Angola**, the **Republic of the Congo** and Gabon major oil producers. Congo/Zaire's coastal and offshore reserves are limited because of its small, 37-km-long coastline. Nevertheless, 70 percent of production in the 1990s was offshore and the remainder near the coast.

Petroleum exploration began in 1956 and commercially exploitable deposits were discovered off the Atlantic coast in 1970 and 1972. Production began offshore in 1975 and onshore in 1979. By the end of 1983, six fields had been discovered, of which four were in production. By 1985, total production had reached 30,000 barrels per day but declined to 25,000 barrels per day by 1995. In the 1980s, positive seismic tests led to exploratory drilling near **Mbandaka** in **Équateur Region**, but no commercially exploitable fields were found and drilling was halted in 1984. Seismic explorations were also undertaken in the **lakes** of the **Great Rift Valley**, leading to the discovery of considerable deposits of natural gas under **Lake Kivu**. However, these have yet to be exploited because of the great depth of the lake and its distance from major markets.

Production was carried out by US, Japanese and Belgian companies in partnership with the Zairian government. At its peak in the mid-1980s, Gulf-Chevron operated 38 wells in Zaire through its subsidiary **Gulf Oil Zaïre**. Sixteen of these were wildcat operations. Production was 18,000 barrels per day in 1994, but the discovery of a new field was expected to raise production by 5,900 barrels per day, leading the company to announce a $500 million exploration program in 1995. Zaïrep, which operates onshore with Belgian participation, announced an $80 million exploration program for 1995.

A refinery, built with Italian participation in 1968 to process imported oil, refines some domestic crude oil. Called the **Société Congo-Italienne de Raffinage (SOCIR)**, the plant has a refining capacity of 17,000 barrels per day. However, because of the high sulfur content of domestic petroleum, very little local crude can be refined by SOCIR. As a result, locally produced crude is exported and lighter crude, primarily from Nigeria, is imported for refining. Two above-ground **pipelines**, the first built in the 1920s and the second completed in the 1950s, carry oil from **Matadi** to **Kinshasa**. A government agency, Petrol-Zaïre, now **Petro-Congo**, distributed refined petroleum products through private dealers until 1985, when it lost its import monopoly. In the early 1990s, **inflation** and a collapsing **currency** caused severe fuel shortages, leading the government of then-Prime Minister Étienne **Tshisekedi** to seize the assets of oil companies. However, they were returned a few months later.

PILLAGES. Literally translated, "lootings," *les pillages* is the name by which Zairians refer to the incidents of looting and violence that occurred in major Zairian cities on several occasions beginning on **September 24-25, 1991**, but especially on January 28, 1993, when 100 people died including the French ambassador. The incidents caused the evacuation of 10,000 expatriates and serious damage to commercial and industrial installations throughout the country. The pillages were a major factor in the 25 percent decline in **gross domestic product** the following two years.

PINZI, ARTHUR. A Congolese politician prominent in the pro-**independence** movement, Pinzi participated in the drafting of the *Conscience Africaine* manifesto in 1956. He helped found the **Mouvement National Congolais (MNC)** in 1958 but split away before independence to form his own party. Elected mayor of Kalamu commune in 1958, Pinzi joined the **Alliance des Bakongo (ABAKO)** and was elected to the **parliament** on its ticket in 1960. He served as finance minister in the Cyrille **Adoula** government from August 2, 1961, to July 10, 1962.

PIPELINES. Two above-ground pipelines carry **petroleum** 350 km from **Matadi** to **Kinshasa** and were built long before petroleum was discovered near the mouth of the **Congo River**. The first, 10 cm (4 in) in diameter, was built in the 1920s. The second, 15 cm (6 in) in diameter, was built in the 1950s. In addition, a 40-cm (16-in) diameter pipeline carries petroleum from an offshore terminal to the coast near Moanda. Slurry pipelines are used in **Katanga Province** to transport unrefined **minerals**.

PLANTATIONS. Large commercial plantations were begun in the 1800s in Congo and were considered to be the primary source of the its wealth after the end of the **slave** trade and before the beginning of the **mining** operations in **Katanga**. During the **colonial era**, hundreds of plantations were established, usually on land grants, for the cultivation of **rubber, timber, sugar** cane, oil **palm, coffee**, tea, and cocoa and for the raising of **livestock**. Following **independence**, many plantations fell into disuse. Others slowly declined because of **transportation** problems, a lack of **government** incentives, and a shortage of **foreign exchange** for inputs. Government statistics indicate more than 1,500 single-crop plantations of 100 to 1,000 hectares were operating in 1970. By 1980, the number of commercial operations had declined by half. However, in 1983, new government policies and a liberalization of domestic prices for **agricultural** products had encouraged a modest upturn, particularly in western Zaire and in **Shaba Region**. The decline of the **mining** sector in the 1990s has added further impetus to the sector, although poor infrastructure continues to hinder growth.

POLICE. During the early **colonial era**, police duties were carried out by the **Force Publique**. Following World War I, a subunit of the Force called the **Troupes en Service Territorial** was formed to police the territory. Following **independence**, the police force of about 3,000 officers largely disintegrated. Nigerian police were brought in to train a new Congolese force, the **Gendarmerie Nationale**, under a **United Nations** program using equipment and funds supplied by the **United States**. In 1966, the **government** enacted a series of laws bringing police operations under the Interior Ministry in a national system called the Police Nationale. This force of 25,000 was charged with **crime** prevention, the apprehension of offenders, the protection of citizens and the maintenance of law and order. It was divided into regional units responsible to the local authorities. Training centers were established with Belgian and US assistance in **Kinshasa** and **Lubumbashi**.

On August 1, 1972, in a move reflecting the growing trend toward centralization of powers, the Police Nationale was dissolved by decree and reabsorbed into the Gendarmerie

Nationale. The move brought policing activities under the defense department and diluted the influence of local authorities over garrisons in the regions. In 1976, the head of the gendarmerie gained the same rank as the chiefs of staff of the army, **navy** and **air force**, and was answerable only to **Mobutu**, who held the defense portfolio and was **armed forces** chief of staff. The gendarmerie began to suffer from a lack of resources following the creation in 1984 of a civilian police force, called the **Civil Guard**, which was trained by **Germany** and **Egypt**.

The Civil Guard was used extensively to repress the **opposition** and after the fall of Mobutu, the Laurent **Kabila** government in June 1997 abolished the Civil Guard and, with **South African** aid, formed a new national police force.

POLITICAL BUREAU. From 1970 until the political reforms of April 1990, the Political Bureau of the **Mouvement Populaire de la Révolution (MPR)** was the most powerful organ of state and ranked immediately below the **president**. Composed of an elite group of veteran political leaders appointed by the president and viewed as close to him, the Political Bureau controlled most of the political process in Zaire. According to the **N'Sele Manifesto**, the Political Bureau "creates policy initiatives which are examined by the Congress of the Party."

During a period of political liberalization in the late 1970s, the composition of the Political Bureau was altered to allow some of its members to be elected by party members. **Mobutu** announced on July 1, 1977, that 12 members would be appointed and 18, two from each region, would be elected. However, the number of appointees was soon increased to 18 with Mobutu, as president of the bureau, holding the tie-breaking vote. By 1980, when the size of the bureau was reduced to 20, the president once again was appointing all its members.

Originally, the Political Bureau chose all candidates for the **Legislative Council**. However, following the liberalization of the 1970s, local party cells were allowed to propose a number of candidates for each given seat in their respective districts. The Political Bureau then "vetted" the candidates. In the legislative elections of 1982, one-half of the candidates proposed by the local cells were approved.

According to the **constitution** of 1974, the Political Bureau could dismiss the president for "deviation from the doctrine" of **Mobutism**, but the "Founder" of the MPR (Mobutu) could not be dismissed. The president had the power to dismiss members of the bureau, but no more than one-third of them during any one term. Under the single-party system, the Political Bureau also controlled the **succession** process. Should the office of the presidency have become vacant, the oldest political commissioner was to assume the office temporarily. The bureau was to schedule an **election** within 30-60 days and nominate the candidate for the presidency. The Political Bureau continued to exist following the transition to multipartyism in 1990, but it was weakened by the departure of many members who left to form their own **political parties** or join the **opposition**. With the appointment of the first government of the **democratic transition**, it ceased to hold any official governing function. *See also* Central Committee.

POLITICAL FORCES OF THE CONCLAVE. *See* CONCLAVE, FORCES POLITIQUES DU.

POLITICAL PARTIES. Political parties proliferated during the first five years of Congolese **independence**, surpassing 100 in number, but were outlawed in 1970 when the **Mouvement Populaire de la Révolution (MPR)** was made the sole legal party. A number of parties continued to oppose the **Mobutu government**, usually from exile. Two parties that remained based in Zaire during the Mobutu years were the **Union pour la Démocratie et le Progrès Social (UDPS)**, which was formed in 1982 by Étienne **Tshisekedi**, and the **Parti Révolutionnaire du Peuple (PRP)**, headed by Laurent **Kabila**, which held a small mountainous area in eastern Congo from the mid-1960s and staged two attacks in **Moba** in 1984 and 1985. After Mobutu announced the **democratic transition** on **April 24, 1990**, the number of political parties grew rapidly and by the mid-1990s had surpassed 400. But the military offensive that sent Mobutu into exile and brought Kabila to power in May 1997 also signaled a potential change in the country's **politics**. Kabila said political parties would be suspended until national **elections**, which he promised to hold in 1999. However, comments by some government members indicated that existing parties were considered part of a corrupt system which was in need major reform. *See also* Alliance des Bakongo (ABAKO); Alliance des Forces Démocratiques pour la Libération du Congo/Zaïre (AFDL); Alliance des Forces Patriotiques (AFP); Association des Baluba du Katanga (BALUBAKAT); Conclave, Forces Politiques du; Confédération des Associations Katangaises (CONAKAT); Confédération Nationale des Associations Congolaises (CONACO); Corps des Activistes pour la Défense de la Révolution (CADR); Dissidents; Fédération Kasaïenne; Front pour la Libération Nationale du Congo (FLNC); Jeunesse du Mouvement Populaire de la Révolution (JMPR); Liboke lya Bangala; Ligue des Jeunes Vigilants (LJV); Mouvement d'Action pour la Résurrection du Congo (MARC); Mouvement National Congolais (MNC); Opposition; Parti de Libération Congolaise (PLC); Parti Démocrate et Social Chrétien (PDSC); Parti Lumumbiste Unifié (PALU); Parti Socialiste Africain (PSA); Parti Solidaire Africain (PSA); Rassemblement des Démocrates Libéraux (RDL); Sacred Union; Union des Démocrates Indépendants (UDI); Union des Fédéralistes et des Républicains Indépendants (UFERI); Union Katangaise; Union Mongo (UNIMO); Union pour la République et la Démocratie (URD).

POLITICS. Political activity was strictly prohibited during the **colonial era**, but following World War II, it began to develop through trade unions, **alumni groups**, **ethnic group** associations and "study" groups. The ban on politics was lifted in preparation for local **elections** in 1959 and **political parties** grew quickly in number, many of them from the ethnic associations. Some attempts were made to form nationally based political parties, but policy disputes and personal rivalries led many to splinter. At **independence**, an estimated 125 parties were in existence. During the legislative elections of 1965, a number of attempts were made to form broad coalitions with names like Rassemblement des Démocrates Congolais (RADECO), Comité Démocratique Africain (CDA), Front Commun National (FCN) and **Confédération Nationale des Associations Congolaises (CONACO)**. CONACO won a majority of the seats in the 1965 elections and succeeded in forming a **government**. However, the apparent trend toward political consolidation was cut short by the

Mobutu coup d'etat of **November 24, 1965**, after which all political activity was banned.

In December 1966, the **Corps des Volontaires de la République (CVR)**, echoing widespread popular dissatisfaction with political partisanship, called for an end to all political parties in order to allow the formation of a single party. The **Mouvement Populaire de la Révolution (MPR)** was formed in 1967 and began to organize while other parties remained banned. The MPR was formally enshrined as the sole legal party in 1970 and its supremacy over the affairs of state and the lives of all Zairians was formalized by the **constitution** of 1974.

In 1977, a degree of liberalization was enacted, permitting multiple candidates within the MPR for legislative seats and the election of some previously appointed members of the Political Bureau. The measures led to the infusion of some new blood into the political hierarchy and the elimination of some of the old guard. By 1980, however, most of the measures had been discarded or circumvented. In 1982, the **Group of Thirteen Parliamentarians** announced the formation of a second political party, an act of treason at that time. They were convicted and sentenced to lengthy prison terms. During the 1980s, they continued to advocate a return to multipartyism, while various other groups opposed the Mobutu government from exile.

On **April 24, 1990**, in the face of rising domestic and international pressure, Mobutu announced the end of the single-party system and declared that three political parties would be allowed. Mobutu said a one-year transition would be observed, to be followed by elections. Observers say the president believed he could continue to control the process and remain in power. However, it quickly became evident he had opened a Pandora's box, as many prominent members of the MPR defected and many exiled **opposition** leaders returned to form their own parties. Everyone except MPR stalwarts began to press for the removal of all restrictions on political activity. Mobutu eventually acquiesced and the restrictions were officially lifted on November 25, 1990. The government sought to control the creation of parties by restricting registration, but that too eventually was abandoned. At the same time, opposition leaders began pressing for a **national conference**, modeled after those being held in a number of West African nations. The purpose was to sweep away laws that concentrated power in the **presidency**, draft a new constitution and organize elections under an independent authority.

The National Conference was convened on August 7, 1991, initially for a period of one month. However, political stalemate and infighting delayed completion of its work until December 1992. Through most of the 1990s, confrontation between pro-Mobutu forces and the opposition stalled the **democratic transition**. On July 30, 1995, it was extended for a third time, until July 9, 1997, by which date elections were to be held. However, the opposition maintained that any elections held within this time frame would be compromised by Zaire's lack of infrastructure and Mobutu's continued control over the state and **security** apparatus. By the mid-1990s, political organizations appeared to have coalesced around three tendencies or alliances: the Forces Politiques du **Conclave (FPC)**, which grouped pro-Mobutu parties; the **Sacred Union**, which grouped the hardline opposition; and the **Union pour la République et la Démocratie (URD)**, which aspired to represent centrist parties.

Mobutu's mandate was due to expire in December 1991 but was extended until the end of the transition. He appeared content to continue as head of state and to preside over the fractious process, but his health deteriorated and he underwent prostate surgery in **Switzerland** in August 1996. A group of small opposition parties in October announced the formation of the **Alliance des Forces Démocratiques pour la Libération du Congo/Zaïre (AFDL)** and launched an offensive to overthrow Mobutu and change the system. The AFDL forces advanced rapidly from the eastern border area and entered **Kinshasa** on May 17, 1997, one day after Mobutu fled into exile. They announced they were suspending political parties that had not participated in their movement, leading to anger by opposition groups over the lack of appreciation for their struggle against Mobutu. The new leaders said they wanted to reform the entire system, which they said had been corrupted by decades of authoritarian rule. The new government promised it would hold elections in 1999 but said meetings and demonstrations by political parties would be banned until then.

POLITIQUE DES GRANDS TRAVAUX / GREAT WORKS POLICY. A program launched by the Zairian government in the early 1970s when, buoyed by high **mineral** prices and encouraged by international lending institutions, **Mobutu** sought to institute the equivalent of an industrial revolution in his country. A number of grandiose projects were initiated, including the **Inga hydroelectric complex**, the **Inga-Shaba power line**, the **Voix du Zaïre** radio/television complex and the **Maluku steel mill**, among others. When completed, these projects struggled to maintain solvency because of high costs for maintenance and raw materials and they severely increased the **government**'s foreign **debt** burden.

POPE JOHN PAUL II. *See* JOHN PAUL II (POPE).

POPULAR LIBERATION ARMY. *See* ARMÉE POPULAIRE DE LIBÉRATION.

POPULAR MOVEMENT FOR THE LIBERATION OF ANGOLA. *See* MOVIMENTO POPULAR DE LIBERTAÇÃO DE ANGOLA (MPLA).

POPULAR REVOLUTIONARY MOVEMENT. *See* MOUVEMENT POPULAIRE DE LA RÉVOLUTION.

POPULATION. The population of **Congo/Zaire** was estimated at 42 million in 1995, although an official count has not been carried out since 1982. The last nationwide census, for the 1982 **elections**, estimated a total population of 29,198,334. The population growth rate from 1980-93 was estimated by **United Nations** agencies to be 3.2 percent per year. The overall percentage of females was 50.5, but in urban areas males outnumbered females. In 1993, an estimated 46.7 percent of the population was under 15 years, while 1.5 percent was above 65 years. Life expectancy at birth was 52 years, up from 49 years in 1982 and 42 years in 1960.

In the 1990s, an estimated 28 percent of the population lived in **urban** areas. **Kinshasa**, with an estimated population of five million, is the largest city. The fastest-growing cities since **independence** have been Kinshasa, **Mbuji-Mayi**, **Bandundu** and **Kikwit**. Average population density in 1990 was 17 persons per square km, up from 9.2 in 1970. Population density is considered low by global standards, but high in comparison to most central and southern African nations.

Rural population density varies considerably, from 1-2 persons per square km in the **Congo River Basin** to more than 30 in parts of the **eastern highlands** and western **Bas-Congo Province**. The higher population densities tend to be located in areas where soil fertility, **rainfall** and **climate** are conducive to farming. The less-populated areas tend to be in the low wetlands where the soils are unable to support intensive farming. Eighty percent of the Zairian population belongs to the **Bantu** family of **ethnic groups**. The remainder is divided between peoples of Sudanese, Nilotic and European origins. More than 250 **languages** and 400 dialects have been identified among the population living in the national territory.

PORTS. Congo/Zaire has three **ports** for ocean going vessels, **Matadi**, **Boma** and **Banana**, all lying on the lower part of the **Congo River**. Banana, nearest the Atlantic Ocean, is linked to Boma and Matadi by **road**. Matadi is linked to the rest of the country primarily by **rail** and **river transportation** networks.

The major river ports on the Congo River are **Kinshasa**, **Mbandaka**, **Bumba**, **Kisangani**, Ubundu and **Kindu**. **Bandundu** and **Ilebo** lie on the **Kasai River**. Zongo is on the **Ubangi River**. And Kongolo and Bukama lie on the **Lualaba** (Upper Congo) **River**. The major lake ports are **Kalemie** on **Lake Tanganyika** and **Goma** on **Lake Kivu**.

PORTUGAL, RELATIONS WITH. Relations between **Congo/Zaire** and Portugal are 500 years old, dating to the 1480s when **Diogo Cão** and other Portuguese **explorers** sailed up the mouth of the **Congo River** and encountered the people of the **Kongo Kingdom**. Initially, relations were close. The Kongo **kings** asked for **missionaries**, technical advisors and, occasionally, military assistance. In exchange they offered **trade** concessions, **ivory** and **slaves**. Subjects of the kingdom went to Portugal to study and represent the kingdom at the Portuguese royal court.

The relationship became primarily a commercial one in the early 1600s, as the Kongo Kingdom began to decay and other European maritime powers began to compete for the region's resources. The arrival of the Belgians following the **Berlin**

Conference of 1885 completed the displacement of the Portuguese as the primary European power in the Congo. However, relations continued to be close because of the proximity of the Portuguese colonies of **Angola** and **Cabinda** and the large number of Portuguese traders and merchants who had established themselves in the territory.

Following **independence**, the Congolese **government** began to support openly the Angolan struggle for independence and the population of Angolan **refugees** in the country grew steadily. These factors strained relations with Portugal. In a speech before the **United Nations** in 1973, **Mobutu** condemned Portugal for blocking independence in Angola and its other African colonies. Later that year, the Portuguese embassy in **Kinshasa** was besieged by an angry mob. The embassy was closed and the Portuguese diplomats went home. The **Zairianization** policies that began that year also dispossessed many Portuguese traders, farmers and businessmen, further straining relations.

Following Angola's independence, relations began to improve and the return of properties nationalized under Zairianization brought some Portuguese back. In the mid-1980s, relations were considered excellent. Mobutu paid a visit to Portugal in 1984 and President Ramalho Eanes reciprocated the same year. During the **pillages** of 1991-92, some Portuguese merchants sustained heavy losses. A significant number left, but many others rebuilt and continued the centuries-old relationship.

POVERTY. Although Congo/Zaire is considered one of the wealthiest nations in sub-Saharan Africa in terms of **mineral** and human resources, poverty is widespread in the country and affects all but a small elite. According to UN figures, one-half the **population** lives below the poverty level, although that figure is believed to have reached as high as 80 percent during the economic crisis of the 1990s. Per-capita **income**, which rose to $200 per year in the early 1970s, fell to $130 by the mid-1990s. These figures place the country among the most impoverished nations in the world. Subsistence **agriculture** is a way of life for most rural dwellers, who constitute 60 percent of the population, but urban dwellers often maintain gardens to supplement their incomes. During the early 1990s, **inflation** and recession reduced **wages** among public sector workers to $5-25 per month. The economic hardships of most citizens contrasted sharply with the conspicuous consumption of the political **élites** who, although they represented less than one percent of the population, controlled most of the wealth in the country.

PRESIDENT. The presidency, as envisioned at **independence** by the **Loi Fondamentale** (Fundamental Law), was meant to be a largely ceremonial office. The power of **government** was to rest largely with the **prime minister** and **parliament**. However, Congo's first president, Joseph **Kasavubu**, repeatedly used his powers to sack his prime ministers and on several occasions caused a constitutional crisis when parliament refused to accept the dismissals.

Following the **coup d'etat** of 1965, **Mobutu** became president with the authority to issue decrees and ordinances with the power of law. With the **constitution** of 1967, and especially that of 1974, power increasingly became concentrated in the presidency until it became the predominant force in **politics** and government. During the 1970s and 1980s, the Bureau du Président (Bureau of the President) was a branch of government that had virtually no budget limitations and was staffed with the best and brightest administrators and *cadres*. The president of Zaire was the president of the **Mouvement Populaire de la Révolution (MPR)** party, which was the supreme institution of state, as well as head of the **armed forces** and six organs of government. Under the 1974 constitution, the president was elected by direct vote and could serve an unlimited number of seven-year terms. Mobutu ran unopposed in 1970, 1977 and 1984 and was elected each time by more than 99 percent of the vote.

With the advent of multipartyism in 1990, the presidency lost some of its influence. **Opposition** parties proliferated and the **National Conference** sought to decentralize political and administrative power and create a **federalist**, parliamentary system. Mobutu initially sought to place himself above politics and even resigned as head of the MPR for a year. However, he returned to marshal his supporters against the opposition. During the **democratic transition**, Mobutu remained the dominant political force in the country and repeatedly blocked the opposition through political patronage, parliamentary maneuvers and, when these failed, the use of force by **security** elements which he ensured remained loyal to him alone.

When the **Alliance des Forces Démocratiques pour la Libération du Congo/Zaïre (AFDL)** took power in May 1997, AFDL leader and the country's new president, Laurent **Kabila**, promised to draft a new constitution and hold **elections** by 1999. The AFDL indicated it favored a system similar to that established by the constitution of 1964, in which parliament played a major role in government. However, with the constitution under revision and political demonstrations banned, it appeared that, initially at least, the presidency would continue to form the backbone of government. *See also* Legislative System.

PRESS. *See* NEWS MEDIA.

PRESSES UNIVERSITAIRES DU ZAÏRE (PUZ). The official printing and publishing house of the **Université Nationale du Zaïre (UNAZA)**, PUZ was established in October 1972 to disseminate monographs, textbooks and studies of the country by Zairian authors and researchers. During its early years, PUZ published hundreds of titles a year. In subsequent years, the number of titles was reduced considerably because of budget constraints. As a result, many academics published their own works or sought publishers outside the country.

PRICE CONTROLS. At various times and to varying degrees the **government** has used price controls in an attempt to control the **economy** and meet popular concerns over **inflation**. However, the controls were dictated more by political concerns than market forces. Prices paid for **agricultural** products traditionally were set low to favor the urban populations and maintain political stability. Prices paid by government marketing boards to miners for **gold**, **diamonds** and other **minerals** also tended to be low, while **petroleum** prices at the pump were usually subsidized. In addition, prices paid to producers of agricultural **exports** were kept low in order to maintain an overvalued **currency** to allow **imports**. These policies tended to encourage the consumption of imported products and discourage farming and the legal marketing of minerals and agricultural produce. They also encouraged

smuggling and undermined official exports and the government tax base.

In mid-1983, the government liberalized many of these policies. Agricultural and mineral prices were still set, but at levels which removed overall subsidies. In the case of fuel, for example, high octane gasoline, used primarily for personal cars, was set high enough to subsidize diesel fuel, which was used primarily for commercial **transportation**. A similar pattern was adopted for agricultural products. In addition, restrictions were lifted on farming and the marketing of minerals by private individuals, leading to significant increases in productivity in these sectors. Controls were furthered loosened in 1987. However, any control over prices disappeared when inflation accelerated to triple-digit levels in the late 1980s and prices began to rise on a daily basis.

PRIME MINISTER. The office of prime minister historically has been the second most powerful political post in the nation, although at **independence** it was meant to be the most powerful position. Under the **Loi Fondamentale** (Fundamental Law) that served as **constitution** from 1960 to 1964, the office of prime minister was considered to be the leading position in **government**, balanced by **parliament** and the power of oversight by the largely ceremonial presidency. Patrice **Lumumba**, Cyrille **Adoula**, Moïse **Tshombe** and Évariste **Kimba** were some of the most notable prime ministers during that period. However, a lack of definition in the division of powers and the absence of legal precedents led to a series of constitutional crisis. These were caused by political standoffs when the **president** tried to dismiss the prime minister but parliament refused to support the dismissal. The paralysis of government that accompanied the crises led to a loss of faith in the system. As a result, the constitution of 1964 gave the president unquestioned power to dismiss the prime minister and cabinet and, with parliamentary approval, appoint a new government.

Following the **coup d'etat** that brought **Mobutu** to power in 1965, the post of prime minister was suspended, then eliminated by decree on October 26, 1966. The constitution of 1967 institutionalized the move, making the president the head of government. In July 1977, as part of a series of liberalization moves aimed at countering international criticism following the first **Shaba** War, the post of prime minister was resurrected but renamed "first state commissioner." The first state commissioner coordinated the activities of the ministries, renamed **departments**, and was the second-ranking official in government. However, the position was overshadowed by the **Mouvement Populaire de la Révolution (MPR)** party, the MPR **Political Bureau** headed by the president, and by the president's position as head of the **Executive Council**, or cabinet. **Mpinga Kasenda, Nguza Karl-I-Bond, Umba di Lutete** and **Kengo wa Dondo** were some of the most notable leaders to serve in the post in the 1980s. Initially at least, they were technocrats and did not remain in the position long enough to assimilate enough power to constitute a threat to the president.

On **April 24, 1990**, under increasing international and domestic pressure for political reform, Mobutu announced the **democratic transition**. **Mulumba Lukoji** was named prime minister to oversee what was to be a one-year process, but he resigned a few months later after the controversial **National Conference** collapsed in chaos. With the election of Étienne **Tshisekedi** by the **Conférence National Souveraine (CNS)** in August 1992, the prime minister's office became a source of **opposition** to and confrontation with the president.

Tshisekedi ordered a number of fiscal reforms that included the dismissal of the governor of the **central bank** and the head of the collections department of customs office. Both were Mobutu allies and their offices reportedly were sources of virtually unlimited cash for the president and his friends. Mobutu refused to accept the dismissals and eventually sent troops to guard the central bank building and prevent Tshisekedi from entering the prime minister's offices. Tshisekedi was dismissed in 1993 and replaced by Faustin **Birindwa**, his former senior advisor. Following a year of political paralysis in which each leader claimed to be the legitimate head of government, Mobutu removed Birindwa and nominated Kengo, who now headed a centrist political alliance.

When troops of the **Alliance des Forces Démocratiques pour la Libération du Congo/Zaïre (AFDL)** took **Kisangani** in a major victory in March 1997, Mobutu dismissed Kengo and reappointed Tshisekedi prime minister. He then dismissed him again after the fall of **Lubumbashi** on April 9 and replaced him with General Likulia Bolongo who fled the country with Mobutu on May 16, the day before the AFDL arrived in Kinshasa. AFDL leader Laurent **Kabila** was sworn in as president on May 29 and named a cabinet that did include a prime minister. *See also* Legislative System.

PRISONS. *See* PENAL SYSTEM.

PRIVATIZATION. A term given to the program in the mid-1980s of reducing state dominance in certain sectors of the Zairian **economy**, in particular **agriculture**, **transportation** and **diamond** and **gold mining**. It should not be confused with **Retrocession**, which was the term used in 1974-75 to return enterprises nationalized under **Zairianization** to private and joint, private/public ownership. In 1994, Léon **Kengo wa Dondo** launched a broader privatization program that envisaged joint ownership by domestic and foreign investors of state-owned companies, including state-owned airlines, river transportation and mining companies. The program, however, was slowed by the fiscal chaos of the mid-1990s and the rebellions of the late 1990s.

PROJET DES SERVICES DES NAISSANCES DÉSIRABLES (PSND) / PROJECT FOR PLANNED BIRTH SERVICES. Organization founded in 1982 to promote **family planning** and **birth control**.

PROJETS SUCRIERS AU ZAÏRE (PSZ). *See* OFFICE NATIONAL DU SUCRE (ONS).

PROPHETS. The name given to religious leaders who developed their own teachings, often based on **Christian** principles, and drew a group of followers who accepted their vision of life and the after-life. Prophets were numerous in early Congolese history and although many played small roles, others developed followings large enough to be considered a danger by the authorities. One of the most famous prophets to incur the wrath of early European missionaries was Dona Beatrice, who lived in the 1700s and came to be called the "Black Joan of Arc." She was burned at the stake by **Portuguese** religious and civilian authorities after she developed a strong following and proclaimed to have delivered a child of virgin birth. Her sect eventually died out.

On the other hand, a 20th-century prophet, Simon **Kimbangu**, developed a following that grew into a major church. Kimbangu was imprisoned in 1921 after reports of his "miracles" began to disturb the colonial authorities. Kimbangu died in prison in 1951, but Kimbanguism continued to grow and was admitted to the World Council of Churches in 1969, the first of several African churches to be recognized by Western church groups.

Although prophets were viewed with some suspicion during the 1970s when **Authenticity** was in force, they were usually tolerated by the **government** if they did not violate the law and social taboos or threaten state **security**. *See also* Kimbanguist Church.

PROTESTANT CHURCH. Protestant **missionaries** arrived in Congo after their Roman Catholic counterparts, founding the first Protestant mission among the **Kongo** in 1878. However, their work expanded quickly. They were responsible for standardizing and developing written forms of numerous Congolese **languages** in order to publish and disseminate the Bible and religious literature in local tongues. The Roman **Catholic Church** was less active in this field since during this period it preferred to have its word interpreted orally by its priests. During the **colonial era**, Belgian authorities in some cases favored Catholic missions, but were nevertheless supportive of the Protestants and, at **independence**, 46 Protestant missionary groups were working in the country, primarily in the areas of **health care**, **education** and training of African church leaders.

The Protestant churches formed the Congo Continuation Committee (CCC) in 1911 to encourage contact and cooperation and to minimize competition among themselves. The CCC became the Congo Protestant Council in 1924 and formally renamed itself the **Église du Christ au Congo (ECC)** in 1934. From 1971 until 1997, it was called the Église du Christ au Zaïre (ECZ). The ECZ claimed 83 member denominations and 10 million members throughout the country in 1982. With the advent of independence, efforts intensified to Africanize the church hierarchy. Rev. Pierre Shaumba was elected the first Congolese secretary-general of the organization and following his retirement was replaced by Rev. (later Archbishop) Jean **Bokeleale**.

During the **Authenticity** period of the early 1970s, the church came under pressure from the Zairian **government** and many foreign missionaries left. Like other religious organizations, the Protestant Church's publications were banned and its youth organization was taken over by the **Jeunesse du Mouvement Populaire de la Révolution (MPR)** in 1972. In 1974, its schools were taken over by the state, its **university** campus at **Kisangani** was absorbed into the **Université Nationale du Zaïre (UNAZA)**, and the public display of religious artifacts was banned. These measures were gradually rescinded in subsequent years and in 1983, **Mobutu** publicly encouraged church groups abroad to return to help reconstruct **social services**.

By the 1990s, many missions, hospitals and schools were again operating. They frequently did so entirely under Zairian religious leaders, despite considerable financial hardships caused by the economic crisis. In 1994, Bokeleale announced he would retire and a commission headed by Vice President Pierre Marini Bohdo began a search for his successor.

PROVINCES. During the **colonial era**, Congo was divided administratively into six provinces, which were retained for a time following **independence**. In June 1963, they were subdivided into 21 provinces in an attempt to dilute regional power bases, address intraregional tensions and strengthen the central **government**. Their number was reduced to 12 in April 1966. Under the administrative reorganization of December 24, 1966, they were further consolidated into eight provinces and the capital district of **Kinshasa**. The provinces were renamed **regions** on July 19, 1972, and their number was increased to 11 in 1988. In 1997, however, following the fall of **Mobutu** and the takeover by the Laurent **Kabila** government, the regions were designated provinces once again as part of the effort to remove symbols of what the new government viewed as an illegal regime.

PYGMIES. The earliest known inhabitants of the **Congo River Basin**, the Pygmies were **forest** dwellers who are best known for their small size and their hunting prowess. Adults usually grow only to about one meter (3-4 feet) in height. Pygmies are thought to be of

Bantu origin, but some anthropologists believe they are more closely related to **Khoisan** speakers of southern and eastern Africa. Seminomadic hunters and gatherers, they traditionally lived in houses of branches and leaves that allowed them to move easily. The reasons for their frequent displacements are a source of much speculation. Some say they avoided other groups which historically had enslaved them. They are known to have adopted the **languages** and customs of their neighbors. Others say the migratory patterns were related to changes in the sources of food. The largest known group in **Congo/Zaire** inhabit the forest and swamps above **Lake Maï-Ndombe** in the northwest. They are part of a larger Pygmy group inhabiting parts of northern **Republic of the Congo**, Gabon and Cameroon. Another major group lives in the northeastern **Ituri Forest** and parts of **Kivu** northeast of the **Lualaba** and **Lomami Rivers**. In the 1990s, some citizens, taking note of the historical discrimination against Pygmies and their increasing assimilation into the general **population**, began to criticize the term, saying Pygmies are merely "short Bantus."

- R -

RADIO. Radio is the most popular of the mass media in Congo/Zaire and there are an estimated four million sets, one for every 10 residents, in the country. Domestic radio is dominated by the **government**-owned La **Voix du Peuple** (formerly La **Voix du Zaïre**), which broadcasts from its national headquarters in central **Kinshasa** and eight regional stations in major urban centers. Historically, news content has been tightly controlled by the government and as a result, many listened to shortwave and satellite programs of international broadcasters such as Voice of America, Radio France Internationale and the British Broadcasting Corporation. In the mid-1990s, the government began to license some small local stations operated by religious and civic groups. A few years later, it allowed private stations to rebroadcast programs of international broadcasters and develop their own news reporting. By 1997, three major stations were operating in Kinshasa: Sango Malamu, Elikya and Radio Message de Vie. *See also* News Media; Radio-Télévision Nationale Congolaise (RTNC).

RADIO-TÉLÉVISION NATIONALE CONGOLAISE (RTNC) / NATIONAL CONGOLESE RADIO AND TELEVISION. The name given to the **government** agency in charge of overseeing the electronic media in Congo, following the installation of the Laurent **Kabila** government in May 1997. The RTNC replaced the **Office Zaïrois de Radio et de Télévision**, which existed until 1997. Its primary purpose was to operate the government-owned television and **radio** stations, the latter renamed La **Voix du Peuple** by the Kabila government to replace La **Voix du Zaïre**. The agency, however, also was responsible for licensing private radio stations, which began to proliferate in the late 1990s. For one week in late 1997, it banned rebroadcasts by local stations of transmission from international broadcasters, but rescinded the order after protests from the international community. *See also* News Media; Telecommunications.

"RADIO TROTTOIRE." Literally translated "sidewalk **radio**," Radio Trottoire was the overactive Congolese rumor mill which even **Mobutu** acknowledged was so influential that it occasionally obliged a response on the part of the government.

RAILWAYS. Five separate railway systems totaling 5,169 km operate in Congo/Zaire. They were owned and operated jointly by **government** agencies and private companies until 1974 when they were nationalized under **Zairianization** and taken over by the newly established Société Nationale des Chemins de Fer Zaïrois (SNCZ) (National Zairian Railway Company). The railways were partly **privatized** in the mid-1990s in an effort to revitalize them after the collapse of most government-operated services during the economic crisis of the early 1990s. From the mid-1970s deteriorating track and rolling stock and a shortage of spare parts and fuel have crippled the operation of most lines.

Railways connecting **river ports** were the main means by which the **colonial era** administration sought to evacuate raw materials from the territory and bring in manufactured goods. They were built at great human and material cost, primarily between the 1890s and 1930s. Thousands of laborers, local and foreign, as well as hundreds of European technicians, died from **disease, malnutrition** and accidents during the construction.

The oldest line was the Chemin de Fer Matadi-Kinshasa (CFMK), which linked the ocean port of **Matadi** to **Kinshasa** and the river and rail network that serviced most of the country. Construction began in Matadi in 1889 on the line to Thysville and was completed in 1898. Construction on the extension to the capital was begun in the 1920s and completed in 1932. The CFMK provided the major land link on national territory between the Atlantic Ocean and 95 percent of the **Belgian Congo** which, because of the cataracts on the **Congo River** between Kinshasa and Matadi, was basically landlocked.

The longest system, the Chemin de Fer Kinshasa-Dilolo-Lubumbashi (KDL), connected the **mining** area of southern **Katanga Province** to the port of **Ilebo** on the **Kasai River** and ultimately to Kinshasa by the Kasai and Congo Rivers. The 1,645-km-long railway did not actually reach Kinshasa, although plans existed from the 1920s for an Ilebo-Kinshasa leg. The first section of the line, from **Elisabethville** to Bukama, which lies on the upper end of the navigable part of the **Lualaba River**, was begun in 1911 and completed in 1918. In 1923, construction of a 1,123-km line connecting Bukama to Ilebo was begun and completed in 1928. The final 522-km leg of the system from **Tenke** to **Dilolo**, was completed in 1931 in order to connect the KDL system to the **Benguela Railway** through **Angola**. The Dilolo-Benguela route was widely used to export **minerals** from Katanga to the Angolan port of **Lobito** on the Atlantic Ocean until the Angolan civil war closed the Benguela Railway in 1975.

In eastern Congo/Zaire, the Chemin de Fer des Grands Lacs (CFL), was a 960-km truncated system that connected the navigable portion of the Lualaba River to the navigable portion of the upper Congo River. The Lualaba flows into the Congo River (and is considered part of the Congo River by local cartographers) but commercial navigation is impeded by cataracts between Kongolo and **Kindu** and between Ubundu and **Kisangani**. The first, 125-km-long section of the line from Kisangani to Ubundu opened in 1906. The second, 355-km section from Kindu to Kongolo was opened in 1911 and extended to Kabalo in 1938. A 275-km branch was later added that extended the system eastward to **Kalemie** on **Lake Tanganyika**, where goods were transshipped across the lake by steamer to **Tanzania** and transported by rail to

Dar es Salaam. In 1956, the CFL system was linked to the KDL system by a 201-km branch from Kabalo to Kamina.

The fourth system, the Chemin de Fer de Mayombe (CFM), was a 140-km line linking the ocean port of **Boma** in **Bas-Congo Province** to the agricultural area of Tshela near **Cabinda**.

The fifth system, the Chemins de Fer Vicinaux du Zaïre (CVZ), was a 1,025-km narrow-gauge railway in northeastern Congo/Zaire which linked agricultural areas in Mugbere and Isiro in the east and Bondo in the north to the port of Aketi on the Itumbiri River, a tributary of the Congo River. The line was extended to **Bumba** on the Congo River in 1973.

A multimillion-dollar plan was announced by the Zairian government in 1984 to rehabilitate and modernize the railways as part of a $135 million dollar project to improve **transportation** infrastructure. However, it was stalled by the government's growing financial insolvency. In 1995, the government of then-Prime Minister **Kengo wa Dondo** opened ownership of some of the lines to foreign investors in order to revive them. A company named **Sizarail** was formed with 49 percent government ownership and 51 percent **Belgian** and **South African** participation and began operating that year. It rehabilitated the Lubumbashi-Ilebo line and the line from Kamina to Kalemie on Lake Tanganyika. Officials said in 1996, the first year of operation, that the company invested $6 million and made a $1 million profit on $66 million gross revenues. Sizarail's operations were disrupted first by the rebellion of the **Alliance des Forces Démocratiques pour la Libération du Congo/Zaïre (AFDL)** in 1997 and by the rebellion of the **Rassemblement Congolais pour la Démocratie (RCD)** beginning in 1998. The Laurent **Kabila** government in 1997 announced a $507 million program aimed at revitalizing the railroads over the coming three years. *See also* National Way.

RAINFALL. Rainfall in Congo/Zaire ranges from 100 to 220 cm (40 to 88 in) per year. The zones of heaviest rainfall are in the **Congo River Basin** and the **eastern highlands**. Zones of least rainfall lie in the savannas of **Katanga** and **Kivu Provinces** and westernmost **Bas-Congo** Province. No region suffers from chronic drought. In addition, the fact that the country straddles the equator means the dry season in the northern part of the country (November through

March) occurs during the southern part's rainy season, and vice versa. As a result, the country's main **rivers** are navigable the entire year. The one notable exception is the **Ubangi River**, which lies entirely north of the equator and is navigable only six months of the year. *See also* Climate.

RAINFOREST. A dense, triple-canopy tropical **forest** covers most of the **Congo River Basin** and the northern third of the territory of Congo/Zaire. Heavy **rainfall**, combined with a thin layer of topsoil, makes the forest a delicate ecological **environment** that is poorly suited to intensive **agriculture**. **Timbering** and **rubber** collection have been widely carried out in the forest, but the large number of natural barriers prevented widespread deforestation of all but the **Mayombe Forest** in **Bas-Congo Province**. Nevertheless, ecologists were concerned in the 1990s over agreements signed between the **government** and various business groups allowing uncontrolled timbering of about one-third of the country's rainforests.

The Congo rainforest is one the least-explored regions on earth. Poor soil and the prevalence of **disease** there make farming and animal husbandry difficult. As a result, it is one of the most sparsely populated regions in the country. The forest is believed to hide interesting archeological artifacts and possibly important **mineral** reserves, but the dense canopy makes aerial surveys difficult. The area has important hydroelectric potential and contains millions of species of flora and fauna which have yet to be studied by science. Environmentalists believe that intense commercial farming is not possible in the area without serious damage to the ecology, but controlled exploitation of such resources as **fish**, nuts, rubber and material for pharmaceutical products, is feasible.

RASSEMBLEMENT CONGOLAIS POUR LA DÉMOCRATIE (RCD) / CONGOLESE RALLY FOR DEMOCRACY. The political wing of a **rebellion** launched on August 2, 1998, by exiled **dissidents**, former members of the Laurent **Kabila** government, and former **Mobutu** supporters. Headed by Ernest **Wamba dia Wamba**, an academic from **Bas-Congo Province** who spent many years in exile in **Tanzania**, the RCD also included among its leaders Bizima **Karaha**, foreign minister in the first Kabila governments, and Arthur **Z'Ahidi Ngoma**, an opposition leader who was subsequently imprisoned by the Kabila government for violating a ban on political activity. RCD military forces were led by Jean-Pierre **Ondekane**, a career officer from **Katanga Province** who commanded the Mobutu forces in **Lubumbashi** until he joined the **Alliance des Forces Démocratiques pour la Libération du Congo/Zaïre (AFDL)** when they took the city in 1997. The RCD was beset by internal rivalries in late 1998 and sought to broaden its base of support by announcing a national assembly in January 1999.

RASSEMBLEMENT DES DÉMOCRATES LIBÉRAUX (RDL) / ASSEMBLY OF LIBERAL DEMOCRATS. An **opposition** party formed in 1990 by Mwamba Mulamba.

REBELLIONS. Since **independence**, Congo/Zaire has experienced a number of rebellions and several secessions. The first rebellion, more accurately described as a mutiny, occurred five days after independence when the **Force Publique** revolted because of frustration over low pay, the lack of advancement opportunities, and the continued presence of Belgian officers. The mutiny was quelled within weeks and led to a more rapid **Africanization** of the officer corps.

On July 11, 1960, Moïse **Tshombe**, angered by the lack of representation of his party in the central **government** and encouraged by private business interests, declared the secession of **Katanga Province** and formed an independent state. The **Katanga Secession** was declared at an end on January 14, 1963.

On August 8, 1960, Albert **Kalonji**, angered by the massacre of **Luba** by government troops and taking advantage of the weakness of the central government, declared the secession of **diamond**-rich southern **Kasai** and formed the Independent Mining State of South Kasai. That secession ended in early 1961 when Kalonji joined the Cyrille **Adoula** government-of-reconciliation.

A third major rebellion occurred in eastern Congo on November 19, 1960, following the dismissal of the Patrice **Lumumba** government by President Joseph **Kasavubu** and the vote by the **United Nations** to seat the Kasavubu delegation instead of the rival Lumumba delegation. The assassination of Lumumba, announced on February 13, 1961, brought an international outcry and helped Lumumba's successor, Antoine **Gizenga**, with support from **China** and the **Soviet Union,** to consolidate a rival government in **Stanleyville**. Several members of the Gizenga government were named to the Adoula government in 1961. Gizenga himself was arrested by Adoula in 1962 but was freed by Tshombe in 1964. He returned to Stanleyville where, on September 7, 1964, he declared the **People's Republic of the Congo (PRC)** (not to be confused with the People's Republic declared in **Congo/Brazzaville** in 1973) in what came to be known as the **Stanleyville Secession**. At its peak the PRC was recognized by 13 foreign governments, but its excesses, which included taking 2,800 foreigners hostage, led to the Belgian-American airdrop on Stanleyville on November 24, 1964, and an offensive by the Congolese army, backed by foreign mercenaries, which reestablished government control over most of the region by 1965. In April 1964, a former lieutenant of Gizenga, Pierre **Mulele**, launched a rebellion in **Kwilu** Province, east of **Leopoldville**, which included bomb attacks in the capital. That rebellion was ended in 1965.

Following the **Mobutu coup d'etat**, there were other smaller rebellions, including a third eastern rebellion sparked by an army mutiny in 1966, the occupation of **Bukavu** in **Kivu** Province for three months in 1967 by **mercenaries** and the **Gendarmerie Katangaise** seeking to restore Tshombe to power, and an uprising in Idiofa, in Kwilu, in 1978. Two uprisings (called "invasions" by the Zairian government) in **Shaba Region** in 1977 and 1978 were led by members of the Gendarmerie Katangaise. These were put down with the help of foreign troops and an air assault on the **mining** center of **Kolwezi** in 1978 by Zairian, French and Belgian troops.

The **Parti de Libération Congolaise (PLC)**, formed in 1984, staged attacks on government installations in northeastern Zaire from bases in the **Ruwenzori Mountains**. In 1984 and 1985, the **Parti Révolutionnaire du Peuple (PRP)**, which had controlled a small portion of territory in the **Mitumba Mountains** of northern Katanga Province since 1964, attacked the town of **Moba** on **Lake Tanganyika**. The PLC abandoned its armed struggle in 1990 and registered as a **political party**. The PRP, however, did not and in October 1996 joined the **Alliance des Forces Démocratiques pour la Libération du Congo/Zaïre (AFDL)** in an offensive that quickly occupied Bukavu and **Goma** and over the next eight months swept west, taking control of **Kinshasa** on May 17, 1997, one day after the flight into exile of Mobutu and most members of his government.

The head of the PRP, Laurent **Kabila**, who emerged during the offensive as the leader of the AFDL, was sworn in as **president** on May 29. The departure of Mobutu was welcomed by most, but dissatisfaction soon set in, especially with the large number of foreign troops that had backed the offensive. These came to be seen as an occupation force. In late 1997, clashes erupted in eastern Congo between local militia and AFDL forces. On August 2, 1998, a group of former Kabila supporters launched a new rebellion and announced the formation of the **Rassemblement Congolais pour la Démocratie (RCD)** on August 12. The rebels advanced quickly and reached the outskirts of Kinshasa on August 26, but they were repelled by government forces reinforced by troops and aircraft from **Angola**, Namibia and Zimbabwe. The RCD, backed by **Rwanda** and **Uganda**, gained control over a vast swath of territory in eastern Congo. *See also* Dissidents; Soumialot, Gaston.

REFUGEES. Since **independence**, Congo/Zaire has been home to hundreds of thousands of refugees, most of them displaced by war and repression in neighboring countries. The first major group fled the war in **Angola** beginning in 1959. They numbered 310,000 in 1990, although repatriation efforts by the Office of the **United Nations** High Commissioner for Refugees had returned more than half of them by the late 1990s. In 1959, hundreds of thousands of Rwandans fleeing preindependence ethnic strife moved into eastern Congo. Others arrived from **Rwanda** and **Burundi** after interethnic fighting in 1975 and 1988. In 1993, 100,000 refugees fled interethnic violence in Burundi in which the recently elected president, Melchior Ndadaye, was assassinated.

In 1994, more than one million Rwandans fled to **Nord-Kivu** after a four-year civil war and the death of Rwandan President Juvenal Habyarimana led to two months of violence in which at least 500,000 were killed. Activities by pro-Habyarimana elements in the refugee camps, which included attacks on local villages and international aid agencies, caused the Zairian **government** to announce in August 1995 that it would repatriate the Rwandan refugees by force if necessary. The government relented under international pressure, but after anti-**Mobutu** forces led by Laurent **Kabila** seized the area in late 1996, 800,000 refugees returned home. An estimated 200,000, said to be members of the Rwandan militia and their families who feared retaliation if they returned, fled deeper into Zaire. Some were eventually repatriated or crossed into **Congo/Brazzaville**. Others were massacred over the ensuing months by Rwandan troops who backed the Kabila offensive.

In addition to these large groups, refugee officials estimated in the late 1990s that there were also 110,000 refugees from southern **Sudan** in the country, 10,000 from **Uganda** and 1,300 from other African nations. *See also* Ethnic Cleansing.

RÉGIE DE DISTRIBUTION D'EAU ET D'ÉLECTRICITÉ (REGIDESO) / WATER AND ELECTRICITY DISTRIBUTION ADMINISTRATION. A **government** agency responsible for water and electric utility administration and development. In 1985, REGIDESO was responsible for 7 million meters of pipe to 202,828 registered clients. It employed 4,180 agents and pumped 1.75 million cubic meters of water during the year. It also furnished electricity provided by small **petroleum**-powered complexes to about 23,000 clients in 40 towns in the interior until 1979 when these operations were turned over to the **Société Nationale d'Électricité (SNEL)**, the national **electrical power** agency. REGIDESO was one of the state-owned companies that weathered the economic crises of the early 1990s relatively well and managed to provide water to customers with relative regularity.

REGIONS. Administrative subdivisions of the territory. These were called **provinces** at **independence** and there were six inherited from the colonial administration: **Leopoldville, Kasai, Équateur, Orientale, Kivu** and **Katanga**. Their number was expanded to 21 in June 1963 and then changed on several occasions, until the administrative reforms of July 19, 1972, when the country was divided into eight regions and the capital district of **Kinshasa**. The regions were **Bas-Zaïre, Bandundu,** Équateur, **Haut-Zaïre, Kasaï Occidental, Kasaï Oriental,** Kivu and **Shaba**. The number was increased to 11 in May 1988 with the division of Kivu into three regions: **Nord-Kivu**, **Sud-Kivu** and **Maniema**. The regions were divided into urban and rural subregions. Rural subregions were further divided into zones which in principle were to contain no more than 200,000 residents.

Under the **constitution** of 1964, the provinces were granted considerable autonomy with their own assemblies and executive branches. With the advent of the **Mobutu** government, however, and the consolidation of power in the presidency in the 1970s, the regions lost most of their powers. Under the constitution of 1974, which institutionalized the single-party system and fused it with the state, the regional assemblies became consultative rather than legislative and laws passed in Kinshasa applied equally to all regions. The military and the administrative, legislative, and judicial branches of government were divided along regional and subregional lines. The regions were administered by governors who wielded considerable power over the local administrations. However, local military commanders and officials of the **Mouvement Populaire de la Révolution (MPR)** party also enjoyed considerable influence.

In the 1970s and 1980s, regional governors and military commanders were routinely assigned to regions other than their home areas in an effort to combat tribalism and prevent them from building personal power bases. However, this policy began to change in the late 1980s and with the advent of multipartyism in 1990 was abandoned. In the 1990s, as the influence and solvency of the central government declined, the regions took on additional responsibilities and autonomy. Many levied their own taxes, retained from local publicly owned companies, paid local **security** forces, and issued their own "visas" to travelers from other parts of the country.

When the government of Laurent **Kabila** was installed after the fall of Mobutu in May 1997, the regions were renamed provinces once again and Bas-Zaïre, Shaba and Haut-Zaïre again became **Bas-Congo**, **Katanga** and **Orientale**.

RELIGION. Citizens of Congo/Zaire are free to practice any religion as long as it is not subversive or abusive to others. Most are deeply religious. The influence of Christian missions has been strong since the 1870s and an estimated three-fourths of the **population** avow some ties with **Christianity**, although their faith may be mixed with traditional practices and beliefs. The remaining people are considered to have been relatively untouched by outside religious influences and adhere to traditional, sometimes called animist, beliefs. An estimated 45 percent of the population practices some form of Roman Catholicism, 25 percent are said to be **Protestant** and 15 percent adhere to smaller Christian-related groups such as the **Kimbanguist Church**, Rosicrucians, Celeste, and others. About 2 percent of the population is Muslim. Figures reported by the churches tend to be higher.

In the early 1970s, the Zairian **government** sought to institute a secular state during a period of intense **nationalism**, called **Authenticity**. In May 1972, Zairians were told to abandon their Christian given names for "authentic" Zairian ones. Later that year, the state took over church schools and **youth** groups and banned religious publications. In 1974, the public display of religious artifacts and symbols was banned. However, these measures were gradually rescinded. Church-owned schools were returned in the 1980s, and by 1990 many Zairians had resumed use of their Christian names. *See also* Catholic Church; Église du Christ au Congo; Islam; Kitawala Movement; Missionaries; Prophets; Spiritualism, Fetishism, Sorcery and Witchcraft.

REPUBLIC OF THE CONGO. *See* CONGO, REPUBLIC OF THE (BRAZZAVILLE); CONGO, REPUBLIC OF THE (KINSHASA).

REPUBLICAN AND FEDERALIST FORCES. *See* FORCES RÉPUBLICAINES ET FÉDÉRALISTES (FRF).

RÉPUBLIQUE DU ZAÏRE. *See* ZAÏRE, RÉPUBLIQUE DU.

RÉPUBLIQUE POPULAIRE DU CONGO (RPC). *See* CONGO, PEOPLE'S REPUBLIC OF THE (PRC).

RETROCESSION. The official name given to the policy, announced on December 30, 1974, of reversing **Zairianization** and returning **nationalized** foreign-owned enterprises to their former owners. Under the program, medium-size businesses, primarily farms and merchant operations, were returned outright, and ownership of up to 40 percent of large enterprises and those operating in certain "strategic" sectors were returned to the private sector. The level of private ownership allowed in these ventures was later increased to 60 percent. The policy was further extended in the 1980s with **privatization**.

RHODES, CECIL (1853 - 1902). British colonizer who extended British influence over parts of southern Africa and competed against the agents of **Leopold II** for control of the **copper** belt that crossed the region of **Katanga** and northern **Zambia**.

RICE. The second most important cereal in cultivation in Congo/Zaire, rice in 1993 was the third-largest food **crop** after **manioc** and **maize**. The country produced 165,000 metric tons per year in the late 1950s, primarily from small landholdings, often of less than one hectare, in the **Congo River Basin**. Production fell drastically following **independence**, however, and in 1965 only 56,000 tons were produced. Production began to rise in the 1970s, reaching 234,000 tons in 1980 and 365,000 tons in 1993, according to **World Bank** figures. Because of the popularity of rice as a staple among urban dwellers, the Zairian **government** historically imported large amounts of rice.

RIVERS. **Congo/Zaire** has more than 12,000 km of navigable rivers. These were the primary means of early exploration and development of the territory. A few rivers form part of the hydrosystem of the **Great Rift Valley lakes** in the east, but most of the country's rivers are part of the **Congo River Basin** system, drained by the **Congo River**, the world's second-largest river after the Amazon in terms of volume of water (120,000 cubic m/sec). The system straddles the equator and drains regions in both the northern and southern hemispheres. Because these have rainy seasons at different times of the year, most of the system is navigable during the entire year. The Congo River, however, is marked by three sets of cataracts which prevent commercial navigation between **Kinshasa** and **Matadi**, Ubundu and **Kisangani** and Kongolo and **Kindu**. Were it not for the cataracts, the Congo River would provide a direct shipping route between the mines of **Katanga**, bordering southern Africa, and the West African Atlantic coast. To circumvent the cataracts, a system of

railways was constructed between 1890 and 1932 which remains today.

The headwaters of the Congo River are formed by the tributaries of the **Lualaba River**, which rises near the border with **Zambia**. Tributaries of the Lualaba, or Upper Congo River as it is called by the government, include the **Lufira**, Luvua, Luama, Elila Rivers in the Katanga and **Kivu Provinces**, and the **Lomami**, Aruwimi and Itimbiri Rivers below Kisangani. One of the major tributaries of the Congo River is the **Kasai River** system, which extends into northern Katanga, the Kasais and southern **Bandundu** Provinces. The **port** of **Ilebo** on the Kasai River is a major transshipment point for **minerals** exported from Katanga via the **National Way**. The Kasai River's major tributaries are the **Kwango**, Kwilu, Lukenie and Sankuru Rivers. A second tributary system drains the southern part of **Équateur** Province via the **Tshuapa**, Lomela and Songela Rivers, which join the Congo River at **Mbandaka**. A third tributary system is the **Ubangi River** system which drains Équateur province via the Lua and Giri Rivers and is navigable only during the rainy season. *See also* Rainfall; Transportation.

ROADS. Congo/Zaire has 145,000 km of roads, most of them built before **independence**. In 1985, the government said 2,600 km of asphalt roads existed in the country and 40,000 km of treated roads were maintained. About one-half of the system consisted of dirt tracks. However, the road system had deteriorated considerably by the mid-1990s because of a lack of maintenance. By then, roads in some areas were being maintained by local governments and private businesses. The rural road system was built primarily to connect **agricultural** and **mineral**-producing areas to the **river** and **rail** systems. Major asphalt highways in western **Zaire** link **Kinshasa** to the sea **ports** of **Boma** and **Matadi** and Kinshasa to **Kikwit**. In the southeast, they link the **mining** centers of **Kolwezi** and **Lubumbashi** to northern **Zambia**. Most other highways are either dirt or gravel. Many of the roads through lowlands are impassable during heavy rains.

In the late 1970s and early 1980s, the governments of the **United States** and **Japan** funded bridge-building and road improvement projects as part of their bilateral aid programs. The Japanese helped build a suspension bridge across the **Congo**

River at Matadi in 1983. In the 1980s, the US Agency for International Development began a program to build bridges in the **Bandundu** area aimed at replacing log-crossings that were considered the weakest links in the system. Another program was launched to repair and refurbish the 300 river ferries in operation in the country.

The **Office des Routes** agency was created by the government in 1972 to oversee road maintenance and construction, but it was largely inoperable in the mid-1990s. Following the military offensive that brought Laurent **Kabila** to power in May 1997, his government announced a major program to improve roads and infrastructure in the country, but particularly in the east, which had suffered from decades of neglect. *See also* Transportation.

ROBERTO, HOLDEN. The leader of the **Frente Nacional de Libertação de Angola (FNLA)**, which fought against the **Portuguese** during the struggle for **Angolan** independence and subsequently fought against the **Movimento Popular de Libertação de Angola (MPLA)** faction during the civil war that followed independence. Roberto, who was **Mobutu**'s son-in-law, received considerable support from the Zairian **government** during the early years of the civil war and reportedly also received covert assistance from the **United States** through the Zairian government. He faded from the international scene following an agreement between the Zairian and Angolan governments in 1978 to end hostilities and cease support for each other's **opposition** movements. FNLA activities resumed on a smaller scale in the early 1980s. In the late 1980s and 1990s, however, most internal opposition to the MPLA government came from the **União Nacional para a Independência Total de Angola (UNITA)**, which also received support from Zaire and the US government.

ROBERTSON, PAT (REVEREND). A prominent pastor and leader of the right-wing Christian Coalition in the **United States**, whose friendship with **Mobutu** led to the formation of the African Development Company, which in the 1990s operated a $300 million **diamond mining** and **forestry** project on concessions granted by the Zairian **government**.

ROGET, LÉON (CAPTAIN). The first commander of the **Force Publique**, Roget was appointed by **Leopold II** in 1886 to form an army for the **Congo Free State**. He forged the Force in two years using a core of European officers and soldiers hired from various African territories.

ROUND TABLE CONFERENCES. Two meetings held in Brussels, **Belgium**, in early 1960 between Congolese leaders and Belgian officials following the riots and political unrest which began on **January 4, 1959**, and the inconclusive **elections** of December 1959. The conference was hastily organized after the Belgian government announced on January 13, 1960, its intention to "form a **democracy**" in the **Belgian Congo**. The Belgian authorities felt the main purpose of the conference was to resolve differences over the timetable for **independence**, which until that time had varied widely among Congolese leaders. Belgium had refused to set a date for independence and as a result some of the most important Congolese parties had boycotted December's local elections and there were threats of renewed violence.

The conference was to open on January 20, but the 45 Congolese delegates, led by Joseph **Kasavubu** and Patrice **Lumumba**, demanded that two preconditions be granted: that a date be set for independence and that the resolutions of the conference be binding. In a move widely interpreted as a victory for the Congolese, the Belgian government agreed. As a result, the date for independence was set for **June 30, 1960**, and the conference opened on January 25. A second Round Table Conference began on April 26, 1960, and continued into May. Its purpose was to examine the financial affairs of the soon-to-be-independent nation and to establish the framework for self-government. The **Loi Fondamentale** (Fundamental Law) was drafted to act as a **constitution** during the initial years of independence and was passed by the Belgian parliament on May 19, 1960. It repealed the **Colonial Charter** and set up a political system modeled on Belgium's.

RUBBER. One of the principal commercial **crops** of Congo/Zaire and, according to the **World Bank**, its third-largest **export** crop, rubber was one of the first exports of the **Congo Free State (CFS)**. The harsh **labor** practices used in its extraction were the main cause of the public outcry that led to the annexation of the Congo by the Belgian parliament, the end of the CFS, and the beginning of the Belgian **colonial** era. Rubber was grown throughout the tropical **forest** area of northern Congo/Zaire, but was a major crop primarily in the **Kisangani** area.

At **independence**, Congo produced 40,000 tons of rubber per year, of which virtually all was exported. Production declined during the political instability of the early 1960s, reaching 20,000 tons in 1965. It began to rise again and in 1973 reached 45,000 tons, of which 30,000 tons were exported. With **Zairianization** and the economic crisis of the mid-1970s, rubber production declined to 17,000 tons in 1982, according to the **central bank**. Production reportedly increased in the late 1980s but a great deal of it was **smuggled** to East Africa and exact figures were not available.

RUSSIA, RELATIONS WITH. *See* SOVIET UNION, RELATIONS WITH.

RUWENZORI MOUNTAINS. The Ruwenzori Mountain range, known as the "Mountains of the Moon" because of its stark, desolate landscape, is located on the border with **Uganda** between **Lake Albert** and **Lake Edward**. The range lies in one of the most remote and sparsely populated regions of Africa and is inhabited primarily by **Pygmies** and Nilotic peoples. Its Margherita Peak reaches an elevation of 5,080 m (16,763 ft) and is the third highest in Africa.

RUZIZI RIVER. A medium-sized **river**, 120 km in length, unnavigable because of cataracts, the Ruzizi flows from **Lake Tanganyika** in eastern **Congo/Zaire** into **Lake Kivu**. Because of the difference in altitudes of the two lakes, the river generates considerable hydroelectric potential, and a 12,600-kilowatt installation near Kamanyola supplies electricity to **Bukavu**.

RWANDA, RELATIONS WITH. One of three former Belgian colonies, Rwanda's ties with **Congo/Zaire** historically have been strong. A small, densely populated country of 8.6 million people, Rwanda lies in the **Great Rift Valley** across **Lake Kivu** from eastern Congo. Rwanda and **Burundi** originally were German colonies that were placed under Belgian trusteeship following World War I. Relations between Rwanda and Congo were good at **independence** but were strained in 1967 when Congolese army units mutinied over the lack of pay and, with support from foreign **mercenaries** and former members of the **Gendarmerie Katangaise**, tried to bring down the central **government**. Loyal troops, also backed by foreign mercenaries, drove the rebels out of the country into Rwanda. The Congolese government's request for extradition was denied, leading to a break in diplomatic relations on January 11, 1968. The **Organization of African Unity** was able to negotiate a compromise and the mercenaries were evacuated by the Red Cross in April 1968.

Relations were restored in February 1969 and strengthened by the establishment, in September 1976, of the **Communauté Économique des Pays des Grands Lacs (CEPGL)** with its seat in Gisenye, Rwanda. Ties remained strong through the mid-1990s, based in large part on the personal friendship between Presidents **Mobutu** and Juvenal Habyarimana.

In October 1990, the historical rivalries between the **Hutu** and **Tutsi ethnic groups** in Rwanda escalated into violence. The Tutsi-dominated Rwandese Patriotic Front (RPF) attacked northern Rwanda from bases in **Uganda**. Zaire sent military units to bolster the Rwandan government forces. Several years of mediation, in which Zaire participated, were leading to multiparty elections when Habyarimana was killed in a suspicious plane accident on April 6, 1994. His death led to two months of violence in which an estimated 500,000 Rwandans were killed. The RPF took control of the country. More than one million **refugees**, fearing retaliation by the new leaders, fled to eastern Zaire and 700,000 took refuge in Burundi and **Tanzania**.

Relations soured as the new government in Kigali accused Zaire of harboring leaders of the former regime, whom it accused of organizing the genocide and of plotting a counteroffensive. The Zairian government claimed neutrality, but in late 1995 it sought to expel the refugees, saying they were straining the local government and were threatening internal stability. Escalating attacks by troops and allied Hutu militia of the Habyarimana regime led to an offensive in October 1996 by the **Alliance des Forces Démocratiques pour la Libération du Congo/Zaïre (AFDL)**. The AFDL, led by Laurent **Kabila**, quickly seized a

1,000-km stretch of territory along the eastern border, causing 800,000 Rwandan refugees to return home in two weeks. Backed by fighters from Rwanda, Uganda, Burundi and **Angola**, the AFDL forces took the country in eight months and entered **Kinshasa** on May 17, 1997, one day after the departure of Mobutu. The Rwandan government was one of the first to recognize the Kabila government after it was sworn in on May 29. Subsequent relations were so close as to lead some citizens to call the Kabila government a Rwandan puppet. They deteriorated, however, when the Kabila government proved unable to halt attacks against Rwanda by Rwandan rebels based in eastern Congo. In July 1998, the Kabila government expelled about 100 Rwandan officers and Rwanda switched support to rebels of the **Rassemblement Congolais pour la Démocratie (RCD)**. *See also* Banyamulenge; Banyarwanda.

- S -

SACRED UNION. Formally known since 1993 as the Union Sacrée de l'Opposition Radicale et Alliés et Société Civile (USORAS) (Sacred Union of the Radical Opposition and Allies and Civil Society), the Sacred Union was formed in early 1991 as alliance of **opposition** parties. Its purpose was to present a united front against attempts by **Mobutu** and the **Mouvement Populaire de la Révolution (MPR)** to manipulate the **democratic transition** and divide the opposition in order to remain in power. By mid-1991, more than 200 parties had joined the group and their number grew to 400 by the mid-1990s. The alliance was dominated by the **Union pour la Démocratie et le Progrès Social (UDPS)** led by Étienne **Tshisekedi**, the **Parti Démocrate et Social Chrétien (PDSC)** of Joseph **Ileo**, and the **Union des Fédéralistes et des Républicains Indépendants (UFERI)** of Jean **Nguza Karl-I-Bond**. It was weakened by defections, most notably of the UFERI when Nguza was appointed **prime minister** on November 28, 1991.

The Sacred Union formally assumed power on August 15, 1992, when Tshisekedi was elected prime minister by the **Conférence Nationale Souveraine (CNS)**. However, he was dismissed by Mobutu in February 1993 and a senior UDPS advisor, Faustin **Birindwa**, was named prime minister. The UDPS and the hardline members of the Sacred Union did not recognize any subsequent government named by Mobutu because they maintained the Tshisekedi government had been dismissed illegally. There were numerous defections and expulsions from the alliance as various parties were drawn into subsequent governments of the **democratic transition**. The group was also beset by internal conflicts between moderates, who wanted to compromise with Mobutu in order to permit the democratic transition to move forward, and hardline members, led by the UDPS, who believed any accommodation with Mobutu would eventually discredit them in the eyes of the people.

Nguza drew several dozen small parties away in 1992 to form the short-lived **Alliance des Forces Patriotiques (AFP)**. Léon **Kengo wa Dondo**, who was not a member of the Sacred Union, succeeded in drawing some of the Sacred Union's minor parties away when he was appointed prime minister in 1994, to form the **Union pour la République et la Démocratie (URD)** alliance.

In late 1996, the Sacred Union, after initial hesitation, announced its support for the **Forces Démocratiques pour la Libération du Congo/Zaïre (AFDL)**, saying it backed the effort to overthrow Mobutu although it did not support the use of force to bring it about. After the AFDL took power in May 1997, newly installed President Laurent **Kabila** met with Tshisekedi and other Sacred Union leaders, but he did not include them in his first **government**, saying he would govern only with **political parties** that had participated in the military struggle against Mobutu. Kabila was able, however, to draw a number of Sacred Union members into subsequent governments, most notably a rival wing of the UDPS led by Frédéric **Kibassa**, and the daughters of two founding fathers, Justine Kasavubu and Julienne Lumumba.

SALARIES. *See* WAGES AND SALARIES.

"SALONGO." A **Lingala** term coined in the early 1970s to denote **labor** holidays set aside for community cleanup activities. Local **political party** leaders were entrusted with organizing this civic activity and prominent leaders were expected to make an appearance. Enthusiasm for the practice, however, waned in the late 1970s and by the 1980s the primary participants were party *cadres*, **students** and other groups organized by the **government**.

SAMBALA. A people of the **Tetela ethnic group** which, through association with the **Afro-Arabs** and Belgians, eventually became identified as a separate group. Sambala was the name given to the people of the Tetela and **Kusu** groups who joined **Ngongo Lutete** to pacify and occupy the **Maniema** region toward the end of the 19th century. Following the end of the war to drive the Afro-Arabs from Congolese territory, they were placed in charge of the area. They led other ethnic groups in the region in access to **education** and economic advancement.

SAMPASSA KAWETA MILOMBE (1942 -). An economist and **government** official long associated with **youth** and **education** during the heyday of the **Mouvement Populaire de la Révolution (MPR)**, Sampassa was born January 23, 1942, at **Likasi** in **Katanga Province**. He was educated in Katanga and received a degree in economic and financial sciences from the Université Officielle du Congo (subsequently renamed the **Université Nationale du Zaïre/Lubumbashi**). He served as minister of youth and sports on a number of occasions from July 12, 1970, until June 1, 1975, when he was appointed secretary-general of the **Jeunesse du Mouvement Populaire de la Révolution (JMPR)**, the youth wing of the party. He was appointed state commissioner (minister) for culture and the arts on February 18, 1981, and state commissioner for secondary and university education on May 7, 1982.

SANGO. A **trade language** used along **Congo/Zaire's** border with the **Central African Republic**.

SANITATION. According to **United Nations** figures, 34 percent of the Zairian **population** in 1991 had access to safe water, defined as treated surface water or uncontaminated water from springs or wells. The figures were 59 percent in urban areas and 17 percent in rural areas. In urban areas, potable water was provided to about one-half of the residents through private connections or primarily through neighborhood standpipes. Others obtained water from wells or streams of varying quality. Less than one-third of urban dwellers had access to public sewage connections. The remainder used pit latrines or public facilities. Garbage collection in urban areas was sporadic. Few rural dwellers had access to public water, sewage or sanitation systems. With the decline of public services in the 1990s, public sanitation, particularly garbage collection, has since deteriorated considerably.

SÃO SALVADOR. The **Portuguese** name for the capital of the **Kongo Kingdom**, located in what is now northern **Angola**. The name was changed from **Mbanza Kongo dia Ntotila** by **Affonso I** after his conversion to **Christianity**.

SATELLITES. Congo/Zaire uses satellites for telephone, telex and telegraph **communications**, relying on a land station at N'Sele outside **Kinshasa** for links to most of the regional capitals and international connections to Europe and the Americas. Automatic dialing service was inaugurated to **Belgium** in 1984, to **France** in 1985 and to the **United States** in 1986. Interregional **telecommunications** rely heavily on satellites because of the decaying network of overland long lines. The service had seriously deteriorated by the 1990s. Most contacts outside the country are now made primarily by privately owned satellite telephones and most contacts within urban areas are made primarily through privately owned cellular phone networks established in Kinshasa beginning in 1991 and later some regional cities like **Goma** and **Mbuji-Mayi**. Satellite service is also used to transmit **radio** and television programs to regional broadcasting stations. The Études des Ressources Terrestres par Satéllite (Study of Terrestrial Resources by Satellite) agency works on mapping the country's **mineral** and **agricultural** resources using data furnished by LANDSAT and other services.

SAVIMBI, JONAS. Leader of the **União Nacional para a Independência Total de Angola (UNITA)** group which fought for **Angola**'s independence from **Portugal** and against the **Movimento Popular de Libertação de Angola (MPLA)** after it took control of Luanda in 1975. Following a peace agreement with the MPLA in 1991, Savimbi ran for president in elections in September 1992 but was defeated by MPLA leader José Eduardo dos Santos. UNITA claimed the elections were fraudulent and resumed its attacks, including a two-week assault on Luanda that left an estimated 1,000 dead. UNITA and MPLA reached another accord in 1995 under which Savimbi was to assume the post of vice president. However, the agreement was shaken by numerous cease-fire violations by both sides. When the **Alliance des Forces Démocratiques pour la Libération du Congo/Zaïre (AFDL)** took power in **Kinshasa** with backing from Angolan troops in May 1997, UNITA's transshipment lines through Congo/Zaire for **diamond** marketing and **arms trafficking** came under threat. Fighting intensified in northeastern Angola between UNITA and MPLA forces, causing several thousand Congolese diamond miners to flee Angola in early 1998 and take refuge in camps in southern **Kasaï Occidental**. Increased clashes led the government in early 1999 to renounce the peace accords.

SCHOOLS. *See* EDUCATION.

SCHRAMME, JEAN (1929 - 1988). A Belgian **mercenary** who participated in the **Katanga secession** of 1960-63 and in 1967 led a revolt in eastern Congo that attempted to restore Moïse **Tshombe** to power. When the rebellion was crushed, Schramme, who had gained a reputation as one of the more ruthless of the foreign mercenaries, disappeared for a time but later resurfaced in Brazil. In April 1986, a Belgian court at Mons convicted Schramme in absentia of murdering a Belgian diamond dealer, Maurice Quintin, in Yumbi in 1967. Schramme said he ordered the murder because the businessman had been spying for the **Mobutu** government. Schramme was sentenced to 20 years at hard labor. However, Brazil refused to extradite him because he was married to a Brazilian citizen. The Brazilian media reported Schramme died in December 1988 of cancer at the age of 59 years.

SCIBE AIRLIFT. One of the major private **air transportation** companies launched in the late 1970s when the **government** monopoly was ended. The company was owned by **Bemba Saolana**, a friend of **Mobutu** and one of the country's wealthiest men. It operated some flights between Congo/Zaire and Europe, but concentrated mostly on domestic routes. One of its planes, reportedly leased through an affiliate, crashed in northern **Angola** in 1995, killing 165 people.

SECESSION. *See* KATANGA SECESSION; REBELLIONS; STANLEYVILLE SECESSION.

SECRET POLICE. *See* INTELLIGENCE SERVICES; SECURITY.

SECURITY. Under the **Mobutu government**, internal security was considered efficient, relying on a large network of informants and foreign technical advisers at different times from **Belgium, France**, the **United States, Morocco**, North Korea, **Israel** and, **South Africa**. A network of several security services operated independently of all other organs and of each other. Each service was endowed with its own **communications** system and reported directly to the **president**. They were credited with unmasking several attempted coups and, reportedly, numerous assassination plots. Security was weakest in the remote rural areas of northern, eastern and southern Congo/Zaire, primarily because of a lack of communications facilities, personnel and material resources in those areas. As a result, some of these areas harbored the most successful antigovernment resistance movements.

The national security service during the 1990s was called the **Service National d'Intelligence et de Protection (SNIP)**. Originally called the Sûreté Nationale at **independence**, it was renamed the Centre National de Documentation (CND) in 1969 and the **Agence Nationale de Documentation (AND)** in the early 1980s. A small, separate wing responsible for external intelligence primarily in neighboring countries was created in 1975. Military intelligence was furnished by the **Service d'Action et de Renseignements Militaire (SARM)**. Border security was provided by the Agence Nationale d'Immigration (ANI). The **Civil Guard** and **Gendarmerie Nationale** also had intelligence units. A shadowy unit called **"Les Hiboux"** ("The Owls") appeared in 1990 and engaged in kidnapping and urban terrorist acts against the **opposition**. Its members possessed automatic firearms and rocket-propelled grenades, leading to speculation that it was a unit of the military. When the **Alliance des Forces Démocratiques pour la Libération du Congo/Zaïre (AFDL)** took power in 1997, it renamed the SNIP the **Agence Nationale**

des Renseignements (ANR) and undertook a major purge of Mobutu's **intelligence services.**

SENDWE, JASON. An early political leader who founded the **Association des Baluba du Katanga (BALUBAKAT)** to represent the **Luba** in **Katanga Province** prior to **independence.** He tried to mediate the conflict between the **Lunda** and Luba in Katanga in 1960-61. He was assassinated in Albertville, now **Kalemie,** in June 1964 during an internal dispute in the BALUBAKAT.

SENGELE. An **ethnic group** living west of **Lake Maï-Ndombe** in **Bandundu Province.** Part of the **Mongo language** group, the Sengele differ from many Mongo groups because of their more complex and hierarchical social structure.

SEPTEMBER 23-24, 1991. On the night of September 23, 1991, elements of the 31st Airborne Division based at the **Centre d'Entraînement des Troupes Aéronautiques (CETA)** at Ndjili **Airport** on the outskirts of **Kinshasa** revolted over low and late **wages** and began looting containers at the airport. The looting quickly spread to Kinshasa's commercial districts and to some wealthy residential areas. Civilians followed soldiers in taking merchandise and equipment from shops, factories and warehouses. The incidents caused **Belgium** and **France** to send troops to evacuate an estimated 10,000 expatriate workers. Similar incidents occurred in other major cities during the following weeks. The looting caused losses estimated at $1 billion and reduced economic productivity by an estimated 20 percent. Political analysts said the violence was also due to popular frustration over the lack of progress by the **National Conference,** which had opened in August to chart the transition to multiparty **democracy** but had collapsed in chaos. It brought a compromise between **Mobutu** and **opposition** parties that led to the reopening of the conference in December. Another wave of looting in January 1993 reached middle-class residential areas and further aggravated the country's economic crisis. *See also* Pillages.

SERVICE D'ACTION ET DE RENSEIGNEMENTS MILITAIRE (SARM) / MILITARY SECURITY AND INTELLIGENCE

SERVICE. The military **intelligence service**, the SARM operated separately from other intelligence services and answered directly to **Mobutu**. The service was credited with discovering a number of anti-Mobutu plots in the 1970s. It was dismantled following the overthrow of the Mobutu government in May 1997. *See also* Security.

SERVICE NATIONAL D'INTELLIGENCE ET DE PROTECTION (SNIP) / NATIONAL INTELLIGENCE AND PROTECTION SERVICE. Zaire's secret **police** in charge of internal **security** and counterespionage and responsible directly to **Mobutu**. The SNIP was called the Sûreté Nationale during the **colonial era** and early post-**independence** years. It was established by the colonial administration originally to watch potential troublemakers and was retained following independence as part of the Interior Ministry to control immigration, supervise resident aliens and protect key **government** figures. The organization was transferred to the Office of the **President** shortly after Mobutu took power in 1965. Headed by Victor **Nendaka** until 1965 and **Singa Boyembe** until 1969, it was feared by Mobutu until he was able to install his allies in 1969 in a reorganization during which it was renamed the Centre National de Documentation (CND). In 1975, the **intelligence services** were reorganized into internal and external sections named the Centre National de Renseignements et d'Investigation (CNRI) and Service National d'**Intelligence** (SNI) respectively. In the early 1980s the service was renamed the **Agence Nationale de Documentation (AND)** before being renamed SNIP in August 1990.

The service was credited with foiling at least a half-dozen coup attempts. Secretive and feared, the SNIP used a large network of informers and its own, separate **communications** system to monitor the activities of **dissidents** and potential challenges to the authority of the president. There were a number of other intelligence services charged with security matters, all of which reported to Mobutu. SNIP underwent a major reorganization and its name was changed to the **Agence Nationale des Renseignements (ANR)** in 1997, following the fall of Mobutu and the takeover by forces under Laurent **Kabila**.

SHABA. Shaba, meaning "**copper**" in Swahili, was the name given to the **mineral**-rich southeastern **province** during the **Mobutu** era, beginning in 1971. (The provinces were renamed **regions** in 1972.) After **Kinshasa**, it was the wealthiest and most developed region in the country and was the scene in 1977 and 1978 of two incursions which shook the Mobutu government and were only suppressed with the help of foreign troops. The original name, **Katanga** Province, was restored following the fall of Mobutu in May 1997.

SHABAIR. One of the first and more successful of the private **air transportation** companies operating in the 1990s. From its base in **Lubumbashi**, Shabair operated daily flights to **Mbuji-Mayi** and **Kinshasa** and in the mid-1990s sought to expand service to Europe and **South Africa**. However, it declined in the mid-1990s and by 1996 was operating only intermittently.

SHI. A group of **Bantu**-related people living in the highlands of **Sud-Kivu Province** near **Bukavu**, between **Lake Tanganyika** and **Lake Kivu**.

SIDA. The French acronym for **Acquired Immune Deficiency Syndrome (AIDS)** by which the **disease** is known in Congo/Zaire. It stands for *Syndrome immunité déficient acquis*. In the 1980s, when the disease first appeared, it was often joked that SIDA stood for *Syndrome inventé pour décourager les amoureux*, "syndrome invented to discourage lovers."

SILVER. A relatively small amount of silver was produced as a by-product of **gold mining** by the **Société Minière et Industrielle du Kivu (SOMINKI)** and the **Générale des Carrières et des Mines (GECAMINES)** in **Katanga Province**. Congo/Zaire produced 4 million ounces of silver per year at **independence**, but production declined to 1.2 million ounces by 1984. No official production has been reported since the 1990s.

SIMBAS. Simba, Swahili for "lion," was the name taken by rebels during the eastern **rebellions** of the early 1960s. The Simbas used potions and incantations which they believed rendered them invulnerable, turned bullets into water, and incapacitated their enemy. The Simbas were primarily young warriors with an average age of 15 years, who were often drugged but who fought with a ferocity that in many battles routed **government** troops. The Simbas engaged in gruesome torture and atrocities against the local population before their rebellions were ended in 1965. *See also* Soumialot, Gaston.

SINGA BOYEMBE MOSAMBAYI (1932 -). One of the supporters of the **coup d'etat** that brought **Mobutu** to power, Singa remained at the senior political and military level in Zaire through the 1980s. Born on October 10, 1932, in Ibembo, **Orientale Province**, Singa was educated in Orientale and **Kasai** Provinces and received military training at the École Royale de Gendarmerie Belge in **Belgium**, and in the **United States** and **Israel**. He was made commissioner (governor) of **Shaba Region** in 1978 following the Shaba invasions and became **armed forces** chief of staff on January 1, 1980. He was named to the **Central Committee** on September 2, 1980.

SIZARAIL. A joint venture of the Zairian **government** and interests in **Belgium** and **South African** formed in 1995 to revive several **railways** in Congo/Zaire. Sizarail invested $66 million to refurbish the lines between **Lubumbashi** and **Ilebo** and between **Kamina** and **Kalemie** in 1996. It reportedly turned a $1 million profit in its first year, but its operations were disrupted in early 1997 by the offensive of the **Alliance des Forces Démocratiques pour la Libération du Congo/Zaïre (AFDL)**, which took control of the operation at one point. After the installation of the AFDL-backed government of Laurent **Kabila**, Sizarail Manager Patrick Claes was arrested in September 1997 on **corruption** charges, but he was released five months later.

SLAVES AND SLAVERY. Slavery was practiced to a certain degree in traditional Congolese **societies**, usually as part of the spoils of war, but it reached mass proportions in the 16th and 17th centuries because of the demand for cheap labor in the Americas. Between 1500 and 1900, when the practice was ended, as many as 30 million Africans are estimated to have been shipped against their will from ports on the central Atlantic coast to markets primarily in Brazil, Central America and the Caribbean. An estimated three million persons were shipped to the Americas from what is now Congo/Zaire and, during the height of the trade, 50,000 were shipped annually. Meanwhile, in eastern Congo, **Afro-Arab** traders exported an estimated 50,000 to 70,000 slaves per year to markets in the east. Territorial wars and the battles fought to capture slaves destroyed a large portion of the region's population. Entire villages were often wiped out in order to capture a few dozen "exportable" slaves.

In the late 18th century, Denmark, Sweden and the Netherlands abolished slavery. England outlawed the trade in 1807 and slavery itself in 1833. **Portugal** followed in 1835 and **France** in 1848. By the mid-19th century, all European countries had abolished the practice, although it continued unofficially for decades afterwards. The importation of slaves was prohibited by the US Congress in 1808 and the **United States** abolished slavery with the Emancipation Proclamation of January 1, 1863, although it was not until the Civil War was ended in 1865 that abolition came into force throughout the nation. Brazil was the last major nation to abolish slavery, in 1888.

The social implications of slavery in African society has been examined in great detail by academicians. Most agree that slavery in the traditional African context did not carry the degree of social and economic dispossession it assumed when it was converted into an **export** industry. In traditional African society, slaves had rights and a heritage and could improve their lot within certain constraints. Under the chattel system, slaves were owned outright by the master, had no legal rights, and could expect nothing better for their descendants.

SMUGGLING. Smuggling of certain **agricultural** and **mineral** products traditionally has been high in Congo/Zaire. **Central Bank** officials estimated in the 1980s that one-half of the country's **diamonds** were being marketed outside official channels. During the economic collapse of the 1990s, that figure is believed to have reached as high as 80 percent. **Gold, ivory, coffee** and tea were other heavily smuggled commodities. A primary reason for smuggling was the low prices paid by **government** marketing boards, heavy taxes and restrictions on private participation in the exploitation of minerals in particular. Another reason has been the weakness of the **currency** and shortages of consumer goods in the remote regions where many of the commodities are produced. Because of these shortages, smugglers in **Kasaï Oriental**, **Katanga** and **Orientale Provinces**, for example, often trade illegally with merchants in neighboring countries for fuel, food, **cloth** and manufactured goods.

SOCIAL SERVICES. A system of welfare and social services was set up at **independence** much along the lines of the colonial system. However, as in many nations, the effectiveness of the system declined over the years because of **inflation**, budget cuts, **corruption** and inefficiency. A pensioner, veteran or, in some cases, a disabled person is entitled to a nominal stipend, but when the individual is able to collect it, the sum rarely provides more than few days' sustenance. As a result, persons in need depend primarily on their extended family, churches, charitable organizations or on occasion a wealthy benefactor.

SOCIALISM. During the height of **Mobutism**, socialism, like **communism** and capitalism, was officially condemned by party ideologists who called it a foreign ideology and advocated instead an **Authenticity**, characterized as Zairian **nationalism** that was "neither to the right nor the left, but forward." However, some aspects of socialism were contained in **government** policies which advocated, for instance, universal **health care**, an end to hunger and a heavy degree of government involvement in the **economy**. Following the economic crisis of the mid-1970s, economic policies began to move away from the centralization and toward **privatization**, with increasing private participation in the **mining**, **agriculture** and **transportation** sectors. These policies were extended further in the 1990s as the government sought funds and technical expertise to revive insolvent state companies.

SOCIÉTÉ BELGO-AFRICAINE DU KIVU (SOBAKI). A **mining** consortium of mixed public and private ownership, which until 1965 was called the Comité National du Kivu. The company was established in 1908, one of the large, privately owned consortia licensed by **Leopold II** and given a virtual monopoly over large tracts of land with the ostensible goal of helping to develop the territory. The company was nationalized under **Zairianization** but was returned to mixed ownership under **Retrocession**.

SOCIÉTÉ CONGO-ITALIENNE DE RAFFINAGE (SOCIR). A company jointly owned by the **government** and private Italian interests which operated Congo/Zaire's sole **petroleum** refinery, completed in 1968 at Kinlao near Moanda on the coast. The installation has a capacity to refine 17,000 barrels per day. However, most Congolese crude is too high in sulfuric content to be processed by the refinery. As a result, locally produced crude is traded for lighter oil, imported primarily from Nigeria, which can be processed. In 1984, SOCIR (then called Société Zaïro-Italienne de Raffinage) refined 183,730 tons of crude but that declined in the 1990s.

SOCIÉTÉ DE DÉVELOPPEMENT INDUSTRIEL ET MINIER DU ZAÏRE (SODIMIZA). The second-largest **copper mining** company in the country, SODIMIZA was formed in 1969 and given mining rights to a 93,000-square-km tract of land in southeastern **Shaba** Region. Copper production from two underground mines at Musoshi and Kinsenda began in 1972 and reached 80,000 tons in 1984, but low prices and the closure of the **Benguela Railway** prevented a large-scale expansion of production. The ore from the mines was processed through a crusher and blender at Musoshi and the semirefined copper was then shipped by **railway** to **Zambia** for smelting and refining. SODIMIZA was owned by the **government** but operated by the Philip Barrett Kaiser Co. of Canada until 1987 when the company was merged with the **Générale des Carrières et des Mines (GECAMINES).**

SOCIÉTÉ DES CIMENTS DU ZAÏRE (CIZA). Owner-operator of one of two major **cement** plants in **Bas-Congo Province**, CIZA produced 630,000 tons of cement per year in the early 1980s despite problems caused primarily by shortages of spare parts and occasional disruptions in the supply of raw materials. During the economic crisis of the early 1990s, production fell drastically.

SOCIÉTÉ DU LITORAL ZAÏROIS. A Belgian company, 15 percent of which was owned by the Zairian **government**, that engaged in **petroleum** production along the coast of Congo/Zaire through the Zaïrep firm.

SOCIÉTÉ GÉNÉRALE DE BELGIQUE (SGB). A large Belgian capital-investment and holding company chartered in 1891 and granted large territorial concessions in the Congo, particularly in **Katanga**. The SGB's parent company, Société Générale, was founded in 1822 by the king of the Netherlands and private members of the aristocracy. The SGB began a massive growth program in 1919-25 and was an influential stockholder in the **Union Minière du Haut-Katanga (UMHK)** until its **nationalization** in 1966. Nevertheless, the SGB's refining subsidiaries, based primarily in **Belgium**, continued to be major purchasers of Zairian **minerals**, particularly the production of the **Générale des Carrières et des Mines (GECAMINES)**, and there were reports in 1996 that it was contemplating entering into an agreement to help revive the GECAMINES operations.

SOCIÉTÉ GÉNÉRALE DES MINÉRAIS (SGM). The former agent for the **Union Minière du Haut-Katanga (UMHK)**, the SGM was a Belgian **mineral** company that processed semirefined **copper** from **Katanga**. When UMHK was nationalized in 1966, the SGM began operating the company under an agreement with the Congolese **government**. Its responsibilities included **mining**, processing, marketing, procurement and staffing. In 1969, a 25-year extension was signed, aimed at eventually compensating SGM for the **Zairianization** of UMHK, which had been renamed the **Générale des Carrières et des Mines (GECAMINES)**, and for operating costs. A revised agreement in 1974 settled the compensation issue and in return SGM agreed to aid with a projected expansion of copper refining in **Shaba** and the establishment of a casting operation in **Bas-Zaïre Region**. However, the agreement was abrogated by the Zairian government later that same year, paving the way for the creation of a government-owned minerals-marketing entity called the **Société Zaïroise de Commercialisation des Minérais (SOZACOM)**, which nevertheless continued to market a great deal of copper through SGM. In 1984 SOZACOM was dissolved and GECAMINES assumed responsibility for marketing its own minerals.

SOCIÉTÉ INTERNATIONALE FORESTIÈRE ET MINIÈRE (FORMINIÈRE). One of three companies formed by the **Société Générale de Belgique** in 1906 to exploit mineral and **agricultural** resources in the **Congo Free State** and later the **Belgian Congo.**

SOCIÉTÉ MINIÈRE DE BAKWANGA (MIBA). Congo/Zaire's second-largest company and its major **diamond mining** entity, MIBA was formed in December 1961 by combining three private companies: the Société Minière du Beceka (MIBEKA), founded in 1919; the Société d'Entreprise et d'Investissements (SIBEKA), owned by the **Société Générale de Belgique (SGB)**; and the Anglo-American Corporation of **South Africa.** MIBA was **nationalized** in 1973, although 20 percent ownership was returned to SIBEKA in 1978. Until the 1990s, MIBA produced most of Zaire's industrial and gemstone diamonds, primarily from alluvial deposits on a concession of 43,000 square km in the southern **Kasai provinces.** At its peak, MIBA production provided two-thirds of the noncommunist world's supply of industrial diamonds.

In 1984, following liberalization in diamond-marketing regulations, MIBA reversed a 20-year decline and in one year nearly doubled production. In 1985, it produced 13.6 million carats of industrial diamonds and 4.8 million carats of gem-quality stones. The figures represented a return to production levels of industrial stones at **independence** and a ten-fold increase in the production of gem-quality stones over the same period. A great deal of the increase, particularly in gemstone production, was attributed to new **government** policies, announced in 1983, which allowed private firms to **trade** in diamonds. It was also attributed to the floating of the Zairian **currency**, which allowed dealers a realistic profit on their transactions. MIBA's production declined in the 1990s because of deteriorating equipment, while artisanal mining in the Kasais and **smuggling** from northern **Angola** raised Zairian production overall. *See also* Société Zaïroise de Commercialisation des Minérais (SOZACOM).

SOCIÉTÉ MINIÈRE DE KISENGE (SMK). Congo/Zaire's major producer of manganese, operating at Kisenge in southwestern **Katanga Province** near the **Angolan** border. The SMK was originally the Société Beceka Manganèse, a holding of the Société Générale founded in 1950. SMK was **nationalized** in 1973. Manganese production peaked in 1960 at 381,000 tons per year and remained above 300,000 tons per year until the closure of the **Benguela Railway** in 1975 and the **Shaba** invasions of 1977-78 caused production to cease. However, considerable stockpiles remain and 15,000 tons of ore were processed in 1984.

SOCIÉTÉ MINIÈRE DE TENKE-FUNGURUME (SMTF). A **copper mining** company formed in 1970 with 20 percent state participation and the remainder owned by a consortium of US, European and Japanese companies. It was granted a concession of 1,425 square km in southern **Shaba Region**, but the operation depended heavily on the reopening of the **Benguela Railway**, which failed to happen, because of the conflict between the **Angolan** government and the **União Nacional para a Independência Total de Angola (UNITA)**. The company was liquidated in October 1984. A consortium led by **South Africa**'s Anglo-American Corporation sought to reopen the mines in the late 1980s but abandoned the project. In November 1996, Canada-based Eurocan Consolidated Ventures announced a joint venture with the **Générale des Carrières et des Mines (GECAMINES)** to resume production by the year 2000. The company said initial production would be 100,000 tons of copper and 8,000 tons of **cobalt** per year, based on an estimated 222 million tons of ore reserves. The agreement was abrogated after the **Alliance des Forces Démocratiques pour la Libération du Congo/Zaïre (AFDL)** took power in May 1997.

SOCIÉTÉ MINIÈRE ET INDUSTRIELLE DU KIVU (SOMINKI). A company of mixed public and private ownership formed on March 25, 1976, by the merger of eight companies, some of them in existence since 1928, engaged primarily in **tin** mining in **Kivu**. The company was owned by the Zairian **government** and a Franco-Belgian company, Empain-Schneider. It was granted a concession area of 9,800-square-km lying in a 90,000-square-km part of the **Kindu** area of what is now **Maniema Province**. Known tin reserves in the area were 29,000 metric tons and estimated resources were 43,700 tons. Output in 1983 was 2,582 tons cassiterite but declined to 1,600 tons in 1990; the company virtually ceased operations in subsequent years. Production and the possible exploitation of known deposits in another area at Twangiza were hindered by transportation problems and low tin prices. SOMINKI also operated a 50-year-old **gold** mine at Mobale with an output in the 1980s of 1,000 troy ounces per month. Total known reserves of gold in the area were 899,700 ounces and estimated reserves were 1,545,000 ounces.

SOCIÉTÉ NATIONALE D'ÉLECTRICITÉ (SNEL). The **government**-owned agency charged with the development and administration of **electrical power** generation in Congo/Zaire. SNEL operates all of the country's electricity generating complexes. The agency's largest project in the 1970s was supervising the construction of the **Inga hydroelectric complex** in **Bas-Zaïre** and the **Inga-Shaba power line** linking the complex to the power grid in **Shaba**. Refurbishment of smaller hydroelectric complexes in Shaba and other parts of Zaire was begun in the late 1970s and plans were launched in the early 1980s for a rural electrification program. SNEL constructed a small hydroelectric complex in the 1980s at Mobayi-Mbongo, near **Mobutu**'s home town of **Gbadolite**. The **pillages** of 1991-92 damaged some facilities. In an interview in December 1995, then-Prime Minister Léon **Kengo wa Dendo** said that SNEL was suffering because of payment arrears by clients in neighboring countries. He said **Zambia** had cleared a one-million-dollar debt but the company was still trying to collect $17 million owed by the government of **Congo/Brazzaville**.

SOCIÉTÉ NATIONALE DES CHEMINS DE FER CONGOLAIS (SNCC). Congo/Zaire's national railroad authority, formed in 1974 as the Société Nationale des Chemins de Fer Zaïrois (SNCZ) by combining a number of **railway** lines. It operates the five major railway systems in the country.

SOCIÉTÉ ZAÏROISE DE COMMERCIALISATION DES MINÉRAIS (SOZACOM). A **government** agency established in June 1974 to market Zairian **minerals**, primarily those produced by the government-owned **Générale des Carrières et des Mines (GECAMINES)**. SOZACOM also took over the marketing of **diamonds** produced by the **Société Minière de Bakwanga**

(MIBA) in 1983, following a dispute with De Beers, which had been the marketing agent since before **independence**. However, SOZACOM was judged to be inefficient and was dissolved in 1984. GECAMINES and MIBA subsequently assumed responsibility for marketing their own minerals.

SOCIETY. The society of **Congo/Zaire** is diverse and complex and is undergoing considerable change. Historically, traditional societal structures have varied considerably among different **ethnic groups**. These were altered by **colonial era** and post-**independence** policies and events. In modern times, differences between urban and rural societies have led many Zairians to lament what they describe as a shredding of the fabric of family and communal life. Many urban dwellers express a sense of aimlessness and a loss of roots. Meanwhile, rural dwellers express despair over falling behind urban dwellers in **education** and **income** levels.

In rural areas, some traditional structures remain. They differ considerably (for example, in matrilineal vs. patrilineal hier-archies, the roles of **chiefs**, and the methods for their selection), but general similarities can be discerned. In traditional society, local communities were often centered around a **descent group**, **clan** or extended family. They usually were headed by a chief, who often represented the spirits, gods or ancestors for the group. In societies with more complex hierarchical systems, a number of chieftaincies might be grouped under a **king** who had authority over and received tribute from the lesser chiefs. The chief often performed religious or ritual functions. The major purpose of these was to protect and better the lives of the followers, whether by increasing fertility and harvests, mediating disputes or directing war strategy. Despite the considerable deference accorded him, the chief rarely acted without consulting advisors such as village elders or senior relatives.

Colonialism considerably affected the chieftaincy structure in the Congo. Colonial authorities granted administrative powers to some traditional chiefs, but most of those chosen to represent the authorities at the village level were selected on the basis of their willingness to cooperate. After independence, **government** administrators were more accommodating toward traditional chiefs and customs. However, the tendency was the same: to encourage the rise of chiefs willing to cooperate in implementing government policies and objectives.

In traditional society, members were distinguished on a scale of worthiness or merit. Age was generally respected as were wealth, political or religious office, and prowess in endeavors such as hunting, warrioring and storytelling. Males were usually accorded higher status than females, although notable exceptions existed. **Slaves** and indentured servants in general had less access to the rights and privileges of their patrons. However, processes usually existed whereby they could rise to some degree in the social stratum.

In urban centers, the extended family and ethnic group remained the pillars of societal structure but were weakened by urban life. A working **class** began to develop in the 1920s and 1930s, but its influence remained low until the trade union movement was allowed to emerge following World War II. The late 1940s and 1950s brought the development of a petty bourgeoisie whose members, sometimes called *évolués*, were primarily salaried white-collar workers like clerks and secretaries in the colonial bureaucracy. Small traders operating low-capital businesses also began to flourish. The lowest urban class, the **unemployed**, also began to grow, although the authorities tried to limit travel to the cities by unemployed Congolese. Independence, and the exodus of expatriate technicians and administrators that accompanied it, altered societal structures and created new classes virtually overnight, as Congolese began to occupy professional and managerial jobs vacated by Europeans.

Four decades after independence, the new structures have evolved and although sociologists differ on their classification, they agree on several general levels. At the highest level in society is the ruling political *élite*, which Georges Nzongola-Ntalaja calls the "state bourgeoisie." Many of its original members were pre-independence *évolués*: clerks and assistants who became ministers and directors. Since independence, members of the *élite* have been joined by educated young *cadres* and political appointees. These newcomers usually owe their positions to political patronage such as a relative in a high position. They usually try to apply their income to build a business that sometimes becomes strong enough to safeguard their position in society if they fall out of political favor.

Some sociologists differentiate between the political *élite* and the large-scale merchants, although individuals in one group are usually related to someone in the other. (It is common for a senior political appointee or manager to launch his wife or children in business.) Lower in status but still respected is the professional class: professors, physicians, intellectuals, military officers and, to a lesser degree, **university students**. They enjoy a measure of affluence although the economic hardships of the 1990s, including high **inflation** and falling purchasing power, forced many of them out of the "**middle class**" income levels. Sometimes called the "*sous-bourgeoisie*" ("under-bourgeoisie"), many survive financially by placing relatives in small trading or farming activities. Small traders can also be placed in this category. They command less respect but frequently are wealthier than their educated compatriots.

Blue-collar wage-earners, including journeymen and semi-skilled workers, are usually classified in the next category. Some analysts group them with small farmers, particularly in income level. However, they usually enjoy a higher status than their rural compatriots because of a proximity to urban centers and their amenities. Cash-**crop** and subsistence farmers are often grouped in a "peasant" class. And lastly, the urban unemployed are viewed as the underclass, the group considered the breeding ground for instability that can threaten the ruling classes. This group is viewed with apprehension. Frequently, authorities in the cities detain the unemployed and indigent and return them to their villages or, if they are young, induct them into the **armed forces**. *See also* Urbanization.

SONGYE. A **Bantu**-speaking people living near Kabinda, in southern **Kasaï Oriental Province** between the Lubufu and **Lomami Rivers**.

SOONDE. One of the **ethnic groups** classified by Jan Vansina as part of the **Lunda** cluster living in western **Katanga** and eastern **Angola**.

SORCERY. *See* SPIRITUALISM, FETISHISM, SORCERY AND WITCHCRAFT.

SOUMIALOT, GASTON. A central figure in the eastern **rebellion** of 1964-65, Soumialot in January 1964 began recruiting young Congolese and **Tutsi** exiles from **Rwanda** and organized them into a fighting force that later came to be called **Simbas**. He launched an offensive in early 1964 that led to the capture of a number of towns in **Kivu** and north **Katanga** and culminated in the taking of **Stanleyville** in August and **Lisala** a few weeks later. By September, Soumialot's forces controlled nearly one-half of Congolese territory. However, their inability to administer the captured territory and growing abuse of local populations led to a decline in popular support. The Congolese **armed forces**, backed by foreign **mercenaries**, launched an offensive which, with the airdrop of Belgian forces on Stanleyville in November 1964, known as "Operation Dragon Rouge," reduced the rebellion to small pockets of resistance by the end of the year. Soumialot sought exile in **Egypt**.

SOUTH AFRICA, RELATIONS WITH. During the years following **independence**, Congo was not in the forefront of the international movement to ostracize South Africa because of the white-led government's policy of apartheid, or racial separateness. Zaire often abstained on **United Nations** resolutions condemning the Pretoria government and did not support the move to expel South Africa from the organization in 1975. However, **Mobutu** condemned the apartheid regime in a speech before the world body in 1973 and, from the late 1970s until the late 1980s, Zaire voted with the African bloc on most anti-South African resolutions at the United Nations and the **Organization of African Unity**. Mobutu also hosted a meeting of southern Africa's frontline states in **Gbadolite** in November 1986.

Nevertheless, Zaire and South Africa found themselves in the same camp on many geopolitical issues. Both governments strongly condemned the **Cuban** and **Soviet Union** presence in Africa, particularly in **Angola** where, during the civil war, they opposed the **Movimento Popular de Libertação de Angola (MPLA)** faction which took power in Luanda in 1975. And they both opposed the resolution at the UN General Assembly equating Zionism with racism.

Despite Zaire's official condemnation of apartheid, it was pragmatic on trade. A primary example was in the **transportation** sector. After the **Benguela Railway** was closed in 1975 by Angola's civil war, as much as one-half of the Zaire's **mineral exports** were shipped through Zimbabwe to the South African port of Durban along the **Southern Way**. The practice continued into the 1990s because of the deterioration of the **National Way** network of **roads** and **railways** within Zaire. During the 1980s, unofficial commercial ties developed, particularly the **import** of South African food and export of Zairian minerals. By the late 1980s, food products from South Africa were found on most grocery shelves in Zairian cities.

On October 1, 1988, then-President Pieter Botha visited Mobutu in Gbadolite. And beginning in 1989, with the dismantling of apartheid, official relations improved and South Africa became an increasingly important trading partner. Zaire exported **coffee**, **timber** and minerals to South Africa and imported South African food, machinery and spare parts. Airline routes developed between **Kinshasa**, **Lubumbashi** and Johannesburg. And a sizable Zairian business community established itself in South Africa.

With the advent of majority-rule in South Africa and the election of Nelson Mandela as president, relations were further enhanced. South African companies entered into a number of joint ventures to rehabilitate mines and transportation networks in Congo/Zaire. Military ties which had been kept secret were enhanced and South African military officers trained elements of the **Division Spéciale Présidentielle (DSP)**, the presidential guard, in **Shaba**. In addition, Mandela hosted mediation talks in May 1997 on a South African ship at Pointe-Noire, **Republic of the Congo**, as forces led by Laurent **Kabila** advanced on Kinshasa in their drive to overthrow the Mobutu government. In June, the South African government announced it was donating $300,000 worth of equipment to help the Kabila government rebuild the **police** force which had been abolished under Mobutu. When the Kabila government was attacked by rebels in August 1998, South Africa remained neutral—unlike several of its neighbors, which supported Kabila militarily—and tried to mediate the conflict.

SOUTH KASAI. The southern **region** of the former province of **Kasai**. At **independence**, ethnic rivalry between the **Luba** and **Lulua** in

SOUTHERN WAY / 395

Kasai and between the Luba and **Lunda** in **Katanga** drove many Luba into South Kasai, tripling its **population** between 1958 and 1963. The presence of large **mineral** deposits, including two-thirds of the noncommunist world's industrial **diamonds**, contributed to the pressures for independence that led Albert **Kalonji** to proclaim the "Independent Mining State of South Kasai" on August 8, 1960. The secession was ended on February 2, 1961, when Kalonji joined the Cyrille **Adoula** government-of-reconciliation. Ethnic tensions remained in the region, however, and the **government** responded to these pressures in 1972 by creating two provinces (later renamed regions), **Kasaï Occidental** dominated by the Lulua, and **Kasaï Oriental** dominated by the Luba. See also Rebellions.

SOUTHERN WAY. The second most economic way to **export** Congo/Zaire's **minerals** from **Katanga Province**, after the **Benguela Railway**. The 3,500-km route traverses **Zambia**, Zimbabwe and **South Africa** to the ports of Durban, East London and Port Elizabeth. Although longer than the more politically favored **National Way**, the route takes less than one-half of the time, about 30 days. During the late 1980s, the Southern Way was used to transport nearly one-half of Katanga's minerals. Use reportedly increased in the 1990s with the deterioration of the **river** and **railway** networks along the National Way.

SOVEREIGN NATIONAL CONFERENCE. See CONFÉRENCE NATIONALE SOUVERAINE (CNS).

SOVIET UNION, RELATIONS WITH. Relations between **Congo/Zaire** and the Soviet Union generally were cool after **independence** and occasionally hostile. The Soviet government viewed the **government** of Congo/Zaire as a Western puppet and the Congolese government saw the Soviet Union as a supporter of local **dissidents** and certain hostile neighbors. Diplomatic relations were established at independence and shortly thereafter Prime Minister Patrice **Lumumba** threatened to ask for Soviet military assistance to help put down the Congo secessions. This threat was one of the reasons for his dismissal by President Joseph **Kasavubu** in 1960, leading to the first constitutional crisis. When **Mobutu** "neutralized" the Kasavubu-Lumumba government on

September 5, 1960, he gave Soviet diplomats 48 hours to leave the country. A low-level mission returned a few years later, only to be expelled by the Moïse **Tshombe** government, which accused it of complicity in the Pierre **Mulele** uprising in **Kwilu**. The Soviet Union criticized Mobutu's **coup d'etat** in 1965 but later moderated its policies when Mobutu adopted nationalistic and nonaligned positions. Relations were normalized in 1967 and ambassadors were exchanged in 1968. However, Soviet diplomats were again expelled in 1970 and 1971 after being accused of encouraging **student** unrest.

Relations were further strained in the 1970s by Soviet support for the **Movimento Popular de Libertação de Angola (MPLA)** faction in **Angola**, which· Zaire opposed, and by suspicion of Soviet responsibility in the **Shaba** invasions of 1977 and 1978 by guerrillas based in Angola. Relations remained cool in the early 1980s. No Soviet representative was invited to the extensive inauguration ceremonies of Mobutu's third presidential term in December 1984. However, a Soviet trade delegation paid a 10-day visit to **Kinshasa** in March 1985 and Soviet officials announced their desire to increase cooperation in the areas of **mining, health care, energy** and fish processing. They said during the visit that Soviet **exports** to Zaire reached $10 million in 1984, four times the level of **trade** the year before. Zairian exports to the Soviet Union historically were negligible.

The collapse of the Soviet Union in December 1991 caused the suspension of most Soviet aid programs in Africa and a significant reduction of the Russian diplomatic presence in all but its closest allies on the continent.

SPECIAL PRESIDENTIAL DIVISION. *See* DIVISION SPÉCIALE PRÉSIDENTIELLE (DSP).

SPEKE, JOHN (1827 - 1864). An English **explorer** who traveled with Richard **Burton** in East Africa and reached **Lake Tanganyika** in 1858. Speke is credited with being the first European to reach the source of the White Nile on **Lake Albert** near Jinja in 1862.

SPIRITUALISM, FETISHISM, SORCERY AND WITCHCRAFT. Many Congolese, like many other Africans, are deeply mystical and some of their traditional rites and beliefs, often called "superstitions" by Westerners, have been borne by the diaspora to Europe, the Middle East and the Americas. The beliefs, sometimes called witchcraft but which would perhaps better be characterized as spiritualism, frequently coexist with equally deep, religious beliefs in **Christianity, Islam** or African adaptations of monotheistic religions, such as **Kimbanguism**. The beliefs range from the honoring and consulting of one's ancestors, to the wearing of protective talismans and the consultation of practitioners to obtain one's wishes or to seek protection from enemies. Ethnographers have observed that beliefs vary from tribe to tribe and even from **clan** to clan within specific **ethnic groups**.

In most **societies** of Congo/Zaire, the spiritual world is often based on one supreme god supported by lesser and subordinate gods, or spirits, and ancestors. The lesser spiritual beings sometimes may communicate with the living, thus providing a link between those in what is considered to be the temporary existence that is life and those in the eternal existence that precedes and follows life. The spirits may be contacted at times by individuals and sometimes with the help of diviners or intermediaries.

Practitioners who invoke the spirits for malevolent purposes, or in some cases to deflect evil from a client to another person, are often called witches or sorcerers. Others who seek the help of the spirits for benign purposes are often called **healers** or physicians. The terms, however, are often interchangeable and since many of the practitioners use tangible items such as fetishes or talismans in their rituals, they are sometimes called fetishists.

SPORTS. As in most countries, sports are popular in Congo/Zaire and closely followed by a large segment of the population. The **government** encourages the development of sports activities and often provides funds for teams and sporting events. Soccer, or football, is considered the national sport, with numerous professional and amateur groups competing at the national and regional level. Boxing, track and field, and, to a lesser degree, basketball, handball and volleyball are also popular. Other activities primarily for the wealthy include motorcycle racing and auto rallying. Historically the country sent a relatively large contingent of athletes to the Olympic Games and to African competitions, although the presence was reduced in the 1990s because of the government's financial problems. Congo/Zaire was one of a dozen African nations that boycotted the 1980 Olympics in Moscow because of the **Soviet** incursion into Afghanistan. It banned sporting ties with **South Africa** until 1990 because of the latter's apartheid policies. The sporting event in the country that drew the most international attention was the world heavyweight boxing championship fight between Mohammed Ali and George Foreman in **Kinshasa** on October 30, 1974.

STANLEY FALLS. The name given during the **colonial era** to the cataracts on the **Congo River** between Ubundu and **Kisangani**, where Henry Morton **Stanley** began his voyage down the Congo River.

STANLEY, HENRY MORTON (1841 - 1904). The journalist-**explorer** who, as a star reporter for the *New York Herald* newspaper, led an expedition into central Africa to find missionary/explorer David **Livingstone** and later explored the **Congo River** for **Belgium**'s King **Leopold II**. Stanley was born in Denbigh, Wales, in 1841. He went to America at an early age, was naturalized a US citizen and later went to work for James Gordon Bennet, Jr., at the *Herald*. He was sent to central Africa in October 1869 on an unlimited budget to find Livingstone, who had not been heard from in two years. Stanley began his trip in March 1871 from Zanzibar. He arrived at the shores of **Lake Tanganyika** later in the year and finally met Livingstone at **Ujiji** on October 28, 1871, with the famous words, "Dr. Livingstone, I presume."

During the trip, he became interested in proving that the **Lualaba River**, which many thought to be the headwater of the Nile, was in fact the headwater of the Congo River, of which little was known. Following Livingstone's death, Stanley set out again to discover the source of the Congo River, the mouth of which had been known to Europeans since the late 15th century. He began in Zanzibar in September 1874. After mapping Lake Victoria and Lake Tanganyika and marching across the **Maniema Forest**, he reached the headwaters of the Congo River at the confluence of the Luama and Lualaba Rivers on October 17, 1876. He sailed down the river to prove the headwaters were indeed those of the Congo River and reached **Kinshasa** on March 9, 1877. After a grueling crossing of the **Crystal Mountains**, he reached **Boma** on August 9, 1877, 999 days after leaving Zanzibar.

In 1878, Stanley was hired by Leopold II to chart and open up the Congo for trade. He left in January 1879 and arrived on August 14, 1879, at **Vivi**, across the river from what is **Matadi** today. From his base at Vivi, he worked his way up the river, building a **road** and establishing trading stations. He reached Stanley Pool (now **Malebo Pool**) at Kinshasa in mid-1881 and negotiated a treaty with the **king** of Ngaliema on the pool's southern bank. Count Pierre Savorgnan de Brazza beat Stanley to the northern bank, and signed a treaty between **France** and the local chief on that side of the river, leading the French to claim what would become **Republic of the Congo**. The road to Vivi was completed by the end of 1881 and Stanley left for Europe.

He returned in December 1882 and sailed up the Congo River to **Stanleyville** (now **Kisangani**), signing more than 450 treaties with local chiefs in the name of Leopold II. Stanley made a final voyage in 1887, ostensibly to rescue a British garrison under siege at Juba, southern **Sudan**, by the forces of the **Mahdi**. The trip lasted three years, but the expedition never reached Juba.

Stanley is credited with opening up the Congo River from Kinshasa to Kisangani to European **trade** and with establishing the treaties with local tribes which Leopold used to take control of most of the **Congo River Basin** when Africa was partitioned among the European powers at the **Berlin Conference** in 1885.

STANLEYVILLE. The name of the trading station that became the major city of northeastern Congo and later the capital of **Orientale Province**. It was established by Henry Morton **Stanley** at the point furthest up the navigable portion of the lower **Congo River**. During the **colonial era**, it was a prosperous trading center, serving the plantations and **timber** mills in the region. It also was a center for the **gold** and **diamond** trade with East Africa. Stanleyville was a center of **opposition** to the central **government** in the 1960s and the seat of the secessionist **People's Republic of the Congo** in 1961 during the eastern **rebellions**. The city was renamed **Kisangani** in 1966. *See also* Stanleyville Secession.

STANLEYVILLE SECESSION. The secession officially began in the capital of northeastern **Orientale Province** on September 7, 1964.

It was ended in 1965, following the deaths of tens of thousands of Congolese and hundreds of foreigners, and a US-supported, Belgian paratroop drop on **Stanleyville**. The troubles, however, began much earlier and lasted much longer. The secession was the most visible outburst of long-standing feelings of disenfranchisement in a remote region that historically held greater ties to the **Great Rift Valley** and East Africa than to **Leopoldville** and the West African coast.

The first break with the central government began as a **rebellion** on November 19, 1960, following the dismissal of Prime Minister Patrice **Lumumba** by President Joseph **Kasavubu** and the vote at the **United Nations** on November 10 to seat the Kasavubu delegation over the rival Lumumba one. Following the death of Lumumba, announced on February 13, 1961, Antoine **Gizenga**, vice president of the Lumumba wing of the **Mouvement National Congolais (MNC)**, announced the formation of a rival government in Stanleyville. Gizenga refused to join the Cyrille **Adoula** government of reconciliation and was arrested in 1962. He was freed from prison in 1964 and returned to Stanleyville. There, he declared the **People's Republic of the Congo**, which was recognized by 13 countries including the **Soviet Union** and **China**. The Stanleyville government at one time controlled nearly two-thirds of Congolese territory and was recognized by the major nations of the Communist bloc.

The excesses of the Gizenga regime, which included atrocities against the local population and the taking of 2,800 foreign hostages, led to a military intervention in which Belgian paratroopers, using US transport planes, dropped on Stanleyville and Paulis on November 24, 1964. The operation launched an offensive by the Congolese **armed forces** that drove the Gizenga forces out of the region in 1965.

STEEL. Zaire's only steel mill is the **Maluku Steel Mill**, located 100 km upriver from **Kinshasa**. Construction was begun in 1972 with financing largely from German and Italian investors. Production began in 1974 with a capacity of 250,000 metric tons per year using a labor force of 1,250 workers at full production. However, the mill was beset with supply and maintenance problems from the beginning and never operated above 10 percent of capacity. It ceased operations in the 1980s.

STRIKES. Congo/Zaire's **labor** movement historically has been weak and during single-party rule, the sole legal trade union, the Union Nationale des Travailleurs Zaïrois (UNTZA), was part of the **Mouvement Populaire de la Révolution (MPR)** party. The Zairian **government** frequently co-opted labor leaders by appointing them to well-paying political positions. When co-option did not succeed, threats, dismissals and force were used. During the 1970s and 1980s, teachers and **civil servants** struck on numerous occasions over low pay, but these strikes were largely ineffective. With the advent of the **democratic transition** in 1990, UNTZA lost its monopoly over the labor movement and more than one dozen trade unions were formed. Civil servants staged lengthy strikes during the 1990s to demand increases in **wages and salaries** whose purchasing power had been seriously eroded by **inflation**. Medical workers in public hospitals staged strikes to protest working conditions. And the **Sacred Union opposition** alliance on a number of occasions paralyzed **Kinshasa** with "*ville morte*" ("dead city") general strikes to apply pressure during the frequent political stalemates between the opposition and the **Mobutu** government. *See also* Union Nationale des Travailleurs Congolais (UNTC).

STUDENTS. Students, particularly **university** students, have often played a political role in Congo/Zaire, whether supporting the **government** during the "revolutionary" days following the **Mobutu coup d'etat** or criticizing the government in the years that followed. Students exerted little influence during the early years following **independence**, but by the mid-1960s they had organized into associations and formed important blocs in certain **political parties**. Many supported Patrice **Lumumba** and were deeply angered by his assassination in 1961. By 1968, two major student organizations had emerged: the **Union Générale des Étudiants Congolais (UGEC)**, with branches on all three campuses and in **Belgium**, and the Association Générale des Étudiants de Lovanium (AGEL), based at **Lovanium University** in **Kinshasa**.

Both were disbanded by the government in 1968 and the **Jeunesse du Mouvement Populaire de la Révolution (JMPR)** wing of the party was proclaimed the only legal **youth** organization. One of the major responsibilities of the JMPR was student mobilization. Many students at first supported Mobutu and opposed Moïse **Tshombe**, whom they linked with the **Katanga secession, mercenaries** and the assassination of Lumumba. They also supported Mobutu's policies of combating tribalism and regionalism and strengthening the authority of the central government. In subsequent years, however, disenchantment grew with the Mobutu government because of mismanagement, declining government support for **education**, the president's growing personal fortune, and his close ties to the **United States** government. Students demonstrated against the visit to Congo/Kinshasa by US Vice President Hubert Humphrey in January 1968.

On June 4, 1969, students at Lovanium demonstrated against low stipends and what they considered to be extravagant government spending. Hundreds of them marched from the campus into the downtown area, breaking through several **police** and military roadblocks. The troops opened fire. Estimates of the number of students killed varied from 40 to 100 although official figures were never published. Thirty-four students were arrested and charged with subversive activities. A number of them fled the country and were given asylum in Bulgaria. Many were tried and given sentences of up to 20 years in prison. They were amnestied on October 14th.

On June 4, 1971, students demonstrating at Lovanium and **Lubumbashi** campuses in memory of the 1969 victims again clashed with security forces. The universities were closed and student leaders were inducted into the **armed forces**. The event was to be repeated in 1977, 1981 and 1982. Following the protests of 1971, a single, national university called the **Université Nationale du Zaïre (UNAZA)**, was created from the three private universities at Lovanium, Lubumbashi and **Kisangani**. On the night of **May 11-12, 1990**, elements of the **Division Spéciale Présidentielle (DSP)** presidential guard entered UNAZA's Lubumbashi campus and attacked students in their dormitories. **Human rights** groups said that between 30 and 100 students were killed. The government claimed that only one died. The incident led to a cutoff of non-humanitarian aid to Zaire by the **European Union**, Canada and the United States.

Students were among the protesters who demonstrated against Laurent **Kabila** in June 1997, after his forces took power in Kinshasa and he declined to name Étienne **Tshisekedi** to his new government.

SUCCESSION. The succession of leadership in most traditional **societies** of Congo/Zaire was delicate and usually occurred upon the death or incapacitation of the **chief**. In some groups, the chief named his own successor on his deathbed. In others, a new chief was chosen by heredity, through consultations with the elders, or by some form of competition.

Under the **Loi Fondamentale** and the **constitution** of 1964, the question of succession of the country's leadership was to be settled by national **elections**. Following the **Mobutu coup d'etat** and during the era of single-party rule, however, it became a topic of possibly dangerous speculation.

The constitution of 1974, which institutionalized the party-state, made provision for the **president** of the republic to be dismissed for deviating from the doctrine of **Mobutism**, but made it impossible to dismiss Mobutu himself as party leader. If the presidency fell vacant, the oldest political commissioner (usually a member of the **Political Bureau**) would assume the office temporarily. The Political Bureau would then set a date for elections to be held within 60 days and would nominate the sole candidate. However, it was clear that Mobutu, by the manner in which he regularly reshuffled his cabinet and purged the senior ranks of the military, intended to govern until his death.

The announcement of the **democratic transition** in April 1990 introduced the possibility that Mobutu could be replaced through national elections and, as a result, a more immediate struggle was launched by the **opposition** to ensure free and fair elections would be held under impartial supervision. This goal was frustrated by obstruction from Mobutu and infighting among opposition **political parties**. The **Haut Conseil de la République / Parlement de la Transition (HCR/PT)** addressed the question of succession in its draft constitution, which called for the president of the Legislative Assembly to assume the presidency temporarily until multiparty elections could be organized.

A referendum on the constitution, however, had yet to be organized when the **Alliance des Forces Démocratiques pour la**

Libération du Congo/Zaïre (AFDL) seized control of the country in May 1997 and installed Laurent **Kabila** as president. Kabila pledged to organize a constitutional referendum by 1998 and hold free elections by 1999, but his government's suspension of political parties and demonstrations and its obstruction of a **United Nations** investigation into massacres in eastern Congo/Zaire did not presage an administration of transparency and civil liberty. For Mobutu, who fled into exile the day before the AFDL arrived in Kinshasa and died of cancer in **Morocco** four months later, the question of succession had been settled, though not for the nation he had dominated for more than three decades and not by constitutional means.

SUDAN, RELATIONS WITH. Relations between **Congo/Zaire** and Sudan were good until 1985, in large part because of the friendship between **Mobutu** and President Gafaar al Nimeiry and their mutual dislike for **Libyan** leader Muammar Khadhafi. Relations cooled after the overthrow of Nimeiry in 1985 and further deteriorated with the advent of the radical Islamic regime of Omar al-Bashir in a coup d'etat in 1989. The civil war in southern Sudan, waged at various levels of intensity from the early 1950s, complicated relations. The **Kinshasa government** historically provided refuge to southern Sudanese fleeing the fighting and supported guerrillas of the Sudan People's Liberation Army. When relations with the government in Khartoum were good, Mobutu tried to mediate the war. In the 1990s, however, reports of atrocities by the Sudanese army against southern civilians and increased activity by Iran in Sudan aggravated relations. Sudan initially was cool toward the Laurent **Kabila** government when it came to power in 1997, because of Khartoum's poor relations with **Uganda**, one of Kabila's main backers. However, it began to support Kabila diplomatically in 1998, after Uganda backed rebels of the **Rassemblement Congolais pour la Démocratie (RCD).**

SUD-KIVU. A **province** in eastern Congo/Zaire that was a subregion of **Kivu Region** until 1988, Sud-Kivu covers an area of 64,789 square km, primarily of heavy **forest**. With an estimated **population** of more than two million in 1994, it is one of the most densely populated regions of the country. The area around the capital of **Bukavu** was overwhelmed in 1994 by an influx of more than 200,000 **refugees** from **Rwanda**'s civil war. The region was the first to be seized by troops of the **Alliance des Forces Démocratiques pour la Libération du Congo/Zaïre (AFDL)** in October 1996 and by forces of the **Rassemblement Congolais pour la Démocratie (RCD)** two years later.

SUGAR. Sugar cane is grown commercially in central **Bas-Congo** and the **Ruzizi River** valley in **Kivu**, an industry that in the 1980s employed 2,500 persons. Production of raw sugar cane, one of the country's major cash **crops**, peaked in 1975 at 614,000 metric tons, declined in subsequent years but began to rise again in the 1980s, reaching 550,000 tons in 1985. Production of refined sugar reached 80,000 tons in 1985. However, **imports** were still required to meet annual consumption of 150,000 tons.

Production began on a commercial scale in 1925 and the first sugar refinery, Moerbek, was built in 1929 in Bas-Congo with an initial capacity of 7,000 tons in 1930, expanded to 40,000 tons in the 1980s. In 1956, a second sugar refinery called Sucrerie et Raffinerie de l'Afrique Centrale (SUCRAF) was created at Klibi in southern Kivu and produced 15,000 tons in 1985. With **Zairianization**, both refineries were grouped under the **Office National du Sucre (ONS)**. However, they were returned to their private owners under **Retrocession**. The ONS was liquidated on May 5, 1978, and the **Projets Sucriers au Zaïre (PSZ)** was established on May 8 to oversee the industry and promote the development of new projects. A third refinery was established under a joint Zairian-**Chinese** venture in 1984 in Yawenda, **Haut-Zaïre** Region, with a planned capacity of 15,000 tons per year. It produced 3,000 tons in 1985. In 1985, the PSZ announced plans to construct four additional refineries: at Mushie-Pentane near **Bandundu**; at Lubilashi in **Shaba** Region; at Luiza in **Bas-Zaïre**; and at Businga in **Équateur** Region. Each refinery was to have an annual production capacity of 15,000 tons.

SUKU. A subgroup of the **Yaka** living in southwestern Congo/Zaire north of Feshi between the Inzia and **Kwilu Rivers**.

SUPREME COURT. *See* JUDICIAL SYSTEM.

SWITZERLAND, RELATIONS WITH. Relations between **Congo/Zaire** and Switzerland have been primarily commercial. Diplomatic relations normally have been correct but were strained in November 1985 when 53 Zairians and six Angolans were deported from Switzerland after local authorities discovered they had applied for political asylum under false identities. Upon their arrival in Zaire, many of the deportees were hospitalized and a number of them reportedly died. Swiss newspapers said the deportees were beaten by Zairian authorities. However, the Zairian **government** said they had been mistreated by Swiss police.

- T -

TANANARIVE CONFERENCE. A conference between various Congolese factions in March 1961 in the capital of Madagascar. The conference adopted a resolution calling for a confederal system of **government** in the Congo. Opposition from the central government in **Leopoldville** led to the **Coquilhatville Conference** in **Équateur Province** in April and May. The Coquilhatville Conference renounced confederalism and called for a **federal** system of government. Neither conference, however, came up with a system of government that was acceptable to the various secessionist groups. After extensive negotiations, **parliament** met in Leopoldville on August 2, with representatives from **Katanga** and **South Kasai** present, and elected Cyrille **Adoula** to head a government of national reconciliation. It would be several more years before the secessions and **rebellions** of the post-**independence** period were ended.

TANGANYIKA, LAKE. *See* LAKE TANGANYIKA.

TANZANIA, RELATIONS WITH. Relations between **Congo/Zaire** and Tanzania officially have been good. During the **Mobutu** era, however, they were strained repeatedly by suspicions in the **government** in **Kinshasa** that Tanzania harbored **opposition** guerrillas. In mid-1975, guerrillas of the **Parti Révolutionnaire du Peuple (PRP)** kidnapped a group of foreign students from a game preserve in Tanzania and held them in eastern Zaire for a number of weeks. In November 1984, the PRP attacked the Zairian port city of **Moba** on **Lake Tanganyika** and held it for two days before government troops recaptured it. The guerrillas attacked Moba again in June 1985 in a less successful action. Zairian authorities said the guerrillas were based in Tanzania and threatened to carry out "hot pursuit" raids into Tanzania if they attacked again. Tanzania denied the charges, saying the guerrillas were based entirely within Zaire.

The poor relations of this period were also blamed in part on personal relations between Mobutu and Tanzanian President Julius **Nyerere**. Nyerere, with his **socialist** policies, friendship with Eastern bloc nations and unassuming lifestyle, differed markedly from Mobutu. When Nyerere retired in 1985, Vice President Ali Hassan **Mwinyi** was elected president of Tanzania. Relations improved markedly, especially after Mwinyi said his government would not allow its territory to be used to destabilize its neighbors. In the 1990s, Mwinyi and Mobutu sought to mediate the civil wars in **Rwanda**, **Burundi** and **Angola**, further reinforcing diplomatic cooperation between their two governments.

Mwinyi was succeeded by Benjamin Mkapa in 1995, who continued the policies of friendship and cooperation and sought to mediate the conflict in eastern Zaire.

In October 1996, the PRP joined the **Alliance des Forces Démocratiques pour la Libération du Congo/Zaïre (AFDL)**, which took Kinshasa in May 1997. Fighters involved in the AFDL offensive were from a number of neighboring countries, including Rwanda, **Uganda** and Angola. There were reports that Tanzanians participated in the offensive, but involvement by the government was never substantiated. Tanzania sought to remain neutral when rebels of the **Rassemblement Congolais pour la Démocratie (RCD)** attacked the Kabila government in 1998.

TEACHERS. *See* EDUCATION.

TEKE. A **Bantu**-speaking people living on both sides of the **Congo River** between **Kinshasa** and the confluence of the **Kasai** and Congo Rivers. Widely believed to have entered the region as early as the 1600s, the Teke was one of the groups that made early contact with the Europeans, beginning with the arrival of

missionary Father de Montesarchio in 1652. They **traded** in tobacco and other **agricultural** goods but became heavily dependent on the **slave** trade in the 18th century. The Teke's traditional political structure has been described as a group of chiefdoms, each with several villages. The villages tended to be small and unstable and there was no centralized defense system. Chieftaincy was hereditary and one of the **chief**'s major duties was to collect tribute for the **king**, who was elected by the village elders and acted as the judicial authority.

TELECOMMUNICATIONS. In 1995, there were an estimated four million **radios** in **Zaire**, 40,000 television sets, 32,000 telephones and 200 telegraph offices. The **government**-operated telephone system was largely dysfunctional by then. However, a joint private US and Zairian company in June 1991 had launched a cellular telephone network in **Kinshasa** and several other cities. Called Telcel, it has 4,000 subscribers. Major humanitarian relief organizations and **missionary** groups operate their own high-frequency radio networks. By the mid-1990s, many businessmen had purchased their own personal **satellite** telephone systems.

A satellite station at N'Sele, linked by microwave towers to Kinshasa, 100 km away, and the **Voix du Peuple** (formerly the **Voix du Zaïre**) complex, provide telecommunications links with the outside world. The station allows the complex to transmit feeds to eight regional stations in **Matadi, Mbandaka, Kisangani, Lubumbashi, Bandundu, Kananga, Mbuji-Mayi** and **Bukavu**. Six other cities reportedly have television stations. Reception is also possible in Kinshasa of television and radio broadcasts from Brazzaville.

The Voix du Zaïre complex was inaugurated on November 24, 1976, and broadcasts in French and the four national **languages**: Kikongo, **Lingala**, Swahili and Tshiluba. The regional stations broadcast in other local languages as well. In the 1990s, the Voix du Zaïre began to receive television and radio feeds primarily from Europe, which it rebroadcast to subscribers. By the 1990s, wealthy residents had purchased satellite dishes and received a variety of direct transmissions from around the world.

Government control of the **news media** historically has been heavy. The print media was liberalized in 1990, although arrests of journalists and attacks on newspapers that overly criticized the government continue to occur. Private broadcasting stations were allowed in 1995 and within two years nearly two dozen stations were in operation. Several private stations began rebroadcasting international stations such as the Voice of America, British Broadcasting Corporation and Radio France Internationale. Pressure continues on radio and television, nevertheless, to avoid antigovernment reporting and rebroadcasts of international stations were briefly prohibited in late 1997.

TELEVISION. *See* TELECOMMUNICATIONS.

TEMBO. A small **ethnic group** living in eastern Congo/Zaire that fought the **Banyarwanda** during the 1990s. *See also* Ethnic Cleansing.

TENKE. A small town in **Katanga Province**, east of **Likasi**, near an area where significant deposits of **copper** and **cobalt** have been found. *See also* Société Minière de Tenke-Fungurume.

TERRITORIAL POLICE. A **police** force formed during the **colonial era**, consisting of about 6,000 men, armed and uniformed, who guarded prisons and public buildings and provided reinforcements to the police when called upon. The force was disbanded following **Mobutu's coup d'etat** in 1965.

TERRITORIAL SERVICE TROOPS. *See* TROUPES EN SERVICE TERRITORIAL (TST).

TERRITORIAL WATERS. Congo/Zaire claims territorial waters extending 12 nautical miles out to sea along its 35-km-long coastline, and an economic zone extending 200 km from the coast. There are offshore **petroleum** deposits and **fishing**, but little other commercial activity in these waters.

TETELA. A **Bantu**-speaking group living between Lusambo and the upper **Congo River** in Sankuru District of **Kasaï Oriental** and **Maniema Provinces**. Ethnologists view the Tetela and **Kusu** as closely related to each other and as distant members of the **Mongo** cluster. The Tetela began to be viewed as a distinct group in the late 1800s with the arrival of the **Afro-Arabs** from the east and the Europeans from the west and south. The Tetela, living in **Kasai**, had less contact with the Afro-Arabs than the Kusu, who in some cases adopted Muslim religion and dress. Belgian colonial authorities separated the two groups when they divided the area into Kasai and **Kivu** Provinces. Patrice **Lumumba** was a Tetela who tried unsuccessfully to unite his people with the Kusu. The Tetela reportedly were the object of a major purge within the **armed forces** in 1975.

THANT, U (1907 - 1974). The Burmese diplomat who became secretary-general of the **United Nations** following the death of Dag **Hammarskjöld** in a plane accident in **Katanga** on September 17, 1961, while trying to mediate an end to the **Katanga Secession**. Thant announced a new plan to end the secession on August 10, 1962. However, lack of progress led to the seizure by UN troops of important Katangan installations on December 28 and the announcement by Moïse **Tshombe** of the end of the secession on January 14, 1963. Thant oversaw the final three years of the UN administration in the Congo. He was replaced by Kurt Waldheim of Austria in 1972.

THEATER. Theatrical arts are vibrant in Congo/Zaire, particularly in **Kinshasa**, where dozens of theater groups flourished even during the recession of the 1970s and 1980s and the **hyperinflation** of the 1990s. Schools, **universities**, and religious and social organizations are major sponsors of acting troupes. Neighborhoods and friends in the artistic community also sponsor plays. Some plays are produced from the domain of international theater but many are written by local playwrights. Writers and producers frequently draw on traditional theater, using African storytelling techniques such as the *griot* or narrator, dream and fantasy sequences, and singing and dancing with drums and musical instruments in the background. The government-sponsored Theatre National (National Theater) tours nationally and internationally.

TIMBER. In the 1990s, Congo/Zaire produced an average of 400,000 cubic meters of timber per year, of which an average of 150,000 cubic meters was exported, according to official figures. The lumber comes primarily from the **Mayombe Forest** in western

Bas-Congo (formerly **Bas-Zaïre**). The remainder comes from the eastern part of the country and is usually exported by road through East Africa. Relatively little of the 1.2 million square km of Zairian forests had been exploited by the mid-1990s. Nevertheless, **environmental** groups place them at risk because timber concessions signed by private companies and the **Mobutu** government cover one-third of the country's forests.

TIN. In the 1940s, the **Belgian Congo** was the second-largest producer of tin in the world, after Bolivia; it produced 14,000 metric tons of the mineral in 1942. Tin in deposits of cassiterite were found primarily along the southern side of the **Lualaba River** in southern **Katanga** and in **Kivu** east of **Bukavu**. A survey by the Bureau de Recherches Géologiques et Minières (BRGM) under a 1969 agreement with the Congolese **government** uncovered estimated reserves of 600,000 metric tons. Beginning in the late 1970s, however, production declined steadily due to low prices and the exhaustion of easily mined deposits. Output of tin contained in ore and concentrate was 3,000 tons in 1983, but declined to 1,600 tons by 1990. Smelter production was 150 tons.

In **Shaba Region** during the 1970s and 1980s, tin was mined by **ZAÏRÉTAIN**, a joint venture that was 50 percent owned by the government and 50 percent by the Belgian GEOMINES company, which operated the mine. Other companies with operations in Shaba in the 1980s included the **Générale des Carrières et des Mines (GECAMINES)** and the Entreprises Minières du Zaïre (EMZ) of mixed ownership. In Kivu, tin deposits were mined by EMZ, Société Minière de Katando (SOMIDO), **Société Minière et Industrielle du Kivu (SOMINKI)** and the Société Minière de Goma, all of mixed public and private ownership. The major deposits in Kivu were located at Manono, Kalimbi and Katondo. By the 1990s, production had virtually ceased and most of the companies were closed.

TIO KINGDOM. A relatively small kingdom established along both sides of the **Malebo Pool** as early as the 16th century. Relatively friendly and anxious to **trade**, the Tio **kings** signed agreements with Henry Morton **Stanley** and Count Savorgnan de Brazza which led to the rapid development of **Leopoldville** and

Brazzaville as the capitals of the Belgian and French colonial empires in central Africa.

TIPPO TIB. The most famous and perhaps most powerful of the **Afro-Arab** traders, whose kingdom at its peak in the late 1800s stretched from **Lake Tanganyika** to central Congo and reputedly employed more than 4,000 agents. Tippo Tib traded primarily in **slaves** and **ivory** taken in raids or purchased from marauding tribes, exchanged for **cloth**, guns and manufactured goods. Tippo Tib came to be regarded as the virtual ruler of eastern Congo and for a brief time was appointed governor of **Orientale Province** by **Leopold II**. However, harassment by the colonial authorities seeking to combat slavery and extend their control into eastern Congo caused Tippo Tib's influence to wane. A protracted war began in the 1880s which drove him and his agents from the region by 1894.

TOGO, RELATIONS WITH. Relations between **Congo/Zaire** and Togo were close from 1967, when Gen. Gnassingbe Eyadema came to power in a coup d'etat. Eyadema was one of the first African leaders to embrace **Mobutu's Authenticity** program and also imitated in many ways the Zairian president's personality cult. Togo under Eyadema traditionally sided with Zaire, Côte d'Ivoire, Cameroon, Senegal and other "moderates" on regional and international issues. Togo contributed troops to the Pan-African Peacekeeping Force sent to **Shaba** in 1978 following the Shaba invasions. During an attempted coup in Lomé in September 1986, the Zairian government sent airborne troops to bolster the Eyadema regime. When Mobutu fled **Kinshasa** on May 16, 1997, one day before the arrival of **opposition** forces led by Laurent **Kabila**, he went to Togo for five days, until **Morocco** granted him exile.

TOPOGRAPHY. **Congo/Zaire** covers a vast territory of 2,344,895 square km (905,365 square miles), the largest nation by territory in sub-Saharan Africa, the third largest in all of Africa and 80 times the size of **Belgium**. The country shares 9,165 km of border with nine countries: **Angola** on the southwest, **Zambia** to the south, **Tanzania**, **Burundi**, **Rwanda** and **Uganda** on the east, **Sudan** to the northeast, the **Central African Republic** to the north, and **Republic of the Congo** on the west and northwest. In addition, Congo/Zaire borders the Angolan enclave of **Cabinda** to the west near the mouth of the **Congo River.**

The country is considered a semienclave since it has only 37 km of coastline on the Atlantic Ocean, north of the mouth of the Congo River. The 4,300-km-long Congo River and its tributaries form the backbone of the national **transportation** infrastructure. They provide the major surface routes despite unnavigable cataracts above **Kisangani** and between **Kinshasa** and the deepwater **port** of **Matadi.** The country straddles the equator and the dry and wet seasons in the northern hemisphere (about one-third of the territory) are virtually opposite the seasons in the southern hemisphere. As a result, the Congo River flows at a relatively constant rate of 30,000 to 80,000 cubic meters per second, making it the second-largest flowing body of water in the world after the Amazon River.

Two-thirds of the territory lies in the low, sometimes marshy, tropical **rainforest** called the **Congo River Basin. Rainfall** in the basin is heavy at 180-220 cm per year. The topsoil of the basin is relatively poor for **agriculture** and the **population** is relatively sparse, as low as 1 person per square km. To the north and south lie high plains covered by savanna and woodlands. The southern high plains, lying primarily in **Katanga Province,** constitute about one-fourth of the total territory. To the east lie highlands bordering the **Great Rift Valley,** with **mountain** ranges rising as high as 5,000 meters. The **lakes** of the Great Rift Valley form part of Congo/Zaire's eastern border. The **eastern highlands** for the most part are covered with thick **forest,** but enjoy arable land and high rainfall, and as a result are relatively densely populated. In the west, between Kinshasa and **Boma,** lies the **Crystal Mountain** range and low-level plains containing land suitable for most farming and some **livestock** raising. From Boma to the Atlantic Ocean are low-lying grasslands and woodlands. *See also* Climate; Volcanoes.

TRADE. Trade was the major reason for the early European exploration and exploitation of Congo, although evangelization and social concerns were the primary motivation of **missionaries** arriving in the **Kongo Kingdom.** When the territory became the **Belgian Congo,** the Belgian government exerted considerable pressure on colonial administrators to balance expenditures for public works and **social services** with revenues from the colony's natural resources. As a result, large corporations were given incentives to invest in **mineral** and **agricultural** enterprises and small- and medium-sized entrepreneurs were allowed to operate with few restrictions.

As in most of colonial Africa, formal trade patterns were primarily with nations in Europe, particularly **Belgium, France, Germany,** and the **United Kingdom,** as well as with the **United States** and, later, **Japan.** These more-developed countries bought **copper, cobalt,** industrial **diamonds, uranium** and some agricultural products and in exchange marketed manufactured goods in the territory. Considerable informal trade also developed with the Congo's neighbors in such items as **cloth,** food and construction materials. These historical patterns continued after **independence.**

During the **Authenticity** period, efforts were made to promote trade with other African nations. The move toward intra-African trade was encouraged by the UN Economic Commission for Africa and the **Organization of African Unity,** which promoted regional trade organizations such as the **Communauté Économique des Pays des Grands Lacs (CEPGL),** the **Union Douanière et Économique de l'Afrique Centrale (UDEAC),** and the **Economic Community of Central African States (ECOCAS).** The government also subscribed to the nonaligned movement's policy of fostering trade with any nation. As a result, trade increased with other nations of Africa and the developing world, in particular, **Morocco, Republic of the Congo** and Brazil. Despite these policies, trade with developing nations in the 1990s remained a fraction of that with the larger economies of the world. *See also* Exports; Imports.

TRANSITIONAL ACT. The document adopted by the **Conférence Nationale Souveraine (CNS)** on August 15, 1992, to govern the nation during a two-year transition period until a new **constitution** could be drafted and national **elections** held. The act called for a figurehead **president,** a **parliament** called the **Haut Conseil de la République (HCR)** to oversee elections, a **prime minister** with full executive powers elected by the HCR, and an independent **judiciary.** The act incorporated the **Compromis Politique Global**

(Comprehensive Political Arrangement) of July 30, 1992, which stated that no institution of state could hinder another from exercising its functions. The reference was to the presidency and the military, but **Mobutu** never formally acknowledged this agreement. *See also* Democratic Transition.

TRANSPORTATION. The size and **topography** of Congo/Zaire, combined with its status as a virtual enclave, have hindered the development of efficient transportation routes. The country's 14,000 km of navigable **waterways** form the backbone of the system, most of which was built during the **colonial era.** Five thousand kilometers of **railways** (five separate systems) circumvent unnavigable portions of the **rivers** and link urban, **mining** and **agricultural** centers to the river and rail systems. Most of the railways were built between 1900 and 1932.

Most of the **roads** were constructed in the decade following World War II. The system deteriorated following **independence** and only two paved roads were constructed: between **Boma** and **Matadi** and between **Kikwit** and **Kinshasa.** In 1983, the Japanese government provided assistance in building a suspension bridge over the **Congo River** at Matadi that improved road links between the breadbasket Bas-Fleuve district and markets in Kinshasa.

Transportation was one of several sectors nationalized under **Zairianization** in 1973 and liberalized during **Retrocession** in 1975. In the 1980s, the Japanese and US governments launched bilateral programs to develop transportation in **Bandundu** and **Bas-Zaïre Regions.** Initial projects included building hundreds of concrete bridges to replace small ferries and log crossings. Ferries on larger rivers were to be refurbished. There were 362,800 **motor vehicles** registered in the country in 1990, of which 175,000 were commercial vehicles and 174,600 were registered in Kinshasa. On January 16, 1997, the **government** announced a reregistration program aimed at raising an estimated $300 million and recovering vehicles stolen during the **pillages** of 1991-93.

Liberalization of **air transportation** in the mid-1980s led to the creation of numerous private air carriers, which competed vigorously with each other and by 1990 had virtually supplanted the money-losing national carrier, **Air Zaïre,** which was reorganized as the **Lignes Aériennes Congolaises** in 1997. *See* *also* Benguela Railway; Eastern Way; National Way; Ports; Southern Way.

TRIBES AND TRIBALISM. *See* ETHNIC GROUPS; ETHNICITY.

TROUPES EN SERVICE TERRITORIAL (TST) / TERRITORIAL SERVICE TROOPS. The name of the **colonial-era police** force created after World War I. In 1959, the troops were renamed gendarmes and one year later were incorporated into the army. *See also* Armed Forces.

TSETSE FLY. A fly common to the wet, low-lying **forest** areas of the **Congo River Basin** that is a major carrier of the sleeping sickness **disease**. Because of the tsetse fly, commercial cattle herding in Congo/Zaire is limited primarily to the plains of **Katanga, Bas-Congo** and **Orientale Provinces**. *See also* Livestock.

TSHIKAPA. A city of about 100,000 inhabitants lying on the **Kasai River** in the heart of the **diamond mining** area of southern **Kasaï Occidental Province**. Many residents of Tshikapa dig and pan for diamonds in the alluvial deposits on the Kasai, Tshikapa, Lovua, Lonaishinie and Lubembe Rivers. In the past, competition for the diamonds sometimes led to clashes between local residents and soldiers who also worked the area. Liberalization of diamond trading in the 1980s and 1990s created an economic boom in the town.

TSHISEKEDI WA MULUMBA, ÉTIENNE (1932 -). One of the founders of the multiparty movement in 1980 who suffered various forms of detention during the 1980s and who, as president of the **Union pour la Démocratie et le Progrès Social (UDPS)**, party in the 1990s, was considered the major hardline opponent of **Mobutu**. Tshisekedi was born on December 14, 1932, in Luluabourg (renamed **Kananga** in 1966), eastern **Kasai Province**, and attended school there. He graduated from **Lovanium University** in 1961 with a degree in law, the first Congolese to do so. Following the Mobutu **coup d'etat**, he was named interior minister from 1965 until 1968, during which time he helped to draft the **N'Sele Manifesto** that was the Magna Carta of the **Mouvement Populaire de la Révolution (MPR)** and the single-party movement. He served as justice minister from 1968 until 1969, and subsequently as ambassador to **Morocco**, deputy-speaker of the **Legislative Council** and chairman of **Air Zaïre**.

In 1980, he was one of the **Group of Thirteen Parliamentarians** who wrote a 52-page open letter to Mobutu condemning **government corruption** and calling for the creation of a multiparty **democracy**. In 1982, he cofounded the UDPS, which in the single-party state was considered a seditious act. He was arrested, convicted of treason and in July 1982 sentenced to 15 years in prison. He was freed under the general **amnesty of 1983**, but when he tried to meet with a US congressional delegation at a major hotel in **Kinshasa** on August 12, 1983, he and other UDPS members were beaten by **security** forces, arrested and banished to their home regions. He was detained and released on a half-dozen subsequent occasions. He was in detention on **April 24, 1990**, when Mobutu announced the end of single-party rule, and he was quickly freed.

The UDPS was one of the first **political parties** to apply for registration and was one of the founders of the **Sacred Union** alliance which, by 1991, grouped more than 200 **opposition** parties. Tshisekedi led the struggle to wrest control of the **democratic transition** from Mobutu and the government. During periods of political stalemate, the UDPS pressed its agenda through **strikes** and acts of civil disobedience and its members were attacked on numerous occasions by security forces. Tshisekedi's residence in the Kinshasa suburb of Limété was attacked on several occasions.

On August 15, 1992, after a year of confrontation and stalemate, the **Conférence Nationale Souveraine** elected Tshisekedi **prime minister**. In December, it adopted the **Transitional Act**, drafted a **constitution**, and formed the **Haut Conseil de la République (HCR)** to oversee the democratic transition. The draft constitution eliminated many decrees of the Mobutu years, restricted the power of the presidency, and abolished such symbols as the flag and national anthem adopted under the MPR government. Mobutu, who had never formally accepted the Transitional Act, rejected the draft constitution and in October convened the disbanded MPR **parliament** to draft a version more to his liking. When Tshisekedi tried to replace the governor of the **central bank** in order to stem a tide of **currency** counterfeiting that had raised **inflation** to 30 percent per day, Mobutu placed soldiers around the central bank and the offices of the prime minister and locked out the Tshisekedi government.

In February 1993, Mobutu dismissed Tshisekedi and named a rival government headed by a former senior UDPS advisor, Faustin **Birindwa**. The HCR refused to recognize the Birindwa government, which was also boycotted by many Western governments. After another year of political stalemate, a compromise was reached, forming the **Haut Conseil de la République / Parlement de Transition (HCR/PT)** by merging the HCR and the MPR parliament. The HCR/PT elected Léon **Kengo wa Dondo** prime minister, but his government was rejected as illegal by Tshisekedi and the Sacred Union, who said the vote was taken without a quorum. Tshisekedi's refusal to compromise caused some supporters, including Zaire's major Western partners, to switch support to more-moderate opposition groups. However, because of his uncompromising opposition to Mobutu, Tshisekedi was regarded by many as the only major opposition leader who could not be corrupted. He told those who criticized his stubbornness that only with the departure of Mobutu could true **democracy** be installed in the country.

Mobutu left power in May 1997 as troops of the **Alliance des Forces Démocratiques pour la Libération du Congo/Zaïre (AFDL)** entered Kinshasa. AFDL leader Laurent **Kabila** met with Tshisekedi after taking the oath of office on May 29, but did not include him in his first cabinet. The exclusion led to demonstrations, which were subsequently banned by the new government. In late 1997, Tshisekedi was briefly detained for attempting to hold a political rally. In January 1998, authorities prevented a meeting at which Tshisekedi was to "present his new year's greetings to the people." On February 12, two days after meeting US civil rights leader Jesse Jackson and as he was making preparations for a speech to mark the 16th anniversary of the UDPS, Tshisekedi was again arrested. The Kabila government, in a gesture that reminded many of the Mobutu government of the 1980s, sent Tshisekedi into internal exile in his home village for a number of months. Tshisekedi supported the Kabila government against the **Rassemblement Congolais pour la Démocratie (RCD)**, but subsequently called for a negotiated end to the **rebellion**. *See also* Dissidents.

TSHOMBE DITENJ, JEAN. A son of former **Prime Minister** Moïse **Tshombe** who was an exiled **dissident** for a number of years until 1984, when he returned under the general **amnesty of 1983**. He was named state secretary (the equivalent of deputy minister) for mines and **energy** in the cabinet reshuffle of January 25, 1985.

TSHOMBE KAPENDA, MOÏSE (1919 - 1969). A controversial Congolese leader who epitomized for some the fractiousness of early Congolese **politics** and the ties of some leaders to foreign interests. For others, however, he was a pragmatic leader who as **prime minister** attempted to unify the country. Tshombe was born on November 10, 1919, at Musamba, the traditional capital of the **Lunda** empire. He was of noble Lunda family, related to the Lunda **king**, and the son of a prominent businessman. He received his primary **education** from Methodist **missionaries** at Sandoa, obtained a teaching diploma at Kanene lez-Kinda, and later received an accounting diploma.

In the 1950s, Tshombe helped found the **Confédération des Associations Katangaises (CONAKAT)** party and became its president-general. He led the CONAKAT delegation to the two **Round Table Conferences** prior to independence. In 1960, he was elected to the national assembly as a delegate from **Katanga** and CONAKAT swept the Katangan provincial assembly. But Tshombe's southern-based supporters failed to obtain enough seats to form a majority in the **parliament** of the central government.

Angered by what he felt was the lack of Katangan representation in the Patrice **Lumumba** cabinet and encouraged by Belgian commercial interests in Katanga, Tshombe declared the **Katanga secession** on July 11, 1960. The secession brought the first **mercenaries** to independent Africa and prompted the **United Nations'** first police action on the continent.

The secession was ended in January 14, 1963, and Tshombe went into exile in Spain. The following year, **President** Joseph **Kasavubu** named him prime minister with a mandate to end the **rebellions** in **Kwilu** and the eastern provinces. The Tshombe government, with a core of leaders from his **Confédération Nationale des Associations Congolaises (CONACO)** coalition, was installed on July 6, 1964. Tshombe held five portfolios. He subsequently infuriated Africanist circles by hiring mercenaries, many of them veterans of the Katanga Secession, to end the eastern rebellions and by authorizing the **Belgian** airdrop on **Stanleyville** on November 24, 1964. Under the constitution of 1964, the prime minister assumed greater powers and the CONACO party scored sizable gains in **elections** in 1965. Kasavubu dismissed him on October 13, 1965, and appointed Évariste **Kimba** to form a government. Kimba's attempt was blocked by Tshombe's supporters, leading to a political stalemate that was one of the major reasons for the military **coup d'etat** on **November 24, 1965**.

Tshombe went into exile in Spain once again. He was condemned to death in absentia for high treason on March 13, 1967, by a high court in **Kinshasa**. On June 30, 1967, as the **Gendarmerie Katangaise** backed by foreign mercenaries tried to restore him to power through a military invasion in eastern Congo, he was kidnapped while on a flight over the Mediterranean and placed under house arrest in Algeria. The Algerian government announced that he had died of a heart attack on June 30, 1969.

TSHOPO RIVER. A small **river** in northeastern Congo/Zaire that flows into the **Congo River** near **Kisangani**. A 12,000-kilowatt hydroelectric complex on the river supplies **electrical power** to the area.

TSHUAPA RIVER. An 800-km-long **river** that rises in northern **Kasaï Oriental Province** near Kataka-Kombe and flows north, then west. It merges with the Lomela River at Boende to become the Busira that subsequently flows into the **Congo River** at **Mbandaka**. It is navigable by shallow-draft boats from Mbandaka to Ikela.

TUCKEY, JAMES (CAPTAIN) (1776 - 1816). A British **explorer** who led an expedition up the **Congo River**, reaching Isangila near what is now **Matadi** in 1816. He is credited with making the first detailed mappings of the **Bas-Congo** region.

TUMBA, LAKE. *See* LAKE TUMBA.

TUTSI. The Tutsi are a group of people living in **Rwanda, Burundi** and parts of eastern **Congo/Zaire** which throughout history has clashed periodically with the **Hutu** group inhabiting the same area. Although usually referred to as an **ethnic group** and classified as such by Belgian colonial authorities, people of the region tend to view the group as more than that, rather as a socioeconomic entity that is differentiated from the Hutu by factors other than **ethnicity**. Descendants of nomadic herders, the Tutsi traditionally dominated the Hutu, who were primarily cultivators. Intermarriage led to a mingling of physical traits and cultural practices. Nevertheless the Tutsi, who made up only 10 percent of the total population of the region, historically ruled over the Hutu majority.

During the **colonial era**, the Tutsi made advances in business and colonial administration and by **independence** were highly influential in the former Belgian colonies. A revolt in Rwanda in 1959 brought the Hutu to power there and sent an estimated two million Tutsi into exile as **refugees**. In neighboring Burundi, however, the Tutsi continued to dominate the military and government. Periodically, the age-old rivalries erupted into violence. There were bloody clashes between the two groups in Rwanda in 1963 and in Burundi in 1972-73 and 1988. In June 1993, multiparty elections in Burundi led to the election of the country's first Hutu president, Melchior Ndadaye, but he was killed in October in an attempted coup d'etat by the Tutsi-dominated Burundian military.

In Rwanda, Tutsi-led guerrillas launched a war against the government in October 1990 that culminated in the death of President Juvenal Habyarimana in a mysterious plane crash in April 1994. Habyarimana's death was followed by two months of violence in which an estimated 500,000 Rwandans were massacred and more than two million were made refugees, primarily in eastern Zaire.

In late 1996, armed supporters of the deposed Habyarimana government based in refugee camps in Zaire staged cross-border attacks into Rwanda and sought to displace local Zairian Tutsi groups, called the **Banyarwanda** and the **Banyamulenge**. The Zairian groups retaliated and in October joined with other opponents of the **Mobutu** government to form the **Alliance des Forces Démocratiques pour la Libération du Congo/Zaïre**

(**AFDL**). In two months they seized a 500-km stretch of territory along the eastern border and took the cities of Uvira, **Bukavu, Goma** and Bunia. The victories caused all but 200,000 hard-core Rwandan refugees to return home. Many of those who remained were massacred by Tutsi members of the advancing AFDL.

Encouraged by the weak defense of the Zairian **armed forces** and the lack of leadership by Mobutu, who was dying of cancer, the AFDL pushed west and took **Kinshasa** on May 17, 1997, one day after Mobutu fled into exile. AFDL leader Laurent **Kabila**, a veteran **dissident**, was installed as **president**. He pledged to hold multiparty elections by 1999, but was also beholden to the well-trained Tutsi troops from Rwanda, **Uganda** and Burundi, who helped him overthrow Mobutu. In subsequent months, popular resentment in **Kinshasa** grew against the foreign troops, which came to be regarded as an occupation force. Kabila's expulsion of 100 Rwandan officers in July 1998 and atrocities against Tutsi in various parts of the country sparked a **rebellion**, backed by Rwanda and Uganda, which emerged as the **Rassemblement Congolais pour la Démocratie (RCD)** in August 1998. *See also* Ethnic Cleansing.

- U -

UBANGI DISTRICT. A district of **Équateur Province** that benefited from the largess of the large number of businessmen, politicians and military leaders who attained power and wealth under the **government** of **Mobutu**, a favorite son.

UBANGI RIVER. A 1,000-km-long **river** that marks **Congo/Zaire's** border with the northern **Republic of the Congo** and southwestern **Central African Republic**. The Ubangi forms where the Boma and **Uele Rivers** join together near Yakoma. It flows past **Mobutu's** home town of **Gbadolite** and the Central African capital of Bangui before joining the **Congo River** about 100 km downriver from **Mbandaka**. The Ubangi is navigable only during the Northern Hemisphere rainy season, usually from June through October.

UELE RIVER. A small, commercially unnavigable **river** in northeastern Congo/Zaire which rises near the border with southern **Sudan**, where it is called the Dungu River, and flows 750 km west into the **Ubangi River** near Yakoma.

UGANDA, RELATIONS WITH. Relations between **Congo/Zaire** and Uganda periodically have been strained because of **smuggling**, troop incursions and rebel activity along their common border. Because of poor **transportation** links between **Kinshasa** and the east, smuggling and illegal **trade** historically flourished across the border. Merchants smuggled **gold**, **diamonds** and some **agricultural** products into East Africa through Uganda in exchange for fuel, manufactured goods, spare parts and consumer items. From 1985, guerrillas of the **Parti de Libération Congolaise (PLC)** staged attacks on **government** installations in eastern Zaire from bases in the **Ruwenzori Mountains**, but these ceased in 1990 when the PLC registered as a **political party** and joined the **democratic transition**. Attacks by Zairian troops in 1992 and 1993 caused 20,000 Zairians to flee into Uganda as **refugees**.

Relations were generally good in the 1970s, during the eight-year regime of Idi Amin Dada, in large part because of his friendship with **Mobutu**. During this period, the two governments changed the names of two **lakes** along their border, **Lake Albert** and **Lake Edward**, to Lake Mobutu and Lake Idi Amin, respectively, though the changes were not recognized by the international community. Amin was driven into exile by opposition forces aided by **Tanzanian** troops in 1979. In January 1989, he surfaced in Zaire and said he planned to return to Uganda with several hundred armed supporters. The Ugandan government requested his extradition in order to try him for atrocities committed during his rule. However, the Mobutu government rejected the request, citing the lack of an extradition treaty between the two countries, but expelled him nine days later. The dispute led the two governments to withdraw their respective ambassadors, but relations were normalized in September of that year.

After the National Resistance Army led by Yoweri Museveni took power in Kampala on January 29, 1986, following a lengthy guerrilla war, relations initially were correct but later cooled. The

Museveni government backed the offensive of the Rwandese Patriotic Front, led by Uganda-based **Tutsi** refugees, which took power in **Rwanda** in 1994 following the death of President Juvenal Habyarimana, a close friend of Mobutu. Mobutu's decision to allow French troops to use Zairian territory as a staging base to help the pro-Habyarimana forces in 1994 created animosity.

Uganda backed the troops of the **Alliance des Forces Démocratiques pour la Libération du Congo/Zaïre (AFDL)**, which deposed Mobutu and took power in Kinshasa on May 17, 1997, thereby considerably enhancing Uganda's influence in central Africa. Relations with the Laurent **Kabila** government which was installed after the AFDL took over, however, quickly soured because of its inability to halt cross-border raids by Ugandan rebels and deteriorating relations with Rwanda, a close ally. Uganda sent troops to back the **rebellion** by the **Rassemblement Congolais pour la Démocratie (RCD)**, beginning in August 1998.

UJIJI. A small **port** city on the eastern shore of **Lake Tanganyika** which was the departure point for many **explorer**'s expeditions into eastern Congo in the 1800s. Henry Morton **Stanley** met David **Livingstone** there in 1871.

ULINDI RIVER. A tributary of the upper **Congo River** that rises in the **Virunga Mountains** west of **Bukavu** and joins the **Congo River** above Lowa, between **Kindu** and Ubundu.

UMBA DI LUTETE (1939 -). A lawyer, diplomat and on several occasions foreign minister, Umba is a technocrat who rose primarily through the executive branch. Born on June 30, 1939, at Kangu in **Bas-Congo Province**, he received a law degree from **Lovanium University** in 1965 and other law certificates in **Belgium** and the **United States**. He served in senior staff positions in the foreign ministry and at the presidency from 1965 to 1967. He was vice foreign minister from 1967 to 1969, minister of **energy** from 1970 to 1971, state commissioner (minister) of mines in 1971-74, state commissioner for foreign affairs in 1974-75, ambassador to the **United Nations** in 1976-77, and state commissioner for foreign affairs again in 1977-79 and 1984-85.

UNEMPLOYMENT. The **government** has issued no official figures for unemployment rates, but economists estimate unemployment in **Kinshasa** and **Lubumbashi** in the 1980s at 40 percent and as high as 80 percent in other regional cities. Following the **pillages** of 1991 and 1993, unemployment rose to 80 percent but declined to 60 percent by 1996. Economists estimate that historically less than one-half of working-age males in the cities participate in the formal economy. That figure fell to 25 percent during the early 1990s. Rural unemployment is estimated at 80 percent or more.

UNIÃO NAÇIONAL PARA A INDEPENDÊNCIA TOTAL DE ANGOLA (UNITA) / NATIONAL UNION FOR THE TOTAL INDEPENDENCE OF ANGOLA. A nationalist **Angolan** guerrilla group, headed by Jonas **Savimbi** and backed by **South Africa** and the **Mobutu government**, UNITA fought a war for independence against the **Portuguese** colonial authorities in the 1960s and 1970s and, in the civil war that followed Angola's independence, fought two rival factions for control of the country. The **Movimento Popular de Libertação de Angola (MPLA)** faction, backed by the **Soviet Union**, seized control of Luanda in 1975 and was recognized by the **United Nations** in 1976. Zaire first backed the **Frente Nacional de Libertação de Angola (FNLA)** led by Holden **Roberto**, a son-in-law of Mobutu, but switched support to UNITA after the FNLA was driven from most Angolan territory in the 1980s. UNITA continued its guerrilla war through the 1990s and controlled significant portions of territory in eastern and southern Angola. It also prevented the operation of the **Benguela Railway**, the most efficient route for **mineral exports** from **Katanga Province**.

UNITA signed a peace agreement with the Angolan government in 1991 and Savimbi ran for president in elections in September 1992. He lost to MPLA leader José Eduardo dos Santos and UNITA resumed fighting. Another agreement was reached in 1995, but sporadic clashes continued and the Benguela Railway remained closed. In December 1996, several UNITA generals assumed their positions in the Angolan military high command as part of moves to unify the rival forces, but clashes continued.

The Angolan government backed the offensive by the **Alliance des Forces Démocratiques pour la Libération du Congo/Zaïre (AFDL)** which took power in **Kinshasa** on May 17, 1997, following the flight of Mobutu into exile. The takeover caused a switch of alliances and as a result, UNITA lost easy access to its supply lines through Congo/Zaire and its forces came under intense pressure from MPLA troops in northern Angola. Increased fighting in late 1998 led UNITA to sever again its peace agreement with the government.

UNIFIED LUMUMBIST PARTY. *See* PARTI LUMUMBISTE UNIFIÉ (PALU).

UNION DES DÉMOCRATES INDÉPENDANTS (UDI) / UNION OF INDEPENDENT DEMOCRATS. A centrist political party formed by Léon **Kengo wa Dondo** in 1990 in an effort to seize the middle ground between the **Mouvement Populaire de la Révolution (MPR)** and the **opposition Sacred Union**, the UDI was composed primarily of businessmen and politicians associated with the **Mobutu government**, often called the "**Dinosaurs.**" Kengo had been **prime minister** on two occasions in the 1980s, during which periods he instituted severe austerity measures in an attempt to stabilize **inflation** and reduce **government** budget deficits, but these were abandoned before they could be completed. In July 1994, when Kengo was again appointed prime minister, the UDI convinced several moderate members of the Sacred Union to defect and join a moderate alliance called the **Union pour la République et la Démocratie (URD).** However, it was dismissed in March 1997 in the final months of the Mobutu regime. *See also* Democratic Transition.

UNION DES ÉTATS DE L'AFRIQUE CENTRALE (UEAC) / UNION OF CENTRAL AFRICAN STATES. *See* UNION DOUANIÈRE ET ÉCONOMIQUE DE L'AFRIQUE CENTRALE.

UNION DES FÉDÉRALISTES ET DES RÉPUBLICAINS INDÉPENDANTS (UFERI) / UNION OF FEDERALISTS AND INDEPENDENT REPUBLICANS. A political party formed by Jean **Nguza Karl-I-Bond** in 1990 with a strong political base in

Shaba Region. UFERI advocated a **federal** system of **government** with considerable autonomy for the regions. During the early 1990s, it built some support in **Bas-Zaïre** because of Nguza's marriage to the daughter of a prominent family in the region, Wivinne N'Landu Kavidi. UFERI was one of three major parties that formed the **Sacred Union** alliance in 1991, but it was expelled when Nguza accepted the post of **prime minister** in November. UFERI subsequently led several dozen members of the Sacred Union into a governing coalition called the **Alliance des Forces Patriotiques (AFP)**. When Nguza was dismissed in 1992 and replaced by Étienne **Tshisekedi**, UFERI militants in Shaba, which they called **Katanga**, began attacking **Luba**-Kasai, who tended to be supporters of Tshisekedi. Thousands were made homeless in the violence of **ethnic cleansing**. An estimated 500 people were killed and more than 100,000 fled to **Kasaï Orientale** over the next two years. Some UFERI leaders joined the Laurent **Kabila** government after it came to power in 1997.

UNION DOUANIÈRE ET ÉCONOMIQUE DE L'AFRIQUE CENTRALE (UDEAC) / CENTRAL AFRICAN CUSTOMS AND ECONOMIC UNION. A French-sponsored customs and tariffs union of former French Equatorial African states. **Mobutu** tried to form a similar organization in 1968, called the Union des États de l'Afrique Centrale (UEAC) with **Chad** and the **Central African Republic (CAR)**. Chad agreed to join, but the CAR declined. Cameroon, **Republic of the Congo** and Gabon, backed by **France**, actively opposed the UEAC and it never reached the operational stage. Zaire joined UDEAC in the early 1980s and Chad, which had dropped out after it joined the UEAC, was readmitted in 1984.

UNION FOR DEMOCRACY AND SOCIAL PROGRESS. *See* UNION POUR LA DÉMOCRATIE ET LE PROGRÈS SOCIAL. (UDPS).

UNION FOR THE COLONIZATION OF KATANGA. *See* UNION POUR LA COLONISATION DU KATANGA.

UNION FOR THE REPUBLIC AND DEMOCRACY. *See* UNION POUR LA RÉPUBLIQUE ET LA DÉMOCRATIE (URD).

UNION GÉNÉRALE DES ÉTUDIANTS CONGOLAIS (UGEC) / GENERAL UNION OF CONGOLESE STUDENTS. A radical and articulate **student** organization of the mid-1960s that criticized imperialism and many Congolese politicians. Although it sympathized with **socialism**, it criticized foreign influence in national affairs and advocated the creation of truly Congolese institutions. Many of its members in 1966 joined the **Corps des Volontaires de la République (CVR)**, which was a major precursor to the **Mouvement Populaire de la Révolution (MPR)**. Some of the UGEC leaders—including its president, N'Kanza Dolomingu—did not choose to join the CVR and were imprisoned. Others were successfully brought into the system, for example, its secretary for international affairs, **Kamanda wa Kamanda**, who was made secretary-general of the presidency. The UGEC was banned from the **universities** in 1968 after the MPR was created in order to facilitate the establishment of the **Jeunesse du Mouvement Populaire de la Révolution (JMPR) youth** wing of the MPR.

UNION KATANGAISE / KATANGAN UNION. A group of primarily Belgian expatriates living in **Katanga Province** which pressed for autonomy for Katanga in the 1950s. Part of the Union pour la Colonisation du Katanga, founded in 1944, the Union Katangaise was accepted into the **Confédération des Associations Katangaises (CONAKAT)** in 1959 and was one of the strongest advocates of an autonomous Katanga within a federal Congolese state. During the **Katanga secession**, the Union became a shadow group, advising officials and occasionally recruiting abroad for it. *See also* Shaba.

UNION MINIÈRE DU HAUT-KATANGA (UMHK). A **mining** consortium of primarily Belgian ownership formed in 1906 to exploit deposits of **copper** ores in **Katanga Province**, which was known as **Shaba Region** under **Mobutu**. Historically the largest company in Congo/Zaire, UMHK was **nationalized** in 1966 and its name was changed to GEOMINES. In 1971 the name was changed to **Générale des Carrières et des Mines (GECAMINES)**. *See also* Mining; Société Générale des Minérais (SGM).

UNION MONGO (UNIMO). A group organized in the 1950s to represent the interests of the **Mongo** people, in particular prior to the **elections** for local councils in 1957. UNIMO sent a delegation, headed by founder Justin **Bomboko**, to the **Round Table Conferences** in 1960 and was represented in the early Congolese **governments**.

UNION NATIONALE DES INTÉRÊTS SOCIAUX CONGOLAIS (UNISCO) / NATIONAL UNION OF CONGOLESE SOCIAL INTERESTS. One of Congo's first **nationalist** organizations, UNISCO was founded in 1946 as an association because of the ban on political activity. Its avowed purpose was to "coordinate activities" of **alumni groups** such as those of the Scheut Fathers, Christian Brothers, Jesuits and Marists.

UNION NATIONALE DES TRAVAILLEURS CONGOLAIS (UNTC) / NATIONAL UNION OF CONGOLESE WORKERS. The trade union formed in the early years of the **Mobutu** government which under the single-party state became Zaire's only trade union. It originally was formed as the Union des Travailleurs Congolais (UTC) in June 1967 and brought together disparate rival unions that existed under the first republic. The move drew protests from some **labor** leaders who feared it would become too closely aligned with the party and **government**. In subsequent years this fear was born out as the union, renamed the Union Nationale des Travailleurs Zaïrois (UNTZA) in 1971, through decrees and the **constitution** of 1974, became part of the party-state.

The Zairian government believed trade unions should serve to mobilize workers behind government policies for the purpose of economic development and the good of the nation. Nevertheless, UNTZA at times demonstrated independence at the grass roots level. And despite opposition from its senior leaders, many of whom held senior party positions, workers staged demonstrations and **strikes** on a number of occasions to protest low **wages** and government austerity measures. In 1990, UNTZA reported 1.1 million registered members, of which 600,000 were employees of the government or state-owned enterprises.

Following Mobutu's announcement of the transition to multipartyism, UNTZA lost its monopoly of the labor movement.

It no longer automatically received dues from all workers employed in the formal **economy** and nearly one dozen rival unions formed along political and professional lines. With the rise of **inflation** in the 1990s and the decline in buying power, strikes became frequent and even UNTZA leaders began to criticize the Mobutu government. Following the fall of Mobutu in 1997, the name was changed to the UNTC.

UNION OF CENTRAL AFRICAN STATES. *See* UNION DES ÉTATS DE L'AFRIQUE CENTRALE (UDEAC).

UNION OF FEDERALISTS AND INDEPENDENT REPUBLICANS. *See* UNION DES FÉDÉRALISTES ET DES RÉPUBLICAINS INDÉPENDANTS (UFERI).

UNION OF INDEPENDENT DEMOCRATS. *See* UNION DES DÉMOCRATES INDÉPENDANTS (UDI).

UNION POUR LA COLONISATION DU KATANGA / UNION FOR THE COLONIZATION OF KATANGA. A group of primarily Belgian inhabitants of **Katanga Province** founded in 1944 to promote the European colonial presence in the **Belgian Congo**. The group advocated Katangan autonomy and some of its leaders belonged to the militant **Union Katangaise**, which was accepted into the **Confédération des Associations Katangaises (CONAKAT)** in June 1959. The group strongly influenced CONAKAT's subsequent positions, advocating Katangan autonomy, a **federalist** system of **government** and, following **independence**, secession.

UNION POUR LA DÉMOCRATIE ET LE PROGRÈS SOCIAL (UDPS) / UNION FOR DEMOCRACY AND SOCIAL PROGRESS. A **political party** founded on February 15, 1982, by the **Group of Thirteen Parliamentarians**, who in 1980 had signed an open letter to **Mobutu** calling for multiparty **democracy**. The UDPS, led by Étienne **Tshisekedi**, became the core of the internally based **opposition** movement in the 1980s. Its rallies and demonstrations pressured the government to end single-party rule in 1990 and it led the hardline opposition of the mid-1990s which rejected any cooperation with Mobutu, maintaining that only when he was removed from power could the country move toward true democracy.

At the time the UDPS was formed, the **Mouvement Populaire de la Révolution (MPR)** was the only legal party and, under the **constitution** of 1974, the formation of a second party was an act of treason. The 13 parliamentarians were arrested, convicted of sedition and in June 1982 sentenced to lengthy prison terms. They were released under the **amnesty of 1983**, but were arrested and placed under various forms of detention on several subsequent occasions, including following an attempt on August 12, 1983, to meet with a delegation of US congressmen visiting **Kinshasa**.

Following Mobutu's announcement of the transition to multiparty democracy on **April 24, 1990**, the UDPS leaders were freed. The UDPS held a rally on April 30 that was suppressed by **security** forces in an incident in which at least two supporters were killed, the first of hundreds of casualties of the **democratic transition**. The UDPS was one of the first opposition parties to be registered after single-party rule was officially ended on November 25, 1990. Its platform advocated building democratic institutions and it was one of the few parties to develop a broad national following. The party was also noted for leading the struggle against what were perceived as Mobutu's attempts to dominate the transition and remain in power. Through **strikes** and popular demonstrations it pressed for a **national conference** to oversee the transition, draft a new constitution, and organize national **elections**.

The UDPS was one of three major parties to form the **Sacred Union** alliance, which by mid-1991 grouped more than 200 opposition parties. After the National Conference was convened on August 7, 1991, the UDPS and Sacred Union led a number of walkouts to protest what was seen as an attempt by pro-Mobutu forces to take control of the body. The protests led to the collapse of the conference eight days later. On September 29, 1991, Tshisekedi was named **prime minister**, one week after the **pillages** in **Kinshasa** which led to the military intervention by **Belgium** and **France** and the evacuation of most expatriate workers. However, his appointment was canceled the following week when he refused to sign an oath of allegiance to the **president**. Mobutu then attempted to divide the Sacred Union by naming as prime minister Jean **Nguza Karl-I-Bond**, who headed another pillar of the alliance, the **Union des Fédéralistes et des Républicains Indépendants (UFERI)**. A period of political confrontation ensued which was only ended in April 1992 when the National Conference reconvened. The conference proclaimed itself the sovereign institution of state and on August 15 elected Tshisekedi prime minister, bringing the UDPS and its allies to power for the first time.

Tshisekedi soon clashed with Mobutu and was dismissed on February 5, 1993, after calling for foreign help to overthrow him. The UDPS's senior economic advisor, Faustin **Birindwa**, accepted the post of prime minister the following month. His appointment led to a period of political stalemate characterized by two rival governments whose leaders were both originally from the same party.

In the mid-1990s, the UDPS still formed the hard, inner core of the Sacred Union, called the Union Sacrée de l'Opposition Radicale et Alliés et Société Civile (USORAS). It viewed the Tshisekedi government of 1992 as the sole legitimate government of the country and rejected all subsequent governments appointed by Mobutu.

When the **Forces Démocratiques pour la Libération du Congo/Zaïre (AFDL)** launched their offensive to overthrow Mobutu in October 1996, the UDPS announced it supported the goals of the AFDL but not its use of force to attain them. After the AFDL took power in Kinshasa and installed Laurent **Kabila** as president on May 29, 1997, senior UDPS leaders were consulted but were not included in the first Kabila government. This exclusion led to protests by UDPS members and raised tensions with the Kabila government, which subsequently banned all political meetings. In subsequent months, a number of UDPS demonstrations were dispersed by **security** forces and their leaders arrested. Tshisekedi was detained on February 12, 1998, days before he was to deliver a speech marking the 16th anniversary of the UDPS. He was sent into internal exile in his home village but was later released. In November 1997, a faction of the UDPS led by Frédéric **Kibassa Maliba**, joined the Kabila government.

UNION POUR LA RÉPUBLIQUE ET LA DÉMOCRATIE (URD) / UNION FOR THE REPUBLIC AND DEMOCRACY. An alliance of centrist parties formed by Léon **Kengo wa Dondo** after he was named **prime minister** in 1994. One of three major alliances in the mid-1990s, the URD positioned itself between the pro-**Mobutu**, Forces Politiques du **Conclave (FPC)** and the **opposition Sacred Union**.

UNION SACRÉE DE L'OPPOSITION RADICALE ET ALLIÉS ET SOCIÉTÉ CIVILE (USORAS). *See* SACRED UNION.

UNIONS. *See* LABOR.

UNITED KINGDOM, RELATIONS WITH. Britain was one of the first European nations in the 1800s to become interested in central Africa and its commercial possibilities. The British government and British associations financed numerous expeditions by **explorers**, particularly of eastern Congo and the **Congo River**. British firms **traded** for a time with merchants in Congo, but following the **Berlin Conference** of 1885, they focused increasingly on the British colonies. Britain was in the forefront of the anti-**slavery** movement and led the international outcry against the harsh **labor** practices of the **Congo Free State**. It was the first European power to grant **independence** to its African colonies, beginning with Ghana in 1957. In the 1990s, the United Kingdom had fewer economic and social ties with **Congo/Zaire** than other industrialized nations such as **Belgium**, the **United States**, **France**, West **Germany**, **Japan** and Italy. However, relations were correct despite British concern over mismanagement, authoritarianism and **human rights** abuses during the **Mobutu** regime. *See also* Rhodes, Cecil.

UNITED NATIONS. The Congo was the stage for the United Nations' first police action in Africa. Faced with deteriorating **security**, the collapse of **government** services, and the perceived threat of Belgian reoccupation following troop landings in **Matadi**, **Elisabethville** and **Luluabourg**, the Congolese government asked for UN military assistance on July 12, 1960, 13 days after **independence**. The United Nations passed a resolution on July 14 agreeing to send UN troops to Congo but limited their responsibilities to "internal" Congolese affairs, namely the **Katanga secession**. It soon became evident, however, that assistance was needed in other areas and the UN contingent in the Congo grew to 20,000 people before the operation ended in July 1964. UN personnel helped set up the Congolese **civil service** and staffed the **police** and **judicial system**, which had been devastated by the sudden departure of Belgian technicians and professionals. UN officials also served for a number of months in a "shadow cabinet" for the Congolese government.

The UN role in Katanga was controversial and the early part of the operation received a great deal of international attention. Faced with the continued inability of the Congolese government to end the secession, the United Nations passed a resolution on February 21, 1961, giving the UN forces the authority to "prevent civil war." The resolution accorded broader powers than that of the previous year and UN officials used it to try to expel foreign **mercenaries** from Katanga in September 1961, causing an outbreak of fighting. The fighting was stopped following the death of UN Secretary-General Dag **Hammarskjöld** in a plane crash while on a trip to Northern Rhodesia to meet Katangan leader Moïse **Tshombe**. However, fighting resumed in December when UN troops moved again to expel the mercenaries. The second operation was more successful and led Tshombe to return to the negotiating table. The UN actions in the Congo were severely criticized by some members, and the **Soviet Union**, for example, refused to contribute funds to the operation.

The controversy contributed to a reluctance on the part of the world body to engage in other police actions on the continent and its decision to concentrate its efforts instead on diplomatic mediations, economic development, and the struggle against drought, **disease** and hunger. On the development front, the United Nations funded numerous development and **social services** programs in Congo/Zaire and also sent humanitarian assistance during periods of crisis and interethnic violence. *See also* International Development Association; International Monetary Fund; Thant, U; World Bank.

UNITED STATES, RELATIONS WITH. The United States has been interested in **Congo/Zaire** since the *New York Herald* newspaper sent Henry Morton **Stanley** to find David **Livingstone** in 1871. The US government initially supported **Leopold II**'s pledge to "civilize" the peoples of the Congo and was the first nation to recognize his **Congo Free State (CFS)** after the **Berlin Conference** in 1885. However, public outcry in the United States and Europe over harsh **labor** practices and atrocities committed against Congolese by agents of the CFS led to the annexation of the territory by the Belgian government in 1908.

During the **colonial era**, US economic interests in the **Belgian Congo** remained considerably smaller than those of **Belgium**, but US churches sent large numbers of **missionaries** to the Congo from 1930 to establish and staff schools, churches and hospitals. Strategic interests, however, were strong. **Uranium** from the Congo was used to make the first atomic bomb in the 1940s and following World War II appreciation grew for the fact that the territory was one of the largest sources in the non-communist world of industrial **diamonds**, **cobalt** and other strategic **minerals**.

Following **independence**, the US government was one of the first to establish diplomatic relations with Congo. The US Agency for International Development and the Peace Corps launched many programs and the US government estimates it provided $1 billion in **foreign aid** during the next 30 years. During the early 1960s, the US government supported the central **government** in **Leopoldville** and opposed the **Katanga secession,** the **Stanleyville secession** and the various **rebellions**. US planes transported the Belgian paratroopers who landed in **Stanleyville** on November 24, 1964, to rescue several hundred European and American hostages being held by **Simba** rebels.

The US government quickly recognized the **Mobutu** government after the **coup d'etat** of **November 24, 1965,** and US investment increased further. Relations cooled somewhat when Mobutu began moving the country toward a single-party state in the late 1960s and they deteriorated further following **Zairianization** and Zaire's diplomatic break with **Israel** in 1973. In June 1975, Mobutu accused the US government of supporting an attempted coup d'etat. Washington denied the charge and recalled its ambassador from **Kinshasa**. Despite the strain in relations, both governments continued to support the **Frente Nacional de Libertação de Angola (FNLA)** and the **União Nacional para a Independência Total de Angola (UNITA)** against the **Movimento Popular de Libertação de Angola**

(MPLA) in Angola's civil war. In the 1980s Zairian territory was used to transship covert US aid to UNITA.

The US government provided transport planes, arms and food to Zairian troops during the Shaba invasions of 1977 and 1978 and accused Cuba and the Soviet Union of complicity in the attack on Kolwezi, in which one US citizen was killed. Following the Shaba wars, Mobutu sought a rapprochement with the United States and other Western nations, where his government was coming under increasing criticism for corruption and human rights violations. Relations were cool during the late 1970s because of the Jimmy Carter administration's emphasis on human rights, but improved considerably under the Ronald Reagan administration, which valued Zaire's strategic location, mineral wealth and support for US policies in the region. In the 1980s, military assistance, which had been reduced to less than $8 million per year, increased to more than $30 million per year. The US Congress continued to criticize authoritarianism and economic mismanagement in Zaire, but the US government expressed support for and pleasure over the economic reforms enacted by the Zairian government and the reestablishment of diplomatic ties with Israel in the mid-1980s. George Bush visited Zaire as vice president in November 1982, George Schultz visited in February of 1987 as secretary of state, and Mobutu visited the United States regularly in private and official capacities.

With Mobutu's announcement of the democratic transition in April 1990, however, relations entered a difficult period. The US Embassy in Kinshasa, headed by Ambassador Melissa Wells, criticized Mobutu's efforts to disrupt the National Conference and pressed Mobutu to allow true political reforms. In 1992, when Mobutu dismissed Étienne Tshisekedi and appointed Faustin Birindwa prime minister, relations entered a period of confrontation. The US government adopted a policy of isolating Mobutu and officials of the rival Birindwa government. As a result, non-humanitarian aid programs were curtailed and members of the Mobutu government were refused visas to the United States, even for medical reasons.

In 1993, frustration over what was perceived as Tshisekedi's hardline opposition to Mobutu and concern over declining living standards caused by Zaire's economic crisis, led to a moderation of this policy. Official contacts were allowed and in 1994 Léon

Kengo wa Dondo, viewed as a political moderate and economic reformer, visited Washington. Official US policy continued to press for an orderly democratic transition and free, multiparty elections, but the view expressed privately by many Zaire watchers in the mid-1990s was that true reform could only occur after the departure of Mobutu.

The US government was among the first to recognize the government of Laurent **Kabila** after the **Forces Démocratiques pour la Libération du Congo/Zaïre (AFDL)** took power in Kinshasa in May 1997, one day after Mobutu's flight into exile. News agencies subsequently reported that US troops had helped train AFDL forces. The US government denied the reports, but acknowledged that US military officers had trained troops in **Rwanda**, which militarily supported the AFDL offensive.

Some major US investors in Congo/Zaire have included **General Motors**, Firestone and Morrison-Knudsen. Others participated in the **mining** and **cement** industries and in **petroleum** exploration. By the 1990s, many of these had been sold or were inactive but a number of companies approached the Kabila government in 1997 with proposals for ventures in the mining and **transportation** sectors. *See also* Central Intelligence Agency.

UNIVERSITÉ NATIONALE DU CONGO (UNC) / NATIONAL UNIVERSITY OF CONGO. During the **Mobutu** era, the sole institution of higher learning other than professional schools. The UNC was created as the Université Nationale du Zaïre (UNAZA) by decree in August 1971, following several years of **student** protests against the **government**. It was created from three **universities**, two of which were run by churches: the **Lovanium University** in **Kinshasa**, the Université Officielle du Congo in **Lubumbashi**, and the Université Libre du Congo in **Kisangani**. All campuses suffered severe declines in the 1980s and 1990s because of low government financial support. Witnesses reported empty libraries and classrooms where students took notes standing because of a lack of desks and chairs. In 1992, the **National Conference** offered to return the campuses to the churches. However, the churches declined initially, citing the high cost of administering them and refurbishing their physical plants.

UNAZA was renamed the UNC after the Laurent **Kabila** government came to power in 1997.

UNIVERSITIES. From 1971 until the 1990s, when higher **education** was liberalized, Congo/Zaire had a single, national university, the Université Nationale du Zaïre (renamed the **Université Nationale du Congo** in 1997) with campuses in **Kinshasa**, **Lubumbashi**, **Kisangani** and, from 1985, **Kananga**. Prior to 1971, the campuses were private universities, run primarily by church groups with financial support from some lay organizations and philanthropic foundations. Total enrollment ranged from 15,000 to 20,000 students. **Lovanium University**, the oldest and perhaps most prestigious campus, was founded in 1954 by the Roman **Catholic Church**. The Lubumbashi campus was first established in 1956 by **Protestant** groups as the Université Officielle du Congo Belge et du Ruanda-Urundi. It became the Université de l'État du Congo in 1960, the Université d'Élisabethville in 1963 and the public Université Officielle du Congo in 1964. The Kisangani campus was founded in 1963 by Protestant missions, but classes were disrupted for a number of years because of the eastern **rebellions**.

Following the creation of UNAZA, the three campuses were maintained in the regional capitals but the administration was centralized in Kinshasa. Although some types of degrees were offered by more than one campus, each campus had a certain degree of specialization: medicine at Kinshasa, for example, philosophy and letters at Kisangani, and natural and social sciences at Lubumbashi. The creation of the fourth campus at Kananga was announced in 1984.

Most educators said the quality of education of the universities was seriously eroded during the 1980s and 1990s by a lack of funds, low **wages** and frequent closings due to **student** protests, usually over poor living and study conditions. However, the universities continued to increase the country's population of university graduates, from 12 at independence, to 167 in 1968, an estimated 2,000 in 1985, and tens of thousands by the 1990s. Graduates of professional and technical schools numbered roughly twice those of the universities.

The **Makanda Kabobi Institute** of the **Mouvement Populaire de la Révolution (MPR)** party provided postsecondary school training to party **cadres**. Two institutions trained teachers, the Institut Pédagogique National-Kinshasa and the Institut Pédagogique National-Bukavu. These institutions offered a five-year program leading to a *license*, the approximate equivalent of a bachelor of arts degree. A number of other institutions offered three-year programs awarding a *graduat* diploma, the approximate equivalent of an associate of arts degree.

In the late 1980s and early 1990s, a number of private universities opened, most notably the Université du **Bas-Zaïre** and Université de **Mbuji-Mayi**, in several regional urban centers. Their number began to grow and, by 1996, had surpassed 120. These institutions frequently lacked teaching facilities and consequently advertised that they taught "theory" only. Few earned international accreditation.

In 1992, the **National Conference** adopted a measure offering to return the nationalized universities to the churches, but the churches initially declined, citing the high cost of refurbishing the physical plants. In 1995, the Protestant Church created the Université Protestante du Zaïre, with faculties in theology and business and economics, on a small campus in Kinshasa.

The universities were frequently a source of **opposition** to the government. A number of demonstrations were harshly repressed by **security** forces in 1969, 1971, 1977, 1981 and 1982. In the 1990s, students were strong supporters of the pro-**democracy** movement. An attack against students in their dormitories at the Lubumbashi campus of UNAZA in May 1990 caused the suspension of non-humanitarian aid by the **United States**, Canada and the **European Union**.

UPEMBA, LAKE. *See* LAKE UPEMBA.

URANIUM. Uranium deposits are known to exist in a number of **copper**-mining areas of **Katanga Province**. However, actual **mining** of the **mineral** occurred only at one location, the Shinkolobwe **gold** mine in southern Katanga, 40 km south of **Likasi**, between 1944 and 1960 by the **Union Minière du Haut-Katanga (UMHK)**. Radium was discovered in gold ore there as early as 1922. The first concentrates were produced from tailings in 1944 and sold to the Combined Development Agency (CDA) of the US and British governments. Uranium bought from the

Belgian Congo by the US government was used in the Manhattan Project that produced the atomic bomb dropped on Japan. From 1944 to 1960, the CDA purchased a total of 32,500 metric tons of (U^{308}) concentrate. The Shinkolobwe mine was closed in April 1960, three months before **independence**.

In 1982, **Zaire** signed an agreement with the French government to undertake surveys and possible production of uranium deposits. The survey of the Shinkolobwe mine showed remaining reserves were too deep to justify reopening the mine. However, surveys of other concessions owned by UMHK's successor, **Générale des Carrières et des Mines (GECAMINES)**, revealed commercially exploitable deposits in **copper** ore.

URBANIZATION. During the **colonial era**, authorities restricted urban **migration** through a system of registration and forced deportations from the cities. After **independence** in 1960, these controls were abandoned and Congo began to experience the same rapid urban growth seen in most African nations. The proportion of people living in urban areas was estimated to have quadrupled from 1960 to 1980. The **United Nations** estimated 27 percent of the **population** in 1980 was living in urban centers and this had risen to 39.8 percent by 1992. Although there are indications that the severe economic recession of the early 1990s has reduced the rate of migration to the cities, the prospect of jobs and access to **health care** and **social services** continues to attract rural inhabitants to the urban centers. The migration has strained the social services and tended to aggravate **unemployment** and **crime**. The **government** at times has forcefully returned homeless and unemployed people to their home regions. It also has inducted jobless **youth** into the **armed forces**.

- V -

VIRUNGA MOUNTAINS. A chain of **mountains** lying in eastern **Congo/Zaire** north of **Lake Kivu** with peaks as high as 5,000 m above sea level. Remote and dense, the Virungas frequently harbored antigovernment guerrillas following **independence** until 1990 and were a haven for bandits at various times throughout.

The Virungas are also home to the country's famous mountain gorillas (of which less than 600 are believed to remain) and the country's largest game park, which are the region's primary tourist attraction. *See also* Volcanoes.

VIVI. First "capital" of **Leopold II**'s Congo, founded by Henry Morton **Stanley** in 1880. Vivi was a small fishing village lying across the **Congo River** from what is now **Matadi**. It was used by Stanley as a base for the arduous overland trek to **Kinshasa**. Kinshasa, which Stanley renamed **Leopoldville**, soon became the political and economic center of the territory because of its strategic position as the main **river port** for the interior.

VOIE NATIONALE. *See* NATIONAL WAY.

VOIX DES SANS-VOIX POUR LES DROITS DE L'HOMME (VSV) / VOICE OF THE VOICELESS FOR HUMAN RIGHTS. Founded by Chiteya Floribert in the 1980s, the Voix des Sans-Voix was one of three major **human rights** organizations operating in Congo/Zaire in the 1990s.

VOIX DU PEUPLE / VOICE OF THE PEOPLE. The name given to the **government**-owned **radio** station after the takeover by the **Alliance des Forces Démocratiques pour la Libération du Congo/Zaïre (AFDL)** in May 1997. Known during the **Mobutu** era as the **Voix du Zaïre**, the station is a subsidiary of the government broadcasting agency, the **Radio-Télévision Nationale Congolaise (RTNC)**, formerly the **Office Zaïrois de Radio et de Télévision (OZRT)**, which is a department of the Ministry of Information. *See also* News Media; Telecommunications.

VOIX DU ZAÏRE / VOICE OF ZAIRE. The **government**-owned **radio** station that was part of an electronic broadcasting complex built with French assistance in 1976 at a reported cost of $1 billion. When Zaire became the **Democratic Republic of the Congo** once again following the departure of **Mobutu** and the installation of Laurent **Kabila** as president, the Voix du Zaïre was renamed the **Voix du Peuple**. *See also* News Media; Telecommunications.

VOLCANOES. A number of volcanoes are active in remote parts of eastern and northeastern Congo/Zaire. The two most notable are located in the **Virunga Mountains**. The Nyirangongo Volcano, altitude 3,500 m, erupted in 1977 and 1994, and the Nyamuragira, altitude 3,000 m, erupted in 1984 and 1994.

VOLUNTEER CORPS OF THE REPUBLIC. *See* CORPS DES VOLONTAIRES DE LA RÉPUBLIQUE (CVR).

VOTING. *See* ELECTIONS.

VUNDUAWE TE PEMAKO. A powerful advisor to **Mobutu** in the 1990s, who during the **democratic transition** period frequently served as chief negotiator between the pro-Mobutu political alliances and the **opposition**. Vunduawe first came to prominence in the late 1970s when, as state commissioner for territorial **administration**, he carried out a major administrative reform. The reform, enacted in 1982, ostensibly decentralized the **government** by setting up a system of regional councils. However, real power was never devolved to these councils and control remained with the party and the **president**. With the overthrow of Mobutu in 1997, Vunduawe reportedly fled to **South Africa**.

VUNGARA. One of two major groups of the **Zande** people living in northernmost Congo/Zaire and speaking a **language** related to the Adamawa-Eastern cluster. The Vungara lived primarily in the eastern part of Zande land near Ango and Faradje, between the **Uele** and **Ubangi Rivers**. They began to arrive in the 18th and 19th centuries when groups of hunters, divided into the Vungara aristocracy and the **Mbomu** commoners, entered northern Congo and conquered the local peoples, some of whom spoke Sudanic languages, others of whom spoke languages of the **Bantu** cluster.

    Chieftaincy among the Vungara was handed down from father to son. However, the son was obliged to vanquish any of his brothers who chose to contest the succession. The vanquished brothers were then expected to leave in order to conquer their own people and found their own lineages. This pattern of succession is said to be one of the major reasons for the mosaic mixture of Sudanic and Bantu cultures in northern Congo. The Vungara in some cases maintained ties with tribes to the north. They fiercely resisted the Belgian colonial authorities until the late 1890s, when they were defeated during a military offensive against followers of the **Mahdi** in southern **Sudan**.

- W -

WAGES AND SALARIES. Wage and salary earners in Congo/Zaire have always been near the bottom of the organized **economy**, while successful businessmen and entrepreneurs have usually occupied the upper levels and senior political officials constitute the *élite*, state bourgeoisie. The minimum wage historically has varied between $30 and $60 per month. Professionals earn two to six times that amount, while ministerial-level, **government** and party officials earn 25 times the minimum wage, not including benefits such as subsidized housing, cars, educational expenses and entertainment allowances.

With the rise of **inflation**, which reached 6,000 percent per year in 1994, the value of wages plummeted and the minimum wage at some points fell as low as $1 per month in real terms. Salaries of workers in the private sector were adjusted for inflation more frequently than those of public employees, but during the 1990s, the minimum wage rarely rose above the equivalent of $15 US.

The country's per-capita **income** has always been low in comparison to equally endowed African countries. This fact is due in part to the large Congolese **population** that lives outside the formal economy, 70 percent of the total population in 1995. It is also due to the active parallel, or informal, economy. Per-capita income peaked at $200 per year in the mid-1970s but fell to $110 dollars by 1995. **Central Bank** figures show that traditionally income levels are highest in **Kinshasa** and **Lubumbashi**, reaching $280 per year in the mid-1970s. **Katanga, Bas-Congo** and **Kasaï Oriental Provinces** follow, in that order, with per-capita income levels averaging one-half to one-fourth of those in the two major cities. From the late 1970s, salaries of professionals in the public sector were usually less than $100 per month, obliging many of these to subsidize their earnings by trading and charging fees for their services.

Indexation of wages to inflation ended in 1976 and the **currency** was floated on the open market beginning in September 1983. These measures pleased donor governments and multilateral lending institutions pressing for free-market reforms. However, they seriously disrupted the purchasing power of wage earners, weakened public confidence in the local currency, and helped create the "inflation mentality" that was partly responsible for **hyperinflation** in 1992-94. Inflation was reduced to less than 400 percent in 1996 but began to rise again in 1997. At that time the salaries of most public servants were less than $10 per month. *See also* Employment.

"WALL STREET." The popular name given to a stretch of road in downtown **Kinshasa** along which traders, sitting on open-air stools and benches, make a vibrant **currency** exchange market. Economists estimate that in the early 1990s "Wall Street," which ironically was located near the US Embassy, accounted for $200-300 million in exchanges per month, roughly 20 percent of the country's total currency transactions. During the period of **hyperinflation**, banks and businesses frequently were obliged to go to "Wall Street" to obtain foreign currency which was unavailable at the **central bank**.

WAMBA DIA WAMBA, ERNEST (1942 -). An opposition figure who emerged in August 1998 as head of the political wing of the rebel **Rassemblement Congolais pour la Démocratie (RCD)**. Wamba was an academic who attended college in the **United States**. He was twice imprisoned by imprisoned by **Mobutu** and spent many years in exile in **Tanzania**.

WATER AND ELECTRICITY DISTRIBUTION ADMINISTRA-TION. *See* RÉGIE DE DISTRIBUTION D'EAU ET D'ÉLECTRICITÉ (REGIDESO).

WATERWAYS. Congo/Zaire's 14,000 km of navigable waterways provide a unique natural **transportation** system. However, parts of the country's major **rivers** are not navigable and the **road** and **railway** systems designed to circumvent them are plagued by swamps, **mountain** ranges and dense **rainforest**. The **Congo River** forms the backbone of the waterway system with 5,000 km of navigable waters which, however, are interrupted by unnavigable cataracts in three places: between **Kinshasa** and **Matadi** on the lower Congo River, and between Kongolo and **Kindu** and between **Ubundu** and **Kisangani** on the upper portion of the river. The **Kasai, Tshuapa** and **Ubangi Rivers** are the major navigable tributaries. Five railway systems circumvent unnavigable portions of the rivers and connect the rivers to areas of commercial **mineral** and **agricultural** production. In the **Great Rift Valley, Lakes Tanganyika, Kivu, Albert** and **Edward**, provide major transportation links with East Africa and points along the eastern Congolese border. *See also* National Way; Ports.

"WAX." The name derived from the method of making patterned **cloth** using dyes and "lost wax" which came to denote the brightly colored cloth that is used for everything from table cloths and curtains to clothes and head coverings. Wax originated in the **Dutch-influenced** areas of Malaysia and Indonesia and was brought to Africa by Dutch traders returning from Asia. The cloth is widely used throughout Africa and has become popular in Europe and America. Most African nations have textile **industries** that manufacture the cloth, although the use of the traditional lost wax method has largely been abandoned. *See also* Dress.

WELFARE. *See* SOCIAL SERVICES.

WEST KASAI PROVINCE. *See* KASAÏ OCCIDENTAL PROVINCE.

WITCHCRAFT. *See* SPIRITUALISM, FETISHISM, SORCERY AND WITCHCRAFT.

WOMEN. In most traditional Congolese **societies,** many of which are matrilineal, women played an important role in lineage and family. An elderly woman could rise to the position of village elder and, in some societies, **chief.** However, male pastimes and vocations such as hunting, **fishing** and warring tended to be regarded as more noble and valorous than the traditional female occupations of cultivating, collecting firewood, cooking and caring for children. Like most African states, Congo/Zaire has enacted laws guaranteeing women equal rights, the vote, property and custodial rights in divorce. The law also outlaws in principle the practice of polygamy. The **civil service** and **armed forces** are open to women. The latter has had its own all-female battalion beginning in 1976. And as many as three ministerial portfolios at one time have been occupied by women.

Following **independence**, a number of women rose to prominence over the years as barristers, professors, physicians and civil servants. Observers note, however, that full equality has yet to be achieved. Significantly fewer women attend and graduate from high schools and **universities** than males. In 1990, the percentage of women above the age of 15 years considered literate was 61 percent, as compared to 84 percent for males, according to **World Bank** statistics. **Literacy** rates in 1985 were 53 percent for women and 79 percent for males. Fewer still rise in the professional ranks and their salaries often are lower than those of males fulfilling similar or less-responsible functions. Others note, however, that with the high incidence of **unemployment**, jobs tend to go to heads of families, who usually are considered to be male despite the increasing number of **urban** families headed by women. Economic decline beginning in the 1980s and the crisis of the 1990s placed additional economic burdens upon women. Traditionally they were most active in the informal **economy**, which became a major source of survival, and as a result many became the major providers for their families when earnings in the formal economy were undercut by rising unemployment and **inflation**.

Sociologists said, given the tendency in family disputes toward recourse to **customary law**, few women are able to draw satisfactory compensation from a divorce if the husband decides to take the children and belongings. In the late 1990s, although the African and Congolese feminist movements were considered young and not as militant as their European and American counterparts, observers noted they had grown since the 1960s and had achieved some progress in the quest for equality.

WORKERS. *See* LABOR.

WORLD BANK. The name commonly used to refer to the International Bank for Reconstruction and Development (IBRD). It was formed following World War II to help rebuild European countries devastated by the war but beginning in the 1960s increasingly turned to financing economic development in newly independent nations of Africa and other parts of the world. The bank was active in Congo virtually from **independence**. It specialized in funding infrastructure projects such as the construction and improvement of **roads, railways** and maritime networks, **telecommunications** facilities and the development of **electrical power** complexes. **Agriculture** and rural **development projects** also received considerable attention. The World Bank provided the **government** of Congo/Zaire with numerous loans to help refinance **debt** payment arrears as part of various stabilization agreements with its sister institution, the **International Monetary Fund (IMF)**. However, Zaire's inability to service its debt in the 1990s led to a shutoff of new funding and the World Bank closed its office in **Kinshasa** in 1993. *See also* International Development Association (IDA); London Club.

WORLD WARS. The **Belgian Congo** provided important human and material resources to **Belgium** and the Allies during the World Wars. Troops of the **Force Publique** fought against German forces in Cameroon and Tanganyika during World War I and against Nazi and Fascist forces in Ethiopia and Nigeria during World War II. In both wars the heroism of the Congolese contingents was praised by the Allied command. In addition, mines in **Katanga** supplied **copper, tin, cobalt** and other **minerals** to the war industry. They also furnished the raw **uranium** used to make the atomic bombs which were dropped on Japan and ended the World War II. Revenues from Congolese **exports** were partly responsible for keeping afloat the treasury of the Belgian government-in-exile during the wars and helped finance the post-World War II reconstruction effort.

- Y -

YAKA. A group of **Bantu**-speaking people which originally lived between the **Kwango** and Wamba Rivers in southwestern Congo/Zaire. Some ethnologists say the **Jaga** invasion, which severely undermined the **Kongo Kingdom** in the 1600s, was actually mounted by the Yaka. A fierce, independent people, the Yaka during the **colonial era** tended to avoid contact with the

Belgian authorities for geographical and political reasons. Yaka residents of **Leopoldville** clashed with **Kongo** groups following **independence** and, during the 1960s, occasionally resisted violently **government** attempts to take control of their lands.

YEKE. A people of the **Bantu** cluster with some Arab influence that live in southern **Katanga Province** between **Kolwezi** and Kazanga near the **Zambian** border. According to Irving Kaplan, the Yeke are descendants of a **kingdom** established in the 1800s by **Tanzania**-based traders called the **Nyamwezi**. Some Yeke joined the **Lunda** in forming the **Confédération des Associations Katangaises (CONAKAT)** party in the late 1950s.

YEMO, MARIE-MADELEINE. **Mobutu**'s mother, affectionately known as "Mama Mobutu," was the model for the "Black Madonna" theme of African motherhood which was prominent in the early stages of the **Authenticity** movement. Following her death on May 18, 1971, **Kinshasa**'s main hospital was named after her and a large monument was erected in her memory at Gemena, in northern Zaire, where she died.

YOUTH. More than half of Congo/Zaire's **population** is below the age of 15 years and two-thirds is younger than 25 years. The growth of the youth population is the result of high birth rates and reduced infant mortality beginning in the 1950s. In the mid-1960s, Congolese cities experienced a dramatic increase in their population of young people, due not only to demographic factors, but also to urban **migration** by youth seeking jobs and the modern life. In the cities, **unemployment** and the decline in influence of the extended family, which traditionally provided support, led to problems of homelessness and juvenile **crime**. The **government**, aware of the potential threat to stability, in 1967 created the **Jeunesse du Mouvement Populaire de la Révolution (JMPR)**, the youth wing of the **Mouvement Populaire de la Révolution (MPR)**. However, the zeal of early JMPR organizers in taking over church and lay youth movements and their property created considerable resentment among the adult population. The resentment waned as the movement matured and became institutionalized.

The lack of **educational** facilities and job prospects later made some youth, particularly university **students**, the most persistent critics of the government. Protests organized by university students and supported by secondary students in 1969 led to clashes with the army in which dozens were killed. Further protests by students commemorating the first clashes led to the **nationalization** of the **universities** in 1971 and the centralization of curricula in 1972 and 1973. Protests in subsequent years led to frequent closings of the universities and secondary schools. Many of the protests focused on poor living and study conditions but some were also against **corruption** and wasteful government spending. The protests also occasionally led to vandalism and looting. They usually prompted a stern response from the authorities, including arrests, suspension of classes and induction of protest leaders into the **armed forces**.

Many student leaders later rose to senior positions in the party and government. Others went into exile and became **dissidents**. In 1990, criticism by students at the **Lubumbashi** campus of the **Université Nationale du Zaïre (UNAZA)** led to an attack by **security** forces on May 11, less than one month after **Mobutu** announced the **democratic transition. Human rights** organizations said as many as 100 students were killed when soldiers invaded their dormitories, although the government said only one was killed. The attack caused the **United States**, Canada and the **European Union** to curtail all non-humanitarian aid to Zaire and marked the beginning of the final withdrawal of support for Mobutu by Western governments.

YOUTH OF THE POPULAR REVOLUTIONARY MOVEMENT. *See* JEUNESSE DU MOUVEMENT POPULAIRE DE LA RÉVOLUTION (JMPR).

- Z -

Z'AHIDI NGOMA, ARTHUR. The leader of a small **political party** called the Forces de l'Avenir (Forces of the Future), Z'Ahidi, who once worked for the **United Nations** Educational, Scientific and Cultural Organization (UNESCO), became the first major prisoner of conscience of the Laurent **Kabila** government, which came to power after the fall of **Mobutu** in May 1997. Z'Ahidi was arrested on November 25, 1997, after he publicly criticized Kabila. Humanitarian organizations pleaded for his release or transfer to house arrest because of his deteriorating health. In early 1998, Z'Ahidi and several other dissidents "escaped" from detention in **Katanga Province**. He was recaptured but later freed. Z'Ahidi emerged in August 1998 as one of the leaders of the **Rassemblement Congolais pour la Démocratie (RCD)** which rebelled against the Kabila government accusing it of favoritism and undemocratic practices. When the RCD established a national assembly in an attempt to broaden its political base in January 1999, Z'Ahidi was named its president but he announced in February that he was leaving the alliance.

ZAIRE. *See* CONGO/ZAIRE; ZAÏRE, RÉPUBLIQUE DU.

ZAIRE COMMITTEE. A group of intellectuals, consisting primarily of Belgian former teachers in Congo/Zaire and exiled Congolese **dissidents** based primarily in **Belgium**. The committee opposed the **Mobutu government** and published occasional newsletters denouncing **corruption**, authoritarianism and **human rights** violations in Zaire. During the 1980s, some exiled politicians allied with the committee and contributed to its work by providing documents and verbal accounts of the excesses of the regime, but most preferred to lead their own dissident groups.

ZAIRE (CURRENCY). The major unit of **currency** from 1967 until 1998, it replaced the Congolese **franc** which had been closely associated with the Belgian franc. One zaire (1Z) equaled 100 makuta (likuta in the singular) and one likuta equaled 100 sengi. Due to the loss of value of the zaire, the makuta and sengi had disappeared from circulation by the 1980s.

When it was introduced, one zaire replaced 1,000 Congo francs and was worth two US dollars. By 1980, according to **central bank** figures, the value of the zaire had declined severalfold and was exchanged officially at 2.8Z to one US dollar. During economic reforms announced in September 1983, the currency was floated on the free market through weekly auctions by the central bank. By 1985, the rate was 50Z to the dollar and by 1990 it was 718Z to the dollar. During the period of

hyperinflation in the 1990s, the zaire declined to 15,587Z to the dollar in 1991, to 645,549Z to the dollar in 1992. By late-1993 one dollar was worth five million zaires, the largest note in circulation.

Monetary reform was decreed on October 22, 1993, during which the name of the currency was changed to the new zaire (NZ), or nouveau zaïre, and 1 NZ, worth nearly two US dollars, was exchanged for three million "old" zaires. The new currency proved to be equally susceptible to the effects of **inflation** and the tendency of the **government** to print banknotes to meet its payroll. By early 1997, one US dollar was worth 180,000 NZ.

When Laurent **Kabila** was installed as president on May 29, 1997, after the overthrow of **Mobutu**, he announced the return of the "cleansed" Congo franc. The reform was formalized on June 30, 1998.

ZAIRE, REPUBLIC OF. *See* ZAÏRE, RÉPUBLIQUE DU.

ZAÏRE, RÉPUBLIQUE DU. The formal name of the nation from October 27, 1971, when it was changed by decree from the République Démocratique du Congo, until May 29, 1997, when it was changed back. Zaire was the name first given to the **Congo River** by Portuguese **explorers**. According to legend, local inhabitants, asked by the explorers what the name of the great **river** was, responded saying "Nzadi," which meant "river" in their dialect. The river and the territory were subsequently renamed "Congo," after the **Kongo** people living near the coast who were the first to enter into contact with the Europeans.

During the **Authenticity** movement, the desire arose to change the name of the republic to an authentic African name that did not evoke a single **ethnic group**, and to remove a painful reminder of the brutality of colonialism and the chaos following **independence**. The name change was also aimed at eliminating confusion with neighboring **Republic of the Congo**, the former French colony. The change was institutionalized by the **constitution** of 1974, which established the party-state.

Under the constitution drafted in August 1996 by the **Haut Conseil de la République / Parlement de la Transition (HCR/PT)**, the name was changed to République Fédérale du Congo. However, after the **Forces Démocratiques pour la**

Libération du Congo/Zaïre (AFDL) came to power on May 29, 1997, the name was changed back to République Démocratique du Congo. In order to avoid confusion, many refer to the country as Congo/Zaire or Congo/Kinshasa. *See also* Belgian Congo; Congo Free State; Congo, Republic of the (Kinshasa); Name Changes.

ZAIRE RIVER. The name given to the **Congo River** by the **Mobutu** government when the country's name was changed to République du **Zaïre** in 1971 under **Authenticity**. The change was not acknowledged by international cartographers. The name "Zaire River" was dropped in May 1997 by the government of Laurent **Kabila**.

ZAÏRÉTAIN. A **tin mining** company established in 1968 to exploit deposits of cassiterite in **Katanga Province**. It was 50 percent owned by the Zairian **government** and 50 percent owned by a Belgian consortium. Production declined in the 1980s and was suspended in the 1990s.

ZAIRIAN RADIO AND TELEVISION AGENCY. *See* OFFICE ZAÏROIS DE RADIO ET DE TÉLÉVISION (OZRT).

ZAIRIANIZATION. The term used to describe the policy of **nationalization** of foreign-owned companies in strategic sectors of the **economy** between 1973 and 1975. On November 30, 1973, amid rising **mineral** prices and at the peak of the **Authenticity** movement, **Mobutu** announced a program aimed at transferring a great deal of Zaire's wealth still in foreign hands to Zairian ownership. The large **mining** companies had already been nationalized in the late 1960s. Zairianization transferred most large and medium-sized companies in the **agricultural** and **transportation** sectors and all companies with gross annual revenues of more than one million **zaires** (at the time roughly equal to one million dollars) to public ownership.

The program most affected Zaire's medium-size and small business owners. Most of them were foreigners of Asian, Arab and southern European nationalities who were perceived as profiteering middlemen. Their companies were turned over to Zairian citizens chosen by the **government**. In many of the more than 100 large enterprises that were Zairianized, the government appointed representatives, called "*délégués*," but retained the original owners as operators or partners. In the smaller businesses, however, there were fewer controls and the new owners in many cases merely sold off the existing assets and abandoned the business. Zairianization also seriously hurt the agricultural sector because the new owners failed to maintain transportation, distribution and marketing infrastructures. In addition, the lack of guidelines for compensation and the favoring of political loyalists brought criticism at the domestic and international levels.

On December 30, 1974, in the face of falling production figures and rising criticism from the international financial community, the Zairian government announced **Retrocession**, a policy which allowed up to 40 percent of the Zairianized properties to be returned to their foreign owners. The proportion was increased to 60 percent nine months later. However, the government retained ownership of what were considered vital industries, namely in **energy**, **timber** and large-scale transportation. *See also* Economy; Nationalization.

ZAMBIA, RELATIONS WITH. Relations between **Congo/Zaire** and Zambia during the years following **independence** were correct for the most part, in large part because of the friendship between **Mobutu** and Zambian President Kenneth Kaunda. However, relations were strained periodically by **smuggling**, border disputes and competition for markets for principal **exports** of **copper** and **cobalt**. Zairian mistrust was aroused during the **Shaba** invasion of 1978 when **Front pour la Libération Nationale du Congo (FLNC)** guerrillas used Zambian territory to cross from bases in **Angola** to Shaba Region, although it was later established that they did so without the consent of the Zambian government.

Relations were strained again in 1983 and 1984 by a series of border clashes in southern Shaba. In one incident, Zairian soldiers raised the Zairian flag over several small villages claimed by both countries. In another, Zairian passengers were abducted from a train in Zambian territory. These incidents and subsequent acts of retaliation were often characterized as acts of banditry by hungry soldiers or as disputes between smugglers. Zambia's expulsion of illegal Zairian immigrants in July 1984 led Zaire to retaliate by ordering the deportation of illegal Zambian immigrants. The order was revoked on August 25. Heavy smuggling, allegedly involving senior military and civilian officials obliged the two governments to impose strict visa controls in 1988. Negotiations led to an agreement on September 18, 1989, ending a long-standing border dispute and leading to an improvement in relations.

Kaunda was defeated in multiparty elections on October 31, 1991, by Frederick Chiluba, who was reelected in 1996. Chiluba tried to mediate the **rebellion** launched in 1998 by the **Rassemblement Congolais pour la Démocratie (RCD)**, in which a half-dozen African nations became militarily involved.

ZANDE. A large cluster of **ethnic groups** of Sudanic origin, speaking **languages** of Adamawa-Eastern origin, that live in northern Congo/Zaire along the **Ubangi** and **Uele Rivers** bordering the **Central African Republic** and **Sudan**. Hunters and warriors, they are believed to have arrived in the **forests** of the **Congo River Basin** in the 1700s and 1800s, although ethnologists are not certain why. They subjugated the people already living in the area and resisted the colonial administration until the early 1920s.

A hierarchical society, the Zande are sometimes divided by ethnologists into an aristocracy called the **Vungara** and commoners called the **Mbomu**. Chieftaincy, generally within the Vungara group, was passed from father to a designated son, who was obliged to vanquish any of his brothers who opposed the **succession**. Vanquished brothers were obliged to leave the **society** and find new people to conquer. The practice was believed to have been a major cause of the intermingling of Zande and **Bantu**-related groups in the area. The group was subdivided into the Vungara, living primarily in the east, and the **Bandiya**, living primarily in the west.

ZIMBABWE, RELATIONS WITH. Relations with Zimbabwe were correct from its independence on April 17, 1980. After the fall of **Mobutu** in 1997, Zimbabwe grew alarmed at the influence and aggressiveness of **Uganda** and **Rwanda** in central Africa. It sent troops—as did **Namibia**, **Angola** and **Chad**—to support the Laurent **Kabila** government when it was attacked by the **Rassemblement Congolais pour la Démocratie (RCD)** in August 1998.

ZINC. Zinc in Congo/Zaire was produced solely by the **Générale des Carrières et des Mines (GECAMINES)** as a by-product of **copper mining** at a single mine at Kipushi, west of **Lubumbashi.** Ore with zinc graded as high as 19 percent was extracted from depths of up to 1,280 m. A plant at Kipushi produced concentrates which were shipped to **Likasi** for roasting and then to the Usine de Zinc de Kolwezi, at **Kolwezi,** where 25-kg ingots of 99.995 percent pure zinc were produced through the electrolytic process. The country's zinc reserves were estimated at 2.2 million metric tons in the late 1980s. Production of concentrate reached 109,182 tons in 1960, declined to 67,000 tons in 1980, but increased again to 80,000 tons in 1984. With the financial deterioration of GECAMINES, production declined steadily in the late 1980s and totaled 20,000 tons in 1992. Production of zinc ingots, primarily for **export,** began in the late 1950s and reached 66,000 tons in 1984.

ZONGO RIVER. A **river** located in **Bas-Congo Province** east of **Matadi** that flows into the **Congo River.** The Zongo is the site of a dramatic waterfall where a 60,000-kW hydroelectric complex, built in 1928, supplies power to **Bas-Zaïre.** The station became less important following the completion of the **Inga hydroelectric complex** in the early 1970s, but remained in operation, the oldest such complex in the country.

BIBLIOGRAPHY

CONTENTS

Introduction

The literature available on Zaire is abundant, as the length of this bibliography testifies. In addition, interest in Great Britain and the United States in the affairs of Zaire since the years of the Congo Free State has contributed to a significant body of literature in the English language. However, a student seeking an advanced or specialized knowledge of the country will find the absence of at least a working knowledge of French to be a serious handicap. This bibliography is devoted primarily to works in English and French. In addition, a few works in Flemish, German, Italian and Portuguese that present new material or a different point of view also have been included.

For the student seeking a general overview of Zaire in English, several works exist. One that is relatively complete, succinct and unopinionated is the *Zaire Area Handbook*, edited by Irving Kaplan as part of the series of country handbooks published by the American University of Washington, DC. This edition, published in 1979, follows events in Zaire through the two Shaba wars, but of course omits the last 20 years of Congolese history. Mention should also be made of the two earlier editions: the US Army's *Area Handbook for the Republic of the Congo (Leopoldville)*, published in 1962, that provides considerably more detail on events leading up to and including independence, and the *Area Handbook for the Democratic Republic of the Congo (Congo-Kinshasa)*, published in 1971, that provides additional detail on the years following independence and the beginnings of Mobutism. In French, *Du Congo au Zaire: 1960-1980*, edited by J. Vanderlinden, takes a similar, long view of political, economic and cultural developments in Zaire.

Other more recent works in English that tend to focus primarily on the Mobutu government include *The Rise and Decline of the Zairian State* by Crawford Young and Thomas Turner, published in 1985; *The Crisis in Zaire: Myths and Realities*, edited by Nzongola-Ntalaja, published in 1986; and *The State-Society Struggle: Zaire in Comparative Perspective* by Thomas M. Callaghy, published in 1984. To varying degrees these works focus on problems such as authoritarianism, centralization, the lack of political freedoms, corruption and declining standards of living that have been among the most recurrent indictments of Mobutism. The Nzongola book, a collection of papers presented at a conference sponsored by Howard University of Washington, DC, contains a revealing segment on how Zairians survive the economic hardships of low wages or unemployment.

Several other specialized works also should be mentioned. Among the bibliographies, the seminal *A Study Guide for Congo-Kinshasa* by Edouard Bustin, published in 1970, is a well-organized collection of virtually all the major material on Zaire through 1968. The listings of the Cataloging Distribution Service of the Library of Congress provide a relatively comprehensive record of monographs published since 1967. Articles in periodicals tend to provide recent, although often slanted material on current Zairian affairs. For recent articles, readers should examine *Africa Report* magazine, which annually publishes a listing of the articles published in its pages in its final issue of the year. Other periodicals with frequent articles on Zaire include *Africa*, *Africa Confidential*, *Africa News* and *West Africa*. Zairian publications include the *Elima* and *Salongo* daily newspapers and *Zaire* magazine. Work on ethnic groups in Zaire has been extensive. Some of the broader publications include *Kingdoms of the Savanna* by Jan Vansina, published in 1966, and in French, *Carte ethnique du Congo: Quart sudest* and *Carte ethnique de la République du Congo: Quart sud-ouest* by Olga Boone, published in 1961 and 1973, respectively. In addition, the series, *Ethnographic Survey of Africa* by the International Africa Institute in the early 1950s provides a broad though dated overview. Finally, the monographs published by the Centre d'Études Ethnographiques de Bandundu (CEEBA) should be mentioned as an example of Zairian efforts to collect, preserve and analyze their traditional societies.

Because of the size of the body of work and the difficulty with which articles in older periodicals are retrieved, this bibliography focuses primarily on monographs. Articles are mentioned when monographs are lacking on a certain subject and in particular for the early days of the Laurent Kabila government, which have yet to receive extensive analysis.

Most scholars agree that the literature on Zaire needs more contributions from Zairian and African scholars. Nevertheless, it should be noted that contributions by Zairians have increased since the 1970s due in large part to the efforts of certain university presses in Zaire, Belgium, Britain and the United States. It is hoped this trend will continue. Initially, Zairian scholars tended to focus on the arts, ethnological and social studies. These are valuable, but also needed are more historical assessments of colonialism and independence by Zairian authors, as well as objective analyses of the Mobutu era and the period after his fall.

Abbreviations and Acronyms in Bibliography

ARSOM	Académie Royale des Sciences d'Outre-Mer
CEDAF	Centre d'Étude et de Documentation Africaines
CEEBA	Centre d'Études Ethnographiques de Bandundu
CEMUBAC	Centre Scientifique et Médicale de l'Université Libre de Belgique en Afrique Centrale
CEPSI	Centre d'Études de Problèmes Sociaux Indigènes

CRISP	Centre de Recherche et d'Information Socio-politiques
IAI	International Africa Institute
INEAC	Institut pour l'Étude Agronomique du Congo
INMZ	Institut des Musées Nationaux du Zaïre
IRCB	Institut Royal Colonial Belge
IRES	Institut de Recherches Économiques et Sociales
JPRS	Joint Publications Research Service
MRAC	Musée Royal de l'Afrique, Tervuren, Belgium
SRBG	Société Royale Belge de Géographie
UNAZA	Université Nationale du Zaïre

I. GENERAL

1. Bibliographies

Belgium. Office de la Coopération au Développement. *Belgium and Cooperation in Development: A Bibliographical Survey*. Brussels: Belgian Information and Documentation Institute, n.d. (1963?).

Biebuyck, Daniel P. *The Arts of Central Africa: An Annotated Bibliography*. Boston: G. K. Hall, 1987.

Boogaerts, M. "L'Enseignement au Congo: Bibliographie," *Cahiers Économique et Sociaux, IRES* 5 no. 2 (1967): 237-65.

Boone, Olga. *Bibliographie ethnographique de l'Afrique subsaharienne*. Tervuren: MRAC, 1960-present (annual, continues work below).

————. *Bibliographie ethnographique du Congo Belge et des regions avoisinantes*. 31 vols. Tervuren: MRAC, 1931-60.

Bustin, Edouard. *A Study Guide for Congo-Kinshasa*. Boston: African Studies Center, Boston University, 1970.

Centre Aequatoria. *Catalogue des doubles: Périodiques et livres conservés à la Bibliothèque du Centre Aequatoria*. Mbandaka: n.d.

Dargitz, Robert E. *A Selected Bibliography of Books and Articles in the Disciples of Christ Research Library in Mbandaka, Democratic Republic of the Congo*. Indianapolis: Department of Africa and Jamaica, United Christian Missionary Society, 1967.

Friedland, William H. *Unions, Labor and Industrial Relations in Africa: An Annotated Bibliography*. Ithaca, NY: Cornell University Press, 1965.

Gaskin, L. J. P. *A Bibliography of African Art*. London: International African Institute, 1965.

————. *A Select Bibliography of Music in Africa*. London: International African Institute, 1965.

Heyse, Théodore. "Bibliographie du Congo Belge et du Ruanda-Urundi, 1939-51." *Cahiers Belges et Congolais*, nos. 4-22 (1953).

————. *Index bibliographique coloniale*. Brussels: Falk, Fils, G. Van Campenhout, 1937.

————. "Le Travail bibliographique colonial belge de 1876 à 1933." *Zaire* (June 1948): 639-56.

Huisman, M. and P. Jacquet. *Bibliographie de l'histoire coloniale 1900-1930: Belgique*. Paris: Société de l'Histoire des Colonies, 1932.

Institut de Recherches Économiques et Sociales (IRES). Université de Lovanium. *Catalogue des archives du Centre d'Études Politiques: Série: Les Provinces du Congo*. Leopoldville, 1966.

Institut Royal Colonial Belge. *Biographie Coloniale Belge*. 5 vols. Brussels: Van Campenhout, 1948.

International African Institute. *African Urbanization: A Reading List of Selected Books, Articles and Reports*. London: IAI, 1965.

————. *West Central Africa*. Africa Bibliography Series. London: IAI, 1966.

Kadima Nzuji Mukala. "Bibliographie littéraire de la République du Zaïre, 1931-72." *Celria* (August 1973). (Also published in *Zaïre-Afrique* no. 87, August-September 1974.)

Lemarchand, René. "Selective Bibliographical Survey for the Study of Politics in the Former Belgian Congo." *American Political Science Review* 56, no. 3 (1960): 715-28.

Liniger-Goumaz, Max. *Préhistoire et protohistoire de la République Démocratique du Congo: Bibliographie*. Geneva: Éditions du Temps, 1969.

————. *République du Zaïre, Kivu-Maniema: Bibliographie*. Geneva: Éditions du Temps, 1977.

Lungu Ndaying Tindel. *Bibliographie sur la productivité du travail dans les secteurs économiques du Zaïre*. Kinshasa: USAID, 1990.

Mitchel, Robert C., Harold W. Turner, and Hans J. Greschat. *A Comprehensive Bibliography of Modern African Religious Movements*. Evanston: Northwestern University Press, 1966.

Musée Royal de l'Afrique Centrale. *Bibliographie géologique du Congo et du Rwanda*. Tervuren: MRAC, 1952-61.

Rossie, Jean Pierre. *Bibliographie commentée de la communauté musulmane au Zaire des origines à 1975*. Brussels: CEDAF, 1976.

Ryelandt, Dominique, ed. "Bibliographie générale des articles et ouvrages politiques sur la République du Congo (Léopoldville)." *Études Congolaises* (special issue, March 1963).

Santos Hernandez, Angel. *Bibliografia Missional*. 2 vols. Santander, Spain: Editorial "Sal Terrae," 1965, pp. 944, 1299.

Smet, A. J. *La Philosophie africaine: Bibliographie sélective*. Kinshasa: UNAZA, 1974.

Vriens, Livinus. *Critical Bibliography of Missiology*. Nijmegen, the Netherlands: Bestelcentrale del V.S.K.B., 1960.

Walraet, Michel. *Bibliographie du Katanga*. 3 vols. Brussels: ARSOM, 1954-60.

Wauters, Alphonse-Jules. *Bibliographie du Congo, 1880-1885*. Brussels: Administration du Mouvement Géographique, 1895.

Williams, Dawn Bastian, Robert W. Lesh, and Andrea L. Stamm. *Zaire*. Oxford: Clio Press, 1995.

Zaretsky, Irving I. *Bibliography on Spirit Possession and Spirit Mediumship on the African Continent*. Berkeley: University of California, Department of Anthropology, 1967.

2. Demographic Statistics

Boute, Joseph. *Demographic Trends in the Republic of Zaire*. Pasadena: Munger Africana Library, California Institute of Technology, 1973.

Boute, Joseph, and Léon de Saint Moulin. *Perspectives démographiques régionales, 1975-1985*. Kinshasa: République du Zaïre, Département du Plan, 1978.

Congo, République Démocratique du. Institut National de la Statistique. *Receuil des rapports et totaux: Recensement en 1970*. Kinshasa: n.d.

————. Ministère du Plan et de la Coordination Économique. Service des Statistiques. Bureau Démographie. *Étude par sondages de la main d'oeuvre à Léopoldville, 1958.* Leopoldville: 1961.

Congo, République Démocratique du, and Institut de Recherches Économiques et Sociales, Lovanium University. *Enquête démographique par sondage, 1955-1957: Analyse générale des résultats statistiques.* Leopoldville: 1961.

De Smets, R. E. *Carte de la densité et de la localisation de la population de l'ancienne province de Léopoldville (République Démocratique du Congo).* Brussels: CEMUBAC, 1966.

————. *Carte de la densité et de la localisation de la population de la Province Orientale (Congo).* Brussels: CEMUBAC, 1962.

Fortems, G. *La densité de la population dans le Bas Fleuve et le Mayombe.* Brussels: ARSOM, 1960.

Gourou, Pierre. "Carte de la densité des populations," in *Atlas Général du Congo Belge.* Brussels: IRCB, 1951.

————. *La densité de la population rurale au Congo Belge.* Brussels: ARSC, 1955.

Huysecom-Wolter, Claudine. *La démographie en Équateur.* Brussels: CEMUBAC, 1964.

Knoop, H. "Some Demographic Characters of a Suburban Squatting Community of Léopoldville: A Preliminary Analysis." *Cahiers Économiques et Sociaux IRES* 4, no. 2 (1966): 119-49.

Lamal, F. *Essai d'étude démographique d'une population du Kwango: Les Basuku du territoire de Feshi.* Brussels: IRCB, 1949.

Neven, M., J. De Potter, and H. Danakpali. *Enquête démographique en milieu azande, Uelé, Congo.* Brussels: ARSOM, 1962.

Ngondo a Pitshandenge, L. de Saint Moulin, and B. Tambashe Oleko. *Perspectives démographiques du Zaïre, 1984-1999, et population d'âge éléctoral en 1993 et 1994.* Kinshasa: Centre d'Études pour l'Action Sociale, 1992.

Pauwels, Jacques. "La répartition de la population dans le territoire de Gungu (Congo)." *Bulletin de la Société Royale Belge de Géographie* (1962). 89-129.

Romaniuk, Anatole. *La Fécondité des populations congolaises.* Paris: Mouton, 1967.

————. *Tableau général de la démographie congolaise: Enquête démographique par sondage, 1955-1957: Analyse générale des résultats statistiques.* Leopoldville: Bureau de la Démographie and IRES, 1961.

Saint Moulin, Léon de. *Atlas des collectivités du Zaïre*. Kinshasa: PUZ, 1976.

Smet, Roger E. de. *Cartes de la densité et de la localisation de la population de la province du Katanga (République du Zaïre)*. Brussels: CEMUBAC, 1971.

United States Agency for International Development. Office of Development Information and Utilization. *Africa, Zaire: Selected Statistical Data by Sex*. Washington: 1981.

Verheust, Thérèse. *Enquête démographique par sondage, 1955-1957: Province Orientale, District de Stanleyville, District du Haut-Uelé*. Brussels: CEDAF, 1978.

Zaire. Ministère du Plan et Aménagement du Territoire. Institut National de la Statistique. *Echanges d'expériences sur le premier recensement scientifique de la population du Zaïre, 1984: De la conception à la publication des données: Actes de la table ronde tenue à Kinshasa le 03 décembre 1992*. Kinshasa: 1994.

————. *Recensement scientifique de la population, 1984: Profil de la femme au Zaïre*. Kinshasa, 1994.

————. *Recensement scientifique de la population 1984: Projections démographiques Zaïre et régions, 1984-2000*. Kinshasa: 1993.

————. *Recensement scientifique de la population, juillet 1984. Caractéristiques démographiques*. Kinshasa: 1991-92.

————. *Recensement scientifique de la population, juillet 1984. Totaux définitifs: Groupements/quartiers*. Kinshasa: 1992.

————. *Recensement scientifique de la population, juillet 1984: Totaux définitifs: Groupements/quartiers, localités*. Kinshasa, 1995.

3. General Information and Interdisciplinary Works

Archer, Jules. *Congo: The Birth of a New Nation*. (Juvenile.) New York: J. Messner, 1979.

Belgium. Office de l'Information et des Relations Publiques pour le Congo Belge et le Ruanda-Urundi. *Belgian Congo*. Translated from French by F. H. Heldt and C. Heldt. Brussels: 1959-60.

Bobb, F. Scott. *Historical Dictionary of Zaire*. Metuchen, NJ: Scarecrow Press, 1988.

British Overseas Trade Board. *Republic of Zaire*. London: 1976.

Brooks, Philip. *Dikembe Mutombo (Mount Mutombo)*. (Juvenile.) Chicago: Children's Press, 1995.

Bustin, Edouard. "The Congo," in *Five African States: Responses to Diversity*, ed. G. M. Carter. Ithaca, NY: Cornell University Press, 1963.

Cambridge History of Africa. Vols. 6-8. Cambridge: Cambridge University, 1979-80.

Carpenter, John Allen. *Zaire*. (Juvenile.) Chicago: Children's Press, 1974.

Centre Aequatoria. *Recherches africanistes au Zaïre: Actes du colloque du cinquantenaire d'Aequatoria, du 11 au 13 octobre, 1987*. Mbandaka: Centre Aequatoria, 1989.

Chapelier, A. *Élisabethville: Essai de géographie humaine*. Brussels: ARSC, 1957.

Comeliau, Christian. *Fonctions économiques et pouvoir politique: La Province de l'Uelé en 1963-1964*. Leopoldville: IRES, 1966.

Congo. 9 vols. (Published annually, various editors.) Brussels: CRISP, 1959-67.

Congo, République Démocratique du. *Bilan, 1965-1970*. Kinshasa: 1970.

———. Armée Nationale. Service d'Education et d'Information. *Le Sixième anniversaire de la République Démocratique du Congo, 30 juin 1966*. Kinshasa: 1966.

———. Haut Commissariat à l'Information. *Le Congo en bref*. Kinshasa: 1966.

Crane, Louise. *The Land and People of the Congo*. (Juvenile.) Philadelphia: Lippincott, 1971.

Dardel, Philippe. *Zaïre*. Paris: Panthéon, 1994.

Diallo, Siradiou. *Zaire Today*. Paris: Éditions J.A., 1977.

Dictionary of African Biography. 2 vols. Algonac, MI: Reference Publications for Encyclopedia Africana, 1979.

Elisofon, Eliot. *Zaire: A Week in Joseph's World*. (Juvenile.) New York: Crowell-Collier Press, 1973.

Encyclopédie du Congo Belge. 3 vols. Brussels: Bieleveld, 1950-53.

First, Ruth. *Power in Africa*. New York: Pantheon, 1970.

Frank, Louis. *Le Congo Belge*. Brussels: La Renaissance du Livre, 1930.

Gann, L. H., and P. Duignan. *White Settlers in Tropical Africa*. Baltimore: Penguin, 1962.

Gappert, Gary, and Garry Thomas, eds. *The Congo, Africa and America*. Syracuse: Syracuse University Press, n.d. (1965?).

Gott, Richard. *Mobutu's Congo*. London: Fabian Society, 1968.

Henderson, Faye. *Zaire: A Country Profile*. Washington: US Agency for International Development, Office for Foreign Disaster Assistance, 1981.

Heyse, Théodore, and Jean Berlage. *Documentation générale sur le Congo et le Ruanda-Urundi, 1953-1960*. 3 vols. (*Cahiers Belges et Congolais*, nos. 26, 31 and 34.) Brussels: Van Campenhout, 1956-60.

Jenike, David. *A Walk through a Rain Forest: Life in the Ituri Forest of Zaire*. (Juvenile.) New York: F. Watts, 1994.

Jewsiewicki, B. *État Indépendant du Congo, Congo Belge, République du Zaïre?* Québec: SAFI Press, 1984.

Kaplan, Irving, ed. *Zaire, a Country Study*. Area Handbook. 3rd ed. Washington: American University, Foreign Area Studies, 1979.

Laman, Karl E. *The Kongo*. Vols. 1-4. Uppsala, Sweden: Studia Ethnographica Upsaliensia, 1953-68.

Laurenty, Jean-Sebastien. *L'Organologie du Zaïre*. Tervuren: MRAC, 1995.

Mabi Mulumba, Mutamba Makombo. *Cadres et dirigeants au Zaïre, qui sont-ils?: Dictionnaire biographique*. Kinshasa: Centre de Recherches Pédagogiques, 1986.

MacGaffey, Wyatt, ed. *Republic of the Congo (Leopoldville)*. Area Handbook. Washington: American University, Foreign Area Studies, 1962.

McDonald, Gordon C., ed. *Democratic Republic of the Congo (Congo-Kinshasa)*. Area Handbook. 2nd ed. Washington: American University, Foreign Area Studies, 1971.

McKowan, Robin. *The Congo: River of Mystery*. (Juvenile.) New York: McGraw-Hill, 1968.

———. *The Republic of Zaire*. (Juvenile.) New York: F. Watts, 1972.

Meditz, Sandra W., and Tim Merrill, eds. *Zaire: A Country Study*. Area Handbook. 4th ed. Washington: Federal Research Division, Library of Congress, 1994.

Newbury, David S. *Vers le passé du Zaïre: Quelques méthodes de recherche historique*. Bukavu: Institut pour la Recherche Scientifique en Afrique Centrale, 1973.

Nzongola-Ntalaja, ed. *The Crisis in Zaire: Myths and Realities*. Trenton, NJ: Africa World Press, 1986.

Siy, Alexandra. *The Efe: People of the Ituri Rain Forest.* (Juvenile.) New York: Dillon Press; Toronto: Maxwell Macmillan; and New York: Maxwell Macmillan International, 1993.
Stefoff, Rebecca. *Republic of Zaire.* Edgemont, PA: Chelsea House Publishers, 1986.
Stewart, Mark. *Dikembe Mutombo.* (Juvenile.) New York: Children's Press, 1996.
Ziegler, Jean. *La Contre-révolution en Afrique.* Paris: Payot, 1963.

4. Periodicals, Newspapers and Mass Media

Berlage, Jean. *Répertoire de la presse du Congo Belge et du Ruanda-Urundi (1920-1958).* Brussels: Commission Belge de Bibliographie, 1959.
Boyoma. (Irregular.) Newspaper published in Kisangani in the early 1990s.
Centre d'Étude et de Documentation Africaine. *Les Périodiques zaïrois (1970-1977).* Brussels: CEDAF, 1978.
Congo, Belgian. *Nsango ya Bisu: Nos nouvelles.* (Semimonthly periodical for the Force Publique.) Leopoldville: 1943-60.
Congo, République du. *La Voix de l'Armée Congolaise: Lolaka ya Armée Congolaise.* (Semimonthly periodical for the armed forces, replaced *Nsango ya Bisu.*) Leopoldville: 1960.
Congo, République du. Bibliothèque Centrale du Congo. *Répertoire des périodiques congolais se trouvant à la Bibliothèque Centrale du Congo.* Leopoldville: 1961.
Congo, République Démocratique du. Ministère de la Culture et des Arts. Direction des Archives et Bibliothèques. *Répertoire alphabétique des périodiques de la Bibliothèque Nationale.* Kinshasa: 1969.
———. *Répertoire des périodiques congolais.* Leopoldville: n.d.
Congo, République Démocratique du. Ministère de l'Education Nationale. *Moniteur congolais.* (Semimonthly.) Leopoldville: 1960-67.
Courier Africain. (Irregular series of monographs.) Brussels: CRISP, 1960-.
Economist Intelligence Unit. *Country Profile: Zaire, Rwanda, Burundi.* London: EIU, annual. (See also *Quarterly Economic Review of Zaire, Rwanda, Burundi* by the same organization.)

Elima. One of Kinshasa's oldest daily newspapers, it became a leading opposition publication in 1990.

Flash. Newspaper published in Kinshasa in the early 1990s.

Jua. Weekly newspaper published in Bukavu in the early 1990s.

Kitchen, Helen, ed. *The Press in Africa.* Washington: Ruth Sloan Associates, 1956.

Kya. Newspaper published in Bas-Congo in the early 1990s.

La Reférence. Daily opposition newspaper published in Kinshasa beginning in 1990.

La Semaine. Weekly newspaper published in Kinshasa beginning in 1990.

Le Cobalt. Newspaper published in Lubumbashi in the early 1990s.

Le Forum des As. Biweekly newspaper published in Kinshasa in the 1990s.

Le Kiosk. Weekly newspaper published in Kisangani in the early 1990s.

Le Lushois. Triweekly newspaper published in Lubumbashi in the 1990s.

Le Phare. Daily opposition newspaper published in Kinshasa beginning in 1990.

Le Potentiel. Daily opposition newspaper published in Kinshasa during the 1990s.

Le Soft. Daily financial newspaper published in Kinshasa in the 1990s.

Lonoh, Malangi Bokelenge. *Agences de presse et information au Zaïre.* Paris: Université de Droit, d'Économie et de Sciences Sociales de Paris, Institut Français de Presse et des Sciences de l'Information, 1982.

Mjumbe. Weekly newspaper published in Lubumbashi in the early 1990s.

Muhindo Misagwe. *Catalogue collectif des périodiques zaïrois et relatifs au Zaïre conservés dans les bibliothèques de la ville de Lubumbashi.* Lubumbashi: Université de Lubumbashi, 1986.

Mukamba, Longesha. *La Cible manquée: Une Étude de la pratique des média dans une ville africaine, Lubumbashi.* Louvain-la-Neuve: Cabay, 1983.

Salongo. Daily pro-MPR newspaper published in Kinshasa beginning in the 1970s.

Simons, Edwine, and Marie Louise Kerremans. *Les Périodiques zaïrois, 1970-1977: Bibliographies.* Brussels: CEDAF, 1978.

Tshionza Mata T., Georges. *Les médias au Zaïre: S'Aligner, ou, se libérer?* Paris: Harmattan, 1996.

Umoja. Daily opposition newspaper published in Kinshasa beginning in 1990.

United States Information Agency. Research Service. *Media Habits of Zairian Priority Audiences.* Washington: 1971.

———. *A Survey of the Print Press of Zaire.* Reston, VA: Center for Foreign Journalists, 1991.

Van Bol, Jean Marie. *La Presse quotidienne au Congo Belge.* Brussels: Pensée Catholique, and Paris: Office Général du Livre, 1959.

Zaire: A Political and Economic Forecast. Syracuse, NY: Political Risk Services, annual.

Zaire. Weekly magazine published in Kinshasa from the early 1970s until the late 1980s.

5. Description, Travel, Maps and Statistical Abstracts

Adamson, Joy. *Queen of Shaba: The Story of an African Leopard.* New York: Harcourt Brace Jovanovich, 1980.

Atlas de la République du Zaïre. Edited by Georges Laclavère. Paris: Éditions J.A., 1978.

Augouard, P. *Vingt-huit années au Congo.* Poitiers: private publisher, 1905.

Belgium. Académie Royale des Sciences d'Outre-Mer. *Atlas général du Congo et du Ruanda-Urundi.* Brussels: 1948-63.

———. Institut Belge d'Information et de Documentation. *Répertoire de l'information en 1972 en République du Zaïre.* Brussels: 1972.

———. Institut National de la Statistique. *Annuaire statistique, 1968-1978.* Kinshasa: 1979.

———. Institut Royal Colonial Belge. *Atlas général du Congo.* Brussels: 1948.

———. Office de l'Information et des Relations Publiques pour le Congo Belge et le Ruanda-Urundi (INFORCONGO). *Congo Belge et Ruanda-Urundi: Guide du voyageur.* 4th ed. Brussels: 1958.

Bradford, Phillips Verner. *OTA: The Pygmy in the Zoo.* New York: St. Martin's Press, 1992.

Burrows, Guy. *The Curse of Central Africa.* London: Everett, 1903.

———. *The Land of the Pygmies.* New York: Thomas Crowell, 1898.

Burton, R. F. *Two Trips to Gorilla Land and the Cataracts of the Congo.* 2 vols. London: Low, Marston and Searle, 1876.

Cameron, Vernay L. *Across Africa*. London: George Philip, 1885.

Capello, H. *De Angola à contra-costa*. Lisbon: 1886.

Capello, H., and R. Ivens. *From Benguella to the Territory of Yacca*. 2 vols. London: Low, 1882.

Caputo, Robert. "Zaire River: Lifeline for a Nation." *National Geographic* 180 (November 1991): 5-35.

Cole, Mary. *Dirt Roads*. Dublin: Gill and Macmillan, 1975.

Congo, Belgian. Institut Géographique. Various maps published from 1946 to 1960. Leopoldville: 1946-60.

Congo, République Démocratique du. *Foire Internationale de Kinshasa*. (International trade fair, June 24 to July 12, 1970.) Kinshasa: 1970.

———. Institut Géographique. Various maps published intermittently. Leopoldville/Kinshasa: 1960-.

Conrad, Joseph. *Heart of Darkness*. London: 1902.

Contact-Kinshasa (association). *Contact Kinshasa: Le Guide de la République du Zaïre*. 3rd ed. Kinshasa: 1975.

Coquilhat, Camille. *Sur le Haut-Congo*. Paris: Lebègue, 1888.

Cornet, Joseph. *Zaïre: Terre de tous les trésors*. Paris: Éditions J.A., 1985.

Crawford, Daniel. *Thinking Black: Twenty-two Years without a Break in the Long Grass of Central Africa*. London: Morgan and Scott, 1912.

Dennet, R. E. *Seven Years among the Fjort*. London: Sampson Low, 1887.

Derkindren, Gaston. *Atlas du Congo Belge et du Ruanda-Urundi*. Brussels: 1955.

Donegan, George J. *Katanga Philatelist: A Specialized Catalogue of the "État du Katanga" Postal Issues*. Springfield, MO: N.p., 1964.

Dorman, Marcus Roberts Phipps. *A Journal of a Tour in the Congo Free State*. Westport, CT: Negro Universities Press, 1970.

Douville, Jean-Baptiste. *Un Voyage au Congo, 1827-1828: Les tribulations d'un aventurier en Afrique equinoxiale*. Paris: La Table Ronde, 1991.

———. *Voyage au Congo et dans l'intérieur de l'Afrique equinoxiale fait dans les années 1828 et 1830*. Stuttgart: Bureau des Nouveautés de la Littérature Française, 1832.

Guinness, Fanny Emma (Fitz Gerald). *Congo Recollections, Edited from Notes and Conversations of Missionaries*. London: Hodder and Stoughton, 1890.

Hilton-Simpson, Melville William. *Land and Peoples of the Kasai*. New York: Negro Universities Press, 1969.

Idoti. *With God in the Congo Forests during the Persecution under Rebel Occupation, as Told by an African Pastor to David M. Davies*. Gerrards Cross, Bucks.: Worldwide Evangelization Crusade, 1971.

Isy-Schwart, Marcel. *Congo safari*. Paris: Éditions G.P., 1973.

Janssens, Emile. *J'étais le Général Janssens*. Brussels: Dessart, 1961.

Jean-Aubry, Georges. *Joseph Conrad in the Congo*. Norwood, PA: Norwood Editions, 1976.

Jeannest, Charles. *Quatre années au Congo*. Paris: G. Charpentier, 1884.

Kabanda, Aloys. *Ali/Forman: Le Combat du siècle à Kinshasa, 29-30 octobre, 1974*. Sherbrooke, Québec: Naaman, 1977.

Kempers, Anne Grimshaw. *Heart of Lightness*. Portsmouth, NH: P. E. Randall, 1993.

Kenney, Lona B. *Mboka: A Congo Memoir*. New York: Crown Publishers, 1973.

Le Marinel, Paul. *Carnets de route dans l'État Indépendant du Congo de 1887 à 1910*. Brussels: Progrès, 1991.

Lederer, André. *Atlas général de la République du Zaïre: Carte des transports de surface*. Brussels: ARSOM, 1976.

Livingstone, David. *The Last Journals of David Livingstone in Africa*. Edited by Horace Waller. London: John Murray, 1874.

———. *Missionary Travels and Researches in South Africa*. London: John Murray, 1857.

———. *The Zambezi Expedition of David Livingstone, 1858-1863*. Edited by J. P. R. Wallis. 3 vols. Oppenheimer Series. London: Chatto and Windus, 1956.

Lumenga-Neso Kiobe. *Kinshasa: Genèse et sites historiques*. Kinshasa: N.p., 1994.

Mark, Joan T. *The King of the World in the Land of the Pygmies*. Lincoln: University of Nebraska Press, 1995.

McKinnon, Arch C. *Kipitene of the Congo Steamship* Lapsley, and Fannie W. McKinnon, *Treasures of Darkness* (published together). Boston: Christopher, 1968.

Michaux, O. *Au Congo: Carnets de campagne; épisodes et impressions de 1889 à 1897.* Namur: Dupagne-Counet, 1913.

Moloney, Joseph A. *With Captain Stairs to Katanga.* London: S. Low, Marston, 1893.

Mopila, Francisco José. *L'Enfance/Mopila: Traduit de l'espagnol par Jaime Castro-Segovia avec la collaboration de Jacques Lanotte.* Kinshasa: Éditions du Mont Noir, 1972.

Nagy, Lazlo. *Katanga.* (Travel atlas.) Lausanne: Rencontre, 1965.

Newman, Gerald. *Zaire, Gabon, and the Congo.* New York: F. Watts, 1981.

Nouveau guide illustré de la ville de Kinshasa. Kinshasa: EDICA, 1973.

Nugent, Rory. *Drums along the Congo: On the Trail of Mokele-Mbembe, the Last Living Dinosaur.* Boston: Houghton Mifflin, 1993.

Prémorel, Raoul de. *Kassai: The Story of Raoul de Premorel, African Trader* (as told to Reginald Ray Stuart). Stockton, CA: Pacific Center for Western Historical Studies, University of the Pacific, 1975.

Répertoire kinois: Édition spéciale, cartes de la ville. Maps. Kinshasa: Hermés, 1986.

Roome, W. J. W. *Tramping through Africa.* London: A. & C. Black, 1930.

Vass, Winifred Kellersberger. *Thirty-one Banana Leaves.* Atlanta: John Knox Press, 1975.

Willaert, Maurice. *Kivu redécouvert.* Brussels: W. Arnold, 1973.

Winternitz, Helen. *East along the Equator: A Journey up the Congo and into Zaire.* New York: Atlantic Monthly Press, 1987.

Yeoman, Guy Henry. *Africa's Mountains of the Moon: A Journey to the Ultimate Sources of the Nile.* New York: Universe Books, 1989.

Zaïre, République du. Bureau du Président. *Profiles of Zaire.* Kinshasa: 1971.

Zaïre, République du. Institut Géographique. Bureau d'Études d'Aménagements Urbains. *Atlas de Kinshasa.* Paris: Institut Géographique National, 1976.

Zaire—In Pictures. Minneapolis, MN: Lerner Publications Company, 1992.

II. HISTORY

1. General History

Buana Kabue. *L'Expérience zaïroise: Du Casque colonial à la toque de léopard.* Paris: Afrique Biblio Club, 1975.

Choprix, Guy. *La Naissance d'une ville: Étude géographique de Paulis (1934-1957).* Brussels: CEMUBAC, 1961.

Congo, Belgian. *Histoire du Congo.* 3 vols. Leopoldville: 1959.

Cornevin, Robert. *Histoire du Congo (Léopoldville).* Paris: Éditions Berger-Levrault, 1963.

———. *Histoire du Congo Léopoldville-Kinshasa: Des Origines préhistoriques à la République du Congo.* Paris: Éditions Berger-Levrault, 1970.

———. *Histoire du Zaïre: Des Origines à nos jours.* 4th ed. Brussels: Hayez, 1989.

Duffy, James. *Portugal in Africa.* Cambridge: Harvard University Press, 1962.

Forbath, Peter. *The River Congo: The Discovery, Exploration and Exploitation of the World's Most Dramatic River.* New York: Harper & Row, 1977.

Galle, Hubert. *Le Congo: De la Découverte à l'indépendance.* Brussels: Éditions J.M. Collet, 1983.

Hauzeur de Fooz, Charles. *Du Congo de Léopold II au Congo-Kinshasa.* Brussels: Imprimerie Mondiale, 1966.

Hennessey, Maurice N. *The Congo.* New York: Praeger, 1961.

———. *Congo: A Brief History and Appraisal.* London: Pall Mall Press, 1961.

Lutumba. *Histoire du Zaïre.* Kinshasa: Okapi, 1972.

Mandjumba Mwanyimi-Mbomba. *Chronologie générale de l'histoire du Zaïre: Des Origines à 1988.* 2nd ed. Kinshasa: Centre de Recherches Pédagogiques, 1989. (First edition published in 1985.)

Martelli, George. *Leopold to Lumumba.* London: Chapman & Hall, 1962.

Mbandaka, hier et aujourd'hui: Eléments d'historiographie locale. Mbandaka: Centre Aequatoria, 1990.

Mendiaux, Édouard. *Histoire du Congo.* Brussels: Dessart, 1961.

Muka. *Evolution du sport au Congo.* Kinshasa: Okapi, 1970.

————. *Vers le sommet du sport zaïrois et africain*. Kinshasa: St. Paul Afrique, 1974.

Peemans, Jean-Philippe. *Le Congo-Zaire au gré du XXe siècle: État, économie, société, 1880-1990*. Paris: Harmattan, 1997.

Tshimanga wa Tshibangu. *Histoire du Zaïre*. Bukavu: Éditions du CERUKI, 1976.

Vanderlinden, J., ed. *Du Congo au Zaire: 1960-1980*. Brussels: CRISP, 1980.

Vellut, J. L. *Guide de l'étudiant en histoire du Zaïre*. Kinshasa: publisher unknown, 1974.

————. "Le Zaïre à la périphérie du capitalisme: Quelques perspectives historiques." *Enquêtes et documents d'histoire africaine* 1 (1975): 114-51.

Verbeek, Léon. *Filiation et usurpation: Histoire socio-politique de la région entre Luapula et Copperbelt*. Tervuren: MRAC, 1987.

Verhaegen, Benoît, ed. *Kisangani, 1876-1976: Histoire d'une ville*. Kinshasa: PUZ, 1975.

Zala L. N'kanza. *Les origines sociales du sous-développement politique au Congo Belge: De Padroado à la loi fondamentale, 1482-1960*. Kinshasa: PUZ, 1985.

2. Pre-Colonial

Anstey, Roger. *The Atlantic Slave Trade and British Abolition, 1760-1810*. Atlantic Highlands, NJ: Humanities Press, 1975.

————. *Britain and the Congo in the Nineteenth Century*. (Reprint of Oxford: Clarendon Press, 1962.) Westport, CT: Greenwood Press, 1981.

————. *Le Royaume du Congo aux XVe et XVIe siècles*. Leopoldville: Éditions de l'Institut National d'Études Politiques, 1963.

Balandier, Georges. *Daily Life in the Kingdom of the Kongo: From the Sixteenth to the Eighteenth Century*. Translated from French by Helen Weaver. London: Allen & Unwin; New York: Pantheon, 1968.

Batsikama ba Mampuya ma Ndwàla, R. *Voiçi les Jagas; ou, L'Histoire d'un peuple parricide bien malgré lui*. Kinshasa: Office National de la Recherche et du Développement, 1971.

Brode, Heinrich. *Tippoo Tib: The Story of his Career in Central Africa*. London: Edward Arnold, 1907.

Ceulemans, P. *La Question arabe et le Congo (1883-1892)*. Brussels: ARSC, 1959.

Curtin, Philip D. *The Atlantic Slave Trade: A Census*. Madison: University of Wisconsin Press, 1969.

Cuvelier, J. *L'Ancien royaume de Congo*. Brussels: Desclée de Brouwer, 1946.

Cuvelier, J., and L. Jadin. L. *L'Ancien Congo d'après les archives romaines, 1518-1640*. Brussels: ARSC, 1954.

Denis, P. *Histoire des Mangbetu et des Matshaga jusqu'à l'arrivée des Belges*. Tervuren: MRAC, 1961.

Denucé, Jean. *L'Afrique au XVIème siècle et le commerce anversois*. Antwerp: De Sikkel, 1937.

Ekholm, Kajsa. *Power and Prestige: The Rise and Fall of the Kongo Kingdom*. Uppsala, Sweden: Skriv Service AB, 1972.

Farrant, Leda. *Tippu Tip and the East African Slave Trade*. New York: St. Martin's Press, 1975.

Filesi, Teobaldo. *San Salvador: Cronache dei re del Congo*. Bologna: E.M.I., 1974.

Friedman, Kajsa Ekholm. *Catastrophe and Creation: The Transformation of an African Culture*. Philadelphia: Harwood Academic Publishers, 1991.

Gamitto, A. C. P. *King Kazembe and the Marave Cheva, Bisa, Bembe, Lunda and other Peoples of Southern Africa*. Translated by Ian Cunnison. 2 vols. Lisbon: Junta de Investigaçoes do Ultramar, 1962.

Goma Foutou, Célestin. *Histoire des civilisations du Congo*. Paris: Anthropos, 1981.

Hall, Richard. *Stanley*. Boston: Houghton Mifflin, 1975.

Harms, Robert W. *River of Wealth, River of Sorrow: The Central Zaire Basin in the Era of the Slave and Ivory Trade, 1500-1891*. New Haven: Yale University Press, 1981.

Hilton, Anne. *The Kingdom of Kongo*. Oxford: Clarendon Press, 1985.

Hilton-Simpson, M. H. *Land and Peoples of the Kasai*. London: Constable, 1911.

Hinde, Sidney Langford. *The Fall of the Congo Arabs*. London: Methuen, and New York: Thomas Whittaker, 1897.

Jadin, Louis. *L'Ancien Congo et l'Angola, 1639-1655: D'Après les archives romaines, portugaises, néerlandaises et espagnoles*. Brussels: Institut Historique Belge de Rome, 1975.

———. *Rivalités luso-néerlandaises au Sohio, Congo, 1600-1675: Tentatives missionaires des récollets flamands et tribulations des capucins italiens, 1670-1675.* Brussels: Institut Historique Belge de Rome, 1966.

Johnston, H. H. (Sir Harry). *George Grenfell and the Congo.* 2 vols. London: Hutchinson, 1908.

———. *The River Congo from its Mouth to Bolobo.* London: Sampson Low, 1884.

Kimena Kekwakwa Kinenge. *Tippo Tip: Traitant et sultan du Manyema.* Kinshasa: Centre de Recherches Pédagogiques, 1979.

Klein, Herbert S. *The Middle Passage: Comparative Studies in the Atlantic Slave Trade.* Princeton, NJ: Princeton University Press, 1978.

Le Fèbre de Vivy, L. *Documents d'histoire précoloniale belge (1861-1865).* Brussels: ARSC, 1955.

Lejeune-Choquet, Adolphe. *Histoire militaire du Congo.* Brussels: Alfred Castaine, 1906.

Massoz, Michel. *Le Congo de Léopold II, 1878-1908: Un Récit historique.* Liège, Belgium: M. Massoz, 1989.

M'Bokolo, Elikia. *Msiri, bâtisseur de l'ancien royaume du Katanga, Shaba.* Paris: ABC, 1976.

Meyers, Joseph. *Le Prix d'un empire.* Brussels: Presses Académiques Européennes, 1964.

Miers, S., and I. Kopytoff, eds. *Slavery in Africa: Historical and Anthropological Perspectives.* Madison: University of Wisconsin Press, 1977.

Operations of the Association Internationale Africaine and of the Comité d'Étude du Haut Congo, from December 1877 to October 1882. London: E. & F. N. Spon, 1883.

Pigafetta, Filippo. *A Report of the Kingdom of the Congo and the Surrounding Countries, Drawn out of the Discourses of the Portuguese by Duarte Lopez (1591).* (Reprint of 1881 edition published in London.) New York: Cass, 1969.

Pinto, Francisco Antonio. *Angola e Congo.* Lisbon: Livraria Ferreira, 1888.

Proyart, l'Abbe. *Histoire de Loango, Kakong et autres royaumes d'Afrique.* Paris: publisher unknown, 1776.

Randles, W. G. L. *L'Ancien royaume du Congo des origines à la fin du XIXe siècle.* Paris: Mouton, 1968.

Reefe, Thomas Q. *The Rainbow and the Kings: A History of the Luba Empire to 1891*. Berkeley: University of California Press, 1981.

Rinchon, Dieudonné. *La Traite et l'esclavage des Congolais par les Européens*. Brussels: Imprimerie De Meester, 1929.

————. *Les Armements négriers au XVIIIème siècle*. Brussels: ARSC, 1956.

Roberts, A. "Nyamwezi Trade," in *Pre-Colonial African Trade*, edited by R. Gray and D. Birmingham. London: publisher unknown, 1970.

Schuler, Monica. *Alas, Alas, Kongo: A Social History of Indentured African Immigration into Jamaica, 1841-1865*. Baltimore: Johns Hopkins University Press, 1980.

Sutton, Smith. *Yakusu: The Very Heart of Africa*. London: publisher unknown, 1910.

Swann, A. J. *Fighting the Slave-Hunters in Central Africa*. (Reprint of 1910 edition.) New York: Cass, 1968.

Thornton, John Kelly. *The Kingdom of Kongo: Civil War and Transition, 1641-1718*. Madison: University of Wisconsin Press, 1983.

Thys, A. *Au Congo et au Kasaï*. Brussels: Weissenbruch, 1888.

Tuckey, J. K. *Narrative of an Expedition to Explore the River Zaire*. London: John Murray; New York: William B. Gilley, 1818.

Vangroenweghe, Daniel. *Du sang sur les lianes*. Brussels: Didier Hatier, 1986.

Vansina, Jan. *The Tio Kingdom of the Middle Congo, 1880-1892*. London: Oxford University Press, 1973.

Verbecken, Auguste. *La Première traversée du Katanga en 1806: Voyage des "pombeiros" d'Angola aux Rios de Sena*. Brussels: IRCB, 1953.

————. *Msiri: Roi du Garenganze*. Brussels: Cuypers, 1956.

Weeks, J. H. *Among the Primitive Bakongo*. London: Seely, Service, 1914.

Womersley, Harold. *Wm. F. P. Burton: Congo Pioneer*. Eastbourne: Victory Press, 1973.

3. Congo Free State

Alexis, M. G. (Gochet, Jean-Baptiste). *La Barbarie africaine et l'action civilisatrice des missions catholiques au Congo et dans l'Afrique équatoriale*. Paris: Procure Générale, 1889.

———. *La Traite des nègres et la croisade africaine*. Liège, Belgium: Dessain, 1889.

———. *Le Congo Belge illustré ou l'État Indépendant du Congo*. Liège: Dessain, 1887.

Ascherson, Neal. *The King Incorporated: Léopold II in the Age of Trusts*. New York: Doubleday, 1964.

Bateman, Charles S. L. *The First Ascent of the Kasai*. London: Philip & Son, 1889.

Bauer, Ludwig. *Léopold the Unloved*. Boston: Little, Brown, 1935.

Belgium. Federaton for the Defense of Belgian Interests Abroad. *The Truth about the Congo Free State*. Brussels: 1905.

Boeck, Guy de. *Les révoltes de la Force Publique sous Léopold II: Congo 1895-1908, Baoni*. Antwerp: Éditions EPO, 1987.

Botinck, François. *Aux Origines de l'État Indépendant du Congo: Documents tirés des archives américains*. Paris: Nauwelaerts, 1966.

Castelein, A. *The Congo State: Its Origin, Rights, and Duties, the Charges of its Accusers*. New York: Negro Universities Press, 1969.

Collins, Robert O. *King Leopold, England and the Upper Nile, 1899-1909*. New Haven, CT: Yale University Press, 1969.

Comeliau, Jean. *Dhanis*. Brussels: Libris, 1943.

———. *Stanley et Léopold II*. Leverville, Belgian Congo: Bibliothèque de l'Étoile, c. 1958.

Conference of Missionary Societies, Representatives of American Organizations Conducting Missionary Work in the Independent State of the Kongo. Washington: Government Printing Office, 1904.

Conference of Missionary Societies, Representatives of American Organizations Conducting Missionary Work in the Independent State of the Kongo. Conditions in the Kongo State. Washington: Government Printing Office, 1905.

Congo, État Indépendant du. *Bulletin Officiel de l'État Indépendant du Congo*. Brussels: 1885-1908.

————. *The Congo: A Report of the Mission of Inquiry Appointed by the Free State Government.* London: G. P. Putnam's Sons, 1906.

————. *Justice Repressive.* Brussels: E. Dory, 1905.

Cookey, S. J. S. *Britain and the Congo Question, 1885-1913.* Ibadan History Series. London: Longmans, 1968; New York: Humanities Press, 1969.

Crowe, Sybil Eyre. *The Berlin West African Conference, 1884-1885.* London: Longmans, Green, 1942.

Delcommune, Alexandre. *Vingt années de vie africaine (1874-1893).* 2 vols. Brussels: Larcier, 1922.

Gann, Lewis H. *The Rulers of Belgian Africa, 1884-1914.* Princeton, NJ: Princeton University Press, 1979.

Gould, Tony. *In Limbo: The Story of Stanley's Rear Column.* London: Hamish Hamilton, 1979.

Harms, Robert. "The End of Red Rubber" *Journal of African History* 16, no. 1 (1975): 73-88.

Institut Royal Colonial Belge. *La Force Publique de sa naissance à 1914.* Brussels: IRCB, 1952.

Keith, Arthur Berriedale. *The Belgian Congo and the Berlin Act.* New York: Negro Universities Press, 1970.

Lerman, Dragutin. *Commissaire Général Dragutin Lerman, 1863-1918: A Contribution to the History of Central Africa,* ed. Aleksander Lopasic. Tervuren: MRAC, 1971.

Lichtervelde, Louis de (Comte). *Léopold II.* (Official biography.) Brussels: publisher unknown, 1935.

Louis, William Roger. *E. D. Morel's History of the Congo Reform Movement.* Oxford: Clarendon Press, 1968.

MacDonnell, John D. *King Leopold Second: His Rule in Belgium and the Congo.* (Reprint of 1905 edition.) New York: Argosy, 1970.

Marchal, Jules. *E. D. Morel contre Léopold II: L'Histoire du Congo, 1900-1910.* Paris: Harmattan, 1996.

————. *L'État Libre du Congo: Paradis perdu: L'Histoire du Congo 1876-1900.* Borgloon: Bellings, 1996.

Massoin, Fritz. *Histoire de l'État Indépendant du Congo.* 2 vols. Namur, Belgium: Imprimerie Picard-Balon, 1912-13.

Massoz, Michel. *Le Congo de Léopold II, 1878-1908: Un Récit historique.* Liège, Belgium: M. Massoz, 1989.

Meyers, Joseph. *Le Prix d'un empire.* Brussels: Presses Académiques Européennes, 1964.

Morel, Edmund Dane. *The Congo Slave State*. Liverpool: J. Richardson & Sons, 1903.

———. *Great Britain and the Congo*. London: Smith, Elder, 1909.

———. *History of the Congo Reform Movement*, ed. W. R. Lewis and Jean Stengers. Oxford: Clarendon Press, 1968.

———. *King Leopold's Rule in Africa*. (Reprint of 1904 edition.) Westport, CT: Negro Universities Press, 1970.

———. *Red Rubber: The Story of the Rubber Slave Trade Flourishing on the Congo in the Year of Grace 1906*. (Reprint of 1906 edition.) New York: Negro Universities Press, 1969.

Presbyterian Reformers in Central Africa: A Documentary Account of the American Presbyterian Congo Mission and the Human Rights Struggle in the Congo, 1890-1918. Leiden, NY: E. J. Brill, 1996.

Reeves, Jesse Siddall. *The International Beginnings of the Congo Free State*. Baltimore: Johns Hopkins Press, 1894.

Roeykens, Auguste. *La Période initiale de l'oeuvre africain de Léopold II (1875-1883)*. Brussels: ARSC, 1957.

———. *La Politique religieuse de l'État Indépendant du Congo: Documents*. Brussels: ARSOM, 1965.

———. *Le Dessein africain de Léopold II (1875-1876)*. Brussels: ARSC, 1956.

———. *Léopold II et la Conférence Géographique de Bruxelles*. Brussels: ARSC, 1956.

———. *Léopold II et l'Afrique, 1855-1880: Essai de synthèse et de mise au point*. Brussels: ARSC, 1958.

———. *Les Débuts de l'oeuvre africain de Léopold II*. Brussels: ARSC, 1955.

———. *L'Initiative africaine de Léopold II et l'opinion publique belge*. Brussels: ARSOM, 1963.

Salmon, Pierre. *Documents inédits de Louis Haneuse, résident aux Stanley Falls: Décembre 1888-février 1889*. Brussels: ARSOM, 1988.

———. *La Révolte des Batetela de l'Expédition du Haut-Ituri, 1897: Témoignages inédits*. Brussels: ARSOM, 1977.

Shaloff, Stanley. *Reform in Leopold's Congo*. Richmond, VA: John Knox Press, 1970.

Slade, Ruth. *King Leopold's Congo: Aspects of the Development of Race Relations in the Congo Independent State*. (Reprint of the edition published by Oxford University Press, London, 1962.) Westport, CT: Greenwood Press, 1974.

Stanley, Henry Morton, Sir. *The Congo and the Founding of Its Free State: A Story of Work and Exploration.* New York: Harper, 1885. (Reprinted, New York: Negro History Press, 1970.)
————. *Exploration Diaries.* Edited by Richard Stanley and Alan Neame. London: Kimber, 1961.
————. *In Darkest Africa.* New York: Scribners, 1890.
————. *Through the Dark Continent, 1874-1877.* London: Sampson, Low, Marston, Searle, 1878.
Starr, Frederick. *Truth about the Congo: The* Chicago Tribune *Articles.* (Reprint of 1907 edition.) New York: Negro Universities Press, n.d.
Sternstein, Jerome L. "King Leopold II, Senator Nelson W. Aldrich, and the Strange Beginnings of American Economic Penetration in the Congo." *African Historical Studies* 2, no. 2 (1969): 189-203.
Stringlhamber, B. E. M., and P. Dresse. *Léopold II au travail.* Brussels: Éditions du Sablon, 1945.
Thompson, R. S. *Fondation de l'État Indépendant du Congo: Un Chapitre de l'histoire du partage de l'Afrique.* Brussels: Office de Publicité, 1933.
Twain, Mark. *King Leopold's Soliloquy.* New York: International Publishers, 1961.
United States. Congress. Senate. *General Act of the Conference of Berlin.* November 1884 to February 1885. (Miscellaneous Document no. 68.) Washington: 1886.
United States. Department of State. *Congo Conference. Message from President Chester Arthur and Report by the Secretary-of-State on Congo Conference at Berlin.* Washington: (January 30) 1895.
————. *Congo Conference.* (Includes protocols of sessions of the Conference at Berlin and related correspondence.) Washington: 1885.
Vandervelde, Émile. *La Belgique et le Congo.* Paris: Félix Alcan, 1911.
————. *Les Derniers jours de l'État Indépendant du Congo.* Mons: Éditions de la Société Nouvelle, 1909.
Verbecken, August. *La Révolte des Batetela en 1895.* Brussels: ARSC, 1958.
Verdick, E. *Les Premiers jours du Katanga (1890-1903).* Brussels: Comité Spécial du Katanga, 1952.
Wack, Henry Wellington. *The Story of the Congo Free State: Social, Political, and Economic Aspects of the Belgian System of*

Government in Central Africa. New York: Argosy-Antiquarian, 1970.

Wauters, Alphonse-Jules. *L'État Indépendant du Congo.* Brussels: Librairie Falk & Fils, 1899.

Willequet, Jacques. *Le Congo belge et la "Weltpolitick" (1894-1914).* Brussels: Presses Universitaires, 1962.

4. Belgian Congo

Anstey, Roger T. *King Leopold's Legacy: The Congo under Belgian Rule, 1908-1960.* London: Oxford University Press, 1966.

Belgium. Ministère des Colonies. *Annuaire Officiel.* 35th ed. Brussels: 1959.

————. *Rapport sur l'Administration de la Colonie du Congo Belge . . . présenté aux Chambres Législatives.* Brussels: annual through 1960.

————. *Receuil à l'usage des fonctionnaires et agents du service territorial au Congo Belge.* Brussels: several editions with addenda.

Belgium. Parti Socialiste Belge. *Congo, 1885-1960: Positions Socialistes.* Brussels: Institut Vendervelde, 1960.

————. *Un Program pour le Congo et le Ruanda-Urundi. (Rapports présentés au Congrès Extraordinaire des 30 juin et 1er juillet 1956).* Brussels: Société d'Édition du Peuple, 1956.

Bertrand, A. "La fin de la puissance Azande." *Bulletin des Séances IRCB* (1943): 264-83.

Bourgeois, René. *Témoignages.* Tervuren: MRAC, 1982.

Brausch, Georges. *Belgian Administration in the Congo.* (Originally published in London: Oxford University Press, 1961.) New York: Greenwood Press, 1986.

Buel, R. L. *The Native Problem in Africa.* 2 vols. (Originally published in New York: Macmillan, 1928.) Hamden, CT: Archon Books, 1965.

Bustin, Edouard. *Lunda under Belgian Rule: The Politics of Ethnicity.* Cambridge: Harvard University Press, 1975.

Comité Spécial du Katanga. *Compte-rendus du Congrès Scientifique d'Élisabethville, 1950.* 8 vols. Brussels: 1951.

Congo, Belgian. Gouvernement Général. *Bulletin administratif / Bestuursblad.* (Published semimonthly in French and Flemish.

Merged with the *Bulletin Officiel* in January 1960 to form *Moniteur Congolais*.) Leopoldville: 1912-59.

———. *Bulletin officiel / Ambjtelijk blad*. (Published monthly and semi-monthly in French and Flemish until merger with *Bulletin Administratif* in 1960. Together, the two publications provide a record of Belgian administration of the colony.) Brussels: 1908-1959.

———. *Conseil du Gouvernement: Compte rendu synthétique des séances*. Leopoldville: annual.

———. *Conseils de Province: Compte-rendus analytiques des séances*. Leopoldville: irregular.

———. *Discours du Gouverneur Général à la séance d'ouverture du Conseil de Gouvernement*. Leopoldville: annual.

———. *Discours / Rede*. (Speeches in French and Flemish with statistical section.) Leopoldville: 1911-59 (annual).

———. *La Charte Coloniale Belge: Commentaire de la loi de gouvernement du Congo Belge éclairé par les discussions parlementaires et la comparaison des législations étrangères*. (Comments by Alexandre Halot-Gevaert.) Brussels: P. Van Fleteren, 1910.

———. *La Charte Coloniale: Commentaire de la loi du 18 octobre 1908 sur le gouvernement du Congo Belge*. (Commentary by Halewyck, Michel.) Brussels: M. Weissenbruch, 1910-19.

Coppens, Paul. *Anticipations Congolaises*. Brussels: Éditions Scientifiques et Techniques, 1956.

Cornet, René Jules. *Maniema: Le Pays des mangeurs d'hommes*. 2nd ed. Brussels: Cuypers, 1955.

Crokaert, Jacques. *Boula matari: Au Congo belge avec le Roi Albert*. Brussels: Collection Nationale, 1929.

Daye, Pierre. *Problèmes congolais*. Brussels: Les Écrits, 1943.

De Bauw, A. *Le Katanga: Notes sur le pays, ses ressources et l'avenir de la colonisation belge*. Brussels: Larcier, 1920.

De Hemptinne, J. *Le Gouvernement du Congo Belge: Projet de réorganisation administrative*. Brussels: Librairie Dewit, 1920.

———. *Le Tournant de notre politique indigène*. Elisabethville: Éditions de la Revue Juridique du Congo Belge, 1935.

Dehoux, Émile. *Le Problème de demain: L'Effort de paix du Congo Belge (colonat blanc et paysannat indigène)*. Brussels: R. Stoops, 1946.

Delcommune, Alexandre. *L'Avenir du Congo Belge menacé*. Brussels: Office de Publicité, 1921.

Delicour, Fernand. *Les Propos d'un colonial belge*. Brussels: Weissenbruch, 1956.

Demuntur, Paul. "Structure de classe et luttes de classes dans le Congo colonial." *Contradictions* 1 (1972): 67-109.

Denuit, Désiré. *Le Congo, champion de la Belgique en guerre*. Brussels: Éditions Frans Van Belle, 1946.

Depage, Henri. *Contributions à l'élaboration d'une doctrine visant à la promotion des indigènes au Congo Belge*. Brussels: ARSC, 1955.

Dessart, Charles. *Le Congo à tombeau ouvert*. Brussels: Dessart, 1959.

Domont, Jean Marie. *Élite noire*. Brussels: Office de Publicité, 1957.

Élisabethville, 1911-1961. Brussels: Cuypers, 1961.

Fetter, Bruce. *The Creation of Élisabethville, 1910-1940*. Stanford: Hoover Institution Press, 1976.

Fonds du Bien-Être Indigène au Congo au Rwanda et au Burundi. *Une Oeuvre de coopération au développement: Quinze années d'activités du Fonds du Bien-Être Indigène . . . 1948-1963*. Ghent: Snoeck-Ducaju, 1964.

Ganshof van der Meersch, W. J. *Congo, Mai-juin 1960: Rapport du ministre chargé des affaires générales en Afrique*. Brussels: Ministère des Affaires Africaines, 1960.

―――. *Fin de la souveraineté belge au Congo*. (Sponsored by the Institut Royal des Relations Internationales.) The Hague: Nijhoff, 1963.

Ganshof van der Meersch, W. J., and François Perin. *Le Droit électoral au Congo Belge*. Brussels: Bruylant, 1958.

Gérard, J. *La Monarchie belge abondonnera-t-elle le Congo?* Brussels: Éditions Europe-Afrique, 1960.

Gilbert, O. P. *L'Empire du silence*. Brussels: Éditions du "Peuple," 1947.

Guebels, L., ed. *Relation complète des travaux de la Commission Permanente pour la Protection des Indigènes au Congo Belge, 1911-1951*. Elisabethville: CEPSI, 1953.

Haleqijck de Heusch, M. *La Charte Coloniale*. 3 vols. Brussels: Weissenbruch, 1914.

―――. *Les Institutions politiques et administratives des pays africains soumis à l'autorité de la Belgique*. (For the Institut Colonial International.) Brussels: Établissements Généraux d'Imprimerie, 1934.

Henige, David P. *Colonial Governors from the Fifteenth Century to the Present.* Madison: University of Wisconsin Press, 1970.

Hostelet, Georges. *Le Problème politique capital au Congo et en Afrique noire.* Brussels: Institut de Sociologie, Université Libre de Belgique, 1959.

————. *L'Oeuvre civilisatrice de la Belgique au Congo, de 1885 à 1953.* Brussels: ARSC, 1954.

————. *Pour éviter l'anarchie puis la dictature, la réalisation de l'indépendance du Congo exige des étapes.* Brussels: private publisher, 1959.

J. K. (Van der Dussen de Kestergat, J.). *André Ryckmans.* Paris: Centurion, 1961.

Jadot, J.M. *Blanc et noirs au Congo Belge: Problèmes coloniaux et tentatives de solutions.* Brussels: Édition de la Revue Sincère, 1929.

Jentgen, P. *Histoire des Secrétaires Généraux du Ministère des Colonies pendant l'occupation.* Brussels: IRCB, 1946.

————. *Les Frontières du Congo Belge.* Brussels: IRCB, 1952.

Jewsiewicki, Bogumil. "African Peasants in the Totalitarian Colonial Society of the Belgian Congo," in Klein, Martin A., ed., *Peasants in Africa: Historical and Contemporary Perspectives*, vol. 4, 45-75. Beverly Hills, CA: Sage Publications, 1980.

————. "Unequal Development: Capitalism and the Katanga Economy, 1919-1940," in Palmer, Robin, and Neil Parsons eds., *The Roots of Cultural Poverty in Central and South Africa*, 317-44. London: Heinemann, 1977.

Joyce, Pierre, and Lewin Rosipe. *Les Trusts du Congo.* Brussels: Société Populaire d'Éditions, 1961.

Kambayi Bwatshia. *Blancs et noirs face à la decolonisation du Congo Belge.* Kinshasa: PUZ, 1992.

Kanyinda Lusanga. *Le Phénomène de la colonisation et l'émancipation des institutions socio-politiques traditionnelles au Zaïre.* Brussels: CEDAF, 1975.

Kestergat, Jean. *Quand le Zaïre s'appelait Congo: L'Aventure coloniale belge.* Brussels: P. Legrain, 1985.

Laxalt, Robert. *A Private War: An American Code Officer in the Belgian Congo.* Reno: University of Nevada Press, 1998.

"L'Évolution politique du Congo Belge et les autorités indigènes," special issue of *Problèmes d'Afrique Centrale*, no. 43 (1959).

Le Rail au Congo Belge. Brussels: Blanchart, 1993.

Lovens, M. *La Révolte de Masisi-Lubutu: Congo Belge, janvier-mai 1944.* Brussels: CEDAF, 1974.

———. *L'Effort militaire de guerre du Congo Belge, 1940-1944.* Brussels: CEDAF, 1975.

Malengreau, Guy. *Les Droits Fonciers Coutumiers chez les indigènes du Congo.* Brussels: IRCB, 1947.

———. "Organization of Native Administration in the Belgian Congo." *Journal of African Administration* 7, no. 2 (1956): 85-88.

Martelli, George. *Leopold to Lumumba: A History of the Belgian Congo, 1877-1960.* London: Chapman and Hall, 1962.

Martynov, V. A. *Congo under the Yoke of Imperialism.* Moscow: Academy of Science, Institute of World Economy and International Relations, 1959.

Maurel, Auguste. *Le Congo de la colonisation belge à l'indépendance.* Paris: Harmattan, 1992.

Merlier, Michel. *Le Congo de la colonisation belge à l'indépendance.* Paris: Maspero, 1962.

Nelson, Samuel Henry. *Colonialism in the Congo Basin, 1880-1940.* Athens: Ohio University Center for International Studies, 1994.

Norton, William B. *A Belgian Socialist Critic of Colonialism: Louis Betrand (1856-1943).* Brussels: ARSOM, 1965.

Paulus, Jean-Pierre. *Congo, 1956-1960.* Brussels: Terre d'Europe, 1961.

———. *Témoignages et Réflexions.* Brussels: Renaissance du Livre, 1976.

Pevée, Albert. *Place aux noirs.* Brussels: Éditions Europe-Afrique, 1960.

Phombeah, Dennis. *Congo: Prelude to Independence.* London: African Research and Publications, 1961.

Pons, Valdo. *Stanleyville: An African Urban Community under Belgian Administration.* London: Oxford University Press, 1969.

Rhodius, Georges. *Congo 1958; ou, Cinquante ans de civilisation.* Brussels: Ministère de la Défense Nationale, Direction de l'Education des Forces Armées, 1959.

Ryckmans, Pierre (former governor-general). *Dominer pour servir.* Brussels: Édition Universelle, 1948.

———. *Étapes et Jalons.* Brussels: Larcier, 1946.

———. *La Politique coloniale.* Brussels: Éditions Rex, 1934.

Salkin, Paul. *Études Africaines.* Brussels: Larcier, 1920.

———. *Le Problème de l'évolution noire, l'Afrique central dans cent ans.* Paris: Payot, 1926.

Sauvy, J. *Le Katanga: Cinquante ans décisifs.* Paris: Société Continentale d'Éditions Modernes Illustrées, 1961.

Sépulchre, Jean. *Propos sur le Congo politique de demain: Autonomie et fédéralisme.* Elisabethville: Éditions de l'Essor du Congo, 1958.

Slade, Ruth M. *The Belgian Congo: Some Recent Changes.* (Sponsored by the Institute of Race Relations.) London: Oxford University Press, 1960.

Sohier, Jean. *La Mémoire d'un policier belgo-congolais.* Brussels: ARSOM, 1974.

Sourdillat, Jacques. *Les Chefferies au Congo Belge.* Paris: Domat-Montchrestien, 1940.

Stengers, J. *Belgique et Congo: Élaboration de la Charte Coloniale.* Brussels: Renaissance du Livre, 1963.

———. *Combien le Congo a-t-il coûté à la Belgique?* Brussels: ARSC, 1957.

———. *Textes inédites d'Emile Banning.* Brussels: publisher unknown, 1955.

Stenmans, Alain. *La Reprise du Congo par la Belgique.* Brussels: Éditions Techniques et Scientifiques, 1949.

Terlinden, Charles, René Jules Cornet, and Michel Walraet. *Le Comité Spécial du Katanga.* Brussels: Cuypers, 1950.

Turner, Thomas. *La Politique indigène du Congo Belge: Le Cas du Sankuru.* Brussels: CEDAF, 1973.

Van Bilsen, A. A. J. *Vers l'Indépendance du Congo et du Ruanda-Urundi: Réflexions sur les devoirs et l'avenir de la Belgique en Afrique centrale.* Kraainem, Belgium: privately printed, 1958.

Van der Kerken, G. *La Politique coloniale belge.* Antwerp: Éditions Zaïre, 1943.

———. *Les Sociétés bantoues du Congo Belge et le problème de la politique indigène.* Brussels: Bruylant, 1920.

Van Grieken, E., and M. Van Grieken-Taverniers. *Les Archives inventoriées au Ministère des Colonies.* Brussels: ARSC, 1958.

Van Zandijcke, A. *Pages de l'histoire du Kasayi.* Namur: Grands Lacs, 1953.

Van Zuylen, Baron Pierre. *L'Échiquier congolais: ou, Le Secret du roi.* Brussels: Dessart, 1959.

Vanden Bossche, Jean. *Sectes et associations indigènes au Congo Belge*. Leopoldville: Gouvernement Générale, AIMO, 1954.

Vanderlinden, Jacques. *À propos de l'uranium congolais*. Brussels: ARSOM, 1991.

———. *Pierre Ryckmans, 1891-1959: Coloniser dans l'honneur*. Brussels: De Boeck University, 1994.

Vandewoude, Émile. *Le voyage du prince Albert au Congo en 1909*. Brussels: ARSOM, 1990.

Vanhove, Julian. *Histoire du Ministère des Colonies*. Brussels: ARSOM, 1968.

Venthemsche, Guy. *Genèse et portée du "plan décennal" du Congo Belge (1949-1959)*. Brussels: ARSOM, 1994.

Verhaegen, Benoît. *Le Centre Extra-Coutumier de Stanleyville (1940-1945)*. Brussels: CEDAF, 1981.

Vermuelen, Victor. *Déficiences et dangers de notre politique indigène*. Brussels: publisher unknown, 1952.

Vers la promotion de l'économie indigène. Brussels: Institut de Sociologie, Université Libre de Belgique, 1956.

Wauters, Alphonse-Jules. *Histoire politique du Congo Belge*. Brussels: P. Van Fleteren, 1911.

Wauthion, R. *Le Congo Belge à un tournant*. Brussels: ARSC, 1959.

Whyms, L. *Léopoldville, son histoire 1881-1956*. Brussels: Office de Publicité, 1956.

5. Independence (1960-1965)

Abi-Saab, Georges. *The United Nations Operation in the Congo, 1960-1964*. Oxford: Oxford University Press, 1978.

African Affairs Research Group. *Save the Congo, Save Africa: The Bleeding Heart of Africa*. N.p.: 1965.

Amalaure, Jean. *Les Pourquois de l'aventure katangaise: Etiologie insolite d'une aventure transcontinentale; essai historique et politique sur des événements encore récents*. Avignon: J. Amalaure, 1983.

Anciaux, Léon. *Le Drame du Congo: La vérité au sujet de la débande de l'Armée Nationale Congolaise*. Brussels: CRAOCA and Fraternelle des Troupes Coloniales 1914-1918, 1960.

Aruffo, Alessandro. *Patrice Lumumba e il panafricanismo*. Rome: Erre Emme, 1991.

Azcoitia, Carlos Eduardo. *La Guerra olvidada: Argentina en la guerra del Congo*. Buenos Aires: Marymar, 1992.

Belgium. Chambre des Représentants. *La Table Ronde Économique, Bruxelles, avril-mai 1960: Compte-rendus et documents*. Brussels, 1960.

———. *Rapport de la Commission Parlementaire chargée de faire une enquête sur les événements qui se sont produits à Léopoldville en janvier 1959*. Brussels: Documents Parlementaires. S. 1958-1959, no. 100/3.

———. *Rapport du Groupe de Travail pour l'Étude du Problème Politique au Congo Belge*. Brussels: Documents Parlementaires. S. 1958-1959, no. 108.

Belgium. Ministère de la Justice. *Congo, July 1960: Evidence*. Brussels: 1960.

Bénot, Yves. *La mort de Lumumba*. Paris: Éditions Chaka, 1989.

Bomandeke Bonyeka. *Le Parlement congolais sous le régime de la loi fondamentale*. Kinshasa: PUZ, 1992.

Bosch, Jean van den. *Pré-Zaire: Le Cordon mal coupé: Document*. Bruxelles: Le Cri, 1986.

Bouvier, Paule. *L'Accession du Congo Belge à l'indépendance*. Brussels: Institut de Sociologie, Université Libre de Belgique, 1966.

Bowett, D. G., et al. *United Nations Forces: A Legal Study of UN Practice*. New York: Praeger, 1964.

Brassinne, Jacques, and Jean Kestergat. *Qui a tué Patrice Lumumba?* Paris: Duculot, 1991.

Burns, A. L., and N. Heathcote. *Peacekeeping by the UN Forces: From Suez to the Congo*. New York: Praeger, 1963.

Cabanès, Bernard. *Du Congo Belge au Katanga*. Paris: Éditions du Fil d'Arianne, 1963.

Calder, Ritchie. *Agony of the Congo*. London: Gollancz, 1961.

Centre de Recherche et d'Information Socio-Politiques. *Congo, 1964: Political Documents of a Developing Nation*. Princeton, NJ: Princeton University Press, 1966.

———. "Le Conditionnement politique de l'Opération 'Dragon Rouge' (Stanleyville, novembre 1964)," *Travaux Africains du CRISP*, no. 38 (1964): 1-20.

———. "Le Kwilu, de la lutte pour l'indépendance à la rébellion muléliste." *Travaux Africains du CRISP*, nos. 30-32 (Feb.-Mar. 1964).

————. "Les Débats de décembre 1964 au Conseil de Sécurité sur l'intervention belgo-américaine à Stanleyville," *Travaux Africains du CRISP*, nos. 42-43 (Feb. 8-15, 1965): 19-21.

Chatterjee, Dwarka Nath. *Storm over the Congo*. Ghaziabad: Vikas, 1980.

Chomé, Jules. *Indépendance congolaise, pacifique conquête*. Brussels: Éditions Remarques Congolaises, 1960.

————. *La Crise congolaise: De l'Indépendance à l'intervention militaire belge (30 juin - 9 juillet 1960)*. Brussels: Éditions Remarques Congolaises, 1960.

————. *Le Drame de Luluabourg*. Brussels: Éditions Remarques Congolaises, 1959.

————. *Le Gouvernement congolais et l'ONU: Un Paradox tragique*. Brussels: Éditions Remarques Congolaises, 1961.

————. *M. Lumumba et le communisme*. Brussels: Éditions Remarques Congolaises, 1961.

————. *Mobutu et la contre-révolution en Afrique*. Waterloo: Tiers-Monde et Révolution, 1967.

————. *Moïse Tshombe et l'escroquerie katangaise*. Brussels: Éditions de la Fondation Joseph Jacquemotte, 1966.

Clarke, Stephen John Gordon. *The Congo Mercenary: A History and Analysis*. Johannesburg: South African Institute of International Affairs, 1968.

Colvin, Ian. *The Rise and Fall of Moïse Tshombe*. London: Leslie Frewin, 1968.

Congo, République Démocratique du. *Constitution de la République Démocratique du Congo*. Kinshasa: Ministère des Affaires Étrangères, 1967.

————. *Constitution de la République Démocratique du Congo. 1er août 1964*. 2nd ed. Coquilhatville: Bureau Presse-Documentation, 1964.

Congo, République du. *De Léopoldville à Lagos*. Leopoldville: 1962.

————. *Documentation technique du gouvernement concernant les résolutions de Coquilhatville*. Leopoldville: 1961.

————. *Les Entretiens Adoula-Tshombe (Second livre blanc du Gouvernement Central sur la séccession katangaise)*. Leopoldville: 1961.

————. Ministère des Affaires Étrangères. *La Province du Katanga et l'indépendance congolaise*. Leopoldville: 1961.

Coquery-Vidrovitch, Catherine, Alain Forest, and Herbert Weiss. *Rébellions-révolution au Zaire, 1963-1965.* 2 vols. Paris: Harmattan, 1987.

Davister, Pierre. *Katanga: Enjeu du monde.* Brussels: Éditions Europe-Afrique, 1960.

Davister, Pierre, and P. Toussaint. *Croisettes et casques bleus.* Brussels: Éditions Actuelles, 1962.

Dayal, Rajeshwar. *Mission for Hammarskjöld: The Congo Crisis.* Princeton, NJ: Princeton University Press, 1976.

De Bosschere, G. *Rescapés de Watsa.* Brussels: Dessart, 1966.

De Coninck, Albert. *Le Drame congolais: Ouvrons le dossier.* Brussels: Éditions "Communisme," 1960.

De Monstelle, Arnaud. *Le Débacle du Congo Belge.* Brussels: Leclerc, 1965.

De Vos, Pierre. *L'Enfer katangais.* Brussels: private publisher, 1973.

————. *Vie et mort de Lumumba.* Paris: Calmann-Lévy, 1961.

Demany, Fernand. *S.O.S. Congo: Chronique d'un soulévement.* Brussels: Labor, 1959.

Dikoba, Simon J. *Matadi sous l'agression des Belges (juillet 1960).* Leopoldville: Indépendance-Imprimerie Kongolaise, 1961.

Dinant, Georges. *L'ONU face à la crise congolaise.* Brussels: Éditions Remarques Congolaises, 1962.

Duchemin, Jacques. *Notre Guerre au Katanga.* Paris: Pensée Moderne, 1963.

Dugauquier, Daphne P. *Congo Cauldron.* London: Jarrolds, 1961.

Dumont, G. H. *La Table Ronde belgo-congolaise.* Paris: Éditions Universitaires, 1961.

Franck, Thomas M., and John Carey, eds. *The Legal Aspects of the United Nations Action in the Congo.* New York: Oceana, 1963.

Gavshon, A. L. *The Mysterious Death of Dag Hammarskjöld.* New York: Walker, 1962.

Gendebien, Paul Henry. *L'Intervention des Nations Unies au Congo, 1960-1964.* Paris: Mouton, 1967.

Gérard-Libais, Jules. "Le Rôle de la Belgique dans l'opération des Nations Unies au Congo, 1960-1964." *Travaux Africains du CRISP*, nos. 68-71.

————. *Séccession au Katanga.* Brussels: Éditions du CRISP, 1963, and Madison: University of Wisconsin Press, 1966.

Gillis, Charles-André. *Kasa-Vubu au coeur du drame congolais.* Brussels: Éditions Europe-Afrique, 1963.

Gordon, King. *The United Nations in the Congo: A Quest for Peace.* New York: Carnegie Endowment for International Peace, 1962.

Hayes, Margaret. *Missing Believed Killed.* London: Hodder & Stoughton, 1966.

Heinz, G., and H. Donnay. *Lumumba: The Last Fifty Days.* (Published originally in French: Brussels: Éditions du CRISP, 1966.) New York: Grove Press, 1969.

Hempstone, Smith. *Rebels, Mercenaries and Dividends: The Katanga Story.* New York: Praeger, 1962.

Henri, P., and J. Marres. *L'État belge responsable en droit du désastre congolais?* Brussels: Éditions R. R. Windfohr, 1961.

Hoare, Michael. *Congo Mercenary.* London: Hale, 1967.

Hoare, Mike. *The Road to Kalamata: A Congo Mercenary's Personal Memoir.* Lexington, MA: Lexington Books, 1989.

Honorin, Michel. *La Fin des mercenaires: Bukavu, novembre 1967.* Paris: Laffont, 1968.

Hoskyns, Catherine. *The Congo: A Chronology of Events, January 1960 - December 1961.* London: Oxford University Press, 1962.

———. *The Congo since Independence.* London: Oxford University Press, for the Royal Institute of International Affairs, 1965.

———. *The Organization of African Unity and the Congo Crisis, 1964-1965: Documents.* Dar es Salaam, Tanzania: Oxford University Press, for the Institute of Public Administration, 1969.

House, Arthur H. *The U.N. in the Congo: The Political and Civilian Efforts.* Washington: University Press of America, 1978.

Ilosono Bekili B'Inkonkoy. *L'Epopée du 24 novembre: Témoignage.* Kinshasa: AS Éditions, 1985.

Ilunga-Kabongo, André, and Baudoin Kalonji. "Les Evénements du Kwilu." *Études Congolaises* 6, no. 3 (1964): 1-21.

Institut de Formation et d'Études Politiques. *À la Redécouverte de Patrice Emery Lumumba.* Kinshasa: 1996.

Jacquemyns, G. *L'ONU au Congo: Ses Interventions vues et jugées par les Belges.* Brussels: INSOC, 1961.

James, Alan. *Britain and the Congo Crisis, 1960-1963.* New York: St. Martin's Press, 1996.

Judd, Charles. *The U.N. and the Congo.* London: United Nations Association, 1961.

Kalb, Madeleine G. "The C.I.A. and Lumumba." *New York Times Magazine,* August 2, 1981, pp. 32-56.

————. *The Congo Cables: From Eisenhower to Kennedy*. New York: Macmillan, 1982.

Kalonji, Albert. *Congo 1960-1964: La Vérité sur la mort de Patrice Lumumba: Documents secrets sur la séccession katangaise et sur Moïse Tshombe: Albert Kalonji révèle et accuse*. Brussels: Éditions du Ponant, 1964.

————. *Ma Lutte au Kasaï pour la vérité au service de la justice*. Barcelona: C.A.G.S.A., 1964.

Kanza, Thomas R. *Conflict in the Congo: The Rise and Fall of Lumumba*. London: R. Collings, 1978, and Boston: G. K. Hall, 1979.

Kapita Mulopo, Léonard. *Congo-Zaire: P. Lumumba, justice pour le héros*. Paris: Harmattan, 1992.

Kasa-Vubu, Joseph. *Receuil des discours, allocutions et messages prononcés de juin 1960 à juin 1965*. Leopoldville: Ministère de l'Information, Bureau de Documentation et des Relations Publiques, 1965.

Kasa-Vubu, Zuzu-Disala Justine M'Poyo. *Joseph Kasa-Vubu, mon père: De la Naissance d'une conscience nationale à l'indépendance*. Brussels: Éditions de Chabassol, 1985.

Kashamura, Anicet. *De Lumumba aux Colonels*. Paris: Buchet-Chastel, 1966.

Katanga, État du. *Livre blanc du gouvernement katangais sur les activitiés des hors-la-loi dans certains territoires baluba*. Elisabethville: 1962.

————. *Livre blanc du gouvernement katangais sur les événements de septembre et décembre 1961*. Elisabethville: 1962.

Katanga, Jean (pseud.). *Le Camp des Baluba: Rapport secret*. Brussels: Dessart, 1962.

Kestergat, J. *Congo, Congo*. Paris: La Table Ronde, 1965.

Kirchmayr, Otto. *Mort d'un affreux*. Paris: Buchet-Chastel, 1967.

Kitchen, Helen, ed. *The Educated African*. New York: Praeger, 1962.

————. *Footnotes to the Congo Story: An "Africa Report" Anthology*. New York: Walker, 1967.

Lagos Study Circle. *The Tragedy of the Congo*. Lagos, Nigeria: 1964.

Lash, Joseph P. *Dag Hammarskjöld*. Garden City, NY: Doubleday, 1961.

Lawson, Richard. *Strange Soldiering*. London: Hodder & Stoughton, 1963.

Le Bailly, J. *Une Poignée de mercenaires*. Paris: Presses de la Cité, 1967.

Le Camp des Baluba: Une Initiative de l'ONU. Brussels: Dessart, 1962.

Le Katanga devra-t-il prendre sa propre indépendance? Elisabethville: A. Decoster, 1959.

Leclerq, Claude. *L'ONU et l'affaire du Congo*. Paris: Payot, 1964.

Lefever, Ernest W. *Crisis in the Congo: A United Nations Force in Action*. Washington: Brookings, 1965.

————. *Uncertain Mandate: Politics of the U.N. Congo Operation*. Baltimore: Johns Hopkins Press, 1967.

Lefever, Ernest W., and Joshua Wynfred. *United Nations Peacekeeping in the Congo, 1960-1964: An Analysis of a Political, Executive and Military Contest*. Washington: Brookings, 1966.

Legum, Colin. *Congo Disaster*. Baltimore: Penguin, 1961.

Longo Mbenza. *Kasa-Vubu, père de l'indépendance du Congo-Zaïre*. Kinshasa: Institut de Formation et d'Études Politiques, 1991.

Lopez-Alvarez, Luis. *Lumumba ou l'Afrique frustrée*. Paris: Cujas, 1964.

Lumumba, Patrice. *Congo, My Country*. New York: Praeger, 1962.

————. *Le Congo, Terre d'Avenir: Est-il menacé?* Brussels: Éditions de l'Office de Publicité, 1961.

————. *Lumumba Speaks: The Speeches and Writings of Patrice Lumumba, 1958-1961*. Translated from French by Helen R. Lane. New York: Little, Brown, 1972.

Lumuna Sando, C. K. *Nord-Katanga, 1960-1964: De la Sécession à la guerre civile: Le Meurtre des chefs*. Paris: Harmattan, 1992.

Mambida-Babinza. *Odyssée des événements de Kisangani-Bukavu, 1960-1967*. Kinshasa: Forces Armées Congolaises, 1967.

Marrés, Jacques, and Pierre De Vos. *L'Equinoxe de janvier*. Brussels: Éditions Eurafrorient, 1959.

Martelli, George. *Experiment in World Government: An Account of the United Nations Operation in the Congo, 1960-1964*. London: Johnson Publications, 1966.

Martens, Ludo. *Pierre Mulele and the Kwilu Peasant Uprising in Zaire*. Translated from the French by Michael Wolfers. London: Zed Books, 1990.

Masson, Paul. *Dix ans de malheurs*. Brussels: Max Arnold, 1970.

————. *La Bataille pour Bukavu: Récits et reportages, mai à octobre 1964*. Brussels: IMPRESOR, 1965.

Mendiaux, Édouard. *Moscou, Accra et le Congo*. Brussels: Dessart, 1960.

Merriam, Alan P. *Congo: Background of Conflict*. Evanston, IL: Northwestern University Press, 1961.

Meynaud, Jean, J. Ladrière, and F. Perin. *La Décision politique en Belgique*. Paris: Colin, 1965.

Michel, Serge. *Uhuru Lumumba*. Paris: Juilliard, 1962.

Monheim, Francis. "La Mutinerie de la Force Publique Congolaise," *Revue Générale Belge* 98, no. 3 (1962): 37-55.

————. *Mobutu, l'homme seul*. Brussels: Éditions Actuelles, 1962.

————. *Réponses à Pierre De Vos au sujet de "Vie et mort de Lumumba."* Antwerp: Imprimerie "De Vlijt," 1961.

Moumié, Félix. *Eyewitness Report on the Congo*. London: Committee of African Organization, 1960.

Muëller, Siegfried Friedrich Heinrich. *The Laughing Man: Confessions of a Murderer, Program of a Regime*. Dresden: Verlag Zeit im Bild, 1966.

————. *Les Nouveaux mercenaires*. Paris: Éditions France-Empire, 1965.

Munongo, Godefroid. *Comment est né le nationalisme katangais*. (Mimeo.) Elisabethville: Service d'Information du Gouvernement Katangais, June 16, 1962. (mimeo.)

Muya Bia Lushiku Lumana. *Les Baluba du Kasaï et la crise congolaise (1959-1966)*. Lubumbashi: Muya Bia Lushiku Lumana, 1985.

Nguya-Ndila, Célestin. *Indépendance de la République Démocratique du Congo et les engagements internationaux antérieurs (succession d'états aux traités)*. Kinshasa: Université de Kinshasa, 1971.

Nicolai, Marie. *Ici Radio Katanga—1960-1961*. Brussels: J. M. Collet, 1987

Niedergang, Marcel. *Tempête sur le Congo*. Paris: Plon, 1960.

Nkrumah, Kwame. *Challenge of the Congo*. New York: International Publishers, 1967.

O'Brien, Conor Cruise. *To Katanga and Back*. New York: Simon and Schuster, 1962.

O'Brien, Conor Cruise, and Felix Topolski. *The United Nations: Sacred Drama*. New York: Ivan Obolensky, 1976.

Odom, Thomas P. *Dragon Operations: Hostage Rescues in the Congo, 1964-1965*. Fort Leavenworth, KS: Combat Studies Institute, US Army Command and General Staff College, 1988.

Okumu, Washington. *Lumumba's Congo: Roots of Conflict*. New York: Ivan Obolensky, 1963.

Olsen, Hal C. *African Heroes of the Congo Rebellion*. Kijabe, Kenya: Africa Inland Mission, 1969.

Orwa, D. K. *The Congo Betrayal: The UN-US and Lumumba*. Nairobi: Kenya Literature Bureau, 1985.

Packham, Eric S. *Freedom and Anarchy*. Commack, NY: Nova Science Publishers, 1995.

Patrice Lumumba. London: Panaf Books, 1973.

Patrice Lumumba, Fighter for Africa's Freedom. Moscow: Progress Publishers, 1966.

Patrice Lumumba: The Truth about a Monstrous Crime of the Colonialists. Moscow: Foreign Languages Publishing House, 1961.

Piguet, Charles. *Liberté pour le Zaïre: Chronique d'une indépendance laborieuse*. Caux, Switzerland: Caux Édition, 1993.

Pradhan, Ram Chandra. *The United Nations and the Congo Crisis*. New Delhi: MANAS Publications, 1975.

Reed, D. *111 Days in Stanleyville*. New York: Harper & Row, 1965.

Reid, Alexander James. *The Roots of Lumumba: Mongo Land*. Hicksville, NY: Exposition Press, 1979.

Ribead, Paul. *Adieu Congo*. Paris: Table Ronde, 1961.

Rikhye, Indar Jit. *Military Adviser to the Secretary-General: U.N. Peacekeeping and the Congo Crisis*. London: Hurst, and New York: St. Martin's Press, 1993.

Rivkin, Arnold. *Africa and the West*. New York: Praeger, 1962.

———. "The Congo Crisis in World Affairs." *Civilizations* 10, no. 4 (1960): 473-79.

Roseveare, Helen. *Doctor among Congo Rebels*. London: Lutterworth, 1965.

Rouch, Jane. *En Cage avec Lumumba*. Paris: Éditions du Temps, 1961.

Rubbens, Antoine. "La Consultation populaire du 22 décembre 1957 à Élisabethville," *Bulletin CEPSI*, no. 42 (Sept. 1958): 77-81.

Russell of Liverpool (Lord). *The Tragedy of the Congo*. Wimbledon, UK: Shamrock Press, 1962.

Schoëller, André. *Congo, 1959-1960: Mission au Katanga, intérim à Léopoldville*. Gembloux: Duculot, 1982.

Schramme, Jean. *La Bataillon Léopard: Souvenirs d'un Africain blanc*. Paris: Éditions J'ai Lu, 1971.

Schuyler, Philippa Duke. *Who Killed the Congo?* New York: Devin-Adair, 1962.

Scott, Ian. *Tumbled House: The Congo at Independence.* London: Oxford University Press, 1969.

Simmonds, R. *Legal Problems Arising from the United Nations Military Operations in the Congo.* The Hague: Martinus Nijhoff, 1968.

Stenmans, Alain. *Les Premiers mois de la République du Congo.* Brussels: ARSOM, 1961.

Struelens, Michel. *The United Nations in the Congo, or O.N.U.C., and International Politics.* Brussels: Max Arnold, 1976.

Taibo, Paco Ignacio, Froilan Escobar, and Felix Guerra. *El Año en que estuvimos en ninguna parte: La Guerrilla africana de Ernesto Che Guevara.* Buenos Aires: Ediciones del Pensamiento Nacional, 1994.

Tournaire, Helène, and Robert Bouteaud. *Livre noir au Congo.* Paris: Librairie Académique, 1963.

Tran-Minh-Tiet. *Le Congo ex-Belge entre l'Est et l'Ouest.* Paris: Nouvelles Éditions Latines, 1962.

Trinquier, R., J. Duchemin, and J. Le Bailly. *Notre guerre au Katanga.* Paris: Éditions la Pensée Moderne, 1963.

Tshombe, Moïse. *Discours prononcé par le Président du Katanga à l'occasion de la fête du 11 juillet 1962.* Elisabethville: Service d'Information du Gouvernement Katangais, 1962.

―――. *Moïse Tshombe parle . . . Les Véritables dessous de l'affair katangaise: L'Avenir du Congo.* Brussels: Éditions du Ponant, 1963.

―――. *Quinze mois de gouvernement du Congo.* Paris: Table Ronde, 1966.

Tully, Andrew. *CIA: The Inside Story.* New York: Morrow, 1962.

Union de Jeunesses Révolutionnaires Congolaises. *Memorandum: L'Agression armée de l'impérialisme américano-belge à Stanleyville et à Paulis.* Brussels: Livre International, 1966.

United Nations. General Assembly. *Report of the Commission of Inquiry into the Events Leading to the Death of Mssrs. Lumumba, Okito and M'polo.* New York: 1961.

United States. "Biographic Data on Members of the Tshombe Government," in *Joint Publications Research Service,* no. 27608, 35-40. Washington: 1964.

————. "Biographic Sketches of Former and Present Congo Ministers," in *Joint Publications Research Service*, no. 33803, 38-47. Washington: 1966.

United States. Congress. House of Representatives. Committee on Foreign Affairs. *Staff Memorandum on the Republic of the Congo.* Washington: (August 24) 1960.

Valahu, Mugur. *The Katanga Circus.* New York: Speller & Sons, 1964.

Van Bilsen, A. A. J. *L'Indépendance du Congo.* Paris: Casterman, 1962.

Van der Haag, Ernest. *The War in Katanga, Report of a Mission: The UN in the Congo.* New York: American Committee for Aid to Katanga Freedom Fighters, 1962.

Van Langenhove, Fernand. *Consciences tribales et nationales en Afrique noire.* The Hague: Nijhoff, 1960.

————. *Le Rôle proéminent du Secrétaire Général dans l'opération des Nations Unies au Congo.* The Hague: Nijhoff, 1964.

Van Lierde, Jean. *La Pensée politique de Patrice Lumumba.* Paris: Éditions Présence Africaine, 1963.

Vanderlinden, Jacques. *1959-1960: La Crise congolaise.* Brussels: Éditions Complexe, 1985.

Vanderstraeten, Louis-François. *Histoire d'une Mutinerie.* Brussels: Académie Royale de Belgique, 1985.

Vanderwalle, Frédéric J. L. A. *L'Ommegang: Odyssée et reconquête de Stanleyville, 1964.* Brussels: Livre Africain, 1970.

————. *Une Ténébreuse affaire, ou Roger Trinquier au Katanga.* Brussels: Tamtam Ommegang, 1979.

Verhaegen, Benoît, ed. "Consultations électorales et élections au Congo, 1957-1959." *Cahiers Économiques et Sociaux IRES* 3, no. 3 (1965): 247-89.

————. "Histoire de Tables Rondes du Congo Indépendant," *Études Congolaises* 1, nos. 2, 4, 5 (1961): 1-14, 1-12, 33-39.

————. *Les Cahiers de Gamboma: Instructions politiques et militaires des partisans congolais (1964-1965).* Brussels: CRISP, 1965.

————. *Rébellions au Congo, I.* Brussels: CRISP, 1966.

————. *Rébellions au Congo, II.* Brussels: CRISP, 1969.

Verhoeven, Jan. *Les Otages de Makondo: Journal de l'époque des Simbas, 1964-1965.* Kessel-Lo, Belgium: Europe-Littérature, 1966.

Von Horn, Carl. *Soldiering for Peace.* New York: McKay, 1967.

Wagoner, Fred E. *Dragon Rouge: The Rescue of Hostages in the Congo.* Washington: National Defense University, 1980.

Wauters, Arthur, ed. *Le Monde communiste et la crise du Congo.* Brussels: Institut de Sociologie, Université Libre de Belgique, 1961.

Welch, Claude E., Jr. *Anatomy of a Rebellion.* Albany: State University of Press of New York, 1980.

Williame, Jean-Claude. *Patrice Lumumba: La Crise congolaise revisitée.* Paris: Karthala, 1990.

Ziegler, Jean. *La Contre-révolution en Afrique.* Paris: Payot, 1963.

6. Post-Independence and Mobutism (1965-1990)

Adelman, Kenneth L. "The Church-State Conflict in Zaire, 1969-1974." *African Studies Review* 18, no. 1 (1975): 102-16.

Association Nationale des Entreprises Zaïroises. *Evolution de la situation socio-économique du Zaïre de 1960 à 1990: Contribution de l'ANEZA à la conférence nationale.* Kinshasa: ANEZA, 1991.

Braeckman, Colette. *Le Dinosaur: Le Zaïre de Mobutu.* Paris: Fayard, 1992.

Callaghy, Thomas M. *The State-Society Struggle: Zaire in Comparative Perspective.* New York: Columbia University Press, 1984.

Centre de Recherche et d'Information Socio-Politiques. *Dans de cadre de l'Authenticité, nouvelles appellations en République du Zaïre.* Brussels: CRISP, 1972.

Chomé, Jules. *L'Ascension de Mobutu: Du Sergent Désiré Joseph au Général Sese Seko.* 2nd ed. Paris: F. Maspero, 1979.

———. *Mobutu, guide suprême.* Brussels: Complexe, 1975.

Comité Zaïre. "Kolwezi '78." *InfoZaïre* 5 (July-August, 1978).

———. *Zaïre—Le Dossier de la recolonisaton.* Paris: Éditions Harmattan, 1978.

Cooper, Rand Richards. "A Zairian Journey: Life under Mobutu, Thief of All Thieves." *Commonweal* 124 (May 9, 1997): 9-12.

Demunter, Paul. *Analyse de la contestation estudiantine au Congo-Kinshasa (juin 1969) et de ses séquelles.* Brussels: CRISP, 1971.

Dungia, Emmanuel. *Mobutu et l'argent du Zaïre: Les Révélations d'un diplomate, ex-agent des Services secrets.* Paris: Harmattan, 1992.

Ekwe-Ekwe, Herbert. *Conflict and Intervention in Africa: Nigeria, Angola, Zaire.* New York: St. Martin's Press, 1990.

Houart, Pierre. *La Pénétration communiste au Congo.* Brussels: Centre de Documentation Internationale, 1960.

————. *Les Événements du Congo.* Brussels: Centre de Documentation Internationale, 1961.

Kabongo-Kongo Kola. *Zaïre: L'Ascension d'une nation engagée.* Kinshasa: PUZ, 1983.

Kalanda, A. Mabika. *La Remise en question: Base de la décolonisation mentale.* Brussels: Éditions Remarques Africaines, 1967.

Kalonda Djessa, Jean-Grégoire. *Du Congo prospère au Zaïre en débacle.* Paris: Harmattan, 1991.

Kalonga, Ali. *Le Mal zaïrois.* Brussels: Éditions Fati, 1978.

Kambembo. *Le Nationalisme congolais, idéologie d'authenticité.* Kinshasa: PUZ, 1971.

Kelly, Sean. *America's Tyrant: The CIA and Mobutu of Zaire.* Washington: American University Press, 1993.

Kestergat, Jean. *Du Congo de Lumumba au Zaïre de Mobutu.* Brussels: P. Legrain, 1986.

Konde Vila-Ki-Kanda. *Mobutu: L'Homme du destin zaïrois.* Kinshasa: Salongo, 1985.

Le Zaïre à la croisée des chemins. Lubumbashi: Mwanga, 1975.

"L'Enlèvement de M. Tshombe le 30 juin 1967." *Travaux Africains du CRISP,* no. 76 (March 12, 1968).

Lezin, Arthur S. "Mobutu and Me." *Foreign Service Journal* 74 (June-July 1997): 38-39.

Marrés, Jacques. *Le Congo assassiné.* Brussels: M. Arnold, 1974.

Mboye Empenge ea Longila. *Le Mobutisme et la rupture du concept ancien.* Kinshasa: PUZ, 1977.

M'Buze-Nsomi Lobwanabi. *Aux Sources d'une révolution.* Kinshasa: Presses Africaines, 1977.

Mobutu Sese Seko. *Discours, allocutions et messages, 1965-1975.* Paris: Éditions J.A., 1975.

————. *Les Grands textes du Mobutisme.* Kinshasa: Institut Makanda Kabobi, 1984.

————. *Mobutu et la guerre de "quatre-vingts jours."* Paris: ABC, 1978.

————. "Speeches and Messages," in *Great African Revolutions.* Romorantin, France: 1976.

Monguya-Mbenga, Daniel. *Histoire secrète du Zaïre*. Brussels: Éditions de l'Espérance, 1977.

Nguza Karl-I-Bond, Jean. *Mobutu: ou, L'Incarnation du mal zaïrois*. London: R. Collings, 1982.

———. *Un Avenir pour le Zaïre*. Brussels: Vie Ouvrière, 1985.

Odom, Thomas P. *Shaba II: The French and Belgian Intervention in Zaire in 1978*. Fort Leavenworth, KS: US Army Command and General Staff College, Combat Studies Institute, 1993.

Okito Bene Bene. *J'ai vu mourir Philippe de Dieuleveult: Un Ex-officier des services secrets du Zaïre parle*. Paris: M. Lafon, 1994.

Ramazani Baya, et al. *1988 au Zaïre*. Kinshasa: Société Zaïroise d'Édition et de Presse (SOZEDIP), 1989.

Remilleux, Jean-Louis. *Mobutu: Dignité pour l'Afrique*. Paris: Albin Michel, 1989.

Schatzberg, Michael G. *The Dialectics of Oppression in Zaire*. Bloomington: Indiana University Press, 1988.

Sergent, Pierre. *La Légion saute sur Kolwezi: Opération Léopard: Le 2e R.E.P. au Zaïre*. Paris: Presses de la Cité, 1978.

Stockwell, John. *In Search of Enemies: A CIA Story*. New York: W. W. Norton, 1978.

Tshonda Omasombo, Jean. *Le Zaïre à l'épreuve de l'histoire immédiate: Hommâge à Benoît Verhaegen*. Paris: Karthala, 1993.

Union des Écrivains Zaïrois. *Authenticité et développement: Actes du Colloque national*. Kinshasa-Gombe: UEZ, and Paris: Présence Africaine, 1982.

Willame, Jean-Claude. *L'automne d'un despotisme: Pouvoir, argent et obéissance dans le Zaïre des années quatre-vingt*. Paris: Karthala, 1992.

Young, Merwin Crawford, and Thomas Turner. *The Rise and Decline of the Zairian State*. Madison: University of Wisconsin Press, 1986.

Zaïre, République du. Département de la Défense Nationale, de la Sécurité du Territoire, et des Anciens Combattants. *Le Bataillon héros: L'Exploit du 311e bataillon para au cours de la deuxième guerre du Shaba*. Paris: ABC, 1979.

Zaïre, République du. Service de Presse de la Présidence. *République du Zaïre: 24 novembre 65 - 24 novembre 90: Paix, unité, démocratie*. Kinshasa: 1990.

7. Multipartyism and Post-Mobutism (1990-)

Association des Moralistes Zaïrois. *Conférence Nationale Souveraine: Contribution de l'AMOZA.* Kinshasa: 1991.

Bakundakwita, Charles. *Il était une fois—: Les refugiés rwandais au Zaïre: Témoignage d'un d'entre eux.* Kinshasa: CEPAS, 1995.

Bolisomi Ebengo, Dieudonné. *Le "Pillage," une stratégie, ou, un handicap pour la démocratie?* Kinshasa: Centre Protestant d'Éditions et de Diffusion, 1993.

Braeckman, Colette. *Terreur africaine: Burundi, Rwanda, Zaïre, les racines de la violence.* Paris: Fayard, 1996.

Conseil des Evêques du Zaïre. *Tous appelés à bâtir la nation: Memorandum et déclaration des evêques du Zaïre.* Kinshasa: Éditions du Secrétariat général de la C.E.Z., 1990.

Digekisa Piluka, Victor. *Le massacre de Lubumbashi, Zaïre, 11-12 mai 1990: Dossier d'un témoin-accuse.* Paris: Harmattan, 1993.

Djungu-Simba Kamatenda. *Le Phénomène Tshisekedi.* Kinshasa: Éditions du Trottoir, 1994.

Dorlodot, Philippe de. *"Marche d'espoir," Kinshasa, 16 février 1992: Non-violence pour la démocratie au Zaïre.* Paris: Harmattan, and Kinshasa: Groupe Amos, 1994.

Gourevitch, Philip. "The Vanishing: How the Congo Became Zaire, and Zaire Became the Congo." *New Yorker* 73 (June 2, 1997): 50-53.

Jewsiewicki, Bogumil, et al. *Naître et mourir au Zaïre: Un Demi-siècle d'histoire au quotidien.* Paris: Karthala, 1993.

Kabungulu Ngoy-Kangoy. *La Transition démocratique au Zaïre: Avril 1990-juillet 1994.* Kinshasa: Centre Interdisciplinaire d'Études et de Documentation en Sciences Sociales, Université de Kinshasa, 1995.

Kankwenda Mbaya, ed. *Zaire, What Destiny?* Translated by Ayi Kwei Armah. Senegal: Codesria, 1993.

"Liberating Zaire Is the Easy Bit." *Economist* 343 (April 12, 1997): 35-36.

Lobho-Lwa-Djugudjugu. *Troisième République au Zaïre: Perestroika, democrature, ou Catastroika?* Kinshasa: Bibliothèque du Scribe, 1991.

Misser, François. "Inside Kabila's Country." *New African* (May 1997): 8-9.

Moore, Will H., and David R. Davis. "Ties That bind? Domestic and International Conflict Behavior in Zaire." *Comparative Political Studies* 31 (February 1998): 45-71.

Mukadi Bonyi. *Quelle sécurité sociale pour la troisième République?: Esquisse d'un modèle sur base des décisions et recommandations de la Conférence Nationale Souveraine.* Kinshasa: Ntobo, 1993.

N'Galamulume, Jean Oscar. *Le processus des réformes démocratiques au Zaïre.* Canada: Éditions New Strategies, 1993.

Ngefa Atondoko Andali, Guillaume. *Pour une bonne observation des élections au Zaïre.* Kinshasa: Association Zaïroise de Défense des Droits de l'Homme, 1993.

Ntombolo Mutuala. *Troisième République du Zaïre: Le Round définitif.* Brussels: Éditions du Souverain, 1991.

Roberts, Renee G. *Inducing the Deluge: Zaire's Internally Displaced People.* Washington: US Committee for Refugees, 1993.

Rosenblum, Peter. "Endgame in Zaire." *Current History* (May 1997): 200-5.

Schatzberg, Michael G. "Beyond Mobutu: Kabila and the Congo." *Journal of Democracy* 8 (October 1997): 70-84.

United States. Congress. House of Representatives. Committee on International Relations. Subcommittee on International Operations and Human Rights. *Refugees in Eastern Zaire and Rwanda* (Hearing on December 4, 1996). Washington, 1996.

Zaire. Conférence Nationale Souveraine. *Le Rapport de la Conférence nationale souveraine.* 32 vols. Kinshasa: 1992-93.

Zaïre, 1992-1996: Chronique d'une transition inachevée. Paris: Harmattan, 1996.

"Zaire: The Last Days of Mobutu." *Economist* (March 22, 1997): 21-22.

III. POLITICS AND GOVERNMENT

1. Constitution, Government and Administration

Belgium. Ministère du Congo Belge et du Ruanda-Urundi. *Constitution 1960: La Loi Fondamentale du 19 mai 1960 relative aux structures du Congo.* Brussels: 1960.

Boissonnade, Euloge. *Le Mal zaïrois.* Paris: Hermés, 1990.

Bokonga Ekanga Botombele. *Cultural Policy in the Republic of Zaire.* Paris: UNESCO, 1980.

Bomandeke Bonyeka. *Le Parlement congolais sous le régime de la Loi Fondamentale.* Kinshasa: PUZ, 1992.

Callaghy, Thomas M. *The State-Society Struggle: Zaire in Comparative Perspective.* New York: Columbia University Press, 1984.

Centre de Recherches et d'Information Socio-Politiques. *Dans le Cadre de l'authenticité, nouvelles appellations en République du Zaïre.* Brussels: 1972.

Congo, Belgian. *La Charte Coloniale: Commentaire de la loi du 18 octobre 1908 sur le gouvernement du Congo Belge.* (Commentary by Michel Halewyck.) Brussels: M. Weissenbruch, 1910-19.

———. *La Charte Coloniale Belge: Commentaire de la loi de gouvernement du Congo Belge éclairé par les discussions parlementaires et la comparaison des législations étrangères.* (Comments by Alexandre Halot-Gevaert.) Brussels: P. Van Fleteren, 1910.

Congo, République Démocratique du. *Constitution de la République Démocratique du Congo.* Kinshasa: Ministère des Affaires Étrangères, 1967.

———. *Constitution de la République Démocratique du Congo, 1er août 1964.* 2nd ed. Coquilhatville: Bureau Presse-Documentation, 1964.

Diambomba, Miala. *Hypotheses for a Training Program for Local Administrators in Zaire and Proposals for Its Realisation.* Québec: Université Laval, Faculté des Sciences de l'Éducation, 1981.

Durieux, André. *Institutions politiques, administratives et judiciaires du Congo Belge et du Ruanda-Urundi.* Brussels: Éditions Bieleveld, 1957.

Dyndo Zabondo, Gaston. *Quel avenir politique et social pour le Congo: De la Necessité d'une "revolution culturelle démocratique."* Paris: Bruyère, 1997.

Fweley Diangitukwa. *Qui gouverne le Zaïre?: La République des copains: Essai.* Paris: Harmattan, 1997.

Gatarayiha Majinya. *Aspects de la réforme administrative au Zaïre: L'Administration publique et la politique de 1965 à 1975.* Brussels: CEDAF, 1976.

Gbabendu Engunduka, A. *Volonté de changement au Zaïre.* Paris: Harmattan, 1991.

Gould, David J. *Bureaucratic Corruption and Underdevelopment in the Third World: The Case of Zaire*. New York: Pergamon Press, 1980.

————. *From Development Administration to Underdevelopment Administration: A Study of Zairian Administration in the Light of Current Crisis*. Brussels: CEDAF, 1978.

————. "Patrons, Clients and the Role of the Military in Zaire," in *The Performance of Soldiers as Governors: African Politics and the African Military*, edited by I. J. Mowe. Washington: University Press of America, n.d.

Gould, David J., and Mwana Elas. "Patrons, Clients and the Politics of Zairianization," in *Political Patronage, Clientalism and Development*, edited by S. N. Eisenstadt, and René Lemarchand. N.p., n.d.

Haleqijck de Heusch, M. *La Charte Coloniale*. 3 vols. Brussels: Weissenbruch, 1914.

————. *Les Institutions politiques et administratives des pays africains soumis à l'autorité de la Belgique*. (For the Institut Colonial International.) Brussels: Établissements Généraux d'Imprimerie, 1934.

International Labor Organization. *Rapport au gouvernement de la République du Zaïre sur l'administration de la sécurité sociale*. Geneva: 1972.

Kambayi Bwatshia L. *Le Mal zaïrois et les dérapages de la transition démocratique au Zaïre*. Kinshasa: Centre de Recherche Eugemonia, 1994.

Kibungi Makola. *Administration publique: Bilan provisoire de la transition*. Kinshasa: Ministère du Plan, Reconstruction et Ravitaillement, 1993.

Kmambo, Isaria. "The Rise of the Congolese State Systems," in *Aspects of Central African History*, edited by T. O. Ranger, pp. 29-48. London: Heinemann, 1968.

La Fontaine, Jean Sybil. *City Politics: A Study of Léopoldville, 1962-1963*. Cambridge: Harvard University Press, 1970.

Lee, J. M. *African Armies and Civil Order*. New York: Praeger, 1969.

Lefever, Ernest. *Spear and Scepter: Army, Police and Politics in Tropical Africa*. Washington: Brookings, 1970.

Lemarchand, René. "Patterns of State Collapse and Reconstruction in Central Africa: Reflections on the Crisis in the Great Lakes Region." *Afrika Spectrum* 32, no. 2 (1997): 173-93.

Leslie, Winsome J. *Zaire: Continuity and Political Change in an Oppressive State*. Boulder, CO: Westview, 1993.

Lihau, Marcel. "La Nouvelle Constitution de la République Démocratique du Congo," *Études Congolaises* 9, no. 3 (1968): 28-70.

Lwamba Bilonda. *Découpages administratifs et territoriaux du Zaïre: Provinces, districts, territoires, zones secteurs et postes*. Lubumbashi: Centre d'Études et Recherches Documentaires sur l'Afrique Centrale, University of Lubumbashi, 1994.

Mbumba Ngimbi. *Kinshasa, 1881-1981, 100 ans après Stanley: Problèmes et avenir d'une ville*. Kinshasa: Centre de Recherches Pédagogiques, 1982.

M'Buze-Nsomi Lobwanabi. *Révolution et humanisme: Essais*. Kinshasa: Presses Africaines, 1974.

McClennan, Barbara N. *Comparative Political Systems*. North Scituate, MA: Duxbury Press, 1975.

Metz, Steven. *Reform, Conflict, and Security in Zaire*. Carlisle Barracks, PA: Strategic Studies Institute, US Army War College, 1996.

Mobutu, Joseph Désiré. *De la Légalité à la légimité*. Kinshasa: Graphica International, for the Haut Commissariat à l'Information, 1968.

————. "Fondement constitutionnel des régimes militaires." *Courrier d'Afrique*, June 11-13, 1966.

————. "Les Problèmes de l'A.N.C." *Eurafrica-Tribune du Tiers Monde* 8, nos. 7-8 (1964): 44-47.

Mokoli, Mondonga M. *The Transition toward Democracy in Post-1990 Zaire: Contradictions and Dilemma*. San Francisco: International Scholars Publications, 1997.

Mpinga-Kasenda. *L'Administration publique du Zaïre: L'Impact du milieu socio-politique sur sa structure et son fonctionnement*. Paris: Pedons, 1973.

Mpinga-Kasenda, and D. J. Gould. *Les Réformes administratives au Zaïre, 1972-1973*. Kinshasa: PUZ, 1975.

Mukamba Kadiata Nzemba. *Le Zaïre à la recherche du renouveau démocratique: Réflexions et échanges*. Paris: Pythagore, 1993.

Mumba M. Shabane, Marcel. *Principes et règles d'organisation des élections libres et démocratiques*. Kinshasa: Centre d'Études pour l'Action Sociale, 1993.

Mupinganayi Kadiakuidi, Bruno. *Vers la faillite de la démocratie en Afrique: Cas du Zaïre*. Kinshasa: Centre Africain de Recherche Industrielle, 1994.

Muyere Oyong. *Impératif du développement et réforme de l'administration locale au Zaïre*. Kinshasa: PUZ, 1986.

Ngefa Atondoko Andali, Guillaume. *Pour une Bonne observation des élections au Zaïre*. Kinshasa: Association Zaïroise de Défense des Droits de l'Homme, 1993.

Nguya-Ndila, Célestin. *Indépendance de la République Démocratique du Congo et les engagements internationaux antérieurs (succession d'états aux traités)*. Kinshasa: Université de Kinshasa, 1971.

Nkulu Kilombo. *Plaidoyer pour une transition démocratique au Zaïre*. Kinshasa: BOPOL, 1993.

Nzongola-Ntalaja, Georges. "Urban Administration in Zaire: A Study of Kananga, 1971-1973." Ph.D. thesis. Madison: University of Wisconsin, 1975.

Promontorio, Victor. *Les Institutions dans la constitution congolaise*. Leopoldville: Concordia, 1965.

Quirini, Pierre de. *Une Constitution pour quoi faire?* Kinshasa: CEPAS, 1990.

Sangmpam, S. N. *Pseudocapitalism and the Overpoliticized State: Reconciling Politics and Anthropology in Zaire*. Aldershot, England: Avebury, 1994.

Tshimanga Mukala Pawuni. *Les Structures matérielles et humaines du Conseil judiciaire*. Boma: Imprimerie CADEMA, 1981.

Turner, Thomas. *Mobutu Sese Seko and the Crisis in Zaire*. Nairobi: N.p., 1992.

Vanderlinden, Jacques. *La République du Zaïre*. Paris: Berger-Levrault, 1975.

Vengroff, Richard. *Development Administration at the Local Level: The Case of Zaire*. Syracuse, NY: Maxwell School of Citizenship and Public Affairs, Syracuse University, 1983.

Vieux, Serge A. *L'Administration zaïroise*. Paris: Berger-Levreut, 1974.

———. *Le Statut de la fonction publique: Le Décret-loi du 20 mars 1965 et ses mesures d'exécution*. Kinshasa: Office National de la Recherche et du Développement, 1970.

Warren, J. *Division Kamanyola*. Paris: Afrique Biblio Club, 1978.

Wembi, Antoine. *La Sécurité sociale au Congo: Origines, possibilités et difficultés de gestion.* Louvain, Belgium: Nauwelaerts, and Leopoldville: IRES, 1966.

Willame, Jean-Claude. *Gouvernance et pouvoir: Essai sur trois trajectoires africaines, Madagascar, Somalie, Zaïre.* Brussels: Institut Africain-CEDAF, and Paris: Harmattan, 1994.

———. "La Seconde guerre du Shaba," in *Enquêtes et Documents d'Histoire Africaine*, vol. 3. Leuven, Belgium: N.p., 1978.

———. *Les Provinces du Congo: Structure et fonctionnement.* Leopoldville: IRES, 1964-65.

Young, Merwin Crawford. *Politics in the Congo: Decolonization and Independence.* Princeton, NJ: Princeton University Press, 1965.

———. "Zaire: The Shattered Illusion of the Integral State." *Journal of Modern African Studies* 32 (June 1994): 247-63.

Young, Merwin Crawford, and Thomas Turner. *The Rise and Decline of the Zairian State.* Madison: University of Wisconsin Press, 1986.

Zaïre, République du. *Constitution de la République du Zaïre: Mise à jour au 1er janvier 1983.* Kinshasa: Journal Officiel, 1983.

———. *Statut du personnel de carrière des services publics de l'état: Loi no. 81-003 du 17 juillet 1981.* Kinshasa: Agence Zaïre Presse, 1981.

Zaïre, République du. Assemblée Nationale. *Annales parlementaires.* Kinshasa: annual.

Zaïre, République du. Bibliothèque Nationale. *Conférence Nationale Souveraine (1991): Quelle politique culturelle pour la troisième république au Zaïre?* Kinshasa: 1993.

Zaïre, République du. Département de la Défense Nationale, de la Sécurité du Territoire et des Anciens Combattants. *Forces armées zaïroises.* Periodical.

2. Politics and Political Parties

Artigue, Pierre. *Qui sont les leaders congolais?* Brussels: Europe-Afrique, 1960.

Bazenguissa-Ganga, Remy. *Les Voies du politique au Congo: essai de sociologie historique.* Paris: Karthala, 1997.

Biebuyck, Daniel, and Mary Douglas. *Congo Tribes and Parties.* London: Royal Anthropological Institute, 1961.

Bolisomi Ebengo, Dieudonné. *Le "Pillage," une stratégie, ou, un handicap pour la démocratie?* Kinshasa: Centre Protestant d'Éditions et de Diffusion, 1993.

Bossassi-Epole Bolya Kodya. *Réflexions critiques pour une authenticité progressiste: L'Expérience zaïroise et les macro-contradictions.* Brussels: R. Venderlinden, 1976.

Buana Kabue. *Citoyen Président: Lettre ouverte au Président Mobutu Sese Seko et aux autres.* Paris: Harmattan, 1978.

Centre de Recherche et d'Information Socio-Politiques. *Les Partis politiques congolais.* Brussels: CRISP, 1964.

Ceulemans, Jacques. *Antoine Gizenga: Hier, aujourd'hui, demain.* Brussels: Remarques Congolaises, 1964.

De Backer, M. C. C. *Notes pour servir à l'étude des "groupements politiques" à Léopoldville.* Brussels: INFORCONGO, 1959.

Demunter, Paul. *Luttes politiques au Zaïre: Le Processus de politisation des masses rurales du Bas-Zaïre.* Paris: Anthropos, 1975.

Djungu-Simba Kamatenda. *Le Phénomène Tshisekedi.* Kinshasa: Éditions du Trottoir, 1994.

Elliot, Jeffrey M., and Mervyn N. Dymally. *Voices of Zaire: Rhetoric or Reality?* New York: Washington Institute Press, 1990.

Institut de Formation et d'Études Politiques. *La Tolérance politique.* Kinshasa: 1996.

Kalanda, Auguste, "À Propos du régime communal au Congo: La Consultation de Luluabourg," *Mouvement Communal,* no. 332 (Sept. 1959): 418-27.

Kalele-Ka-Bila. *Les Idéologies régionalistes.* Lubumbashi: Labossa, 1989.

Kalonga, Ali. *Le Mal zaïrois.* Brussels: Éditions Fati, 1978.

Kamitatu-Massamba, Cléophas. *La Grande mystification du Congo-Kinshasa: Les Crimes de Mobutu.* Paris: Maspero, 1971.

———. *Le Pouvoir à la portée du peuple.* Paris: Harmattan, 1977.

Kanza, Thomas. *Congo 196. . . ?* Brussels: Remarques Congolaises, 1962.

———. *Éloge de la révolution.* Brussels: Remarques Congolaises, 1968.

———. *Le Congo à la veille de son indépendance: ou, Propos d'un Congolais désillusioné.* Brussels: private publisher, 1959.

———. *Propos d'un Congolais naïf: Discours sur la vocation coloniale dans l'Afrique de demain.* Paris: Présence Africaine, 1959.

———. *Tôt ou tard . . . Ata ndele.* Brussels: Le Livre Africain, 1959.

Kasa-Vubu, Joseph. *Receuil des discours, allocutions et messages prononcés de juin 1960 à juin 1965.* Leopoldville: Ministère de l'Information, Bureau de Documentation et des Relations Publiques, 1965.

Kashamura, Anicet. *Culture et aliénation en Afrique.* Paris: Édition du Cercle, 1971.

Labrique, Jean. *Congo politique.* Leopoldville: Éditions de l'Avenir, 1957.

Larock, Victor, ed. *Le P.S.B. avait raison: Positions socialistes au sujet du Congo, 1959-1960.* Brussels: Institut Émile Vandervelde, 1960.

Le Pari Congolais. Brussels: Dessart, 1960.

Lemarchand, René. "Patrice Lumumba," in *African Political Thought: Lumumba, Nkrumah and Touré.* Edited by W. A. E. Skurnik. pp. 13-64. Denver: Social Science Foundation and Graduate School of International Studies, 1967-68.

———. *Political Awakening in the Belgian Congo.* (Originally published by University of California Press, Berkeley, 1964.) Westport, CT: Greenwood Press, 1982.

Lobho-Lwa-Djugudjugu. *Troisième République au Zaïre: Perestroika, democrature, ou catastroika?* Kinshasa: Bibliothèque du Scribe, 1991.

Lumumba, Patrice. *Congo, My Country.* New York: Praeger, 1962.

———. *Le Congo, terre d'avenir: Est-il menacé?* Brussels: Éditions de l'Office de Publicité, 1961.

———. *Lumumba Speaks: The Speeches and Writings of Patrice Lumumba, 1958-1961.* (Translated from French by Helen R. Lane.) New York: Little, Brown, 1972.

"M. Gizenga et la fondation du PALU (Parti Lumumbiste Unifié)." *Courrier Africain du CRISP*, no. 37 (November 19, 1964): 22.

Mabaya Ma Mbongo. *Autopsie de l'univers néo-colonial au Zaïre: L'Exil à perpétuité.* Sartrouville, France: Éditions Kolwezi, 1985.

———. *Le Fascisme au Zaïre.* Sartrouville, France: Éditions Kolwezi, 1984.

Manya K'Omalowete a Djonga. *Patrice Lumumba, le Sankuru et l'Afrique: Essai.* Lutry, Switzerland: J.-M. Bouchain, 1985.

Mobutu Sese Seko. *Discours, allocutions et messages, 1965-1975.* Paris: Éditions J.A., 1975.

———. "Speeches and Messages," in *Great African Revolutions.* Romorantin, France: N.p., 1976.

Monnier, Laurent. "Notes sur l'ABAKO et le nationalisme Kongo." *Geneva-Africa* 5, no. 2 (1966): 51-61.

Mouvance Progressiste du Congo, Zaïre. *Congo, Zaïre: Démocratie neo-coloniale, ou, deuxième indépendance?* Paris: Harmattan, 1992.

Mouvement Populaire de la Révolution. *Glossaire idéologique du M.P.R.* Kinshasa: FORCAD, 1986.

———. *MPR, 1967-1982: Quinze ans au service de la dignité humaine.* Kinshasa: Agence Zaïre Presse, 1982.

———. *Rapport d'activité 1967-1972.* Kinshasa: N.p., n.d.

———. *Statut du M.P.R.* Kinshasa: N.p., n.d.

Mudimbe, V. Y. *Parables and Fables: Exegesis, Textuality, and Politics in Central Africa.* Madison: University of Wisconsin Press, 1991.

N'Galamulume, Jean Oscar. *Le processus des réformes démocratiques au Zaïre.* Canada: Éditions New Strategies, 1993.

N'Gbanda Nzambo-ko-Atumba, Honoré. *La Transition au Zaïre: Le Long tunnel.* Kinshasa: NORAF, 1995.

Ngefa Atondoko Andali, Guillaume. *Pour une Bonne observation des élections au Zaïre.* Kinshasa: Association Zaïroise de Défense des Droits de l'Homme, 1993.

Nguza Karl-I-Bond, Jean. *Mobutu, ou, l'incarnation du mal zaïrois.* London: R. Collings, 1982.

———. *Un avenir pour le Zaïre.* Brussels: Vie Ouvrière, 1985.

Nkamany-A-Baleme, Kabamba. *Pouvoirs et ideologies tribales au Zaïre.* Paris: Harmattan, 1997.

Ntombolo Mutuala. *Troisième République du Zaïre: Le Round définitif.* Brussels: Éditions du Souverain, 1991.

Nzongola-Ntalaja, Georges. "The Bourgeoisie and Revolution in the Congo." *Journal of Modern African Studies* 8, no. 4 (1970): 511-30.

Oyatambwe, Wamu. *Église Catholique et pouvoir politique au Congo-Zaïre: La Quête démocratique.* Paris: Harmattan, 1997.

Parti Communiste de Belgique. *La Lutte pour l'indépendance du Congo: Rapport d'activité du Comité Central du P.C. de Belgique au XIVème Congrès.* Brussels: 1963.

Perin, François. *Les Institutions politiques du Congo indépendant au 30 juin 1960*. Leopoldville: Institut Politique Congolais, 1960.

Ryckbost, J. *Essai sur les origines et le développement des premières associations professionnelles au Congo (1940-1944)*. Leopoldville: IRES, 1962.

Schatzberg, Michael G. "Fidelité au guide: The J.M.P.R. in Zairian Schools." *Journal of Modern African Studies* 16, no. 3 (1978): 417-31.

————. *Politics and Class in Zaire*. New York: Africana, 1980.

Tcha-Malenge, Kibwe. *Who Will Win in Congo-Kinshasa?* Toronto: Norman Bethune Institute, 1976.

Tshombe, Moïse. *Discours prononcé par le Président du Katanga à l'occasion de la fête du 11 juillet 1962*. Elisabethville: Service d'Information du Gouvernement Katangais, 1962.

————. *Moïse Tshombe parle . . . Les Véritables dessous de l'affair katangaise: L'Avenir du Congo*. Brussels: Ponant, 1963.

————. *Quinze mois de gouvernement du Congo*. Paris: Table Ronde, 1966.

Turner, Thomas. *Le Vandisme (Sankuru-Zaïre) et sa signification politique*. Brussels: CEDAF, 1974.

Union de Jeunesses Révolutionnaires Congolaises. *Memorandum: L'Agression armée de l'impérialisme américano-belge à Stanleyville et à Paulis*. Brussels: Livre International, 1966.

Van der Steep, Daniel. *Élections et Réformes de la composition des organes politiques*. Brussels: CEDAF, 1978.

Van Lierde, Jean. *La Pensée politique de Patrice Lumumba*. Paris: Présence Africaine, 1963.

Van Reyn, Paul. *Le Congo Politique*. Brussels: Europe-Afrique, 1960.

Verbeek, Roger. *Le Congo en question*. Paris: Présence Africaine, 1965.

Verhaegen, Benoît, ed. *ABAKO 1950-1960*. CRISP, 1963.

————. "Consultations électorales et élections au Congo, 1957-1959." *Cahiers Économiques et Sociaux IRES* 3, no. 3 (1965): 247-89.

————, ed. *Les Cahiers de Gamboma: Instructions politiques et militaires des partisans congolais (1964-1965)*. Brussels: CRISP, 1965.

Weiss, Herbert P. *Political Protest in the Congo: The Parti Solidaire Africain during the Independence Struggle*. Princeton, NJ: Princeton University Press, 1967.

Weiss, Herbert, and Benoît Verhaegen, eds. *P.S.A.: Parti Solidaire Africain*. Brussels: CRISP, 1963.
Welch, Claude E. *Soldier and State in Africa*. Evanston, IL: Northwestern University Press, 1970.
Willame, Jean Claude. *Patrimonialism and Political Change in the Congo*. Stanford: Stanford University Press, 1972.
Young, Crawford. *Politics of Cultural Pluralism*. Madison: University of Wisconsin Press, 1976.
Zaire. Conférence Nationale Souveraine. *Le Rapport de la Conférence Nationale Souveraine*. 32 vols. Kinshasa: 1992-93.

3. Law and Human Rights

Amnesty International. *Memorandum to the Head of State Concerning Amnesty International's Mission to Zaire in July 1981*. New York: Amnesty International, 1981.
———. *Political Imprisonment in Zaire: An Amnesty International Special Briefing*. New York: Amnesty International, 1983.
———. *Zaire: Reports of Torture and Killings Committed by the Armed Forces in Shaba Region*. London: Amnesty International, 1986.
Association Nationale des Entreprises Zaïroises. *Code du travail*. Kinshasa: ANEZA, 1972.
Bakajika, Banjikila Thomas. *Épuration éthnique en Afrique: Les Kasaïens: Katanga 1961-Shaba 1992*. Paris: Harmattan, 1997.
Baldo, Suliman, and Peter Rosenblum. *Zaire: Transition, War and Human Rights*. New York: Human Rights Watch, 1997.
Balleger, Lois. "La Protection légale du mariage monogamique au Congo Belge." *CEPSI Bulletin*, no. 11 (1950): 87.
Banza, D. S. R. "Du Barreau et de la représentation en justice en République Démocratique du Congo," *Revue Congolaise d'Administration*, no. 3 (July-August 1968).
Baumer, Guy. *Les Centres indigènes extra-coutumiers au Congo Belge*. Paris: Domat-Monchrestien, 1939.
Biebuyck, Daniel. *Right in Land, Its Resources among the Nyanga (Republic of the Congo-Leopoldville)*. Brussels: ARSOM, 1966.
Bolongo, Likulia (General). *Droit pénal militaire zaïrois*. Paris: Librairie Générale de Droit et de Jurisprudence, 1977.

Braudo, Serge. "Les Établissements pénitentiaires au Congo (Léopoldville)," *Penant* 76 (January-March 1966): 55-72.

Buabua wa Kayembe Mubadiate. *Traité de droit fiscal zaïrois: Constats et propositions sur les contributions et la douane.* Kinshasa: PUZ, 1993.

Campbell, Scott. *What Kabila Is Hiding: Civilian Killings and Impunity in Congo.* New York: Human Rights Watch, 1997.

Cikuru Batumike. *Une liberté de moins: Témoignage de prison et autres rubriques.* Langenthal, Switzerland: Éditions Mosaïque, 1986.

Congo, Belgian. *Code du Travail.* 2 vols. Brussels: Éditions du Marais, 1953.

———. *Code Économique du Congo Belge: Mise à jour début 1954.* Brussels: Agence Économique et Financière, 1954.

———. *Commentaire du Code pénal congolais.* Edited by Mineur, G. 2nd ed. Brussels: F. Larcier, 1953.

———. *Rapport de la Commission pour l'Étude du Problème Foncier.* 4 vols. Leopoldville: Gouvernement Générale, 1957.

Congo, République Démocratique du. Ministère du Travail. *Code du Travail.* Kinshasa: Éditions CADICEC, 1967.

Crabb, John H. *The Legal System of Congo-Kinshasa.* Charlottesville, VA: Michie, 1970.

De Quirini, Pierre. *Le Pouvoir réglementaire en droit public colonial belge.* Brussels: IRCB, 1952.

———. *Le Problème juridique des dettes du Congo Belge et l'État du Congo.* Brussels: ARSOM, 1961.

———. *Les Lois que tout citoyen doit connaître.* Kinshasa-Gombe: CEPAS, 1983.

———. *Souveraineté et communauté belgo-congolaise.* Brussels: ARSC, 1959.

Digekisa Piluka, Victor. *Le Massacre de Lubumbashi, Zaïre, 11-12 mai 1990: Dossier d'un témoin-accuse.* Paris: Harmattan, 1993.

Falmagne, Étienne. *Code du Travail du Katanga: Présentation des textes actuellement en vigueur, accompagnée des notices publiées et d'extraits inédits de jurisprudence, et d'un commentaire par articles.* Elisabethville: Société d'Études Juridiques du Katanga, 1962.

Ganshof van der Meersch, W. J., and François Perin. *Le Droit électoral au Congo Belge.* Brussels: Bruylant, 1958.

Grévisse, F. *La Grande pitié des juridictions indigènes.* Brussels: IRCB, 1949.

———. *Le Centre Extra-Coutumier d'Élisabethville.* Brussels: IRCB, 1951.

———. *Notes sur le droit coutumier des Balebi.* Elisabethville: Éditions de la Revue Juridique du Congo Belge, 1934.

Heyse, Théodore. *Congo Belge et Ruanda-Urundi: Notes de droit public et commentaires de la Charte Coloniale.* Brussels: G. Van Campenhout, 1952-54.

———. *Grandes lignes du régime des terres du Congo Belge et du Ruanda-Urundi et leurs applications (1940-1946).* Brussels: IRCB, 1947.

———. *Problèmes fonciers et régimes des terres (aspects juridiques, économiques et sociaux).* Brussels: CEDESA, 1960.

Human Rights Watch. *Prison Conditions in Zaire.* New York: January 1994.

Human Rights Watch and Fédération Internationale des Ligues des Droits de l'Homme. *Zaire—Forced to Flee: Violence Against the Tutsis in Zaire.* New York: N.p., July 1996.

Idzumbuir Assop, Joséphine. *La Justice pour mineurs au Zaïre: Realités et perspectives.* Kinshasa: Éditions Universitaires Africaines, 1994.

———. *La Place de la convention relative aux droits de l'enfant en droit zaïrois.* Kinshasa: UNICEF, 1994.

Kalala Ilunga. *Commentaire de la loi relative au nom des personnes physiques.* Publisher unknown: 1974.

Kalambay Lumpungu, G. *Droit civil.* Kinshasa: PUZ, 1985.

Kalanda, Mabika. *Le Code de la famille à l'épreuve de l'authenticité.* Kinshasa: Laboratoire d'Analyses Sociales de Kinshasa; and Paris: Harmattan, 1990.

Kalongo Mbikayi. *Responsabilité civile et socialisation des risques en droit zaïrois: Étude comparative du droit zaïrois et des systèmes juridiques belge et français.* Kinshasa: PUZ, 1974.

Kambale Kalume, Pascal. *Connaissez-vous votre état civil?: Importance, notions et procédures en matière d'établissement d'actes de l'état-civil.* Kinshasa: Association Zaïroise de Défense des Droits de l'Homme, 1994.

Katuala Kaba-Kashala. *Jurisprudences des cours et tribunaux, 1965-1974.* Kinshasa: N.p., 1992.

Kengo-wa-Dondo. "Considérations sur le project du nouveau Code de la Famille." (Speech opening Supreme Court on October 4, 1975.) Kinshasa: Cour Suprême de Justice de la République du Zaïre, 1976.

―――. "La Confiscation." (Speech opening Supreme Court on October 20, 1973.) Kinshasa: Cour Suprême de Justice de la République du Zaïre, 1973.

―――. *Vers une Société sans prison*. Kinshasa: Cour Suprême de Justice de la République du Zaïre, 1975.

Lamy, Émile. *Le Droit privé zaïrois*. Kinshasa: PUZ, 1975.

Lawyers Committee for Human Rights. *Zaire: Repression as Policy: A Human Rights Report*. New York: Lawyers Committee for Human Rights, 1990.

Lierde, Chr. van. *Éléments de droit civil Zaïrois*. Kinshasa: Centre de Recherches Pédagogiques, 1990.

Likulia Bolongo. *Droit pénal spécial zaïrois*. Paris: Librairie Générale de Droit et de Jurisprudence, 1976.

―――. *Méthodes d'approche de la qualification des faits en droit pénal*. Kinshasa: PUZ, 1982.

Longman, Timothy, and Alison DesForges. *"Attacked by All Sides": Civilians and the War in Eastern Zaire*. New York: Human Rights Watch, 1997.

Louwers, Octave. *Lois en vigueur dans l'État Indépendant du Congo*. Brussels: P. Weissenbruch, 1905.

Lukombe Nghenda. *Règles relatives aux organes des sociétés commerciales en droit zaïrois*. Kinshasa: PUZ, 1981.

Malengreau, Guy. *Les Droits fonciers coutumiers chez les indigènes du Congo*. Brussels: IRCB, 1947.

M'pelekwa Yomputy Yeyele. *Index alphabétique du Code pénal et de divers textes de loi: À l'Usage des juges de police et des officiers de police judiciaire*. Mbanza-Ngungu, Zaire: Parquet de la Sous-Région des Cataractes, 1976.

Mpengo Lofonge. *Guide pratique de la législation sociale au Zaïre*. Kinshasa: Jomo, 1988.

Muepu Mibanga. *Songye: Le Recueil de jurisprudence de l'État Indépendant du Congo jusqu'à 1967*. Kinshasa: Renapi, 1987.

Mukusa, Jean C. "Le Problème de l'unification et de l'intégration du droit congolais." *Problèmes Sociaux Congolais*, nos. 75-76 (1966-67): 55-61.

Nkulu Butombe, J. I. *La Question du Zaïre et ses répercussions sur les juridictions ecclésiastiques, 1865-1888.* Kinshasa: Faculté de Théologie Catolique, 1982.

Ntoto Aley Angu. *La rupture pour faute lourde en droit zaïrois du travail.* Lubumbashi: Impala, 1991.

Nyabirungu Mwene Songa. *Droit pénal général zaïrois.* 2nd ed. Kinshasa: Éditions Droit et Société, 1995.

Paulus, Jean-Pierre. *Droit publique du Congo Belge.* Brussels: Institut de Sociologie Solvay, Université Libre de Belgique, 1959.

Pauwels, Johan M. *La Législation zaïroise relative au nom: Droit et authenticité africaine.* Brussels: ARSOM, 1983.

————. *Répertoire de droit coutumier congolais: Jurisprudence et doctrine, 1954-1967.* Kinshasa: Office National de la Recherche et du Développement, 1970.

Pindi-Mbensa Kifu, Gilbert. *Le Droit zaïrois de la consommation.* Kinshasa: CADICEC, 1995.

Piron, P., J. De Vos, et al. *Codes et lois du Congo Belge.* 3 vols. Brussels: Larcier, 1959-60.

Quirini, Pierre de. *Démocratie et droits de la personne humaine.* Kinshasa: CEPAS, 1993.

Riddell, James C., Jeswald W. Salacuse, and David Tabachnick. *The National Land Law of Zaire and Indigenous Land Tenure in Central Bandundu, Zaire.* Madison: University of Wisconsin, Land Tenure Center, 1987.

Roberts, Renee G. *Inducing the Deluge: Zaire's Internally Displaced People.* Washington: US Committee for Refugees, 1993.

Rubbens, Antoine. *Dettes de Guerre.* Elisabethville: Éditions "L'Essor du Congo," 1945.

————. *Le Droit judiciaire congolais.* 3 vols. Kinshasa: Université Lovanium, 1965-68.

————. *L'Indépendance des magistrats dans la République Démocratique du Congo.* Brussels: ARSOM, 1966.

————. *L'Instruction criminelle et la procédure pénale.* Brussels: Larcier, and Leopoldville: Lovanium, 1965.

Schatzberg, Michael G. *The Dialectics of Oppression in Zaire.* Bloomington: Indiana University Press, 1988.

Simmonds, R. *Legal Problems Arising from the United Nations Military Operations in the Congo.* The Hague: Martinus Nijhoff, 1968.

Sohier, A. *Traité élémentaire de droit coutumier du Congo Belge*. 2nd ed. Brussels: Maison Ferdinand Larcier, 1954.

Touchard, G., and O. Louwers. *Jurisprudence de l'État Indépendant du Congo*. Brussels: Weissenbruch, 1905-10.

Tribunal Permanent des Peuples. *Session sur le Zaïre: Rotterdam, 18, 19 et 20 septembre 1982: Sentence*. Rotterdam: Tribunal Permanent des Peuples, 1982.

Tshiyembe Mwayila. *Invention de l'état de droit et projet de société démocratique en Afrique: Le Cas du Zaïre*. Paris: D. de Selliers, 1992.

United States. Department of Labor. *Labor Law and Practice in the Republic of Zaire*. Washington: Department of Labor, 1972.

United States Institute of Peace. "Zaire, Predicament and Prospects: A Report to the Minority Rights Group (USA)." Washington: USIP, 1996.

Verstraete, M. *La Nationalité congolaise*. Brussels: ARSC, 1959.

Wekerle, Anton. *Guide to the Text of the Criminal Law and Criminal Procedure Codes of Burundi, Rwanda, and Zaire*. Washington: Library of Congress, Law Library, 1975.

Yett, Sheldon. *Masisi, Down the Road from Goma: Ethnic Cleansing and Displacement in Eastern Zaire*. Washington: Immigration and Refugee Services of America, 1996.

Zaïre, République du. *Code des contributions de la République du Zaïre*. Kinshasa: Chambre de Commerce de Kinshasa, 1972.

———. Court Suprême. *Bulletin des arrêts de la Cour suprême de justice*. Kinshasa, unknown frequency.

Zaïre, République du. Département de la Justice. *Le Code pénal zaïrois: Dispositions législatives et réglementaires mises à jour au 31 mai 1982*. Kinshasa: 1983.

Zaïre, République du. Ministère du Travail et de la Prévoyance Sociale. *Code du travail*. Kinshasa-Gombe: CADICEC, 1981.

———. *Gérants d'entreprise, ce que vous devez savoir . . . du chèque en droit congolais*. Kinshasa: CADICEC, 1971.

———. *La Représentation des travailleurs dans l'entreprise: Code congolais du travail*. Kinshasa: CADICEC, 1971.

———. *Le Régime général des biens au Zaïre: Loi no. 021 du 20 juillet 1973*. Kinshasa: Agence Zaïre Presse, 1974.

Zaïre, République du. Tribunal de Centre, Ilebo. *Receuil de jurisprudence du Centre d'Ilebo*. Kinshasa: Office National de la Recherche et du Développement, 1973.

4. Foreign Relations and Foreign Assistance

American Council of Voluntary Agencies for Foreign Service. Technical Assistance Information Clearing House. *Development Assistance Programs of US Non-Profit Organizations in Zaïre*, New York: N.p., 1974.

Ball, George. *The Elements in Our Congo Policy*. (Based on an address before Town Hall in Los Angeles, CA, on December 19, 1961.) Washington: US Department of State, no. 7826, African Series 25, 1961.

British National Export Council. Africa Committee. *Trade Mission to the Democratic Republic of the Congo*. London: BNEC, 1970.

Clos, Max. "The Chinese Role in the Congo: Fact or Fiction?" *Africa Report* 19, no. 1 (1965): 18-19.

Conflit belgo-zaïrois: Fondements historiques, politiques, économiques et culturelles. Paris: Présence Africaine, 1990.

Gappert, Gary, and Garry Thomas, eds. *The Congo, Africa, and America*. Syracuse, NY: Maxwell Graduate School of Citizenship and Public Affairs, Syracuse University, 1965.

Gibbs, David N. *The Political Economy of Third World Intervention: Mines, Money, and US Policy in the Congo Crisis*. Chicago: University of Chicago Press, 1991.

Gildea, Tara. *A Case Study of Zaire's Foreign Policy: Shaba I and II*. Geneva: Institut Univérsitaire de Hautes Études Internationales, 1990.

Hakim, Najib J., and Richard P. Stevens. "Zaire and Israel: An American Connection." *Journal of Palestine Studies* 12 (Spring 1983): 41-53.

Helmreich, Jonathan E. *United States Relations with Belgium and the Congo, 1940-1960*. Newark: University of Delaware Press, and London: Associated University Presses, 1998.

Hilsman, Roger. "The Congo Crisis." in *To Move a Nation: The Politics of Foreign Policy in the Administration of John F. Kennedy*. New York: Doubleday, 1967.

Kalb, Madeleine G. *The Congo Cables*. New York: Macmillan, 1982.

Kelly, Sean. *America's Tyrant: The CIA and Mobutu of Zaire*. Washington, DC: American University Press, 1993.

Lee, Brady. "Peacekeeping, the Congo, and Zones of Peace." *Peace Review* 9 (June 1997): 189-91.

Lemarchand, René. *American Policy in Southern Africa: The Stakes and the Stance.* Washington: University Press of America, 1978.

Lewellen, Ted C. "State Terror and the Disruption of Internal Adaptations by CIA Covert Actions." *Scandinavian Journal of Development Alternatives* 9 (June-September 1990): 47-65.

Lumumba-Kasongo, Tukumbi. *The Dynamics of Economic and Political Relations between Africa and Foreign Powers: A Study in International Relations.* Westport, CT: Praeger, 1998.

Maganga-Boumba. *Le Congo et L'OUA.* Paris: Harmattan, 1989.

Meynaud, Jean, J. Ladrière, and F. Perin. *La Décision politique en Belgique.* Paris: Colin, 1965.

Moshje, Luc. *La Pénétration américaine au Congo.* Brussels: Remarques Congolaises, 1963.

Piniau, Bernard. *Congo-Zaïre, 1874-1981: La Perception du lointain.* Paris: Harmattan, 1992.

Rodrigues, J. H. *Brazil and Africa.* Berkeley: University of California Press, 1965.

Rusk, Dean. "U.S. Policy in the Congo." *Department of State Bulletin* 46:1180 (February 5, 1962): 216-18. (Text of statement before the Africa Subcommittee, Committee on Foreign Relations, US Senate, on January 18, 1962.)

Schatzberg, Michael G. "Military Intervention and the Myth of Collective Security: The Case of Zaire." *Journal of Modern African Studies* 27 (1989): 315-40.

———. *Mobutu or Chaos?: The United States and Zaire, 1960-1990.* Lanham, MD: University Press of America, 1991.

Tripathy, Amulya Kumar. *U.S. Foreign Policy: A Study of CIA and External Intervention in Central Africa.* Delhi, India: Discovery, 1989.

United Nations. Development Programme. Office of the Resident Representative (Democratic Republic of the Congo). *Technical Co-operation Programmes of the United Nations and its Specialized Agencies in the Democratic Republic of the Congo during 1966.* Kinshasa: 1967.

United States. Agency for International Development. *Field Budget Submission for Zaire.* Washington: annual.

———. *U.S. Overseas Loans and Grants and Assistance from International Organizations.* Washington: annual.

United States. Congress. House. Committee on Foreign Affairs. Subcommittee on Africa. *Expressing the Sense of the Congress with Respect to the Situation in Sudan; Concerning the Movement toward Democracy in the Federal Republic of Nigeria; and Concerning Democracy for Zaire.* Washington: 1995.

———. Congress. House. Committee on Foreign Affairs. Subcommittee on Africa. *Zaire, a Country in Crisis: Hearing before the Subcommittee on Africa of the Committee on Foreign Affairs, October 26, 1993.* Washington: 1995.

———. Congress. House. Committee on International Relations. Subcommittee on Africa. *Zaire: Collapse of an African giant?* (Hearing on April 8, 1997.) Washington: 1997.

———. Congress. House. Committee on International Relations. Subcommittee on Human Rights and International Organizations. *The Human Rights Situation in South Africa, Zaire, Horn of Africa, and Uganda:* (Hearing June 21 to August 9, 1984). Washington: 1985.

———. Congress. House. Committee on International Relations. Subcommittee on International Security and Scientific Affairs. *Congressional Oversight of War Powers Compliance: Zaire Airlift.* (Hearing of August 10, 1978, on Shaba airlift.) Washington: 1978.

———. Congress. Senate. Committee on Foreign Relations. Subcommittee on African Affairs. *Emergency Situation in Zaire and Somalia.* February 5, 1992. Washington: 1992.

———. Congress. Senate. Committee on Foreign Relations. Subcommittee on African Affairs. *Security Supporting Assistance for Zaire.* Washington: 1975.

———. Congress. Senate. Committee on Foreign Relations. Subcommittee on African Affairs. *The Situation in Zaire.* November 6, 1991. Washington: 1992.

———. Congress. Senate. Committee on Foreign Relations. Subcommittee on African Affairs. *U.S. Policies toward Liberia, Togo, and Zaire: Hearing before the Subcommittee on African Affairs of the Committee on Foreign Relations.* Washington: 1993.

———. Congress. Senate. Committee on Housing and Urban Affairs. Subcommittee on International Finance. *U.S. Loans to Zaire.* (Hearing on request for guarantees by US Export-Import Bank for additional funds for the Inga-Shaba power transmission line.) Washington: 1979.

United States Library of Congress. *The United States and Africa.* (Bibliography of official US publications compiled by Julian W. Witherell.) Washington: 1978.

Villers, Gauthier de. *De Mobutu à Mobutu: Trente ans de relations Belgique-Zaïre.* Brussels: De Boeck University, 1995.

———. *Zaïre, 1990-1991: Faits et dits de la société d'après le regard de la presse.* Brussels: CEDAF, 1992.

Weissman, Stephen R. *American Foreign Policy in the Congo, 1960-1964.* Ithaca, NY: Cornell University Press, 1974.

Willame, Jean-Claude. *La Politique africaine de la Belgique à l'épreuve: Les Relations belgo-zaïroises, 1978-1984.* Brussels: Centre d'Étude et de Documentation Africaines, 1985.

Williams, Mennan (Soapy). "The Urgent Need for Congo Reconciliation." *Department of State Bulletin* 47:1222 (November 26, 1962): 803-05. (Text of address before Jefferson Society of the University of Virginia, Charlottesville, VA, November 1962.)

Woodward, Bob. *Veil: The Secret Wars of the CIA, 1981-1987.* New York: Simon & Schuster, 1987.

Zaire. *Report of the Seminar on the Problems of Refugees in Zaire.* (Seminar sponsored jointly with the Office of the UN High Commissioner for Refugees, held in Kinshasa, April 19-25, 1982.) Geneva: UNHCR, 1982.

Zaïre, 1885-1985: Cent ans de regards belges. (Documents of an exhibition from May 9 to June 30, 1985.) Brussels: European Economic Community Cultural Center, 1985.

IV. ECONOMY

1. General Economic

Annuaire: Trois milles contacts professionnels au Zaïre, au Burundi et au Rwanda. Kinshasa: annual.

Belgium. Direction Études Économiques, Statistique et Documentation. *Statistique des mouvements de capitaux au Congo Belge et au Ruanda-Urundi de 1887-1956.* Brussels: 1958.

————. Ministère des Colonies. *La Situation économique du Congo Belge et du Ruanda-Urundi.* (Yearly reports, 1950-59.) Brussels: 1951-60.

Bézy, Fernand. *Problèmes stucturels de l'économie congolaise.* Paris: Nauwelaerts, 1957.

Bongoma. *Indépendance économique et révolution.* Kinshasa: Léopard-Okapi, 1969.

Buabua wa Kayembe Mubadiate. *La Fiscalisation de l'économie informelle au Zaïre.* Kinshasa: PUZ, 1995.

Carael, M. *Le Kivu montagneux: Surpopulation, sousnutrition, érosion du sol.* Brussels: CEDAF, 1979.

Carrol, Douglas F. *Basic Data on the Economy of the Democratic Republic of the Congo (Kinshasa).* Washington: US Bureau of International Commerce, 1968.

Conjoncture Économique. Kinshasa: annual.

Cornell University. Food and Nutrition Policy Program. Équipe de Recherche sur la Consommation et la Pauvreté. *Bibliographie annotée sur la consommation et la pauvreté: Villes de Kinshasa et Bandundu.* Kinshasa: 1990.

Diambomba, Miala. *Analyse exploratoire des effets de la dépendance sur l'évolution des économies africaines: L'Example du Zaïre.* Québec: Université Layal, Faculté des Sciences de l'Éducation, 1981.

Fédération des Entreprises Congolaises. *The Congolese Economy on the Eve of Independence.* Brussels: FEC, 1960.

Gamela Nginu Diamuangana, Kioni-Kiabantu Tomasikila, and Maphana ma Nguma. *Évolution et transformation des structures de l'économie zaïroise, 1970-1984.* Kinshasa: Presses de l'Université de Kinshasa, 1987.

Gran, Guy, and Galen Hull, eds. *Zaire: The Political Economy of Underdevelopment.* New York: Praeger, 1979.

Herdt, Tom. *De l'Économie informelle au Zaïre: (Sur)vie et pauvreté dans la période de transition.* Brussels: Institut Africain, 1996.

Houyoux, Joseph. *Budgets ménagers, nutrition et mode de vie à Kinshasa (République du Zaïre).* Kinshasa: PUZ, 1973.

Indicateurs Économique et fiscal: République du Zaïre. Periodical. Kinshasa: AZEX.

International Bank for Reconstruction and Development (World Bank). *Zaire: Current Economic Situation and Constraints.* Washington: 1980.

Jewsiewicki, Bogumil. "The Great Depression and the Making of the Colonial Economic System in the Belgian Congo." *African Economic History* 4 (1977): 153-76.

———. *Histoire économique d'une ville coloniale, Kisangani: 1877-1960.* Brussels: CEDAF, 1978.

Kalele-Ka-Eila. *Le F.M.I. et la situation sociale au Zaïre: Basusu na bisengo, basusu na mawa.* Lubumbashi: Laboratoire des Sciences Sociales Appliquées, 1984.

Kankwenda Mbaya. *Sur les Conditions du décollage économique au Zaïre.* Kinshasa-Gombe: Presses de l'Institut de Recherche Scientifique, 1981.

Kibungi Makola. *L'Incidence des variables explicatives de l'inflation.* Kinshasa: Ministère du Plan, 1995.

Klein, Carolyn K. *Basic Data on the Economy of the Republic of Zaire.* Washington: US Bureau of International Commerce, 1972.

Le Fèvre, Jacques. *Structures économiques du Congo Belge et du Ruanda-Urundi.* Brussels: Treurenberg, 1955.

Leclercq, Hughes. *Conjoncture financière et monétaire au Congo.* 2 vols. Leopoldville: IRES Lovanium, 1960-61.

Léonard, Charles. *Profils de l'Économie du Zaïre: Années 1955-1987.* Kinshasa: République du Zaïre, Département de l'Économie Nationale et de l'Industrie, 1987.

Lokota Ekot'e Panga. *La Crise de l'industrialisation, la problématique des activités informelles et les perspectives du développement endogène en Afrique subsaharienne: Cas du Zaïre.* Louvain: CIACO, 1994.

Lutumba-Lu-Vilu na Wundu. *De la Zaïrianisation à la rétrocession et au dialogue nord-sud: Une Tentative de libération intégrale du peuple zaïrois, 1973-1975.* Brussels: Office International de Librairie, 1976.

MacGaffey, Janet, et al. *The Real Economy of Zaire: An Anthropological Study.* Philadelphia: University of Pennsylvania Press, 1991.

Munkeni Lakup Tier, Florent. *Fondements méthodologiques à une mesure du coût réel de la vie au Zaïre.* Kinshasa: Institut de Recherches Économiques et Sociales, University of Kinshasa, 1990-95.

Muteba-Tshitenge. *Zaïre: Combat pour la deuxième indépendance.* Paris: Harmattan, 1985.

Peemans, Jean-Philippe. *Diffusion du progrès économique et convergence des prix: Le Cas Congo-Belgique, 1900-1960: La Formation de système des prix et salaires dans une économie dualiste*. Louvain: Nauwelaerts, 1968.

Stolper, Wolfgang F. *Report to Ambassador Vance and Acting Director Kelly on Certain Problems of the Zairian Economy*. Washington: Agency for International Development, 1972.

Zaïre, Banque du. *Bulletin de statistiques*. Kinshasa: annual.

————. *Bulletin mensuel de statistiques*. Kinshasa: monthly.

Zaïre, République du. Département des Finances. *Conjoncture Économique*. Kinshasa: 1983.

Zaïre, République du. Département du Plan. Institut National de la Statistique. *Bulletin trimestriel de statistiques*. Kinshasa: quarterly.

————. *Le Zaïre en chiffres*. Kinshasa: 1988.

————. *L'Impact de la crise du golfe persique sur l'économie zaïroise*. Kinshasa: 1990.

————. *Prix et indice des prix à la consommation familiale*. Kinshasa: monthly.

————. *Synthèse économique, 1976*. Kinshasa: 1977.

Zaïre. Ministère du Plan et Aménagement du Territoire, Institut National de la Statistique. *Secteur artisanal et comptabilité nationale au Zaïre: Résultats d'une enquête légère sur le secteur informel de la production et des services*. Kinshasa: 1991.

2. Agriculture and Livestock

Belgium. Administration Générale de la Coopération au Développement. *Le Cotonnier au Zaïre*. Brussels: 1992.

Belgium. Ministère des Colonies. *Aperçu sur l'économie agricole de la province de Léopoldville*. Brussels: 1955.

Biebuyck, Daniel, ed. *African Agrarian Systems*. London: Oxford University Press, 1963.

Brixhe, A. *Le Coton au Congo Belge*. Brussels: Ministère des Colonies, 1958.

————. *Les Parasites du cotonnier en Afrique centrale: Tableaux de détermination*. Brussels: Ministère des Affaires Etrangères et du Commerce Exterieur, Service des Publications de l'Assistance Technique, 1961.

Bruens, F. *La Culture maraîchère dans la Province du Kivu.* Brussels: Ministère du Congo Belge et du Ruanda-Urundi, Direction de l'Agriculture, Forêts et Élevage, 1960.

Bulletin Agricole du Congo Belge. (Note especially "L'Agriculture, les forêts, l'élevage, la chasse et la pêche de 1885 à 1958" in Jubilee Volume, 1960.) Brussels: Periodical published four times per year from 1910 until 1953 and six times per year from 1954 until 1961.

Cardwell, Lucy. *Transport Cost and Other Determinants of the Intensity of Cultivation in Rural Zaire.* New Haven: Economic Growth Center, Yale University, 1975.

Chambon, R., and M. Alofs. *Le District agricole du Tanganyika.* Brussels: Ministère des Colonies, 1958.

Collart, A. *Pêche artisanale et pêche industrielle au Lac Tanganyika.* Brussels: Ministère du Congo Belge et du Ruanda-Urundi, 1958.

Cornet, René Jules. *Les Phares verts.* Brussels: L. Cuypers, 1965.

De Halleux, B., et al. *Bibliographie analytique pour l'agronomie tropicale, Zaïre, Rwanda, Burundi.* Tervuren: Centre d'Informatique Appliquée au Développement et à l'Agriculture Tropicale, MRAC, 1972.

De Schlippe, Pierre. *Shifting Cultivation in Africa: The Zande System of Agriculture.* London: Routledge & Paul, 1956.

De Wildeman, Émile. *Les Caféiers: Étude publiée sous les auspices de l'État Indépendant du Congo.* Brussels: Veuve Monnom, 1901.

Deramée, O. *L'Élevage du mouton en Afrique centrale.* Brussels: CEDESA, 1967.

Devred, R. *Récolte, collection et conservation des végétaux au Congo Belge et au Ruanda-Urundi.* Brussels: Ministère du Congo Belge et du Ruanda-Urundi, 1958.

D'Hendencourt, Roger. *L'Élevage au Katanga.* Bruges: Desclée De Brouwer, 1953.

Diamond, R. B., et al. *Supplying Fertilizers for Zaire's Agricultural Development.* (Prepared for the US Agency for International Development.) Muscle Shoals, AL: Tennessee Valley Authority, 1975.

Drachoussolf, V. "Agricultural Change in the Belgian Congo." *Stanford University Food Research Institute Studies* 5, no. 2 (1965): 137-201.

Goorts, P., N. Magis, and J. Wilmet. *Les Aspects biologiques, humains et économiques de la pêche dans le lac de retenue de la Lufira (Katanga).* Liège: FULREAC, 1961.

Goossens, Frans. *Nourrir Kinshasa: L'Approvisionnement local d'une métropole africaine*. Leuven, Belgium: Katholieke Universiteit Leuven, and Paris: Harmattan, 1994.

Guldentorps, R. E., and L. Scuvie. *Recherche de la densité optimale du palmier à huile planté en allées*. Brussels: INEAC, 1968.

Hall, Gordon E., et al. *An Evaluation of Proposed USAID Project for Improvement of Lake Tanganyika's Fishery Resources in Zaire*. N.p., 1975.

Harms, Robert. *Land Tenure and Agricultural Development in Zaire, 1895-1961*. Madison: Land Tenure Center, University of Wisconsin, 1974.

Hathcock, J. S. *A Study of Agricultural Conditions in the Belgian Congo and Ruanda-Urundi*. Paris: Office of the US Special Representative in Europe, Food and Agriculture Division, 1952.

Hecq, J., et al. *Agriculture et structures économiques d'une société traditionnelle au Kivu (Congo)*. Brussels: INEAC, 1963.

Hirsch, Hans G. *Credit for Agriculture through Cooperatives in the Democratic Republic of the Congo*. Kinshasa: US Department of Agriculture, Economic Research Services, 1971.

Institut de Recherches Économiques et Sociales. *Étude d'orientation pour la relance agricole*. Kinshasa: Haut Commissariat au Plan et à la Reconstruction Nationale, July 1966.

Institut pour l'Étude Agronomique du Congo Belge (INEAC). Division de Phytopathologie et d'Entomologie Agricole. *Normes de main d'oeuvre pour les travaux agricoles au Congo Belge*. Brussels: 1958.

———. *Précis des maladies et des insectes nuisible recontrés sur les plantes cultivées au Congo, au Rwanda et au Burundi*. Brussels: 1962.

Jewsiewicki, Bogumil. *Agriculture nomade et économie capitaliste: Histoire des essais de modernisation de l'agriculture africaine au Zaïre à l'époque coloniale*. 2 vols. Lubumbashi: UNAZA, 1975.

———. "Contributions to a History of Agriculture and Fishing in Central Africa." *African Economic History*, special issue, 1979.

Jones, William. *Manioc in Africa*. Stanford: Stanford University Press, 1959.

Kazadi-Tshamala. *La Formation du capital dans l'agriculture du Zaïre post-colonial: Situation et perspectives*. Brussels: CEDAF, 1983.

Leplae, Edmond. *La Crise agricole coloniale et les phases du développement de l'agriculture dans le Congo central.* Brussels: IRCB, 1932.

Likaka, Osumaka. *Rural Society and Cotton in Colonial Zaire.* Madison: University of Wisconsin Press, 1997.

Lumumba, Tolenga Emery. *Le Rôle de l'agriculture dans les pays du tiers monde, particulièrement au Zaïre.* Budapest: Institut d'Économie Mondiale de l'Académie des Sciences de Hongrie, 1976.

Malengreau, Guy. *Vers un paysannat indigène: Les Lotissements agricoles au Congo Belge.* Brussels: IRC, 1949.

Mbuki Mwamufiya, and James B. Fitch. "Maize Marketing and Distribution in Southern Zaire." Occasional paper. Mexico City: International Maize and Wheat Improvement Center, 1976.

Miracle, Marvin P. *Agriculture in the Congo Basin: Tradition and Change in African Rural Economies.* Madison: University of Wisconsin Press, 1967.

———. *Maize in Tropical Africa.* Madison: University of Wisconsin Press, 1966.

Mulambu-Mvuluya, Faustin. *Cultures obligatoires et colonisation dans l'ex-Congo Belge.* Brussels: CEDAF, 1974.

Muzinga Kanzila. *Prospection des arbres et arbustes fourragers naturels dans la communauté économique des pays des grands lacs (Burundi, Rwanda, Zaïre).* Gitega, Burundi: Institut de Recherche Agronomique et Zootechnique de la C.E.P.G.L., 1991.

Ngoy Amba Lokwa. *Processus d'exploitation et de commercialisation du café au Zaïre: Cas de l'OZACAF, 1980-1985.* Kinshasa: Université de Kinshasa, Faculté des Sciences Économiques, 1987.

Ochse, J. J., et al. *Tropical and Subtropical Agriculture.* 2 vols. New York: Macmillan, 1961.

Peeters, Gérard. *Essai sur l'économie de l'élevage du bovidé au Congo.* Leopoldville: Éditions de l'Université, 1960.

Popelier, G. H. *Nature et évolution de l'agriculture zaïroise (1958-1975).* Brussels: CEDAF, 1977.

Schmitz, Jean-Louis. *L'Éleveur et son bétail: L'Élevage bovin villageois dans l'ouest du Zaïre.* Brussels: Coopération Technique Belge, and Kinshasa: INADES-Formation-Zaïre, 1985.

Shapiro, David. *The Agricultural Development of Zaire.* Aldershot, Hants, England: Avebury, and Brookfield, VT: Ashgate, 1992.

Sorenson, L. Orlo. *Maize Marketing in Zaire*. (Prepared for the US Agency for International Development.) Manhattan, KS: Food and Grain Institute, Kansas State University, 1975.

Tollens, Eric F. *Problems of Micro-Economic Data Collection on Farms in Northern Zaire*. East Lansing: Department of Agricultural Economics, Michigan State University, 1975.

Tondeur, G. *L'Agriculture nomade au Congo Belge*. Brussels: Ministère des Colonies, 1957.

Tshibaka, Tshikala B. *Food Production in a Land-Surplus, Labor-Scarce Economy: The Zairian Basin*. Washington: International Food Policy Research Institute, 1989.

United States Agency for International Development. *Central Shaba Agricultural Development Project: Project paper*. Kinshasa: 1986.

Vallaeys, G. *Les Caféiers au Congo Belge: La Pratique de la taille du caféier Robusta*. Brussels: Ministère du Congo Belge et du Ruanda-Urundi, 1959.

Wilmet, Jules. *Systèmes agraires et techniques agricoles au Katanga*. Brussels: ARSOM, 1963.

Zaïre, République du. Centre de Documentation Agricole. *Index: Agriculture, 1960-1976*. Kinshasa: 1977.

Zaïre, République du. Département de l'Agriculture et du Développement Rural. *Analyse sommaire des principales contraintes au développement de l'agriculture zaïroise*. Kinshasa: 1987.

————. *Plan de relance agricole: 1982-1984*. Kinshasa: 1982.

————. Service d'Études et Planification. *Situation actuelle de l'agriculture zaïroise*. Kinshasa, 1987.

————. *Synthèse de la situation actuelle de l'agriculture zaïroise, juillet 1986*. Kinshasa, 1986.

Zaïre, République du. Ministère de l'Agriculture. Animation Rurale et Développement Communautaire. *Plan directeur du développement agricole et rural*. Kinshasa: 1991.

————. Service National des Statistiques Agricoles. *Recensement général de l'agriculture, 1988-1990: Résultats définitifs*. Kinshasa: 1991.

Zaïre, République du. Présidence de la République. Commissariat Général au Plan. *Production vivrière face aux besoins alimentaires de la région de l'Équateur: Évaluation et types d'actions*. Mbandaka: 1981.

3. Business, Commerce and Finance

Altvater, Elmar, ed. *The Poverty of Nations: A Guide to the Debt Crisis from Argentina to Zaire*. Translated by Terry Bond. London: Zed Books, 1990.

Association Nationale des Entreprises du Zaïre. *Colloque ANEZA sur le libéralisme concerté*. (Colloquium at N'Sele, November 12-14, 1987.) Kinshasa: ANEZA, 1987.

Azama Lana. *Droit fiscal zaïrois: Exposé, commentaire et analyse critique des dispositions légales et réglementaires*. Kinshasa: CADICEC, 1986.

Belliveau, Nancy. "Heading Off Zaire's Default." *Institutional Investor* (March 1977): 23-28.

Bézy, Fernand. *Accumulation et sous-développement au Zaïre, 1960-1980*. Louvain-la-Neuve: Presses Universitaires de Louvain, 1981.

Bouët-Williaumez, L. E. *Commerce et traite des noirs aux côtes occidentales d'Afrique*. Paris: Imprimerie Nationale, 1848.

Buhendwa bwa Mushaba, Joseph. *La Banque centrale et l'économie zaïroise*. Kinshasa: Saint Paul, 1996.

Centre de Recherche et d'Information Socio-Politiques. *L'Investissement privé étranger et national du Zaïre*. Brussels: CRISP, 1972.

Centre de Recherches Économiques et Sociales. *Morphologie des groupes financiers*. Brussels: CRISP, 1962.

Congo, République Démocratique du. Banque Nationale du Congo. *Rapport Annuel*. (Annual reports of the central bank, issued until the bank was renamed Banque du Zaïre.) Kinshasa: 1967-1970.

Duban, Marie Paule. *Un Instrument de développement: Le Mouvement coopératif de crédit au Kivu: Ses Activités en milieu rural et urbain*. Sherbrooke, Québec: Centre d'Études en Économie Coopérative, Université de Sherbrooke, 1976.

Dupriez, Pierre. *Contrôle des changes et structures économiques: Congo, 1960-1967*. The Hague: Mouton, 1970.

Facultés Catholiques de Kinshasa. *Naissance, vie et mort des projets de développement: Actes du Vème séminaire scientifique, Kinshasa, du 27 au 29 mars 1992*. Kinshasa: F.C.K., 1994.

Gozo, K. M. *Le secteur non structuré de Kinshasa: Caractéristiques des entreprises et de la main d'oeuvre: Potentialités d'emploi et de distribution de revenu.* Addis Ababa: International Labor Organization, 1985.

Gray, Richard, and David Birmingham, eds. *Pre-Colonial African Trade: Essays on Trade in Central and Eastern Africa before 1900.* London: Oxford University Press, 1970.

Ibula Mwana Katakanga. *La consolidation du management public au Zaïre* . Kinshasa: PUZ, 1987.

La Problématique de la P.M.E. informelle au Zaïre: Approche socio-économique. Kinshasa: CADICEC, 1988.

Louwers, O. *Le Problème financier et le problème économique au Congo Belge en 1932.* Brussels: IRCB, 1933.

Lukama Nkunzi. *Service de la dette publique du Zaïre, 1908-1975: Considérations théoriques, analyse et discussion des modes et procédés techniques de réduction et/ou extinction de la dette publique.* Kinshasa: UNAZA, IRES, 1978.

Lukieni Lu Nyimi. *Comment créer une P.M.E. au Zaïre?: Formalités juridiques essentielles.* Kinshasa: Centre de Recherches Interdisciplinaires sur la Gestion et le Développement, 1992.

Mabi Mulumba. *Les Banques commerciales face aux mutations structurelles de l'économie zaïroise.* Kinshasa: Centre de Recherches Pédagogiques, UNAZA, 1983.

MacGaffey, Janet. *Entrepreneurs and Parasites: The Struggle for Indigenous Capitalism in Zaire.* Cambridge: Cambridge University Press, 1987.

Mahaniah, Kimpianga. *Repenser le commerce au Manianga: Un Milieu rural au Bas-Zaïre.* Kinshasa: Centre de Vulgarisation Agricole, 1990.

Michelini, Philip. *Marketing in Zaire.* Washington: Overseas Business Reports of the US Department of Commerce, 1977.

Mulumba Lukoji. *Le Service de la dette publique de l'ex-Congo Belge: Le Cas des dettes financières.* Brussels: CEDAF, 1973.

Mutamba Lukusa. *Déséquilibre macro-économique et ajustements au Zaïre, 1976-1987.* Kinshasa: PUZ, 1990.

Mutwale-Muyimbwe. *Les Sources publiques de financement de l'État Indépendant du Congo, 1885-1907: Essai d'analyse économique.* Brussels: CEDAF, 1973.

Nguyen Chanh Tam, et al. *Guide juridique de l'entreprise.* Kinshasa: Faculté de Droit, UNAZA, 1973.

Nzeza zi Nkanga. *Les Enquêtes sur les budgets des ménages en milieu urbain en République du Zaïre*. Kinshasa: Institut National de la Statistique, 1972.

Parisis, Albert. *Les Finances communales et urbaines au Congo Belge*. Brussels: ARSOM, 1960.

"Popular Monetarism: Zaire." *Economist* 342 (April 5, 1997): 69-70.

Ryelandt, Bernard. *L'Inflation en pays sous-développé: Origines, mécanismes de propagation, et effets des pressions inflatoires au Congo, 1960-1969: Interactions entre phénomènes monétaires et réels*. Paris: Mouton, 1970.

Simonis, Raymond. *Une Banque centrale éphémère: La Banque Centrale du Congo Belge et du Ruanda-Urundi, 1951-1961*. Brussels: Centre d'Études Financières, 1981.

Tshiunza Mbiye. *Le Zaïre face à l'indépendance monétaire*. Kinshasa: Sodimca, 1973.

———. *Le Zaïre-monnaie, de l'étalon-dollar à l'étalon D.T.S.* Kinshasa: PUZ, 1975.

United States. Agency for International Development. *Towards Design of a Mission Strategy for Development of Zaire's Savings and Credit Cooperative Movement*. Kinshasa: 1990.

Zaïre, Banque du. *Rapport annuel*. (Annual reports of Zaire's central bank, formerly the Banque Nationale du Congo, issued from 1971 until the present.) Kinshasa: 1973-1997.

———. *Rapport final des travaux relatifs au projet de reaménagement de la politique monétaire*. Kinshasa: 1993.

Zaïre, République du. *Ordonnance-loi régissant la protection de l'épargne et le contrôle des intermédiaires financières*. Kinshasa: 1972.

Zaïre, République du. Département de l'Économie Nationale. *Enquête sur les entreprises, 1969-1970*. Kinshasa: 1973.

———. Institut National de la Statistique. *Annuaire des statistiques du commerce extérieur*. Kinshasa: annual.

———. *Direction des Statistiques Économiques et Financières*. Kinshasa: 1982.

Zaïre, République du. Ministère du Plan et Aménagement du Territoire, Institut National de la Statistique. *L'Inflation dans les regions du Zaïre en 1990*. Kinshasa: 1991.

4. Planning and Development

Badika Nsumbu Lukau. *Promotion du développement endogène: Réalité ou utopie?: Cas de la région du Bas-Zaïre*. Mbanza-Ngungu: APRODEC, 1992.

Belgium. Académie Royale des Sciences d'Outre-Mer. *L'Apport scientifique de la Belgique au développement de l'Afrique centrale: Livre Blanc*. 3 vols. Brussels: 1962-63.

―――. Ministère des Colonies. *Le Plan décennal pour le développement économique et social du Congo*. 2 vols. Brussels: Éditions De Visscher, 1949.

Bézy, Fernand. *Principes pour l'orientation du développement économique au Congo*. Leopoldville: Université Lovanium, 1959.

Breitengross, J. P., ed. *Planification et développement économique au Zaïre*. Hamburg: Deutches Institut fur Afrika Forschung, n.d.

Centre de Recherches Universitaires du Kivu (CERUKI). *Le Problématique du développement au Kivu: Actes du troisième colloque au CERUKI, Bukavu, 17-21 avril 1978*. Bukavu: CERUKI, 1983.

Centre d'Études pour l'Action Sociale. *Chronique d'une société civile en formation au Sud-Kivu*. Kinshasa: CEPAS, 1994.

Ciamala Kanda. "Éléments de blocage du développement rural au Zaïre: Cas Luba du Kasaï." *Cahiers Économiques et Sociaux* 16, no. 3 (Sept. 1978): 334-71.

Ciparisse, Gérard. "An Anthropological Approach to Socioeconomic Factors of Development: The Case of Zaire." *Current Anthropology* 19, no. 1 (March 1978): 34-41.

Coméliau, Christian. *Conditions de la planification du développement: L'Example du Congo*. The Hague: Mouton, 1969.

Congo, Belgian. Commissariat au Plan Décennal. *Plan décennal pour le développement économique et social du Congo Belge: Rapport annuel 1955*. Leopoldville: 1956.

Congo, République Démocratique du. Haut Commissariat du Plan et à la Réconstruction Nationale. *Plan intérimaire de relance agricole*. Kinshasa: 1967.

―――. Institut de Recherches Économiques et Sociales. *Études d'orientation pour le plan de développement et de diversification industriels*. 2 vols. Kinshasa:, July 1966.

―――. *Indépendance, inflation et développement: L'Économie congolaise de 1960 à 1965*. Paris: Mouton, 1968.

Étude du développement intègre de la zone d'influence du complèxe hydroelectrique d'Inga. Rome: Società di Ingegneria e Consulenza Attivitaè Industriali, 1964.

Fleischle-Jaudas, Waltraud. *Répertoire de développement: Zaïre 1985.* Kinshasa: Centre d'Études pour l'Action Sociale, 1985.

Gouverneur, Jacques. *Productivity and Factor Proportions in Less Developed Countries: The Case of Industrial Firms in the Congo.* Oxford: Clarendon Press, 1971.

Gran, Guy. *Development by People.* New York: Praeger, 1983.

Kankuenda M'baya. *Les Industries du pôle de Kinshasa: Réflexion sur la stratégie des pôles de croissance en pays africains.* Brussels: CEDAF, 1977.

La Promotion des communautés rurales au Zaïre: Réalisations, méthodologie, réflexions: Projets de promotion sociale dans les régions de Bandundu et Bas-Zaïre. Paris: Agence de Coopération Culturelle et Technique, 1985.

Lacroix, Jean-Louis. *Industrialisation au Congo: La Transformation des structures économiques.* Paris: Mouton, 1967.

Leslie, Winsome J. *The World Bank and Structural Transformation in Developing Countries: The Case of Zaire.* Boulder, CO: L. Rienner, 1987.

Lombeya Bosongo, L. *Organisation coopérative et développement rural.* Kinshasa: PUZ, 1985.

Lwamba Katansi. *Le Plan de développement économique, social, et culturel du Zaïre: Que sera-t-il, impératif ou indicatif?* Kinshasa: publisher unknown, 1977.

Mahaniah, Kimpianga. *Les coopératives au Zaïre: Cas du Manianga, un milieu rural du Bas-Zaïre.* Kinshasa: Centre de Vulgarisation Agricole, 1992.

Masala Loka Mutombo, Hubert-Alphonse. *L'Expérience zaïroise en matière de planification socio-économique à travers le premier plan quinquennal, 1986-1990 et quelques suggestions pour la gestion économique rationnelle de la Troisième République.* Kinshasa: B.E.P.I., 1992.

Masamba Makela. *Droit économique: Cadre juridique du développement au Zaïre.* Kinshasa: CADICEC, 1995.

Miquel, Pierre. *Les Villes secondaires: Diagnostic et propositions, gestion urbaine, économie urbaine, équipements.* Kinshasa: Ministère des Travaux Publics, Urbanisme et Habitat, 1991.

Mitchnik, David A. *The Role of Women in Rural Zaire and Upper Volta: Improving Methods of Skill Acquisition.* Oxford: OXFAM, 1978.

Mokoli, Mondonga M. *State against Development: The Experience of Post-1965 Zaire.* Westport, CT: Greenwood, 1992.

Muteba-Tshitenge. *Zaïre: Combat pour la deuxième indépendance.* Paris: Harmattan, 1985.

Okitundu Avoki, René. *Les Petites organisations communautaires comme espace de développement local et base de la maîtrise du processus du développement national: Perspectives et limites: Cas de la communauté de base au Zaïre.* Louvain: CIACO, 1994.

Peemans, Jean-Philippe. *The Political Economy of Zaire in the Seventies.* Document 7406. Louvain: Institut d'Étude des Pays en Voie de Développement, Université Catholique de Louvain, 1974.

————. "The Social and Economic Development of Zaire since Independence: An Historical Outline." *African Affairs*, no. 295 (1975): 148-79.

Piret, Baudoin. "L'Aide Belge du Congo et le développement inégal du capitalisme monopoliste d'état." *Contradictions*, no. 1 (1972): 111-37.

————. "Le Sous-développement du Zaïre vu à travers la balance des paiements Belgique-Zaïre," *Contradictions*, nos. 15-16 (1978): 187-205.

Quirini, Pierre de. *Les Zones urbaines et les collectivités rurales au service des citoyens.* Kinshasa: CEPAS, 1987.

Recherches sur le développement rural en Afrique centrale. Liège: FULREAC, 1968.

Segers, Joseph. *Actions pour le développement en République du Zaïre.* Kinshasa-Gombe: Centre d'Études pour l'Action Sociale, 1971.

Shikayi Luboya. *Initiatives de développement local et pouvoir paysan: étude d'une dynamique locale de développement: Le Rôle des associations villageoises, des organisations non-gouvernementales des micro-projets dans la vallée de la Ruzizi (1978-1989), Sud-Kivu, Zaïre.* Louvain: CIACO, 1994.

Tiker-Tiker. "Le Concept du 'développement rural' dans le processus du développement économique du Zaïre." *Cahiers Économiques et Sociaux* 16, no. 3 (September 1978): 243-57.

Vianda-Kioto Luzolo. *Tradition et développement en milieu rural au Bas-Zaïre.* Ottawa: Institut de Coopération Internationale, Université d'Ottawa, n.d.

Wendjo Okitandjeka, Pascal. *Pour un renouveau de l'effort de développement à la base.* Kinshasa: NORAF, 1994.

Zaïre, République du. Département du Plan. *Premier plan quinquennal de développement économique et social: 1986-1990.* Kinshasa: 1986.

——. *Programme intérimaire de réhabilitation économique, 1983-1985.* Kinshasa: 1983.

——. *Rapport relatif au Séminaire National d'Information et de Sensibilisation sur l'Élaboration du Plan Quinquennal 1986-1990, du 13 août au 3 novembre 1984.* Kinshasa: 1984.

Zaïre, République du. Ministère des Travaux Publics, Urbanisme et Habitat. *Aménagement du territoire, Schéma national: Potentialités naturelles.* Kinshasa: 1990.

——. *Armature urbaine du Shaba: Annexe: dossiers, diagnostic.* Kinshasa: 1990.

——. *Rapport national sur le développement social: Presenté au Sommet mondial pour le développement social, Copenhague, Danemark, mars 1995.* Kinshasa: 1995.

——. *Schéma régional d'aménagement: Bas-Zaïre.* Kinshasa, 1990.

——. *Schéma régional d'aménagement: Maniema, Nord-Kivu, Sud-Kivu, document préliminaire.* Kinshasa: 1992.

Zaïre, République du. Ministère du Plan, Reconstruction et Ravitaillement. *Programme d'investissement public, P.I.P. prioritaire, 1992-1994.* Kinshasa: 1992.

5. Mining

Bézy, Fernand. *Changements de structure et conjoncture de l'industrie minière au Congo, 1938-1960.* Leopoldville: IRES, Lovanium University, 1961.

De Kun, Nicolas. *The Mineral Resources of Africa.* Amsterdam: Elsevier, 1965.

Deliens, Michel. *Les Minéraux secondaires d'uranium du Zaïre.* Tervuren: MRAC, 1981.

——. *Les Oxydes hydratés de cobalt du Shaba méridional, République du Zaïre.* Tervuren: MRAC, 1974.

Derriks, J. J. *Le Gîte d'uranium de Shinkolobwe: État actuel des connaissances du point de vue géologie et métallogénie.* N.p., 1955.

D'Ydewalle, Charles. *L'Union Minière du Haut Katanga: De l'Âge colonial à l'indépendance*. Paris: Plon, 1960.

Générale des Carrières et des Mines (GECAMINES). *La Gécamines à vingt ans*. Lubumbashi: 1987.

————. *Rapport Annuel*. Lubumbashi: annual.

Groupe Wajingaji. *Industrie minière et développement au Zaïre*. Vol. 1. Kinshasa: PUZ, 1973.

Ilunga Ilunkamba. *Propriété publique et conventions de gestion dans l'industrie du cuivre au Zaïre*. Brussels: CEDAF, 1984.

International Bank for Reconstruction and Development (World Bank). *Appraisal of GECAMINES Expansion Project, Zaire*. Report nos. 576-aCK and P-1551-CK, December and January 1974.

Katzenellenbogen, Simon E. *Railways and the Copper Mines of Katanga*. Oxford: Clarendon Press, 1973.

Lefebvre, J. J., and T. Tshauka. *Altérations associées à la minéralisation uranifère de Musoshi (Shaba, Zaïre)*. Tervuren: MRAC, 1986.

Lukieni Lu Nyimi. *Étude générale sur le cuivre*. Louvain-la-Neuve, Belgium: Université Catholique de Louvain, Faculté de Droit, 1982.

Marthoz, A. *L'Industrie minière et métallurgique au Congo Belge*. Brussels: ARSC, 1955.

Mining Yearbook. London: Financial Times, annual.

Misser, François. "The Diamond Wars: A Power Shift in the Diamond Industry Is the Key to the Recent Series of Conflicts That Are Changing Governments in West and Central Africa." *Index on Censorship* 27 (January-February 1998): 25-29.

Morgan, George A. *Zaire*. Washington: US Department of the Interior, Bureau of Mines, 1985.

Mulumba Lukoji, et al. *Industrie minière et développement au Zaïre*. Kinshasa: PUZ, 1973.

Mutshipayi Manianga. *Comment apprécier les entreprises minières*. Kinshasa: PUZ, 1988.

Panou, G. *Le Gisement de Bukena: Un Cas particulier d'estimation des réserves*. Brussels: ARSOM, 1974.

Prigogine, A. *Accroissement de la production du cuivre dans la République du Zaïre: Rôle joué par les concentrateurs*. Brussels: ARSOM, 1973.

Radmann, Wolf. "The Nationalization of Zaire's Copper: From Union Minière to GECAMINES," *Africa Today* 25, no. 4 (1978): 25-47.

Schaar, Georges. *Les Mines d'or du 5ème parallèle*. Brussels: ARSC, 1959.

Union Minière du Haut-Katanga. *L'Union Minière du Haut Katanga, 1906-1956*. Brussels: Cuypers, 1956.

————. *Union Minière du Haut Katanga, 1950*. Elisabethville: 1950.

————. *Union Minière du Haut Katanga, 1964*. Brussels: 1964.

United Nations Economic Commission for Africa (ECA). *Le Rôle des sociétés transnationales dans l'industrie du cuivre au Zaïre*. Addis Ababa: 1982.

United States. Department of the Interior. Bureau of Mines. *Mineral Industries of Africa*. Washington: 1976.

————. *Minerals Yearbook*. Pittsburgh, PA: 1988.

Vanderlinden, Jacques. *À Propos de l'uranium congolais*. Brussels: ARSOM, 1991.

Zaïre, République du. Département des Mines. *Industrie minière du Zaïre*. Kinshasa: annual.

6. Other Industry

Bézy, Fernand. *L'Industrie manufacturière à Léopoldville et dans le Bas-Congo et ses problèmes d'approvisionnement, 1960-1961*. Leopoldville: IRES, Université de Lovanium, 1962.

Colloque national sur le développement industriel, Kinshasa, Zaïre, 1971. (Conference held June 14-17, 1971.) Kinshasa: Kinshasa Chamber of Commerce, 1971.

Kankuenda M'baya. *Les Industries du pôle de Kinshasa: Réflexion sur la stratégie des pôles de croissance en pays africains*. Brussels: CEDAF, 1977.

Kayitenkore wa Sangano. *L'Industrie de la construction et le développement*. Kinshasa: PUZ, 1978.

Musa Galu. *Les déterminants de la performance du secteur manufacturier au Zaïre*. Kinshasa: Centre d'Analyse et de Prospective Économique, IRES, 1996.

Mutombo, Pierre Sylvain. *Les Fibres de coton en République Démocratique du Congo et l'industrie textile*. Kinshasa: Office National de la Recherche et du Développement, 1970.

Zaïre, République du. Présidence. Commissariat Général au Plan. *Séminaire national sur l'importance et les possibilités de développement de l'industrie chimique au Zaïre*. Kinshasa: 1981.

7. Labor

Association Nationale des Entreprises Zaïroises. *Code du travail.* Kinshasa: ANEZA, 1972.

CADICEC. *Gérants d'entreprise, ce que vous devez savoir . . . du chèque en droit congolais.* Kinshasa: 1971.

————. *La Représentation des travailleurs dans l'entreprise: Code congolais du travail.* Kinshasa: 1971.

Doucy, Arthur, and Pierre Feldheim. *Problèmes du travail et politique sociale au Congo Belge.* Brussels: Librairie Encyclopédique, 1952.

————. *Travailleurs indigènes et productivité du travail au Congo Belge.* Brussels: Institut de Sociologie, Université Libre de Belgique, 1958.

Friedland, William H. *Unions, Labor and Industrial Relations in Africa: An Annotated Bibliography.* Ithaca, NY: Cornell University Press, 1965.

Gassana Muhirwa. *Le Syndicalisme et ses incidences socio-politiques en Afrique: Le Cas de l'UNTZa.* Kinshasa: PUZ, 1982.

Higginson, John. *A Working Class in the Making: Belgian Colonial Labor Policy, Private Enterprise, and the African Mineworker, 1907-1951.* Madison: University of Wisconsin Press, 1989.

International Labor Organization. *Formation, recyclage et perfectionnement du personnel de la REGIDESO.* Geneva: 1981.

————. *Rapport sur les salaires dans la République du Congo.* Geneva: 1960.

————. *Réflexions pour une politique de l'emploi Zaïre: Alternatives pour les secteurs rural et non-structuré.* (Report by a special commission of the Programme des Emplois et des Compétences Techniques pour l'Afrique, May-June 1984.) Addis Ababa: 1984.

Isaffo, Jean R. *La Gestion des ressources humaines: Un Nouveau défi pour l'entreprise Zaïroise.* Kinshasa: CADICEC-UNIAPAC-Zaïre, 1990.

Kazadi wa Dile, Jacques S. *Politiques et techniques de rémunération dans l'entreprise au Congo: Leurs Implications quant au développement économique.* Kinshasa: IRES, 1970.

Luwenyema Lule. *Précis de droit du travail zaïrois.* Kinshasa: Éditions Lule, 1985.

Lux, André. *Le Marché du travail en Afrique noire.* Louvain, Belgium: Nauwelaerts, 1963.

McCabe, James L. *Distribution of Labor Income in Urban Zaire.* (Report for USAID.) New Haven: Economic Growth Center, Yale University, 1973.

Motoulle, L. *Politique sociale de l'Union Minière du Haut Katanga pour sa main d'oeuvre indigène et ses résultats au cours de vingt années d'application.* Brussels: IRCB, 1946.

Northrup, David. *Beyond the Bend in the River: African Labor in Eastern Zaire, 1865-1940.* Athens: Ohio University, Center for International Studies, 1988.

Perin-Hockers, Maryse. *L'Absentéisme des travailleurs africains et l'instabilité dans les entreprises de la région d'Élisabethville, 1957-1958.* Brussels: Institut de Sociologie, Université Libre de Belgique, and Elisabethville: CEPSI, 1959.

Perrings, Charles. *Black Mineworkers in Central Africa.* London: Heinemann, 1979.

Phanzu-Nianga di Mazanza. *Introduction à l'arbitrage commercial.* Kinshasa: Soprodar, 1981.

Poupart, R. *Facteurs de productivité de la main d'oeuvre autochtone à Élisabethville.* Brussels: Institut de Sociologie, Université Libre de Belgique, 1960.

————. *Première esquisse de l'évolution du syndicalisme au Congo.* Brussels: Institut de Sociologie, Université Libre de Belgique, 1960.

Schwantz, Alf. "Croissance urbaine et chômage à Kinshasa." *Manpower and Unemployment Research in Africa* 2, no. 1 (1969): 37-44.

————. "Illusion d'une émancipation et alienation réelle de l'ouvrière zaïroise." *Canadian Journal of African Studies* 6, no. 2 (1972): 183-212.

Tshibaka, Tshikala B. *Labor in the Rural Household Economy of the Zairian Basin.* Washington: International Food Policy Research Institute, 1992.

United States. Department of Labor. Bureau of International Labor Affairs. *Foreign Labor Information: Labor in the Belgian Congo.* Washington: 1959.

————. *Labor Law and Practice in the Republic of Zaire.* Washington: 1972.

————. *Zaire.* Washington: annual.

Wolter, R., L. Devreux, and R. Régnier. *Le Chômage au Congo Belge: Rapport d'enquête 1957.* Brussels: Institut de Sociologie, Université Libre de Belgique, 1959.

Zaïre, République du. *Code du travail, mesures d'applications: Textes officiels depuis le 9 août 1967 jusqu'en juin 1994.* 16th ed. Kinshasa: CADICEC, 1994.

8. Transportation, Communications and Energy

American ORT Federation. *Training for Road Construction Repairs and Maintenance, Republic of Zaire, Office des Routes: Final Report.* Geneva: 1975.

Benguela Railway. Benguela, Angola: Companhia do Caminho de Ferro de Benguela, 1960.

Berenschot-Bosboom, N.V. *Study of Ports and River Transport: Democratic Republic of the Congo.* Washington: International Bank for Reconstruction and Development, 1970.

Bokonga Ekanga Botombele. *Communications Policies in Zaire: A Study.* Paris: UNESCO, 1980.

Borgniez, G. *Donnés pour la mise en valeur du gisement de méthane du Lac Kivu.* Brussels: ARSOM, 1960.

Campus, F. *L'Aménagement hydroélectrique du fleuve Congo à Inga.* Brussels: ARSC, 1958.

Cavallaro, Evaldo. *Infrastrutture e decollo economico: Il Caso dello Zaire.* Rome: Istituto Italo-Africano, 1976.

Chelman, W. *Le Marché pétrolier au Congo Belge et au Ruanda-Urundi.* Leopoldville: IRES, 1959.

Clerfayt, A. *Le Développement énergique du Congo Belge et du Ruanda-Urundi.* Brussels: ARSOM, 1960.

Comité des Transporteurs au Congo Belge. *Transports au Congo Belge.* Leopoldville: 1959.

Compagnie du Chemin de Fer du Bas-Congo au Katanga, 1906-1956. Brussels: Compagnie du Chemin de Fer du Bas-Congo au Katanga, 1956.

Cornet, René Jules. *La Bataille du Rail.* Brussels: Cuypers, 1958.

Guth, Herbert J. *Civil Aviation in the Republic of Zaire.* (Prepared for USAID.) Washington: USAID, 1972.

Huybrechts, André. *Transports et structures de développement au Congo: Étude du progrès économique de 1900 à 1970*. Paris: Mouton, 1970.

Katzenellenbogen, Simon E. *Railways and the Copper Mines of Katanga*. Oxford: Clarendon Press, 1973.

Keating, Robert B., and John T. Howell. *A Transport Reconnaissance of the Northeast Congo Region*. (Prepared for USAID.) Washington: USAID, 1970.

Lederer, André. *Histoire de la navigation au Congo*. Tervuren: MRAC, 1965.

———. *L'Évolution des transports à l'ONATRA durant les années 1960 à 1977*. Brussels: ARSOM, 1978.

———. *L'Exploitation des affluents du Zaïre et des ports de l'intérieur de 1960 à 1971*. Brussels: ARSOM, 1973.

"Les Relations SABENA - Air Congo, 1960-1968." *Études Africaines du CRISP*, nos. 90-91 (March 1969).

Malu wa Kalenga. *Implications Énergétiques de l'exode rural et de l'explosion démographique en Afrique au sud du Sahara*. Kinshasa: PUZ, 1985.

———. *Les Solutions possibles du problème du déficit énergétique de la région du Shaba en République du Zaïre*. Kinshasa: Office National de la Recherche et du Développement, République du Zaïre, 1972.

———. *Recherches nucléaires et développement du Zaïre: Vingt-cinq ans d'activités*. Kinshasa: Presse du Commissariat Général à l'Énergie Atomique de la République du Zaïre, 1985.

Mission franco-belge pour l'étude préliminaire d'un port en eau profonde. (Joint study in cooperation with the Congolese government's Ministère des Affaires Étrangères, de la Coopération et du Commerce Extérieur.) Paris: Ovaty, 1971.

Muamba Mukebayi, Joseph. *Le Zaïre maritime et multimodal*. Kinshasa: Services Maritimes Zaïrois, 1992.

Ngamilu Awiry, B. Romain. *L'aviation civile et militaire zaïroise*. Braine-l'Alleud: J. M. Collet, 1993.

Research and Development Consulting Engineers. *République du Zaïre, services routiers, 1969-1971*. N.p., 1972.

Rochon, Paul-André. *Étude sur la possibilité de réduire la demande en combustibles ligneux à Kinshasa à partir de mesures d'économie d'énergie: Bois*. Ottawa: Institut de Développement International et de Coopération, Université d'Ottawa, 1983.

Société Nationale des Chemins de Fer Zaïrois. *Rapport annuel*. Lubumbashi: annual.

———. *Rapport au Secrétaire d'État Belge à la Coopération*. Lubumbashi: 1983.

Willame, Jean-Claude. *Zaïre, l'épopée d'Inga: Chronique d'une prédation industrielle*. Paris: Harmattan, 1986.

9. Foreign Trade and Investment

Bongoy Mpekesa. *Investissements mixtes au Zaïre: Joint ventures pour la période de transition*. Kinshasa: PUZ, 1974.

Contracting Parties to the General Agreement on Tariffs and Trade. *Protocol for the Accession of the Democratic Republic of the Congo to the Agreement of October 30, 1947: Done at Geneva August 11, 1971*. Washington: US Government Printing Office, 1972.

Fédération des Industries Belges. *La Belgique et le développement du Tiers-Monde: Livre blanc*. Brussels: FIB, 1967.

Kabala Kabunda, M. K. K. "Multinational Corporations and the Installation of Externally-Oriented Economic Structures in Contemporary Africa: The Example of the Unilever-Zaire Group," in *Multinational Corporations in Africa*, edited by Carl Widstrand. New York: Africana, 1976.

Lofumbwa Bokila. *Les Régimes fiscaux visant à encourager les investissements directs et de portefeuille dans les pays en voie de développement: L'Interaction du système fiscal zaïrois et des régimes préférentiels des pays de l'O.C.D.E.*. Brussels: Bruylant, 1981.

Lumumba-Kasongo, Tukumbi. *The Dynamics of Economic and Political Relations between Africa and Foreign Powers: A Study in International Relations*. Westport, CT: Praeger, 1998.

Mangungu Ekombe Endambo. *Une Communauté autour des grands lacs africaines: Zaïre-Rwanda-Burundi*. Bukavu: République du Zaïre, 1977.

Phanzu-Nianga di Mazanza. *Doing Business in Zaire: A Summary of Business Law, Quinquennial Plan, and Natural Resources*. Kinshasa: African Business Consultants Association, 1988.

———. *Legal and Fiscal Guide for the Foreign Investor in Zaire*. 2nd ed. Kinshasa: Imprimerie Kassale, 1977.

Pile et face: Bilan de la coopération belgo-zaïroise. Brussels: Revue Nouvelle, 1989.

Tshitenge, J. P. "Le Commerce extérieur de la République Démocratique du Congo, 1965-1968." *Cahiers Économiques et Sociaux IRES* 7, nos. 2-3 (1969): 243-63.

United Nations. Economic Commission for Africa. *Report by the ECA Mission on Economic Cooperation in Central Africa.* New York: 1966.

United States. *Agricultural Commodities: Agreement between the United States of America and the Democratic Republic of the Congo modifying the Agreement of October 21, 1969, signed at Kinshasa, March 24 and July 7, 1970.* Washington: US Government Printing Office, 1970.

————. *Agricultural Commodities: Agreement between the United States of America and the Democratic Republic of the Congo, signed at Kinshasa, August 12, 1968.* Washington: US Government Printing Office, 1968.

————. Department of Commerce, International Trade Administration. *Zaire.* Washington: annual.

Van der Steen, Daniel. *Échanges économiques extérieurs du Zaïre: Dépendance et développement.* Brussels: CEDAF, 1977.

Widstrand, Carl, ed. *Multinational Firms in Africa.* Uppsala: Scandinavian Institute of African Studies, 1975.

Zaïre, République du. Département de l'Économie Nationale. *Investir au Zaïre: L'Industrie de transformation.* Kinshasa: 1975.

————. *Le Guide de l'Investisseur.* Kinshasa: 1974.

V. SOCIETY

1. Anthropology, Ethnology and Traditional Societies

Actualité et inactualité des "Études Bakongo" du P. Van Wing: Actes du colloque de Mayidi du 10 au 12 avril, 1980. Inkisi, Zaire: République du Zaïre, Grand Séminaire Mayidi, 1983.

Bailey, Robert Converse. *The Behavioral Ecology of Efe Pygmy Men in the Ituri Forest, Zaire.* Ann Arbor: Museum of Anthropology, University of Michigan, 1991.

Baxter, P. T. W., and A. Butt. *The Azande and Related Peoples of the Anglo-Egyptian Sudan and Belgian Congo*. Part 9 of *Ethnographic Survey of Africa, East Central Africa*. London: International African Institute, 1953.

Bergmans, Lieven. *Les Wanande*. Butembo, Zaire: Éditions A.B.B., n.d.

Biebuyck, Daniel P. "Fondements de l'organisation politique des Lunda du Mwaan tayaav," *Zaïre*, no. 11 (October 1957): 787-817.

———. *Lega Culture: Art, Initiation, and Moral Philosophy among a Central African People*. Berkeley: University of California Press, 1973.

———. *Mitambas: A System of Connected Marriages among the Babembe of Fizi Territory, Kivu Province, Congo Republic*. Brussels: ARSOM, 1962.

———. "On the Concept of Tribe." *Civilization* 16, no. 4 (1966): 500-15.

———. *Right in Land and its Resources among the Nyanga (Republic of the Congo-Leopoldville)*. Brussels: ARSOM, 1966.

———. *Symbolism of the Lega Stool*. Philadelphia: Institute for the Study of Human Issues, 1977.

Bittremieux, Leo. *La Société secrète des Bakhimba au Mayombe*. Brussels: IRCB, 1936.

———. *Symbolisme in de Negerkunst*. Brussels: Vroman, 1937.

Bleeker, Sonia. *The Pygmies: Africans of the Congo Forest*. London: Dobson, 1971.

Boaz, Noel Thomas. *Evolution of Environments and Hominidae in the African Western Rift Valley*. Martinsville: Virginia Museum of Natural History, 1990.

Boelaert, E. *L'État indépendant et les terres indigènes*. Brussels: ARSC, 1956.

———. *Nsona Lianja: L'Épopée nationale des Nkundo-Mongo*. Antwerp: Kongo-Overzee, 1949.

Boone, Olga. *Carte ethnique de la République du Zaïre: Quart sud-ouest*. Tervuren: MRAC, 1973.

———. *Carte ethnique du Congo: Quart sud-est*. Tervuren: MRAC, 1961.

Boulanger, André. *Société et religion des Zela (Rép. du Zaïre)*. Bandundu: CEEBA, 1985.

Bourgeois, Arthur P. *The Yaka and Suku*. Leiden: E. J. Brill, 1985.

Burssens, H. *Les Peuplades de l'Entre Congo-Ubangi*. Tervuren: MRAC, and London: IAI, 1958.

Bwakasa, Tulu Kia Mpansu. *L'Impense du discours: "Kindoki" et "Nkisi" en pays kongo du Zaïre*. Kinshasa: PUZ, 1973.

Bylin, Eric. *Basakata: Le Peuple de l'entrefleuves Lukenie-Kasaï*. Lund, Sweden: Berlingska Boktryckeriet, 1966.

Centre d'Études Ethnographiques de Bandundu. *L'Organisation sociale et politique chez les Yansi, Teke et Boma*. (Papers of the 4th seminar organized by the CEEBA.) Bandundu: CEEBA, 1968.

Colle, P. *Les Baluba (Congo Belge)*. Brussels: A. de Wit, 1913.

Costermans, J. *Mosaïque Bangba: Notes pour servir à l'étude des peuplades de l'Uelé*. Brussels: IRCB, 1953.

Crine, Bruno. *La Structure sociale des Foma*. Brussels: CEDAF, 1972.

———. *L'Avant-tradition zaïroise*. Kinshasa: Office National de la Recherche et du Développement, 1974.

Cunnison, Ian G. *The Luapula Peoples of Northern Rhodesia: Custom and History in Tribal Politics*. Manchester: Manchester University Press, 1959.

Daye, Pierre. *Le Miroir du Congo Belge*. Brussels: Éditions N.E.A., 1929.

De Beaucorps, R. *Les Basongo de la Luniungu et de la Gobari*. Brussels: IRCB, 1941.

———. *Les Bayansi du Bas-Kwilu*. Louvain: Éditions de L'Aucam, 1933.

———. *L'Évolution économique chez les Basongo de la Luniungu et de la Gobari*. Brussels: IRCB, 1951.

De Beir, L. *Les Bayaka de M'Nene N'toombo Lenge-lenge*. St. Augustin, West Germany: Anthropos-Institut, 1975.

De Cleene, Natal. *Introduction à l'ethnographie du Congo Belge et du Ruanda-Urundi*. Antwerp: De Sikkel, 1957.

———. *Le Clan matrilinéal dans la société indigène*. Brussels: IRCB, 1946.

De Mahieu, Wauthier. *Qui a obstrué la cascade?: Analyse sémantique du rituel de la circoncision chez les Komo du Zaïre*. Cambridge: Cambridge University Press, 1985.

De Plaen, G. *Les Structures d'autorité des Bayanzi*. Paris: Éditions Universitaires, 1974.

De Sousberghe, L. *L'Indissolubilité des unions entre apparentés au Bas-Zaïre*. Uppsala: Institutionen for Allmaën-och Jaëmfoërande Ethnografi vid Uppsala Universitet, 1976.

————. *Structures de parenté et d'alliance d'après les formules pende.* Brussels: ARSC, 1955.

Delhaise, C. *Les Warega.* Brussels: A. de Wit, 1909.

Denis, Jacques. *Les Yaka du Kwango: Contribution à une étude ethno-démographique.* Tervuren: MRAC, 1964.

Devisch, René. *L'Institution rituelle khita chez les Yaka au Kwango du nord: Une analyse séméiologique.* Leuven, Belgium: Katholieke Uniêversiteit te Leuven, 1976.

————. *Weaving the Threads of Life: The Khita Gynecological Healing Cult among the Yaka.* Chicago: University of Chicago Press, 1993.

Dias de Carvalho, H. *Expedição ao Muatiamvu: Ethnographia e historia dos povos da Lunda.* Lisbon: Adolpho Modesto, 1890.

Dictionnaire des rites. Bandundu: CEEBA, 1985.

Douglas, Mary. *The Lele of the Kasai.* London: Oxford University Press, 1963.

————. *Purity and Danger.* New York: Praeger, 1966.

Doutreloux, Albert. *L'Ombre des fétiches: Société et culture Yombe.* Louvain, Belgium: Nauwelaerts, 1967.

Droogers, André. *The Dangerous Journey: Symbolic Aspects of Boys' Initiation among the Wagenia of Kisangani, Zaire.* The Hague: Mouton, 1980.

Duffy, Kevin. *Children of the Forest.* New York: Dodd, Mead, 1984.

Elshout, Pierre. *The Batwa People of the Ekonda Group in Kiri Territory.* Washington: Joint Publications Research Service, 1965.

Evans-Pritchard, E. E. *The Azande: History and Political Institutions.* Oxford: Clarendon Press, 1971.

————. *Essays in Social Anthropology.* New York: Free Press of Glencoe, 1962.

————. *Witchcraft, Oracles, and Magic among the Azande.* Oxford: Clarendon Press, 1976.

————. *The Zande Trickster.* Oxford: Clarendon Press, 1967.

Fabian, Johannes. *Moments of Freedom: Anthropology and Popular Culture.* Charlottesville: University Press of Virginia, 1998.

Franham, Kay. *The Pygmies of the Ituri Forest: An Adventure in Anthropology.* Agincourt, Ont.: Gage Education Publications, 1972.

Fu-Kiau, André. *M'Kongo ye Nza Yakun Zungidila; Nza Kongo: Le Mukongo et le monde qui l'entourait; cosmogonie-Kongo.* (In

Kikongo and French.) Kinshasa: Office National de la Recherche de Développement, 1969.

Gelders, V. *Le Clan dans la société indigène.* Brussels: IRCB, 1943.

Goemaere, Alphonse. *Notes sur l'histoire, la religion, les institutions sociales et la jurisprudence chez les Ndengese et les Ohendo (Rép. du Zaïre).* Bandundu: CEEBA, 1988.

Gusimana Wa Mama. *Les Origines et guerres pende.* Bandundu: Gusimana Wa Mama, 1984.

Halkin, Joseph. *Les Ababua.* Brussels: A. de Wit, 1911.

Hallet, Jean-Pierre. *Pygmy Kitabu.* New York: Random House, 1973.

Haveaux, G. *La Tradition historique des Bapende orientaux.* Brussels: IRCB, 1954.

Hiernaux, Jean. "Cultures préhistoriques de l'âge des métaux au Ruanda Urundi et au Kivu." Part 1. *Bulletin des Séances ARSC,* no. 2 (1956).

————. *Cultures préhistoriques de l'âge des métaux au Ruanda Urundi et au Kivu.* Part 2. Brussels: ARSOM, 1960.

————. *Diversité humaine en Afrique subsaharienne: Recherches biologiques.* Brussels: Institut de Sociologie, Université Libre de Belgique, 1968.

Hochegger, Hermann. *Le Langage des gestes rituels.* Bandundu: CEEBA, 1981.

————. *Mort, funérailles, deuil et culte des ancêtres chez les populations du Kwango/Bas-Kwilu.* Bandundu: CEEBA, 1969.

————. *Normes et pratiques sociales chez les Buma.* Bandundu: CEEBA, 1975.

Hubbard, Maryinez. *À la Recherche des Mangbetu, Haut-Zaïre.* Brussels: CEDAF, 1975.

Hulstaert, G. *Éléments pour l'histoire mongo ancienne.* Brussels: ARSOM, 1984.

————. *General Survey of the Mongo People in Congo-Leopoldville.* Washington: Joint Publications Research Service, 1965.

————. *Le Marriage des Nkondo.* Brussels: IRCB, 1938.

————. *Les Mongo: Aperçu général.* Tervuren: MRAC, 1961.

Hutereau. A. *Histoire des peuplades de l'Uelé de l'Ubangi.* Brussels: Bibliothèque Congo, 1922.

Iyeki. *Essai sur la Psychologie Bonto.* Kinshasa: Office National de Recherche et de Développement, 1970.

Ize-Senze. *Symbolique verbale et rituelle chez les Sakata, Lelé, Wongo, Kuba, Lulua, Mbole et Vira (République du Zaïre)*. Bandundu: CEEBA, 1984.

Janni, Pietro. *Etnografia e mito: La storia dei pigmei*. Rome: Edizioni dell'Ateneo & Bizzarri, 1978.

Kalanda, Mabika. *Baluba et Lulua: Une Ethnie à la recherche d'un nouvel équilibre*. Brussels: Remarques Congolaises, 1959.

Kamainda, Thomas. *The Cult of the Dead among the Balambo in the Congo (Leopoldville)*. Washington: Joint Publications Research Service, 1964.

Kayemba-Buba. *Histoire et signification du Djalelo*. Kinshasa: Imprimerie de Kinshasa, n.d.

Kezembe XIV, Mwata. *My Ancestors and My People*. London: Bantu Heritage Series, 1951.

Kimpianga Mahaniah. *La Mort dans la pensée kongo*. Kinsantu, Zaire: Centre de Vulgarisation Agricole, 1980.

Kopytoff, Igor. "Family and Lineage among the Suku of the Congo," in *The Family Estate in Africa*, edited by R. F. Gray and P. H. Gulliver, pp. 83-116. Boston: Boston University Press, 1964.

———. "The Suku of Southwestern Congo," in *Peoples of Africa*, edited by James L. Gibbs, pp. 441-78. New York: Holt, Rinehart & Winston, 1965.

Krzywicki, Janusz. *Contes Didactiques Bira (Haut-Zaïre)*. Rome: Instituto Italo-Africano, 1985.

Lagae, C. R. *Les Azande ou Niam-Niam*. Brussels: Vromant, 1926.

Lehuard, Raoul. *Les Phemba du Mayome*. Arnouville, France: Arts d'Afrique, 1977.

Lemal, F. *Basuku et Bayaka des districts Kwango et Kwilu au Congo*. Tervuren: MRAC, 1965.

Lotar, L. *La Grande chronique de l'Ubangi*. Brussels: IRCB, 1937.

———. *La Grande chronique de l'Uelé*. Brussels: IRCB, 1946.

Louillet, L. *Le "Lusalo"; ou, Mariage monogame par l'échange de sang*. Elisabethville: Éditions de la Revue Juridique du Congo Belge, 1936.

Lucas, Stephen A. *L'Organisation politique des Baluba du Katanga*. Elisabethville: Université Officielle du Congo, Faculté de Droit, 1964.

Lumbwe Mudindaambi. *Objets et techniques de la vie quotidienne mbala*. Bandundu: CEEBA, 1976.

MacGaffey, Wyatt. *Customs and Government in the Lower Congo.* Berkeley: University of California Press, 1970.

Maes, Joseph, and O. Boone. *Les Peuplades du Congo Belge.* Brussels: Veuve Monnom, 1935.

Masson, Paul. *Trois Siècles chez les Bashi.* Tervuren: MRAC, 1960.

Matadiwamba Kamba Mutu. *Espace Lunda et les Pelende-Khobo: Récit historique.* Bandundu: CEEBA, 1988.

McCulloch, Merran. *The Southern Lunda and Related Peoples.* Part 1 of Ethnographic Survey of Africa: West Central Africa. London: IAI, 1951.

Merriam, Alan P. *An African World: The Basongye Village of Lupupa Ngye.* Bloomington: Indiana University Press, 1974.

Mertens, Pierre Joseph. *Les Badzing de la Kamtsha.* 3 vols. Brussels: IRCB, 1935-39.

————. *Les Chefs couronnés chez les Bakongo orientaux.* Brussels: IRCB, 1942.

Middleton, John. *Lugbara Religion: Ritual and Authority among an East African People.* London: Oxford University Press (for IAI.), 1960.

Miller, Joseph C. *Cokwe Expansion, 1850-1900.* Madison: University of Wisconsin, African Studies Committee, Occasional Papers, no. 1 (1969). Second revised printing, 1974.

————. "Kings, Lists and History of Kasanje." *History of Africa* 6 (1979: 51-96.

Mitchell, J. C., and J. F. Barnes. *The Lamba Village.* Capetown: University of Capetown, 1950.

Mokaka Mwa Bomunga, Justin-Robert. *Solidarité traditionnelle chez les peuples de la "Sud-Ngiri" et amour théologal.* Louvain, Belgium: Academia, 1994.

Mudiji-Malamba Gilombe. *Formes et fonctions symboliques des masques mbuya des Phende: Essai d'iconoloqie et d'herméneutique.* Louvain-la-Neuve, Belgium: Université Catholique de Louvain, Institut Supérieur de Philosophie, 1981.

Mulyumba wa Mamba, Itongwa. *Aperçu sur la structure politique des Balega-Basile.* Brussels: CEDAF, 1978.

Mune, Pierre. *Le Groupement du petit-Ekonda.* Brussels: ARSC, 1959.

Mve Ondo, Bonaventure. *L'Owani et le Songa: Deux jeux de calculs africains.* Libreville, Gabon: Centre Culturel Français Saint-Exupéry, 1990.

Myanga Gangambi. *Les Masques pende de Gatundo.* Bandundu: CEEBA, 1974.

Ndambi Munamuhega. *Les Masques pende de Ngudi.* Bandundu: CEEBA, 1975.

Ngolo Kibango. *Minganji, danseurs de masques pende.* Bandundu: CEEBA, 1976.

Ngoma, Ferdinand. *L'Initiation ba-kongo et sa signification.* Lubumbashi: CEPSI, 1965.

Nkiere Bokuna Mpa-Osu. *La Parenté comme système idéologique: Essai d'interprétation de l'ordre lignager chez les Basakata.* Kinshasa: Faculté de Théologie Catholique, 1984.

———. *L'Organisation politique traditionnelle des Basakata en République du Zaïre.* Brussels: CEDAF, 1975.

Nkudi, Kalala. *Le Lilwakoy des Mbole du Lomami: Essai d'analyse de son symbolisme.* Brussels: CEDAF, 1979.

N'Sanda Wamenka. *Récits épiques des Lega du Zaïre.* Niamey, Niger: Agence de Coopération Culturelle et Technique, 1992.

Nzamba. *Gandanda initiation et mythes pende.* Bandundu: CEEBA, 1974.

Obenga, Théophile. *Le Zaïre: Civilisations traditionnelles et culture moderne: Archives Culturelles d'Afrique centrale.* Paris: Présence Africaine, 1977.

Packard, Randall M. *Chieftanship and Cosmology: An Historical Study of Political Competition.* Bloomington: Indiana University Press, 1981.

Phillippe, René. *Inongo: Les Classes d'âge en région de la Lwafa (Tsuapa).* Tervuren: MRAC, 1965.

Plancquaert, M. *Les Jaga et les Bayaka du Kwango.* Brussels: IRCB, 1932.

———. *Les Sociétés secrètes chez les Bayaka.* Louvain, Belgium: Kuyl-Otto, 1930.

Roy, Hubert van. *Les Byaambvu du Moyen-Kwango: Histoire du royaume luwa-yaka.* Berlin: D. Reimer, 1988.

Ryckmans, André. *Droit coutumier africain: Proverbes judiciaires kongo.* Mbandaka: Aequatoria, 1993.

Salmon, Pierre. *Récits historiques zande.* Brussels: CEMUBAC, 1965.

Schebesta, Paul. *Among the Congo Pigmies.* (Translated from German by Gerald Griffin.) New York: AMS Press, 1977.

———. *My Pygmy and Negro Hosts.* (Translated from German by Gerald Griffin.) New York: AMS Press, 1978.

Sendwe, Jason. "Traditions et coutumes ancestrales du Baluba Shankadj." *Bulletin CEPSI*, no. 24 (1954): 87-120, and no. 31 (1955): 57-84.

Smith, H. Sutton. *Yakusu*. London: Marshall Bros., 1912.

Soret, Marcel. *Les Kongo nord-occidentaux*. Paris: Presses Universitaires de France, 1959.

Southall, Aidan. *Alur Society: A Study in the Types and Processes of Domination*. Cambridge: Heffer, 1956.

Tango Muyay. *Leur Bouche crache du feu: Agressions verbales yansi*. Bandundu: CEEBA, 1978.

Tayaya Lumbombo. *Réparation de l'infidelité conjugale chez les Yansi, République du Zaïre*. Bandundu: CEEBA, 1981.

Tempels, Placide. *Bantu Philosophy*. Paris: Présence Africaine, 1959.

Theuws, Jacques A. Th. *Word and World: Luba Thought and Literature*. St. Augustin, West Germany: Verlag des Anthropos-Instituts, 1983.

Thiry, Edmond. *Une Introduction à l'éthnohistoire des Hema du sud, Haut-Zaïre*. Tervuren: MRAC, 1996.

Thomas, Jacqueline. *Les Ngbaka de la Lobaye*. Paris: Mouton, 1963.

Thuriaux-Hennebert, Arlette. *Les Zande dans l'histoire du Bahr-el-Ghazal et de l'Equatoria*. Brussels: Institut de Sociologie de L'Université Libre de Belgique, 1964.

Torday, Émil. *Notes ethnographiques sur les peuples communément appelés Bakuba, ainsi que sur les peuplades apparentées, les Bushongo*. Brussels: Ministère des Colonies, 1910.

———. *On the Trail of the Bushongo*. New York: Negro Universities Press, 1969; reprint of 1925 edition.

Towles, Joseph A. *Asa: Myth of Origin of Blood-Brotherhood among the Mbo, Ituri Forest*. Tervuren: MRAC, 1993.

———. *Nkumbi Initiation: Ritual and Structure among the Mbo of Zaire*. Tervuren: MRAC, 1993.

Tshinkela. *Le Miroir Mukongo*. Kinshasa: Procure des Frères, 1965.

Tshiswaka Lumembo. *Les Ethnies en démographie: L'Exemple du Zaïre: Du Regroupement des tribus à la définition de la catégorie ethnique: Problèmes posés par l'utilisation de la notion ethnie dans les enquêtes ethno-démographiques en Afrique noire*. Paris: AMIRA, 1985.

Turnbull, Colin M. *The Forest People*. New York: Simon and Schuster, 1961. (Republished in New York: Holt, Rinehart, and Winston, 1983.)

————. *The Mbuti Pygmies: Change and Adaptation.* New York: Holt, Rinehart, and Winston, 1983.

————. *Wayward Servants: The Two Worlds of the African Pygmies.* Westport, CT: Greenwood Press, 1976.

Turner, V. W. *Schism and Continuity in an African Society: A Study of Ndembu Village Life.* Manchester: Manchester University Press, 1957.

Valdy, Jacques. *Bakongo.* Aalter: André de Rache, 1955.

Van der Kerken, G. *Le Mésolithique et le Néolithique dans le Bassin de l'Uelé.* Brussels: IRCB, 1942.

————. *L'Ethnie Mongo.* 2 vols. Brussels: IRCB, 1944.

Van Dorpe, Walter. *Origine et migrations des Yeke (de la Tanzanie au Zaïre).* Bandundu: CEEBA, 1978.

Van Everbroeck, Nestor. *Ekmond'e mputela: Histoire, croyance, organisation clanique, politique, sociale et familiale des Bkonda et de leurs batoa.* Tervuren: MRAC, 1974.

————. *Mbomb'Ipolu, le seigneur à l abîme: Histoire, croyances, organisation clanique, politique, judiciaire, vie familiale des Bolia, Sengele et Ntomb'e njale.* Tervuren: MRAC, 1961.

Van Geluwe, H. *Les Bali et les peuplades apparentées (Ndaka, Mbo, Beke, Lika, Budu, Nyari).* Part 5 of *Ethnographic Survey of Africa: Central Africa.* London: IAI, 1960.

————. *Les Bira et les peuplades limitrophes.* Tervuren: MRAC, 1956.

————. *Mamvu-Mangutu et Balese-Mvuba.* London: IAI, 1957.

Van Overbergh, Cyrille, and E. De Jonghe. *Les Bangala.* Brussels: A. de Wit, 1907.

————. *Les Basonge.* Brussels: A. de Wit, 1908.

————. *Les Mangbetu.* Brussels: A. de Wit, 1909.

————. *Les Mayombe.* Brussels: W. de Wit, 1907.

Van Riel, J. *L'eau en milieu rural centre africain.* Brussels: ARSOM, 1964.

Van Roy, H. *Proverbes Kongo.* Tervuren: MRAC, 1963.

Van Wing, J. *Études Bakongo.* 2 vols. 2nd ed. Bruges, Belgium: Desclée de Brouwer, 1959.

Vandeqoude, Emiel J. L. M. *Documents pour servir à la connaissance des populations du Congo Belge: Aperçu historique de l'étude des populations autochtones, par les fonctionnaires et agents du Service Territorial, suivi de l'inventaire des études historiques, ethnographiques et linguistiques conservées aux Archives du*

Congo Belge. Leopoldville: Section Documentation, Archives du Congo Belge, 1958.

Vansina, Jan. *The Children of Woot: A History of the Kuba Peoples.* Madison: University of Wisconsin Press, 1978.

———. *Introduction à l'ethnographie du Congo.* Brussels: CRISP, 1966.

———. *Kingdoms of the Savanna.* Madison: University of Wisconsin Press, 1966.

———. *Le Royaume Kuba.* Tervuren: MRAC, 1964.

———. *Les Tribus Ba-kuba et les peuplades apparentées.* Tervuren: ARSAF, 1954.

———. *Paths in the Rainforest.* N.p., n.d.

Verhaegen, P. *Le Problème de l'Habitat rural en Afrique noire.* Brussels: CEDESA, 1960.

Verhulpen, E. *Baluba et Balubaisés du Katanga.* Antwerp: L'Avenir Belge, 1936.

Whitely, W., and J. Slaski. *The Bemba and Related Peoples of Northern Rhodesia.* Part 2 of *Ethnographic Survey of Africa: East Central Africa.* London: IAI, 1951.

Widman, Ragnar. *The Niombo Cult among the Babwende.* Stockholm: Etnografiska Museet, 1967.

Winter, E. H. *Bwamba.* Cambridge: W. Heffer (for the East African Institute of Social Research), 1956.

Wolfe, Alvin W. *In the Ngombe Tradition.* Evanston, IL: Northwestern University Press, 1961.

Yanga, Tshimpaka. *La Parenté égyptienne des peuples du Zaïre: Racines millénaires d'une vie socio-culturelle commune.* Lubumbashi: Cactus, 1989.

Yoder, John Charles. *The Kanyok of Zaire: An Institutional and Ideological History to 1895.* Cambridge: Cambridge University Press, 1992.

Yogolelo Tambwe ya Kasimba. *Introduction à l'histoire des Lega: Problèmes et méthode.* Brussels: CEDAF, 1975.

2. Education

American Council on Education. *Survey of Education in the Democratic Republic of the Congo.* Washington: ACE, 1969.

Babudaa Malibato. *Education et instruction civiques: Le Citoyen dans la communauté nationale: Troisième secondaire.* Kinshasa: BEC, 1974.

————. *Le Citoyen dans le développement national: Quatrième secondaire, manuel conforme au programme de la République du Zaïre.* Kinshasa: Mayaka Esongama Nsa, 1975.

————. *Le Citoyen et la conscience nationale, africaine, internationale.* Kinshasa: Éditions Bobiso, 1981.

Barden, John Glenn. *A Suggested Program of Teacher Training for Mission Schools among the Batetela.* (Originally published, New York: Bureau of Publications, Teachers College, Columbia University, 1941.) New York: AMS Press, 1972.

Belgium. Ministère des Colonies. *La Réforme de l'enseignement au Congo Belge: Mission pédagogique Coulon-Deneyn-Benson.* Brussels: Éditions du Conseil Supérieur de l'Enseignement, 1954.

Bureau de l'Enseignement National Catholique. *Les Études Supérieures en République Démocratique du Congo.* Kinshasa-Kalina: BENC, 1971.

Centre Polyvalent pour l'Éducation Permanente. *Éducation socio-économique: Naissances désirables: Manuel à l'intention des instructeurs d'alphabétisation.* Kinshasa: 1978.

Chuma Basukura, et al. *Profil des professions et des études en République du Zaïre: Guide à l'intention des diplômés d'état.* Kinshasa: PUZ, 1973.

Cornet, C. M., M. D. Vandenbulcke, and Kalonji Mutambayi. *Bantu?: Proverbes africains à l'usage de l'enseignement secondaire.* Brussels: A. De Boeck, 1976.

Delvaux, Jean Paul. *L'Examen de l'intelligence des écoliers de Kinshasa.* Kinshasa: Université Lovanium, 1970.

École Nationale de Droit et d'Administration. Leopoldville: Imprimerie de l'Avenir, 1962.

Ekwa, Martin. *Le Congo et l'éducation: Réalisations et perspectives dans l'enseignement national catholique.* Leopoldville-Kalina: Bureau de l'Enseignement National Catholique, 1965.

————. *Pour une société nouvelle, l'enseignement national: Textes et discours, 1960-1970.* Kinshasa: BEC, 1971.

Erny, Pierre. *Sur les sentiers de l'université: Autobiographies d'étudiants zaïrois.* Paris: Pensée Universelle, 1977.

Fullerton, Gary. *L'UNESCO au Congo.* Paris: UNESCO, 1964.

Gasibirege Rugema Simon. *Brève histoire de la formation du personnel enseignant au Zaïre.* Kinshasa: Maison de l'Éducation au Zaïre, 1982.

George, Betty G. (Stein). *Educational Developments in the Congo (Leopoldville).* Washington: US Department of Health, Education and Welfare, Office of Education, 1966.

Georgis, P. *Essai d'acculturation par l'enseignement primaire au Congo.* Brussels: CEMUBAC, 1962.

Georgis, P., and Baudoin Agbiano. *L'Enseignement au Congo depuis l'indépendance.* Brussels: CEMUBAC, 1966.

Golan, Tamar. *Educating the Bureaucracy in a New Polity: A Case Study of l'École Nationale de Droit et d'Administration (ENDA), Kinshasa, Congo.* New York: Columbia University Teachers' College Press, 1968.

Hull, Galen. *Université et État: L'UNAZA-Kisangani.* Brussels: CEDAF, 1976.

International Bank for Reconstruction and Development. *Zaire: Education Sector Memorandum.* (Report by the Consultative Group for Zaire.) Memorandum ZA 77-5. Washington: 1977.

Kapuku Mudipanu. *Étude comparative des systèmes d'évaluation des élèves en techniques professionnelles dans les écoles d'infirmiers/ères de Kinshasa et du Bas-Zaïre, 1980-1982.* Québec: Université Laval, Faculté des Sciences de l'Éducation, 1984.

———. *La Valeur prédictive des concours d'admission et des examens de contrôle organisés à l'Institut Supérieur des Techniques Médicales (I.S.T.M.) de 1974 à 1980: Le Cas de l'enseignement et administration des soins infirmiers à Kinshasa.* Québec: Université Laval, Faculté des Sciences de l'Éducation, 1983.

Kasongo Ngoyi Makita Makita. *Les Étudiants et les élèves de Kisangani (1974-1975): Aspirations, opinions et conditions de vie.* Brussels: CEDAF, 1977.

Kita Kyankenge Masandi. *Colonisation et enseignement: Cas du Zaïre avant 1960.* Bukavu: CERUKI, 1982.

Knapen, Marie-Thérèse. *L'Enfant mukongo: Orientations de base du système éducatif et développement de la personalité.* Louvain, Belgium: Nauwelaerts, 1962.

Koivukari, Mirjami. *Rote Learning, Comprehension, and Participation by the Learners in Zairian Classrooms.* Jyväskyla, Finland: Jyväskylaën Yliopisto, 1982.

Magabe, M., ed. *Éducation préscolaire dans la ville de Bukavu, Zaïre: Étude exploratoire.* Bukavu: CERUKI, 1987.

Mulier, Freddy. *La Coopération technique belge dans l'enseignement zaïrois.* Brussels: CEDAF, 1979.

Presses Universitaires du Zaïre. *Recherche et publications scientifiques à l'UNAZA.* Kinshasa: 1972.

Rideout, William M. *Survey of Education in the Democratic Republic of the Congo.* Washington: American Council on Education, Overseas Liaison Committee, 1969.

Rimlinger, Gaston V. *Education and Modernization in Zaire: A Case Study.* Houston: Rice University, Program of Development Studies, 1974.

Sack, Richard, et al. *La Langue d'instruction et ses incidences sur les écoliers zaïrois: Cas du Nord-Kivu.* Kisangani: UNAZA, Centre de Recherches Interdisciplinaires pour le Développement de l'Éducation, 1976.

Shomba Kinyamba, Sylvain. *Les Sciences sociales en question: Un Aperçu panoramique et une approche critique.* Lubumbashi: Presses Universitaires de Lubumbashi, 1993.

Université Libre du Congo. *Université Libre du Congo, République Démocratique du Congo, Kisangani.* Kisangani: ULC, 1970.

Université Nationale du Zaïre. Centre de Recherches Interdisciplinaires pour le Développement et l'Éducation. *Rapport général des travaux du Premier Congrès des Professeurs Nationaux de l'Enseignement Supérieur et Universitaire.* (Report of congress held at N'Sele, 1971.) Kinshasa: PUZ, 1971.

Verhaegen, Benoît. *L'Enseignement universitaire au Zaïre: De Lovanium à l'UNAZA, 1959-1979.* Paris: Harmattan, 1978.

Verheust, Thérèse. *L'Enseignement en République du Zaïre.* Brussels: CEDAF, 1974.

Zaïre, République du. Ministère de l'Enseignement Supérieur et Universitaire. *Annuaire statistique de l'Éducation.* Kinshasa: annual.

———. *Enseignement supérieur et universitaire du Zaïre: Essaimage et perspectives d'avenir.* Kinshasa: PUZ, 1994.

3. Religion, Missions and Traditional Beliefs

Abel, Armand. *Les Musulmans noirs du Maniema*. Brussels: Centre pour l'Étude des Problèmes du Monde Musulman Contemporain, 1960.

Anciaux, Léon. *Le Problème musulman dans l'Afrique belge*. Brussels: George Van Campenhout, 1949.

Andersson, Efraim. *Messianic Popular Movements in the Lower Congo*. Uppsala: Almquist & Wiksells, 1958.

Annuaire Catholique du Congo, du Ruanda et de l'Urundi. Brussels: Oeuvre Pontificales Missionaires, 1960-61.

Archidiocèse de Kinshasa. Commission Diocésaine des Implantations Pastorales. *Connaissez-vous Kinshasa et son église?* Kinshasa: 1990.

Arnot, Frederick Stanley. *Garenganze; or, Seven Years' Pioneer Mission Work in Central Africa*. London: Cass, 1969.

———. *Missionary Travels in Central Africa*. Bath: Office of Echoes of Service, 1914.

Arnout, Alexandre. *Les Pères blancs aux sources du Nil*. Paris: Librairie Missionnaire, 1953.

Asch, Susan. *L'Église du Prophète Kimbangu: De ses Origines à son rôle actuel au Zaïre, 1921-1981*. Paris: Éditions Karthala, 1983.

Axelson, Sigbert. *Culture Confrontation in the Lower Congo: From the Old Congo Kingdom to the Congo Independent State with Special Reference to the Swedish Missionaries in the 1880s and 1890s*. Stockholm: Gummesson, 1970.

Balandier, Georges. "Messianisme des Ba-Kongo." *Encyclopédie Mensuelle d'Outre-Mer*, August 1951.

———. *Sociologie actuelle de l'Afrique noire*. Paris: Presses Universitaires de France, 1955.

Baptist Missionary Society. *1878-1978: One Hundred Years of Christian Mission in Angola and Zaire*. London: BMS, 1978.

Bentley, William Holman. *Pioneering on the Congo*. New York: Johnson Reprint Corp., 1979.

Bernard, Guy. "The Nature of a Sociological Research: Religious Sects in the West of the Congo." *Cahiers Économiques et Sociaux IRES* 2, no. 3 (1964): 261-69.

Bernard, Guy, and P. Caprasse. "Religious Movements in the Congo: A Research Hypothesis." *Cahiers Économiques et Sociaux IRES* 3, no. 1 (1965): 49-60.

Bockie, Simon. *Death and the Invisible Powers: The World of Kongo Belief.* Bloomington: Indiana University Press, 1993.

Bontinck, François. *Jean-François de Rome: La Fondation de la Mission des Capucins au Royaume du Congo (1648).* Louvain, Belgium: Nauwelaerts, 1964.

Braekman, E. M. *Histoire de Protestantisme au Congo.* Brussels: Librairie des Éclaireurs Unionistes, 1961.

Brashler, Peter J. *Change: My Thirty-Five Years in Africa.* Wheaton, IL: Tyndale House, 1979.

Buluku, C. *Dieu, idoles et sorcelleries.* Bandundu: CEEBA, 1968.

Burton, William Frederick Padwick. *Luba Religion and Magic in Custom and Belief.* Tervuren: MRAC, 1961.

Centre d'Études Ethnographiques de Bandundu. *Dieu, idoles et sorcellerie dans la région Kwango/Bas-Kwilu: Rapports et compte rendu de la Deuxième Semaine d'Études Ethnopastorales, Bandundu, 1966.* Bandundu: CEEBA, 1968.

Chinapah, Vinayagum. *Swedish Missions and Education in the Republic of Zaire: A Description and Diagnosis.* Stockholm: University of Stockholm, Institute of International Education, 1981.

Chomé, Jules. *La Passion de Simon Kimbangu.* Brussels: Les Amis de Présence Africaine, 1959.

Commission Diocésaine des Jeunes de Kinshasa. *Option fondamentale: Thèmes et chants de l'initiation à l'option fondamentale des Bilenge ya Mwinda.* Kinshasa: St. Paul Afrique, 1978.

Conférence Episcopale du Zaïre. *Réconciliation et pénitence dans la mission de l'Église: Contribution de l'Épiscopat du Zaïre au synode romain 1983.* Kinshasa-Gombe: CEZ, 1984.

Coppo, Salvatore. *A Truly African Church.* Eldoret, Kenya: Gaba Publications, AMECA, 1987.

Crawford, John Richard. *Protestant Missions in Congo, 1878-1969.* N.p., 1969. (English translation of *Témoignage protestant au Zaïre, 1878-1970.* Kinshasa: Centre Protestant d'Éditions et de Diffusion, 1972.)

Cuvelier, J. *Documents sur une mission française au Kakongo, 1766-1776.* Brussels: IRCB, 1953.

————. *L'Ancien royaume de Congo.* Brussels: Desclée de Brouwer, 1946.

————. *Relations sur le Congo du Père Laurent de Lucques, 1700-1717.* Brussels: IRCB, 1953.

Cuvelier, J., and L. Jadin. *L'Ancien Congo d'après les archives romaines, 1518-1640.* Brussels: ARSC, 1954.

D'Anna, Andrea. *Da Cristo a Kimbangu. "Chiese nere" e sincretismi pagano-cristiani in Africa.* Bologna: Éditions "Nigrizia," 1964.

Davies, David Morgan. *The Captivity and Triumph of Winnie Davies.* London: Hodder & Stoughton, 1968.

Dawson, David. *Trapped!* Ventura, CA: Regal Books, 1982.

De Beir, L. *Religion et magie des Bayaka.* St. Augustin, West Germany: Anthropos-Institut St. Augustin, 1975.

De Boeck, André. *Contribution à l'étude du système moral de la jeunesse zaïroise.* Brussels: Vander, 1975.

De Craemer, Willy. *The Jamaa and the Church: A Bantu Catholic Movement in Zaire.* Oxford: Clarendon Press, 1977.

De Rome, Jean-François. *La Fondation de la mission des Capuciors au Royaume du Congo (1648).* (Translated by François Botinck.) Louvain, Belgium: Nauwelaerts, 1964.

De Thier, Franz M. *Singhitini: La Stanleyville musulmane.* Brussels: Centre pour l'Étude des Problèmes du Monde Musulman Contemporain, 1963.

Delhez, Charles. *La Bienheureuse anuarité et le Pape Jean-Paul II.* Kinshasa: St. Paul Afrique, 1985.

Denis, L. *Les Jésuites belges au Kwango.* Brussels: Universelle, 1943.

Dequeker, Paul. *Églises Tropicales.* Kinshasa: CEP., 1984.

Devant les Sectes non-chrétiennes: Rapports de compte-rendus de la 31ème semaine de missiologie. Bruges: Desclée De Brower, 1961.

Dialembonkebi Diebo Makani-Ma-Nsi. *Le droit de l'homme à l'existence: Au Regard de la métaphysique négro-africaine.* Kinshasa: Lokole, 1988.

Dieu, Léon. *Dans la brousse congolaise: Les Origines des missions de Scheut au Congo.* Liège: Maréchal, 1946.

Egbulem, Nwaka Chris. *The Power of Africentric Celebrations: Inspirations from the Zairean Liturgy.* New York: Crossroad, 1996.

Fabian, Johannes. *Jamaa: A Charismatic Movement in Katanga.* Evanston, IL: Northwestern University Press, 1971.

Facultés Catholiques de Kinshasa. Séminaire Scientifique Régional de Philosophie. *La Ville africaine et ses urgences vitales: Actes du Quatrième séminaire scientifique régional de philosophie, Kinshasa, du 16-19 juin 1988.* Kinshasa: FCK, 1991.

Fourche, T. *Une Bible noire.* Brussels: M. Arnold, 1973.

Fuller, Millard. *Bokotola.* New York: Association Press, 1977.

Gérard, Robert. *Les Fondements syncrétiques du Kitawala.* Brussels: CRISP, 1969.

Gillis, Charles-André. *Kimbangu, fondateur d'église.* Brussels: Librairie Encyclopédique, 1960.

Harris, John Hobbis, Sir. *The Christian Church and the Congo Question.* London: Edward Hughes, 1909.

Heintze-Flad, Wilfred. *L'Église Kimbanguiste, une église qui chante et prie: Les "Chants captés" kimbanguistes.* Lieden: Interuniversitair Institut voor Missiologie en Oecumenica, 1978.

Janzen, John M., and Wyatt MacGaffey. *An Anthology of Kongo Religion: Primary Texts from Lower Zaire.* Lawrence: University of Kansas, 1974.

Kabongo-Mbaya, Philippe B. *L'Église du Christ au Zaïre: Formation et adaptation d'un protestantisme en situation de dictature.* Paris: Karthala, 1992.

Kaké, Ibrahima Baba. *Dona Béatrice: La Jeanne d'Arc congolaise.* Paris: ABC, 1976.

Kasonga-Tshiosha, Patrice. *Statuts du clergé diocésain au Zaïre (1936-1962-1980).* Kinshasa: Éditions Universitaires Africaines, 1993.

Kasongo, Michael. *History of the Methodist Church in the Central Congo.* Lanham, MD: University Press of America, 1997.

Keidel, Levi O. *War to Be Won.* Grand Rapids, MI: Zondervan Publishing House, 1977.

Kimplianga Mahaniah. *L'Impact du Christianisme sur le Manianga, 1880-1980.* Kinshasa: Centre de Vulgarisation Agricole, 1981.

Lagerborg, Mary Beth. *Though Lions Roar: The Story of Helen Roseveare, Missionary Doctor to the Congo.* Fort Washington, PA: Christian Literature Crusade, 1995.

Lagergren, David. *Mission and State in the Congo: A Study of the Relations between Protestant Missions and the Congo Independent State Authorities with Special Reference to the Equator District, 1885-1903.* Lund, Sweden: Gleerup, 1970.

Lanternari, V. *The Religions of the Oppressed: A Study of Messianic Cults.* New York: A. A. Knopf, 1963.

Lory, Marie-Joseph. *Face à l'avenir: L'Église au Congo Belge et au Ruanda-Urundi*. Paris: Casterman, 1958.

Lufualabo, François. *La Notion luba-bantoue de l'être*. Paris: Casterman, and Louvain: Église Vivante, 1964.

———. *Orientation pre-chrétienne de la conception bantoue*. Kinshasa: Centre d'Études Pastorales, 1964.

———. *Vers une théodicée bantoue*. Tournai, Belgium: Casterman, 1962.

MacGaffey, Wyatt. *Astonishment and Power*. Washington: Smithsonian Institution Press, 1993.

———. "Comparative Analysis of Central African Religions." *Africa* 42, no. 1 (1972): 21-31.

———. "Cultural Roots of Kongo Prophetism." *History of Religions* 17, no. 2 (November 1977): 177-93.

———. *Modern Kongo Prophets: Religion in a Plural Society*. Bloomington: Indiana University Press, 1983.

———. "Oral Tradition in Central Africa." *International Journal of African Historical Studies* 7, no. 3 (1975): 417-26.

———. *Religion and Society in Central Africa: The BaKongo of Lower Zaire*. Chicago: University of Chicago Press, 1986.

Makanzu Mavumilusa. *L'Histoire de l'Église du Christ au Zaïre: Nous n'avons pas trahi l'Évangile de Jesus-Christ*. Kinshasa: Centre Protestant d'Éditions et de Diffusion, 1973.

Malula, Joseph (Cardinal). *Directoire de la Pastorale du mariage et de la famille*. Kinshasa: Archidiocèse de Kinshasa, 1984.

———. *Priests for the Year 2000: Our Hopes and Expectations*. Bamenda, Cameroon: Archdiocese of Bamenda, 1996.

Markowitz, Marvin D. *Cross and Sword: The Political Role of Christian Missions in the Belgian Congo, 1908-1960*. Stanford, CA: Hoover Institution Publications, 1973.

Masamba ma Mpolo. *Sorcellerie et pastorale*. Kinshasa: Centre Protestant d'Éditions et de Diffusion, 1977.

McGavran, Donald Anderson. *Zaire: Midday in Missions*. Valley Forge, PA: Judson Press, 1979.

Mosmans, Guy. *L'Église à l'heure de l'Afrique*. Paris: Casterman, 1961.

Mukoso Ng'ekieb, Fernand. *Les Origines et les débuts de la mission du Kwango (1879-1914)*. Kinshasa: Facultés Catholiques de Kinshasa, 1993.

Mulago, G. C. M. *La Religion traditionelle des bantous et leur vision du monde*. Kinshasa: PUZ, 1973.

Mulago, Vincent, and T. Theuws. *Autour du mouvement de la "Jamaa."* Leopoldville-Limété: Centre d'Études Pastorales, 1960.

Ndaywel e Nziem, Isidore. *La Société zaïroise dans le miroir de son discours religieux (1990-1993)*. Brussels: CEDAF, 1993.

Nelson, Jack E. *Christian Missionizing and Social Transformation: A History of Conflict and Change in Eastern Zaire*. New York: Praeger, 1992.

Nelson, Robert, G. *Congo Crisis and Christian Mission*. St. Louis, MO: Bethany Press, 1961.

Ngandu Nkashama, Pius. *Églises nouvelles et mouvements religieux: L'Exemple zaïrois*. Paris: Harmattan, 1990.

Ngokwey, Ndolamb. *Le Désenchantement enchanteur; ou, D'un Mouvement religieux à l'autre*. Brussels: CEDAF, 1978.

Ntedika Konde. *La Faculté de Théologie et l'avenir de l'Église en Afrique*. Kinshasa: Faculté de Théologie Catholique de Kinshasa, 1975.

Nyeme Tese. *Munga, éthique en un milieu africain: Gentilisme et christianisme*. Ingenbohl, Switzerland: Imprimerie du Père Théodose, 1975.

Okolo Okonda w'Oleko. *Pour une philosophie de la culture et du développement: Recherches d'herméneutique et de praxis africaines*. Kinshasa: PUZ, 1986.

Pierson, Robert H. *Angels over Elisabethville: A True Story of God's Providence in Time of War*. Mountain View, CA: Pacific Press Publishers Association, 1975.

Prouty, Robert. *Scar across the Heart*. Boise, ID: Pacific Press Publishers Association, 1986.

Ramsbottom, Fred. *African Plenty: A Missionary Life of Miracles*. Basingstoke, Hants, England: M. Pickering, 1987.

Religieux et religieuse en République du Zaïre, 1985. Kinshasa: ASUMA, 1985.

Rencontre des Moralistes Zaïrois. *Morale et société zaïroise: Actes de la première rencontre des moralistes zaïrois, du 1er au 4 novembre 1978*. Tshumbe-Wembonyama, Zaire: Centre d'Études et de Recherches Anthropologiques du Sankuru, 1982.

Rodeheaver, Homer Alvan. *Singing Black: Twenty Thousand Miles with a Music Missionary*. New York: AMS Press, 1975 (reprint of the 1936 edition published by Rodeheaver Co., Chicago).

Scheitler, Marcel. *Histoire de l'église catholique au Kasayi, 1891-1938*. 2nd ed. Kananga: Éditions de l'Archidiocèse, 1991.

Sizemore, Bill. "Taken for a Ride: TV Preacher Pat Robertson Used Operation Blessing's Airplanes for Diamond Mining Operations in Zaire, Former Pilots Say." *Church and State* (June 1997): 4-6.

Taylor, John V., and Dorothea A. Lehmann. *Christians of the Copper-Belt*. London: SCM Press, 1961.

Tempels, Placide. *Aux origines de la Philosophie bantoue: La Correspondance Tempels-Hulstaert, 1944-1948*. (Translated by François Bontinck.) Kinshasa: Faculté de Théologie Catholique, 1985.

Toews, John B. *The Mennonite Bretheren Church in Zaire*. Fresno, CA: Mennonite Bretheren Publishing House, 1978.

Truby, David W. *Congo Saga: An Authentic Record of Heroes of the Cross during the Simba Rising*. London: Unevangelized Fields Mission, 1964.

————. *Regime of Gentlemen: Personal Experiences of Congolese Christians during the 1964 Rebellion*. London: Marshall, Morgan & Scott, 1971.

Tshibangu Tshishiku. *Le Cardinal Malula, pasteur et prophète (1917-1989): Temoignages de la presse nationale et internationale*. Kinshasa: Fondation Cardinal Malula, 1992.

————. *Le Propos d'une théologie africaine*. Kinshasa: PUZ, 1974.

Van Caeneghem, R. *La Notion de Dieu chez les BaLuba du Kasaï*. Brussels: ARSC, 1956.

Verbeek, Léon. *Le Monde des esprits au sud-est du Shaba et au nord de la Zambie: Recueil de textes oraux*. Rome: LAS, 1990.

Verner, Samuel P. *Pioneering in Central Africa*. Richmond, VA: Presbyterian Committee of Publications, 1903.

Vivez donc votre vie!: Les GEN au Zaïre disent leurs expériences. Kinshasa: St. Paul Afrique, 1981.

Wharton, E. T. *Led in Triumph: Sixty Years of Southern Presbyterian Mission in the Belgian Congo*. Nashville, TN: Board of World Missions, Presbyterian Church, 1952.

Womersley, Harold. *Congo Miracle: Fifty Years of God's Working in Congo (Zaire)*. Eastbourne: Victory Press, 1974.

4. Sociology, Urbanization and Migration

Baeck, L. "An Expenditure Study of the Congolese 'Évolués' of Léopoldville, Belgian Congo," in *Social Change in Modern Africa*, edited by Adian J. Southall, pp. 159-81. London: Oxford University Press, 1961.

————. "Une Société rurale en transition: Étude socio-économique de Thysville." *Zaïre* 11, no. 2 (1957): 115-86.

Benoit, Jacqueline. *La Population africaine à Élisabethville à la fin de 1957: Son état, sa structure, ses movements et ses perspectives d'évolution prochaine*. Elisabethville: CEPSI, 1962.

Bernard, Guy. *Ville africaine, famille urbaine: Les Enseignants de Kinshasa*. Paris: Mouton, 1969.

Buakasa, Gérard. *Reinventer l'Afrique: De la Tradition à la modernité au Congo-Zaïre*. Paris: Harmattan, 1996.

Capelle, Emmanuel. *La Cité indigène de Léopoldville*. Leopoldville: Centre d'Études Sociales Africaines, 1947.

Caprasse, P. *Leaders africains en milieu urbain*. Elisabethville, CEPSI, 1959.

Centner, T. *L'Enfant africain et ses jeux*. Elisabethville: CEPSI, 1963.

Chronique d'une société civile en formation au Sud-Kivu. Kinshasa: CEPAS, 1994.

Comhaire-Sylvain, Suzanne. *Femmes de Kinshasa hier et aujourd'hui*. Paris: Mouton, 1968.

De Maximy, René. *Kinshasa, ville en suspens: Dynamique de la croissance et problèmes d'urbanisme: Étude socio-politique*. Paris: Éditions de l'Office de la Recherche Scientifique et Technique Outre-mer, 1984.

De Thier, Franz M. *Le Centre extra-coutumier de Coquilhatville*. Brussels: Institut de Sociologie, Université Libre de Belgique, 1956.

————. *Singhitini, la Stanleyville musulmane*. Brussels: Centre pour l'Étude des Problèmes du Monde Musulman Contemporain, 1963.

Denis, Jacques. *Le Phénomène urbain en Afrique centrale*. Brussels: ARSC, 1958.

Dethier, Robert. *Une Famille de citadins du Katanga*. Liège: Institut de Sociologie de la Faculté de Droit, 1961.

Facultés Catholiques de Kinshasa. *O.N.G., valeurs démocratiques et développement dans le Kivu et les pays des grands-lacs:*

Séminaire-atelier international, Murhesa (Bukavu) du 02 au 04 novembre 1992. Kinshasa: FCK, 1994.

Gondola, Charles Didier. *Villes miroirs: Migrations et identités urbaines à Kinshasa et Brazzaville, 1930-1970.* Paris: Harmattan, 1996.

Grinker, Roy Richard. *Houses in the Rain Forest: Ethnicity and Inequality among Farmers and Foragers in Central Africa.* Berkeley: University of California Press, 1994.

Jacobson-Widding, Anita. *Marriage and Money.* Uppsala: Institutionen for Allmaën och Jaëmfoërande Etnografi, 1967.

Kalele-Ka-Bila. *Sociologie du développement; ou, Plaidoirie en faveur du sous-développement: Une Critique des théories sociologiques classiques.* Lubumbashi: Labossa, 1986.

Kaufmann, Robert. *Millénarisme et Acculturation.* Brussels: Institut de Sociologie, Université Libre de Belgique, 1964.

Kazintenkore, E. "La Construction dans les zones de squatting de Kinshasa." *Cahiers Économiques et Sociaux, IRES* 5, no. 3 (1967): 327-53.

La Fontaine, Jean S. "The Free Women of Kinshasa: Prostitution in a City in Zaire," in *Choice and Change: Essays in Honour of Lucy Mair,* edited by J. Davis, pp. 89-113. New York: Humanities Press, 1974.

Leblanc, Michel. *Lubumbashi: Un Écosystème urbain tropical.* Lubumbashi: Centre International de Sémiologie, UNAZA, 1978.

———. *Personalité de la Femme Katangaise.* Paris: Béatrice-Nauwelaerts, 1960.

Lejeune, Émile. "Les Classes sociales au Congo." *Remarques Africaines* (1966): 259.

Liniger-Goumaz, Max. *Villes et problèmes urbains de la République Démocratique du Congo: Bibliographie.* Geneva: Les Éditions de Temps, 1968.

Lumpungu Kamanda. *Les Pygmées aussi ont des droits: Une Analyse de la situation des pygmées au Zaïre.* Kinshasa: UNICEF, 1995.

Lux, André. "Luluabourg: Migration, accroissement et urbanisation de la population congolaise de Luluabourg." *Zaïre* 12, nos. 7-8 (1958): 819-77.

Masamba ma Mpolo. *Les personnes agées et leurs familles dans une société rurale changeante: Le Cas de la République du Zaïre.* Kinshasa: Centre de Vulgarisation Agricole, 1986.

————. *Older Persons and Their Families in a Changing Village Society: A Perspective from Zaire.* Washington: International Federation on Ageing, and Geneva: World Council of Churches, Office of Family Education, 1984.

Masiala Ma Solo. *Les Enfants de personne: Étude clinique et de phénomènologie sociale sur l'enfance et la jeunesse défavorisées.* Kinshasa: Éditions Enfance et Paix, 1990.

Mianda, Gertrude D. M. *Femmes africaines et pouvoir: Les Maraîchières de Kinshasa.* Paris: Harmattan, 1996.

Minon, Paul. *Katuba: Étude quantitative d'une communauté urbaine africaine.* Liège: Institut de Sociologie de la Faculté de Droit, 1960.

Moeller de Laddersous, A. *Les Grandes lignes de migration des Bantous de la Province Orientale du Congo Belge.* Brussels: IRCB, 1936.

Mpase Nselenge Mpeti. *L'Évolution de la solidarité traditionnelle en milieu rural et urbain au Zaïre: Cas des Ntomba et des Basengele du Lac Mai-Ndome.* Kinshasa: PUZ, 1974.

Mpinga, H. "La Coexistence des pouvoirs 'traditionnel' et 'moderne' dans la ville de Kinshasa." *Cahiers Économiques et Sociaux IRES* 7, no. 1 (1969): 67-90.

————. "Les Mécanismes de la croissance urbaine en République Démocratique du Congo." *Études Congolaises*, 11, no. 3 (1968): 95-103.

Mulambu Mvuluya. *Migrations et structure des groupements dans la zone de Miabi: Mythes et réalités.* Kinshasa: Saint Paul, 1991.

Muyengo Mulombe. *Enfants du ciel, misères de la terre: Cent récits vrais.* Kinshasa: Saint Paul Afrique, 1992.

Ngimbi Bamweneko, Marie-Josiane A. *La dynamique de la famille Yombe face au travail salarié de la femme.* Kinshasa: Facultés Catholiques de Kinshasa, 1994.

Njuma Ekundanayo. *Analyse de la situation des femmes et enfants pygmées du Zaïre.* Kinshasa: N.p., 1993.

Nlandu-Tsasa, Cornelis. *La rumeur au Zaïre de Mobutu: Radio-Trottoir à Kinshasa.* Paris: Harmattan, 1997.

Nzuzi, Lelo. *Urbanisation et aménagement en Afrique noire.* Paris: Sedes, 1989.

Parpart, Jane L., and Kathleen A. Staudt. *Women and the State in Africa.* Boulder, CO: L. Rienner, 1989.

Piérard, J. P. "La Dot congolaise: Sa Situation actuelle et son avenir." *Bulletin des Séances ARSOM*, no. 3 (1967): 468-95.

Raymaekers, Paul. "Juvenile Pre-delinquency and Delinquency in Leopoldville." *Bulletin of the International African Labour Institute* 10, no. 3 (1963): pp. 329-57.

————. *L'Organisation des zones de squatting, elément de résorption du chômage structurel dans les milieux urbains en voie de développement*. Brussels: Éditions Univérsitaires, 1964.

Richelle, Marc. *Aspects psychologiques de l'acculturation: Recherches sur les motifs de la stabilisation urbaine au Katanga*. Elisabethville: CEPSI, 1960.

Roelants, Frank. *Un Lieu d'espérance: Le Récit d'une experience avec les enfants de la rue de Kinshasa au Zaïre*. Bandundu: CEEBA, 1996.

Roels-Ceulemans, M. J. *Problèmes de la jeunesse à Léopoldville: Analyse quantitative de la population juvénile*. Leopoldville: IRES, Lovanium, 1961.

Schatzberg, Michael G. *Politics and Class in Zaire: Bureaucracy, Business, and Beer in Lisala*. New York: Africana, 1980.

Shomba Kinyamba. *La Prostitution, son vrai visage au Zaïre*. Lubumbashi: Éditions Africa, 1987.

Smal, Guy A., and Joseph W. Mbuyi. *Femme africaine, réveille-toi!* Paris: La Pensée Universelle, 1973.

Sohier, J. *Essai sur la criminalité dans la Province de Léopoldville*. Brussels: ARSC, 1959.

————. *Quelques traits de la physionomie de la population européene d'Élisabethville*. Brussels: IRCB, 1953.

Streiffeler, Friedhelm, and Mbaya Mudimba. *Village, ville et migration au Zaïre: Enquête psycho-sociologique sur le mouvement des populations de la sous-région de la Tshopo à la ville de Kisangani*. Paris: Harmattan, 1986.

Tshibanda Wamuela Bujitu. *Femmes libres, femmes enchaînées: La Prostitution au Zaïre*. Lubumbashi: St. Paul Afrique, 1986.

Turnbull, Colin M. *The Lonely African*. New York: Simon and Schuster, 1962.

Verhaegen, Benoît. *Femmes zaïroises de Kisangani: Combats pour la survie*. Louvain-la-Neuve, Belgium: Centre d'Histoire de l'Afrique, 1990.

Vincent, J. F. *Femmes africaines en milieu urbain*. Paris: N.p., 1966.

Warkentin, Raija. *Our Strength Is in Our Fields: African Families in Change*. Dubuque, IA: Kendall/Hunt, 1994.

Zaïre, République du. Département des Travaux Publics et de l'Aménagement du Territoire. *Les Villes du Shaba: Indicateurs de développement urbain*. Kinshasa, 1986.

————. Ministère du Plan, Reconstruction et Ravitaillement. *Programme d'action national pour la survie, la protection et la promotion du couple mère-enfant au Zaïre, d'içi l'an 2000*. Kinshasa: 1992.

VI. SCIENCE

1. Archeology

Boaz, Noel T. *Evolution of Environments and Hominidae in the African Western Rift Valley*. Martinsville, VA: Virginia Museum of Natural History, 1990.

Brabant, H. *Excavations à Sanga: Contribution odontologique à l'étude des ossements trouvés dans la nécropole protohistorique de Sanga*. Tervuren: MRAC, 1965.

Cahen, Daniel. *La Site archéologique de la Kamoa (Région du Shaba, République du Zaïre) de l'âge du fer*. Tervuren: MRAC, 1975.

Cahen, Daniel, and G. Mortelmans. *Un Site tshitolien sur le plateau des Bateke, République du Zaïre*. Tervuren: MRAC, 1973.

Cahen, Daniel, and Philippe Martin. *Classification formelle automatique et industries lithiques: Interprétation des hachereaux de la Kamoa*. Tervuren: MRAC, 1972.

Leroy, Pierre. *Matériaux pour servir à la préhistoire de l'Uelé: Le Dallage d'Afrique mégalithe d'Obeledi*. Brussels: ARSOM, 1961.

Nenquin, Jacques. "Dimple-based pots from Kasai, Belgian Congo." *Man* 59, no. 242 (1959): 153-55.

————. *Excavations at Sanga, 1957: The Protohistoric Necropolis*. Tervuren: 1963.

————. "Notes on Some Early Pottery Cultures in Northern Katanga." *Journal of African History* 4, no. 1 (1963): 19-32.

————, ed. *Inventaria Archaeologica Africana*. Tervuren: MRAC, 1964.

Van Noten, Francis. *The Uelian: A Culture with a Neolothic Aspect, Uele-Basin (N.E. Congo Republic), An Archaeological Study.* Tervuren: MRAC, 1968.

2. Geology

Cahen, L. *Géologie du Congo Belge.* Liège: Vaillant-Carmann, 1954.
Cahen, L., and N. J. Snelling. *The Geochronology of Equatorial Africa.* Amsterdam: North Holland Publishing, 1966.
Carrol, Paul. *Congo: Études sols pour la plaine de Kinshasa.* Washington: US Department of Agriculture, 1969.
Congo, République Démocratique du. Service Géologique. *Bulletin.* (Replaced the Service Géologique du Congo Belge in 1960.) Leopoldville: 1945-1970.
Danse, A. "Genèse organo-chimique de la latération et de l'argilisation dans les paysages latéritiques." *Bulletin de Service Géologique du Congo Belge* 9, no. 1 (March 1959): 1-8.
Davreux, L. "Quelques considérations sur le bassin hydrographique du Congo." *Bulletin du Société Royale Belge de Géographie* 81, no. 1-2 (1957): 67-79.
De Heinzelin de Braucort, J. *Le Paléolithique aux abords d'Ishango.* Brussels: Institut des Parcs Nationaux, 1961.
Denaeyer, Marcel E. *Le Glacis des volcans actifs au nord du Lac Kivu, République du Zaïre.* Paris: Éditions du Muséum, 1975.
Devroey, E. J. *Annuaire Hydrologique du Congo Belge et du Ruanda-Urundi (1951-1959).* 9 vols. Brussels: ARSOM, 1952-1960.
Egoroff, Boris. *L'Éruption du Volcan Mihaga en 1954.* Brussels: Institut des Parcs Nationaux du Congo, 1965.
Evrard, Carlo. *Le Prix de revient des cartes des sols et de la végétation au Congo.* Leopoldville, N.p., 1961.
————. *Les Recherches géophysiques et géologiques et les travaux de sondage dans la cuvette congolaise.* Brussels: ARSC, 1957.
François, Armand. *La Couverture katangienne: Entre les Socles de Zilo et de la Kabompo, République du Zaïre, région de Kolwezi.* Tervuren: MRAC, 1981.
Gautier, A. *Fossil Fresh Water Mollusca of the Lake Albert-Lake Edward Rift, Uganda.* Tervuren: MRAC, 1970.

————. *Geological Investigation in the Sinda-Mohari (Ituri, NE-Congo): A Monograph on the Geological History of a Region in the Lake Albert Rift.* Ghent: 1965.

Greenwood, Peter Humphry. *Neogene Fossil Fishes from the Lake Albert-Lake Edward Rift (Zaïre).* London: British Museum (Natural History), 1975.

Herrinck, P. *Seismicité du Congo Belge: Compilation des séismes observés aux stations climatologiques entre 1909 et 1954.* Brussels: ARSC, 1959.

Lavreau, J. *Étude géologique du Haut-Zaïre: Genèse et évolution d'un segment lithosphérique archéen.* Tervuren: MRAC, 1982.

Lepersonne, Jacques. *Structure géologique du bassin intérieur du Zaïre.* Brussels: ARSOM, 1978.

Mulder, M. de. *The Karisimbi Volcano (Virunga).* Tervuren: MRAC, 1985.

Pecrot, A., et al. *L'Altération des sols au Kivu.* Brussels: INEAC, 1962.

Pire, J., M. Berreux, and J. Quiodbach. *L'Intensité des pluies au Congo Belge et au Ruanda-Urundi.* Brussels: ARSOM, 1960.

Robert, M. *Géologie et géographie du Katanga, y compris l'étude des ressources et de la mise en valeur.* Brussels: publisher unknown, 1956.

Sahama, Thure George. *The Nyiragongo Main Cone.* Tervuren: MRAC, 1978.

Sys, C., et al. *La Cartographie des sols au Congo: Ses Principes et ses méthodes.* Brussels: INEAC, 1961.

Taverne, Louis. *Les Téléostéens fossiles du crétacé moyen de Kipala (Kwango, Zaïre).* Tervuren: MRAC, 1976.

Tazieff, Haroun. *Nyiragongo: The Forbidden Volcano.* (Translated from French by J. F. Bernard.) New York: Barron's/Woodbury, 1979.

Tibbitts, G. Chase. *Ground-water Resources Investigation Program for the Kinshasa Area, Democratic Republic of the Congo.* (Prepared by the US Geological Survey in cooperation with Democratic Republic of the Congo under the auspices of USAID.) Kinshasa: USAID, 1968.

United States Agency for International Development. Bureau for Technical Assistance. *Developing Country Coverage of Earth Resource Technology Satellite ERTS-1: July 1972 - June 1973, Zaire.* Washington: 1973.

Van Oosterwyck-Gastuche, M. C. *Étude des silicates de cuivre du Katanga*. Tervuren: MRAC, 1967.

Varlamoff, N. *Les Gisements de tungstène au Congo Belge et au Ruanda-Urundi*. Brussels: ARSC, 1958.

Wood, Roger Conant. *Fossil Marine Turtle Remains from the Paleocene of the Congo*. Gautier, Achilles, and Dirk Van Damme. *A Revision of the Miocene Freshwater Molluscs of the Mohari Formation. Sinda Mohari, Ituri, N.E. Zaire*. (Published together.) Tervuren: MRAC, 1973.

3. Geography

Annaert, J. *Contribution à l'étude géographique de l'habitat et de l'habitation indigènes en milieu rural dans les Provinces Orientale et du Kivu*. ARSOM, 1960.

Béguin, H. *La Mise en valeur du sud-est du Kasaï: Essai de géographie agricole et de géographie agraire et ses possibilités d'application pratique*. Brussels: INEAC, 1960.

Choprix, Guy. *La Naissance d'une ville: Étude géographique de Paulis (1934-1957)*. Brussels: CEMUBAC, 1961.

Kama Funzi Mudindambi. *La République du Zaïre: Géographie, troisième secondaire, programme officiel*. Paris: Hatier, 1973.

Mountjoy, A. B., and C. Embleton. *Africa: A New Geographical Survey*. New York: Praeger, 1967.

Nicolai, Henri. *Le Kwilu*. Brussels: CEMUBAC, 1963.

———. *Luozi: Géographie régionale d'un pays du Bas-Congo*. Brussels: ARSOM, 1961.

———. *Progrès de la connaissance géographique au Congo, au Ruanda et au Burundi en 1964, 1965 et 1966*. Brussels: CEMUBAC, 1967.

Nicolai, Henri, and J. Jacques. *La Transformation des paysages congolais par le chemin de fer: L'Example du B.C.K.* Brussels: IRCB, 1954.

Peeters, Leo. *La Géographie du pays Logo au sud d'Aba*. Brussels: CEMUBAC, 1963.

Raucq, P. *Notes de géographie sur le Maniema*. Brussels: IRCB, 1952.

Robert, M. *Contribution à la géographie du Katanga*. Brussels: IRCB, 1954.

Thompson, B. W. *The Climate of Africa*. Nairobi: Oxford University Press, 1965.

Verbeken, Auguste. *Contribution à la géographie historique du Katanga et des régions voisines*. Brussels: ARSC, 1954.

Zaïre, République du. Institut Géographique. *Rapport annuel, Institut Géographique du Zaïre*. Kinshasa: annual.

4. Medicine, Health and Diet

Anderson, Barbara, and James McCabe. "Nutrition and the Fertility of Younger Women in Kinshasa." *Journal of Development Economics* 4 (1977) 343-63.

Association Zaïroise pour le Bien-Être Familial. *Plan triennal, 1992-1994*. Kinshasa: 1991.

Bakutuvwidi Makani. *Planification familiale, fécondité et santé familiale au Zaïre, 1982-1984: Rapport sur les résultats d'une enquête régionale sur la prévalence contraceptive*. Kinshasa-Gombe: Institut National de la Statistique, and Columbia, MD: Westinghouse Public Applied Systems, 1985.

Batangu Mpesa. *APHARZA, Association des Pharmaciens Zaïrois: Cinq ans après*. Kinshasa: APHARZA, 1976.

Bertrand, Jane T. *Family Planning Success in Two Cities in Zaire*. Washington: World Bank, 1992.

Bervoets, W., and M. Lassance. *Modes et coutumes alimentaires des Congolais en milieu rural*. Brussels: ARSC, 1959.

Centre de Recherches Industrielles en Afrique Centrale. *Enquête alimentaire au Shaba: Contribution du CRIAC*. Lubumbashi: 1977.

Christakis, Nicholas A. "The Ethical Design of an AIDS Vaccine Trial in Africa." *Hastings Center Report* 18 (June-July 1988): 31-37.

Clerck, M. de. *Le Traitement du diabète en Afrique*. Kinshasa: St. Paul Afrique, 1988.

Colbourne, Michael. *Malaria in Africa*. London: Oxford University Press, 1966.

Cornet, René Jules. *Bwana muganga: Hommes en blanc en Afrique noire*. Brussels: ARSOM, 1971.

De Craemer, Willy, and Renée C. Fox. *The Emerging Physician: A Sociological Approach to the Development of the Congolese Medical Profession*. Stanford: Hoover Institution, 1968.

Derryberry, Mayhen, et al. *Maternal and Child Health Care Service in the Kinshasa Area.* American Public Health Association for USAID. Washington: 1971.

D'Heer, A. *Une Nourriture saine.* Kananga, Zaire: Projet-Soya, 1976(?).

Diocèse d'Idiofa. *Comment le clan se nourrit: ou, Bien manger, est-ce possible?: De la Vie ancestrale à une vie nouvelle assumée.* Idiofa, Zaire: Diocèse d'Idiofa, 1982.

Duren, A. *L'Organisation médicale Belge en Afrique.* Brussels: ARSC, 1955.

Ebola Virus Haemorrhagic Fever. (Proceedings of International Colloquium on Ebola Virus Infection and Other Haemorrhagic Fevers, held in Antwerp, Belgium, December 6-8, 1977.) Amsterdam: Elsevier/North-Holland Biomedical Press, 1978.

Ermans, A. M., et al. *Role of Cassava in the Etiology of Endemic Goitre and Cretinism.* Ottawa: International Development Research Centre, 1980.

Feierman, Steven, and John M. Janzen, eds. *The Social Basis of Health and Healing in Africa.* N.p., n.d.

Feldmeier, Hermann. "The Ebola Epidemics in Zaire and Gabon." *Swiss Review of World Affairs* (July 1996): 29-30.

Fountain, Daniel E. *Infirmier, comment bâtir la santé: Manuel de santé communautaire.* Kangu-Mayumbe, Zaire: Bureau d'Études et de Recherches pour la Promotion de la Santé, and Kinshasa: Centre Médical de Vange-Bandundu, 1982.

Gelfand, Michael. *A Clinical Study of Intestinal Bilharziosis (Schistosoma Mansomi) in Africa.* London: Arnold, 1967.

"Human Immunodeficiency Virus Infection among Employees in an African Hospital." *New England Journal of Medicine* 319 (October 27, 1988): 1123-27.

Hurley, Suzanne M., Leo Morris, and Jay S. Friedman. *1991 Zaire National Immunization Survey Further Analysis of Data: Family Planning Module.* Atlanta: Center for Disease Control and Prevention, 1993.

Iteke, E. B., and A. M. Ermans, eds. *Nutritional Factors Involved in the Goitrogenic Action of Cassava.* Ottawa: International Development Research Centre, 1982.

Janzen, John M. *The Quest for Therapy in Lower Zaire.* Berkeley: University of California Press, 1978.

Jelliffe, D. B. *Child Health in the Tropics: A Practical Handbook for Medical and Paramedical Personnel.* London: Arnold, 1968.

Kapita M. Bila. *SIDA en Afrique: Maladie et phénomène social.* Kinshasa: Centre de Vulgarisation Agricole, 1988.

Kayembe Lunganga. *Rapport general sur les indicateurs de mortalité infantile et juvenile au Zaïre.* Kinshasa: USAID, 1990.

Kikhela, D. Nzita. *Techniques for Collection and Analysis of Data on Perinatal Mortality in Kinshasa, Zaire.* Ottawa: International Development Research Centre, 1989.

Lambrechts, A., et al. "Enquête alimentaire parmi les populations rurales du Haut-Katanga." *Problèmes Sociaux Congolais,* no. 51 (1960): 7-25.

Laurent, Raymond F. *Contribution à l'histoire de l'herpétologie congolaise et bibliographie générale.* Brussels: ARSOM, 1965.

———. *Le Genre Leptopelis Guënther (Salientia) au Zaïre.* Tervuren: MRAC, 1973.

Lerberghe, W. van. *Kasongo: Child Mortality and Growth in a Small African Town.* London: Smith-Gordon, 1990.

Lyons, Maryinez. *The Colonial Disease: A Social History of Sleeping Sickness in Northern Zaire, 1900-1940.* Cambridge: Cambridge University Press, 1992.

Malanda Dem. *Le Développement mental des enfants sourds-muët à Bandundu, Zaïre.* Kinshasa: PUZ, 1974.

Mukoko Matondo. *Plantes médicinales et leurs usages.* Kinshasa: Centre de Vulgarisation Agricole, 1991.

Nlandu Mangani. *La Promotion des naissances désirables au Bas-Zaïre.* New Orleans: Tulane University, and Kinshasa: Communauté Baptiste du Zaïre-Ouest, 1994.

Parent, J. "Le Nourrisson au Katanga." *Problèmes Sociaux Congolais,* no. 50 (1960): 5-25.

———. "Le Nouveau-né au Katanga." *Problèmes Sociaux Congolais,* no. 48 (1960): 45-48.

"The Prevalence of Infection with Human Immunodeficiency Virus over a Ten-Year Period in Rural Zaire." *New England Journal of Medicine* 318 (February 4, 1988): 276-79.

Rotsart de Hertaing, I. *Nutrition: L'Éducation nutritionnelle dans la pratique journalière.* Kangu-Mayombe, Zaire: Bureau d'Études et de Recherches pour la Promotion de la Santé, 1975.

Sala-Kiakanda, Mpembele. *Social Science Research for Population Policy Design: Case Study of Zaire.* Liège: IUSSP, 1982.

Schwetz, Jacques. *L'Évolution de la médecine au Congo Belge.* Brussels: Office de Publicité, 1946.

United States. Department of Health, Education and Welfare. Division of International Health. *Republic of the Congo: A Study of Health Problems and Resources.* Washington: 1960.

————. *Syncrisis: The Dynamics of Health, Zaire.* Washington: 1975.

Van Dooren, F., and M. Rogowsky. *Étude cardio-circulatoire de l'indigène du Congo Belge et du Ruanda-Urundi.* Brussels: ARSC, 1959.

Vincent, Marc. *Les Problèmes de protection maternelle et infantile au Congo Belge et au Ruanda-Urundi.* 2 vols. Brussels: FOREAMI, 1959.

Zaire River Expedition. (1974-75) Medical Research Team. *Onchocerciasis in Zaire: A New Approach to the Problem of River Blindness,* edited by F. C. Rodger. Oxford: Pergamon Press, 1977.

5. Natural Science and Zoology

Belgium. Comité Exécutif de la Flore du Congo Belge et Jardin Botanique de l'État. *Flore du Congo Belge et du Ruanda Urundi: Spermatophytes.* Brussels, 1958.

————. Division de Phytopathologie et d'Entomologie Agricole. *Précis des maladies et des insectes nuisibles rencontrés sur les plantes cultivées au Congo, au Ruanda et au Burundi.* Brussels: INEAC, 1962.

————. Institut National pour l'Étude Agronomique du Congo (Belge). *Carte des sols et de la végétation du Congo et du Ruanda-Urundi.* Brussels: INEAC, 1955-58.

————. Office de l'Information et des Relations Publiques du Congo Belge et du Ruanda-Urundi (INFORCONGO). *Monographie des principales essences forestières exploités au Congo Belge.* Brussels: 1958.

Berg, A. *Rôle écologique des eaux de la Cuvette Congolaise sur la croissance de la jacinthe d'eau.* Brussels: ARSOM, 1961.

Bose, M. N. *Mesozoic Sporae Dispersae from Zaire.* Tervuren: MRAC, 1976.

————. *Some Mesozoic Plants from Western Congo.* Lakhanpal, R. N. *Some Middle Tertiary Plant Remains from South Kivu, Congo.* (Published together.) Tervuren: MRAC, 1966.

Bultot, F. *Estimations . . . des moyennes vraies journalières, diurnes et nocturnes de la température et de l'humidité de l'air du Congo, au Rwanda et au Burundi.* Brussels: INEAC, 1961.

Crabbé, Marcel. *La nébulosité et la visibilité au Zaïre.* Brussels: ARSOM, 1986.

Curry-Lindahl, Kai. *Contribution à l'étude des vertébrés terrestres en Afrique tropicale.* Brussels: IPN, 1961.

————. *Ecological Studies of Mammals, Birds, Reptiles and Amphibians in the Eastern Belgian Congo.* Tervuren: MRAC, 1960.

De Witte, Gaston F. *Genera des serpents du Congo et du Ruanda-Urundi.* Tervuren: MRAC, 1962.

Dirsh, V. M. *Acridoidea of the Congo (Orthoptera).* Tervuren: MRAC, 1970.

Doumenge, Charles. *La conservation des écosystèmes forestiers du Zaïre.* Gland, Switzerland: IUCN Tropical Forests Program (ECC), 1990.

Dowsett, Robert J., and Alexandre Prigogine. *L'Avifaune des Monts Marungu, The Avifauna of the Marungu Highlands.* Brussels: Cercle Hydrobiologique de Bruxelles, 1974.

Du Soleil, G., and N. Vanderlest. *Annuaire météorologique du Congo Belge et du Ruanda-Urundi, 1957-1961.* 5 vols. Brussels: ARSOM, 1957-60.

Elzius, Claude Cornet d'. *Écologie, structure et évolution des populations des grands mammifères du secteur central du Parc National des Virunga (Parc National Albert), Zaïre (Congo Belge).* Brussels: Fondation pour Favoriser les Recherches Scientifiques en Afrique, 1996.

Fouarge, Joseph. *Essais physiques, mécaniques et de durabilité de bois de la République Démocratique du Congo.* Brussels: Institut National pour l'Étude Agronomique du Congo, 1970.

Germain, R. *Les Biotopes alluvionaires herbeux et les savanes intercalaires du Congo equatorial.* Brussels: ARSOM, 1965.

Gillardin, J. *Les Essences forestières du Congo Belge et du Ruanda-Urundi: Leurs dénominations indigènes, leur distribution et leur habitat.* Brussels: Ministère du Congo Belge et du Ruanda-

Urundi, Division de L'Agriculture, des Forêts et de l'Élevage, 1959.

Harris, W. Victor. *Termites: Their Recognition and Control*. London: Longmans, 1961.

Hayman, R. W. *The Bats of the Congo and of Rwanda and Burundi*. Tervuren: MRAC, 1966.

Henry, J. M. *Analyse d'acclimatation de végétaux en zone équatoriale zaïroise de basse altitude*. Brussels: Centre d'Informatique Appliquée au Développement et à l'Agriculture Tropical, 1976.

Inger, Robert, and Hyman Marx. *The Food of Amphibians*. Brussels: IPN, 1961.

Institut National de Recherche et d'Action Pédagogiques (Congo). Département de l'Enseignement Secondaire. Section Sciences Naturelles. *Écologie: Étude de milieux naturels du Congo*. Brazzaville: 1975-78.

Institut National pour l'Étude Agronomique du Congo. *Carte des sols et de la végétation du Congo Belge et du Ruanda-Urundi*. Brussels: 1954.

Kabala Matuka. *Aspects de la conservation de la nature au Zaïre*. Kinshasa: Lokole, 1976.

Lakhanpal, Rajendra Nath. *Cenozoic Plants from Congo*. Tervuren: MRAC, 1970.

Lambert, J. *Contribution à l'étude des poissons de la forêt de la Cuvette congolaise*. Tervuren: MRAC, 1961.

Léonard, A. *Les Savanes herbeuses du Kivu*. Brussels: INEAC, 1962.

Magis, Noël. *Nouvelle contribution à l'étude hydrobiologique des lacs de Mwadingusha, Koni et N'Zilo*. Liège: PULREAC, Université de Liège, 1961.

Malaisse, François. *Carte de la végétation du bassin de la Luanza; Vegetation Map of the Luanza Drainage Area*. Brussels: Cercle Hydrobiologique de Bruxelles, 1975.

————. *Écologie de la Rivière Luanza; Ecology of the Luanza River*. Brussels: Cercle Hydrobiologique de Bruxelles, 1976.

Maldague, M. E. *Relations entre le couvert végétal et la microfaune: Leur Importance dans la conservation biologique des sols tropicaux*. Brussels: INEAC, 1961.

Palaeozoic Sporae Dispersae from Congo. 5 vols. Tervuren: MRAC, 1966.

Pierlot, Roger. *Structure et composition des forêts denses d'Afrique équatoriale, specialement celles du Kivu.* Brussels: ARSOM, 1966.

Poll, Max. *Les Poissons du Stanley-Pool.* Tervuren: Musée du Congo Belge, 1938.

Robyns, Walter, ed. *Flore iconographique des champignons du Congo.* Brussels: Ministère de l'Agriculture, Jardin Botanique de l'État, n.d.

Schaller, George B. *The Year of the Gorilla.* Chicago: University of Chicago Press, 1988.

Schelpe, Edmund. *Ptéridophytes; Pteridophyta.* Brussels: Cercle Hydrobiologique de Bruxelles, 1973.

Schmitz, A. *La Végétation de la plaine de Lubumbashi (Haut Katanga).* Brussels: Institut National pour l'Étude Agronomique du Congo, 1971.

——. *Révision des groupements végétaux décrits du Zaïre, du Rwanda et du Burundi.* Tervuren: MRAC, 1988.

Schoutheden, H. *Contribution à l'ornithologie de la République du Congo.* 8 vols. Tervuren: MRAC, 1961-65.

Shadab, Mohammad Umar. *A New Genus of Pseudophloeine Bugs from the Democratic Republic of the Congo (Heteroptera, Coreoidea).* New York: American Museum of Natural History, 1972.

Staner, Pierre. *Les Eriosema de la flore congolaise.* Tervuren: Musée du Congo Belge, 1934.

Witte, John. "Deforestation in Zaire: Logging and Landlessness." *Ecologist* 22 (March-April 1992): 58-64.

Zaïre, République du. *Reconnaissance des ressources hydro-électriques dans le Nord-Est.* Kinshasa: 1972.

VII. CULTURE

1. Fine Arts

African-American Institute. *Art in Zaire.* New York: AAI, 1975.

Association Internationale des Critiques d'Arts. *Trésors de l'art traditionnel.* Kinshasa: AICA-Zaïre, 1973.

Bamba Ndombasi Kufimba and Musangi Ntemo. *Anthologie des sculpteurs et peintres zaïrois contemporains*. Paris: Nathan, 1987.

Bantje, Han. *Kaonde Song and Ritual*. Gansemans, Jos. *La Musique et son rôle dans la vie sociale et rituelle Luba*. (Published together.) Tervuren: MRAC, 1978.

Barbier, Jean, ed. *Art pictural des pygmées*. Geneva: Musée Barbier-Mueller, 1990.

Biebuyck, Daniel P. *The Arts of Zaire*. 2 vols. Berkeley: University of California Press, 1985-86.

———. *La Sculpture des Lega*. Paris: Galérie Helène & Philippe Leloup, 1994.

———. *Statuary from the pre-Bembe Hunters: Issues in the Interpretation of Ancestral Figurines Ascribed to the Basikasingo-Bembe-Boyo*. Tervuren: MRAC, 1982.

Bissek, Nicolas. *Les peintres du fleuve Congo*. Saint-Maur, France: Sepia, 1995.

Bokonga Ekanga Botombele, ed. *Cultural Policy in the Republic of Zaire: A Study*. Paris: UNESCO Press, 1976.

Brandel, Rose. *The Music of Central Africa, An Ethnomusicological Study: Former A.E.F., Former Belgian Congo, Ruanda-Urundi, Uganda, Tanganyika*. The Hague: Nijhoff, 1961.

Breuil, Henri. *Les Figures incisées et ponctuées de la grotte de Kiantapo (Katanga)*. Mortelmans, G. *Les Dessins rupestres gravés, ponctués et peints du Katanga: Essai de synthèse*. (Published together.) Tervuren: MRAC, 1952.

Bustin, Marie-Louise. *Art Décoratif Tschokwe*. 2 vols. Lisbon: Subsidios para a Historia, Arqueologia Ethnografia dos Povos da Lunda, 1961.

Caraway, Caren. *African Designs of the Congo*. Owings Mills, MD: Stemmer House, 1986.

Centre d'Études Ethnologiques de Bandundu. *Les Masques pende*. Bandundu: CEEBA, n.d.

Coart, Émile Jean Baptiste. *Vannerie et tissage*. Brussels: Renaissance d'Occident, 1926.

Cornet, Joseph. *Art from Zaire; L'Art du Zaïre: One Hundred Masterworks from the National Collection*. (Exhibition of traditional art from the Institut des Musées Nationaux du Zaïre.) New York: African-American Institute, 1975.

———. *Art of Africa: Treasures from the Congo*. (Translated from French by Barbara Thompson.) London: Phaedon, 1971.

————. *Pierres sculptées du Bas-Zaïre*. Kinshasa: Institut des Musées Nationaux du Zaïre, 1978.

————. *A Survey of Zairian Art: The Bronson Collection*. (Translated by Matt McGaughey.) Raleigh: North Carolina Museum of Art, 1978.

Dequeker, Paul. *L'Architecture tropicale: Théorie et mise en pratique en Afrique tropicale humide*. Kinshasa: Centre de Recherches Pédagogiques, 1992.

Duvelle, Charles. *Musique Kongo: Ba-Bembe, Ba-Kongo, Ba-Kongo Nseke, Ba-Lari*. (LP record with annotations.) Ocora LP OCR 35k, 1967.

Elisofon, Eliot. *The Sculpture of Africa*. New York: Hacker Art Books, 1978.

Enquête sur la vie musicale au Congo Belge, 1934-1935: Questionnaire Knosp. Tervuren: MRAC, 1968.

Fagg, William. *The Congo Basin Tribes*. Vol. 2 of *African Tribal Sculpture*. New York: Tudor, 1966.

Felix, Marc Leo. *Ituri: The Distribution of Polychrome Masks in Northeast Zaire; die Verbreitung Polychromer Masken in Nordost-Zaire*. Munich: Verlag F. Jahn, 1992.

————. *One Hundred Peoples of Zaire and Their Sculpture: The Handbook*. Brussels: Zaire Basin Art History Research Foundation, 1987.

Galerie Kamer. *Congo*. (Exhibition catalogue.) New York: 1969.

Hampton University Museum. *A Taste for the Beautiful: Zairian Art from the Hampton University Museum*. Hampton, VA: University of Hampton, 1993.

Harris, Elizabeth. *Late Beads in the African Trade*. Lancaster, PA: Center for Books on Beads, 1984.

Herreman, Frank, and Petridis Constantijn, eds. *Face of the Spirits: Masks from the Zaire Basin*. Ghent: Snoeck-Ducaju, and Washington: National Museum of African Art, 1993.

Institut des Musées Nationaux du Zaïre. *Trésors de l'art traditionnel*. (Catalogue for an exhibition in Kinshasa from September 13 to October 18, 1973.) Kinshasa: IMNZ, 1973.

Janzen, John M. *Lemba, 1650-1930: A Drum of Affliction in Africa and the New World*. New York: Garland, 1982.

Jewsiewicki, Bogumil. *Art pictural zaïrois*. Sillery, Québec: Septentrion, 1992.

Kanza Matondo ne Mansangaza. *Musique zaïroise moderne*. (Excerpts from a seminar delivered at Kinshasa campus of UNAZA in 1969.) Kinshasa: CNMA, 1972.

Kinzanza. *Mon Manuel de musique congolaise moderne*. Kinshasa: Institut National des Arts, 1971.

La Naissance de la peinture contemporaine en Afrique centrale, 1930-1970. Tervuren: MRAC, 1992.

Lehuard, Raoul. *Art Bakongo: Les Centres de style*. Arnouville, France: Arts d'Afrique Noire, 1989.

Lema Gwete. *L'Art et le pouvoir dans les sociétés traditionnelles*. Kinshasa: UNDP/UNESCO, 1986.

Les Arts au Congo Belge et au Rwanda-Urundi. Brussels: C.I.D., 1950.

Lévi-Strauss, Claude. *La Voie des ancêtres: En Hommage*. Paris: Dapper, 1986.

Lonoh, Malangi Bokelenge (Michel). *Essai de commentaire de la musique congolaise moderne*. Kinshasa: St. Paul, 1969.

———. *Négritude, africanité et musique africaine*. Kinshasa: Centre de Recherches Pédagogiques, 1990.

———. *Négritude et musique: Regards sur les origines et l'évolution de la musique négro-africaine de conception congolaise*. Kinshasa: République Démocratique Congolaise, 1971.

Low, John. *Shaba Diary: A Trip to Rediscover the "Katanga" Guitar Styles and Songs of the 1950s and '60s*. Vienna: E. Stiglmayr, 1982.

Mack, John. *Émil Torday and the Art of the Congo, 1900-1909*. Seattle: University of Washington Press, 1990.

Maquet, J. N. *Note sur les instruments de musique congolaise*. Brussels: ARSC, 1956.

Maurer, Evan M., and Allen F. Roberts. *Tabwa: The Rising of a New Moon, a Century of Tabwa Art*. Ann Arbor: University of Michigan Museum of Art, 1985.

Mobyem, M. K.-Mikanza. *Je fais du théatre*. Paris: Harmattan, 1984.

Musée Dapper. *Au Royaume du signe: Appliqués sur toile des Kuba, Zaïre*. (Catalogue of Exhibition from May 25 to September 24, 1988.) Paris: A. Biro, 1988.

Myanga Gangambi. *Les Masques pende de Gatundo*. Bandundu: CEEBA, 1974.

Ndambi Munamuhega. *Les Masques pende de Ngudi*. Bandundu: CEEBA, 1975.

Newbury, David S. *Kings and Clans: Ijwi Island and the Lake Kivu Rift, 1780-1840*. Madison: University of Wisconsin Press, 1991.

Neyt, François. *Approche des arts Hemba*. Villiers-le-Bel, France: Arts d'Afrique Noire, 1975.

————. *Arts traditionnels et histoire au Zaïre: Cultures forestières et royaumes de la savane*. Translated into English by Scott Bryson. Brussels: Société d'Arts Primitifs, 1981.

————. *Luba: To the Sources of the Zaire*. Translated by Murray Wyllie. Paris: Musée Dapper, 1994.

Ngolo Kibango. *Minganji, danseurs de masques pende*. Bandundu: CEEBA, 1976.

Olbrechts, Frans M. *Congolese Sculpture*. New Haven, CT: Human Relations Area Files, 1982.

————. *Les Arts plastiques au Congo Belge*. Brussels: Erasme, 1959.

Ortolani, Sante. *Initiation esthétique à l'art zaïrois contemporain*. Kinshasa: Institut des Sciences et Techniques de l'Information, 1976.

Otten, Rik. *Le Cinéma dans les pays des grands lacs: Zaïre, Rwanda, Burundi*. Paris: Harmattan, 1984.

Ramirez, Francis. *Histoire du cinéma colonial au Zaïre, au Rwanda et au Burundi*. Tervuren: MRAC, 1985.

Schildkrout, Enid, et al. *African Reflections: Art from Northeastern Zaire*. Seattle: University of Washington Press, 1990.

Sidoff, Phillip G. *Art of the Congo*. Milwaukee, WI: Milwaukee Public Museum, 1974.

Soëderberg, R. *Les Instruments de musique au Bas-Congo et dans les régions avoisinantes*. Stockholm: Ethnographical Museum of Sweden, 1956.

Sousberghe, Léon de. *L'Art pende*. Brussels: Palais des Académies, 1959.

Strother, Z. S. *Inventing Masks: Agency and History in the Art of the Central Pende*. Chicago: University of Chicago Press, 1998.

Syra Dji; visages et racines du Zaïre. (Exhibit organized in Paris from May 7 to August 30, 1982, under the auspices of the Zairian government's Département de la Culture et des Arts.) Paris: Musée des Arts Décoratifs, 1982.

Tchebwa, Manda. *Terre de la chanson: La Musique zaïroise, hier et aujourd'hui*. Louvain-la-Neuve, Belgium: Duculot, 1996.

Thieme, Darius L. *African Music: A Briefly Annotated Bibliography.* Washington: Library of Congress, Reference Department, Music Division, 1964.

Thompson, Robert Farris. *African Art in Motion.* Los Angeles: University of California, 1974.

Thompson, Robert Farris, and Joseph Cornet. *The Four Moments of the Sun.* (Catalogue of an exhibition of Kongo sculpture at the National Gallery of Art, Washington, DC, in 1981.) Washington: National Gallery of Art, 1981.

Thompson, Robert Farris, and Serge Bahuchet. *Pygmées?: Peintures sur écorce battue des Mbuti (Haut-Zaïre).* Paris: Musée Dapper, 1991.

Wannyn, Rob L. *L'Art ancien du métal au Bas-Congo.* Champles par Wavre, Belgium: Vieux Planquesaule, 1961.

Washburn, Dorothy Koster. *Style, Classification, and Ethnicity: Design Categories on Bakuba Raffia Cloth.* Philadelphia: American Philosophical Society, 1990.

Wingert, Paul S. *The Sculpture of Negro Africa.* New York: Columbia University Press, 1961.

2. Languages and Linguistics

Ayibite, P. *Initiation à l'enseignement des langues zaïroises: Première et deuxième années secondaires.* Lubumbashi: Centre de Linguistique Théorique et Appliquée, 1982.

Balegamire Bazilashe, J., and Rusimbuka J. M. Ngoboka. *Langue et culture en Afrique: Le Cas de Bahavu du Zaïre: Mélanges à la mémoire d'Aramazani Birusha A. (1943-1987).* Kinshasa: NORAF, 1991.

Bentley, William Holman. *Dictionary of the Kongo Language.* London: Baptist Missionary Society, 1887.

Bryan, M. A. *The Bantu Languages of Africa.* Handbook of African Languages. London: IAI, 1959.

Burssens, A. *Introduction à l'étude des langues bantoues congolaises.* Antwerp: Kongo-Overzee, 1955.

Carrington, J. F. "The Drum Language of the Lokele Tribe." *African Studies* 3, no. 2 (June 1944).

———. *Talking Drums of Africa.* London: Carey Kinsgate Press, 1949.

585 / Bibliography • Languages and Linguistics

Centre de Linguistique Théorique et Appliquée. *Linguistique et sciences humaines*. Kinshasa: semiannual.

Clarke, R. T. "The Drum Language of the Tumba Tribe." *American Journal of Sociology* 40 (1934).

Dalby, David, ed. *Language and History in Africa*. New York: Africana, 1970.

De Rop, Albert J. *Introduction à la linguistique bantoue congolaise*. Brussels: Mimosa, 1963.

Devisch, Renaat. *Se Recréer femme: Manipulation sémantique d'une situation d'infécondité chez les Yaka du Zaïre*. Berlin: D. Reimer, 1984.

Fabian, Johannes. *History from Below: The Vocabulary of Elisabethville by André Yav: Texts, Translation, and Interpretative Essay*. (With assistance from Kalundi Mango and linguistic notes by W. Schicho.) Amsterdam: J. Benjamins, 1990.

―――. *Language and Colonial Power: The Appropriation of Swahili in the Former Belgian Congo, 1880-1938*. Cambridge: Cambridge University Press, 1986; Berkeley: University of California Press, 1991.

―――. *Power and Performance: Ethnographic Explorations through Proverbial Wisdom and Theater in Shaba, Zaire*. Madison: University of Wisconsin Press, 1990.

Falk, Sully, et al. *La Francophonie au Zaïre*. Lubumbashi: Impala, 1988.

Gouala, Pierre Macaire. *Problems of Learning English in the Congo Due to Mother-Tongue Interference*. Nairobi: African Curriculum Organisation Project, 1981.

Goyvaerts, D. L. *Language and History in Central Africa*. Wilrijk, Belgium: University of Antwerp, 1986.

Gusimana. *Dictionnaire Pende-Français*. Bandundu: CEEBA, 1972.

Guthrie, Malcolm. *Comparative Bantu: An Introduction to the Comparative Linguistics and Prehistory of the Bantu Languages*. 4 vols. Farnborough: Gregg Press, 1967-72.

Haddad, Adnan. *L'Arabe et le Swahili dans la République du Zaïre: Études islamiques*. Paris: Société d'Édition d'Enseignement Supérieur, 1983.

Hulstaert, G. *Au Sujet de deux cartes linguistiques du Congo Belge*. Brussels: IRCB, 1954.

―――. *Carte linguistique du Congo Belge*. Brussels: publisher unknown, 1950.

Kaji, Shigeki. *Deux mille phrases de Swahili tel qu'il se parle au Zaïre.* Tokyo: Institute for the Study of Languages and Cultures of Asia and Africa, 1985.

Le Zaïre, deuxième pays francophone du monde? Québec: Centre International de Recherche sur le Bilinguisme, 1977.

Mahieu, Wauthier de. *Qui a obstrué la cascade?: Analyse sémantique du rituel de la circoncision chez les Komo du Zaïre.* Cambridge: Cambridge University Press, 1985.

Matumele Maliya Mata Bonkoba. *La Recherche en lexicologie politique au Zaïre.* Lubumbashi: Centre de Linguistique Théorique et Appliquée, UNAZA, 1975.

Mayaka. *Quelques belgicismes en République du Zaïre.* Kinshasa: Société Nationale des Linguistes du Zaïre, 1974.

Muyunga, Yacioko Kasengulu. *Lingala and Ciluba Audiometry.* Kinshasa: PUZ, 1979.

Ndolo, Pius. *Vocabulaire mbala.* Tervuren: MRAC, 1972.

Ndomba Kanyinda. *Structure syllabique du vocabulaire élémentaire du Français et du Ciluba: Étude comparative.* Lubumbashi: Centre de Linguistique Théorique et Appliquée, UNAZA, 1973.

Polomé, E. "Cultural Languages and Contact Vernaculars in the Republic of the Congo." *University of Texas Studies in Literature and Language* 4, no. 4 (Winter 1963): 499-511.

Sesep N'Sial Bal-a-Nsien. *Langage, normes et répertoire en milieu urbain africain: L'Indoubill.* Québec: Centre International de Recherche en Aménagement Linguistique, 1990.

Sumaili, N'gaye Lussa. *Documents pour une étude des particularités lexico-sémantiques du Français au Zaïre.* Lubumbashi: Centre de Linguistique Théorique et Appliquée, UNAZA, 1974.

United States. Department of Defense. *Lingala-English Dictionary.* Washington: 1962.

———. Department of State. Foreign Service Institute. *Lingala: Basic Course.* Washington: 1963.

Van Buick, G. *Les Deux cartes linguistiques du Congo Belge.* Brussels: IRCB, 1952.

———. *Les Recherches linguistiques au Congo Belge.* Brussels: IRCB, 1948.

———. *Manuel de linguistique bantoue.* Brussels: IRCB, 1949.

Vass, Winifred Kellersberger. *The Bantu Speaking Heritage of the United States.* Los Angeles: Center for Afro-American Studies, 1979.

Verbeke, Ronald. *Études psychométriques en milieu africain: La Compréhension du vocabulaire dans l'apprentissage d'une langue étrangère.* Kinshasa: UNAZA, 1970.

Verbeken, Auguste. "Le Tambour-téléphone chez les indigènes de l'Afrique centrale." *Congo* (1920).

Wtterwulghe, Georges-François. *Vocabulaire à l'usage des fonctionnaires se rendant dans les territoires du district de l'Uelé et de l'enclave Redjai-Lado.* Brussels: État Indépendant du Congo, 1903.

3. Literature and Oral Folklore

Aardema, Verna. *Traveling to Tondo: A Tale of the Nkundo of Zaire.* New York: Knopf, 1991.

Biebuyck, Daniel. *Hero and Chief: Epic Literature from the Banyanga (Zaire Republic).* Berkeley: University of California Press, 1978.

Bokoko, Elolo, ed. *Anthologie de poésie de Bandundu.* Bandundu: CEEBA, 1983.

Bol, V. P., and J. Allary. *Littérateurs et poètes noirs.* Leopoldville: Bibliothèque de l'Étoile, 1964.

Colldén, Lisa, ed. *Trésors de la tradition orale Sakata: Proverbes, mythes, légendes, fables, chansons et devinettes de Sakata.* Uppsala: University of Stockholm, 1979.

Comhaire-Sylvain, Suzanne, ed. *Jetons nos couteaux: Contes des garçonnets de Kinshasa et quelques parallèles haïtiennes.* Bandundu: CEEBA, 1974.

De Decker, J. M. *Les Clans Ambuun (Bambunda) d'après leur littérature orale.* Brussels: IRCB, 1950.

De Rop, Albert Jozef. *La Littérature orale: Synthèse et bibliographie.* (Mongo tales.) Brussels: CEDAF, 1974.

————, ed. *Versions et fragments de l'épopée mongo.* Brussels: ARSOM, 1978.

De Rop, Albert Jozef, and E. Ecelaert, eds. *Versions et fragments de l'épopée mongo, Nsong'a Lianja. Partie II.* (Companion to *Versions et fragments de l'épopée mongo.*) Mbandaka, Zaire: Aequatoria, 1983.

Djungu-Simba Kamatenda, ed. *Autour du feu: Contes d'inspiration lega.* Kinshasa: Saint Paul, 1984.

Dzokanga, A., ed. *Chansons et proverbes lingala.* Paris: Conseil International de la Langue Française, EDICEF, 1978.

Frobenius, Leo, ed. *Mythes et contes populaires des riverains du Kasaï.* (Translated into French from German by Claude Murat.) Wiesbaden: Franz Steiner Verlag GMEB, 1983.

Gisaangi, Sona, ed. *Dieu nous a tout confié excepté cette forêt.* Bandundu: CEEBA, 1974.

Goemaere, Alphonse. *Donne-moi ton beau vêtement: Littérature orale et notes sur l'histoire des Ndengese (Rép. du Zaïre).* (Translated from Dutch by Jean van Zeeland.) Bandundu: CEEBA, 1989.

Halen, Pierre. *Le Petit Belge avait vu grand: Une Littérature coloniale.* Brussels: Labor, 1993.

Hochegger, Herman. *Allons, tuons la mort: Mythes sakata.* Bandundu: CEEBA, 1974.

———. *Cendrillon en Afrique: Versions zaïroises proches des contes de Grimm: Traditions orales de 1906 a 1993.* Bandundu: CEEBA, 1993.

———. *Femme, pourquoi pleures-tu?: Mythes buma.* Bandundu: CEEBA, 1972.

Hulstaert, G. *Contes Mongo.* Brussels: ARSOM, 1965.

Ilunga Bamuyeja. *Deux griots de Kamina: Chants et poèmes.* Kinshasa: Centre Africain de Littérature, 1974.

Jadot, J. M. *Les Écrivains africains du Congo Belge et du Ruanda-Urundi: Une Histoire, un bilan, des problèmes.* Brussels: ARSC, 1959.

Jones, A. M. *Studies in African Music.* London: Oxford University Press, 1959.

Kadima Nzuji Mukala. *La Littérature zaïroise de langue française, 1945-1965.* Paris: Karthala, 1984.

Kalonji, M. T. Zezeze. *Une Écriture de la passion chez Pius Ngandu Nkashama.* Paris: Harmattan, 1992.

Katende, Cyovo, ed. *Voilà la nouvelle lune! Dansons! Chansons populaires de la zone de Gandajika.* Bandundu: CEEBA, 1977.

Kavutirwaki, Kambale. *Contes folkloriques nande.* Tervuren: MRAC, 1975.

Kishwe. *Anthologie des écrivains congolais moderne.* Kinshasa: SNEC (Lokole), 1969.

Knappert, Jan. *Myths and Legends of the Congo.* Nairobi: Heinemann Educational Books, 1971.

La Littérature coloniale: De l'Amour aux colonies, de son récit. Brussels: Le Cri, 1994.

Labi Tawaba and Tamundel Mubele, eds. *Qui la sortira de cette pierre?: Mythes yansi.* Bandundu: CEEBA, 1974.

Lumbwe Mudindaambi, ed. *Mange ces dents!* (Mbala tales.) Bandundu: CEEBA, 1972.

———. *Mythes mbala.* Bandundu: CEEBA, n.d.

———. *Pourquoi le coq ne chante plus?* Bandundu: CEEBA, 1973.

Lumbwe Mudindaambi and Kimbungu, eds. *Ma Femme n'est pas ton gibier.* (Mbala tales.) Bandundu: CEEBA, 1977.

Maalu-bungi, C. *Contes populaires du Kasaï.* Kinshasa: Mont Noir, 1974.

Manzanga Kaladi and Makumar Mpang Brick. *Ne me tue pas, épouse-moi!: Mythes dinga.* Bandundu: CEEBA, 1977.

Mbuya Bangu. *Le Père dans la peau du lion.* (Pelende tales.) Bandundu: CEEBA, 1977.

Monsengo Osantwene and Ipasso Lokope, eds. *Le Père qui ne voulait pas de fille: Mythes nkundu et tere.* Bandundu: CEEBA, 1974.

Mulyumba wa Mamba, Itongwa. *Les Proverbes, un langage didactique dans les sociétés africaines traditionnelles: Le Cas des Balega-Bashile.* Brussels: CEDAF, 1973.

Munongo, A. (Mwenda II). "Chants historiques des Bayeke, traduits en Français et expliqués." *Bulletins Juridictions Indigènes et du Droit Coutumier Congolais* 16 (1948): 280-94, and 20 (1952): 305-16.

N'Sanda Wamenka. *Contes du Zaïre: Contes des montagnes, de la savane et de la forêt au pays du fleuve Zaïre.* Paris: Conseil International de la Langue Française EDICEF, 1975.

Nziata Mulenge. *Pour la guérir, il faut ton coeur!: Mythes pende.* Bandundu: CEEBA, 1974.

Nzuji Madija, C. *Devinettes tonales: Tusumwinu.* Paris: SELAF, 1976.

———. *Kasala: Chant héroïque luba.* Lubumbashi: PUZ, 1974.

Nzungu Mavinga Lelo di Kimbi Kiaku. *Santé et tradition: Proverbes et coutumes relatifs à la santé.* Kangu-Mayombe, Zaire: Bureau d'Études et de Recherches pour la Promotion de la Santé, 1975.

Quaghebeur, Marc, and Émile Van Balberghe, eds. *Papier blanc, encre noire: Cent ans de culture francophone en Afrique centrale: Zaïre, Rwanda et Burundi.* Brussels: Labor, 1992.

Ritiy Mutz. *Elle ne mangea que des oiseaux: Mythes ruund.* Bandundu: CEEBA, 1979.

Roland, Hadelin. *Quarante contes de la région des Basanga*. Brussels: Artes Africanae, 1937.

Ross, Mabel, and Barbara Walter, eds. *"On Another Day . . .": Tales Told among the Nkundo of Zaire*. Hamden, CT: Archon Books, 1979.

Schicho, Walter, and Mbayabo Ndala. *Le Groupe Mufwankolo*. Vienna: Afro-Pub, 1981.

Stanley, Sanna. *Monkey Sunday: A Story from a Congolese Village*. New York: Farrar, Straus and Giroux, 1998.

Stappers, Léonard, and Jacques Vinke. *Textes Luba: Contes d'animaux*. Tervuren: MRAC, 1962.

Sumaili N'gaye-Lussa. *Chronologie des oeuvres littéraires zaïroises*. Kinshasa: Comité Directeur de l'Union des Écrivains Zaïrois, 1981.

Tito Yisuku Gafudzi. *Négritude et tendances de la poésie zaïroise contemporaine*. Kinshasa: La Grue Couronnée, 1976.

Van Coppenolle, Renée. *Contes de Muakudi l'Africaine*. Waterloo, Belgium: Fichermont, 1975.

Wannyn, Rob L. *Les Proverbes anciens du Bas-Congo*. Brussels: Vieux Planquesaule, 1983.

TABLES

TABLE 1: ADMINISTRATIVE REGIONS BY AREA AND POPULATION *(in thousands)* 1970, 1982 AND 1995

Regions	Area (sq. km)	Population 1970	1982	1995 (est.)
Kinshasa	2,016	1,308	2,124	5,105
Bandundu	295,658	2,601	4,141	5,798
Bas-Zaïre	61,869	1,519	1,726	2,417
Équateur	403,293	2,432	3,288	4,607
Haut-Zaïre	503,239	3,356	4,524	6,334
Kasaï Occidental	156,967	2,434	2,933	4,007
Kasaï Oriental	168,216	1,872	2,335	3,270
Maniema*	132,250	623	764	1,070
Nord-Kivu*	59,563	1,473	1,862	2,607
Shaba	496,975	2,754	3,762	5,268
Sud-Kivu*	64,849	1,265	1,739	2,430
TOTAL	2,344,895	21,637	29,198	42,913

* *Note:* Kivu was divided into Maniema, Nord-Kivu and Sud-Kivu Regions in 1988.

Source: Government of Zaire, Bureau de la Statistique, and Makanda Kabobi Institute.

TABLE 2. KEY ECONOMIC INDICATORS
($ US millions unless otherwise noted)

Item	1980	1985	1990	1995
GENERAL				
Gross Domestic				
Product	6,519	7,124	7,376	4,656
Exchange rate				
($1 US = zaires)	2.8	50	718	7,024 *
TRADE AND BALANCE OF PAYMENTS				
Total Exports	2,269	1,853	2,138	1,100
Total Imports	1,519	1,247	1,539	600
Current Account	-292	-289	-643	-700
EXTERNAL PUBLIC DEBT				
Total Debt	4,770	6,171	10,270	12,336 **
Total Debt Service	542	497	348	66 **
Principal	277	228	200	5 **
Interest	265	269	148	61 **

* New zaires, which were exchanged for 3 million zaires each (about $1.50 US) in October 1993.
** Figures for 1994.

Note: Economic data for Zaire during the early 1990s was imprecise for several reasons. Official government figures were not released on a number of occasions. The International Monetary Fund ceased publication of some data. And hyperinflation and fluctuating foreign exchange rates hindered the compilation of data in constant terms.

Sources: Banque du Zaïre, International Monetary Fund, *Economist* Intelligence Unit.

TABLE 3: ECONOMIC INDICATORS DURING THE 1990s
(period of high inflation)

INFLATION RATE (percent)

1991	1992	1993	1994	1995	1996
2,154	4,130	2,000	6,000	600	1,000

CURRENCY EXCHANGE RATE
(US $1 = zaires)

1991	1992	1993	1994	1995	1998
15,587	645,549	5 million	1,194	7,024	3.4

GOVERNMENT FINANCES (billions of zaires)

Item	1991	1992	1993	1994	1995
Revenue	312	183,542	2,830*	208	1,778
Expenditures	600	885,173	13,269*	315	1,884
Balance	-288	-701,631	-10,446*	-108	-106

* Trillions (thousands of billions) of zaires.

Note: Figures from 1994 are in new zaires (NZ), exchanged for 3 million zaires each on October 22, 1993. Figures for 1998 are in Congolese francs, exchanged for 100,000 NZ each on June 30, 1998.

Source: Banque du Zaïre, Ministry of Finance, International Monetary Fund.

TABLE 4: PRODUCTION OF MAJOR MINERALS
(in metric tons unless otherwise specified)

Minerals	1960	1980	1990	1995
Coal	163,000	287,000	126,000	n/a
Cobalt	8,222	14,482	10,000	4,100
Copper	302,252	425,700	335,500	35,000
Diamonds				
(1,000 carats)	13,455	10,235	19,500	20,000*
Gold	9.771	1.271	5,200	900*
Manganese	381,630	6,321	N/A	N/A
Petroleum				
(1,000 barrels)	0	6,566	10,679	10,950
Silver	123.3	85.01	N/A	N/A
Zinc	109,182	67,000	38,200	2,700*

* Estimate.
Sources: US Bureau of Mines, GECAMINES, *Economist* Intelligence Unit.

TABLE 5: PRODUCTION OF MAJOR CROPS
(in 1,000 metric tons)

Crop	1959	1976	1987	1992
Coffee, Arabica	10	20	19	20
Coffee, Robusta	52	88	76	70
Cotton	63	11	14*	13*
Maize	115	128	850	1,052
Manioc	1,780	819	16,820	20,210
Palm kernel	61	23	45*	50*
Palm oil	244	128	165	180
Plantains	N/A	N/A	1,880	2,224
Rice	110	137	330	440
Rubber	40	28	17	7
Sugar cane	277	614	1,150*	1,180*
Timber (sawed)	212	81	N/A	114

* Estimate.
Sources: Banque du Zaïre, World Bank, *Economist* Intelligence Unit.

TABLE 6: TRADE WITH MAJOR TRADING PARTNERS
(millions of US dollars)

EXPORTS TO

Country	1976	1985	1990	1994
Benelux	174.5	499.4	452.5	158.0
United States	94.0	376.8	151.8	66.6
South Africa*	0	0	0	36.9
Italy	84.2	121.6	55.9	31.8
Japan	11.2	46.2	21.0	27.7

IMPORTS FROM

Country	1976	1985	1990	1994
Benelux	126.1	259.7	168.3	53.6
South Africa*	0	0	22.2	38.2
Germany	74.3	97.4	68.9	26.0
Hong Kong	5.2	13.8	16.1	23.7
Nigeria	0	0	16.8	18.1

* Officially, Zaire did not trade with South Africa until the South African government began to dismantle apartheid.

Note: Official trade figures with African nations are negligible, but informal trade, particularly with Angola, Congo, Rwanda and Uganda, is considered extensive because of smuggling.

Sources: International Monetary Fund, Economist Intelligence Unit.

ABOUT THE AUTHOR

F. Scott Bobb is a journalist who has been reporting on and writing about the Democratic Republic of the Congo (formerly Republic of Zaire) since the mid-1970s. Brought up by missionaries in the Congo from 1954 until 1971, he joined the Voice of America in 1977 as a reporter-broadcaster. In 1982, Bobb became a foreign correspondent for VOA. He served as West Africa correspondent from 1982 to 1985, South America correspondent from 1985 to 1990, and East Africa correspondent from 1990 to 1993. He returned to Washington to become chief of correspondents in 1993 and chief of the VOA News Division in 1996. In 1998, Bobb returned overseas, as VOA Middle East correspondent. Aside from the first edition of this volume, published in 1988, Bobb has written for a number of publications and occasionally works as a consultant.